P·O·C·K·E·T·S

FRENCH DICTIONARY

FRENCH · ENGLISH
ENGLISH · FRENCH

DORLING KINDERSLEY

London • New York • Moscow • Sydney

A DORLING KINDERSLEY BOOK

www.dk.com

First published in Great Britain in 1997
by Dorling Kindersley Limited,
80 Strand, London WC2R 0RL

PAGE*One* team   Chris Clark, Matthew Cook,
Bob Gordon, Helen Parker

DK Managing editor   Jane Yorke

German editors   Anke Kornmüller
Christa Wiseman

Copyright © 1997 Dorling Kindersley Ltd., London
8 10 9 7

This edition published in 2002

A CIP catalogue record for this book is available from
the British Library

ISBN 0 7513 5686 7

This edition revised by Dorling Kindersley

Printed and bound by LegoPrint, Italy

THE IMITATED PRONUNCIATION

If the syllables given are pronounced as if they formed part of an English word, the speaker will probably be understood. However the real sounds of the French language can be achieved by remembering a few simple rules:

r   (italic) not to be pronounced at all.

ng   (italic) not to be pronounced at all. It merely indicates that the preceding vowel has a nasal sound; ah*ng* is pronounced like **au** in "aunt", a*ng* like **ang** in "fang", o*ng* like **ong** in "wrong", and u*ng* like **ung** in "lung".

r   (bold type) pronounced more strongly than in English – rrroll it on the tongue.

sh   (bold) like **s** in "measure".

eh   like **e** in "bed".

er   like **u** in "fur".

er   (bold) is the same sound, but longer and with the **r** sounded.

er   like **e** in "her", but more closed.

ah   like **a** in "far", but shorter.

ai or ay   like **ai** in "fair".

E, EE   represent the sound of the French **u**: say "tree" with lips rounded as when whistling, and the terminal sound of **ee** is the one required.

oo   like **oo** in "book", "look", "took".

There is practically **no stress** in French words; the same value should be given to all syllables.

LA PRONONCIATION FIGURÉE

Prononcer chaque syllabe comme si elle appartenait à un mot français, mais en tenant compte des indications suivantes:

a entre	a extrêmement bref. Dans certains mots (**have, had, has, man, hat** etc), l'**a** de "bal" et l'**è** de "complète".

a, eu o son indistinct et sourd, analogue à celui d'**e** dans "me", "de", "que". Ce son est souvent indiqué par une apostrophe dans la prononciation figurée de certaines finales anglaises: **lesson**, less -'n.

o son très bref, entre **eu** dans "fleur" et **a** dans "lac". Par exemple: **but**, botte (son presque comme "batte").

oa désigne un son qu'on reproduira avec une exactitude suffisante en prononçant à peu près, et d'une seule émission de voix, comme **au** dans "laure", "Fauré".

r à la fin d'un mot ou d'une syllabe, ne se fait sentir que très faiblement, à moins qu'il ne soit immédiatement suivi d'une voyelle.

h cette lettre s'aspire toujours distinctement.

th (dur=*ts*, et doux=*dz*). Prononcer *is* et *dz* en mettant le bout de la langue entre les dents comme lorsqu'on zézaie.

L'**e** muet à la fin d'une syllabe ne doit jamais se prononcer.

ACCENT TONIQUE

En anglais, l'accentuation d'une syllabe est donnée dans la prononciation figurée par le symbole ´ placé après la syllabe accentuée.

ABBREVIATIONS

a	adjective	poss	possessive
abbr	abbreviation	pp	past participle
adv	adverb	prep	preposition
aero	aeronautics	pres part	present participle
art	article	pron	pronoun
auto	car	psych	psychology
Brit	British	refl	reflexive
chem	chemistry	s	singular
com	commercial	TM	trademark
comput	computing	v	verb
conj	conjunction	vulg	vulgar
eccl	ecclesiastical		
f	feminine noun		
fam	familiar		
fin	financial		
fig	figurative sense		
geog	geographical		
hair	hairdressing		
inf	infinitive		
interj	interjection		
interrog	interrogative		
jur	legal		
m	masculine noun		
mech	mechanical		
med	medical		
mil	military		
mus	musical		
n	noun		
naut	nautical		
num	numeral		
pers	persons		
phr	phrase		
pl	plural		
pop	popular		

ABRÉVIATIONS

abbr	abbréviation	poss	possessif
adj	adjectif	pp	participe passé
adv	adverbe	prep	préposition
aero	aéronautique	pres part	participe présent
art	article	pron	pronom
auto	auto	psych	psychologie
Brit	britanique	refl	réflechi
chem	chimie	s	singulier
com	commercial	v	verbe
comput	informatique	vulg	vulgaire
conj	conjonction	TM	marque déposée
eccl	ecclésiastique		
f	nom féminin		
fam	familier		
fig	figuré		
fin	financier		
geog	géographique		
hair	coiffure		
inf	infinitif		
interj	interjection		
interrog	interrogatif		
jur	juridique		
m	nom masculin		
mech	mécanique		
med	médical		
mil	militaire		
mus	musical		
n	nom		
naut	nautique		
num	chiffre		
pers	personnes		
phr	expression		
pl	pluriel		
pop	populaire		

FRENCH · ENGLISH
FRANÇAIS · ANGLAIS

à, ăh, *prep* to; at; in; within; on; by; for; from; according to.

a, ăh, *v* has.

abaissement, ăh-bayss-mahng, *m* lowering; fall; diminution; disgrace.

abaisser, ăh-bayss-eh, *v* to lower; to pull down; **s'–,** to humble oneself; to stoop.

abandon, ăh-bahng-dong, *m* abandonment; desertion; ease. **à l'–,** neglected space.

abandonné, e, ăh-bahng-donn-eh, *pp* & *a* deserted; depraved; profligate; neglected; disused.

abandonner, ăh-bahng-donn-eh, *v* to abandon; to desert; to give up; to

let go; **s'–,** to indulge (**à,** in); to let oneself go.

abasourdir, ăh-băh-zoohr-deer, *v* to stun.

abatage, abattage, ăh-băh-tăhsh, *m* cutting down; slaughter.

abâtardir, ăh-bah-tăhr-deer, *v* to debase; to corrupt.

abat-jour, ăh-băh-shoohr, *m* reflector; lamp shade.

abattement, ăh-băht-mahng, *m* prostration.

abattis, ăh-băh-te, *m* felling; giblets.

abattoir, ăh-băh-to'ăhr, *m* slaughter house.

abattre, ăh-băh-tr, *v* to bring down; to cut down. **s'–,** to fall.

abattu, e, ăh-băh-tE, *pp* & *a* brought down;

depressed.

abat-vent, ăh-băh-vahng, *m* wind-screen.

abbaye, ăh-bay-yee, *f* abbey.

abbé, ăh-beh, *m* abbot; priest.

abbesse, ăh-bess, *f* abbess.

abcès, ăhb-say, *m* abscess.

abdiquer, ăhb-de-keh, *v* to abdicate.

abdomen, ăhb-doh-menn, *m* abdomen.

abeille, ăh-bay'e, *f* bee.

abhorrer, ăh-bor-eh, *v* to abhor; to loathe.

abîme, ăh-beem, *m* abyss.

abîmer, ăh-bee-meh, *v* to spoil; to damage.

abject, e, ăhb-sheckt, *a* base; mean.

abjection, ăhb-sheck-se-ong, *f* vileness.

abjurer, ăhb-shE-reh, *v* to renounce.

ablution, ăhb-lE-se-ong, *f* washing.

abnégation, ăhb-neh-găh-se-ong, *f* self-denial.

aboi, ăh-boăh, *m*

aboiement, ăh-boăh-mahng, *m* bark; barking.

abois, ăh-boăh, *mpl* **aux abois,** oh-z'–, at bay; desperate situation.

abolir, ăh-bol-eer, *v* to abolish.

abominable,* ăh-bomm-e-năh-bl, *a* abominable.

abomination, ăh-bomm-e-năh-se-ong, *f* abomination.

abondamment, ăh-bong-dăh-mahng, *adv* plentifully.

abondant, e, ăh-bong-dahng, *a* abundant.

abonder, ăh-bong-deh, *v* to abound (**en,** in, with).

abonné, e, ăh-bonn-eh, *mf* subscriber; season ticket holder.

abonnement, ăh-bonn-mahng, *m* subscription; **carte d'–,** kăhrt d–, season ticket.

abonner (s'–),săh-bonn-eh, *v* to subscribe.

abord, ăh-bor, *m* access (à); at first; **–s,** surroundings.

aborder, ăh-bor-deh, *v* to land; to approach; to accost; to run foul of; to collide with.

aborti-f, ve, ăh-bor-tiff, *a* abortive.

aboutir, ăh-boo-teer, *v* to achieve (a result); to lead (à, to).

aboutissant, ăh-boo-tiss-ahng, *m* abuttal. **tenants et –s,** ter-nahng z'eh–, ins and outs.

aboyer, ăh-bo'ăh-yeh, *v* to

bark.

abrégé, ăh-breh-sheh, *m* summary; synopsis.

abréger, ăh-breh-sheh, *v* to shorten.

abreuver, ăh-brer-veh, *v* to water animals; *fig* to soak. **s'–,** to drink plentifully.

abreuvoir, ăh-brer-vo'ăhr, *m* watering place.

abréviation, ăh-breh-ve-ah-se-ong, *f* abbreviation.

abri, ăh-bre, *m* shelter.

abricot, ăh-bre-ko, *m* apricot.

abriter, ăh-bre-teh, *v* to shelter.

abroger, ăh-bro-sheh, *v* to repeal.

abrupt, e,* ăh-brEpt, *a* abrupt; steep; rugged.

abrutir, ăh-brE-teer, *v* to stupefy; to daze; **s'–,** to make a beast of oneself.

absent, e, ăh-sahng, *a* absent.

absenter(s'), săh-sahng-teh, *v* to absent oneself

absinthe, ăh-sangt, *f* wormwood; absinthe.

absolument, ăhb-sol-E-mahng, *adv* absolutely.

absolution, ăhb-sol-E-se-ong, *f* absolution; pardon.

absorber, ăhb-sor-beh, *v*

to absorb; to engross.

absorption, ăhb-sorp-se-ong, *f* absorption.

absoudre, ăhb-soo-dr, *v* to absolve.

abstenir(s'), săbhs-ter-neer, *v* to abstain.

abstinence, ăhbs-te-nahngss, *f* abstinence; fasting.

abstraire, ăhbs-trair, *v* to abstract.

abstrait, e,* ăhbs-tray, *a* abstract; abstruce; obscure.

absurde,* ăhbss-EErd, *a* absurd; silly.

absurdité, ăhbss-EEr-de-teh, *f* absurdity; nonesense.

abus, ăh-bE, *m* abuse; **– de confiance,** – der-kong-fe-ahngss, breach of confidence.

abuser, ăh-bE-zeh, *v* to deceive; to abuse.

abusi-f, ve,* ăh-bE-ziff, *a* improper (use of word); excessive.

académie, ăh-kăh-deh-mee, *f* academy.

acajou, ăh-kăh-shoo, *m* mahogany.

acariâtre, ăh-kăh-re-ah-tr, *a* bad-tempered; cantankerous.

accablant, e, ăh-kăh-blahng, *a* overwhelming;

oppressive; unbearable.

accablement, ăh-kăh-bler-mahng, m depression; dejection.

accabler, ăh-kăh-bleh, v to overwhelm; to crush; to overcome (**de,** with).

accaparer, ăh-kăh-păh-reh, v to monopolize.

accéder, ăhck-seh-deh, v to accede; to comply (**à,** with).

accélérateur, ăhck-seh-leh-răh-ter, **m** accelarator.

accélérer, ăhck-seh-leh-reh, v auto to accelerate; to hasten.

accent, ăhck-sahng, m accent; tone; stress.

accentuer, ăhck-sahng-tE-eh, v to accentuate; to emphasize.

acceptation, ăhck-sehp-tăh-se-ong, f acceptance.

accepter, ăhck-sehp-teh, v to accept.

acception, ăhck-sehp-se-ong, f meaning (of word).

accès, ăhck-say, m access (**à,** to); fit.

accessoire, ăhck-sess-o'ăhr, m detail; perk; pl properties; a accessory.

accident, ăhck-se-dahng, m accident; mishap.

accidenté, e, ăhck-se-dahng-teh, a eventful; uneven; victim (of accident); injured.

accise, ăhck-seez, f excise.

acclamer, ăh-klăh-meh, v to acclaim.

acclimater, ăh-kle-măh-teh, v to acclimatise.

accolade, ăh-kol-ăhd, f embrace.

accommodant, e, ăh-komm-odd-ahng, a easy to deal with.

accommodement, ăh-komm-odd-mahng, m settlement.

accommoder, ăh-komm-od-eh, v to suit; to do up (food); s'– à, to adapt oneself to; s'– de, to put up with.

accompagnement, ăh-kong-păhn'yer-mahng, m attendance; accessory; accompaniment.

accompagner, ăh-kong-păhn'yeh, v to accompany.

accompli, e, ăh-kong-ple, pp & a accomplished; thorough.

accomplissement, ăh-kong-pliss-mahng, m completion; fulfilment.

accord, ăh-kor, m agreement; consent; tuning; d'–, agreed; **tomber d'–,** tong-beh

d–, to come to an agreement; **mettre d'–,** met-tr-d–, to conciliate.

accordage, ăh-kor-dăhsh, m tuning.

accorder, ăh-kor-deh, v to accord; to grant; to tune; to reconcile; s'–, to agree.

accoster, ăh-koss-teh, v to accost (a person); to come alongside.

accoter, ăh-kot-eh, v to stay; s' –, to lean.

accoucher, ăh-koo-sheh, v to give birth; to deliver a child.

accoucheur, ăh-koo-sher, m obstetrician.

accoucheuse, ăh-koo-sher-z, f midwife.

accouder (s'), săh-koo-deh, v to lean on one's elbow.

accoupler, ăh-koo-pleh, v to couple; to yoke; to pair.

accourcir, ăh-koohr-seer, v to shorten.

accoutrement, ăh-koo-trer-mahng, m garb.

accoutrer, ăh-koo-treh, v to rig out.

accoutumer, ăh-koo-tE-meh, v to accustom; s'– à, to get used to.

accréditer, ăh-kreh-de-teh, v to accredit; to

credit.

accroc, ăh-kro, *m* tear; *fig* hitch.

accrocher, ăh-kro-sheh, *v* to hook on; to catch; **s'–**, to cling.

accroire, ăh-kro'ăhr, *v* (used infinitive only and with **faire**), to make believe; **en faire –**, ahng fayr –, to impose (à, upon).

accroissement, ăh-kro'ahss-mahng, *m* increase.

accroître, ăh-kro'ăh-tr, *v* to increase; **s'–**, to grow.

accroupir, (**s'**), săh-kroo-peer, *v* to squat.

accru, e, ăh-krE, *pp* increased.

accueil, ăh-ker'e, *m* reception; welcome.

accueillir, ăh-ker-yeer, *v* to receive; to welcome.

accumulateur, ăh-kE-mE-lăh-ter, *m* accumulator; storage battery.

accumuler, ăh-kE-mE-leh, *v* to accumulate; to heap.

accusation, ăh-kE-zăh-se-ong, *f* accusation; charge.

accusé, e, ăh-kE-zeh, *mf* accused person; **– de réception**, – der reh-sep-se-ong,

acknowledgement of receipt.

accuser, ăh-kE-zeh, *v* to accuse; to indict.

acerbe, ăh-sairb, *a* sour; harsh.

acéré, e, ăh-seh-reh, *a* sharp; steeled.

achalandé, e, ăh-shăh-lahng-deh, *a* well-stocked (of shop).

acharnement, ăh-shăhr-ner-mahng, *m* relentlessness; desperate eagerness.

acharner (s'), săh-shăhr-neh, *v* to be relentless; to persist in something.

achat, ăh-shăh, *m* purchase.

acheminement, ăsh-meen-mahng, *m* dispatch; transporting; routing.

acheminer, ăhsh-me-neh, *v* to despatch; **s'–**, to set out; to proceed.

acheter, ăhsh-teh, *v* to buy; **s'–**, to be bought; to be purchased.

acheteur, ăhsh-ter, *m* purchaser.

achever, ăhsh-veh, *v* to finish.

achoppement, ăh-shop-mahng, *m* stumbling; **pierre d'–**, pe'air d–, stumbling block.

acide, ăh-seed, *m* acid; *a* sour; sharp.

acier, ăh-se-eh, *m* steel.

aciérie, ăh-se-eh-ree, *f* steel works.

acné, ăhck-neh, *m* acne.

acolyte, ăh-kol-eet, *m* acolyte; accomplice.

acompte, ăh-kongt, *m* instalment.

à-côtés, ăh-koht-eh *mpl* perk.

acoustique, ăh-kooss-tick, *f* acoustics; *a* acoustic.

acquérir, ăh-keh-reer, *v* to acquire.

acquiescer, ăh-ke-ess-eh, *v* to acquiesce (à, in).

acquis, e, ăh-ke, *pp* acquired; *m* knowledge; experience.

acquisition, ăh-ke-ze-se-ong, *f* acquisition; purchase.

acquit, ăh-ke, *m* receipt; discharge; **– à caution**, **– t'ah** koh-se-ong, permit (Customs); **pour –**, poohr –, received with thanks.

acquittement, ăh-kit-mahng, *m* payment; *jur* acquittal.

acquitter, ăh-ke-teh, *v* to clear; to pay; to receipt; to acquit (an accused person); **s'– de**, to carry out.

1 4

âcre, ahkr, *a* acrid; sour.

âcreté, ah-krer-teh, *f* acridity.

acrimonie, ăh-kre-monn-ee, *f* acrimony.

acrobate, ăh-kro-băht, *mf* acrobat.

acrobatie, ăh-krob-ăh-see, *f* acrobatics.

acte, ăhckt, *m* act; action; deed; certificate; faire – de, fair – der, to show proof of.

ac-teur, -trice, ăhck-ter, *mf* actor; actress.

actif, ăhck-tiff, *m* assets.

acti-f, ve, * ăhck-tiff, *a* active.

action, ăhck-se-ong, *f* act; deed; share; *pl* stock.

actionnaire, ăhck-se-onn-air, *mf* shareholder.

actionner, ăhck-se-onn-eh, *v* to set in motion; to sue.

activer, ăhck-te-veh, *v* to urge on; to activate.

activité, ăhck-te-ve-teh, *f* activity.

actualité, ăhck-tE-ăh-lee-teh, *f* reality; event; les –s, leh z–, the news; newsreel.

actuel, le, * ăhck-tE-ell, *a* present; real.

acuité, ăh-kE-e-teh, *f* acuteness.

adage, ăh-dăhsh, *m* saying; adage.

adapter, ăh-dăhp-teh, *v* to adapt; to fit; to apply; s'–, to be suitable (à, for).

additif, ăh-de-teef, *m* additive.

addition, ăh-de-se-ong, *f* addition; (restaurant) bill.

additionnel, le, ăh-de-se-onn-ell, *a* additional.

adepte, ăh-dept, *a* adept.

adhérer, ăh-deh-reh, *v* to adhere; s'–, to join (party).

adhésion, ăh-deh-se-ong, *f* adhesion; joining (of party).

adieu, ăh-de-er, *m* farewell; *adv* good-bye; farewell.

adjacent, ăh-dăh-shăh-sahng, *a* adjacent; contiguous.

adjectif, ăhd-sheck-teef, *m* adjective.

adjoindre, ăhd-sho'ang-dr, *v* to adjoin; s'–, to take as an associate; to join.

adjoint, ăhd-sho'ang, *m* assistant; deputy mayor.

adjudant, ăhd-shE-dahng, *m* adjutant.

adjudicataire, ăhd-shE-de-kăh-tair, *m* highest bidder.

adjugé! ăhd-shE-sheh, *pp* gone! (in auctions).

adjuger, ăhd-shE-sheh, *v* to award; to knock down (at auctions); s'–, to appropriate to one's use.

adjurer, ăhd-shE-reh, *v* to adjure; to beseech.

admettre, ăhd-met-tr, *v* to admit; to allow.

administrateur, ăhd-me-niss-trăh-ter, *m* administrator; manager; director; trustee.

administré, e, ăhd-me-niss-treh, *pp* & *n* administered; person under one's jurisdiction.

administrer, ăhd-me-niss-treh, *v* to administrate; to administer.

admira-teur, -trice, ăhd-me-răh-ter, *mf* admirer.

admirer, ăhd-me-reh, *v* to admire.

admission, ăhd-miss-e-ong, *f* admission; admittance.

admonester, ăhd-monn-ess-teh, *v* to reprimand.

admonition, ăhd-monn-e-se-ong, *f* warning.

adolescence, ăh-doll-ess-sahngss, *f* adolescence.

adolescent, e, ăh-doll-ess-sahng, *a* & *n* adolescent.

adonner (s'), săh-donn-eh, *v* to addict oneself to; to devote oneself to.

adopter, ăh-dop-teh, *v* to adopt.

adorable, ăh-do-răh-bl, *a* adorable; charming.

adora-teur, -trice, ăh-dor-ăh-ter, *mf* worshipper.

adorer, ăh-do-reh, *v* to adore; to be passionately fond of.

adosser, ăh-dohss-eh, *v* to lean (against).

adoucir, ăh-doo-seer, *v* to soften; **s'–,** to grow softer.

adoucissement, ăh-doo-siss-mahng, *m* softening; alleviation.

adresse, ăh-dress, *f* address; skill.

adresser, ăh-dress-eh, *v* to address; to direct; **s'–,** to apply; to be directed.

adroit, e,* ăh-dro'ăh, *a* handy; skilful; artful.

aduler, ăh-dE-leh, *v* to fawn upon; to adulate.

adulte, ăh-dEElt, *a* adult, grown up.

adultère, ăh-dEEl-tair, *a* & *n* adulterous; adulterer; adultery.

advenir, ăhd-ver-neer, *impers v* to happen; to befall.

adverbe, ăhd-vairb, *m* adverb.

adversaire, ăhd-vair-sair, *m* opponent; foe.

adverse, ăhd-vairss, *a* adverse.

adversité, ăhd-vair-se-teh, *f* misfortune; adversity.

aéré, ăh-eh-reh, *a* aired; airy; aerated.

aérobic, ăh-eh-ro-bik, *m* aerobics.

aérodrome, ăh-eh-ro-drohm, *m* aerodrome; airport.

aérogare, ăh-eh-ro-gahr, *f* air terminal.

aéroport, ăh-eh-ro-por, *m* airport.

aérosol, ăh-eh-ro-sol, *m* aerosol.

affable,* ăh-făh-bl, *a* affable.

affaiblir, ăh-fay-bleer, *v* to weaken.

affaire, ăh-fair, *f* affair; business; matter; thing; action; work; scrape; **avoir – à,** ăh-vo'ăhr – ăh, to have to do with; **faire des –s,** fair day z'–, to do business; **faire l'–de,** fair l– der, to suit; **homme d'–s,** omm d–, *n* business man; **se tirer d'–,** ser -te-reh-d–, *v* to get out of a scrape; **j'en fais mon –,** shahng -fay-monn –, I take it upon myself.

affairé, e, ăh-fay-reh, *a* busy.

affaissé, e, ăh-fess-eh, *pp* sunk down; depressed.

affaisser (s'), săh-fess-eh, *v* to sink, to flag.

affamé, e, ăh-făh-meh, *pp* & *a* starved; starving.

affamer, ăh-făh-meh, *v* to starve.

affectation, ăh-feck-tăh-se-ong, *f* affectation; simulation; assignment.

affecté, e, ăh-feck-teh, *a* affected; conceited.

affecter, ăh-feck-teh, *v* to feign; to set apart; **s'–,** to be moved; affected.

affection, ăh-feck-se-ong, *f* affection; fondness; disease.

affectionner, ăh-feck-se-onn-eh, *v* to be fond of.

afférent, e, ăh-feh-rahng, *a* pertaining to.

affermer, ăh-fair-meh, *v* to rent; to lease.

affermir, ăh-fair-meer, *v* to strenghten.

afféterie, ăh-feh-tree, *f* affectation.

affichage, ăh-fe-shăhsh, *m* bill-posting.

affiche, ăh-feesh, *f* placard; poster.

afficher, ăh-fe-sheh, *v* to stick up; to make a show of; to expose.

affiler, ăh-fe-leh, *v* to sharpen.

affilié, e, ăh-fe-le-eh, *a* affiliated.

affiner, ăh-fe-neh, *v* to refine.

affirmer, ăh-feer-meh, *v* to assert; to affirm.

affleurer, ăh-fler-reh, *v* to level.

affliger, ăh-fle-sheh, *v* to afflict; to grieve.

affluent, ăh-flE-ahng, *m* tributary; *a* affluent.

affluer, ăh-flE-eh, *v* to flow; to run; to abound.

affolé, e, ăh-foll-eh, *a* distracted; panic-stricken; spinning (compass).

affoler, ăh-foll-eh, *v* to drive mad; **s'–,** to become infatuated (**de,** with); to panic.

affranchi, e, ăh-frahng-she, *pp* & *a* freed; prepaid.

affranchir, ăh-frahng-sheer, *v* to free; to prepay; to stamp (letter).

affranchissement, ăh-frahng-shiss-mahng, *m* emancipation; prepayment; postage.

affréter, ăh-freh-teh, *v* to charter; to freight.

affreu-x, se,* ah-frer, *a* hideous; dreadful; shocking (news).

affriander, ăh-free-ahng-deh, *v* to entice.

affront, ăh-frong, *m* insult; disgrace.

affronter, ăh-frong-teh, *v* to confront; to dare; to face.

affubler, ăh-fE-bleh, *v* to muffle up; **s'–,** to rig oneself out.

affût, ăh-fE, *m* lying in wait (for game); carriage (gun); **être à l'–,** ay-tr ăh l–, to be on the watch (**de,** for).

affûter, ăh-fE-teh, *v* to sharpen.

afin, ăh-fang, *conj* **– de,** in order to; **– que,** in order that.

agacement, ăh-găhss-mahng, *m* annoyance.

agacer, ăh-găh-seh, *v* to set on edge; to irritate; to provoke; to tease.

agacerie, ăh-găhss-ree, *f* provocation; *pl* allurement.

âge, ahsh, *m* age; old age; period; generation.

âgé, e, ah-sheh, *a* aged; old.

agence, ăh-shahngss, *f* agency.

agencement, ăh-shahngss-mahng, *m* arrangement (of house); *pl* fittings; fixtures.

agenda, ăh-shang-dăh, *m* memorandum book; diary.

agenouiller (s'), săhsh-noo'e-yeh, *v* to kneel.

agent, ăh-shahng, *m* agent; middleman; policeman; **– de voyages,** – der-vo'ăh-yăhsh travel agent.

agglomérer (s'), săh-glomm-eh-reh, *v* to agglomerate.

agglomérer (s'), săh-glomm-eh-reh, *v* to agglomerate.

aggravation, ăh-grăh-văh-se-ong, *f* aggravation; worsening.

aggraver, ăh-grăh-veh, *v* to aggravate; to make worse; to increase; **s'–,** to become worse.

agile,* ăh-shill, *a* nimble; quick.

agir, ăh-sheer, *v* to act; to do; to work; **de quoi s'agit-il?** der kwăh săh-she-till? what is the matter? **il s'agit de ...,** ill săh-she der ... the matter, thing, or question is (about, to) ...

agiter, ăh-she-teh, *v* to agitate; to shake; to toss; to wave; **s'–,** to exert oneself; to fret; to swell; to get disturbed.

agneau, ăhn-yoh, *m* lamb.

agonie, ăh-gonn-ee, *f* death-struggle; anguish;

great pain. **à l'–**, ăh-l–, dying.

agonisant, ăh-gonn-e-zahng, *a* dying.

agrafe, ăh-grăhf, *f* hook; clasp; staple.

agrafeuse, ăh-grăh-ferz, *f* stapler.

agraire, ăh-grair, *a* agrarian.

agrandir, ăh-grahng-deer, *v* to enlarge; to expand; to magnify; **s'–**, to become larger; to become richer.

agrandissement, ăh-grahng-diss-mahng, *m* enlargement.

agréable,* ăh-greh-ăh-bl, *a* agreeable; pleasing; acceptable.

agréé, ăh-greh-eh, *m* solicitor; attorney.

agrégation, ăh-greh-găh-se-ong, *f* competitive exam conducted by the State for admission to teaching posts.

agrégé, e ăh-greh-sheh, *mf* holder of the aggrégation.

agrément, ăh-greh-mahng, *m* consent; favour; pleasure; *pl* charms.

agrés, ăh-gray, *m pl* rigging; tackle.

agresseur, ăh-grayss-er, *m* aggressor.

agreste, ăh-gresst, *a* rustic.

agricole, ăh-gre-kol, *a* agricultural.

agriculteur, ăh-gree-kEEl-ter, *m* agriculturist; farmer.

agripper, ăh-gre-peh, *v* to clutch.

aguerrir, ăh-ghay-reer, *v* to inure to war; to harden; to accustom; **s'–**, to become inured to war; hardened; accustomed.

aguets, ăh-ghay, *mpl* **aux –**, oh z'–, on the watch.

ahurir, ăh-E-reer, *v* to astound; to confuse.

ahurissement, ăh-E-riss-mahng, *m* flurry; bewilderment.

aide, ayd, *mf* helper; assistant.

aide, ayd, *f* help; assistance; **à l'–!** ăh l–! help!

aider, ay-deh, *v* to assist; to help.

aïe, ăh-e, *int* oh dear! oh! (pain).

aïeul, ăh-yerl, *m* grandfather

aïeule, ăh-yerl, *f* grandmother.

aïeux, ăh-yer, *mpl* ancestors; forefathers.

aigle, ay-gl, *m* eagle; lectern; *f* standard.

aiglon, ay-glong, *m* eaglet.

aigre,* ay-gr, *a* sour; acid; tart.

aigrefin, ay-grer-fang, *m* swindler; haddock.

aigrelet, te, ay-grer-lay, *a* sourish.

aigrette, ay-grett, *f* egret; tuft.

aigreur, ay-grer, *f* sourness; acrimony; ill-feeling; spite.

aigrir, ay-greer, *v* to sour; to irritate; to envenom; **s'–**, to become sour; to become embittered.

aigu, ë, ay-ghE, *a* sharp; pointed; acute; shrill.

aiguille, ay-gwee-yer, *f* needle; hand (of clock, watch); index; spire; switch; point (rail).

aiguillette, ay-gwee-yet, *f* tagged-lace; slice of flesh.

aiguilleur, ay-gwee-yer, *m* pointsman.

aiguillon, ay-gwee-yong, *m* goad; sting; prickle; thorn; spur.

aiguillonner, ay-gwee-yonn-eh, *v* to goad; to spur on.

aiguiser, ay-gwee-zeh, *v* to whet; to sharpen.

ail, ăh'e, *m* garlic.

aile, ayl, *f* wing; sail; aisle; flank (of army, of fleet).

ailé, e, ay-leh, *a* winged.

aileron, ayl-rong, *m* pinion; small wing; fin.

ailette, ay-lehtt, *f* winglet.

ailleurs, ăh'e-yer, *adv* elsewhere; **d'–,** moreover.

aimable,* ay-măh-bl, *a* amiable; lovable; kind; pleasing.

aimant, ay-mahng, *m* loadstone; magnet.

aimant, e, ay-mahng, *a* loving; affectionate.

aimanter, ay-mahng-teh, *v* to magnetize.

aimer, ay-meh, *v* to love; to like; to be fond of; to enjoy; **s'–,** to love each other.

aine, ayn, *f* groin.

aîné, e, ay-neh, *a & n* elder; eldest.

aînesse, ayness, *f* primogeniture; **droit d'–,** dro'ăh d–, birthright.

ainsi, ang-se, *adv & conj* so, thus; therefore, – **que,** – ker, as well as; – **de suite,** – der sweet, so on; – **soit-il,** – so'ăh-till, amen!

air, air *m* air; wind; look; appearance; likeness; tune; **avoir l'– de,** ăh-vo'ăhr l– der, to look like; **en l'–,** ahng l–, in the air; upward; at random.

airain, ay-rang, *m* brass; **d'–,** d–, pitiless; hard.

aire, air, *f* area; threshing-floor; zone.

ais, ay, *m* plank; board.

aisance, ay-zahngss, *f* ease; comfort; competency; **être dans l'–,** ay-tr dahng l–, to be well off.

aise, ayz, *f* ease; comfort; enjoyment; **à l'–,** ăh l–, comfortable.

aise, ayz, *a* glad; pleased (**de,** of, with).

aisé, e,* ay-zeh, *a* easy; well off; comfortable.

aisselle, ayss-ell, *f* armpit.

ajonc, ăh-shong, *m* furze; gorse.

ajourner, ăh-shoohr-neh, *v* to postpone; to put off; to defer; to summon; **s'–,** to adjourn.

ajouter, ăh-shoo-teh, *v* to add; **s'–,** to be added.

ajuster, ăh-shEES-teh, *v* to adjust; to fit; to arrange; to reconcile; to aim at; **s'–,** to be adjusted; adapted; to adapt oneself; to fit.

alanguir, ăh-lahng-gheer, *v* to make languid; to enfeeble; to weaken.

alarme, ăh-lăhrm, *f* alarm.

alarmer, ăh-lăhr-meh, *v* to alarm; **s'–,** to take fright.

albâtre, ăhl-bah-tr, *m* alabaster; snowy whiteness.

albumine, ăhl-bE-meen, *f* albumen.

alcali, ăhl-kăh-le, *m* alkali.

alcool, ăhl-kohl, *m* alcohol; spirits.

alcoolique, ăhl-koll-eeck, *mf* alcoholic.

alcoolisme, ăhl-koh-lissm, *m* alcoholism.

alcôve, ăhl-kohv, *f* alcove; recess.

alcyon, ăhl-se-ong, *m* king fisher; halcyon.

aléa, ăh-leh-ăh, *m* risk, chance.

aléatoire, ăh-leh-ăh-to'ăhr, *a* risky; hazardous.

alêne, ăh-laynn, *f* awl.

alentour, ăh-lahng-toohr, *adv* around; about.

alentours, ăh-lahng-toohr, *mpl* neighbourhood; surroundings; outskirts.

alerte, ăh-layrt, *f* alarm; alert.

alerte, ăh-layrt, *a* alert; sharp; quick; nimble.

algue, ăhl-gh, *f* alga; seaweed.

aliénable, ăh-le-eh-năh-bl, *a* transferable.

aliénation, ăh-le-eh-năh-se-*ong*, *f* transfer; estrangement; madness.

aliéné, e, ăh-le-eh-neh, *n* & *a* lunatic; mad(man).

aliéner, ăh-le-eh-neh, *v* to transfer; to alienate; to estrange.

aligner, ăh-leen-yeh, *v* to set in a line; **s'–,** to fall in.

aliment, ăh-le-mah*ng*, *m* food.

alimentaire, ăh-le-mah*ng*-tair, *a* dietary; nutritious, alimentary.

alinéa, ăh-le-neh-ăh, *m* paragraph.

alité, e, ăh-le-teh, *pp* & *a* laid up; bed-ridden.

aliter, ăh-le-teh, *v* to confine to bed; **s'–,** to take to one's bed.

allaiter, ăh-lay-teh, *v* to suckle; to nurse.

allant, ăh-lah*ng*, *pres part* & *a* going; active; stirring.

allécher, ăh-leh-sheh, *v* to allure; to entice.

allée, ăh-leh, *f* going; alley; passage; lane; path; **–s et venues,** –z'eh ver-nE, coming and going; running about.

allége, ăh-laysh, *f* barge; tender; sill (window).

alléger, ăh-leh-sheh, *v* to

lighten; to unload; to ease.

allégre, * ăh-lay-gr, *a* lively; cheerful.

allégresse, ăhl-leh-gress, *f* cheerfulness; glee.

alléguer, ăhl-leh-gheh, *v* to allege.

allemand, e, ăhl-mah*ng*, *a* & *n* German.

aller, ăh-leh, *v* to go; to get on; to become; to fit; to suit; **comment allez-vous?** komm-ahng t'ăh-leh voo? how are you?; **cette veste vous va bien,** set-vaysst-voo-văh-be-ang, this jacket suits you (or fits you) well; **s'en –,** sahng n'–, to go away.

aller, ăh-leh, *m* **billet d'– et retour,** bee-yay d–eh-rer-toor, return ticket.

allergie, ăh-lair-shee, *f* allergy.

allergique (à), ăh-lair-sheeck, *a* allergic.

alliage, ăh-le-ăhsh, *m* alloy.

alliance, ăh-le-ahngss, *f* alliance; match; wedding-ring.

allier, ăh-le-eh, *v* to ally; to match; to blend; to mix; to alloy; **s'–** to combine; to unite (**à,**

with); to intermarry; to harmonize with.

allô!, ăh-loh *int* hello (on phone).

allocation, ăh-lock-ăh-se-*ong*, *f* allowance; grant.

allocution, ăh-lock-E-se-*ong*, *f* short speech.

allonge, ăh-long*sh*, *f* (table) extension.

allonger, ăh-long-sheh, *v* to lengthen; to prolong; **s'–,** to grow longer; to lie down.

allouer, ăh-loo-eh, *v* to allow; to grant.

allumer, ăh-lE-meh, *v* to light; to kindle; **s'–,** to light up; to catch fire.

allumette, ăh-lE-mett, *f* match.

allumeur, ăh-lE-mer, *m* igniter; lamplighter.

allure, ăh-lEEr, *f* gait; pace; manner; aspect.

allusion, ăhl-lE-ze-*ong*, *f* allusion; **faire – à,** fayr – ăh, to allude to.

aloi, ăh-lo'ăh, *m* standard; quality; condition; **de bon –,** der-bong–, genuine.

alors, ăh-lor, *adv* then; at that time; in that case.

alouette, ăh-loo-ett, *f* lark.

alourdir, ăh-loor-deer, *v* to render heavy; **s' –,** to become heavy.

aloyau, ăh-lo'ăh-e-oh, *m* sirloin.

alpestre, ăhl-pess-tr, *a* Alpine.

alphabet, ăhl-făh-bett, *m* alphabet.

alpinisme, ăhl-pe-nism *m* mountaineering.

altérable, ăhl-teh-răh-bl, *a* liable to (negative) change.

altérant, e, ăhl-teh-rahng, *a* alterative; producing thirst.

altération, ăhl-teh-răh-se-ong, *f* change; deterioration; misrepresentation; falsification; faltering; thirst.

altercation, ăhl-tayr-se-ong, *f* wrangling.

altéré, e, ăhl-teh-reh, *a* altered; thirsty.

altérer, ăhl-teh-reh, *v* to alter; to impair; to debase; to misrepresent; to falsify; to make thirsty; **s'–,** to become worse.

alternati-f, -ive, * ăhl-tair-năh-tiff, *a* alternative; alternating; **-ive,** *f* alternative.

alterner, ăhl-ter-neh, *v* to alternate; to take turns.

altesse, ăhl-tess, *f* Highness.

altitude, ăhl-tee-tEEd, *f* altitude.

alto, ăhl-to, *m* tenor violin.

alun, ăh-lung, *m* alum.

alvéole, ăl-veh-ol, *f* cell; socket.

amabilité, ăh-măh-be-le-teh, *f* pleasantness; kindness.

amadouer, ăh-măh-doo-eh, *v* to coax.

amaigrir, ăh-may-greer, *v* to make thin; to emaciate.

amaigrissant, e, ăh-may-gre-ssahng, *a* slimming.

amande, ăh-mahngd, *f* almond.

amandier, ăh-mahng-de-eh, *m* almond tree.

amant, e, ăh-mahng, *mf* lover; suitor; sweetheart.

amarrer, ăh-măh-reh, *v* to moor; to fasten; to lash.

amas, ăh-măh, *m* heap; pile; mass.

amasser, ăh-măhss-eh, *v* to amass; to heap up; **s'–,** to gather.

ama-teur, -trice, ăh-măh-ter, *mf* amateur; lover; admirer; enthusiast; fan.

amazone, ăh-măh-zohn, *f* amazon; horse woman; *m* riding-habit; the Amazon river.

ambassade, ăhng-băhss-

ăhd, *f* embassy.

ambassa-deur, -drice, ăhng-băhss-ăh-der, *mf* ambassador; ambassadress.

ambiance, ahng-be-ahngss, *f* atmosphere (of surroundings; environment etc.).

ambiant, e, ahng-be-ahng, *a* surroundings; ambient.

ambigu, ë, ahng-be-ghE, *a* ambiguous; obscure.

ambitieu-x, se, * ahng-be-se-er, *a* ambitious; pretentious; *n* ambitious person.

ambition, ahng-be-se-ong, *f* ambition.

ambre, ahng-br, *m* amber.

ambulance, ahng-bE-lahngss, *f* ambulance.

ambulancier, ahng-bE-lahngss-e-eh, *m* ambulanceman; orderly.

ambulant, e, ahng-bE-lahng, *a* itinerant; strolling; travelling (circus, etc.).

âme, ahmm, *f* soul; mind; spirit; life; feeling; ghost; heart; essence; core; creature; bore (of gun); valve.

améliorer, ăh-meh-le-o-reh, *v* to improve; to make better; **s'–,** to get better.

aménagement, ăh-meh-năhsh, *m* fitting; disposition; *pl* fittings; accommodation.

aménager, ăh-meh-năh-sheh, *v* to arrange; to fit up (a house).

amende, ăh-mahngd, *f* fine; penalty; costs; – **honorable,** –onn-or-ăh-bl, apology.

amendement, ăh-mahngd-mahng, *m* amendment; improvement.

amender, ăh-mahng-deh, *v* to improve.

amener, ăhm-neh, *v* to bring; to introduce; to bring in, on or about; **mandat d'–,** mahng-dăh d–, warrant for arrest; capias.

am-er, ère, * ăh-mair, bitter.

américain, e, ăh-meh-re-kang, *a & mf* American.

amertume, ăh-mair-tEEm, *f* bitterness.

ameublement, ăh-mer-bler-mahng, *m* furniture.

ameuter, ăh-mer-teh, *v* to train to hunt together; to excite; **s'–,** to rebel; to riot.

ami, e, ăh-me, *mf* friend; **chambre d'–,** shahng-br d–, spare room; *a* friendly to; fond of.

amiable, ăh-me-ăh-bl, *a* amicable; **à l'–,** ăh l–, amicably; by private contract.

amical, e, * ăh-me-kăhl, *a* friendly; kind.

amidon, ăh-me-dong, *m* starch.

amincir, ăh-mang-seer, *v* to make thinner; **s'–,** to become thinner.

amiral, ăh-me-răhl, *m* admiral; **contre –,** kong-tr' –, rear admiral.

amirauté, ăh-me-roh-teh, *f* admiralty.

amitié, ăh-me-te-eh, *f* friendship; *pl* kind regards; compliments; love.

ammoniaque, ăh-monn-e-ăhck, *f* ammonia.

amnésie, ăh-meh-nee-zee, *f* loss of memory; amnesia.

amnistie, ăhm-niss-tee, *f* amnesty; general pardon.

amoindrir, ăh-mo'ang-dreer, *v* to diminish.

amollir, ăh-moll-eer, *v* to soften; to mollify; to enervate.

amonceler, ăh-mongss-leh, *v* to heap up.

amont, ăh-mong, *m* head waters; **en –,** ang –, upstream.

amorce, ăh-morss, *f* bait; priming; cap.

amortir, ăh-mor-teer, *v* to deaden; to pay off; to redeem; **s'–,** to grow weak or faint.

amortissable, ăh-mor-tiss-ăh-bl, *a* redeemable.

amortissement, ăh-mor-tiss-mahng, *m* paying off; redemption; (radio) damping.

amortisseur, ăh-mor-tiss-er, *m* shock-absorber.

amour, ăh-moohr, *m* love; passion; **--propre,** – pro-pr, self-love; self-esteem.

amourette, ăh-moo-rett, *f* petty love affair; passing fancy.

amoureu-x, se, * ah-moo-rer, *a* in love; enamoured.

amovible, ăh-mov-ee-bl, *a* removable.

ampère, ahng-pair, *m* ampere.

ampèremètre, ahng-pair-met-tr, *m* ammeter.

amphibie, ahng-fe-bee, *a* amphibious.

ample, * ahng-pl, *a* ample; spacious; large; copious.

ampleur, ahng-pler, *f* ampleness; largeness; fullness.

ampliation, ahng-ple-ăh-se-ong, *f* duplicate; true

copy; **pour –**, poohr –, a true copy.

amplification, ahng-ple, fe-käh-se-ong, *f* enlargement.

amplifier, ahng-ple-fe-eh, *v* to enlarge upon.

amplitude, ahng-ple-tEEd, *f* amplitude.

ampoule, ahng-pool, *f* blister; phial; (electric light) bulb.

ampoulé, e, ahng-pool-eh, *a* blistered; bombastic.

amputer, ahng-pE-teh, *v* to amputate.

amuser, äh-mE-zeh, *v* to amuse; to entertain; to deceive; **s'–,** to enjoy oneself.

amuse-gueule, äh-mEEz-gherl, *m* cocktail snack.

amygdale, äh-meegh-dähl, *f* tonsil.

an, ahng, *m* year, **jour de l'–, s**hoohr der l–, New Year's day.

analogue äh-näh-log, *a* analogous.

analyser, äh-näh-le-zeh, *v* to analyze; to parse; to criticize.

ananas, äh-näh-näh, *m* pineapple.

anarchie, äh-nähr-shee, *f* anarchy.

anathème, äh-näh-taym, *m* anathema.

ancêtre, ahng-say-tr, *m* ancestor.

anchois, ahng-sho'äh, *m* anchovy.

ancien, ahng-se-ang, *m* elder; senior.

ancien, ne, * ahng-se-ang, *a* ancient; old; past; former; retired.

ancienneté, ahng-se-enn-teh, *f* antiquity; seniority; age.

ancre, ahng-kr, *f* anchor; **lever l'–,** ler-veh l–, to weigh anchor; **– de salut,** – der säh-lE, sheet anchor.

andouille, ahng-doo'e-yer, *f* chitterlings; idiot

andouilette, ahng-doo'e-yette, *f* small sausage.

âne, ahn, *m* donkey; dunce.

anéantir, äh-neh-ahng-teer, *v* to annihilate; to destroy; to tire out.

anéantissement, äh-neh-ahng-tiss-mahng, *m* annihilation; utter exhaustion; self-humiliation.

anèmie, äh-neh-mee, *f* anaemia.

anémique, äh-neh meeck, *a med* anaemic.

ânerie, ahn-ree, *f* stupidity; gr**o**ss ignorance; blunder.

anesthésie, äh-ness-teh-ze, *f* anaesthesia.

anesthésiste, äh-ness-teh-zist, *m* anaesthetist.

anévrisme, äh-neh-vrissm, *m* aneurism.

ange, ahngsh, *m* angel; **être aux–,** ay-tr oh z' –, to be overjoyed.

angine, ahng-**s**heen, *f* sore-throat.

anglais, ahng-glay, *a* English (language); *n* English *m*.

angle, ahng-gl, *m* angle; corner.

Angleterre, ahng-gler-tair, *f* England.

angliciser, ahng-gle-se-zeh, *v* to anglicize.

anglicisme, ahng-gle-sissm, *m* anglicism.

angoisse, ahng-gwähss, *f* anguish; pang.

anguille, ahng-ghee-yer, *f* eel; **– sous roche,** – soo rosh, a snake in the grass.

anicroche, äh-ne-krosh, *f* hitch.

animal, äh-ne-mähl, *n* & *a* animal; sensual; brutal.

animer, äh-ne-meh, *v* to animate; to enliven; to cheer; to excite; to jazz up; **s'–,** to become excited, warm, angry; to encourage each other.

anis, ăh-ne, *m* aniseed.

ankylose, ahng-ke-lohz, *f* stiffness.

anneau, ăh-noh, *m* ring.

année, ăh-neh, *f* year; crop; vintage.

annelé, e, ăhn-leh, *a* ringed.

annexe, ăh-nex, *f* annex; rider; schedule.

annihilation, ăhn-ne-ee-lăh-se-ong, *f* annihilation.

anniversaire, ăh-ne-vair-sair, *m* & *a* anniversary; birthday.

annonce, ăh-nongss, *f* announcement; advertisement.

annoncer, ăh-nong-seh, *v* to announce; to foretell; **s'– bien,** s– be-ang, to look promising.

annoter, ăhn-no-teh, *v* to annotate.

annuaire, ăhn-nE-air, *m* year-book; almanac; calendar; directory.

annulaire, ăhn-nE lair, *m* ring-finger, *a* annular.

annulation, ăhn-nE-lăh-se-ong, *f* cancelling.

annuler, ăhn-nE-leh, *v* to annul, to cancelling.

anoblir, ăh-nob-leer, *v* to ennoble.

anodin, e, ăh-nod-ang, *a* & *m* mild; pain killer.

anomalie, ăh-nomm-ăh-lee, *f* anomaly.

ânon, ah-nong, *m* little donkey.

ânnoner, ah-nonn-eh, *v* to falter, to mumble.

anonyme, * ** ăh-nonn-eem, *a* anonymous; **société –, soss-e-eh-teh –, joint-stock company.

anorak, ăh-noh-răhck, *m* anorak.

**anormal, e, * ** ăh-nor-măhl, *a* abnormal.

anse, ahngss, *f* handle; cove.

antan, ahng-tahng, *m* yesteryear.

antécédent, ahng-teh-seh-dăhng, *a* & *m* previous; antecedent.

antenne, ahng-tenn, *f* antenna; feeler; horn; (radio) aerial.

**antérieur, e,* ** ahng-teh-re-er, *a* former; past; front.

antériorité, ahng-teh-re-o-re-teh, *f* priority.

anthère, ăhng-tair, *f* anther; tip.

anthropophage, ahng-trop-of-ăhsh, *a* & *m* cannibal.

antibiotique, ahng-te-be-oh-teeck, *a* & *m* antibiotic.

anticonceptionnel, le ahng-te-kong-sep-se-ong-nell, *a* contraceptive.

antidérapant, ahng-te-deh-răh-pahng, *a* non-skid (tyre).

antidote, ahng-te-dott, *m* antidote.

antienne, ahng-te-enn, *f* anthem.

antihistaminique, anng-te-iss-tăh-me-neeck *m* antihistamine.

antiquaire, ahng-te-kair, *m* antique dealer; antiquarian.

antiquité, ahng-te-ke-teh, *f* antiquity; *pl* antiques.

antiseptique, ahng-te-sayp-tick, *a* & *m* antiseptic.

antre, ahng-tr, *m* cave; den.

anxiété, ahngk-se-eh-teh, *f* anxiety.

**anxieu-x, se,* ** ahngk-se-er, *a* anxious; uneasy.

août, ăh'oo, or oo, *m* August.

apache, ăh-păhsh, *m* Apache; hooligan.

apaiser, ăh-pay-zeh, *v* to appease; **s' – ,** to subside; to abate; to compose oneself.

apanage, ăh-păh-năhsh, *m* appanage; attribute; lot.

aparté, ăh-păhr-teh, *m* words spoken aside.

apartheid, ah-păhr-teh-eed *m* apartheid.

apercevoir, ăh-pair-ser-vo'ăhr, *v* to perceive; **s'–** (de or que), to notice.

apercu, ăh-pair-SE, *m* glance; summary view.

apéritif, ăh-peh-re-teef *m* apéritif.

aphthe, ăhft, *m* mouth ulcer.

apitoyer, ăh-pe-to'ah-e-eh, *v* to move to compassion; **s' –**, to pity.

aplanir, ăh-plăh-neer, *v* to level; to smooth.

aplatir, ăh-plăh-teer, *v* to flatten.

aplomb, ăh-plong, *m* perpendicularity; self-possession; audacity; **d' –**, upright.

apogée, ăh-po-sheh, *m* apogee; greatest height; peak.

apologie, ăh-poll-o-shee, *f* apology; vindication.

apostat, ăh-poss-tăh, *m* apostate.

aposter, ăh-poss-teh, *v* to set on watch (a spy).

apostolat, ăh-poss-toll-ăh, *m* apostleship.

apostrophe, ăh-poss-trof, *f* apostrophe; address; reproach.

apostropher, ăh-poss-trof-eh, *v* to address; to challenge.

apothicaire, ăh-po-te-kair, *m* apothecary; **compte d' –**, kongt d–, exorbitant bill.

apôtre, ăh-poh-tr, *m* apostle.

apparaître, ăh-păh-ray-tr, *v* to appear.

apparat, ăh-păh-răh, *m* pomp; state; **d' –**, formal.

appareil, ăh-păh-ray'e, *m* preparation; display; apparatus; appliance.

appareiller, ăh-păh-ray'e-eh, *v* to match; to set sail.

apparemment, ăh-păh-răh-mahng, *adv* apparently.

apparence, ăh-păh-rahngss, *f* appearance.

apparent, e, ăh-păh-rahng, *a* apparent.

apparenté, e, ăh-păh-rahng-teh, *a* related.

apparition, ăh-păh-re-se-ong, *f* appearance; publication; ghost.

appartement, ăh-păhr-ter-mahng, *m* suite of rooms; flat.

appartenir, ăh-păhr-ter-neer, *v* to belong to; to concern.

appas, ăh-pah, *mpl* attractions; charms.

appât, ăh-pah, *m* bait; allurement.

appauvrir, ăh-poh-vreer, *v* to impoverish.

appel, ăh-pell, *m* call; appeal; muster.

appeler, ăhp-leh, *v* to call; to appeal; to name; **s' –**, to be called.

appendice, ăh-pang-diss, *m* appendix; appendage.

appendicite, ăh-pang-de-sit, *f* appendicitis.

appesantir, ăh-per-zahng-teer, *v* to make heavy; **s' –**, to become heavy; to dwell (**sur**, upon).

appesantissement, ăh-per-zahng-tiss-mahng, *m* heaviness; dullness.

appétissant, e, ăh-peh-tiss-ahng, *a* appetising; tempting.

appétit, ăh-peh-te, *m* appetite; hunger; **l'–vient en mangeant**, l– ve-*ang* t'ahng mahng-shahng, the more one has, the more one wants.

applaudir, ăh-ploh-deer, *v* to applaud; to commend; **s'– (de**, on), to congratulate oneself.

applaudissement, ăh-ploh-diss-mahng, *m*

applause; cheering.

application, ăh-ple-käh-se-ong, f application; attention; diligence; appropriation.

applique, ăh-pleek, f bracket; inlaid work.

appliqué, e, ăh-ple-keh, pp & a applied; studios; diligent.

appliquer, ăh-ple-keh, v to apply; to lay on; to adapt; to devote; **s' –**, to be applied; to be applicable to; to apply oneself.

appoint, ăh-po'ang, m balance; odd money.

appointements, ăh-po'angt-mahng, mpl salary.

apport, ăh-por, m share of capital; pl vendor's shares.

apporter, ăh-por-teh, v to bring (something portable).

apposer, ăh-poh-zeh, v to affix; to append; to add.

apposition, ăh-poh-ze-se-ong, f affixing; apposition.

apprécier, ăh-preh-se-eh, v to appreciate; to value.

appréhender, ăh-preh-ahng-deh, v to apprehend; to arrest; to fear.

appréhension, ăh-preh-ahng-se-ong, f apprehension; fear.

apprendre, ăh-prahng-dr, v to learn; to hear; to teach; to inform.

apprenti, ăh-prahng-te, m apprentice; novice.

apprentissage, ăh-prahng-tiss-ähsh, m apprenticeship.

apprêt, ăh-pray, m preparation; dressing of food; affection.

appris, e, ăh-pre, pp learnt; taught; **malappris,** măh-lăh-pre, ill-bred.

apprivoiser, ăh-pre-vo'äh-zeh, v to tame.

approba-teur, trice, ăh-pro-băh-ter, mf approver; a approving, of approval.

approbati-f, ve,* ăh-pro-băh-tiff, a approbatory, of approval.

approbation, ăh-pro-băh-se-ong, f approval.

approchant, e, ăh-pro-shahng, a near; like; approximate; adv thereabouts.

approche, ăh-prosh, f approach; access.

approcher, ăh-pro-sheh, v to approach; to bring near; **s'–**, to come near.

approfondi, e, ăh-pro-fong-de, a profound; thorough.

approfondir, ăh-pro-fong-deer, v to deepen; to sift.

approprier, ăh-pro-pre-eh, v to appropriate; to adapt; **s' –**, to appropriate to oneself.

approuver, ăh-proo-veh, v to approve.

approvisionnement, ăh-pro-ve-ze-onn-mahng, m victuals; supply; stores.

approvisionner, ăh-pro-ve-ze-onn-eh, v to provide; **s'–**, to provide oneself (**de,** with); to lay in store.

approximati-f, ve,* ăh-prock-se-mäh-tiff, a approximate; rough.

appui, ăh-pwe, m support; sill.

appuyer, ăh-pwe-yeh, v to support; to prop; to insist; **s'–**, to lean; to rely (**sur,** on).

âpre, ah-pr, a rough; harsh; severe.

après, ăh-pray, prep after; adv afterwards; **d'–**, from, according to; et –?eh–? what then?

après-demain, ăh-prayd-mang, adv the day after tomorrow.

après-dîner, ăh-pray-de-neh, *m* after dinner.

après-midi, ăh-pray-me-de, m & *f* afternoon.

âpreté, ah-prer-teh, *f* roughness; harshness; greediness.

apte, ăh-pt, *a* fit, capable, qualified (**à,** of, for).

aptitude, ăhp-te-tEEd, *f* aptitude, fitness (**à,** to; **pour,** for).

apurer, ăh-pE-reh, *v* to audit.

aquarelle, ăh-ko'ăh-rell, *f* water-colour.

aquarium, ăh-ko'ăh-re-omm, *m* aquarium.

aquatique, ăh-ko'ăh-tick, *a* aquatic.

aqueduc, ăhck-dEEk, *m* aqueduct.

aquilin, ăh-ke-lang, *a* aquiline.

aquilon, ăh-ke-long, *m* north wind; cold wind.

arable, ăh-răh-bl, *a* arable; tillable.

arachide, ăh-răh-sheed, *f* ground-nut.

araignée, ăh-rayn-yeh, *f* spider.

aratoire, ăh-răh-to'ăhr, *a* agricultural.

arbalète, ăhr-băh-lett, *f* cross-bow.

arbitrage, ăhr-be-trăhsh, *m* arbitration.

arbitraire,* ăhr-be-trayr, *a* arbitrary; despotic.

arbitre, ăhr-bee-tr, *m* arbitrator; umpire; master; **libre –,** lee-br' –, free will.

arborer, ăhr-bor-eh, *v* to set up; to hoist; to don.

arbre, ăhr-br, *m* tree; shaft; axle.

arbrisseau, ăhr-bre-soh, *m* small tree.

arbuste, ăhr-bEEst, *m* shrub.

arc, ăhrk, *m* bow; arc; arch.

arcade, ăhr-kăhd, *f* row of arches; arcade.

arc-boutant, ăhrk-boo-tahng, *m* buttress.

arceau, ăhr-soh, *m* arch; vault.

arc-en-ciel, ăhr-kahng-se-ell, *m* rainbow.

archange, ăhr-kahngsh, *m* archangel.

arche, ăhrsh, *f* arch; ark.

archaéologie, ăhr-keh-o-lo-shee *f* archaeology.

archéologue, ăhr-keh-o-log, *m* archeologist.

archer, ăhr-sheh, *m* bowman.

archet, ăhr-shay, *m* bow; fiddlestick.

archevêque, ăhr-sher-vayk, *m* archbishop.

archidiacre, ăhr-she-de-

ăh-kr, *m* archdeacon.

archiduc, ăhr-she-dEEk, *m* archduke.

archiduchesse, ăhr-she-dE-shess, *f* archduchess.

archipel, ăhr-she-pell, *m* archipelago.

architecte, ăhr-she-teckt, *m* architect.

architecture, ăhr-she-teck-tEEr, *f* architecture.

archives, ăhr-sheev, *fpl* archives; records; recording office.

arçon, ăhr-song, *m* saddlebow.

ardemment, ăhr-dăh-mahng, *adv* ardently; eagerly; passionately.

ardent, e, ăhr-dahng, *a* burning; glowing; eager.

ardeur, ăhr-der, *f* ardour; eagerness; heat; spirit.

ardoise, ăhr-do'ăhz, *f* slate.

ardoisière, ăhr-do'ăh-ze-air, *f* slate-quarry.

ardu, e, ăhr-dE, *a* arduous; difficult.

are, ăhr, *m* unit of land measure in the French metrical system, (equal to 100 square metres, or 119.60 square yards).

arène, ăh-rain, *f* arena; ring.

arène, ăh-rayt, *f* fish-bone; edge; ridge.

argent, ăhr-**shahng,** *m* silver; money; cash; – **comptant,** –kong-tahng, ready money;– **fou,** – foo, lots of money.

argenté, e, ăhr-shahng-teh, *a* silvered; silver-white.

argenter, ăhr-shahng-teh, *v* to plate.

argenterie, ăhr-shahng-tree, *f* silver plate; plate.

argille, ăhr-sheel, f clay.

argileu-x, se, ăhr-she-ler, *a* clayey.

argot, ăhr-gho, *m* slang.

arguer, ăhr-ghE-eh, *v* to argue; to infer; to accuse.

argument, ăhr-ghE-mahng, *m* argument; reasoning; plea; summary.

argumenter, ăhr-ghE-mahng-teh, *v* to argue; to infer (**de,** from).

argus, ăhr-ghEEss, *m* argus; clear-sighted person; second-hand car price guide.

argutie, ăhr-ghE-see, *f* quibble.

aride,* ăh-reed, *a* arid; dry; barren.

aridité, ăh-re-de-teh, *f* aridity; dryness; barrenness.

aristocratie, ăh-riss-to-krăh-see, *f* aristocracy.

arithmétique, ăh-reet-meh-tick, *f* arithmetic.

arlequin, ăhr-ler-kang, *m* harlequin.

arlequinade, ăhr-ler-ke-năhd, *f* harlequinade; buffoonery.

armateur, ăhr-măh-ter, *m* ship-owner.

armature, ăhr-măh-tEEr, *f* iron-work; framework; fittings.

arme, ăhrm, *f* weapon; arm; **maître d'** –, may-tr d–, fencing master; **faire des–s,** fair day z'–, to fence.

armée, ăhr-meh, *f* army; multitude.

armement, ăhr-mer-mahng, *m* armament.

armer, ăhr-meh, *v* to arm (**de,** with); to set against (**contre,** kong-tr); to cock; to equip; **s'**–, to arm oneself (**de,** with); to summon up.

armoire, ăhr-mo'ăhr, *f* cupboard; wardrobe.

armoiries, ăhr-mo'ăh-ree, *fpl* arms; coat of arms.

armorial, ăhr-mo-re-ăhl, *m* book of heraldry.

armure, ăhr-mEEr, *f* armour.

armurier, ăhr-mE-re-eh, *m* gunsmith.

arnica, ăhr-ne-kăh, *mf* arnica.

aromatiser, ăh-ro-măh-te-zeh, *v* to aromatise; to perfume.

arome, ăh-rohm, *m* aroma; flavouring.

aronde, ăh-rongd, *f* **en queue d'–,** ahng ker d–, dovetailed.

arpège, ăhr-paish, *m* arpeggio.

arpent, ăhr-pahng, *m* acre.

arpentage, ăhr-pahng-tăhsh, *m* land surveying.

arpenter, ăhr-pahng-teh, *v* to survey; to stride along.

arpenteur, ăhr-pahng-ter, *m* land surveyor.

arquer, ăhr-keh, *v* to arch; to bend; **s'**–, to become curved.

arrache-pied (d'), dăh-răhsh-pe-eh, *adv* at a stretch; without interruption.

arracher, ăh-răh-sheh, *v* to force out; to pull out; to pluck out; to snatch; to tear away; to wrest; **s'** –, to tear oneself away; to break away (**à,** from).

arrangement, ăh-rahngsh-mahng, *m* arrangement; preparation; adjustment; accommodation.

arranger, ăh-rahng-sheh, *v*

to arrange; to settle; to repair; to suit; to trim up; **s' –**, to make shift (**de**, with); to come to an arrangement (**avec**, with).

arrérages, ăh-reh-răhsh, *mpl* arrears.

arrestation, ăh-ress-tăh-se-ong, *f* arrest; custody.

arrêt, ăh-ray, *m* decree; stop; catch.

arrêté, ăh-ray-teh, *m* decision; order; decree.

arrêter, ăh-ray-teh, *v* to stop; to detain; to restrain; to arrest; to fix; to resolve; to book; to engage; to conclude; **s'–**, to stop; to resolve (**à**, on).

arrhes, ăhr, *fpl* deposit (of money).

arrière, ăh-re-air, *m* back part; stern; *adv* behind; *interj* away!; **en –**, ahng n'–, backward; **–pensée**, – pahng-seh, *f* ulterior motive; **–plan**, – plahng, *m* background; **–saison**, – say-zong, *f* end of autumn; closing season.

arriéré, ăh-re-eh-reh, *m* arrears.

arriéré, e, ăh-re-eh-reh, *a* in arrears; backward (mentally).

arrimer, ăh-re-meh, *v* to stow.

arrimeur, ăh-re-mer, *m* stevedore.

arrivage, ăh-re-văhsh, *m* arrival (of cargo, goods).

arrivée, ăh-re-veh, *f* arrival.

arriver, ăh-re-veh, *v* to arrive (**à**, at); to come; to reach; to occur; to succeed; (with **de**) to become of; **arrive que pourra**, ăh-reev ker poo-răh, happen what may.

arriviste, ăh-re-visst, *m & f* pushy person; climber (social).

arrogamment, ăh-ro-găh-mahng, *adv* arrogantly.

arrogance, ăh-ro-gahngss, *f* arrogance.

arrogant, e, ăh-ro-gahng, *a* arrogant; haughty.

arroger (s'), săh-ro-sheh, *v* to arrogate to oneself; to assume.

arrondir, ăh-rong-deer, *v* toround; **s' –**, to become round; to increase.

arrondissement, ăh-rong-diss-mahng, *m* rounding; administrative district; borough.

arrosage, ăh-ro-zăhsh, *m* watering.

arroser, ăh-ro-zeh, *v* to water; to sprinkle; to

wet; to baste.

arrosoir, ăh-ro-zo'ăhr, *m* watering can; sprinkler.

arsenal, ăhr-ser-năhl, *m* arsenal; dockyard.

arsenic, ăhr-ser-nick, *m* arsenic.

art, ăhr, *m* art.

artère, ăhr-tair, *f* artery.

artériole, ăhr-teh-re-ol, *f* small artery.

artésien, ăhr-teh-ze-ang, *a* artesian.

arthrite, ăhr-treet, *f* arthritis.

artichaut, ăhr-te-shoh, *m* artichoke.

article, ăhr-tee-kl, *m* article; subject; thing; paragraph; item; goods; **–de fond**, – der fong, leading article.

articulation, ăhr-te-kE-lăh-se-ong, *f* articulation; joint.

articulé, e, ăhr-te-kE-leh, *a* articulated.

articuler, ăhr-te-kE-leh, *v* to utter; to pronounce; to set forth.

artifice, ăhr-te- fiss, *m* contrivance; deceit; **feu d' –**, fer d –, fireworks.

artificiel, le, * ăhr-te-fe-se-ell, *a* artificial.

artificieu-x, se, * ăhr-te-fe-se-er, *a* artful.

artillerie, ăhr-tee-yer-ree,

f artillery.

artilleur, ăhr-tee-yer, *m* artilleryman.

artisan, ăhr-te-zahng, *m* artisan; craftsman.

artiste, ăhr-tisst, *m* artist; actor; performer.

as, ahss, *m* ace; *fig* one who excels in some part.

asbeste, ăhz-best, *m* asbestos.

ascendance, ăhss-sahng-dahngss, *f* ascending line; ascendency.

ascendant, ăhss-sahng-dahng, *m* ascendency, *pl* fore-fathers.

ascendant, e, ăhss-sahng-dahng, *a* ascending.

ascenseur, ăhss-sahng-ser, *m* lift; hoist.

ascension, ăhss-sahng-se-ong, *f* ascension; ascent; Ascension day.

ascète, ăhss-sett, *m* ascetic; hermit.

ascétisme, ăhss-seh-tism, *m* asceticism.

asile, ăh-zeel, *m* asylum; shelter; refuge; sanctuary.

aspect, ăhss-pay, *m* aspect; view; appearance.

asperge, ăhss-pairsh, *f* asparagus.

asperger, ăhss-pair-sheh, *v* to sprinkle (**de,** with).

aspérité, ăhss-peh-re-teh, *f* roughness.

aspersion, ăhss-pair-se-ong, *f* aspersion; sprinkling.

asphalte, ăhss-făhlt, *m* asphalt.

asphyxier, ăhss-feek-se-eh, *v* to asphyxiate; to suffocate.

aspic, ăhss-pick, *m* asp; spike lavender; cold meat in jelly.

aspirant, ăhss-pe-rahng, *m* candidate.

aspirant, e, ăhss-pe-rahng, *a* suction (pump, etc).

aspiration, ăhss-pe-răh-se-ong, *f* inhalation; suction; *fig* longing.

aspirer, ăhss-pe-reh, *v* to inhale; to exhaust; to suck up; *fig* to long for.

aspirine, ăhss-pe-reen *f* aspirin.

assaillant, e, ăhss-sah'e-ahng, *n & a* assailant.

assaillir, ăhss-sah'eer, *v* to assail; to attack.

assainir, ăhss-ay-neer, *v* to make healthy.

assaisonnement, ăhss-ay-zonn-mahng, *m* seasoning; salad dressing.

assaisonner, ăhss-ay-zonn-eh, *v* to season; to dress (salad).

assassin, ăhss-ăh-sang, *m* murderer.

assaut, ăhss-oh, *m* assault; attack; fencing match.

assemblage, ăhss-ahng-blăsh, *m* assemblage; gathering; medley; joining.

assemblée, ăhss-ahng-bleh, *f* assembly; congregation; party; meeting.

assembler, ăhss-ahng-bleh, *v* to collect; to convoke; to join together; s' –, to meet; **qui se ressemble s'assemble,** kee ser rerss-ahng-bl săhss-ahng-bl, birds of a feather flock together.

asséner, ăhss-eh-neh, *v* to strike; to deal (a blow).

assentiment, ăhss-ahng-te-mahng, *m* assent.

asseoir, ăhss-o'ăhr, *v* to seat; s'–, to sit down.

assermenter, ăhss-air-mahng-teh, *v* to swear in.

assertion, ăhss-air-se-ong, *f* assertion.

asservir, ăhss-air-veer, *v* to enslave; to subdue.

asservissement, ăhss-air-viss-mahng *m* enslavement; slavery.

assesseur, ăhss-ess-er, *m* assessor; assistant; judge.

assez, ăhss-eh, *adv*

enough; fairly; rather.

assidu, e, ăhss-e-dE, *a* assiduous; diligent; attentive.

assiduité, ăhss-e-dwe-teh, *f* assiduity; regular attendance; *pl* assiduous attentions.

assidûment, ăhss-e-dE-mahng, *adv* assiduously; diligently.

assiégeant, e, ăhss-e-eh-shahng, *n* & *a* besieger.

assiéger, ăhss-e-eh-sheh, *v* to besiege; to dun (**de,** with).

assiette, ăhss-e-ett, *f* plate; situation; assessment.

assignable, ăhss-een-yăh-bl, *a* assignable.

assignation, ăhss-een-yăh-se-ong, *f* assignment; summons; writ; subpoena; appointment.

assigner, ăhss-een-yeh, *v* to assign; to allot; to summon; to appoint.

assimiler, ăhss-e-me-leh, *v* to assimilate (**to,** with).

assis, e, ăhss-e, *pp* seated.

assise, ăhss-eez, *f* course; layer; foundation; *pl* assizes.

assistance, ăhss-iss-tahngss, *f* attendance; audience; help.

assistant, e, ăhss-iss-tahng *mf* & *a* person present;

helper; *pl* those present.

assister, ăhss-iss-teh, *v* to attend; to be present; to help.

association, ăhss-o-se-ăh-se-ong, *f* association; partnership.

associé, e, ăhss-o-se-eh, *mf* associate; partner.

associer, ăhss-o-se-eh, *v* to associate; **s' –,** to join (**à, avec,** with); to enter into partnership; to share (**à, in**).

assombrir, ăhss-ong-breer, *v* to darken; **s' –,** to become gloomy.

assommant, e, ăhss-omm-ahng, *a* boring.

assommer, ăhss-omm-eh, *v* to knock down; to bore to death.

assommoir, ăhss-omm-o'ăhr, *m* bludgeon; (fig.) sleazy pub.

assomption, ăhss-ongp-se-ong, *f* Assumption.

assortiment, ăhss-or-te-mahng, *m* assortment; set; stock; match.

assortir, ăhss-or-teer, *v* to assort; to stock; to match; **s' –,** to harmonize (**à, avec,** with).

assoupir, ăhss-oo-peer, *v* to make drowsy; to hush up; **s' –,** to doze; to die

away.

assoupissant, e, ăhss-oo-piss-ahng, *a* soporific.

assoupissement, ăhss-oo-piss-mahng, *m* drowsiness; indolence.

assouplir, ăhss-oo-pleer, *v* to make supple; **s' –,** to become supple.

assourdir, ăhss-oohr-deer, *v* to deafen; to muffle.

assourdissant, e, ăhss-oohr-diss-ahng, *a* deafening.

assouvir, ăhss-oo-veer, *v* to satiate; to glut.

assujettir, ăhss-E-shayt-eer, *v* to subdue; to bind; to fasten; **s' –,** to subject oneself.

assujettissement, ăhss-E-shayt-iss-mahng, *m* subjection.

assumer, ăhss-E-meh, *v* to assume.

assurance, ăhss-E-rahngss, *f* assurance; reliance; boldness; insurance.

assuré, e, ăhss-E-reh, *pp* & *a* assured; insured; secured; confident.

assurément, ăhss-E-reh-mahng, *adv* certainly; assuredly.

assurer, ăhss-E-reh, *v* to assure; to insure; to secure; to assert; **s' –,** to make sure (**de,** of; **que,**

that).

assureur, ăhss-E -rer, *m* insurer; underwriter.

asthme, ăhssm, *m* asthma.

asticot, ăhss-te-ko, *m* maggot.

asticoter, ăhss-te-kot-eh, *v fam*, to worry; to tease.

astiquer, ăhss-te-keh, *v* to polish.

astral, e, ăhss-trăhl, *a* stellar; astral.

astre, ăhss-tr, *m* star.

astreindre, ăhss-trang-dr, *v* to subject; to compel.

astringent, e, ăhss-trang-shahng, *a* astringent.

astrologie, ăhss-tro-lo-shee *f* astrology.

astrologue, ăhss-troll-og, *m* astrologer.

astronome, ăhss-tronn-omm, *m* astronomer.

astronaute, ăhss-tro-noht *mf* astronaut.

astuce, ăhss-tEEss, *f* cunning; astuteness; witticism.

astucieu-x, se,* ăhss-tE-se-er, *a* artful; crafty; witty.

atelier, ăh-ter-le-eh, *m* workshop; office; studio; gang; **chef d'–**, shayf d–, overseer.

atermoiement, ăh-tair-mo'ăh-mahng, *m* respite.

athée, ăh-teh, *mf* atheist.

athlète, ăht-lett, *m* athlete; champion.

athlétique, ăht-leh-teeck *a* athletic.

atlas, ăht-lăhss, *m* atlas.

atmosphère, ăht-moss-fair, *f* atmosphere.

atome, ăh-tom, *m* atom.

atomique, ăh-to-mick, *a* atomic.

atomiseur, ăh-to-me-zer, *m* atomiser; spray.

atours, ăh-toohr, *mpl* attire; finery.

atout, ăh-too, *m* trump card.

âtre, ăh-tr, *m* hearth.

atroce,* ăh-tross, *a* atrocious; heinous; excruciating.

atrocité, ăh-tross-e-teh, *f* atrocity; eyesore.

atrophié, e, ăh-trof-e-eh, *a* wasted; withered.

attabler (s'), săh-tăh-bleh, *v* to sit down to table.

attachant, e, ăh-tăh-shahng, *a* attractive; engaging.

attache, ăh-tăhsh, *f* tie; bond; fastening; leash.

attaché, ăh-tăh-sheh, *m* attaché (of an Embassy).

attaché, e, ăh-tăh-sheh, *pp & a* attached.

attachement, ăh-tăhsh-mahng, *m* affection.

attacher, ăh-tăh-sheh, *v* to

attach; to fasten; to bind; to interest; to endear; **s'–**, to cling.

attaque, ăh-tăhck, *f* attack; fit; stroke.

attaquer, ăh-tăh-keh, *v* to attack; to begin; to sue; **s'– à**, to attack.

atteindre, ăh-tang-dr, *v* to reach; to attain; to strike; to injure.

atteinte, ăh-tangt, *f* blow; injury; violation.

attelage, ăht-lăhsh, *m* team; (way of) harnessing.

atteler, ăht-leh, *v* to put to; to yoke.

attenant, e, ăht-nahng, *a* adjoining.

attendant (en), ahng n'ăh-tahng-dahng, *adv* meanwhile.

attendre, ăh-tahng-dr, *v* to wait for; to expect; to look forward to; **s'– à**, to expect, to rely upon.

attendrir, ăh-tahng-dreer, *v* to make tender; to move; **s'–**, to be moved.

attendrissement, ăh-tahng-driss-mahng, *m* emotion; feeling of pity.

attendu, e, ăh-tahng-dE, *pp* expected; *prep* considering.

attentat, ăht-tahng-tăh, *m* criminal attempt;

outrage.

attente, ăh-tahngt, *f* waiting; expectation.

attenter, ăh-tahng-teh, *v* to make a criminal attempt.

attenti-f,-ve,* ăh-tahng-tiff, *a* attentive.

attention, ăh-tahng-se-ong, *f* attention; care; kindness.

atténuer, ăht-teh-nE-eh, *v* to weaken; to extenuate.

atterrer, ăh-tay-reh, *v* to thrown down; to astound.

atterrir, ăh-tay-reer, *v* to land.

atterrissage, ăh-tay-riss-ăhsh, *m* landing.

attestation, ăh-tess-tăh-se-ong, *f* certificate; testimonial.

attester, ăh-tess-teh, *v* to attest; to take to witness.

attiédir, ăh-te-eh-deer, *v* to cool; **s'–,** to cool down.

attirail, ăh-te-rah'e, *m* apparatus; paraphernalia.

attirant, e, ăh-te-rahng, *a* attractive; alluring.

attirer, ăh-te-reh, *v* to attract; to draw; to bring on; **s'–,** to bring on oneself; to attract each other.

attiser, ăh-te-zeh, *v* to stir up; to poke; to store.

attitré, e, ăh-te-treh, *a* regular; appointed; official.

attitude, ăh-te-tEEd, *f* attitude.

attouchement, ăh-toosh-mahng, *f* touch; feeling.

attraction, ăh-trăhck-se-ong, *f* attraction.

attrait, ăh-tray, *m* attraction; charm.

attrape, ăh-trăhp, *f* catch; trick; hoax; trap; **–** **nigaud,** – ne-goh, booby-trap; con game.

attraper, ăh-trăh-peh, *v* to entrap; to catch; to cheat; to get.

attrayant, e, ăh-tray'e-ahng, *a* attractive.

attribuer, ăht-tre-bE-eh, *v* to attribute; to assign; to impute; **s' –,** to claim.

attribution, ăht-tre-bE-se-ong, *f* attribution; prerogative.

attrister, ăh-triss-teh, *v* to sadden; **s'–,** to grieve.

attroupement, ăh-troop-mahng, *m* gathering; mob.

attrouper, ăh-troo-peh, *v* to assemble; **s'–,** to crowd.

au *sing,* **aux** *pl,* oh,

contraction of **à le, à les.**

aubaine, oh-bayn, *f* windfall; godsend.

aube, ohb, *f* dawn.

aubépine, oh-beh-peen, *f* hawthorn.

auberge, oh-bairsh, *f* inn; **– de (la) jeunesse,** – der (lah) sher-ness, youth hostel.

aubergine, oh-bair-sheen, *f* aubergine; eggplant.

aubergiste, oh-bair-shisst, *m* innkeeper.

aucun, e, oh-kung, *a* any; no; none; *pron* anyone; no one.

aucunement, oh-kEEn-mahng, *adv* by no means; not at all.

audace, oh-dăhss, *f* audacity; insolence; daring.

audacieu-x, se*, oh-dăh-se-er, *a* audacious; impudent; bold.

au-dessous, oh-der-soo, *adv* below; underneath.

au-dessus, oh-der-sEE, *adv* above.

audience, oh-de-ahngss, *f* audience; hearing; court; sitting.

audiencier, oh-de-ahngss-e-eh, *m* usher; crier of a court.

audi-teur, trice, oh-de-

ter, *mf* hearer; listener.

auditi-f, ve, oh-de-tiff, *a* auditory.

audition, oh-de-se-ong, *f* hearing; audition.

auditoire, oh-de-to'ăhr, *m* audience; auditorium.

auge, ohsh, *f* trough; hod; spout.

augmentation, og-mahng-tăh-se-ong, *f* increase; rise.

augmenter, og-mahng-teh, *v* to increase; to raise; **s'–,** to increase.

augure, oh-ghEEr, *m* omen; augur.

augurer, oh-ghE-reh, *v* to augur; to surmise.

auguste, oh-ghEEst, *a* august.

aujourd'hui, oh-shoohr-dwe, *adv* today; nowadays.

aumône, oh-mohn, *f* alms; charity.

aumônier, oh-moh-ne-eh, *m* chaplain.

aune, ohn, *m* alder; *f* ell.

auparavant, oh-păh-răh-vahng, *adv* before; previously; once; first.

auprès, oh-pray, *adv* near; beside; close.

auprès de, oh-pray der, *prep* near; close to; in comparison with.

auréole, oh-reh-ol, *f* halo;

glory; crown; nimbus.

auriculaire, oh-re-kE-lair, *m* the little finger; *a* auricular.

aurifère, oh-re-fair, *a* auriferous.

aurifier, oh-re-fe-eh, *v* to fill teeth with gold.

aurore, oh-ror, *f* dawn.

ausculter, ohss-kEEl-teh, *v* to have one's chest examined by a doctor.

auspice, oss-piss, *m* auspice.

aussi, ohss-e, *adv* too; also; likewise; so; as; as much. *conj* therefore; consequently; **–...que, –** ker, as...as.

aussitôt, ohss-e-toh, *adv* immediately; **–que, –** ker, as soon as.

austère,* ohss-tair, *a* stern; rigid.

autant, oh-tahng, *adv* as much; as many; so much; so many; **d'–mieux,** d– me-er, all the better; **d'– moins,** d– mo'ang, all the less; **d' – que,** d– ker, more especially as.

autel, oh-tell, *m* altar.

auteur, oh-ter, *m* author; writer; **droit d'–,** dro'ăh d–, copyright.

authenticité, oh-tahng-te-se-teh, *f* authenticity;

genuineness.

autobiographe, oh-toh-be-oh-grăhf, *m* autobiographer.

autobiographie, oh-toh-be-oh-grăh-fee, *f* autobiography.

autobus, oh-toh-bEEs, *m* bus.

autocratie, oh-toh-krăh-see, *f* autocracy.

autographe, oh-toh-grăhf, *m* autograph.

automate, oh-toh-măht, *m* automation.

automatique,* oh-toh-măh-tick, *a* automatic.

automne, oh-tonn, *m* autumn.

automobile, oh-toh-mo-beel, *f* car, *a* self-moving; **canot –,** kăh-no –, motor-boat.

automobilisme, oh-toh-mo-be-lissm, *m* motoring.

automobiliste, oh-toh-mo-be-lisst, *mf* motorist.

autopsie, oh-top-see, *f* post-mortem examination; autopsy.

autorisation, oh-toh-re-zăh-se-ong, *f* authority; permission.

autoriser, oh-toh-re-zeh, *v* to authorize.

autorité, oh-toh-re-teh, *f* authority; power;

control.

autoroute, oh-toh-root, *f* motorway.

autour, oh-toohr, *adv* round about.

autour de, oh-toohr der, *prep* around; about.

autre, oh-tr, *pron* another; *a* other; different; **tout** –, too t'–, quite different; anybody else; **nous –s, vous –s, noo** z'–, voo z'–, we, you, ourselves, yourselves; **à d'–,** ăhd d–, nonsense!

autrefois, oh-trer-fo'ăh, *adv* formerly.

autrement, oh-trer-mahng, *adv* otherwise.

autruche, oh-trEEsh, *f* ostrich.

autrui, oh-trwe, *pron & m* others.

auvent, oh-vahng, *m* penthouse; shed.

aux, oh, *m & fpl* to the; at the.

auxiliaire, ohk-se-le-air, *a & m* auxiliary.

aval, ăh-văhl, *m* guarantee; endorsement; lower part; **en –,** ahng n'–, down the river.

avaler, ăh-văh-leh, *v* to swallow; *fig* to pocket.

avance, ăh-vahngss, *f* advance; money advanced; **d'–,** d–,

beforehand.

avancement, ăh-vahngss-mahng, *m* progress; rise.

avancer, ăh-vahngss-eh, *v* to advance; to promote; to hasten; to hold forth; to proceed; to progress; (clock) to be fast; **s'–,** to come forward.

avanie ăh-văh-nee, *f* outrage, affront.

avant, hă-vahng, *adv* far; deep; forward; *prep* before; *m* forepart; bow; **en –,** ahng n'–, in front; **– de que,** before; **– dernier,** – dair-ne-se-eh, last but one; **––hier,** – t'e-air, the day before yesterday; **––première,** – prer-me-air, *f* preview. **––propos,** – pro-poh, foreword; **––veille,** –vay'e, two days before.

avantage, ăh-vahng-tăhsh, *m* advantage; perk.

avantageu-x, se,* ăh-vahng-tăhsh-er, *a* advantageous.

avare, ăh-văhr, *m* miser; *a* avaricious.

avarice, ăh-văh-riss, *f* avarice.

avarie, ăh-văh-ree, *f* damage; average.

avarier, ăh-văh-re-eh, *v* to damage; to spoil; **s'–,** to get damaged.

avec, ăh-veck, *prep* with; by.

avenant, ăh––nahng, *m* additional clause (to an insurance policy).

avenant, e, ăhv-nahng, *a* prepossing; **à l'–,** ăh-l–, in keeping with.

avènement, ăh-vane-mahng, *m* accession; coming.

avenir, ăhv-neer, *m* future; prospects; posterity; **à l' –,** ăhl-, in future.

avent, ăh-vahng, *m* advent.

aventure, ăhv-nahng-tEEr, *f* adventure; love affair; **à l'–,** ăhl-, at random.

aventuré, e, ăh-vahng-tE-reh, *a* hazardous.

aventurer, ăh-vahng-tE-reh, *v* to venture; **s'–,** to take a chance.

aventureu-x, se,* ăh-vahng-tE-rer, *a* adventuresome.

aventuri-er, ère, ăh-vahng-tE-re-eh, *mf* adventurer, adventuress.

avenue, ăhv-nE, *f* avenue.

avérer, ăh-veh-reh, *v* to aver; **s'–,** to be proved.

averse, ăh-vairss, *f* heavy shower.

aversion, ăh-vair-se-ong, *f* dislike (**pour,** of, for).

averti, e, ăh-vair-te, *a* experienced; wide-awake.

avertir, ăh-vair-teer, *v* to warn; to inform.

avertissement, ăh-vair-tiss-mahng, *m* warning; notice; preface.

aveu, ăh-ver, *m* admission; avowal; **homme sans –,** omm sahng z' –, vagabond.

aveugle, ăh-ver-gl, *a* blind.

aveuglément, ăh-ver-gleh,mahng, *adv* blindly; implicitly.

aveugler, ăh-ver-gleh, *v* to blind; **s'–,** to be blind (**sur,** to).

aveuglette, (à l'), ăh-lăh-ver-glett, *adv* in the dark; blindly.

aviateur, ăh-ve-ăh-ter, *m* airman.

aviation, ăh-ve-ăh-se-ong, *f* flying; Air Force.

avide,* ăh-veed, *a* greedy; eager.

avilir, ăh-ve-leer, *v* to degrade; **s'–,** to degrade oneself; to depreciate.

avilissement, ăh-ve-liss-mahng, *m* degradation; debasement.

avion, ăh-ve-ong, *m* aeroplane.

aviron, ăh-ve-rong, *m* oar;

l'–, rowing (sport).

avis, ăh-ve, *m* opinion; advice; caution; news.

avisé, e, ăh-ve-zeh, *a* advised; far-seeing; circumspect.

aviser, ăh-ve-zeh, *v* to perceive; to advise; to see to it; **s'–,** to take it into one's head (**de,** to).

aviver, ăh-ve-veh, *v* to brighten; to quicken; to polish.

avocat, ăh-vo-kăh, *m* barrister; counsel; lawyer.

avocat, ăh-vo-kăh, *m* avocado.

avoine, ăh-vo'ăhn, *f* oats.

avoir, ăh-vo'ăhr, *v* to have; to get; to be; *m* property; **qu'avez-vous?** kăh-veh-voo? what is the matter with you? **j'ai chaud,** shay-shoh, I am warm; **il y a,** ill-e-ăh, there is; there are; **– un an, –** ung-ahng, one year ago; **j'ai vingt ans,** shay-vang-ahng, I'm twenty.

avoisiner, ăh-vo'ăh-ze-neh, *v* to be near.

avortement, ăh-vor-ter-mahng, *m* abortion.

avorter, ăh-vor-teh, *v* to miscarry; **se faire –,** to have an abortion.

avorton, ăh-vor-tong, *m* abortive child or animal.

avoué, ăh-voo-eh, *m* solicitor; attorney.

avouer, ăh-voo-eh, *v* to confess; acknowledge.

avril, ăh-vreel, *m* April.

axe, ăhks, *m* axis; axle.

ayant-droit, ay-yahng-dro'ăh, *m* rightful owner; beneficiary.

azote, ăh-zot, *m* nitrogen.

azur, ăh-zEEr, *m* azure; blue.

azyme, ăh-zeem, *a* unleavened.

B

baba, băh-băh, *m* baba, spongy plum-cake; **– au rhum,** – oh romm, sponge cake moistened with rum syrup.

babillage, băh-bee-yăsh, *m* prattling.

babillier, băh-bee-yeh, *v* to prattle.

babine, băh-been, *f* lip of animal; chops (of animals).

babiole, băh-be-ol, *f* bauble; toy; knick-knack.

bâbord, bah-bor, *m* port side.

babouin, băh-boo-ang, *m* baboon.

bac, băhck, *m* ferry-boat; tank; vat.

baccalauréat, băh-kăh-loh-reh-ăh, *m* school leaving certificate.

bâche, bahsh, *f* awning; hot-bed frame; tank.

bachelier, băh-sher-le-eh, *m* one who has passed school leaving certificate.

bachot, băh-sho, *m fam* baccalauréat.

bacille, băh-sill, *m* bacillus.

bâcler, bah-kleh, *v* to hurry over.

badaud, e, băh-doh, *a & mf* idler; saunterer.

badigeonner, băh-de-shonn-eh, *v* to colour-wash; to paint.

badin, e, băh-dang, *a & mf* playful; joker.

badinage, băh-de-năhsh, *m* banter.

badiner, băh-de-neh, *v* to joke.

badminton, băhd-min-tong, *m* badminton.

bafouer, băh-foo-eh, *v* to scoff at.

bagage, băh-găhsh, *m* luggage; **plier –,** ple-eh –, to pack up; make off.

bagarre, băh-găhr, *f* fight; brawl.

bagatelle, băh-găh-tell, *f* trifle; trinket.

bagne, băhn-yer, *m* convicts' prison.

bagnole, băhn-yoll, *f fam* banger (car).

bague, băhg, *f* ring.

baguette, băh-ghett, *f* wand; rod; stick; long stick of bread.

bah! băh, *interj* nonsense! indeed!

bahut, băh-E, *m* chest; cupboard.

bai, e, bay, *a* bay.

baie, bay, *f* bay; berry; opening.

baigner, bain-yeh, *v* to bathe; **se –,** to bathe.

baignoire, bain-yo'ăhr, *f* bath tub; (theatre) box.

bail, bah'e, *m* lease.

bâillement, bah'e-mahng, *m* yawning; gaping.

bâiller, bah'e-eh, *v* to yawn; to gape.

bailleur, bah'e-er, *m* lessor.

bailli, bah'e-yee, *m* bailiff.

bâillon, bah'e-yong, *m* gag.

bâillonner, bah'e-yonn-eh, *v* to gag.

bain, bang, *m* bath; **salle de –,** sähl-der –, *f* bathroom.

bain-marie, bang-mäh-ree, *m* (cooking) double saucepan.

baïonnette, bäh'e-onn-ett, *f* bayonet.

baiser, bay-zeh, *m* kiss.

baisse, bess, *f* fall; decline; drop.

baisser, bess-eh, *v* to lower; to let down; to decline; **se –,** to stoop.

bal, bähl, *m* ball.

balade, bäh-lähd, *f* stroll; ramble.

balader (se), ser bäh-läh-deh, *v fam* to take a stroll.

baladin, bäh-läh-dang, *m* mountebank; buffoon.

balafre, bäh-läh-fr, *f* gash; scar.

balai, bäh-lay, *m* broom; brush.

balance, bäh-lahngss, *f* scale; pair of scales; Libra.

balancer, bäh-lahng-seh, *v* to balance; to weigh; to hesitate; to swing; *fam* to turn out; to dismiss.

balancier, bäh-lahng-se-

eh, *m* pendulum; pole; beam.

balançoire, bäh-lahng-so'ähr, *f* see-saw; swing.

balayer, bäh-lay-yeh, *v* to sweep.

balayures, bäh-lay-yEEr, *fpl* sweepings.

balbutier, bäh-bE-se-eh, *v* to stammer; to mumble.

balcon, bähl-kong, *m* balcony.

baldaquin, bähl-däh-kang, *m* canopy.

baleine, bäh-lain, *f* whale.

baleinier, bäh-lay-ne-eh, *m* whaler; **– de sauvetage,** – der sohv-tähsh, lifeboat.

balise, bäh-leez, *f* beacon; buoy.

ballade, bäh-lähd, *f* ballad; ballade.

ballant, e, bäh-lahng, *a* swinging; dangling.

balle, bähl, *f* ball, bullet; bale; **prendre la – au bond** prahng-dr-läh – oh-bong, to seize the opportunity.

ballet, bäh-lay, *m* ballet.

ballon, bäh-long, *m* balloon; football.

ballot, bäh-loh, *m* bale.

ballottage, bäh-lot-ähsh, *m* second ballot; shaking.

ballotter, bäh-lot-eh, *v* to

toss; to ballot.

balnéaire, bähl-neh-air, *a* bathing; **station –,** stäh-se-ong –, seaside; health resort.

balourdise, bäh-loohr-deez, *f* stupid thing; blunder.

balsamique, bähl-zäh-mick, *a* balsamic.

balustre, bäh-lEEs-tr, *m* railing; balustrade.

bambin, e, bahng-bang, *mf* little child; tiny tot.

bambocheur, bahng-boh-sher, *m* debauchee.

bambou, bahng-boo, *m* bamboo.

ban, bahng, *m* proclamation; banishment.

banal, e,* bäh-nähl, *a* commonplace; banal.

banane, bäh-nähn, *f* banana.

banc, bahng, *m* bench.

bancal, e, bahng-kähl, *a &* n bandy-legged.

bandage, bahng-dähsh, *m* bandaging; truss; tyre.

bande, bahngd, *f* strip; wrapper; gang; lot; tyre.

bandeau, bahng-doh, *m* head-band; bandage.

bandelette, bahngd-lett, *f* headband; small bandage.

bander, bahng-deh, *v* to

bandage; to bind up; to stretch; to blind fold.

banderole, bahngd-rol, *f* streamer.

bandit, bahng-de, *m* bandit.

bandoulière, bahng-doo-le-air, *f* shoulder-belt; **en** –, ahng –, slung over the shoulder.

banlieue, bahng-le-er, *f* suburbs.

bannière, băh-ne-air, *f* banner; flag.

bannir, băh-neer, *v* to banish.

banque, bahngk, *f* bank; banking.

banqueroute, bahngk-root, *f* bankruptcy.

banquet, bahng-kay, *m* feast; banquet.

banquette, bahng-kett, *f* bench; seat.

banquier, bahng-ke-eh, *m* banker.

banquise, bahng-keez, *f* ice-bank, -floe.

baptême, băh-taym, *m* baptism.

baptiser, băh-te-zeh, *v* to christen.

baquet, băh-kay, *m* tub; bucket.

baragouiner, băh-răh-gwee-neh, *v* to talk gibberish.

baraque, băh-răhck *f* shed;

hovel; hut.

baratter, băh-răh-teh, *v* to churn.

barbare, băhr-băhr, *a* & *mf* barbarian; barbarous.

barbe, băhrb, *f* beard.

barbecue, băhr-ber-kE, *m* barbecue.

barbelé, băhr-ber-leh, *a* barbed; *n* barbed wire.

barbiche, băhr-beesh, *f* tuft of beard.

barbier, băhr-be-eh, *m* barber.

barboter, băhr-bot-eh, *v* to dabble; to paddle.

barbouiller, băhr-boo'e-yeh, *v* to daub; to scribble.

barbu, e, băhr-bE, *a* bearded.

barème, băh-raym, *m* ready-reckoner; price scale.

barguigner, băhr-gheen-yeh, *v* to hum and haw; to hesitate.

baril, băh-re, *m* barrel; cask; keg.

bariolage, băh-re-o-lăhsh, *m* medley (of colours).

bariolé, băh-re-o-leh, *a* gaudy; of many colours.

barman, băhr-măhn, *m* barman.

baromètre, băh-roh-met-tr, *m* barometer.

baron, băh-rong, *m* baron.

baronne, băh-ronn *f* baroness.

baronnet, băh-ro-nay, *m* baronet.

baroque, băh-rock, *a* odd, quaint; baroque (style).

barque, băhrk, *f* boat.

barrage, băh-răhsh, *m* stoppage; dam; barrage.

barre, băhr, *f* bar; tiller; stroke.

barreau, băh-roh, *m* bar; profession of the law.

barrer, băh-reh, *v* to bar; to cross out.

barrette, băh-rehtt, *f* hair slide; small bar.

barrière, băh-re-air, *f* barrier; gate.

bas, bah, *adv* low down; bottom; stocking.

bas, se, * bah, *a* low; mean; base.

basané, e, băh-zăh-neh, *a* sunburnt; swarthy.

bas-côté, bah-koh-teh, *m* aisle (side).

bascule, băhss-kEEl, *f* see-saw; weighing-machine.

base, bahz, *f* basis; base.

base-ball, bez-boll, *m* baseball.

baser, bah-zeh, *v* to base; to ground.

basilic, băh-ze-leeck, *m* basil.

bas-fond, bah-fong, *m* low ground.

basque, băhsk, f flap (coat, etc); a & mf Basque.

basse, bahss, f bass; violoncello.

basse-cour, bahss-koohr, f poultry-yard.

bassesse, bahss-ess, f baseness; meanness.

bassin, băhss-ang, m basin; dock; pelvis.

bassiner, băhss-e-neh, v to warm (a bed); to bathe (wound etc.).

bassinoire, băhss-e-no'ăhr, f warming pan.

basson, bahss-ong, m bassoon.

baste! băhsst! interj nonsense!

bastingage, băhss-tang-găhsh, m netting.

bastringue, băhss-trang-gh, m sleazy dancing place.

bas-ventre, bah-vahng-tr, m lower abdomen.

bât, bah, m pack-saddle.

bataille, băh-tah'e, f battle.

bataillon, băh-tah'e-ong, m battalion; host.

bâtard, e, bah-tăhr, n & a illegitimate; bastard; French loaf of bread.

bateau, băh-toh, m boat.

bateleur, băht-ler, m juggler; tumbler.

batelier, băh-ter-le-eh, m boatman.

bâti, bah-te, m tacking; frame; pp built.

batifoler, băh-te-foll-eh, v to play; to romp.

bâtiment, bah-te-mahng, m building; ship.

bâtir, bah-teer, v to build; to erect; to tack.

bâtisse, bah-tiss, f building; masonry.

batiste, băh-tisst, f cambric; lawn.

bâton, bah-tong, m stick; club; **à –s rompus**, ăh–rong-pE, by fits and starts; **mettre des –s dans les roues**, met-tr day–dahng lay roo, to put a spoke in one's wheel.

bâtonner, bah-tonn-eh, v to cudgel.

battage, băh-tăhsh, m beating; churning; threshing.

battant, băh-tahng, m (door) leaf; (bell) clapper.

battant, e, băh-tahng, a beating; pelting.

battement, băht-mahng, m beat(ing); throb(bing); clapping.

batterie, băht-ree, f fight; percussion; battery; set; **– de cuisine**, – de kwee-

zeen, kitchen utensils.

battoir, băh-to'ăhr, m beater; paddle; bat.

battre, băh-tr, v to beat; to thrash; to coin; to churn; to thresh; to shuffle; **se –**, to fight.

baudet, boh-day, m donkey; idiot.

bauge, bohsh, f lair (of wild boar); dirty hovel; squirrel's nest.

baume, bohm, m balm; balsam.

bavard, e, băh-văhr, mf chatterbox; a talkative.

bavardage, băh-văhr-dăhsh, m chit-chat.

bavarder, băh-văhr-deh, v to chatter.

baver, băh-veh, v to dribble.

bavoir, băh-vo'ăhr, m bib.

bazar, băh-zăhr, m bazaar.

béant, e, beh-ahng, a gaping; **bouche –e**, boosh-beh-ahngt, agape.

béat, e,* beh-ăh, a sanctimonious; blissful.

beau, boh, m beautiful; beauty; best; fine weather.

beau (before vowel or a mute h: **bel**, bell); boh; m; **belle,*** bell, f, a beautiful; handsome; fine fair; **avoir –**, ăh-vo'ăhr–, to... in vain; **de**

plus belle, der-plE-bell, more (or worse) than ever.

beaucoup, boh-koo, *adv* much; many; a great deal.

beau-fils, boh-fiss, *m* stepson; son-in-law.

beau-frère, boh-frair, *m* brother-in-law.

beau-père, boh-pair, *m* father-in-law; stepfather.

beauté, boh-teh, *f* beauty.

beaux-parents, boh-păh-rahng, *mpl* parents-in-law.

bébé, beh-beh, *m* baby.

bec, beck, *m* beak; snout.

bécarre, beh-kăhr, *m* (music) natural.

bécasse, beh-kăhss, *f* woodcock.

bécassine, beh-kăhss-een, *f* snipe; silly girl.

bec-de-lièvre, beck der le-ay-vr, *m* harelip.

béchamel, beh-shăh-mell, *f* cream sauce.

bêche, baish, *f* spade.

bêcher, bay-sheh, *v* to dig.

becqueter, bayk-teh, *v* to peck; to kiss.

bedaine, ber-denn, *f* paunch; belly.

bedeau, ber-doh, *m* beadle.

bée, beh, *af* open, gaping; **bouche –**, boosh –,

open-mouthed.

beffroi, beh-fro'ăh, *m* belfry.

bégayer, beh-ghay-yeh, *v* to stammer; to stutter.

bègue, baygh, *n* & *a* stammerer; stammering.

bégueule, beh-gherl, *f* haughty prude.

beige, baish, *a* unbleached; natural; beige.

beignet, bayn-yay, *m* fritter.

bêler, bay-leh, *v* to bleat.

bélier, beh-le-eh, *m* ram; battering-ram.

belle-fille, bell fee-ye, *f* daughter-in-law; stepdaughter.

belle-mère, bell mair, *f* mother-in-law; stepmother.

belle-soeur, bell ser, *f* sister-in-law.

belliqueu-x, se,* bell-le-ker, *a* warlike.

bémol, beh-mol, *m* (music) flat.

bénédicité, beh-neh-de-se-teh, *m* grace before meals.

bénédiction, beh-neh-dick-se-ong, *f* blessing.

bénéfice, beh-neh-fiss, *m* benefit; profit; living.

benêt, ber-nay, *a* & *m* simpleton; silly.

bénévole,* beh-neh-vol, *a* voluntary; unpaid.

béni, e, beh-ne, *a* blessed.

béni-n, gne, beh-nang, *a* benign; kind.

bénir, beh-neer, *v*, to bless.

bénitier, beh-ne-te-eh, *m* holy-water basin.

benzine, bang-zeen, *f* benzine.

béquille, beh-kee-ye, *f* crutch.

bercail, bair-kah'e, *m* (sing. only) sheepfold; fold.

berceau, bair-soh, *m* cradle; arbour; cradle vault.

bercer, bair-seh, *v* to rock; to lull; to delude.

berceuse, bair-serz, *f* rocking-chair; lullaby.

béret, beh-ray, *m* beret; cap.

berge, bairsh, *f* steep bank of a river.

berg-er, ère, bair-sheh, *mf* shepherd.

bergère, bair-shair, *f* easy chair.

bergerie, bair-sher-ree, *f* sheep-fold.

berlue, bair-lE, *f* dimness of sight; false vision.

berner, bair-neh, *v* to toss in a blanket; to fool.

besace, ber-zăhss, *f*

double-bag carried by beggars.

besogne, ber-zon-yer, *f* work; task; labour.

besogneu-x, se, ber-zon-yer, *a* needy; necessitous.

besoin, ber-zo-ang, *m* need; want; necessity. **au –,** oh –, in case of need.

bestial, e,* bess-te-ăhl, *a* beastly; brutish.

bestiaux, bess-te-oh, *mpl* cattle.

bétail, beh-tah'e, *m* cattle; livestock.

bête, bayt, *f* beast; animal; *a** stupid; **– noire,** –no'ăhr, aversion.

bêtise, bay-teez, *f* stupidity; stupid thing.

béton, beh-tong, *m* concrete.

betterave, bett-răhv, *f* beetroot.

beugler, ber-gleh, *v* to bellow; to bawl.

beurre, ber, *m* butter.

beurrer, ber-reh, *v* to butter.

bévue, beh-vE, *f* blunder; mistake.

biais, be-ay, *m* slant; expedient; **en –,** ahng–, on the cross.

biaiser, be-ay-zeh, *v* to slope; to shuffle.

bibelot, beeb-lo, *m* trinket; knickknack.

biberon, beeb-rong, *m* feeding-bottle.

bible, bee-bl, *f* bible.

bibliophile, be-ble-off-eel, *m* lover of books.

bibliothécaire, be-ble-o-teh-kair, *m* librarian.

bibliothéque, be-ble-o-teck, *f* library; bookcase.

biche, bish, *f* hind; doe.

bicoque, be-kock, *f* paltry town; hut; hovel.

bicyclette, be-se-klett, *f* bicycle.

bidon, be-dong, *m* can.

bidonville, be-dong-veel, *m* shanty town.

bielle, be-ell, *f* connecting-rod.

bien, be-ang, *adv* well; quite; very; okay; *m* good; property; welfare; **–que, –ker,** although; **tout va –,** too văh–, all is well.

bien-aimé, e, be-ang n'ay-meh, *a* beloved.

bien-être, be-ang n'ay-tr, *m* comfort; welfare.

bienfaisant, e, be-ang-fer-zahng, *a* kind; charitable.

bienfait, be-ang-fay, *m* kindness; favour; boon.

bienfai-teur, trice, be-ang-fay-ter, *mf* benefactor;

benefactress.

bien-fonds, be-ang-fong, *m* landed property; real estate.

bienheureu-x, se, be-ang-ner,rer, *a* blessed; happy.

bienséance, be-ang-seh-ahngss, *f* decorum; propriety.

bientôt, be-ang-toh, *adv* soon; shortly.

bienveillance, be-ang-vay'e-yahngss, *f* kindness; goodwill.

bienveillant, e, be-ang-vay'e-yahng, *a* kind; benevolent.

bienvenu, e, be-angv-nEE, *a* & n welcome.

bienvenue, be-angv-nEE, *f* welcome.

bière, be-air, *f* beer; coffin; bier.

biffer, be-feh, *v* to strike out; to cancel.

bifteck, beef-teck, *m* beefsteak.

bifurquer (se), ser be-fEEr-keh, *v* to fork.

bigarré, e, be-găh-reh, *a* motley; streaked.

bigorneau, be-gor-noh, *m* winkle.

bigot, e, be-gho, *mf* bigot; *a* bigoted.

bigoudi, be-goo-de, *m* curler (hair).

bijou, be-shoo, *m* jewel,

trinket; *fig* darling.

bijouterie, be-**shoot**-ree, *f* jewellery.

bijoutier, be-**shoo**-te-eh, *m* jeweller.

bikini, be-ke-ne, *m* bikini.

bilan, be-lahng, *m* balance-sheet; schedule.

bile, beel, *f* bile; gall; anger.

bilieu-x, se, be-le-er, *a* bilious; irritable.

bilingue, be-langg, *a* bilingual.

billard, bee-yǎhr, *m* billiards; billiard-room.

bille, bee-ye, *f* ball; marble; log.

billet, bee-yay, *m* bill; note; ticket; – **de banque,** – der bahngk, bank-note; – **simple,** – sang-pl, single ticket; – **d'aller et retour,** – dǎh-leh-eh rer-toohr, return ticket.

billevesée, bill-ver-zeh, *f* nonsense.

billion, bill-e-ong, *m* billion.

billot, bee-yo, *m* block.

bimensuel, -le, be-mǎhng-sE-ell, *a* fortnightly.

binette, be-nett, *f* hoe; *pop* face.

binocle, be-nock-kl, *m* pince-nez.

biographie, be-og-rǎh-fee,

f biography.

bipède, be-payd, *a* & *m* biped; two-legged.

biplan, be-plahng, *m* biplane.

bique, bick, *f* she-goat.

bis, biss, *adv* twice; again; encore!

bis, e, be, *a* brown.

bisaïeul, e, be-zǎh-yerl, *mf* great-grandfather; great-grandmother.

biscornu, e, biss-kor-nE, *a* odd; queer.

biscotte, biss-kot, *f* rusk.

biscuit, biss-kwe, *m* biscuit.

bise, beez, *f* north wind; cold blast; *fam* kiss.

biseau, be-zoh, *m* bevel.

bisque, beesk, *f* shellfish soup; vexation.

bisquer, bees-keh, *v fam* to be vexed.

bisser, biss-eh, *v* to encore.

bissextile, be-secks-teel, *af* used only in **Année** –, Leap Year.

bistré, e, biss-treh, *a* tawny; swarthy.

bizarre,* be-zǎhr, *a* odd; whimsical; eccentric.

blafard, e, blǎh-fǎhr, *a* dim; wan; pale.

blague, blǎhg, *f* tobacco-pouch; *fam* joke.

blaguer, blǎh-gheh, *v fam*

to joke; to hoax.

blaireau, blay-roh, *m* badger; shaving brush.

blâme, blahm, *m* blame; censure.

blâmer, blah-meh, *v* to blame; to find fault with.

blanc, blahng, *m* white; blank; white (man); **blanche,** blahngsh, *f* white (woman).

blan-c, che, *a* white; clean; blank; pale; **nuit blanche** nwe blahngsh, sleepless night.

blanchaille, blahng-shah'e, *f* whitebait.

blanchâtre, blahng-shah-tr, *a* whitish.

blancheur, blahng-sher, *f* whiteness.

blanchir, blahng-sheer, *v* to whiten; to bleach; to grow white.

blanchissage, blahng-shiss-ǎhsh, *m* washing.

blanchisserie, blahng-shiss-re, *f* laundry; laundering.

blanquette, blahng-kett, *f* stew with white sauce.

blaser, blah-zeh, *v* to blunt; to pall; **se** –, ser–, to get tired of (**de**); to become blasé.

blason, blah-zong, *m* heraldry; coat-of-arms.

blasphème, blăhss-faym, *m* blasphemy.

blé, bleh, *m* corn; wheat; grain.

blême, blaym, *a* pallid; ghastly; wan.

blémir, bleh-meer, *v* to grow pale.

blessant, e, bless-ahng, *a* offensive (**pour,** to); hurtful.

blessé, bless-eh, *m* wounded man; *pp* & *a* wounded.

blesser, bless-eh, *v* to wound; to hurt; to injure; to offend; **se –,** to hurt oneself; to be offended (**de,** at, with).

blessure, bless-EEr, *f* wound; injury.

blet, te, blay, *a* overripe.

bleu, e, bler, *a* blue; *m* bruise.

bleuâtre, bler-ah-tr, *a* bluish.

bleuet, bluet, bler-ay, blE-ay, *m* cornflower.

bleuir, bler-eer, *v* to make blue; to turn blue.

blindé, blang-deh, *a* steel-plated; iron-clad.

bloc, block, *m* block; lump; log; **en –,** ahng –, in a lump.

blocus, block-EEss, *m* blockade.

blond, e, blong, *a* & *n* blond; fair; light.

bloquer, block-eh, *v* to blockade; to block up.

blottir (se) serblot-eer, *v* to crouch; to snuggle down.

blouse, blooz, *f* frock; smock-frock; pinafore; (billiards) pocket.

blouser, bloo-zeh, *v* to dupe; **se –,** ser –, *fam* to blunder.

bluette, blE-ayt, *f* spark; literary trifle.

boa, bo'ăh, *m* boa; fur tippet.

bobard, bo-bahr, *m fam* tall story; lie.

bobine, bob-een, *f* bobbin; spool; reel; coil.

bobo, bob-o, *m* slight hurt.

bocage, bock-ăhsh, *m* grove; copse.

bocal, bock-ăhl, *m* glass bowl; wide-mouthed bottle.

bock, bock, *m* beer-glass; glass of beer.

bœuf, berf, *m* bullock; beef.

boghei, bo-gay, *m* buggy (carriage).

bohémien, ne, bo-eh-me-ang, *mf* Bohemian; gipsy.

boire, bo'ăhr, *v* to drink; to soak up (paper, etc.).

boire (beaucoup), bo'ăhr- (boh-koo), *v fam* booze.

bois, bo'ăh, *m* wood; timber; (deer) horns.

boisé, e, bo'ăh-zeh, *a* wooded; wainscoted.

boiserie, bo'ăhz-ree, *f* wainscot.

boisseau, bo'ăhss-oh, *m* bushel.

boisson, bo'ăhss-ong, *f* drink; beverage; drinking; **– non alcoolisée, –** nong-ăhl-koll-e-seh, soft drink.

boîte, bo'ăh, *f* box; case; tin; **– aux lettres,** –oh lay-tr, letter box; **en –,** ahng –, *a* tinned; **– de vitesses, –** derve-tess, gear box.

boiter, bo'ăh-teh, *v* to limp.

boiteu-x, -se, bo'ăh-ter, *mf* cripple; *a* lame; limping.

bol, boll, *m* bowl; basin.

bombance, bong-bahngss, *f* feasting.

bombarder, bong-băhr-deh, *v* to bombard.

bombe, bongb, *f* bomb; shell.

bomber, bong-beh, *v* to make convex; to bulge out.

bon, bong, *m* good; good quality; bond; order; cheque.

bon, ne, bong, *a* good;

kind; advisable; right.

bonasse, bonn-ăhss, *a* simple; silly; credulous.

bonbon, bong-bong, *m* sweet.

bonbonnière, bong-bonn-e-air, *f* sweet box.

bond, bong, *m* bound; leap; jump; **faire faux –,** fair foh –, to fail.

bonde, bongd, *f* plughole; bunghole; sluice.

bondir, bong-deer, *v* to bound; to spring; to skip.

bondon, bong-dong, *m* bung; Neufchâtel cheese.

bonheur, bonn-**er** *m* happiness; delight; luck.

bonhomie, bonn-omm-ee, *f* good nature; simplicity.

bonhomme, bonn-omm, *m* good-natured man; old man; fellow.

bonification, bonn-e-fe-kăh-se-ong, *f* improvement; allowance.

bonifier, bonn-e-fe-eh, *v* to improve.

boniment, bonn-e-mahng, *m* salesman's speech; claptrap.

bonjour, bong- shoor, *m* good morning.

bonne, bonn, *f* maid-servant; nursemaid.

bonnement, bonn-mahng, *adv* simply; plainly.

bonnet, bonn-ay, *m* cap; **gros –,** groh –, big wig; magnate.

bonneterie, bonn-tree, *f* hosiery.

bonnetier, bonn-te-eh, *m* hosier.

bonsoir, bong-so'ăhr, *m* goodevening; good night.

bonté, bong-teh, *f* goodness; kindness **(pour,** to).

bord, bor, *m* border; edge; rim; side; bank; shore; **– du trottoir, –** dE-trot-o'ăhr, kerb.

bordée, bor-deh, *f* volley; broadside.

border, bor-deh, *v* to border; to edge; to hem; to tuck up.

bordereau, bor-der-roh, *m* schedule; detailed account; memorandum.

bordure, bor-dEEr, *f* border; edge; kerb.

boréal, e, bor-eh-ăhl, *a* northern.

borgne, born-yer, *a* blind in one eye; *fig* shady.

borne, born, *f* boundary; milestone; terminal.

borné, e, bor-neh, *pp* & *a* limited; narrow; shortwitted.

borner, bor-neh, *v* to bound; to limit; to confine.

bosquet, boss-kay, *m* grove; thicket.

bosse, boss, *f* hump; bump; embossment.

bosseler, boss-leh, *v* to emboss; to dent; to batter.

bossu, e, boss-E, *mf* hunchback; *a* hunchbacked.

bot, bo, *n* & *a* used only in **pied-bot,** pe-eh-bo, clubfoot; club-footed.

botanique, bot-ăh-nick, *f* botany; *a* botanical.

botte, bott, *f* boot; high boot; bundle; hank; thrust; **à propos de –s,** ăh pro-poh de –, without any reason.

botter, bott-eh, *v* to help one with his boots; *fam* to suit; to boot; to kick.

bottier, bott-e-eh, *m* bootmaker.

bottin, bott-ang, *m* French telephone directory.

bottine, bott-een, *f* half-boot; lady's boot; boot.

bouc, book, *m* he-goat; **– émissaire,** –eh-miss-air, scape-goat.

boucanier, boo-kăh-ne-eh, *m* buccaneer.

bouche, boosh, *f* mouth;

opening.

bouchée, boo-sheh, *f* mouthful.

boucher, boo-sheh, *v* to stop; to obstruct; to cork.

bouch-er, èr, boo-sheh, *mf* butcher.

boucherie, boosh-ree, *f* butcher's shop or trade; shambles; slaughter.

bouchon, boo-shong, *m* cork; stopper; ale-house.

boucle, boo-kl, *f* buckle; ring; curl; – **d'oreille**, –doh-ray'e, ear-ring.

boucler, boo-kleh, *v* to buckle; to ring; to curl.

bouclier, boo-kle-eh, *m* shield; buckler.

bouder, boo-deh, *v* to pout; to sulk.

boudin, boo-dang, *m* black pudding.

boue, boo, *f* mud; mire; dirt.

bouée, boo-eh, *f* buoy.

boueur, or boueux, boo-er, *m* dustman.

boueu-x, se, boo-er, *a* muddy.

bouffant, e, boo-fahng, *a* puffed; baggy.

bouffée, boo-feh, *f* puff; whiff.

bouffer, boo-feh, *v* to puff out; *pop* to eat greedily.

bouffi, e, boo-fe, *pp & a* puffed up; inflated; (**de**, with).

bouffon, boo-fong, *m* buffoon; jester.

bouffon, ne, boo-fong, *a* comical; droll.

bouge, boosh, *m* hovel; den; bulge.

bougeoir, boo-sho'ăhr, *m* flat candlestick.

bouger, boo-sheh, *v* to stir; to budge; to move.

bougie, boo-shee, *f* wax candle; sparking-plug.

bougonner, boo-ghonn-eh, *v* to grumble.

bougran, boo-grahng, *m* buckram.

bouillabaisse, boo'e-yăh-bess, *f* highly-seasoned fish soup.

bouillant, e, boo'e-yahng, *a* boiling; hot-tempered.

bouilli, boo'e-yee, *a* boiled.

bouillie, boo'e-yee, *f* baby cereal; gruel.

bouillir, boo'e-yeer, *v* to boil.

bouilloire, boo'e-yo'ăhr, *f* kettle.

bouillon, boo'e-yong, *m* broth; soup; stock; bubble.

bouillonner, boo'e-yonn-eh, *v* to bubble up; to boil.

bouillotte, boo'e-yot, *f* hot water bottle; (cardgame) bouillotte.

boulangerie, boo-lahng sh-ree, *f* baker's shop.

boule, bool, *f* ball; **jeu de –s, sher–der–**, game of bowls.

bouleau, boo-loh, *m* birchtree.

boulet, boo-lay, *m* cannon-ball; shot; small ovoid coal.

boulette, boo-lett, *f* meat ball; pellet; blunder.

boulevard, bool-văhr, *m* boulevard.

bouleversement, bool-vair-ser-mahng, *m* overthrow; confusion.

bouleverser, bool-vair-seh, *v* to overthrow; to upset.

boulier, boo-lee-eh, *m* abacus; scoring board.

boulon, boo-long, *m* bolt; pin.

boulonner, boo-lonn-eh, *v* to bolt; *fam* to work hard.

bouquet, boo-kay, *m* bunch; nosegay; aroma; crowning piece; prawn.

bouquin, boo-kang, *m fam* book.

bouquiner, boo-ke-neh, *v fam* to read.

bouquiniste, boo-ke-nisst, *m* dealer in secondhand

books.

bourbe, boohrb, *f* mud; mire; dirt.

bourbier, boohr-be-eh, *m* slough; mire.

bourde, boohrd, *f* fib, sham.

bourdon, boohr-dong, *m* bumble-bee; great bell; drone bass.

bourdonner, boohr-donn-eh, *v* to hum; to buzz.

bourg, boohr, *m* market town; borough.

bourgade, boohr-gǎhd, *f* small town or large village.

bourgeois, -e, boohr-sho'ǎh, *mf* citizen; middleclass man or woman; bourgeois; **les petits –,** lay per te –, the lower middle class; master; *a** middle class; common.

bourgeoisie, boohr-sho'ǎh-zee, *f* middle class.

bourgeon, boohr-shong, *m* bud; shoot; *fam* pimple.

bourgeonné, e, boohr-shonn-eh, *a* in bud; pimply.

bourgmestre, boohrg-mess-tr, *m* burgomaster.

bourgogne, boohr-gonn-yer, *m* Burgundy wine.

bourrade, boo-rǎhd, *f* cuff; hard blow.

bourrasque, boo-rǎhsk, *f* gust of wind.

bourre, boohr, *f* flock; wadding.

bourreau, boo-roh, *m* executioner; tormentor, tyrant.

bourreler, boohr-leh, *v* to prick; to sting; to torment.

bourrelet, boohr-lay, *m* pad; padding; cushion; *fam* rolls of fat.

bourrelier, boohr-le-eh, *m* harness-maker.

bourrer boo-reh, *v* to stuff; to cram; (**de,** with); to thrash.

bourriche, boo-reesh, *f* basket; hamper.

bourru, e, boo-rE, *a* surly; rough.

bourse, boohrs, *f* purse; scholarship; Stock Exchange.

boursier, boohr-se-eh, *a* & *n* exhibitioner; speculator on the Stock Exchange.

boursoufler, boor-soo-fleh, *v* to bloat; to puff up.

bousculer, boos-kE-leh, *v* to jostle; to hustle.

bouse, booz, *f* cow-dung; manure.

boussole, boo-sol, *f* sea compass; compass.

bout, boo, *m* end; tip; **à –,** ǎh –, exhausted; **au – du compte,** oh – dE kongt, after all.

boutade, boo-tǎhd, *f* whim; freak; sally.

boute-en-train, boot-ahng-trang, *m* life and soul of a party.

bouteille, boo-tay'e, *f* bottle.

boutique, boo-teeck, *f* shop; boutique; stall.

boutiqui-er, -ère, boo-te-ke-eh, *mf* shopkeeper.

bouton, boo-tong, *m* bud; button; handle; knob; stud; pimple; **– de manchettes,** – der mahng-shett, *m* cufflink.

boutonner, boo-tonn-eh, *v* to button; to bud.

boutonnière, boo-tonn-e-air, *f* button-hole.

bouture, bou-tEEr, *f* slip; cutting (of plant).

bouvreuil, boo-vrer'e, *m* bullfinch.

boxe, box, *f* boxing.

boyau, bo'ǎh-yoh, *m* bowel; gut; hose; long narrow passage

bracelet, brǎhss-lay, *m* bracelet.

braconnier, brǎh-konn-e-eh, *m* poacher.

braguette, brah-ghett, *f* fly

(of trousers).

brailler, brah'e-yeh, *v* to bawl; to squall.

braire, brair, *v* to bray.

braise, brayz, *f* embers; live coals.

braisé, e, bray-zeh, *a* stewed; braised.

brancard, brahng-kähr, *m* stretcher; shaft.

brancardier, brahng-kähr-de-eh, *m* stretcher-bearer.

branche, brahngsh. *f* branch; bough; division.

brancher, brahng-sheh, *v* to branch; to plug in; to connect; to put through; to roost, to perch.

branchies, brahng-shee, *fpl* gills.

brandir, brahng-deer, *v* to brandish.

branlant, e, brahng-lahng, *a* shaking; tottering; loose.

branle, brangl, *m* swinging; impulse; motion; **donner le –,** donn-eh ler –, to set going.

branle-bas, brahngl-bah, *m* upset; clearing the decks for action.

branler, brahng-leh, *v* to swing; to totter; to be loose.

braquer, bräh-keh, *v* to aim (**sur,** at); to change direction (of car, etc.).

bras, bräh, *m* arm; handle; bracket; power; labour; **– dessus – dessous, –** der-*se* – der-soo, arm in arm.

brasier, bräh-ze-eh, *m* red-hot coal-fire; brazier.

brassard, brähss-ähr, *m* armlet; arm-band.

brasse, brähss, *f* fathom; stroke; breast stroke.

brassée, brähss-eh, *f* armful; stroke.

brasser, brähss-eh, *m* to brew; to concoct.

brasserie, brähss-ree, *f* brewery; café; restaurant.

brasseur, brähss-er, *m* brewer

bravade, bräh-vähd, *f* bravado; bluster.

brave,* brähv, *a* brave; honest; good; smart; **un homme –,** ung n'omm –, a brave man; **un – homme,** ung – omm, a worthy man.

braver, bräh-veh, *v* to brave; to face; to dare.

bravoure, bräh-voohr, *f* bravery; courage; gallantry.

brebis, brer-be, *f* sheep; ewe; **– galeuse,** – gäh-lerz, black sheep (of the family).

brèche, braysh, *f* breach; gap; notch.

bredouille, brer-doo'e-yer, *a* empty-handed; **être –,** to have failed.

bredouiller, brer-doo'e-yeh, *v* to mumble.

bref, brayf, *adv* briefly; in short.

br-ef, ève, *a* brief; short.

breloque, brer-lock, *f* trinket; charm.

brème, braym, *f* bream.

bretelle, brer-tell, *f* strap; *pl* braces.

breuvage, brer-vähsh, *m* drink; draught; beverage.

brevet, brer-vay, *m* patent; licence; warrant; commission; diploma.

breveter, brerv-teh, *v* to patent; to grant a patent; to commission.

bréviaire, breh-ve-air, *m* breviary.

bribe, breeb, *f* scrap.

bric-à-brac, breeck-äh-brähck, *m* curios; odds and ends; junk.

bricole, bree-kol, *f* breast harness; *fpl* odds and ends; trifles.

bricoler, bree-ko-leh, *v* to put breast harness on horse; to do odd jobs; to potter about; to do DIY.

bricoleur, bree-ko-ler, *a* & *n* handy; handy-man.

bride, breed, *f* bridle; reins; string (of bonnet etc.); treble (crochet); **tourner –,** toohr-neh –, to turn back.

brider, bre-deh, *v* to bridle; to restrain; to tie up.

brie, bree, *m* Brie cheese.

brièvement, bre-ayv-mahng, *adv* briefly.

brièveté, bre-ayv-teh, *f* briefness.

brigade, bre-găhd, *f* brigade; gang; **– de sûreté,** –der sEEr-teh, detective force.

brigadier, bre-găh-de-eh, *m* corporal; bombardier; sergeant; foreman.

brigand, bre-ghahng, *m* thief; robber.

brigue, breegh, *f* aspire to; cabal.

briguer, bre-gheh, *v* to intrigue for; to solicit.

brillamment, bree-yăh-mahng, *adv* brilliantly.

brillant, e, bree-yahng, *a* bright; brilliant; shining. *n* brilliancy; shine; diamond.

briller, bree-yeh, *v* to shine; to be conspicuous.

brimborion, brang-bo-re-

ong, *m* bauble; trinket.

brimer, bree-meh, *v* to rag; to persecute.

brin, brang, *m* bit; blade; sprig.

brioche, bre-osh, *f* bun.

brique, brick, *f* brick.

briquet, bre-kay, *m* cigarette lighter; **pierre à –,** pe-ayr ah–, *f* lighter flint.

briqueterie, brick-tree, *f* brick-works.

bris, bre, *m* wreck.

brisant, bre-zahng, *m* breaker; reef.

brise, breez, *f* breeze.

briser, bre-zeh, *v* to break; **se –,** to break up.

broc, brock, *m* jug; jar.

brocanter, brock-ahng-teh, *v* to deal in second-hand goods.

brocant-eur, -euse, brock-ahng-ter, *mf* dealer in second-hand goods; broker.

brocard, brock-ăhr, *m* taunt; jeer; scoff.

brocart, brock-ăhr, *m* brocade.

broche, brosh, *f* spit; brooch.

broché, e, brosh-eh, *pp* & *a* (books) paperbacked.

brochet, brosh-ay, *m* pike.

brochette, bro-shett, *f* skewer; small spit.

brochure, brosh-EEr, *f* pamphlet, brochure.

broder, brod-eh, *v* to embroider; *fig* to embellish (a story).

broderie, brod-ree, *f* embroidery; *fig* embellishment.

broiement, bro'ăh-mahng, *m* pounding; crushing.

broncher, brong-sheh, *v* to stumble; to trip; **sans –,** sahng –, without flinching.

bronches, brongsh, *fpl* bronchia.

bronchite, brong-sheet, *f* bronchitis.

bronzage, brong-zăhsh, *m* suntan.

bronze, brongz, *m* bronze.

bronzer, brong-zeh, *v* to bronze; to tan.

brosse, bross, *f* brush.

brosser, bross-eh, *v* to brush.

brou, broo, *m* husk; hull.

brouet, broo-ay, *m* thin broth.

brouette, broo-ett, *f* wheel-barrow; hand cart.

brouhaha, broo-ăh-ăh, *m* uproar; hubbub.

brouillamini, broo'e-yăh-me-ne, *m fam* confusion.

brouillard, broo'e-yăhr, *m* fog; haze; rough book;

blotting-paper.

brouille, broo'e-ye, *f* disagreement; quarrel.

brouiller, broo'e-yeh, *v* to mix up; to confuse; **se –,** to fall out; to quarrel.

brouillon, broo'e-yong, *m* rough draft; rough book.

brouillon, ne, broo'e-yong, *n* & *a* blundering; muddle-headed.

broussailes, broo-sah'e, *fpl* brushwood.

brouter, broo-teh, *v* to graze.

broyer, bro'ăh-yeh, *v* to pound; to crush.

bru, brE, *f* daughter-in-law.

bruine, brween, *f* drizzling rain.

bruire, brweer, *v* to rustle; to murmur.

bruissement, brweess-mahng, *m* rustling; rumbling.

bruit, brwee, *m* noise; din; rumour; sound.

brûlant, e, brE-lahng, *a* burning; scorching; fervent; impassioned.

brûle-pourpoint (à), ăh brEEl poohr-po'ang, *adv* point-blank.

brûler, brE-leh, *v* to burn; to blow; to pass without stopping (traffic lights, etc).

brûlure, brE-lEEr, *f* burn; scald.

brume, brEEm, *f* mist; haze.

brun, e, brung, brEEn, *a* & *n* brown; dusky; dark.

brunâtre, brE-nah-tr, *a* brownish.

brune, brEEn, *f* dusk; dark complexioned woman.

brunir, brE-neer, *v* to brown; to burnish; to tan.

brusque,* brEEsk, *a* blunt; rough; abrupt; sudden.

brusquer, brEEss-keh, *v* to be blunt with; hurry on (of events).

brusquerie, brEEss-ker-ree, *f* bluntness; abruptness.

brut, e, brEt, *a* raw; rough; abrupt; coarse; gross.

brutal, e,* brE-tăhl, *a* brutal; brutish.

brutaliser, brE-tăhl-e-zeh, *v* to treat brutally; to bully.

brutalité, brE-tăhl-e-teh, *f* roughness; brutishness.

brute, brEt, *f* brute.

bruyamment, brE-yăh-mahng, *adv* noisily; loudly.

bruyant, e, brE-yahng, *a* noisy; loud.

bruyère, brE-yair, *f* heather.

buanderie, bE-ahngd-ree, *f* laundry (place).

bûche, bEEsh, *f* log; *fig* blockhead; hard work; Christmas log (cake).

bûcher, bEE-sheh, *m* wood-shed; funeral pyre; stake.

bûcheron, bEEsh-rong, *m* wood-cutter; logger.

bûch-eur, -euse, bEE-sher, *mf fam* plodder; swotter; hard worker.

budget, bEEd-shay, *m* budget.

buée, bE-eh, *f* steam; vapour; blur.

buffet, bE-fay, *m* sideboard; buffet; refreshment room.

buffle, bEE-fl *m* buffalo; buff-leather.

buis, bwe, *m* box-wood; box tree.

buisson, bweess-ong, *m* bush; thicket; **faire l'école buissonière,** fair leh-kol bweess-onn-e-air, to play truant.

bulle, bEEl, *f* bubble.

bulletin, bEEl-tang, *m* report; bulletin; ticket; ballot paper.

buraliste, bE-răh-lisst, *mf* office-keeper; tobacconist.

bureau, bE-roh, *m* office; writing-desk; board.

bureaucrate, bE-roh-

krâht, *m* bureaucrat; *fam*
red-tapist.

bureaucratie, bE-roh-
krâhss-ee, *f* bureaucracy;
fam red-tape.

burette, bE-rayt, *f* cruet;
can; flagon.

burlesque, bEEr-lessk, *a*
burlesque; ludicrous.

burnous, bEEr-nooss, *m*
burnous; Arab cloak.

busc, bEEsk, *m* busk;
whalebone.

buse, bEEz, *f* buzzard; *fig*
blockhead.

buste, bEEst, *m* bust.

but, bE, *m* mark; aim; goal;
end; purpose.

buter, bE-teh, *v* to butt; to
prop; to stumble; **se –**,
ser –, to be bent (à, on).

buté, bE-teh, *a* fixed;
obstinate.

butin, bE-tang, *m* plunder;
booty.

butor, bE-tor, *m fig* lout.

butte, bEEt, *f* mound;
knoll; **en – à,** ahng – ăh,
exposed to.

buvable, bE-văh-bl, *a*
drinkable.

buvard, bE-văhr, *m*
blotting-pad; **papier –,**
păh-pe-eh –, blotting-
paper.

buveu-r, -se, bE-ver, *mf*
drinker.

ça, săh, *pron* contraction of **cela,** ser-lăh, that.

çà, săh, *adv* hither; – **et là,** – eh lăh, here and there.

cabale, kăh-băhl, *f* cabal.

cabane, kăh-băhnn, *f* hut; cabin.

cabanon, kăh-băh-nong, *m* cell; padded cell.

cabaret, kăh-băh-ray, *m* cabaret.

cabas, kăh-bah, *m* rush basket; bag.

cabestan, kăh-bess-tahng, *m* capstan; windlass.

cabillaud, kăh-bee-yoh, *m* (fresh) codfish.

cabine, kăh-been, *f* cabin; beach hut; cubicle (at pool); phone box; – **d'essayage,** –deh-seh-yăhsh, *m* changing room (shop).

cabinet, kăh-be-ney, *m* small room; closet; office; practice; WC; chambers; cabinet (politics).

câble, kah-bl, *m* cable; rope.

câbler, kah-bleh, *v* to cable; to twist (strands).

câblogramme, kah-blo-grahmm, *m* cablegram.

caboche, kăh-bosh, *f fam* head.

cabosser, kăh-bo-sseh, *v* to bump; to dent.

cabotage, kăh-bot-ăhsh, *m* coasting.

caboter, kăh-bot-eh, *v* to coast.

cabotin, kăh-bot-ang, *m* bad actor; strolling player; show off.

cabrer (se), ser kăh-breh,

v to rear; to fire up.

cabriole, kăh-bre-ol, *f* caper; leap; somersault.

cabriolet, kăh-bre-oll-ay, *m* convertible (car).

cacahuète, kăh-kăh-wait, *f* peanut.

cacao, kăh-kăh-o, *m* cocoa.

cacatoes, kăh-kăh-to'es, *m* cockatoo.

cachalot, kăh-shă-lo, *m* sperm-whale.

cache, kăhsh, *f* hiding-place.

cache-cache, *m* hide-and-seek.

cache-nez, kăhsh-neh, *m* muffler; scarf.

cacher, kăh-sheh, *v* to hide; to conceal.

cachet, kăh-shay, *m* seal; *med* style; tablet; fee (show business).

cacheter, kăhsh-teh, *v* to seal (up).

cachette, kăh-shett, *f* hiding-place; **en –,** ahng –, secretly.

cachot, kăh-sho, *m* cell; dungeon; prison.

cachotterie, kăh-shot-ree, *f* affected secretiveness.

cadavre, kăh-dah-vr, *m* corpse; dead body.

cadeau, kăh-doh, *m* present; gift.

cadenas, kăhd-nah, *m*

padlock.

cadenasser, kăhd-năhss-eh, *v* to padlock.

cadence, kăh-dahngss, *f* cadence; rhythm.

cadet, te, kăh-day, *a* & *n* younger; least; youngest.

cadran, kăh-drahng, *m* dial.

cadre, kah-dr, *m* frame; plan; managerial staff; staff.

cadrer, kah-dreh, *v* to agree; to tally.

cadu-c, que, kăh-dEEk, *a* lapsed; obsolete; null and void.

caducité, kăh-dE-se-teh, *f* decrepitude.

cafard, kăh-făhr, *m* cockroach; **avoir le –**, *v* *fam* to be down (in the dumps).

cafarder, kăh-făhr-deh, *v* to sneak.

café, kăh-feh, *m* coffee; café; **– au lait**, – oh lay, coffee with milk; **– noir**, – no'ăhr, black coffee.

cafétéria, kăh-feh-teh-re-ăh, *f* cafeteria.

cafetière, kăhf-te-air, *f* coffee-pot.

cage, kăhsh, *f* cage; coop; frame.

cagneu-x, se, kăhn-yer, *a* knock-kneed.

cagot, e, kăh-go, *n* & *a*

hypocrite.

cahier, kăh-yeh, *m* copy-book; exercise-book.

cahin-caha, kăh-ang kăh-ăh, *adv* so so; middling.

cahot, kăh-o, *m* jolt; road shock.

cahoter, kăh-ot-eh, *v* to jolt; to bump along.

cahute, kăh-EEt, *f* hut; hovel.

caille, kah'e, *f* quail.

cailler, kah'e-yeh, *v* to curdle; to clot.

caillot, kah'e-o, *m* clot.

caillou, kah'e-yoo, *m* pebble; flint; stone.

caisse, kess, *f* cash desk; check out; case; box; chest; cash-box; fund; (carriage) body; drum; **– d'épargne**, – deh-păhrn'yer, savings bank.

caissi-er, ère, kess-e-eh, *mf* cashier.

cajoler, kăh-sholl-eh, *v* to wheedle; to coax.

calamité, kăh-lăh-me-teh, *f* calamity.

calandre, kăh-lahng-dr, *f* calender; mangle.

calcaire, kăhl-kair, *m* limestone; *a* calcareous.

calciner, kăhl-se-neh, *v* to calcine; to burn up.

calcul, kăhl-kEEl, *m* calculation; arithmetic; calculus; stone (in

bladder, etc).

calculer, kăhl-kE-leh, *v* to calculate; to reckon; to compute.

cale, kăhl, *f* wedge; (ship) hold.

calé e, kăh-leh, *a* wedged up; stalled; *fam* learned.

caleçon, kăhl-song, *m* men's underpants; bathing trunks.

calembour, kăh-lahng-boohr, *m* pun.

calembredaine, kăh-lahng-brer-dayn, *f* foolery; nonsense.

calendrier, kăh-lahng-dre-eh, *m* calendar.

calepin, kăhl-pang, *m* memorandum-book; notebook.

caler, kăh-leh, *v* to wedge up; to jam; to stall.

calfeutrer, kăhl-fer-treh, *v* to make snug; to make draught-proof; **se –**, to shut oneself up cosily.

calibre, kăh-lee-br, *m* calibre; size; diameter.

calice, kăh-liss, *m* chalice; calyx.

calicot, kăh-le-ko, *m* calico.

califourchon (à), ăh kăh-le-foohr-shong, *adv* astride.

câlin, e, kah-lang, *a* caressing.

câliner, kah-le-neh, v to caress; to fondle.

calleu-x, se, käh-ler, a callous; horny.

calmant, kähl-mahng, m sedative.

calmant, e, kähl-mahng, a soothing.

calmar, kähl-mähr m squid.

calme, kählm, m calm; stillness; a quiet; calm.

calmer, kähl-meh, v to calm; to quiet; to still.

calomnie, käh-lomm-nee, f calumny; slander.

calomnier, käh-lomm-ne-yeh, v to calumniate; to slander.

calorie, käh-lo-re, f calorie.

calorifère, käh-lor-e-fair, a heat-conveying; m heating installation.

calorifuger, käh-lo-re-fE-sheh, v to insulate; to lag.

calotte, käh-lott, f skullcap; cap; slap; fam priesthood.

calotter, käh-lott-eh, v to box the ears of.

calque, kählk, m tracing; copy.

calquer, kähl-keh, v to trace; to copy.

calvaire, kähl-vair, m calvary; fig martyrdom.

calvitie, kähl-vee-see, f baldness.

camarade, käh-mäh-rähd, m comrade; pal; friend.

camaraderie, käh-mäh-rähd-ree, f close friendship; comradeship.

camard, e, käh-mähr, a flat-nosed.

cambouis, kahng-boo-e, m dirty oil or grease.

cambrer, kahng-breh, v to bend; to arch; se –, ser –, to camber.

cambriolage, kahng-bre-ol-ähsh, m burglary.

cambrioleur, kahng-bre-ol-er, m burglar.

came, kähm, f cam; arbre à –, ahr-br äh–, m camshaft.

camée, käh-meh, m cameo.

camelote, kähm-lot, f cheap goods; trash; stuff.

caméra, käh-meh-räh, f cine-camera; film, TV camera.

caméscope, käh-meh-skop, m camcorder.

camion, käh-me-ong, m lorry; wagon.

camionnage, käh-me-onn-ähsh, m carting; carriage (of goods).

camionnette, käh-me-onn-ett, f van.

camisole, käh-me-zol, f

camisole; straight jacket.

camouflage, käh-moo-flähsh, m camouflage.

camouflet, käh-moo-flay, m affront; insult.

camoufler, käh-moo-fleh, v to disguise; to camouflage; se –, to hide.

camp, kahng, m camp.

campagnard, e, kahng-pähn-yähr, n & a countryman, countrywoman; rustic.

campagne, kahng-pähn-yer, f country; campaign.

campement, kahngp-mahng, m encampment; camping.

camper, kahng-peh, to camp.

camphre, kahng-fr, m camphor.

camping, kahng-peeng, m campsite.

campus, kang-pEss, m campus.

camus, e, käh-mE, a flat-nosed.

canaille, käh-nah'e, f scoundrel.

canal, käh-nähl, m canal; channel; pipe; conduit.

canapé, käh-näh-peh, m sofa; open sandwich.

canard, käh-nähr, m duck;

drake; false news; rag (newspaper).

cancan, kahng-kahng, *m* gossip; cancan.

cancaner, kahng-käh-neh, *v* to gossip.

cancer, kahng-sair, *m* cancer.

cancéreu-x, se kahng-seh-rer, *a* cancerous; *n* cancer patient.

cancre, kahng-kr, *m* crab-fish; *fig* dunce.

candélabre, kahng-deh-läh-br, *m* candelabrum; street-lamp.

candeur, kahng-der, *f* candour; frankness.

candidat, kahng-de-däh, *m* candidate.

candide, * kahng-deed, *a* candid; open; frank.

cane, kähn, *f* (female) duck.

caneton, kähn-tong, *m* duckling.

canevas, kähn-vah, *m* canvas; sketch.

caniche, käh-neesh, *m* poodle.

canif, käh-niff, *m* penknife.

canin, käh-nang, *a* canine.

canine, käh-neen, *f* canine tooth.

caniveau, käh-ne-voh, *m* gutter.

cannabis, käh-näh-beess,

m cannabis.

canne, kähn, *f* cane; walking-stick; rod.

cannelle, käh-nell, *f* cinnamon.

cannelure, kähn-lEEr, *f* groove.

canon, käh-nong, *m* cannon; gun.

canot, käh-no, *m* canoe; – **de sauvetage**, –der sohvtahsh, lifeboat.

canotage, käh-not-ähsh, *m* boating.

canotier, käh-not-e-eh, *m* oarsman; boater hat.

cantaloup, kahng-täh-loo, *m* cantaloup melon.

cantatrice, kahng-täh-triss, *f* professional singer.

cantharide, kahng-täh-reed, *f* Spanish fly.

cantine, kahng-teen, *f* canteen.

cantique, kahng-tick, *m* canticle; sacred song.

canton, kahng-tong, *m* sub-district; canton.

cantonade, kahng-tonn-ähd, *f* (theatre) wings; à **la** –, äh läh –, for all to hear.

cantonnier, kahng-tonn-e-eh, *m* road-mender.

caoutchouc, käh-oot-shoo, *m* india-rubber; mackintosh.

cap, kähp, *m* cape.

capable, käh-päh-bl, *a* able; efficient; qualified.

capacité, käh-päh-se-teh, *f* capacity; capaciousness; qualification.

cape, kähp, *f* cape; cloak with a hood.

capitaine, käh-pe-tayn, *m* captain.

capital, e, käh-pe-tähl, *a* capital; principal; chief.

capital, käh-pe-tähl, *m* capital; stock.

capitale, käh-pe-tähl, *f* (city) capital.

capiteu-x, se, käh-pe-ter, *a* heady; strong (of wines).

capitonner, käh-pe-tonn-eh, *v* to stuff; to pad.

capituler, käh-pe-tE-leh, *v* to capitulate; to come to terms.

capon, käh-pong, *m* coward.

caporal, käh-por-ähl, *m* corporal.

capote, käh-pot, *f* great coat; hooded cloak; hood (of car); *fam* condom.

câpre, käh-pr, *f* caper.

caprice, käh-priss, *m* caprice; whim; fancy.

capsule, kähp-sEEl, *f* capsule; cap.

capter, kähp-teh, *v* to pick

up (radio signal); to harness (water).

captieu-x, se, * kăhp-se-er, *a* captious.

capti-f, ve, kăhp-tiff, *a* captive; *n* prisoner.

capture, kăhp-tEEr, *f* capture; booty; arrest.

capturer, kăhp-tE-reh, *v* to capture; to arrest.

capuchon, kăh-pE-shong, *m* hood; cover.

capucin, kăh-pE-sang, *m* capuchin; friar.

capucine, kăh-pE-seen, *f* nasturtium.

caque, kăhck, *f* keg; barrel.

caquet, kăh-kay, *m* cackle.

caqueter, kăhck-teh, *v* to cackle; to chatter.

car, kăhr, *conj* for; because; as.

car, kăhr, *m* coach (motor).

carabine, kăh-răh-been, *f* rifle.

carabinier, kăh-răh-be-ne-eh, *m* rifleman.

caracoler, kăh-răh-koll-eh, *v* to wheel about; to prance.

caractère, kăh-răhck-tair, *m* character (personality); temper; type; print.

carafe, kăh-răhf, *f* decanter; water-bottle;

carafe.

carafon, kăh-răh-fong, *m* small decanter.

carambolage, kăh-rahng-boh-lăhsh, *m auto* pileup.

caramel, kăh-răh-mell, *m* burnt sugar; caramel; toffee.

carapace, kăh-răh-păhss, *f* carapace; shell.

carat, kăh-răh, *m* carat.

caravane, kăh-răh-văhn, *f* caravan.

carbonate, kăhr-bonn-ăht, *m* carbonate.

carbone, kăhr-bonn, *m* carbon.

carboniser, kăhr-bonn-e-zeh, *v* to carbonize; to char.

carburateur, kăhr-bE-rah-ter, *m* carburettor.

carbure, kăhr-bEEr, *m* carbide.

carcasse, kăhr-kăhss, *f* carcass; framework.

cardiaque, kăhr-de-ăhck, *a & mf* cardiac.

cardinal, e, kăhr-de-năhl, *a* cardinal; principal; chief.

Carême, kăh-raym, *m* Lent.

carence, kăh-rahngss, *f* deficiency.

carène, kăh-rain, *f* keel; bottom; careen.

caressant, e, kăh-rayss-ahng, *a* caressing; tender.

caresser, kăh-rayss-eh, *v* to caress; to stroke; to cherish.

cargaison, kăhr-gay-zong, *f* cargo freight.

cari, kăh-re *m* curry.

caricature, kăh-re-kăh-tEEr, *f* caricature.

carie, kăh-ree, *f* decay; –dentaire, dahng-tair, dental decay; cavity.

carillon, kăh-ree-ong, *m* chime; peal.

carmin, kăhr-mang, *m* crimson.

carnage, kăhr-năhsh, *m* slaughter.

carnassier, kăhr-năhss-e-eh, *a* carnivorous.

carnaval, kăhr-năh-văhl, *m* carnival.

carnet, kăhr-nay, *m* note-book.

carnivore, kăhr-ne-vor, *a* carnivorous.

carotte, kăh-rot, *f* carrot; *fam* humbug.

carotter, kăh-rot-eh, *v fam* to dupe; to cheat.

carpe, kăhrp, *f* carp.

carpette, kăhr-pett, *f* rug.

carré, kăh-reh, *m* square; landing.

carré, e, kăh-reh, *a* square; straight;

peremptory.

carreau, kăh-roh, *m* square; pane; tile; diamonds (cards).

carrefour, kăh-foohr, *m* crossroads.

carreler, kăh-leh, *v* to pave with brick or tile.

carrément, kăh-reh-mahng, *adv* squarely; boldly; straightforwardly.

carrer, kăh-reh, *v* to square; **se –** to strut.

carrière, kăh-re-air, *f* quarry; career.

carriole, kăh-re-ol, *f* light covered cart.

carrosse, kăh-ross, *m* coach (horse-drawn).

carrosserie, kăh-ross-re, *f* bodywork of car.

carrure, kăh-rEEr, *f* breadth of shoulders.

cartable, kăhr-tabl, *m* school satchel.

carte, kăhrt, *f* card; ticket; map; menu; **– bancaire,** --bahng-kair, cheque card; **– de crédit,** –der-kreh-de, credit card; **– de retrait,** –der-rer-treh, cash card; **– de vins,** –der-vang, wine list; **– grise,** –greez, car registration document .

cartilage, kăhr-te-lăhsh, *m* cartilage; *fam* gristle.

carton, kăhr-tong, *m* cardboard; carton; hat-box; cardboard box.

cartouche, kăhr-toosh, *f* cartridge; carton (of cigarettes); refill.

cas, kah, *m* case; matter; event; **en cas de,** ahng – der, in case of.

casani-er, ére, kăh-zăh-ne-eh, *a* home-loving.

cascadeur, kăhss-kăh-der, *m* stunt-man.

case, kahz, *f* hut; cabin; pigeonhole; square (on game board).

caser, kah-zeh, *v* to place; to find a situation for.

caserne, kăh-zairn, *f* barracks.

casier, kah-ze-eh, *m* set of pigeonholes; **– judiciaire,** –shE-de-se-air, police record.

casino, kăh-ze-noh, *m* casino.

casque, kăhssk, *m* helmet.

casquette, kăhss-kett, *f* cap.

cassant, e, kăhss-ahng, *a* brittle; blunt; sharp.

cassation, kăhss-ah-se-ong, *f* annulment; quashing; appeal.

casse, kăhss, *f* breakage.

casse-cou, kahss-koo, *m* break-neck; daredevil.

casse-noisettes, kahss-

no'äh-zett, *m* nut-cracker.

casse-tête, kahss-tayt, *m* club; tomahawk; puzzle; brainteaser.

casser, kahss-eh, *v* to break; to crack; to quash; to discharge.

casserole, kăhss-rol *f* saucepan.

cassette, kăhss-ett, *f* cassette; **lecteur de –,** leck-*ter* der, *m* cassette player.

cassis, kahss-iss, *m* black currant.

cassure, kahss-EEr, *f* broken place; crack; fracture.

caste, kăhsst, *f* caste.

castor, kăhss-tor, *m* beaver.

casuel, kăh-zE-ell, *m* perquisites; perk.

casuel, le,* kăh-zE-ell, *a* casual; accidental.

catalogue, kăh-tăh-log *m* catalogue; list.

cataplasme, kăh-tăh-plăhssm, *m* poultice.

catarrhe, kăh-tăhr, *m* catarrh.

catastrophe, kăh-tăhss-trof, *f* catastrophe.

catéchisme, kăh-teh-shissm, *m* catechism.

catégorie, kăh-teh-go-re, *f* category; order; class.

cathédrale, kăh-teh-drăhl, f cathedral.

catholique, kăh-toll-eeck, a & mf Catholic.

cauchemar, kohsh-măhr, m nightmare; bugbear.

cause, kohz, f cause; motive; case; trial; **à – de**, ăh – der, on account of.

causer, koh-zeh, v to cause; to chat.

causerie, kohz-ree, f talk; chat; chattering.

causeuse, koh-zerz, f settee.

caustique, kohss-tick, a caustic.

cauteleu-x, se,* koht-ler, a cunning; crafty.

cautériser, koh-teh-re-zeh, v to cauterize; to burn.

caution, koh-se-ong, f bail; security; **sujet à –**, SE-**shay** t'ăh –, not to be trusted.

cautionnement, koh-se-onn-mahng, m bail; surety; security.

cautionner, koh-se-onn-eh, v jur to stand surety for.

cavalerie, kăh-văhl-ree, f cavalry.

cavali-er, ère, kăh-văh-le-eh, mf horseman; horsewoman; rider; partner; a blunt; offhand.

cavalièrement, kăh-văh-le-air-mahng, adv bluntly; unceremoniously.

cave, kăhv, f cellar; vault; a hollow.

caveau, kăh-voh, m cellar; vault.

caverne, kăh-vairn, f cavern; cave; den.

cavité, kăh-ve-teh, f cavity; hollow.

CD, seh-deh, m abbr CD.

CD ROM, seh-deh-romm, m abbr CD ROM.

ce, cet, m; **cette**, f ser, sett, a this; that.

ceci, ser-se, pron this; this thing.

cécité, seh-se-teh, f blindness.

céder, seh-deh, v to yield; to give up; to hand over.

cédille, seh-dee-ye, f cedilla.

cèdre, say-dr, m cedar.

ceindre, sang-dr, v to enclose; to surround; to gird; to wreathe (**de**, with).

ceinture, sang-tEEr, f girdle; belt; waist; enclosure; zone; circle.

ceinturon, sang-tE-rong, m sword-belt.

cela, ser-lăh, or slăh, pron that.

célèbre, seh-lay-br, a celebrated; famous.

célébrer, seh-leh-breh, v to celebrate.

céler, ser-leh, v to hide; to conceal (**à**, from).

céleri, seh-ler-re, m celery.

célérité, seh-leh-re-teh, f speed; swiftness.

céleste, seh-laist, a celestial; heavenly.

célibat, seh-le-băh, m celibacy.

célibataire, seh-le-băh-tair, m bachelor; f single woman; a unmarried; single.

cellier, say-le-eh, m cellar; storeroom.

cellulaire, say-lE-lair, a cellular.

cellule, say-lEEl, f cell.

celui, m **celle**, f ser-lwe, sell, pron he; she; him; her; the one; that.

cendre, sahng-dr, f ash; ashes; cinder.

cendré, e, sahng-dreh, a ash-coloured.

cendrier, sahng-dre-eh, m ash-tray.

cendrillon, sahng-dree-yong, f Cinderella.

cène, sayn, f Lord's Supper.

censé, e, sahng-seh, a

reputed; supposed.

censeur, sahng-ser, *m* censor; critic.

censure, sahng-sEEr, *f* censorship; censure.

censurer, sahng-sE-reh, *v* to censure; to blame.

cent, sahng, *m* & *a* one hundred; hundred.

centaine, sahng-tain, *f* hundred; une –, EEn –, about a hundred.

centenaire, sahngt-nair, *m* centenary; *a* & *mf* centenarian.

centiare, sahng-te-ähr *m* centiare (a square metre).

centième, sahng-te-aym, *m* the hundredth part; *a* hundredth.

centigrade, sahng-te-grähd, *m* centigrade.

centigramme, sahng-te-grähm, *m* centigramme.

centime, sahng-teem, *m* centime.

centimètre, sahng-te-met-tr, *m* centimetre, *m* centimetre; *fam* tape measure; (hundredth part of a metre).

central, e, sahng-trähl, *a* central.

centralisation, sahng-trähle-zäh-se-ong, *f* centralisation.

centre, sahng-tr, *m* centre;

middle; – **de la ville**, – der-läh-veel town centre; – **de zone urbaine**, – der-zohn-EEr-bayn, inner-city; – **médical**, – meh-de-kähl, clinic; –**ville**, – veel, town centre.

centrifuge, sahng-tre-fEE sh, *a* centrifugal.

centupler, sahng-tE-pleh, *v* to increase a hundredfold.

cep, sayp, *m* vine-stock.

cependant, ser-pahng, *adv* meanwhile; *conj* yet; however.

céramique, seh-räh-meek, *a* ceramic; *f* ceramics; pottery.

cerceau, sair-soh, *m* hoop.

cercle, sair-kl, *m* circle; ring; hoop; club.

cercueil, sair-ker-e, *m* coffin.

céréale, seh-reh-ähl, *f* cereal.

céréales, seh-reh-ähl, *fpl* cereals; corn crops.

cérébral, e, seh-reh-brähl, *a* cerebral.

cérémonial, seh-reh-monn-e-ähl, *m* ceremonial.

cérémonie, seh-reh-monn-ee, *f* ceremony.

cérémonieu-x, se,* seh-reh-monn-e-er, *a*

ceremonious, formal.

cerf, sair, or sairf, *m* stag; deer; hart; – **volant**, – voll-ahng, stag-beetle; kite.

cerfeuil, sair-fer'e, *m* chervil.

cerise, ser-reez, *f* cherry.

cerisier, ser-re-ze-eh, *m* cherry tree.

cerneau, sair-noh, *m* green walnut.

cerné, e, sair-neh, *pp* & *a* surrounded; (eyes) black-ringed.

cerner, sair-neh, *v* to surround; to trap.

certain, e,* sair-tang, *a* certain, sure; *pl* (before a noun) some.

certes, sairt, *adv* most certainly.

certificat, sair-te-fe-käh, *m* certificate; testimonial.

certifier, sair-te-fe-eh, *v* to certify; to testify.

certitude, sair-te-tEEd, *f* certitude; certainty; assurance.

cerveau, sair-voh, *m* brain; mind; intellect.

cervelas, sair-ver-lah, *m* saveloy.

cervelle, sair-vell, *f* brains; head; intelligence.

ces, say (*pl* of ce) *mf a* these; those.

cessation, sess-äh-se-ong, f discontinuance.

cesse, sayss, f ceasing; respite.

cesser, sayss-eh, v to cease; to come to an end.

cessez-le-feu, says-eh-ler-fer, m ceasefire.

cessible, sayss-ee-bl, a jur transferable.

cession, sayss-e-ong, f jur transfer.

c'est-à-dire, sayt-ah-deer, conj that is to say.

chacal, shäh-kähl, m jackal.

chacun, e, shäh-kung, pron everyone; each; each one.

chafouin, e, shäh-foo-ang, n & a mean-looking; mean; sly-looking (person).

chagrin, shäh-grang, m grief, sorrow; trouble; (leather) shagreen.

chagrin e shäh-grang, a sorrowful; gloomy; peevish.

chagrinant, e, shäh-gre-nahng, a grievous; sad; vexing.

chagriner, shäh-gre-neh, v to grieve; to vex.

chahut, shäh-EE, m uproar; noise; **faire du –,** fair dE –, to make row.

chaîne, shain, f chain; line; pl fetters.

chaînon, shay-nong, m link (of chain).

chair, shair, f flesh; meat; pulp; **– de poule,** – der pool, goose-bumps.

chaire, shair, f pulpit; desk; professorship.

chaise, shayz, f chair; seat.

chaise longue, shayz long-gh, f deck-chair; chaise-longue; couch.

chaland, shäh-lahng, m lighter; barge.

châle, shahl, m shawl.

chalet, shah-lay, m Swiss cottage; chalet.

chaleur, shäh-ler, f heat; warmth; zeal; heat (of animals); **en –,** ahng –, a randy.

chaleureu-x, se,* shäh-ler-rer, a warm; ardent.

chaloupe, shäh-loop, f long-boat; launch.

chalumeau, shäh-lE-moh, m reed; blowpipe.

chalut, shäh-lE, m trawl-net.

chalutier, shäh-lE-te-eh, m trawler.

chamailler (se), ser shäh-mah'e-yeh, v to squabble; to quarrel.

chambranle, shahng-brahngl, m door frame.

chambre, shahng-br, f

bedroom; chamber;– **à une lit,** – äh-ung-lee f single room; **– pour une personne,** –poohr-En-pair-sonn, single room.

chambrée, shahng-breh, f roomful.

chameau, shäh-moh, m camel.

chamelier, shäh-mer-le-eh, m camel driver.

chamois, shäh-mo'äh, m chamois; wild goat; chamois leather; a buff.

champ, shahng, m field; ground; subject; scope; **surle–,** sEErler –, immediately; **à tout bout de –,** äh-too-boo der –, every moment.

champagne, shahng-pähn-yer, m champagne.

champêtre, shahng-pay-tr, a rural; rustic.

champignon, shahng-peen-yong, m mushroom.

champion, shahng-pe-ong, m champion.

chance, shahngss, f chance; luck.

chancelant, e, shahngs-lahng, a tottering.

chanceler, shahngss-leh, v to totter; to stagger.

chancelier, shahng-ser-le-eh, m chancellor.

chancellerie, shahng-sell-ree, f chancellery.

chanceu-x, se, shahng-ser, a lucky; risky.

chancre, shahng-kr, m canker.

chandeleur, shahngd-ler, f Candlemas.

chandelier, shahng-der-le'eh, m candlestick.

chandelle, shahng-dell, f candle.

change, shahngsh, m change; exchange; **agent de –,** ăh-shahng der –, stockbroker; exchange broker.

changeant, e, shahng-shahng, a changeable; fickle.

changement shahngsh-mahng, m change; alteration.

changer, shahng-sheh, v to change; to alter; to exchange; to shift.

changeur, shahngsh-er, m moneychanger.

chanoine, shăh-no'ăhn, m canon.

chanson, shahng-song, f song; ballad.

chansonnette, shahng-sonn-ett, f little song; ditty.

chansonnier, shahng-sonn-e-eh, m song-writer (esp satirical); song-book.

chant, shahng, m singing; song; strain; canto.

chantage, shahng-tăhsh, m blackmail.

chantant, e, shahng-tahng, a singing; tuneful.

chanter, shahng-teh, v to sing; to celebrate; fam to say; **faire –,** fair –, to blackmail.

chanteu-r, se, shahng-ter, mf singer.

chantier, shahng-te-eh, m yard; timber-yard; dockyard; building site.

chantonner, shahng-tonn-eh, v to hum a tune.

chanvre, shahng-vr, m hemp.

chaos, kăh-o, m chaos.

chape, shăhp, f cope; cover.

chapeau, shăh-poh, m hat.

chapelain, shăhp-lang, m chaplain.

chapelet, shăhp-lay, m chaplet; rosary.

chapeli-er, ère, shăh-per-le-eh, mf hatter.

chapelle, shăh-pell, f chapel.

chapellerie, shăh-pell-ree, f hat-making; hat-shop.

chapelure, shăhp-lEEr, f bread crumbs.

chaperon, shăhp-rong, m hood; chaperon.

chaperonner, shăhp-ronn-

eh, v to chaperon; to put a hood on.

chapiteau, shăh-pe-toh, m big top; marquee; capital; crest.

chapitre, shăh-pe-tr, m chapter; heading; chapter-house.

chapitrer, shăh-pe-treh, v to lecture; to reprimand.

chapon, shăh-pong, m capon.

chaque, shăhck, a each; every.

char, shăhr, m car; chariot; hearse.

charabia, shăh-răh-be-ăh, m gibberish.

charbon, shăhr-bong, m coal; charcoal; carbuncle.

charbonnage, shăhr-bonn-ăhsh, m colliery.

charbonner, shăhr-bonn-eh, v to blacken; to char.

charbonnier, shăhr-bonn-e-eh, m coal-man; charcoal-burner.

charcuterie, shăhr-kEEt-ree, f pork butcher's shop; delicatessen.

chardon, shăhr-dong, m thistle.

chardonneret, shăhr-donn-ray, m goldfinch.

charge, shăhrsh, f load; burden; expense; office;

charge.

chargement, shăhr-sher-mahng, *m* loading; cargo.

chargé, e, shăhr-sheh, *pp* & *a* full; laden; heavy (of stomach); **–** **d'affaires,** – dăh-fair, deputy ambassador.

charger, shăhr-sheh, *v* to load; to charge; to entrust (**de,** with); **se –,** to take upon oneslf.

chargeur, shăhr-sher, *m* loader; shipper.

chariot, shăh-re-o, *m* (supermarket) trolley; waggon; cart; truck; carriage (of typewriter).

charitable,* shăh-re-tăh-bl, *a* charitable.

charité, shăh-re-teh, *f* charity; alms; benevolence.

charivari, shăh-re-văh-re, *m* hurlyburly; deafening noise.

charlatan, shăhr-lăh-tahng, *m* quack; charlatan.

charmant, e, shăhr-mahng, *a* charming; delightful.

charme, shăhrm, *m* charm; spell; attraction.

charmer, shăhr-meh, *v* to charm.

charnel, le, shăhr-nell, *a* carnal; sensual.

charnière, shăhr-ne-air, *f* hinge; **à la – de,** at the meeting point between.

charnu, e, shăhr-nE, *a* fleshy.

charogne, shăh-ronn-yer, *f* carrion.

charpente, shăhr-pahngt, *f* frame-work.

charpentier, shăhr-pahng-te-eh, *m* carpenter.

charpie, shăhr-pee, *adv* **en –,** in shreds.

charretée, shăhr-teh, *f* cart-load.

charretier, shăhr-te-eh, *m* carter.

charrette, shăh-rett, *f* cart.

charrier, shăh-re-eh, *v* to cart; to drift; *fam* to poke fun at; to exaggerate.

charron, shăh-rong, *m* wheelwright; cartwright.

charrue, shăh-rE, *f* plough; **mettre la – devant les bœufs,** met-tr lăh–der-vahng lay ber, to put the cart before the horse.

charte, shăhrt, *f* charter.

chartreuse, shăhr-trerz, *f* Chartreuse (Carthusian monastery); chartreuse (liqueur).

chas, shah, *m* eye of a needle.

châsse, shahss, *f* shrine;

frame.

chasse, shăhss, *f* chase; hunting; shooting; sport; pursuit.

chasse-neige, shăhss-naysh, *m* (*inv in pl*) snow-plough; (skiing) stem.

chasser, shăhss-eh, *v* to hunt; to drive away; to shoot; to discharge.

chasseur, shăhss-er, *m* hunter; sportsman; footman.

châssis, shahss-e, *m* frame; sash; chassis.

chaste,* shăhsst, *a* chaste; pure; modest.

chasteté, shăhss-ter-teh, *f* chastity; purity.

chat, te, shăh, *mf* cat; **– huant,** –E-ahng, *m* tawny owl; brown owl.

châtaigne, shah-tain-yer, *f* sweet chestnut.

châtain, e, shah-tang, *a* chestnut.

château, shah-toh, *m* castle; mansion.

châteaubriant, shah-toh-bre-ahng *m* thick grilled fillet-steak.

châtelain, e, shaht-lang, *mf* owner of a manor or castle.

châtier, shah-te-eh, *v* to chastise; to punish; to correct.

châtiment, shah-te-mahng; *m* chastisement; punishment.

chatoiement, shäh-to'äh-mahng, *m* glistening; play of colours.

chaton, shäh-tong, *m* kitten; setting of stone.

chatouiller, shäh-too'e-yeh, *v* to tickle.

chatouilleu-x, se, shäh-too'e-yer, *a* ticklish; touchy.

chatoyer, shä-to'äh-yeh, *v* to glisten; to shimmer.

châtrer, shah-treh, *v* to castrate; to prune.

chatterie, shätt-ree, *f* (usually in *pl*) coaxing way.

chaud, shoh, *m* heat; warmth; **avoir –,** äh-vo'ähr –, to be hot.

chaud, e,* a hot; warm; new (of news).

chaudière, shoh-de-air, *f* copper; boiler.

chaudron, shoh-drong, *m* kettle; caldron; *fam* bad piano.

chaudronnier, shoh-dronn-e-eh, *m* boilermaker; brazier.

chauffage, shoh-fäsh, *m* warming; heating; **– central,** – sahng-trähl, *m* central heating.

chauffe, shohf, *f* heating; furnace.

chauffe-eau, shohf-oh, *m* water; heater.

chauffer, shoh-feh, *v* to warm; to heat; to get hot.

chauffeur, shoh-fer, *m* stoker; driver; chauffeur.

chaume, shohm, *m* stubble; thatch.

chaumière, shoh-me-air, *f* thatched house; cottage.

chausse-pied, shohss-pe-eh, *m* shoehorn.

chaussée, shohss-eh, *f* causeway; carriageway; road.

chausser, shohss-eh, *v* to put shoes or boots on; to supply with shoes or boots.

chaussette, shohss-ett, *f* sock.

chausson, shohss-ong, *m* slipper; babies' bootees; **– de dance,** – der dahngss, ballet shoes.

chaussure, shohss-EEr, *f* shoes; foot-gear; **–s de sport,** – der-spor *fpl* trainers.

chauve, shohv, *a* bald.

chauve-souris, shohv-soo-re, *f* bat.

chauvin,e, shoh-vang, *a, mf* chauvinist.

chauvinisme, shoh-ve-nissm, *m* chauvinism.

chaux, shoh, *f* lime; **blanc de –,** blahng der –, white-wash.

chavirer, shäh-ve-reh, *v* to capsize.

chef, sheff.; *m* ; chef; head-cook; chief; boss; **de son –,** der song –, on one's responsibility.

chef-d'œuvre, shay-der-vr, *m* masterpiece.

chef-lieu, sheff-le-er, *m* chief town (of country).

chemin, sher-mang, *m* way; road; path; **– de fer,** – der fair, railway; **en –,** ahng –, on the way.

chemineau, sher-me-no, *m* tramp.

cheminée, sher-me-neh, *f* chimney; fireplace; mantelpiece; funnel.

cheminer, sher-me-neh, *v* to walk; to jog on.

cheminot, sher-me-no, *m* railwayman.

chemise, sher-meez, *f* shirt; **– de nuit,** – der nwee, nightdress; case; folder.

chemisier, sher-me-ze-eh, *m* shirt-maker; woman's blouse or shirt.

chenal, sher-nähl, *m* channel.

chenapan, sher-näh-pahng, *m* scamp; wretch.

chêne, shain, *m* oak.

chéneau, sheh-noh, *m* eaves; gutter.

chenet, sher-nay, *m* firedog.

chenil, sher-ne, *m* kennel.

chenille, sher-nee-ye, *f* caterpillar.

chèque, sheck, *m* cheque; – **barré,** – băh-reh, crossed cheque; – **de voyage,** – der-voăh-yăhsh, traveller's cheque.

cher, shair, *adv* dear; at a high price.

ch-er, ère,* shair, *a* dear; beloved; costly.

chercher, shair-sheh, *v* to seek; to look for; **envoyer –,** ahng-vo'ăh-yeh –, to send for.

chercheur, shair-sher, *m* seeker; inquirer.

chère, shair, *f* living; fare; cheer; **faire bonne –,** fair bonn –, to live well; to feast.

chéri, e, sheh-re, *a* darling; beloved; favourite; *m* dear one; dearest.

chérir, sheh-reer, *v* to cherish; to love.

cherté, shair-teh, *f* high price; dearness.

chérubin, sheh-rE-bang, *m* cherub.

chéti-f, ve,* sheh-tiff, *a* puny; paltry; weak.

cheval, sher-văhl, *m* horse; – **vapeur,** – văh-per, horsepower.

chevaleresque, sher-văhl-resk, *a* chivalrous.

chevalerie, sher-văhl-ree, *f* chivalry; knighthood.

chevalet, sher-văh-lay, *m* support; stand.

chevalier, sher-văh-le-eh, *m* knight; – **d'industrie,** – dang-dEEs-tree, wheeler dealer.

chevaucher, sher-voh-sheh, *v* to ride; to overlap.

chevelu, e, sherv-lE, *a* hairy.

chevelure, sherv-lEEr, *f* head of hair.

chevet, sher-vay, *m* bolster; bedside.

cheveu, sher-ver, *m* hair (a single); **les –x,** lay –, the hair.

cheville, sher-vee-ye, *f* ankle; peg; pin; bolt.

chèvre, shay-vr, *f* she-goat; **ménager la – et le chou,** meh-năh-sheh lăh – eh ler shoo, to run with the hare and hunt with the hounds.

chevreau, sher-vroh, *m* kid.

chèvrefeuille, shay-vrer-

fer'e, *m* honeysuckle.

chevrette, sher-vrett, *f* doe.

chevreuil, sher-vrer'e, *m* roe(–deer).

chevrier, sher-vre-eh, *m* goatherd.

chevron, sher-vrong, *m* rafter.

chevrotant, sher-vrot-ahng, *a* quivering; tremulous.

chevrotin, sher-vrot-ang, *m* kid-leather.

chewing-gum, shoo'eng-gomm, *m* chewing-gum.

chez, sheh, *prep* at; to; with; among; in; at or to the house of.

chic, sheeck, *m* stylishness; knack; *a* smart; stylish; *fam* fine!; a sport (of person).

chicane, she-kăhn, *f* chicanery.

chicaner, she-kăh-neh, *v* to quarrel over; to shuffle; to quibble.

chicanerie, she-kăhn-ree, *f* chicanery.

chiche,* sheesh, *a* stingy; *interj* I dare you!

chicorée, she-kor-eh, *f* chicory; endive.

chicot, she-ko, *m* stump.

chien, she-ang, *m* dog; (gun) cock.

chienne, she-enn, *f* she-dog; bitch.

chiffe, sheef, f flimsy stuff; weak man.

chiffon, she-fong, m rag; scrap; duster; pl finery.

chiffonné, e, she-fonn-eh, pp & a crumpled; of irregular but agreeable features.

chiffonner, she-fonn-eh, v to rumple; to vex.

chiffonnier, she-fonn-e-eh, m rag-and-bone man.

chiffre, shee-fr, m figure, number; total; cipher; **en –s connus,** ahng – konn-E, in plain figures; **– d'affaires,** – dăh-fair, turnover.

chiffrer, she-freh, v to cipher; to reckon.

chignon, sheen-yong, m (hair) bun.

chimère, she-mair, f chimera; idle fancy; fantasy.

chimérique, she-meh-reeck, a chimerical.

chimie, she-mee, f chemistry.

chimique,* she-meeck, a chemical.

chimiste, she-meesst, m (scientific) chemist.

chimpanzé, shang-pahng-zeh chimpanzee.

chiper she-peh, v fam to

nick; to swipe.

chipoter she-pot-eh, v to haggle.

chique, sheeck, f wad of tobacco.

chiquenaude, sheeck-nohd, f fillip; flick of finger.

chiquer she-keh, v to chew (tobacco).

chirurgie, she-rEEr-shee, f surgery.

chirurgien, she-rEEr-she-ang, m surgeon.

chlore, klor, m chlorine.

chlorure, klor-EEr, m chloride.

choc, shock, m shock; collision; clash; knock.

chocolat, shock-oll-ăh, m chocolate; a chocolate coloured.

chœur, ker, m choir; chorus; choristers; chancel.

choir, sho'ăhr, v to fall.

choisi, sho'ăh-ze, pp & a chosen; selected; choice.

choisir, sho'ăh-zeer, v to choose; to select (**dans, entre, parmi,** from).

choix, sho'ăh, m choice; selection; election.

choléra, koll-eh-răh, m cholera.

cholestérol, koh-lays-teh-rol, m cholesterol.

chômage, shoh-măhsh, m

unemployment.

chômage, shoh-măhsh, m unemployment; time spent without work.

chômer, shoh-meh, v to stand idle; to be out of work; to keep as a holiday.

chômeur, shoh-mer, m unemployed.

chopper, shop-eh, v to stumble; to trip up.

choquant, e, shock-ahng, a offensive (**pour,** to); shocking; unpleasant.

choquer, shock-eh, v to shock; to strike; to touch; to displease; **se –,** to take offence (**de,** at); to be shocked.

chose, shohz, f thing; matter; affair; **bien des – s à,** be-ang deh – ăh, my best regards to.

chou, shoo, m cabbage; dear; pet; **–fleur, –fler** cauliflower.

choucroute, shoo-kroot, f sauerkraut.

chouette, shoo-ait, f owl; a fam fantastic; great; marvellous.

choyer, sho'ăh-yeh, v to fondle; to pet.

chrétien, ne,* kreh-te-ang, a & mf Christian.

chrétienté, kreh-te-ang-teh, f Christendom.

christ, krisst, *m* Christ;
crucifix.

christianisme, krisst-e-ăh-
nissm, *m* Christianity.

chrome, krohm, *m*
chromium; chrome.

chronique, kronn-eeck, *f*
chronicle; *a* chronic.

chronomètre, kronn-
omm-ay-tr, *m*
chronometer.

chrysalide, kre-zăh-leed, *f*
chrysalis.

chrysanthème, kre-zahng-
taym, *m*
chrysanthemum.

chuchoter, shE-shot-eh, *v*
to whisper.

chut, shEEt, *interj* hush!
shush!

chute, shEEt, *f* fall;
downfall; failure.

ci, se, *adv* here; this; ~
joint, –sho'ang,
enclosed; **comme –
comme ça,** komm –
komm săh, so, so;
middling.

cible, see-bl, *f* target.

ciboulette, se-boo-lett, *f*
chives.

cicatrice, se-kăh-triss, *f*
scar.

cidre, see-dr, *m* cider.

Cie (for **Compagnie**),
kong-păhn-yee, *f* "Co.".

ciel, se-ell, *m* heaven; sky;
climate.

cierge, se-airsh, *m* candle.

cigale, se-găhl, *f* cicada.

cigare, se-găhr, *m* cigar.

cigarette, se-găh-rett, *f*
cigarette.

cigogne, se-gonn-yer, *f*
stork.

cil, seel, *m* eyelash.

cime, seem, *f* summit, top,
crest.

ciment, se-mahng, *m*
cement.

cimenter, se-mahng-teh, *v*
to cement.

cimetière, seem-te-air, *m*
cemetery; churchyard.

cimier, se-me-eh, *m* crest;
buttock of beef.

cinéaste, se-neh-ăhsst, *m*
film maker.

cinéma, se-neh-măh, *m*
cinema; **faire du –,** fair
dE –, to act in films.

cingler, sang-gleh, *v* to
lash; to sail.

cinglé, sang-gleh, *a fam*
nuts; crackers.

cinq, sangk, *a* five.

cinquantaine, sang-kahng-
tain, *f* about fifty.

cinquante, sang-kahngt, *a*
fifty.

cinquantenaire, sang-
kahngt-nair, *m* fiftieth
anniversary.

cinquantième, sang-
kahng-te-aym, *a* fiftieth.

cinquième, sang-ke-aym,

m & *a* fifth.

cintre, sang-tr, *m* semi-
circle; arch; coat hanger.

cintré, e, sang-treh, *pp* & *a*
arched; fitted (of coat,
etc).

cirage, se-răhsh, *m*
polishing; shoe polish.

circoncire, seer-kong-seer,
v to circumcise.

circoncision, seer-kong-
se-ze-ong, *f*
circumcision.

circonférence, seer-kong-
feh-rahngss, *f*
circumference.

circonflexe, seer-kong-
flex, *a* circumflex.

circonscription, seer-
kongss-krip-se-ong, *f*
district.

circonscrire, seer-kongss-
kreer, *v* to circumscribe.

circonspect, e, seer-
kongss-peckt, or seer-
kongss-pay, *a*
circumspect; wary.

circonspection, seer-
kongss-peck-se-ong, *f*
cautiousness.

circonstance, seer-kongss-
tahngss, *f* circumstance;
occasion.

circonstancier, seer-
kongss-tahng-se-eh, *v* to
state fully.

circonvenir, seer-kongv-
neer, *v* to circumvent;

to deceive.

circonvoisin, seer-kong-vo'ăh-*zang*, *a* circumjacent; neighbouring.

circuit, seer-kwe, *m* circuit; roundabout way.

circulaire, seer-kE-lair, *f* circular; *a* circular.

circulation, seer-kE-lăh-se-*ong*, *f* circulation; currency; traffic.

circuler, seer-kE-leh, *v* to circulate; to move.

cire, seer, *f* wax.

cirer, se-reh, *v* to wax; to polish (shoes, floors, etc); to spread about.

cirque, seerk, *m* circus.

ciseau, se-zoh, *m* chisel; *pl* scissors; shears.

ciseler, seez-leh, *v* to carve; to chisel.

citadelle, se-tăh-dell, *f* citadel.

citadin, e, se-tăh-*dang*, *mf* townsman; townswoman.

citation, se-tăh-se-*ong*, *f* quotation; subpoena.

cité se-teh, *f* city; town.

citer, se-teh, *v* to quote; to mention; to summon; to subpoena.

citerne, se-tairn, *f* cistern; tank; reservoir.

cithare, se-tăhr, *f* zither.

citoyen, ne, se-to'ăh-yang,

mf & *a* citizen; freeman; inhabitant.

citrate, se-trăht, *m* citrate.

citron, se-trong, *m* lemon; citron; *a* lemon-coloured.

citronade, si-tro-năhd, *f* lemonade.

citrouille, see-troo'e-yer, *f* pumpkin; gourd.

cives, seev, *fpl* chives.

civet, se-vay, *m* game; stew; – **de lièvre,** – der le-ay-vr, jugged hare.

civière, se-ve-air, *f* stretcher.

civil, se-vill, *m* civilian; layman.

civil, e,* se-vill, *a* polite; civil.

civilisation, se-ve-le-zăh-se-ong, *f* civilization.

civiliser, se-ve-le-zeh, *v* to civilize.

civilité, se-ve-le-teh, *f* civility.

civique, se-veeck, *a* civic.

claie, klay, *f* hurdle; screen.

clair, klair, *m* light; light part.

clair, e,* klair, *a* clear; bright; light; evident.

claire-voie, klair-vo'ăh, *f* opening; lattice; skylight.

clairière, klai-re-air, *f* glade.

clairon, klai-rong, *m* clarion; bugle; bugler.

clairsemé, e, klair-ser-meh, *a* thinly sown; sparse; scattered.

clairvoyance, klair-vo'ăh-yahngss, *f* clairvoyance; clear-sightedness.

clairvoyant, e, klair-vo'ăh-yahng, *n* & *a* clairvoyant; judicious.

clameur, klăh-mer, *f* clamour; outcry.

clan, klahng, *m* clan; clique.

clandestin, e,* klahng-dess-*tang*, *a* clandestine.

clapet, klăh-pay, *m* clapper; valve.

clapier, klăh-pe-eh, *m* burrow; warren; hutch.

clapoter, klăh-pot-eh, *v* to lap; to ripple.

clapotis, klăh-pot-e, *m* ripple; splashing.

clapper, klăh-peh, *v* to smack; to click.

claque, klăhck, *m* opera-hat; *f* slap; hired applauders.

claquemurer, klăhck-mE-reh, *v* to shut up; to confine.

claquer, klăh-keh, *v* to clap; to smack.

claqueur, klăh-ker, *m* hired applauder.

clarifier, klăh-re-fe-eh, *v*

to clarify; **se –,** to get clear.

clarinette, klăh-re-nett, *f* clarinet.

clarté, klăhr-teh, *f* clearness; light; brightness.

classe, klahss, *f* class; order; rank; form; school; classroom.

classement, klahss-mahng, *m* classification; filing.

classeur, klăhss-**er,** *m* files; filing cabinet.

classifier, klăhss-e-fe-eh, *v* to classify.

classique, klăhss-eeck, *m* classic; *a* classical.

clause, klohz, *f* clause; condition.

claustration, klohs-trăh-se-ong, *f* cloistering; confinement.

clavecin, klăhv-sang, *m* harpsichord.

clavicule, klăh-ve-kEEl, *f* collarbone.

clavier, klăh-ve-eh, *m* keyboard.

clef, or **clé,** kleh, *f* key; wrench; lever; key-stone; **fermer à –,** fair-meh ăh –, to lock.

clémence, kleh-mahngss, *f* clemency; mercy.

clerc, klair, *m* clerk; *eccl* cleric; scholar. **faire un pas de –,** fair ung pah

der –, to make a blunder.

clerge, klair-sheh, *m* clergy.

clérical, e, kleh-re-kăhl, *a* clerical.

cliché, kle-sheh, *m* stereotype; block; negative; stereotyped phrase.

client, e, kle-ahng, *mf* client; patient; customer.

clientèle, kle-ahng-tell, *f* clients; customer.

cligner, clignoter, kleen-yeh, kleen-yot-eh, *v* to wink; to blink; to flicker.

clignotant, kleen-yot-ahng, *m* winker, flash-light indicator.

climat, kle-măh, *m* climate; clime; atmosphere.

climatérique, kle-măh-teh-reeck, *a* climatic.

climatisé, kle-măh-te-zeh, *a* air-conditioned.

climatiseur, kle-măh-te-zer, *m* air conditioner.

clin d'œil, klang-der'e, *m* wink; twinkling of an eye.

clinique, kle-neeck, *f* clinical hospital; nursing home; surgery; *a* clinical.

clinquant, klang-kahng, *m* tinsel; glitter.

clique, kleeck, *f* gang; set; clan.

cliquetis, kleeck-te, *m* clank; clashing; jingle.

clivage, kle-văhsh, *m* cleavage.

clochard, klo-shar, *m* tramp; homeless person.

cloaque, klo'ăhck, *m* sewer; cesspool.

cloche, klosh, *f* bell; bell-glass; cover; blister; *fam* idiot; twit.

cloche-pied (à), ăh klosh-pe-eh, *adv* hopping on one leg.

clocher, klosh-eh, *v* to limp; *fam* to be wrong.

clocher, klosh-eh, *m* steeple; bell-tower.

clochette, klosh-ett, *f* hand-bell; bell-flower; blue bell.

cloison, klo'ăh-zong, *f* partition.

cloître, klo'ăh-tr, *m* cloister; monastery.

clopin-clopant, klop-ang klop-ahng, *adv* hobbling along.

clos, e, klo, *pp* & *a* closed; finished.

clos, klo, *m* close; enclosure; vineyard.

clôture, kloh-tEEr, *f* enclosure; seclusion;

closing.

clôturer, kloh-tE-reh, *v* to enclose; to close down.

clou, kloo, *m* nail; boil; chief attraction; **– de girofle**, – der she-rofl, clove.

clouer, kloo-eh, *v* to nail; to rivet; to clench.

clouter, kloo-teh, *v* to stud.

clown, kloon, *m* clown.

club, klEEb, *m* club.

clystère, kliss-tair, *m* enema.

coacquéreur, ko'äh-keh-rer, *m* joint purchaser.

coadministrateur, ko'ähd-me-niss-träh-ter, *m* codirector.

coaguler, ko'äh-ghE-leh, *v* to coagulate; **se –**, to curdle.

coaliser (se), ser ko'äh-le-zeh, *v* to join forces; to form a coalition.

coasser, ko'ähss-eh, *v* to croak.

coassocié, e, ko'äh-soss-e-eh, *mf* co-partner.

cocagne (pays de), pay-yee der kock-ähn-yer, land of plenty; **mât de –**, mah der –, greasy pole.

cocarde, kock-ährd, *f* cockade.

cocasse, kock-ähss, *a* funny; droll.

coccinelle, kock-se-nell, *f* ladybird.

coche, kosh, *m* coach; barge; *f* notch; sow.

cocher, kosh-eh, *m* coachman; driver.

cochon, kosh-ong, *m* hog; pig; porker; swine; pork; **– de lait**, – der lay, sucking pig; **– d'Inde**, – dangd, guinea pig.

cochonnerie, kosh-onn-ree, dirtiness; indecent action or language; *fam* dirty trick.

coco, kock-o, *m* coconut; *fam* pet.

cocon, kock-ong, *m* cocoon.

cocotier, kock-ot-e-eh, *m* coconut palm.

cocotte, kock-ot, *f* cast-iron casserole; **– minute**, – me-nEEt, pressure cooker; *fam* ducky; darling; child's word for chicken.

code, kod, *m* code; law.

coefficient, ko-eh-fe-se-ahng, *m* coefficient.

coercition, ko-air-se-se-ong, *f* coercion.

cœur, ker, *m* heart; soul; love; courage; core; **avoir mal au –**, äh-vo'ähr mähl oh –, to feel sick.

coffre, kofr, *m* trunk;

chest; box; **–fort, – for** safe.

coffrer, kof-reh, *v fam* to lock up.

coffret, kof-ray, *m* small chest; jewelbox.

cognac, kon-yähck, *m* (Cognac) brandy.

cognée, kon-yeh, *f* hatchet.

cogner, kon-yeh, *v* to knock; to strike; to drive in.

cohérent, e, ko-eh-rahng, *a* coherent.

cohéritier, ko-eh-re-te-eh, *m* joint-heir.

cohésion, ko-eh-ze-ong, *f* cohesion.

cohue, koE, *f* crowd; mob; rout; uproar.

coi, coite, *f* ko'äh, ko'äht, *a* quiet; still.

coiffe, ko'ähf, *f* head-dress.

coiffer, ko'ähf-eh, *v* to put on the head; to do someone else's hair; **se –**, to do one's hair.

coiffeur, -euse, ko'ähf-er, *mf* hairdresser.

coiffeuse, ko'äh-ferz, dressing table.

coiffure, ko'ähf-EEr, *f* headdress; hair style.

coin, ko-ang, *m* corner; angle; wedge.

coincer, ko-ang-seh, *v* to

wedge up; to jam.

coïncider, ko-ang-se-deh, *v* to coincide.

coing, ko-ang, *m* quince.

col, kol, *m* collar; neck; pass.

colère, koll-air, *f* anger; passion; rage; wrath; ire.

colérique, koll-eh-reeck, *a* angry; quick tempered; irascible.

colibri, koll-e-bre, *m* hummingbird.

colifichet, koll-e-fe-shay, *m* trifle; bauble.

colimaçon, koll-e-măh-song, *m* snail.

colin-maillard, koll-angmah'e-yăhr, *m* blindman's buff.

colique, koll-eeck, *f* stomach cramps.

colis, koll-e, *m* package; parcel.

collabora-teur, trice, kollăh-bor-ăh-ter, *mf* collaborator; assistant; contributor.

collaborer, kol-lăh-boreh, *v* to work together.

collage, koll-ăhsh, *m* sticking; pasting; gluing.

collant, e, koll-ahng, *a* sticking; tight; *m* pair of tights.

collation, koll-ăh-se-ong, *f* collation; light meal.

collationner, koll-ăh-se-

onn-eh, *v* to collate; to compare; to lunch.

colle, kol, *f* paste; glue; size.

collecte, koll-leckt, *f* collection.

collecti-f, ve,* koll-leckteeff, *a* collective.

collectionner, koll-leckse-onn-eh, *v* to collect (paintings, etc).

collège, koll-aysh, *m* secondary school.

collégien, koll-eh-sheang, *m* school-boy.

coller, koll-eh, *v* to stick; to glue; to adhere.

collet, koll-ay, *m* collar; snare; – **monté,** – mongteh, strait-laced.

colleur, koll-er, *m* billsticker; paper-hanger.

collier, koll-e-eh, *m* collar; necklace; ring.

colline, koll-een, *f* hill; hillock.

colloque, koll-lock, *m* conference; symposium.

collusoire, koll-lE-zo'ăhr, *a* collusive.

colombe, koll-ongb, *f* dove.

colombier, koll-ong-be-eh, *m* dovecote; pigeonhole.

colon, koll-ong, *m* colonist; planter; settler.

côlon, kohll-ong, *m* colon.

colonel, koll-onn-ell, *m*

colonel.

colonie, koll-onn-ee, *f* colony; settlement.

colonnade, koll-onn-ăhd, *f* colonnade.

colonne, koll-onn, *f* column; pillar; – **vertébrale,** – vair-tehbrăhl, spine; backbone.

colorer, koll-or-eh, *v* to colour; to stain.

coloris, koll-or-e, *m* colouring; hue.

colosse, koll-oss, *m* colossus; giant.

colporter, koll-por-teh, *v* to hawk about; to spread (news).

colporteur, koll-por-ter, *m* pedlar; hawker.

combat, kong-băh, *m* fight; battle; contest; **hors de –,** or **der –,** disabled.

combattre, kong-băh-tr, *v* to fight; to contest; to contend (**contre,** with).

combien, kong-be-ang, *adv* how much; how many how; – **de temps,** – der tahng, how long?

combinaison, kong-benay-zong, *f* combination; petticoat; slip; contrivance; – **de plongée,** – der-plongsheh, wetsuit.

combine, kong-been, *f fam*

scheme; arrangement;
fiddle.

combiner, kong-be-neh, *v*
to combine; to contrive.

comble, kong-bl, *m*
(measure) heaped;
summit; acme; *pl* attic;
loft; **de fond en –,** der
fong t'ahng –, from top
to bottom; **pour – de,**
poohr – der, to crown;
to complete.

comble, kong-bl, *a*
crowded; full; heaped
up.

combler, kong-bleh, *v* to
fill; to heap; to cover; to
overwhelm (**de,** with);
to fulfil.

combustible, kong-bEEs-
tee-bl, *m* fuel; *a*
combustible.

comédie, komm-eh-dee, *f*
comedy; play; theatre.

comédien, ne, komm-eh-
de-ang, *mf* actor; actress.

comestibles, komm-ess-
tee-bl, *mpl* provisions;
food.

comète, komm-ett, *f*
comet.

comice, komm-iss, *m*
agricultural or electoral
meeting.

comique, komm-eeck, *m*
comic actor; comic art;
a comic; comical.

comité, komm-e-teh, *m*

board; committee.

commandant, komm-
ahng-dahng, *m*
commander; major;
commanding officer.

commande, komm-ahngd,
f order.

commander, komm-ahng-
deh, *v* to command; to
order; to overlook.

commanditaire, komm-
ahng-de-tair, *m* sleeping
partner.

commandite, komm-ahng-
deet, *f* limited
partnership.

comme, komm, *adv* as;
like; as if; almost; how;
conj as; since; because.

commençant, e, komm-
ahng-sahng, *mf*
beginner.

commencement, komm-
ahngss-mahng, *m*
beginning.

commencer, komm-
ahngss-eh, *v* to begin.

comment, komm-ahng,
adv how; why! what! **–
donc!** – dong! to be
sure!

commentaire, komm-
mahng-tair, *m*
commentary; comment;
remark.

commenter, komm-ahng-
teh, *v* to comment; to
criticise; to pass

remarks.

commerçant, -e, komm-
air-sahng, *mf* trader;
tradesman; dealer; *a*
commercial; business.

commerce, komm-airss, *m*
trade; business.

commère, komm-air, *f*
gossip; busybody.

commettre, komm-et-tr, *v*
to commit; to entrust;
appoint; to make (a
mistake).

commis, komm-e, *m* clerk;
shop assistant; **–
voyageur,** –vo'ăh-yăh-
sher, commercial
traveller.

commissaire, komm-iss-
air, *m* commissioner;
commissary; steward;
(police) superintendent;
– priseur, – pre-zer,
auctioneer.

commissariat, komm-iss-
săh-re-ăh, *m* (police)
station.

commission, komm-iss-e-
ong, *f* commission;
message; errand;
committee; commission
agency; **–ner** *v* to
commission.

commissionnaire, komm-
iss-e-onn-air, *m* porter;
messenger; commission
agent.

commode, komm-odd, *f*

chest of drawers; *a* convenient; suitable; handy.

commodité, komm-odd-e-teh, *f* convenience.

commotion, komm-moss-e-ong, *f* disturbance; concussion.

commun, komm-ung, *m* generality; commonplace; lower class; menials; *pl* domestic offices.

commun, e, komm-ung, komm-EEn, *a* common; ordinary; trivial; vulgar.

communal, e, komm-E-năhl, *a* communal.

communauté, komm-E-noh-teh, *f* community; convent; corporation.

commune, komm-EEn, *f* commune; parish.

communément, komm-E-neh-mahng, *adv* commonly.

communicant, e, komm-E-ne-kahng, *a* communicating.

communication, komm-E-ne-kăh-se-ong, *f* communication; message; cognizance; telephone call.

communier, komm-E-ne-eh, *v* to receive the sacrament.

communion, komm-E-ne-ong, *f* communion; sacrament; fellowship.

communiqué, komm-E-ne-keh, *m* official statement.

communiquer, komm-E-ne-keh, *v* to communicate; to impart; to infuse.

communisme, komm-E-nissm, *m* communism.

communiste, komm-E-neest, *a* & *mf* communist.

compact, e, kong-păhckt, *a* compact; dense.

compagne, kong-păhn-yer, *f* female companion; partner; playmate.

compagnie, kong-păhn-yee, *f* company; society; companionship; **fausser –,** foh-seh –, to give the slip.

compagnon, kong-păhn-yong, *m* companion; partner; mate; playmate.

comparable, kong-păh-răh-bl, *a* comparable.

comparaison, kong-păh-ray-zong, *f* comparison.

comparaître, kong-păh-ray-tr, *v* to appear (in court).

comparant, kong-păh-rahng, *a* appearing (in court).

comparer, kong-păh-reh, *v* to compare.

compartiment, kong-păhr-te-mahng, *m* compartment; division.

comparution, kong-păh-rE-se-ong, *f* appearance (in court).

compas, kong-pah, *m* compass; compasses.

compassé, e, kong-păhss-eh, *a* formal; stiff.

compasser, kong-păhss-eh, *v* to measure; to regulate; to lay out.

compassion, kong-păhss-e-ong, *f* compassion; pity.

compatible, kong-păh-tee-bl, *a* compatible.

compatir, kong-pah-teer, *v* to sympathize (à, with).

compatissant, kong-pah-tiss-ahng, *a* compassionate.

compatriote, kong-păh-tre-ot, *mf* compatriot.

compenser, kong-pahng-seh, *v* to compensate.

compère, kong-pair, *m* announcer (theatre); accomplice; chum.

compétati-f, kong-peh-te-teef, *a* competitive

compétence, kong-peh-tahngss, *f* competence; jurisdiction; sphere.

compétent, e, kong-peh-tahng; *a* competent.

compéti-teur, trice, kong-peh-te-ter, *mf* competitor.

compétition, kong-peh-te-se-ong, *f* competition; rivalry; contest.

compilateur, kong-pe-lǎh-ter, *m* compiler.

compiler, kong-pe-leh, to compile.

complainte, kong-plangt, *f* lament; ballad.

complaire (à), kong-plair-ǎh, *v* to please; **se –,** to delight (**à, dans,** in).

complaisamment, kong-play-zǎh-mahng, *adv* obligingly.

complaisance, kong-play-zahngss, *f* obligingness; kindness; complacency.

complaisant, kong-play-zahng, *m* flatterer.

complaisant, e, kong-play-zahng, *a* obliging; kind.

complément, kong-pleh-mahng, *m* complement; (grammar) object; remainder.

complet, kong-play, *m* full number; suit (of clothes).

compl-et, ète,* kong-play, *a* complete; full; utter.

compléter, kong-pleh-teh, *v* to complete; to make complete.

complexe, kong-plex, *a* complex; complicated.

complexion, kong-plex-e-ong, *f* constitution; disposition.

complexité kong-plex-e-teh, *f* complexity.

complication, kong-ple-kǎh-se-ong, *f* complication.

complice, kong-pliss, *mf & a* accomplice; co-respondent.

compliment, kong-ple-mahng, *m* compliment; *pl* congratulations.

complimenter, kong-ple-mahng-teh, *v* to congratulate.

compliqué, e, kong-ple-keh, *a* complicated.

compliquer, kong-ple-keh, *v* to complicate.

complot, kong-plo, *m* plot; conspiracy; scheme.

comploter, kong-plot-eh, *v* to plot.

comporter, kong-por-teh, *v* to permit; to admit; to comprise; **se –,** to behave.

composé, kong-poz-eh, *m* compound.

composé, e, kong-poz-eh, *a* composed; compound.

composer, kong-poz-eh, *v* to compose; to compound; to settle; to

dial (a number).

composi-teur, trice, kong-poz-e-ter, *m* composer; compositor.

composition, kong-poz-e-se-ong, *f* composition; agreement; examination; essay; **de bonne –,** der bonn –, easy to deal with.

compote, kong-pot, *f* stewed fruit; **en –,** ahng – stewed; *fig* bruised.

compréhensible, kong-preh-ahng-see-bl, *a* understandable.

compréhensi-f, ve, kong-preh-ahng-siff, *a* comprehensive.

compréhension, kong-preh-ahng-se-ong, *f* comprehension.

comprendre, kong-prahng-dr, *v* to understand; to include.

compression, kong-press-e-ong, *f* compression.

comprimé, kong-pre-meh, *m* tablet.

comprimé, e, kong-pre-meh, *pp & a* compressed.

comprimer, kong-pre-meh, *v* to compress; to condense; to restrain.

compris, e, kong-pre, *pp & a* understood; included; **y –, e –,** including; **non**

–, nong –, excluding.

comprometant, e, kong-promm-ett-ahng, *a* compromising.

compromettre, kong-promm-et-tr, *v* to compromise; to imperil.

compromis, kong-promm-e, *m* compromise.

comptabilité, kong-tăh-be-le-teh, *f* accountancy; book-keeping; accounts; accountant's office.

comptable, kong-tăh-bl, *m* accountant; **expert – ecks-pair –,** *m* chartered accountant; *a* accountable; responsible.

comptant, kong-tahng, *a* ready (money); cash; **au – oh –,** for cash.

compte, kongt, *m* account; reckoning; amount; right number; **en fin de –,** ahng fangd –, after all; **se rendre – de,** ser rahng-dr – der, to realize.

compte-rendu, kongt rahng-dE, *m* account; report; minutes (of meeting).

compter, kong-teh, *v* to count; to reckon; to intend; to rely.

compteur, kong-ter, *m* speedometer; meter; recorder.

comptoir, kong-to'ăhr, *m* counter; counting-house; branch; bar.

compulser, kong-pEEl-seh, *v* to examine (documents, etc).

comte, kongt, *m* count; earl.

comté, kong-teh, *m* county; earldom.

concasser, kong-kăhss-seh, *v* to pound; to crush.

concave, kong-kăhv, *a* concave.

concéder, kong-seh-deh, *v* to concede; to grant; to allow.

concentration, kong-sahng-trăh-se-ong, *f* concentration.

concentré, kong-sahng-treh, *m* extract; concentration.

concentrer, kong-sahng-treh, *v* to concentrate; to hold back (feelings).

concept, kong-sept, *m* concept.

conception, kong-sep-se-ong, *f* conception; thought.

concernant, kong-sair-nahng, *prep* relating to.

concerner, kong-sair-neh, *v* to concern; to belong to.

concert, kong-sair, *m* concert; concord; **de –,** der–, in concert; jointly.

concerter, kong-sair-teh, *v* to concert; to contrive; **se –,** to plan together.

concession, kong-sess-e-ong, *f* concession; grant; claim.

concessionnaire, kong-sess-e-onn-air, *m* concessionnaire; contractor; grantee.

concevable, kongss-văh-bl, *a* conceivable.

concevoir, kongss-vo'ăhr, *v* to conceive; to understand; to imagine.

concierge, kong-se-airsh, *mf* hall-porter; caretaker.

conciergerie, kong-se-air-sher-ree, porter's lodge.

conciliable, kong-se-le-ăh-bl, *a* reconcilable.

conciliabule, kong-se-le-ăh-bEEl, *m* conventicle; secret meeting; *fam* confabulation.

conciliant, e, kong-se-le-ahng, *a* conciliatory.

concilia-teur, trice, kong-se-le-ăh-ter, *mf & a* peacemaker, conciliator; conciliatory.

concilier, kong-se-le-eh, *v* to reconcile; **se –,** to win over.

concis, e, kong-se, *a*
concise; brief.

concision, kong-se-ze-ong,
f concision.

concitoyen, ne, kong-se-
to'äh-yang, *mf* fellow
citizen.

conclave, kong-klăv, *m*
conclave.

concluant, e, kong-klE-
ahng, *a* conclusive.

conclure, kong-klEEr, *v* to
conclude; to close; to
infer; to prove; to move.

conclusi-f, ve, * kong-klE-
zeeff, *a* conclusive.

conclusion, kong-klE-ze-
ong, *f* conclusion;
inference; motion;
verdict.

concombre, kong-kong-br,
m cucumber.

concordance, kong-kor-
dahngss, *f* agreement;
concord; (Bible)
concordance.

concorder, kong-kor-deh,
v to live in concord; to
agree; to compound.

concourir, kong-koo-reer,
v to concur; to
converge; to compete;
to co-operate.

concours, kong-koohr, *m*
co-operation;
competitive
examination; concourse;
competition; meeting.

concre-t, ète, kong-kray, *a*
concrete.

concubine, kong-kE-been,
f concubine.

concupiscence, kong-kE-
piss-ahngss, *f*
concupiscence; lust.

concurremment, kong-
kEEr-răh-mahng, *adv*
concurrently; in
competition.

concurrence, kong-kEEr-
rahngss, *f* competition;
concurrence; **jusqu'à –
de,** shEEs-kăh – der, to
the amount of.

concurrentiel, kong-kE-
rahng-se-ell, *a*
competitive (prices).

concurrent, e, kong-kEEr-
rahng, *mf* competitor.

condamnable, kong-dăh-
năh-bl, *a* reprehensible;
condemnable.

condamnation, kong-dăh-
năh-se-ong, *f*
condemnation;
sentence; conviction.

condamnè, e, kong-dăh-
neh, *pp & mf*
condemned; convict.

condamner, kong-dăh-
neh, *v* to condemn; to
convict; to sentence; to
block up.

condenser, kong-dahng-
seh, *v* to condense.

condescendance, kong-

dess-sahng-dahngss, *f*
condescension.

condescendre, kong-dess-
sahng-dr, *v* to
condescend; to yield; to
comply.

condiment, kong-de-
mahng, *m* condiment.

condisciple, kong-de-see-
pl, *m* schoolmate.

condition, kong-de-se-
ong, *f* condition;
position; term.

conditionnel, le, * kong-
de-se-onn-ell, *a*
conditional.

conditionner, kong-de-se-
onn-eh, *v* to condition.

condoléance, kong-doll-
eh-ahngss; *f* condolence.

conduc-teur, trice, kong-
dEEk-ter, *mf* driver;
conductor; leader; guide;
a conducting; leading.

conduire, kong-dweer, *v*
to conduct; to lead; to
guide; to drive; to steer;
to carry; to manage; **se
–,** to behave.

conduit, kong-dwe, *m*
pipe; tube; way.

conduite, kong-dweet, *f*
conduct; behaviour;
management; care;
driving; channel;
changer de –,

cône, kohn, *m* cone.

confection, kong-feck-se-

ong, f making;
manufacture; ready-
made clothes; –neur, m
ready-made clothing
manufacturer; maker.

confédération, kong-feh-
deh-răh-se-ong f
confederacy.

confédéré e, kong-feh-
deh-reh, a confederate.

confédérer, kong-feh-deh-
reh, v to unite together.

conférence, kong-feh-
rahngss, f lecture;
conference; **maître de
–s,** may-tr der –,
lecturer.

conférencier, kong-feh-
rahng-se-eh, m lecturer.

conférer, kong-feh-reh, v
to confer (à, upon); to
grant; to compare; to
consult together.

confesser, kong-fayss-eh, v
to confess; to
acknowledge.

confession, kong-fayss-e-
ong, f confession.

confiance, kong-fe-ahngss,
f confidence; trust;
reliance.

confiant, e, kong-fe-ahng,
a confident; confiding;
assured.

confidemment, kong-fe-
dăh-mahng, adv in
confidence.

confidence, kong-fe-

dahngss, f confidence;
secret.

confidentiel, le, * kong-fe-
dahng-se-ell, a
confidential

confier, kong-fe-eh, v to
confide; to entrust; **se –,**
to confide (à, in).

confiner, kong-fe-neh, v
to confine; to border
upon.

confins, kong-fang, mpl
confines; borders.

confire, kong-feer, v to
preserve; to pickle.

confirmati-f, ve, kong-
feer-măh-teeff, a
confirmatory.

confirmer, kong-feer-meh,
v to confirm; **se –,** to be
confirmed.

confiscation, kong-fiss-
kăh-se-ong, f
confiscation; forfeiture.

confiserie, kong-feez-ree, f
confectionery;
preserving; sweetshop.

confiseur, kong-fe-zer, m
confectioner.

confisquer, kong-fiss-keh,
v to confiscate.

confit, kong-fe, a
preserved; candied.

confiture, kong-fe-tEEr, f
preserve; jam.

conflagration, kong-flăh-
grăh-se-ong, f
conflagration.

conflit, kong-fle, m
conflict; clash.

confluent, kong-flE-ahng,
m confluence.

confondre, kong-fong-dr, v
to confound; to confuse;
to overwhelm; **se–,** ser–,
to become indistinct; to
be mistaken.

conformation, kong-for-
măh-se-ong,
f conformation.

conforme, kong-form, a in
accordance;
conformable; consistent
(à, with); **pour copie –,**
poohr kop-e –, certified
copy.

conformément, kong-for-
meh-mahng, adv in
accordance (à, with).

conformer, kong-for-meh,
v to conform; **se–,** to
comply (à, with).

conformite', kong-for-me-
teh, f conformity.

confort, kong-for, m
comfort, ease.

confortable, * kong-for-
tăh-bl, a comfortable;
easy.

conforter, kong-for-teh, v
to comfort; to
strengthen.

confraternité, kong-frăh-
tair-ne-teh, f
brotherhood.

confrère, kong-frair, m

colleague; fellow-member; brother; (newspapers) contemporary.

confronter, kong-frong-teh, v to confront; to compare.

confus, e, kong-fE, a confused; embarrassed; overwhelmed.

confusion, kong-fE-ze-ong, f confusion; disorder; trouble; shame.

congé, kong-sheh, m leave; notice to quit; dismissal; holiday.

congédier, kong-sheh-de-eh, v to discharge; to dismiss; to pay off.

congélateur, kong-sheh-lãh-ter, m deep-freeze.

congélation, kong-sheh-lãh-se-ong, f freezing.

congeler, kongsh-leh, v to congeal; to freeze.

congestion, kong-shess-te-ong, f congestion.

congre, kong-gr, m congereel.

congrégation, kong-greh-gãh-se-ong, f congregation.

congrés, kong-gray, m congress.

conique, koh-neeck, a conic, conical.

conjecturer, kong-sheck-tE-reh, v to conjecture;

to surmise; to guess.

conjoindre, kong-sho'ang-dr, v to join; to unite.

conjoint, e, * kongsho'ang, pp & a joined, united; –s, mpl husband and wife.

conjonction, kong-shongk-se-ong, f conjunction; union.

conjugaison, kong-shE-gay-zong, f conjugation.

conjugal, e, * kong-shE-gãhl, a conjugal; married.

conjuguer, kong-shE-gheh, v to conjugate.

conjuration, kong-shE-rãh-se-ong, f conspiracy; entreaty (in pl).

conjuré, kong-shE-reh, m conspirator, plotter.

conjurer, kong-shE-reh, v to conspire; to implore; to ward off.

connaissance, konn-ayss-ahngss, f knowlegde; acquaintance; senses; learning; sans –, sahng–, unconscious.

connaisseur, konn-ess-er, m connoisseur.

connaître, konn-ay-tr, v to know, to be acquainted with; to be aware of; ne rien – à, ner-re-ang – ãh, to be ignorant of something; se – (à or

en), to be a good judge (of); chiffres connus, shee-fr konn-E, plain figures.

connexe, konn-ecks, a connected (à, with).

connexion, konn-eck-se-ong, f connection.

connivence, konn-ne-vahngss, f connivance.

connu, konn-E, a known; bien –, be-ang –, well-known.

conquérant, kong-keh-rahng, m conqueror.

conquérant, e, kong-keh-rahng, a conquering.

conquérir, kong-keh-reer, v to conquer; to gain.

conquête, kong-kayt, f conquest.

consacrer, kong-sãh-kreh, v to consecrate; to devote.

conscience, kong-se-ahngss, f conscience; conscientiousness; consciousness; awareness.

conscription, kongs-krip-se-ong, f conscription.

conscrit, kongs-kre, m conscript.

consécration, kong-seh-krãh-se-ong, f consecration; dedication.

consécuti-f, ve,* kong-

seh-kE-teeff, *a*
consecutive.

conseil, kong-say'e, *m*
advice; council;
deliberation; counsel;
adviser; –
d'administration,
–dăhd-me-niss-trăh-se-ong, board of directors; –
de guerre, – der ghair,
court-martial.

conseiller, kong-say'e-eh,
m councillor; adviser.

conseiller, kong-say'e-eh,
v to advise; to counsel.

consentement, kong-sahngt-mahng, *m*
consent; assent.

consentir, kong-sahng-teer, *v* to consent; to
agree.

conséquemment, kong-seh-kăh-mahng, *adv*
consequently;
accordingly.

conséquence, kong-seh-kahngss, *f* consequence;
inference; importance;
en –, ahng –,
consequently; **sans** –,
sahng –, immaterial.

conséquent, e, kong-seh-kahng *a* consequent;
consistent; **par** –, păhr
–, ïn consequence.

conserva-teur, trice,
kong-sair-văh-ter, *mf* &
a guardian; keeper;

commissioner;
preservative;
conservative.

conservation, kong-sair-văh-se-ong, *f*
preservation;
guardianship;
(mortgages) registration.

conservatoire, kong-sair-văh-to'ăhr, *m*
conservatory; museum;
academy of music.

conserve, kong-sairv, *f*
preserve; pickled food,
tinned food; **en** –, ahng
–, *a* tinned.

conserver, kong-sair-veh,
v to preserve; to
conserve (food); take
care of; to retain.

considérable,* kong-se-deh-răh-bl, *a*
considerable.

considération, kong-se-deh-răh-se-ong, *f*
consideration; regard;
esteem; **en** – **de,** ahng –,
der, out of regard for.

considérer, kong-se-deh-reh, *v* to consider; to
examine; to value; to
regard.

consignataire, kong-seen-yăh-tair, *m* consignee;
trustee.

consigna-teur, trice,
kong-seen-yăh-ter, *mf*
consignor.

consignation, kong-seen-yăh-se-ong, *f*
consignment; deposit.

consigne, kong-seen-yer, *f*
orders; cloak-room; left
luggage office.

consigner, kong-seen-yeh,
v to deposit; to record;
to confine.

consistance, kong-siss-tahngss, *f* firmness;
consistency; stability;
credit.

consister, kong-siss-teh, *v*
to consist (à, dans, in,
of).

consolation, kong-soll-ăh-se-ong, *f* consolation;
comfort.

console, kong-sol, *f*
bracket; console.

consoler, kong-soll-eh, *v*
to console; to comfort.

consomma-teur, trice,
kong-somm-ăh-ter, *mf*
consumer; customer.

consommation, kong-somm-ăh-se-ong, *f*
consummation;
consumption; a drink
(in café, etc).

consommé, kong-somm-eh, *m* stock; clear soup.

consommer, kong-somm-eh, *v* to consume; to
complete.

consomption, kong-songp-se-ong, *f* consumption.

consonne, kong-sonn, *f*
consonant.

conspirateur, kongs-pe-
räh-ter, *m* conspirator.

conspiration, kongs-pe-
räh-se-ong, *f* conspiracy;
plot.

conspirer, kongs-pe-reh, *v*
to conspire.

conspuer, kongs-pE-eh, *v*
to hoot; to hiss.

constamment, kongs-täh-
mahng, *adv* constantly.

constance, kongs-tangss, *f*
constancy; persistence.

constant, e, kongs-tahng,
a constant, steadfast.

constatation, kongs-täh-
täh-se-ong, *f*
establishment (of fact);
certified statement.

constater, kongs-täh-teh,
v to ascertain; to prove;
to state; to report.

constellation, kongs-tell-
läh-se-ong, *f*
constellation.

consternation, kongs-tair-
näh-se-ong, *f*
consternation.

consterné, e, kongs-tair-
neh, *a* dismayed.

consterner, kongs-tair-
neh, *v* to dismay.

constipation, kongs-te-
päh-se-ong, *f*
constipation.

constipé, e, kongs-te-peh,

a constipated.

constituant, e, kongs-te-
tE-ahng, *a* constituent.

constituer, kongs-te-tE-eh,
v to constitute; to
appoint; to assign; **se –
prisonnier,** ser – pre-
zonne-eh, to give
oneself up.

constitution, kongs-te-tE-
se-ong, *f* constitution;
settlement.

constitutionnel, le, kongs-
te-tE-se-onn-ell, *a*
constitutional.

constricteur, kongs-trick-
ter, *m* constrictor.

constructeur, kongs-trEEk-
ter, *m* builder; –
mécanicien, – meh-käh-
ne-se-ang, engineer.

construction, kongs-trEEk-
se-ong, *f* construction;
building; structure.

construire, kongs-trE-eer,
v to construct; to build;
to construe.

consul, kong-sEEl, *m*
consul.

consulaire, kong-sE-lair, *a*
consular.

consulat, kong-sE-läh, *m*
consulate.

consultant, kong-sEEl-
tahng, *a* consulting;
avocat –, äh-vock-äh –,
Chamber counsel;
médecin –, mehd-sang –,

consulting physician.

consultation, kong-sEEl-
täh-se-ong, *f*
consultation.

consulter, kong-sEEl-teh, *v*
to consult; to refer to; to
give consultations; **se –,**
to consider.

consumer, kong-sE-meh, *v*
to consume; to destroy;
to squander.

contact, kong-tähckt, *m*
contact; touch;
connection.

contagieu-x, se, kong-täh-
she-er, *a* contagious;
infectious; catching.

contagion, kong-täh-she-
ong, *f* contagion;
infection.

contaminer, kong-täh-me-
neh, *v* to contaminate.

conte, kongt, *m* tale; story;
yard; **– à dormir debout,**
–äh-dor-meer der-boo,
cock and bull story; **– de
fées,** – der feh, fairy tale.

contemplation, kong-
tahng-pläh-se-ong, *f*
contemplation;
meditation.

contempler, kong-tahng
pleh, *v* to contemplate;
to meditate.

contemporain, e, kong-
tahng-por-ang, *a*
contemporary.

contenance, kongt-

nahngss, f countenance;
look; capacity.

contenir, kongt-neer, v to
hold; to contain; to
restrain.

content, kong-tahng, a
contented; satisfied;
pleased.

contentement, kong-
tahngt-mahng, m
satisfaction.

contenter, kong-tahng-
teh, v to satisfy; to
please.

contentieux, kong-tahng-
se-er, m disputed claims;
legal business; a in
dispute; litigious.

contention, kong-tahng-
se-ong, f intensity of
thought.

contenu, kongt-nE, m
contents; subject.

conter, kong-teh, v to tell;
to relate; **en –** (à), to
tell a tall story.

contestable, kong-tess-
tăh-bl, a open to
dispute; questionable.

contestation, kong-tess-
tăh-se-ong, f contest;
dispute.

contester, kong-tess-teh, v
to contest; to dispute.

conteu-r, se, kong-ter, mf
storyteller.

contexte, kong-text, m
context.

contexture, kong-tex-tEEr,
f contexture; structure.

contigu, ë, kong-te-ghE, a
adjoining; contiguous.

contiguïté, kong-te-gwe-
teh, f contiguity;
proximity.

continent, kong-te-nahng,
m continent.

continental, e, kong-te-
nahng-tăhl, a
continental.

contingent, kong-tang-
shahng, m share;
proportion; quota.

contingent, e, kong-tang-
shahng, a contingent;
casual.

continu,* e, kong-te-nE, a
continued; continuous.

continuel, le, * kong-te-
nE-ell, a continual.

continuer, kong-te-nE-eh,
v to continue.

continuité, kong-te-nwe-
teh, f continuity.

contondant, e, kong-tong-
dahng, a blunt.

contorsion, kong-tor-se-
ong, f contortion.

contour, kong-toohr, m
outline; circuit.

contourner, kong-toohr-
neh, v to outline; to
distort; to twist; to go
round; med bypass.

contraceptif, kong-trăh-
sep-teef, m

contraceptive.

contracepti-f, ve, kong-
trăh-sep-teef, a
contraceptive.

contractant, e, kong-
trăhck-tahng, mf & a
contracting party;
contracting.

contracter, kong-trăck-
teh, v to contract; to
acquire; to catch; **se –,**
to shrink; to be
contracted.

contradictoire, kong-trăh-
dick-to'ăhr, a
contradictory.

contraindre, kong-trang-
dr, v to constrain; to
compel; **– en justice, –**
ahngshEEs-teess, to sue.

contraint, e, kong-trang, a
constrained; unnatural.

contrainte, kong-trangt, f
compulsion; restraint.

contraire, kong-trair, a &
a contrary; reverse; **au –,**
oh –, on the contrary;
on the other hand.

contraire, * kong-trair, a
adverse; opposed;
injurious.

contrariant, e, kong-trăh-
re-ahng, a vexing;
provoking.

contrariété, kong-trăh-re-
eh-teh, f contrariness;
anno yance.

contraste, kong-trăhst, m

contrast; opposition.

contrat, kong-träh, *m* contract; deed; agreement; indenture; covenant.

contravention, kong-träh-vahng-se-ong, *f* offence; breach of regulations; *fam* fine.

contre, kong-tr, *prep* against; versus; near; *adv* par –, pähr –, on the other hand; *m* opposite side.

contre-amiral, kong-träh-me-rähl, *m* rear-admiral.

contrebalancer, kong-trer-bäh-lahng-seh, *v* to counterbalance.

contrebande, kong-trer-bahngd, *f* smuggling; smuggled goods.

contrebandier, kong-trer-bahng-de-eh, *m* smuggler.

contrebas (en), ahng kong-trer-bah, *adv* downwards; at lower level.

contrebasse, kong-trer-bahss, *f* double bass.

contrecarrer, kong-trer-käh-reh, *v* to thwart.

contrecœur (à), äh kong-trer-ker, *adv* reluctantly.

contrecoup, kong-trer-koo, *m* rebound; consequence.

contredire, kong-trer-deer, *v* to contradict.

contredit (sans), sahng kong-trer-de, *adv* unquestionably.

contrée, kong-treh, *f* country; region; district; land.

contre-épreuve, kongtr-eh-prerv, *f* counter-proof.

contrefaçon, kong-trer-fäh-song, *f* forgery; counterfeit; piracy; infringement.

contrefacteur, kong-trer-fähck-ter, *m* forger; counterfeiter.

contrefaire, kong-trer-fair, *v* to counterfeit; to imitate; to mimic; to disguise; to infringe.

contrefait, kong-trer-fay, *pp* & *a* counterfeited.

contrefort, kong-trer-for, *m* buttress; spur; stiffener.

contre-jour (à), äh kong-trer-shoohr, *adv* in a false light.

contremaître, kong-trer-may-tr, *m* foreman; overseer.

contremander, kong-trer-mahng-deh, *v* to countermand.

contremarque, kong-trer-mährk, *f* check.

contrepartie, kong-trer-pähr-tee, *f* counterpart; opposite view.

contre-pied, kong-trer-pe-eh, *m* contrary; reverse.

contrepoids, kong-trer-po'äh, *m* counterpoise.

contrepoil (à), äh kong-trer-po'ähl, *adv* against the grain; the wrong way.

contrepoint, kong-trer-po'ang, *m* counterpoint.

contrepoison, kong-trer-po'äh-zong, *m* antidote.

contresens, kong-trer-sahngss, *m* misinterpretation; wrong way.

contresigner, kong-trer-seen-yeh, *v* to countersign.

contretemps, kong-trer-tahng, *m* mishap; disappointment; out of time; à –, äh –, inopportunely.

contre-torpilleur, kong-trer-tor-pee-yer, *m* destroyer.

contrevenant, kong-trerv-nahng, *m* offender.

contrevenir, kong-trerv-neer, *v* to infringe; to transgress.

contrevent, kong-trer-vahng, *m* shutter.

contre-vérité, kong-trerveh-re-teh, f statement contrary to the truth; irony; satire.

contribuable, kong-tre-bEăh-bl, m tax-payer; a tax-paying.

contribuer, kong-tre-bEeh, v to contribute; to be conducive.

contribution, kong-tre-bEong, f contribution; tax; rate; part.

contrister, kong-triss-teh, v to grieve; to sadden.

contrit, e, kong-tre, a contrite; penitent.

contrôle, kong-trohl, m register; list; hall-mark stamp; checking; censure; control.

contrôler, kong-troh-leh, v to inspect; to verify; to monitor; se –, to control oneself.

contrôleu-r, se, kong-troh-ler, mf inspector; ticket collector.

controuvé, e, kong-trooveh, pp & a invented; false.

controverse, kong-trov-airs, f controversy.

contusion, kong-tE-ze-ong, f bruise.

convaincant, e, kong-vang-kahng, a convincing.

convaincre, kong-vang-kr,

v to convince; to convict.

convaincu, e, kong-vang-kE, pp & a convinced; convicted.

convalescence, kong-văhlayss-ahngss, f convalescence.

convenable, * kongv-năhbl, a proper; fit; suitable.

convenance, kongv-nahngss, f fitness; convenience; pl good manners; propriety.

convenir, kongv-neer, v to agree (avec, with; de, on); to acknowledge; to suit; to be expedient.

convention, kong-vahng-se-ong, f convention; agreement; condition.

conventionnel, le, * kong-vahng-se-onn-ell, a conventional.

convenu, kongv-nE, pp agreed.

converger, kong-vair-sheh, v to converge.

conversation, kong-vair-săh-se-ong, f conversation.

converser, kong-vair-seh, v to converse; to talk.

conversion, kong-vair-se-ong, f conversion; wheeling.

converti, e, kong-vair-te, mf & a convert;

converted.

convertir, kong-vair-teer, v to convert; to turn; se –, to become converted (à, to).

convexe, kong-vex, a convex.

conviction, kong-vick-se-ong, f conviction; convincing proof.

convier, kong-ve-eh, v to invite; to prompt.

convive, kong-veev, m guest (at meal).

convocation, kong-vockăh-se-ong, f convocation; requisition; summons.

convoi, kong-vo'ăh, m funeral procession; train; convoy.

convoiter, kong-vo'ăh-teh, v to covet.

convoitise, kong-vo'ăhteez, f covetousness.

convoquer, kong-vock-eh, v to convoke; to call; to summon; to assemble.

convulsion, kong-vEEl-se-ong, f convulsion.

convulsi-f, ve, * kong-vEEl-seef, a convulsive.

coopéra-teur, trice, ko-op-eh-răh-ter, mf cooperator.

coopérer, ko-op-eh-reh, v to co-operate.

coordonner, ko-or-donn-eh, *v* to arrange; to coordinate.

copain, kop-ang, *m* chum.

copeau, kop-oh, *m* chip; shaving.

copie, kopee, *f* copy; manuscript; reproduction; imitation.

copier, kop-e-eh, *v* to copy; to imitate; to mimic.

copieu-x, se, * kop-e-er, *a* copious; plentiful.

copropriétaire, kop-rop-re-eh-tair, *m* joint-owner.

coq, kock, *m* cock; cockerel; weather-cock; –à-l'âne, – äh lahn, abrupt change of subject.

coque, kock, *f* shell; cockle; hull.

coquelicot, kock-le-ko, *m* poppy.

coqueluche, kock-LEEsh, *f* whooping-cough; (person) favourite.

coquerico, kock-re-ko, *m* cock-a-doodle-doo.

coquet, te, * kock-ay, *a* coquettish; elegant.

coquetier, kock-te-eh, *m* egg-cup.

coquetterie, kock-ett-ree, *f* coquetry; flirtation.

coquillage, kock-ee-yähsh, *m* empty shell; shell-fish.

coquille, kock-ee-ye, *f* shell.

coquin, e, kock-ang, *a* rogue; rascal; *fam* naughty.

coquinerie, kock-een-ree, *f* michieviousness.

cor, kor, *m* horn; (on the foot) corn.

corail, kor-ah'e, *m* coral.

Coran, kor-ahng, *m* Koran.

corbeau, kor-boh, *m* raven; crow.

corbeille, kor-bay'e, *f* basket; wedding presents; flower-bed; – à papier, – äh pah-pe-eh –, waste paper basket.

corbillard, kor-bee-yähr, *m* hearse.

cordage, kor-dähsh, *m* rope.

corde, kord, *f* string; cord; rope; **la – sensible,** läh – sahng-see-bl, the tender spot; **tenir la –,** ter-neer läh –, to have the best chance.

cordeau, kor-doh, *m* line; cord.

corder, kor-deh, *v* to cord; to twist.

cordial, e, * kor-de-ähl, *a* hearty.

cordon, kor-dong, *m* twist; string; cord; – **bleu,**

–bler, first-rate cook.

cordonnerie, kor-donn-ree, *f* shoe-making; cobbler's shop.

cordonnet, kor-donn-ay, *m* twist; string; braid.

cordonnier, kor-donn-e-eh, *m* cobbler.

coriace, kor-e-ähss, *a* tough (of meat, etc); *fam* hard (of person).

cormoran, kor-mor-ahng, *m* cormorant.

cornaline, kor-näh-leen, *f* cornelian stone.

corne, korn, *f* horn; feeler (of snail); shoe-horn; (books) dog-eared.

corneille, kor-nay'e, *f* crow.

cornemuse, kor-ner-mEEz, *f* bagpipe.

cornet, kor-nay, *m* horn; cornet; ice cream cone; ear-trumpet.

corniche, kor-neesh, *f* cornice; coast road.

cornichon, kor-ne-shong, *m* gherkin; (person) ninny.

cornu, e, kor-nE, *a* horned.

corollaire, kor-oll-lair, *m* corollary.

corps, kor, *m* body; frame; corps; corpse; substance.

corpulent, e, kor-pE-lahng, *a* stout;

corpulent.

correct, e, * kor-reckt, *a* correct; proper.

correcteur, kor-reck-ter, *m* proofreader.

correction, kor-reck-se-ong, *f* correction; accuracy; correctness; punishment.

corrélati-f, ve,* kor-reh-läh-teeff, *a* correlative.

correspondance, kor-ress-pong-dahngss, *f* correspondence; connection (between trains); **petite –,** per-teet –, personal column.

correspondant, e, kor-ress-pong-dahng, *mf* & *a* correspondent; pen friend; guardian; corresponding.

corridor, kor-e-dor, *m* corridor; passage.

corrigé, kor-e-sheh, *m* corrected copy; key to a book.

corriger, kor-e-sheh, *v* to correct; to mark (exercise etc); to chastise.

corroboration, kor-rob-or-äh-se-ong, *f* strengthening.

corroder, kor-rod-eh, *v* to corrode.

corrompre, kor-ong-pr, *v* to corrupt; to bribe.

corrompu, e, kor-ong-pE, *pp* & *a* corrupted; bribed; putrid

corrup-teur, trice, kor-EEp-ter, *mf* & *a* corrupter; briber; corrupting.

corruptible, kor-EEp-tee-bl, *a* corruptible.

corruption, kor-EEp-se-ong, *f* corruption.

corsage, kor-säsh, *m* bodice.

corsé, e, kor-seh, *a* full-bodied.

corser, kor-seh, *v* to give volume to; *fig* to thicken.

corset, kor-say, *m* corset.

cortège, kor-taysh, *m* procession; retinue.

corvée, kor-veh, *f* drudgery; unpleasant job; chore.

coryphée, kor-e-feh, *m* leader; chief.

cosaque, koz-ähck, *m* cossack.

cosmétique, koss-meh-teeck, *m* & *a* cosmetic.

cosmique, koss-meeck, *a* cosmic.

cosmopolite, koss-mop-oll-eet, *mf* & *a* cosmopolitan.

cosse, koss, *f* shell; husk; pod.

cossu, e, koss-E, *a* well off.

costume, koss-tEEm, *m* costume; suit (man's); **grand –,** grahng –, full dress.

costumier, koss-tE-me-eh, *m* costumier; master of wardrobe.

cote, kot, *f* mark; share; quota.

côte, koht, *f* rib; hill; coast; shore; **– à –, –äh–,** side by side.

côté, koht-eh, *m* side; way; part; direction; **à –,** äh –, near; **de ce –,** der ser –, this way; **mauvais –,** moh-vay –, wrong side.

coteau, kot-oh, *m* hill-side; slope.

côtelette, koht-lett, *f* cutlet; chop.

coter, kot-eh, *v* to assess; to quote; to number.

coterie, kot-ree, *f* set; circle; clique.

côtier, kot-te-eh, *m* coasting vessel; *a* coasting; coastal.

cotillon, kot-ee-yong, *m* petticoat.

cotisation, kot-e-zäh-se-ong, *f* contribution; subscription.

cotiser, kot-e-zeh, *v* to rate; **se –,** to club together; to open a subscription.

coton, kot-ong, *m* cotton; down; cotton.

cotonnade, kot-onn-ăhd, *f* cotton; cotton goods.

côtoyer, koh-to'ăh-yeh, *v* to skirt; to border on.

cottage, kot-ăhsh, *m* cottage.

cou, koo, *m* neck.

couard, koo-ăhr, *mf & a* coward; cowardly.

couchant, koo-shahng, *m* sunset; west; decline; *a* setting.

couche, koosh, *f* couch; bed; layer; confinement; nappy; **– à jeter,** – ăh-sher-teh, disposable nappy; **–culotte,** –kE-lot, *f* disposable nappy.

couché, koo-sheh, *pp & a* lying down; in bed.

coucher, koo-sheh, *m* bedtime; sunset.

coucher, koo-sheh, *v* to lay down; to put to bed; **se –** to go to bed.

couchette, koo-shett, *f* crib; berth; sleeper (on trains etc.).

couci-couça, koo-se koo-să, *adv fam* so so.

coucou, koo-koo, *m* cuckoo; cuckoo clock; cowslip.

coude, kood, *m* elbow; bend; angle.

coudée, kood-eh, *f* –s

franches, – frahngsh, elbow room.

cou-de-pied, kood-pe-eh, *m* instep.

coudoyer, koo-do'ăh-yeh, *v* to elbow; to jostle.

coudre, koo-dr, *v* to sew; to stitch; to tack.

couenne, koo-ăhn, *f* rind (of bacon).

coulage, koo-lăhsh, *m* leakage; pouring; casting.

coulant, e, koo-lahng, *a* flowing; running; fluent; (person) accommodating.

coulée, koo-leh, *f* flow; casting.

couler, koo-leh, *v* to flow; to glide; to run (of liquid); to cast; to sink.

couleur, koo-ler, *f* colour; paint; (cards) suit.

couleuvre, koo-ler-vr, *f* grass snake; *fig* bitter pill.

coulis, koo-le, *m* jelly; meat or vegetable broth; *a* vent –, vahng –, thin draught.

coulisse, koo-leess, *f* groove; slide; wing of theatre; (Stock Exchange) outside brokers.

couloir, koo-lo'ăhr, *m* passage; corridor; lobby.

coup, koo, *m* blow; stroke; hit; kick; knock; rap; thrust; cast; cut; stab; lash; wound; shot; report; toll; beat; clap; peal; throw; haul; event; deed; outburst; trick.

coupable, koo-păh-bl, *mf & a* culprit; guilty.

coupage, koo-păhsh, *m* mixing; diluting; cutting.

coupant, e, koo-pahng, *a* cutting; sharp.

coupe, koop, *f* cut; cup; section.

couper, koo-peh, *v* to cut; to mix; to dilute; to cut off.

couperet, koop-ray, *m* chopper; knife (for meat).

couperose, koop-rohz, *f* blotchiness (of complexion).

coupeur, koo-per, *m* cutter.

couplage, koo-plăhsh, *m* coupling; connecting.

couple, koo-pl, *m* pair; couple; *f* brace; couple.

coupler, koo-pleh, *v* to couple.

couplet, koo-play, *m* verse; stanza.

coupole, koo-pol, *f* cupola.

coupon, koo-pong, *m*

remnant; short length; coupon; ticket.

coupure, koo-pEEr, f cut; suppression; small bank note; cutting.

cour, koohr, f yard; court; courtship.

courage, koo-rǎhsh, m courage.

courageu-x, se,* koo-rǎhsh-er, a courageous; spirited; brave.

couramment, koo-rǎh-mahng, adv fluently; generally.

courant, koo-rahng, m current; stream; course; **au – de,** oh – der, conversant with; **mettre au –** met-tr-oh–, to inform; a current; running; ordinary; present.

courbature, koohr-bǎh-tEEr, f stiffness in the joints; ache.

courbaturé,e koohr-bǎh-tE-reh, a stiff; aching.

courbe, koohrb, f curve; bend; curb.

courbé, koohr-beh, pp & a curved; bent; crooked.

courbette, koohr-bett, f servile bow; cringing.

courbure, koohr-bEEr, f curvature; bend.

coureur, koo-rer, m runner; racer; fam

womanizer; a running.

courge, koohrsh, f marrow.

courgette, koohrsh-ett, f courgette.

courir, koo-reer, v to run; to go about; to pursue; to hunt; to flow.

courlis, koohr-le, m curlew.

couronne, koo-ronn, f crown; coronet; wreath.

couronné, koo-ronn-eh, pp & a crowned; rewarded with a prize.

couronnement, koo-ronn-mahng, m coronation; crowning.

courrier, koo-re-eh, m courier; mail; post; messenger.

courroie, koo-ro'ǎh, f strap; belt.

courroucer, koo-roo-seh, v to irritate; to incense.

courroux, koo-roo, m wrath.

cours, koohrs, m course; flow; vent; currency; market price; course of lessons; lectures.

course, koohrs, f running; run; race; drive; ramble; errand; pl shopping.

coursier, koohr-se-eh, m steed.

court, e, koohr, a short; limited; m court; **– de**

tennis, – der-teh-neess m tennis court.

courtage, koohr-tǎhsh, m brokerage.

courtaud, e, koohr-toh, a thick-set.

court-circuit, koohr-seer-kwe, m short circuit.

courtepointe, koohr-ter-po'angt, f counterpane.

courtier, koohr-te-eh, m broker.

courtisan, koohr-te-zahng, m courtier.

courtisane, koohr-te-zǎhn, f courtesan.

courtiser, koohr-te-zeh, v to court.

courtois, e, * koohr-to'ǎh, a courteous.

courtoisie, koohr-to'ǎh-zee, f courtesy.

couru, e, koo-rE, pp & a run; sought after; popular; fam dead certainty.

cousin, koo-zang, m gnat.

cousin, e, koo-zang, mf cousin.

coussin, kooss-ang, m cushion; bolster.

coussinet, kooss-e-nay, m pad; small cushion; bearing.

cousu, e, koo-zE, pp sewed; sewn; covered.

coût, koo, m cost; expense; charge.

coût de la vie, koo-der-läh-ve, *m* cost-of-living.

coûtant, koo-tahng, *a* used only in **à prix –,** ăh pre –, cost price.

couteau, koh-toh, *m* knife.

coutelas, koot-lah, *m* cutlass.

coutellerie, koo-tell-ree, *f* cutlery (trade).

coûter, koo-teh, *v* to cost.

coûteu-x, se, * koo-ter, *a* expensive.

coutil, koo-te, *m* ticking.

coutume, koo-tEEm, *f* custom; practice.

coutumier, koo-tEE-me-eh, *a* customary; usual.

couture, koo-tEE, *f* seam; needlework; sewing.

couturi-er, ère, koo-tE-re-eh, *mf* dressmaker.

couvée, koo-veh, *f* brood.

couvent, koo-vahng, *m* convent.

couver, koo-veh, *v* to brood; to sit on; to hatch out; to smoulder; **– des yeux,** – day z'e-er, to look fondly on.

couvercle, koo-vair-kl, *m* cover; lid; cap.

couvert, koo-vair, *m* place setting; cover charge (in restaurant); cover; shelter; **mettre le –,** met-tr ler –, to lay the table.

couvert, koo-vair, *a* covered; overcast (weather); clad.

couverture, koo-vair-tEEr, *f* cover; blanket; rug; security.

couvre-chef, koo-vrer-sheff, *m* hat; *fam* cap.

couvre-feu, koo-vrer-fer, *m* curfew.

couvre-lit, koo-vrer-le, *m* bed spread.

couvreur, koo-vrer, *m* slater; roofer.

couvrir, koo-vreer, *v* to cover (**de,** with); to conceal; to screen; **se –,** to put one's hat on; to clothe oneself.

cow-boy, ko-boy, *m* cowboy.

crabe, krahb, *m* crab.

crachat, krăh-shăh, *m* spittle; sputum.

craché, krăh-sheh, *pp & a;* **tout –,** too –, the very image of; the dead spit of.

cracher, krăh-sheh, *v* to spit; *fam* to fork out.

crachoir, krăh-sho'ăhr, *m* spittoon.

craie, kray, *f* chalk.

craindre, krang-dr, *v* to fear; to dread.

crainte, krangt, *f* fear; dread.

crainti-f, ve, * krang-teeff, *a* timorous; fearful.

cramoisi, e, krăh-mo'ăh-ze, *a* crimson.

crampe, krahngp, *f* cramp.

crampon, krahng-pong, *m* clamp; stud; crampon; *fam* bore.

cramponner, krahng-ponn-eh, *v* to cramp; **se – à,** to cling to.

cran, krahng, *m* notch; cog; peg; *fam* pluck.

crâne, krahn, *m* skull; *a* plucky; swaggering.

crânerie, krahn-ree, *f* pluck; swagger.

crapaud, krăh-poh, *m* toad.

crapule, krăh-pEEl, *f* debauchery; *fam* foul person.

crapuleu-x, se, krăh-pE-ler, *a* sordid.

craquelin, krăhck-lang, *m* cracknel.

craquement, krăhck-mahng, *m* cracking; crackling.

craquer, krăh-keh, to crack; to crackle.

crasse, krăhss, *f* dirt; filth; stinginess; *a* gross, crass.

crasseu-x, se, krăhss-er, *a* filthy; nasty; sordid.

cratère, krăh-tair, *m* crater.

cravache, krăh-văhsh, *f*

riding crop.

cravate, krăh-văht, *f* neck-tie; scarf.

crayeu-x, se, kray-e-er, *a* chalky.

crayon, kray-yong, *m* pencil.

crayonner, kray-yonn-eh, *v* to sketch; to draw.

créance, kre-ahngss, *f* credit; trust; debt; credence.

créancier, kreh-ahngss-e-eh, *m* creditor.

créateur, kreh-ăh-ter, *m* creator, maker; *a* creative.

création, kreh-ăh-se-ong, *f* creation; production.

créature, kreh-ăh-tEEr, *f* creature.

crécelle, kreh-sell, *f* rattle.

crèche, kraysh, *f* creche; crib.

crédence, kreh-dahngss, *f* side-board.

crédit, kreh-de, *m* credit; trust; loan; influence; esteem.

créditer, kreh-de-teh, *v* to credit (**de**, with).

credo, kreh-do, *m* creed, belief.

crédule, kreh-dEEl, *a* credulous.

crédulité, kreh-dE-le-teh, *f* credulity.

créer, kreh-eh, *v* to create;

to invent; to establish.

crémaillère, kreh-mah'e-air, *f* rack; *fam* **pendre la –**, pahng-dr lăh –, to have a house warming.

crémation, kreh-măh-se-ong, *f* cremation.

crématorium, kreh-măh-to-re-Em, *m* crematorium.

crème, kraym, *f* cream; custard; best.

crémerie, krehm-ree, *f* milk-shop; dairy.

crémi-er, ère, kreh-me-eh, *mf* dairyman; dairywoman.

créneau, kreh-noh, *m* battlement.

crénelé, e, krehn-leh, *a* notched; crenelated.

créneler, krehn-leh, *v* to cog; to mill.

crénelure, krehn-lEEr, *f* indentation.

crêpe, krayp, *m* crêpe; *f* pancake.

crêper, kray-peh, *v* to frizz; to crisp.

crépi, kreh-pe, *m* roughcast.

crépir, kreh-peer, *v* to roughcast; to crimp.

crépine, kreh-peen, *f* fringe (on upholstery).

crépiter, kreh-pe-teh, *v* to crackle.

crépu, e, kreh-pE, *a*

woolly; fuzzy.

crépuscule, kreh-pEEss-kEEl, *m* twilight; decline.

cresson, krehss-ong, *m* cress; water-cress.

crétacé, e, kreh-tăhss-eh, *a* cretaceous.

crête, krayt, *f* crest; top; ridge; comb (of a cock).

crétin, kreh-tang, *m* idiot.

crétinisme, kreh-te-nissm, *m* idiocy.

creuser, krer-zeh, *v* to dig; to hollow; to scoop out; to fathom.

creuset, krer-zay, *m* crucible; *fam* test.

creux, krer, *m* hollow cavity; cast; bass voice.

creu-x, se, kr, krer, *a* hollow; empty; unsubstantial; off-peak.

crevaison, krer-veh-zong, *f* puncture; bursting.

crevasse, krer-văhss, *f* crevice; chink; crack.

crève-cœur, krayv-ker, *m* heart-breaking thing.

crever, krer-veh, *v* to burst; to pierce; to puncture; **se –**, to burst.

crevette, krer-vett, *f* shrimp; prawn.

cri, kre, *m* cry; shout; shriek; scream; clamour; **le dernier –**, ler dair-ne-eh –, the latest fashion.

criailler, kree-ah'e-yeh, *v*

to bawl.

criant, e, kree-ahng, *a* crying; shameful.

criard, e, kree-ăhr, *c.* clamorous; shrill; loud; gaudy.

crible, kree-bl, *m* sieve; riddle.

cribler, kree-bleh, *v* to sift; to riddle; to pierce with holes.

cric, kre, *m* carjack.

cricket, kre-kay, *m* (game) cricket.

cri-cri, kre-kre, *m* (insect) cricket.

criée, kree-eh, *f* auction.

crier, kree-eh, *v* to cry; to shout; to shriek; to proclaim.

crieur, kree-er, *m* crier; auctioneer; town-crier.

crime, kreem, *m* crime.

criminalité, kre-me-năh-le-teh, *f* criminality.

criminel, le, kre-me-nell, *mf* & *a** criminal; culprit.

crin, krang, *m* horsehair; **les –s,** lay –, mane and tail.

crinière, kre-ne-air, *f* mane; *fam* thick head of hair.

crique, kreeck, *f* creek.

criquet, kre-kay, *m* locust; *fam* cricket.

crise, kreez, *f* crisis; fit;

attack.

crisper, kriss-peh, *v* to shrivel; to clench; **se –,** to contract.

crisser, kriss-eh, *v* to grate; to grind.

cristal, kriss-tăhl, *m* crystal; cut-glass.

cristallin, kriss-tăh-lang, *a* crystalline.

cristalliser, kriss-tăh-le-zeh, *v* to crystallise.

critérium, kre-teh-re-omm, *m* criterion.

critique, kre-teeck, *m* critic; *f* criticism; censure; *a** critical.

critiquer, kre-te-keh, *v* to criticise.

croasser, kro'ăhss-eh, *v* to croak; to caw.

croc, kro, *m* hook; canine tooth; tusk; fang.

croche, krosh, *f* quaver.

crochet, krosh-ay, *m* hook; picklock; clasp; bend; crochet.

crocheter, krosh-teh, *v* to pick (a lock).

crochu, e, krosh-E, *a* hooked; crooked.

crocodile, krock-odd-eell, *m* crocodile.

crocus, krock-EEss, *m* crocus; saffron.

croire, kro'ăhr, *v* to believe; to think; to trust to.

croisade, kro'ăh-zăhd, *f* crusade.

croisé, kro'ăh-zeh, *m* crusader; twill; *pp* & *a* crossing; double-breasted.

croisée, kro'ăh-zeh, *f* crossing; casement window; transept.

croisement, kro'ăhz-mahng, *m* crossing.

croiser, kro'ăh-zeh, *v* to crossbreed; to thwart; to cruise.

croiseur, kro'ăh-zer, *m* cruiser.

croisière, kro'ăh-ze-air, *f* cruise.

croissance, krwăhss-ahngss, *f* growth; increase.

croissant, krwăhss-ahng, *m* crescent; croissant.

croissant, e, krwăhss-ahng, *a* growing.

croître, kro'ah-tr, *v* to grow; to increase; to lengthen.

croix, kro'ăh, *f* cross.

croquant, krock-ahng, *m* *fam* peasant; poor wretch; *a* crisp.

croque-mitaine, krock-me-tain, *m* *fam* bogeyman.

croque-mort, krock-mor, *m* undertaker's man.

croquer, krock-eh, *v* to

crunch; to munch; to sketch.

croquette, krock-ett, *f* croquette; rissole.

croquignole, krock-een-yol, *f* cracknel.

croquis, krock-e, *m* sketch; outline.

crosse, kross, *f* crozier; butt-end; hockey stick.

crotte, krot, *f* dung; dropping (of animal dirt).

crotté, e, krot-eh, *a* dirty; muddy.

crotter, krot-eh, *v* to dirty.

crottin, krot-ang, *m* horse or sheep dung.

croulant, e, kroo-lahng, *a* sinking; tottering; tumbledown.

crouler, kroo-leh, *v* to fall; to sink; to crumble.

croup, kroop, *m* croup.

croupe, kroop, *f* rump; buttocks.

croupier, kroo-pe-eh, *m* croupier.

croupière, kroo-pe-air, *f* crupper.

croupion, kroo-pe-ong, *m* rump; tail base; *fam* parson's nose.

croupir, kroo-peer, *v* to stagnate; to wallow.

croupissant, e, kroo-piss-ahng, *a* stagnating; putrescent.

croustillant, e, krooss-tee-yahng, *a* crisp.

croûte, kroot, *f* crust; scab; casser une –, kähss-ehEEn –, to take a snack.

croûton, kroo-tong, *m* crust-end; crouton.

croyable, kro'äh-yäh-bl, *a* credible; likely.

croyance, kro'äh-yahngss, *f* belief; creed; faith.

croyant, e, kro'äh-yahng, *mf* believer; *pl* the faithful.

cru, krE, *m* vineyards; vintage.

cru, e, krE, *a* raw; crude; coarse.

cruauté, krE-oh-teh, *f* cruelty.

cruche, krEEsh, *f* pitcher; blockhead.

cruchon, krE-shong, *m* jug; stone bottle.

crucial, e, krE-se-ähl, *a* crucial.

crucifier, krE-se-fe-eh, *v* to crucify.

crucifix, krE-se-fe, *m* crucifix.

crudité, krE-de-teh, *f* crudity; crudeness; rawness; coarseness.

crue, krEE, *f* rise; swelling; flood.

cruel, le, * krE-ell, *a* cruel; sore; annoying.

crûment, krEE-mahng, *adv*

bluntly.

crustacé, krEEss-tähss-eh, *m & a* crustacean; crustaceous.

crypte, kree-pt, *f* crypt.

cube, kEEb, *m* cube; toy building block; *a* cubic.

cueillette, ker'e-yett, *f* picking; gathering; mixed cargo.

cueillir, ker'e-yeer, *v* to gather; to pick; to pluck.

cuiller or **cuillère**, kwee-yair, *f* spoon.

cuillerée, kwee-yer-reh, *f* spoonful.

cuir, kweer, *m* skin; hide; leather; strop.

cuirasse, kwee-rähss, *f* cuirass; breastplate; armour-plating.

cuirassé, kwee-rähss-eh, *m* battleship.

cuirassé, e, kwee-rähss-eh, *a* armoured.

cuirassier, kwee-rähss-e-eh, *m* cuirassier.

cuire, kweer, *v* to cook; to bake; to roast; to stew; to smart.

cuisant, e, kwee-zahng, *a* sharp; acute; burning.

cuisine, kwee-zeen, *f* kitchen; cooking; cookery.

cuisiner, kwee-ze-neh, *v* to cook; *fam* to concoct (scheme, etc).

cuisini-er, ère, kwee-ze-ne-eh, *mf* cook; *f* cooker.

cuisse, kweess, *f* thigh; leg of bird.

cuisson, kweess-ong, *f* cooking; baking; firing (of bricks, etc); smarting.

cuissot, kweess-o, *m* haunch.

cuit, e, kwee, *pp* & *a* cooked; done; drunk; done for.

cuivre, kwee-vr, *m* copper; –**jaune,** –shohn, brass.

cuivreu-x, se, kwee-vrer, *a* coppery.

cul, kE, *m* (vulgar, except in compounds), bottom; back; rump.

culbute, kEEl-bEEt, *f* somersault; fall; tumble; failure; ruin.

culbuter, kEEl-bE-teh, *v* to topple over; to tumble down.

culinaire, kE-le-nair, *a* culinary.

culminant, e, kEEl-me-nahng, *a* highest; prominent.

culot, kE-lo, *m* bottom; plug; **avoir le –,** *fam* to have the cheek.

culotte, kE-lot, *f* buttock (of beef); knickers; short trousers; breeches.

culotter, kE-lot-eh, *v* to breech.

culpabilité, kEEl-păh-be-le-teh, *f* guilt.

culte, kEElt, *m* worship; creed; cult; veneration.

cultivateur, kEEl-te-văh-ter, *m* grower; agriculturist; farmer.

cultiver, kEEl-te-veh, *v* to cultivate.

culture, kEEl-tEEr, *f* cultivation; culture.

cumuler, kE-mE-leh, *v* to hold several offices; to cumulate.

cupide, kE-peed, *a* covetous; greedy.

curage, kE-răhsh, *m* picking (of teeth); clearing; cleaning.

curatelle, kE-răh-tell, *f* guardianship; trusteeship.

cura-teur, trice, kE-răh-ter, *mf* guardian; curator; trustee.

cure, kEEr, *f* cure; treatment; living; vicarage; parish.

curé, kE-reh, *m* parish priest.

cure-dent, kEEr-dahng, *m* tooth-pick.

curer, kE-reh, *v* to pick (teeth etc); to clean out.

curieux, kE-re-er, *m* inquisitive person; looker-on; curious thing or fact.

curieu-x, se,* kE-re-er, *a* curious; inquisitive; singular.

curiosité, kE-re-ohz-e-teh, *f* curiosity; inquisitiveness; curio.

cutané, e, kE-tăh-neh, *a* cutaneous.

cuve, kEEv, *f* vat; tub; copper.

cuvée, kE-veh, *f* vatful; vintage.

cuver, kE-veh, *v* to ferment; to settle; – **son vin, – song vang,** to sleep "booze" off.

cuvette, kE-vett, *f* basin; washing-up bowl.

cuvier, kE-ve-eh, *m* wash-tub.

cyanure, se-ăh-nEEr, *m* cyanide.

cycle, see-kl, *m* cycle.

cycliste, see-kleest, *mf* cyclist.

cygne, seen-yer, *m* swan.

cylindre, se-lang-dr, *m* cylinder; roller.

cymbale, sang-băhl, *f* cymbal.

cynique, se-neeck, *m* cynic; *a** cynical.

cynisme, se-nissm, *m* cynicism.

cyprès, se-pray, *m* cypress.

cystite, se-steet, *f* cystitis.

cytise, se-teez, *m* cytisus; laburnum.

dactylographe, dăhck-te-log-răhf, *mf & a* typist.

dactylographie, dăhck-te-log-răh-fee, *f* typewriting.

dada, dăh-dăh, *m* hobby-horse; hobby; pet subject.

dague, dăhg, *f* dagger.

daigner, dayn-yeh, *v* to deign.

daim, dang, *m* deer; buck; suede.

dais, day, *m* canopy.

dalle, dăhl, *f* flag-stone; slab.

daltonisme, dăhl-tonn-issm, *m* colour-blindness.

damas, dăh-mah, *m* damask.

dame, dăhm, *f* lady; queen (cards); a king at draughts; *pl* game of draughts.

dame! dăhm! *interj* why! well! indeed!

damer, dăh-meh, *v* to crown (at draughts); *fam* – le pion à, – ler pe-ong ăh, to outdo.

damier, dăh-me-eh, *m* draught-board.

damner, dah-neh, *v* to damn.

damoiselle, dăh-mo'ăh-zell, *f obs* damsel.

dandin, dahng-dang, *m* ninny.

dandiner (se), ser dahng-de-neh, *v* to waddle; to strut.

danger, dahng- sheh, *m* danger.

dangereu-x, se,* dahng-sher-rer, *a* dangerous.

dans, dahng, *prep* in, into; within; according to.

danse, dahngss, *f* dance; dancing.

danseu-r, se, dahng-ser, *mf* dancer.

dard, dăhr, *m* dart; sting; dace.

darder, dăhr-deh, *v* to dart; to shoot; to beam.

darne, dăhrn, *f* slice of fish.

dartre, dăhr-tr, *f* skin trouble (scurf, etc).

date, dăht, *f* date.

dater, dăh-teh, *v* to date.

datif, dăh-tiff, *m* dative.

datte, dăht, *f* (fruit) date.

dattier, dăh-te-eh, *m* date-tree.

daube, dohb, *f* stew.

dauber, doh-beh, *v* to cuff; to jeer; to stew.

dauphin, doh-fang, *m* dolphin; dauphin.

davantage, dăh-vahng-tăhsh, *adv* more.

de, der, *prep* of; from; out of; by; with; as; than; to; upon; since; some; any.

dé, deh, *m* thimble; die.

débâcle, deh-bah-kl, *f* breaking-up; downfall.

déballage, deh-băh-lăhsh, *m* unpacking; *fam* show-down.

déballer, deh-băh-leh, *v* to unpack.

débandade, deh-bahng-dǎhd, *f* stampede; **à la —,** ǎh lǎh —, helter-skelter.

débander, deh-bahng-deh, *v* to unbend; to uncover. to disband; **se—,** to disband; to disperse; to run away; to relax.

débaptiser, deh-bǎh-te-zeh, *v* to change the name of.

débarbouiller, deh-bǎhr-boo'e-yeh, *v* to wash the face of; to clean; **se —,** to wash one's face; to extricate oneself.

débarcadère, deh-bǎhr-kǎh-dair, *m* landing-place.

débarder, deh-bǎhr-deh, *v* to unload.

débardeur, deh-bǎhr-der, *m* docker.

débarquement, deh-bǎhr-ker-mahng, *m* landing; arrival; unloading.

débarquer, deh-bǎhr-keh, *v* to land; to disembark; to unload.

débarras, deh-bǎh-rǎh, *m* riddance; **chambre de —,** shahng-br der —, lumber-room.

débarrasser, deh-bǎh-rǎhss-eh, *v* to clear; to rid; **se —,** to get rid (**de,** of).

débat, deh-bǎh, *m* debate; *pl* pleadings; trial; case.

débattre, deh-bǎh-tr, *v* to debate; to discuss; **se —,** to struggle.

débauche, deh-bohsh, *f* debauch; debauchery.

débaucher, deh-boh-sheh, *v* to debauch; to entice away; **se —,** to go astray.

débilé,* deh-beell, *a* weak; feeble; dim-witted.

débilité, deh-be-le-teh, *f* debility; weakness.

débiliter, deh-be-le-teh, *v* to weaken; to debilitate; to demoralize.

débine, deh-been, *f fam* distress; destitution; straits.

débiner, deh-be-neh, *v fam* to disparage; to run down; **se —,** to make off; to run away.

débit, deh-be, *m* sale; market; retail shop; flow; utterance; output; delivery.

débit, deh-be, *m* debit.

débitant, deh-be-tahng, *m* dealer.

débiter, deh-be-teh, *v* to retail; to sell; to cut up; to recite; to debit (**de,** with).

débi-teur, trice, deh-be-ter, *mf & a* debtor; debit.

déblai, deh-blay, *m* excavation; clearing; *pl* rubble.

déblayer, deh-blay-yeh, *v* to clear away.

débloquer, deh-block-eh, *v* to raise the blockade of; to unclamp; to free.

déboire, deh-bo'ǎhr, *m* vexation; disappointment.

déboiser, deh-bo'ǎh-zeh, *v* to deforest.

déboîter, deh-bo'ǎh-teh, *v* to dislocate; to disconnect.

débonnaire, deh-bonn-air, *a* good-natured; meek; gentle.

débordement, deh-bor-der-mahng, *m* overflowing; *fam* dissoluteness.

déborder, deh-bor-deh, *v* to overflow; to project; to untuck.

débotter, deh-bot-eh, *v* to pull boots off; **au —, oh —,** immediately on arrival.

débouché, deh-boo-sheh, *m* outlet; market; issue.

déboucher, deh-boo-sheh, *v* to open; to uncork; to unblock; to emerge; to run into.

déboucler, deh-boo-kleh, *v* to unbuckle; to uncurl.

débourber, deh-boohr-beh, *v* to clean; to extricate from the mud.

déboursés, débours, deh-boohr-seh, deh-boohr, *mpl* expenses; disbursements.

débourser, deh-boohr-seh, *v* to disburse; to lay out.

debout, der-boo, *adv* upright; standing.

débouter, deh-boo-teh, *v* to dismiss.

déboutonner, deh-boo-tonn-eh, *v* to unbutton.

débraillé, e, deh-brah'e-yeh, *a* untidy; disarrayed.

débrayage, deh-bre-yash, *m auto* disengaging; declutching.

débrayer, deh-bray-yeh, *v* to declutch; to disengage.

débrider, deh-bre-deh, *v* to unbridle; to stop; **sans –,** without stopping.

débris, deh-bre, *m* remains; debris; rubbish.

débrouillard, e, deh-broo'e-yăhr, *mf* & *a fam* resourceful; capable.

débrouiller, deh-broo'e-yeh, *v* to disentangle; to unravel; **se –,** to cope.

début, deh-bE, *m* beginning; first appearance; lead.

débutant, e, deh-bE-tahng, *mf* & *a* beginner; performer appearing for the first time.

débuter, deh-bE-teh, *v* to begin; to make one's first appearance.

deçà, der-săh, *adv* on this side.

décacheter, deh-kăhsh-teh, *v* to unseal.

décadence, deh-kăh-dahngss, *f* decay; decline.

décaisser, deh-kayss-eh, *v* to unpack; to disburse.

décaler, deh-cah-leh, *v* to unwedge; to alter (time); to displace.

décalquer, deh-kăhl-keh, *v* to transfer a tracing; to trace

décamper, deh-kahng-peh, *v* to move off; to bolt.

décanter, deh-kahng-teh, *v* to decant.

décapiter, deh-kăh-pe-teh, *v* to behead.

décéder, deh-seh-deh, *v* to die; to decease.

déceler, dehss-leh, *v* to disclose; to reveal; to defect.

décembre, deh-sahng-br, *m* December.

décemment, deh-săh-mahng, *adv* decently.

décence, deh-sahngss, *f* decency; propriety.

décent, e, deh-sahng, *a* decent; becoming; proper.

déception, deh-sep-se-ong, *f* disappointment; setback.

décerner, deh-sair-neh, *v* to award; to issue (writ, etc).

décès, deh-say, *m* death; decease.

décevant, deh-ser-vahng, *a* misleading; disappointing.

décevoir, deh-ser-vo'ăhr, *v* to disappoint.

déchaîné, deh-shay-neh, *pp* & *a* unchained; furious; mad.

déchaîner, deh-shay-neh, *v* to unchain; to let loose.

déchanter, deh-shahng-teh, *v* to become disillusioned.

décharge, deh-shăhrsh, *f* discharge; discharging; unloading; acquittal; à –, ăh –, for the defence.

décharger deh-shăhr-sheh, *v* to unload; to relieve; to clear.

déchargeur, deh-shăhr-sher, *m* docker.

décharné, deh-shăhr-neh, *a* emaciated.

déchaussé, e, deh-shohss-eh, *pp* & *a* barefooted; shrinking (of gums).

dèche, daysh, *f pop* destitution.

déchéance, deh-sheh-ahngss, *f* forfeiture; downfall.

déchet, deh-shay, *m* waste; loss.

décheveler, deh-sherv-leh, *v* to dishevel; to tousle.

déchiffrer, deh-she-freh, *v* to decipher; to sight-read (music).

déchiqueter, deh-shick-teh, *v* to cut up; to slash; to tear.

déchirant, e, deh-she-rahng, *a* piercing; heartrending.

déchirement, deh-sheer-mahng, *m* tearing; anguish; excruciating pain.

déchirer, deh-she-reh, *v* to tear; to rend; to break.

déchirure, deh-she-rEEr, *f* tear; rip.

déchoir, deh-sho'ähr, *v* to fall; to decline; to decay.

décidé, e, deh-se-deh, *pp* & *a* decided; determined.

décidément, deh-se-deh-mahng, *adv* decidedly.

décider, deh-se-deh, *v* to decide; to determine; to persuade; **se –,** to make

up one's mind.

decimal, deh-se-mahl, *a* decimal.

décimale, deh-se-mahl, *f* decimal (fraction).

décisi-f, ve,* deh-se-zeeff, *a* decisive.

décision, deh-se-ze-ong, *f* decision; resolution.

déclamer, deh-kläh-meh, *v* to declaim; to recite.

déclaration, deh-kläh-räh-se-ong, *f* declaration; affidavit; verdict.

déclarer, deh-kläh-reh, *v* to declare; to proclaim; to certify.

déclassé, e, deh-klähss-eh, *mf* & *a* one who has lost social position.

déclencher, deh-klahng-sheh, *v* to unlock; to loosen; to disconnect; (*fam*) to launch; to set in motion.

déclinaison, deh-kle-nay-zong, *f* declination (of compass, star, etc); declension.

décliner, deh-kle-neh, *v* to decline; to deviate.

déclivité, deh-kle-ve-teh, *f* declivity.

déclouer, deh-kloo-eh, *v* to pry open.

décocher, deh-kosh-eh, *v* to shoot; to let fly.

décoiffer, deh-ko'äh-feh, *v*

to take off hat; to disarrange hair.

décollage, deh-ko-lash, *m* unsticking; take-off (of plane).

décoller, deh-koll-eh, *v* to unstick; to take off (of plane.

décolleté, e, deh-koll-teh, *a* low-cut; low-necked; *m* neck-line.

décolorer, deh-koll-or-eh, *v* to discolour; to bleach.

décombres, deh-kong-br, *mpl* rubbish.

décommander, deh-komm-ahng-deh, *v* to countermand; to cancel.

décomposer, deh-kong-poz-eh, *v* to decompose.

décomposition, deh-kong-poz-e-se-ong, *f* decomposition; discomposure; analyzing.

décompte, deh-kongt, *m* deduction; disappointment.

décompter, deh-kong-teh, *v* to deduct; to be disappointed.

déconcerter, deh-kong-sair-teh, *v* to disconcert; to confuse; to baffle.

décongeler, deh-kong-sher-leh, *v* to thaw; to defrost (food).

déconseiller, deh-kong-say'e-yeh, *v* to advise

against.

déconsidérer, deh-kong-se-deh-reh, v to bring into discredit.

décontenancer, deh-kongt-nahngss-eh, v to disconcert.

décontracté, deh-kong-trahck-teh, a relaxed.

décontracter (se), ser deh-kong-trahck-teh, v to relax.

déconvenue, deh-kongv-nE, f mishap; bad luck; disappointment.

décor, deh-kor, m decoration; pl stage-scenery.

décorateur, deh-kor-ăh-ter, m decorator.

décoration, deh-kor-ăh-se-ong, f decoration; medal.

décoré, e, deh-kor-eh, a decorated; wearing a decoration.

décorer, deh-kor-eh, v to embellish; to confer a decoration on.

découcher, deh-koo-sheh, v to sleep out; to stay out all night.

découdre, deh-koo-dr, v to unpick.

découler, deh-koo-leh, v to drop; to trickle; to follow (**de**, from).

découper, deh-koo-peh, v to cut up; to cut out; to carve.

découplé, deh-koo-pleh, pp & a uncoupled; **bien** –, be-ang –, strapping.

découpure, deh-koo-pEer, f indentations.

décourageant, deh-koo-rah-shahng, a discouraging; disheartening.

découragement, deh-koo-răhsh-mahng, m discouragement; despondency.

décourager, deh-koo-răh-sheh, v to discourage; to deter; **se** –, to lose heart.

décousu, e, deh-koo-zE, pp & a unsewed; unconnected; desultory.

découvert, deh-koo-vair, m deficit; overdraft.

découvert, e, deh-koo-vair, pp & a uncovered; open; **à** –, ăh –, openly; unsecured; exposed.

découverte, deh-koo-vairt, f discovery.

découvrir, deh-koo-vreer, v to uncover; to discover; to unmask; to find out; **se** –, to take off one's hat; to come to light; (weather) to clear up.

décrasser, deh-krăhss-eh, v to clean; to get dirt

off.

décréditer, deh-kreh-de-teh, v to bring into discredit.

décrépit, e, deh-kreh-pe, a decrepit; senile.

décret, deh-kray, m decree; order.

décréter, deh-kreh-teh, v to decree.

décrier, deh-kre-eh, v to run down; to decry.

décrire, deh-kreer, v to describe.

décrocher, deh-krosh-eh, v to unhook; to take off.

décroissance, deh-kro'ăhss-ahngss, f decrease.

décroître, deh-kro'ăh-tr, v to decrease; to diminish.

décrotter, deh-krot-eh v to clean mud off (boots, etc); to brush.

décrottoir, deh-krot-o ăhr, m scraper.

déçu, e, deh-sE, pp & a disappointed.

décupler, deh-kE-pleh, v to increase tenfold.

dédaigner, deh-dayn-yeh, v to disdain.

dédaigneu-x, se,* deh-dayn-yer, a disdainful; scornful.

dédain, deh-dahng, m disdain; scorn.

dedans, der-dahng, adv

inside; in; in it; in them;
m inside; interior.

dédicace, deh-de-kähss, *f*
dedication.

dédier, deh-de-eh, *v* to
dedicate.

dédire, deh-deer, *v* to
retract a statement.

dédit, deh-de, *m* forfeit.

dédommagement, deh-
domm-ähsh-mahng, *m*
compensation;
indemnification.

dédommager deh-domm-
äh-**sheh,** *v* to
compensate; (**de,** for).

dédouaner, deh-doo-ah-
neh, *v* to clear luggage
through customs.

dédoubler, deh-doo-bleh,
v to take the lining out
of; to diminish by half;
to divide in two.

déduction, dah-dEEk-se-
ong, *f* deduction;
inference; – **faite de, –**
fayt der, after deducting.

déduire, deh-dweer, *v* to
deduct; to deduce; to
infer.

déesse, deh-ess, *f* goddess.

défaillance, deh-fah'e-
yahngss, *f* faint;
faltering; failing.

défaillir, deh-fah'e-yeer, *v*
to faint; to falter; to fail.

défaire, deh-fair, *v* to
undo; to break; to

defeat; **se – de,** to get rid
of.

défait, e, deh-fay, *pp* & *a*
undone; dishevelled;
defeated.

défaite, deh-fayt, *f* defeat;
pretext.

défalcation, deh-fähl-käh-
se-ong, *f* deduction.

défaut, deh-foh, *m* defect;
fault; default; **à – de,** äh
– der, for want of; **faire
–,** fair –, to fail.

défaveur, deh-fäh-ver, *f*
disgrace; disfavour.

défavorable, * deh-fäh-
vor-äh-bl, *a*
unfavourable.

défecti-f, ve, deh-feck-
teeff, *a* defective.

défection, deh-feck-se-
ong, *f* desertion;
disloyalty.

défectueu-x, se, * deh-
feck-tE- er, *a* defective;
faulty.

défectuosité, deh-feck-tE-
oz-e-teh, *f* defect;
blemish; faultiness.

défend-eur, eresse, deh-
fahng-der, *mf* defendant.

défendre, deh-fahng-dr, *v*
to defend; to forbid.

défense, deh-fahngss, *f*
defence; prohibition; *pl*
tusks.

défenseur, deh-fahng-ser,
m defender.

défensi-f, ve, * deh-fahng-
seeff, *a* defensive.

déférence, deh-feh-
rahngss, *f* deference.

déférer, deh-feh-reh, *v* to
bestow; to bring before;
to comply (**à,** with); to
defer; (oath) to tender.

déferler, deh-fair-leh, *v* to
unfurl; to break.

défi, deh-fe, *m* defiance;
challenge.

défiance, deh-fe-ahngss, *f*
distrust; diffidence.

défiant, e, deh-fe-ahng, *a*
distrustful; suspicious.

déficeler, deh-fiss-leh, *v* to
untie.

défier, deh-fe-eh, *v* to
challenge; to defy; **se –
(de),** to mistrust.

défigurer, deh-fe-ghE-reh,
v to disfigure.

défilé, deh-fe-leh, *m*
straight; march past.

défini, e, deh-fe-ne, *pp* &
a defined; definite;
precise.

définir, deh-fe-neer, *v* to
define.

définissable, deh-fe-niss-
äh-bl, *a* definable.

définiti-f, ve, * deh-fe-ne-
teeff, *a* definitive;
positive; **en –ve,** ahng –,
finally.

définition, deh-fe-ne-se-
ong, *f* definition; clue

(of crossword).

défoncer, deh-fongss-eh, *v* to smash up; to break up.

déformer, deh-for-meh, *v* to put out of shape; to distort.

défraîchi, e, deh-fray-she, *a* no longer fresh; tatty.

défrayer, deh-fray-yeh, *v* to defray the expense of.

défricher, deh-fre-sheh, *v* to clear; to reclaim (of land).

défroque, deh-frock, *f* cast-off clothes (usu in *pl*; of monk, etc).

défroqué, deh-frock-eh, *a & m* unfrocked (priest etc); ex-priest.

défunt, e, deh-fung, *a* deceased.

dégagé, e, deh-gäh-sheh, *pp & a* redeemed; free; easy; off hand; private.

dégager, deh-gäh-sheh, *v* to redeem; to clear; to release.

dégaine, deh-gain, *f* ungainliness; awkward gait.

dégainer, deh-gay-neh, *v* to unsheathe.

dégarnir, deh-gähr-neer, *v* to strip; to dismantle; **se – de,** to part with; to get short of.

dégât, deh-gah, *m* damage;

havoc; waste.

dégel, deh-shell, *m* thaw.

dégénérer, deh-sheh-neh-reh, *v* to degenerate.

dégingandé, e, deh-shang-gahng-deh, *a & mf* ungainly.

dégivrer, deh-she-vreh, *v* to de-ice; to defrost.

dégivreur, deh-she-vrer, *m* de-icer.

dégommer, deh-gomm-eh, *v* to unstick; *fam* to give the sack to.

dégonfler, deh-gong-fleh, *v* to reduce; to bring down; to defiate; **se –,** to collapse (tyre, balloon, etc); *fam* to get into a funk.

dégorger, deh-gor-sheh, *v* to disgorge; to clear; to scour.

dégourdi, e, deh-goohr-de, *a* sharp; acute (of person).

dégourdir, deh-goohr-deer, *v* to revive; to stretch; to sharpen; **se –,** to get sharp.

dégoût, deh-goo, *m* dislike; disgust; loathing.

dégoûtant, e, deh-goo-tahng, *a* sickening; disgusting.

dégoûté, e, deh-goo-teh, *pp & a* disgusted; fastidious; squeamish.

dégoutter, deh-goot-eh, *v* to drip; to trickle.

dégrader, deh-gräh-deh, *v* to degrade; to debase; to damage.

dégrafer, deh-gräh-feh, *v* to unhook; to unclasp.

dégraisser, deh-grayss-eh, *v* to scour; to clean; to remove the grease from; to skim fat off.

degré, der-greh, *m* degree; step; stage.

dégringoler, deh-grang-goll-eh, *v* to tumble down.

dégriser, deh-gre-zeh, *v* to sober.

dégrossir, deh-gross-eer, *v* to smooth rough edges of; *fig* to knock the rough edges off.

déguenillé, e, deh-gher-nee-yeh, *a* ragged.

déguerpir, deh-gair-peer, *v* to pack off; to clear out.

déguisement, deh-gheez-mahng, *m* disguise.

déguiser, deh-ghee-zeh, *v* to disguise; to conceal.

déguster, deh-ghEEs-teh, *v* to taste; to sample; to eat or drink with relish.

déhanché, deh-ahng-sheh, *a* swaying; ungainly.

dehors, der-or, *adv* without; outside; *m*

outside; exterior;
appearances.

déjà, deh-shǎh, *adv*
already; yet; then;
before; as far back as; to
begin with.

déjeuner, deh-sher-neh, *m*
lunch; **petit –,** per-te –,
breakfast.

déjeuner, deh-sher-neh, *v*
to breakfast; to lunch.

déjouer deh-shoo-eh, *v* to
baffle; to thwart.

déjuger (se), ser deh-shE-
sheh, *v* to change one's
opinion.

delà der-lǎh, *prep* beyond;
on the other side of;
farther than; **au – de** oh
– der beyond.

délabré, e, deh-lǎh-breh, *a*
tattered; dilapidated; in
ruins.

délabrement, deh-lǎh-
brer-mahng, *m* ruin;
decay; dilapidation.

délai, deh-lay, *m* interval;
delay; **dans un – de,**
dahng z'ung – der,
within.

délaissement, deh-layss-
mahng, *m*
abandonment;
relinquishment.

délaisser, deh-layss-eh, *v*
to forsake; to abandon.

délassement, deh-lǎhss-
mahng, *m* relaxation;

rest.

déla-teur, trice, deh-lǎh-
ter, *mf* informer.

délation, deh-lǎh-se-ong, *f*
information;
denunciation.

délayer, deh-lay-yeh, *v* to
mix with water; to thin
out; to spin out.

délecter (se), ser deh-
leck-teh, *v* to delight (à,
in).

délégation, deh-leh-gǎh-
se-ong, *f* delegation;
assignment; proxy.

délégué, deh-leh-gheh, *m*
delegate; deputy; shop
steward; union
representative.

déléguer, deh-leh-gheh, *v*
to delegate; to assign.

délétère, deh-leh-tair, *a*
deleterious.

délibérément, deh-le-beh-
reh-mahng, *adv*
deliberately.

délibérer, deh-le-beh-reh,
v to deliberate; to
resolve.

délicat, e, * deh-le-kǎh, *a*
delicate; dainty;
scrupulous; tricky;
difficult.

délicatesse, deh-le-kǎh-
tess, *f* delicacy; nicety;
scrupulousness.

délicieu-x, se, * deh-le-se-
er, *a* delicious;

delightful.

délictueu-x, se, deh-lick-
tE- er, *a* unlawful;
offensive.

délié, deh-le-eh, *pp & a*
untied; loose; easy;
slender; sharp.

délier, deh-le-eh, *v* to
untie; to unbind; to
release; to absolve.

délimiter, deh-le-me-teh,
v to fix the limits of.

délinquant, deh-lang-
kahng, *m* offender;
delinquent.

délirant, e, deh-le-rahng,
a delirious; frenzied;
rapturous.

délire, deh-leer, *m*
delirium; frenzy.

délit, deh-le, *m*
misdemeanour; offence;
en flagrant –, ahng flǎh-
grahng –, in the very
act; **le corps du –,** ler
kor dE –, the charge.

délivrance, deh-le-
vrahngss, *f* deliverance;
release; rescue;
confinement.

délivrer, deh-le-vreh, *v* to
deliver; to rid; to
release; to set free.

déloger, deh-losh-eh, *v* to
dislodge; to turn out;
fam to clear out; **– sans
tambour ni trompette, –**
sahng tahng-boohr ne

trong-payt, to steal away.

déloyal, e, * deh-lo'ăh-yăhl, *a* disloyal; dishonest; unfair.

déloyauté, deh-lo'ăh-yoh-teh, *f* dishonesty.

déluge, deh-LEE sh, *m* flood.

déluré, e, deh-lE-reh, *a* sharp; resourceful.

demain, der-mang, *adv* to-morrow; **après –,** ăh-pray –, the day after to-morrow.

démancher, deh-mahng-sheh, *v* to take the handle off; to dislocate.

demande, der-mahngd, *f* question; request; prayer; *pl* enquiries; orders.

demander, der-mahng-deh, *v* to ask; to beg; to claim; to want; to demand; to require; **se –,** to wonder.

demand-eur, eresse, der-mahng-der, *mf* plaintiff; applicant.

démangeaison, deh-mahng- shay-zong, *f* itching; longing.

démanger, deh-mahng-sheh, *v* to itch; to long.

démantibuler, deh-mahng-te-bE-leh, *v* to put out of order.

démaquillant, deh-măh-

kee-yahng, *m* makeup remover.

démaquiller, deh-măh-kee-yeh, *v* to remove make-up.

démarche, deh-mahrsh, *f* gait; walk; step; measure; attempt; application.

démarquer, deh-măhr-keh, *v* to unmark; to mark down (goods).

démarrage, deh-măh-răhsh, *m* unmooring; start.

démarrer, deh-măh-reh, *v* to start up; to cast off.

démarreur, deh-mah-rer, *m* starter (in car).

démasquer, deh-măhss-keh, *v* to unmask; to show up.

démêlé, deh-may-leh, *m* (usu *pl*) dispute; differences.

démêler, deh-may-leh, *v* to disentangle.

démêloir, deh-may-lo'ăhr, *m* large-tooth comb.

démembrer, deh-mahng-breh, *v* to dismember.

déménagement, deh-meh-năhsh-mahng, *m* moving (house); removal.

déménager, deh-meh-năh-sheh, *v* to remove; to move house.

démence, deh-mahngss, *f* madness; insanity.

démener (se), ser deh-mer-neh, *v* to struggle.

démenti, deh-mahng-te, *m* flat denial.

démentir, deh-mahng-teer, *v* to refute; to contradict.

démérite, deh-meh-reet, *m* demerit.

démériter, deh-meh-re-teh, *v* to deserve censure.

démesuré, e, deh-mer-ZEE-reh, *a* immoderate; excessive.

démettre, deh-met-tr, *v* to dislocate; to dismiss; **se –,** to resign.

démeubler, deh-mer-bleh, *v* to unfurnish.

demeurant, der-mer-rahng, *pp* residing; **au –,** oh –, after all.

demeure, der-mer, *f* residence; **à – , ăh –,** permanently; **mettre en –,** met-tr'ahng –, to call upon.

demeurer, der-mer-reh, *v* to reside; to live; to stay; to stand; **en – là,** ahng –lăh, to go no farther.

demi, der-me, *m* & *a* half; *fam* a glass of beer.

démission, deh-miss-e-ong, *f* resignation;

donner sa démission, donn-eh säh –, to give one's resignation.

démobiliser, deh-mob-e-le-zeh, *v* to demobilise.

démocratie, deh-mock-räh-see, *f* democracy.

démodé, e, deh-mod-eh, *a* out of fashion.

demoiselle, der-mo'äh-zell, *f* young lady; miss; single; **– d'honneur, –** donn-**er,** bridesmaid.

démolir, deh-moll-eer, *v* to pull down.

démon, deh-mong, *m* demon; devil; an imp (of child).

démoniaque, deh-monn-e-ähck, *a* demonic.

démonstration, deh-mongss-träh-se-ong, *f* demonstration.

démontable, deh-mong-täh-bl, *a* that can be dismantled.

démonter, deh-mong-teh, *v* to dismount; to take apart; to put out; **se –,** to lose face.

démontrer, deh-mong-treh, *v* to demonstrate; to prove.

démoraliser, deh-mor-äh-le-zeh, *v* to demoralise.

démordre, deh-mor-dr, *v* to let go; to desist.

démouler, deh-moo-leh, *v* to remove from mould.

démunir (se), ser deh-mE-neer, *v* to part **(de,** with).

dénaturé, e, deh-näh-tE-reh, *pp* & *a* altered; distorted; unnatural; depraved.

dénégation, deh-neh-gäh-se-ong, *f* denial.

dénicher, deh-ne-sheh, *v* to take out of its nest; to find out.

dénier, deh-ne-eh, *v* to deny.

dénigrer, deh-ne-greh, *v* to disparage.

dénombrement, deh-nong-brer-mahng, *m* numbering; enumeration; census.

dénommer, deh-nomm-eh, *v* to name.

dénoncer, deh-nongss-eh, *v* to denounce.

dénonciateur, deh-nongss-e-äh-ter, *m* informer.

dénoter, deh-not-eh, *v* to denote; to show.

dénouement, deh-noo-mahng, *m* outcome; issue; end; ending.

dénouer, deh-noo-eh, *v* to untie; to undo; to unravel; to loose; to solve.

denrée, dahng-reh, *f* ware; provision; *pl* produce;

commodities; **–s alimentaires, –** äh-le-mahngt-air, food products.

dense, dahngss, *a* dense.

densité, dahng-se-teh, *f* thickness; density.

dent, dahng, *f* tooth; notch; cog; prong.

dentaire, dahng-tair, *a* dental.

dentelé, e, dahngt-leh, *a* indented; notched; jagged.

dentelle, dahng-tell, *f* lace; lace-work.

dentier, dahng-te-eh, *m* denture.

dentifrice, dahng-te-freess, *m* toothpaste.

dentiste, dahng-teesst, *m* dentist.

dentition, dahng-te-se-ong, *f* teeth.

dénuder, deh-nE-deh, *v* to denude; to strip.

dénué, e, deh-nE-eh, *pp* & *a* destitute; devoid of.

dénûment, deh-nEE-mahng, *m* destitution; penury.

déodorant, deh-oh-doh-rahng, *m* deodorant.

dépannage, deh-pah-nash, *m* breakdown service.

dépanner, deh-pah-neh, *v* to repair (broken down cars); *fam* to help out.

dépaqueter, deh-păhck-teh, *v* to unpack.

dépareillé, e, deh-păh-ray'e-yeh, *pp & a* unmatched; odd; incomplete.

déparer, deh-păh-reh, *v* to strip; to disfigure; to spoil the look of.

départ, deh-păhr, *m* departure.

département, deh-păhr-ter-mahng, *m* department; county.

départir, deh-păhr-teer, *v* to allot; to bestow; **se – de,** to give up.

dépasser, deh-păhss-eh, *v* to pass; to go beyond; to exceed; to outrun; to rise above.

dépayser, deh-pay-yee-zeh, *v* to send from home.

dépaysé, deh-pay-yee-zeh, *a* disoriented; **se sentir –,** not to feel at home.

dépêche, deh-paysh, *f* despatch; telegram.

dépêcher, deh-pay-sheh, *v* to dispatch; **se –,** to hurry.

dépeindre, deh-pang-dr, *v* to depict.

dépendance, deh-pahng-dahngss, *f* dependence; dependency; *pl* outbuildings.

dépendre, deh-pahng-dr, *v* to depend; to result; to belong to; to unhang.

dépens, deh-pahng, *mpl* (legal) expenses, costs; **au – de,** at the expense of.

dépense, deh-pahngss, *f* expense; expenditure.

dépenser, deh-pahngss-eh, *v* to spend (money or time).

dépensi-er, ére, deh-pahngss-e-eh, *mf* spend thrift; *a* extravagant; prodigal.

déperdition, deh-pair-de-se-ong, *f* loss; waste.

dépérir, deh-peh-reer, *v* to pine away.

dépêtrer, deh-pay-treh, *v* to disentangle; to extricate.

dépeupler, deh-per-pleh, *v* to depopulate.

dépister, deh-piss-teh, *v* to track; to throw off the scent.

dépit, deh-pe, *m* frustration; vexation; **en – de,** ahng – der, in spite of.

dépiter, deh-pe-teh, *v* to vex; to spite.

déplacé, e, deh-plăhss-eh, *pp & a* in the wrong place; improper; uncalled for; displaced

(of person).

déplacement, deh-plăhss-mahng, *m* removal; change of place; **frais de –,** fray der –, travelling expenses.

déplacer, deh-plăhss-eh, *v* to displace **se –,** to move; to travel.

déplaire, deh-plair, *v* to displease; to offend; **se – à,** to dislike (a place, etc)

déplaisant, e, deh-play-zahng, *a* disagreeable; unpleasant.

déplier, deh-ple-eh, *v* to unfold.

déplisser, deh-pliss-eh, *v* to unpleat.

déploiement, deh-plo'ăh-mahng, *m* unfolding; display.

déplorer, deh-plor-eh, *v* to deplore.

déployer, deh-plo'ăh-yeh, *v* to unfold; to display; to exert; to deploy.

déplumer, deh-plE-meh, *v* to pluck; to pick.

déporté, deh-por-teh, *m & a* deported; transported convict.

déportements, deh-por-ter-mahng, *mpl* misconduct.

déporter, deh-por-teh, *v* to depart; to transport.

déposant, deh-poh-zahng, *m* depositor; witness.

déposer, deh-poh-zeh, *v* to deposit; to put down; to lodge; to give evidence; to depose; to leave; **marque déposée,** mahrk –, registered trademark.

dépositaire, deh-poh-ze-tair, *m* depositary; trustee.

déposition, deh-poh-ze-se-ong, *f* evidence.

déposséder, deh-poss-eh-deh, *v* to dispossess.

dépôt, deh-poh, *m* deposit; depositing; trust; store; warehouse; jail; sediment.

dépouille, deh-poo'e-ye, *f* (animal) skin; (human) remains.

dépouillement, deh-poo'e-yer-mahng, *m* stripping; abstract; perusal; counting.

dépouiller, deh-poo'e-yeh, *v* to deprive; to strip; to skin.

dépourvoir, deh-poohr-vo'ăhr, *v* to leave unprovided for; to strip.

dépourvu, e, deh-poohr-VE, *pp* & *a* destitute; unprovided; **au –,** oh –, unprepared.

dépraver, deh-prăh-veh, *v* to deprave.

déprécier, deh-preh-se-eh, *v* to depreciate; to under-value.

dépression, deh-preh-se-ong, *f* depression; dejection; **– nerveuse, –** nair-verz, nervous breakdown.

déprimer, deh-pre-meh, *v* to depress; to disparage.

depuis, der-pwe, *adv* & *prep* since; ever since; from; **– peu, –** per, lately; **– quand? –** kahng, how long?

député, deh-pE-teh, *m* representative; member of the French Parliament.

députer, deh-pE-teh, *v* to delegate; to send a deputation.

déraciner, deh-răh-se-neh, *v* to uproot.

déraillement, deh-rah'e-mahng, derailment.

dérailler, deh-rah'e-yeh, *v* to derail.

déraisonnable, deh-ray-zonn-ăh-bl, *a* unreasonable.

déraisonner, deh-ray-zonn-eh, *v* to rave; to talk nonsense.

dérangement, deh-rahng sh-mahng, *m* derangement; disturbance; trouble;

disorder; upset.

déranger, deh-rahng-sheh, *v* to displace; to put out of order; to disturb; to upset; to lead astray; **se –,** to get out of order; to get into bad ways; to put oneself out.

déraper, deh-răh-peh, *v* to trip; to skid.

déréglé, e, deh-reh-gleh, *pp* & *a* put out of order; irregularly; disorderly; dissolute.

déréglement, deh-ray-gler-mahng, *m* disorder; irregularity; dissoluteness.

dérégler, deh-reh-gleh, *v* to unsettle; to put out of order; **se –,** to get out of order; to lead a disorderly life.

dérider, deh-re-deh, *v* to unwrinkle; to cheer; **se – to** brighten up.

dérision, deh-re-ze-ong, *f* derision; mockery.

dérisoire, * deh-re-zo'ăhr, *a* derisive.

dérive, deh-reev, *f* drift; lee-way; **à la –,** ăh lăh –, adrift.

dériver, deh-re-veh, *v* to drift; to be derived; to derive.

derni-er, ère, dair-ne-eh, *a* last; latter; utmost;

final; youngest; latest.

dernièrement, dair-ne-air-mahng, *adv* lately.

dérobé, e, deh-rob-eh, *pp* & *a* stolen; concealed; **à la dérobée,** ăh lăh–, stealthily.

dérober, deh-rob-eh, *v* to steal; to rob; to hide; to shield; **se –,** to steal away; to shun.

dérouiller, deh-roo'e-yeh, *v* to rub the rust off; **se –,** to polish up (a subject).

dérouler, deh-roo-leh, *v* to unroll.

déroute, deh-root, *f* rout; disorder.

dérouter, deh-root-eh, *v* to lead astray; to baffle; to divert.

derrière, dayr-e-air, *adv* & *prep* behind; at the back.

derrière, dayr-e-air, *m* back; hindquarters; *fam* bottom; rear.

dès, day, *prep* from; since; on; even; in; **– que,** – ker, as soon as.

désabuser, deh-zăh-bEzeh, *v* to disabuse; disillusion.

désaccord, deh-zăh-kor, *m* disagreement; discord.

désaccorder, deh-zăh-kordeh, *v* to put out of tune; to set at variance.

désaffection, deh-zăhfeck-se-ong, *f* disaffection.

désagréable, * deh-zahgreh-ăhbl, *a* disagreeable; unpleasant.

désagréger, deh-zăh-grehsheh, *v* to disintegrate.

désagrément, deh-zăhgreh-mahng, *m* unpleasantness; inconvenience; defect; nuisance.

désaltérer, deh-zăhl-tehreh, *v* to quench the thirst of.

désapproba-teur, trice, deh-zăh-prob-ăh-ter, *a* disapproving.

désapprouver, deh-zăhproo-veh, *v* to disapprove of.

désarmer, deh-zăhr-meh, *v* to disarm; to appease; to pay off.

désarroi, deh-zăh-ro'ăh, *m* disarray; confusion.

désastre, deh-zăhss-tr, *m* disaster.

désavantage, deh-zăhvahng-tăhsh, *m* disadvantage.

désaveu, deh-zăh-ver, *m* disavowal.

désaveugler, deh-zăh-vergleh, *v* to disabuse.

désavouer, deh-zăh-voo-

eh, *v* to disavow; to disown.

desceller, deh-sell-eh, *v* to unseal.

descendance, deh-sahngdahngss, *f* descent; lineage.

descendre, deh-sahng-dr, *v* to descend; to come or go down; to dismount; to alight; to stop or stay; to put up (at hotel, etc); to make a search; to take down.

descente, deh-sahngt, *f* descent; taking down; rupture; run (skiing).

description, dehss-kreepse-ong, *f* description.

désembarquer, deh-zahngbăhr-keh, *v* to disembark; to land.

désemparer, deh-zahngpăh-reh, *v* to quit; to disable; **sans –,** sahng –, without stopping.

désenchanter, deh-zahngshahng-teh, *v* to disenchant; to disillusion.

désenfler, deh-zahng-fleh, *v* to let the gas out; to subside.

désennuyer, deh-zahngnwe-yeh, *v* to amuse; to enliven.

déséquilibré, deh-zeh-ke-le-breh, *a* mentally

unbalanced; out of balance.

désert, deh-zair, *m* wilderness; desert.

déserter, deh-zair-teh, *v* to desert; to forsake.

désespéré, e, deh-zess-peh-reh, *mf* & *a* a desperate; desperado.

désespérer, deh-zess-peh-reh, *v* to despair.

désespoir, deh-zess-po'ăhr, *m* despair.

déshabiller, deh-zăh-bee-yeh, *v* to undress.

déshériter, deh-zeh-re-teh, *v* to disinherit.

déshonnête, deh-zonn-ayt, *a* indecent.

déshonneur, deh-zonn-er, *m* dishonour; disgrace.

déshonorer, deh-zonn-or-eh, *v* to dishonour; to disgrace.

désignation, deh-zeen-yăh-se-ong, *f* designation; indication; nomination.

désigner, deh-zeen-yeh, *v* to point out; to denote; to appoint.

désillusion, deh-zill-lE-ze-ong, *f* disillusion.

désinfecter, deh-zang-feck-teh, *v* to disinfect.

désintéressement, deh-zang-teh-ress-mahng, *m* disinterestedness.

désintéresser, deh-zang-teh-ress-eh, *v* to indemnify; **se –,** to lose interest.

désintéressé, deh-zang-teh-ress-eh, *a* not involved; unbiased; unselfish.

désinvolte, deh-zang-vollt, *a* casual free and easy.

désinvolture, deh-zang-voll-tEEr, *f* casual manner.

désir, deh-zeer, *m* desire; wish.

désirer, deh-ze-reh, *v* to desire; to wish.

désister (se), ser deh-ziss-teh, *v* to desist; to waive.

désobéir, deh-zob-eh-eer, *v* to disobey.

désobéissance, deh-zob-eh-iss-ahngss, *f* disobedience.

désobligeance, deh-zob-le-shahngss, *f* unkindness.

désobliger, deh-zob-le-sheh, *v* to disoblige.

désœuvré, e, deh-zer-vreh, *a* idle.

désolant, e, deh-zoll-ahng, *a* distressing; grievous; annoying.

désolation, deh-zoll-ăh-se-ong, *f* grief; desolateness.

désolé, deh-zoll-eh, *a* desolate (area); **je suis**

–, sher swee –, I'm sorry.

désoler, deh-zoll-eh, *v* to lay waste; to distress; **se –,** to lament; to grieve.

désopilant, e, deh-zop-e-lahng, *a* funny; laughable.

désopiler (se – la rate), ser deh-zop-ee-leh lăh răht, (*fam*) to laugh immoderately.

désordonné, e, deh-zor-donn-eh, *pp* & *a* disorderly; untidy.

désordre, deh-zor-dr, *m* disorder; disturbance; licentiousness; **en –, ahng –,** *a* messy.

désorienter, deh-zor-e-ahng-teh, *v* to put out; to bewilder.

désormais, deh-zor-may, *adv* henceforth.

désosser, deh-zohss-eh, *v* to bone.

dessaisir, deh-say-zeer, *v* to dispossess; **se –,** to part (**de,** with).

dessaler, deh-săh-leh, *v* to remove salt; to soak.

dessécher, deh-seh-sheh, *v* to dry up.

dessein, deh-sang, *m* design; plan.

desserrer, deh-say-reh, *v* to loosen.

dessert, deh-sair, *m* dessert.

desservant, deh-sair,-vah*ng*, *m* officiating priest or clergyman.

desservir, deh-sair, *v* to clear the table; to play a dirty trick on; to officiate; to serve (of trains, etc).

dessiller (les yeux), deh-see-yeh lay ze'er, *v* to open someone's eyes.

dessin, deh-sa*ng*, *m* drawing; design; pattern.

dessinateur, deh-se-näh-ter, *m* draughtsman; sketcher

dessiner, deh-se-neh, *v* to draw; to sketch; to outline; **se** –, to become perceptible.

dessous, der-soo, *m* underneath; disadvantage; worst.

dessous, der-soo, *adv* & *prep* under; underneath.

dessus, der-sE, *adv* & *prep* on; above; uppermost; upon; over.

dessus, der-sE, *m* upper part; top; top; right side; advantage.

destin, dess-tang, *m* destiny; fate; lot.

destinataire, dess-te-näh-tair, *m* receiver; consignee; addressee.

destination, dess-te-näh-se-ong, *f* destination;

object; end.

destinée, dess-te-neh, *f* destiny; fate.

destiner, dess-te-neh, *v* to destine; to intend; to fate.

destitué, dess-te-tE-eh, *pp* & **a** dismissed; destitute; devoid.

destituer, dess-te-tE-eh, *v* to dismiss.

destitution, dess-te-tE-se-ong, *f* dismissal; removal.

destruction, dess-trEEk-se-ong, *f* destruction.

désuétude, deh-sE-eh-tEed, *f* disuse.

désunion, deh-zE-ne-ong, *f* separation; disunion.

désunir, deh-zE-neer, *v* to separate; to disunite.

détaché, e, deh-täh-sheh, *pp* & *a* detached; unconnected; indifferent; disinterested.

détachement, deh-tähsh-mah*ng*, *m* detachment; indifference.

détacher, deh-täh-sheh, *v* to untie; to detach; to undo; to separate; **se** –, to break away (**de**, from).

détail, deh-tah'e, *m* detail; particular; trifle; retail.

détailler, deh-tah'e-yeh, *v*

to cut up; to retail; to relate in detail.

déteindre, deh-tang-dr, *v* to take the colour out of; to discolour; to fade; to run (of colour).

détendre, deh-tahng-dr, *v* to unbend; to relax; to slacken.

détendu, deh-tahng-dEE, *a* slack; relaxed.

détenir, deh-ter-neer, *v* to detain; to keep back.

détente, deh-tahngt, *f* relaxation; slackening; expansion; trigger.

déten-teur, trice, deh-tahng-ter, *mf* holder.

détention, deh-tahng-se-ong, *f* detention; imprisonment.

détenu, deh-ter-nE, *m* prisoner.

détériorer, deh-teh-re-or-eh, *v* to damage; to impair; to deface.

déterminé, e, deh-tair-me-neh, *pp* & *a* determined; resolute.

déterminer, deh-tair-me-neh, *v* to determine; to decide; to bring on; **se** –, to resolve.

déterrer, deh-tay-reh, *v* to dig up; to unearth; to discover

détester, deh-tess-teh, *v* to detest; to hate; to abhor.

détoner, deh-tonn-eh, *v* to detonate; to explode.

détonner, deh-tonn-eh, *v* to be out of tune.

détordre, deh-tor-dr, *v* to untwist.

détour, deh-toohr, *m* turn; bend; winding; wile; roundabout way; subterfuge; **sans** –, sahng –, straightforward.

déourné, e, deh-toohr-neh, *pp & a* out of the way; embezzled.

détournement, deh-toohr-ner-mahng, *m* turning aside; embezzlement; abduction; hijacking.

détourner, deh-toohr-neh, *v* to lead astray; to turn away; to avert; to divert; to deter; to embezzle; to abduct; to hijack.

détracteur, deh-trähck-ter, *m* slanderer.

détraction, deh-trähck-se-ong, *f* slander; calumny.

détraquer, deh-träh-keh, *v* to put out of order.

détremper, deh-trahng-peh, *v* to water; to dilute; to soften.

détresse, deh-trayss, *f* distress.

détriment, deh-tre-mahng, *m* detriment; prejudice.

détritus, deh-tre-tEEss, *m* detritus; remains.

détroit, deh-tro'äh, *m* strait; straits; pass.

détromper, deh-trong-peh, *v* to disabuse; to correct someone's mistake.

détrôner, deh-troh-neh, *v* to dethrone.

détrousser, deh-trooss-eh, *v* to rob; to untuck.

détruire, deh-trweer, *v* to destroy.

dette, dett, *f* debt.

deuil, der'e, *m* mourning; sorrow; grief; mourners.

deux, der, *m & a* two; both; second (the).

deuxième,* der-ze-aym, *a &m* second.

dévaler, deh-väh-leh, *v* to descend; to rush down.

dévaliser, deh-väh-le-zeh, *v* to rob; to plunder.

devancer, deh-vahng-seh, *v* to get ahead of; to outrun; to precede; to anticipate.

devanci-er, ère, der-vahng-se-eh, *mf* predecessor.

devant, der-vahng, *prep & adv* before; opposite; in front; ahead; *m* front; forepart; **aller au** – **de,** äh-leh oh – der, to go to meet.

devanture, der-vahng-

tEEr, *f* front; shop-front; facade.

dévaster, deh-vähss-teh, *v* to devastate.

déveine, deh-vain, *f* run of bad luck.

développement, deh-ver-lop-mahng, *m* unfolding; development; growth; extent.

développer, deh-ver-lop-eh, *v* to unfold; to develop; to expand; to explain; **se** –, to spread out.

devenir, derv-neer, *v* to become.

dévergondage, deh-vair-gong-dähsh, *m* licentious life-style.

dévergondé, e, deh-vair-gong-deh, *a* shameless.

dévergonder (se), ser deh-vair-gong-deh, *v* to lose all sense of shame.

déverser, deh-vair-seh, *v* to incline; to pour; to throw.

dévêtir, deh-vay-teer, *v* to undress.

déviation, deh-ve-a-se-ong, *f* deviation; diversion.

dévider, deh-ve-deh, *v* to unwind.

dévier, deh-ve-eh, *v* to deviate.

deviner, der-ve-neh, *v* to

guess.

devinette, der-ve-nett, *f* puzzle; riddle.

devis, der-ve, *m* estimate.

dévisager, deh-ve-zăh-sheh, *v* to stare at.

devise, der-veez, *v* device; motto; currency.

deviser, der-ve-zeh, *v* to chat.

dévisser, deh-viss-eh, *v* to unscrew.

dévoiler, deh-vo'ăh-leh, *v* to unveil; to reveal.

devoir, der-vo'ăhr, *v* to owe; to be bound to; to have to; **je crois –, sher** kro'ăh **–,** I think it my duty to.

devoir, der-vo'ăhr, *m* duty; task; exercise; *pl* homework; **se mettre en – de,** ser met-tr'ahng– der, to set about.

dévorant, e, deh-vor-ahng, *a* devouring; ravenous; burning.

dévorer, deh-vor-eh, *v* to devour.

dévot, e, * deh-vo, *a & mf* devout; pious person.

dévotion, deh-vos-e-ong, *f* devotion; piety.

dévoué, e, deh-voo-eh, *pp & a* devoted; loving; **votre tout –,** vot-rer too **–,** yours faithfully.

dévouement, deh-voo-

mahng, *m* devotedness; self-sacrifice.

dévouer, deh-voo-eh, *v* to devote.

dévoyé, e, deh-vo'ăh-yeh, *a* delinquent.

dextérité, decks-teh-re-teh, *f* dexterity; skill.

diabète, de-ăh-bett, *m* diabetes.

diable, de-ăh-bl, *m* devil; mischievous child; **tirer le – par la queue,** te-reh ler – păhr lăh ker, to struggle hard for a living; **un pauvre –,** ung poh-vr **–,** a poor wretch.

diablement, de-ăh-bler-mahng, *adv fam* deucedly; fiendishly.

diabolique, * de-ăh-boll-eeck, *a* diabolical.

diacre, de-ăh-kr, *m* deacon.

diagnostic, de-ăhg-noss-teeck, *m* diagnosis.

diagonal, e, * de-ăh-gonn-ăhl, *a* diagonal.

dialecte, de-ăh-leckt, *m* dialect.

dialogue, de-ăh-log, *m* dialogue.

diamant, de-ăh-mahng, *m* diamond.

diamètre, de-ăh-met-tr, *m* diameter.

diapason, de-ăh-păh-zong, *m* pitch; tuning-fork.

diaphane, de-ăh-făhn, *a* transparent.

diapositive, de-ah-poh-ze-teev, *f* (photo) transparency; (colour) slide.

diarrhée, de-ăh-reh, *f* diarrhoea.

dictateur, dick-tăh-ter, *m* dictator.

dictature, dick-tăh-tEEr, *f* dictatorship.

dictée, dick-teh, *f* dictation.

dicter, dick-teh, *v* to dictate.

dictionnaire, dicks-e-onn-air, *m* dictionary.

dicton, dick-tong, *m* saying.

dièse, de-ayz, *m* (music) sharp.

diète, de-ett, *f* diet.

dieu, de-er, *m* God.

diffamant, e, de-făh-mahng, *a* defamatory.

diffamation, de-făh-măh-se-ong, *f* libel slander.

diffamer, de-făh-meh, *v* to defame; to slander.

différence, de-feh-rahngss, *f* difference.

différencier, de-feh-rahng-se-eh, *v* to distinguish.

différend, de-feh-rahng, *m* difference; dispute.

différent, de-feh-rahng, *a* different; unlike;

various.

différentiel, le, de-feh-rahng-se-ell, *mf & a* differential.

différer, de-feh-reh, *v* to defer; to postpone; to differ (**de,** from).

difficile, * de-fe-seell, *a* difficult; particular; *fam* choosy.

difficulté, de-fe-kEEl-teh, *f* difficulty; obstacle; objection.

difforme, de-form, *a* deformed; ugly.

difformité, de-for-me-teh, *f* deformity.

diffus, e, de-fE, *a* diffuse; prolix.

diffuser, de-fE-zeh, *v* to diffuse; to broadcast.

diffusion, de-fE-ze-ong, *f* diffusion; diffuseness; **radio –,** rãh-de-o –, broadcasting.

digérer, de-sheh-reh, *v* to assimilate; to digest.

digestion, de-shess-te-ong, *f* digestion.

digital, e, de-she-tãhl, *a* digital.

digitale, de-she-tãhl, *f* foxglove.

digne, * deen-yer, *a* worthy; deserving; dignified.

dignité, deen-yee-teh, *f* dignity; title; stateliness.

digue, deeg, *f* dike; dam; embankment.

dilapider, de-lãh-pe-deh, *v* to dilapidate; to squander.

dilater, de-lãh-teh, *v* to dilate; to enlarge.

dilatoire, de-lãh-to'ãhr, *a* dilatory.

dilemme, de-lemm, *m* dilemma.

diligence, de-le-shahngss, *f* diligence; speed; stage-coach.

diluer, de-lE-eh, *v* to dilute; to water down.

dimanche, de-mahngsh, *m* Sunday.

dimension, de-mahng-se-ong, *f* dimension; size; measurement.

diminuer, de-me-nE-eh, *v* to diminish; to lessen; to abate.

diminution, de-me-nE-se-ong, *f* decrease; abatement.

dinde, dangd, *f* female turkey.

dindon, dang-dong, *m* male turkey; *fig* goose.

dindonneau, dang-donn-o, *m* young turkey.

dîner, de-neh, *v* to dine; *m* dinner.

dînette, de-nett, *f* informal meal; doll's tea party.

diocèse, de-oss-ayz, *m* diocese.

diplomate, de-plomm-ãht, *m* diplomat.

diplomatie, de-plomm-ãh-see, *f* diplomacy.

diplômé,-e de-ploh-meh, *mf & a* graduate.

dire, deer, *v* to say; to tell; to speak; to mean; **dites donc!** deet dong, by the way! well!

dire, deer, *m* saying; statement.

direct, e, * de-reckt, *a* direct; straight; through express (of train); live (of television).

direc-teur, trice de-reck-ter, *mf* director; manager; headteacher; manageress.

direction, de-reck-se-ong, *f* management; manager's office; steering; direction.

dirigeable, de-re-shãh-bl, *m* airship; *a* manageable.

diriger, de-re-sheh, *v* to direct; to manage; to run; to guide; **se –,** to go (**vers, sur,** towards).

discerner, diss-air-neh, *v* to discern; to distinguish.

disciple, diss-ee-pl, *m* disciple; follower.

discipline, diss-e-pleen, *f*

discipline.

disc-jockey, deesk-**sho**-keh, *m* disc jockey.

discontinuer, diss-kong-te-nE-eh, *v* to discontinue.

disconvenance, diss-kongv-nahngss, *f* unsuitableness; incongruity; disproportion.

discorde, diss-kord, *f* discord; disagreement.

discourir, diss-koo-reer, *v* to discourse.

discours, diss-koohr, *m* speech; lecture; talk.

discourtois, e, * diss-koohr-to'ăh, *a* discourteous.

discrédit, diss-kreh-de, *m* discredit; disrepute.

discréditer, diss-kreh-de-teh, *v* to discredit.

discr-et, ète, * diss-kray, *a* discreet; quiet.

discrétion, diss-kreh-se-ong, *f* discretion.

disculper, diss-kEEL-peh, *v* to exonerate.

discussion, diss-kEEss-e-ong, *f* discussion; debate; dispute.

discuter, diss-kE-teh, *v* to discuss; to debate.

disert, e, de-zair, *a* fluent; eloquent.

disette, de-zett, *f* dearth; scarcity.

disgrâce, diss-grahss, *f* disgrace; misfortune.

disgracié, e, diss-grăhss-e-eh, *pp & a* unfortunate; out of favour. out of favour.

disgracier, diss-grăhss-e-eh, *v* to put out of favour.

disgracieu-x, se, * diss-grăhss-e-er, *a* ungraceful.

disjoindre, diss-sho-ang-dr, *v* to take apart.

disloquer, diss-lock-eh, *v* to dislocate.

disparaître, diss-păh-ray-tr, *v* to disappear.

disparate, diss-păh-răht, *a* incongruous; ill-assorted.

disparition, diss-păh-re-se-ong, *f* disappearance.

disparu, e, diss-păh-rE, *pp* disappeared; missing.

dispensaire, diss-pahng-sair, *m* clinic; out-patients' clinic.

dispense, diss-pahngss, *f* dispensation; exemption; license.

disperser, diss-pair-seh, *v* to scatter; to disperse.

disponibilité, diss-ponn-e-be-le-teh, *f* availability; *pl* funds available.

disponible, diss-ponn-ee-bl, *a* disposable; available; unengaged.

dispos, diss-poh, *a* active; nimble; lively; **frais et –,** fray-eh –, fresh.

disposé, e, diss-poz-eh, *pp & a* disposed; inclined; willing.

disposer, diss-poz-eh, *v* to dispose; to have at command; to induce.

dispositif, diss-poz-e-tiff, *m jur* purview; (technology) apparatus; *fig* plan of action.

disposition, diss-poz-e-se-ong, *f* arrangement; frame of mind; tendency; aptitude.

disproportionné e, diss-prop-or-se-onn-eh, *a* disproportionate.

dispute, diss-pEet, *f* dispute; quarrel.

disputer, diss-pE-teh, *v* to dispute; **se –,** to quarrel; to vie.

disque, deesk, *m* disc; (computer) disk; record.

dissemblable, diss-sahng-blăh-bl, *a* dissimilar.

dissension, diss-sahng-se-ong, *f* dissension.

dissentiment, diss-sahng-te-mahng, *m* dissent.

disséquer, diss-seh-keh, *v* to dissect.

dissertation, de-sair-tăh-se-ong, *f* dissertation; essay.

dissident, diss-se-dahng, *m* dissenter.

dissimulé, e, diss-se-mE-leh, *pp* & *a* deceptive; concealed.

dissimuler, diss-se-mE-leh, *v* to dissimulate; to conceal.

dissiper, diss-se-peh, *v* to dissipate; to waste; to dispel; **se –,** to vanish; to be naughty (at school).

dissolu, e, diss-soll-E, *a* dissolute.

dissoluble, diss-soll-EE-bl, *a* dissolvable; soluble.

dissolvant, diss-soll-vahng, *m* & *a* solvent; nail- varnish remover.

dissoudre, diss-soo-dr, *v* to dissolve.

dissuader, diss-sE-ăh-deh, *v* to dissuade.

distance, diss-tahngss, *f* distance.

distancer, diss-tahngss-eh, *v* to distance.

distant, e, diss-tahng, *a* distant; remote.

distendre, diss-tahng-dr, *v* to distend.

distillerie, diss-till-ree, *f* distillery.

distinct, e,* diss-tang-kt, *a* distinct.

distinction, diss-tangk-se-ong, *f* distinction; refinement.

distingué, e, diss-tang-gheh, *a* distinguished; refined.

distinguer, diss-tang-gheh, *v* to distinguish; to perceive.

distraction, diss-trăhck-se-ong, absent-mindedness; entertainment; recreation.

distraire, diss-trayr, *v* to distract; to separate; to amuse; to abstract.

distrait, e,* diss-tray, *a* inattentive; absent-minded.

distribuer, diss-tre-bE-eh, *v* to distribute.

distributeur, diss-tre-bE-ter, *m* deliverer; distributor; – **automatique,** – oh-tomm-ăh-teeck –, vending machine.

distribution, diss-tre-bE-se-ong, *f* distribution; delivery; handling.

dit, dee, *m* saying.

dit, e, dee, *pp* & *a* told; agreed; alias; **autrement** –, oh-trer-mahng–, in other words.

dito, de-to, *adv* ditto.

divaguer, de-văh-gheh, *v* to wander; to ramble.

divan, de-vahng, *m* divan; sofa.

diverger, de-vair-sheh, *v* to diverge.

divers, de-vair, *mpl* sundries.

divers, e, de-vair, *a* different; various; several; varied.

divertir, de-vair-teer, *v* to amuse; to divert.

divertissant, e, de-vair-tiss-ahng, *a* entertaining.

divertissement, de-vair-tiss-mahng, *m* amusement; entertainment.

dividende, de-ve-dahngd, *m* dividend.

divin, e,* de-vang, *a* divine; heavenly; exquisite.

diviniser, de-ve-ne-zeh, *v* to deify.

diviser, de-ve-zeh, *v* to divide.

divisionnaire, de-ve-ze-onn-air, *a* divisional; of a division.

divorce, de-vorss, *m* divorce; separation.

divulguer, de-vEEl-gheh, *v* to divulge.

dix, deess, (before a consonant, dee), *m* & *a* ten; tenth.

dixième, de-ze-aym, *m* & *a* tenth.

dizaine, de-zain, *f* ten; about ten.

do, do, the note C.

docile,* doss-eell, *a* docile; tractable.

docteur, dock-ter, *m* doctor.

doctorat, dock-tor-ăh, *m* doctorate.

doctrine, dock-treen, *f* doctrine.

document, dock-E-mahng, *m* document.

documentaire, dock-E-mahng-tair, *m* & *a* documentary.

documenter, dock-E-mahng-teh, *v* to document.

dodo, dod-o, *m* (baby talk) sleep; **aller faire –,** ăh-leh-fair –, to go bye byes.

dodu, e, dod-E, *a* plump.

dogmatiser, dog-măh-te-zeh, *v* to dogmatize.

dogme, dogm, *m* dogma.

dogue, dog, *m* large watchdog.

doigt, do'ăh, *m* finger; **à deux –s de,** ăh der – der, within an inch of.

doigter, doigté, do'ăh-teh, *m* fingering.

doit, do'ăh, *m* debit.

doléance, doll-eh-ahngss, *f* complaint; grievance.

dolent, e, doll-ahng, *a* doleful; painful.

domaine, domm-ain, *m* domain; estate; property; *fam* province; department; sphere.

dôme, dohm, *m* dome; canopy.

domesticité, domm-ess-te-se-teh, *f* servants; domesticity.

domestique, domm-ess-teeck, *mf* & *a* servant; domestic; private; tame.

domicile, domm-e-seell, *m* domicile; residence; abode.

domicilié, e, domm-e-se-le-eh, *a* domiciled; resident.

dominant, e, domm-e-nahng, *a* dominant; ruling; prevailing.

dominer, domm-e-neh, *v* to rule; to domineer; to govern; to overlook.

dominical, e, domm-e-ne-kăhl, *a* dominical; *f* **oraison –e,** or-ay-zong –, the Lord's Prayer.

dommage, domm-ăhsh, *m* damage; loss; **c'est –** say –, it is a pity.

dompter, dong-teh, *v* to tame; to subdue.

dompteu-r, se, dong-ter, *mf* tamer; animal trainer.

don, dong, *m* gift; present; talent.

dona-teur, trice, donn-ăh-ter, *mf* donor.

donc, dong (and dongk at the beginning of a sentence and before a vowel), *conj* then; therefore.

donjon, dong- shong, *m* dungeon; keep; turret.

donne, donn, *f* (cards) deal.

donnée, donn-eh, *f* notion; *pl* data.

donner, donn-eh, *v* to give; to strike; to look; to shine; to yield (of trees, etc); to deal; to charge; **s'en –,** sahng –; to enjoy oneself.

dont, dong, *pron* whose; of whom; from whom; by whom; of which; with whom or which.

doré, e, dor-eh, *pp* & *a* gilded; gilt; golden.

dorénavant, dor-eh-năh-vahng, *adv* henceforth.

dorer, dor-eh, *v* to gild; to glaze (pastry).

dorloter, dor-lot-eh, *v* to coddle.

dormant, e, dor-mahng, *a* sleeping; dormant; dull.

dormeur, dor-mer, *m* sleeper.

dormir, dor-meer, *v* to sleep; to be dormant.

dorsal, dor-săhl, *a* dorsal.

dortoir, dor-to'ăhr, *m* dormitory.

dorure, dor-EEr, *f* gilding; (pastry) glaze.

dos, doh, *m* back.

dosage, doh-zăhsh, *m* dosage.

dose, dohz, *f* dose.

doser, doh-zeh, *v* to dose.

dossier, doh-se-eh, *m* back (of chair, etc) brief; file of notes; dossier.

dot, dott, *f* dowry; marriage settlement.

dotal, e, dot-ăhl, *a* of the dowry.

doter, dot-eh, *v* to endow (**de**, with).

douairière, doo-ay-re-air, *f & a* dowager.

douane, doo-ăhn, *f* customs.

douanier, –iere, doo-ăh-ne-eh, *m & f* customs officer.

doublage, doo-blăhsh, *m* doubling; dubbing (film).

double,* doo-bl, *a* double; *m* duplicate; replica; double.

doubler, doo-bleh, *v* to double; to line (**de**, with); to dub (film); to understudy; to overtake (on road).

doublure, doo-blEEr, *f* lining; substitute.

douceâtre, dooss-ah-tr, *a* sweetish.

douceur, dooss-er, sweetness; softness; charm; gentleness; *pl* sweets; pleasant things.

douche, doosh, *f* shower; douche.

doué, doo-eh, *a* gifted.

douer, doo-eh, *v* to endow (with qualities).

douille, doo-ye, *f* socket (electricity).

douillet, te,* doo'e-yay, *a* delicate; tender.

douleur, doo-ler, *f* pain; grief; sorrow.

douloureu-x, se,* doo-loo-rer, *a* painful; mournful; grievous.

doute, doot, *m* doubt.

douter, doo-teh, *v* to doubt; **se –,** to suspect; to have some notion (**de** or **que,** of or that).

douteu-x, se,* doo-ter, *a* doubtful; questionable.

douve, doov, *f* moat; open ditch.

dou-x, ce,* doo, dooss, *a* sweet; soft; kind; gentle; smooth; mild.

douzaine, doo-zain, *f* dozen.

douze, dooz, *a* twelve; (the) twelfth.

douzième, doo-ze-aym, *mf* & *a* twelfth.

doyen, do'ah-yang, *m* dean; senior; elder.

dragée, drăh-sheh, *f* sugared almond; sugar-coated pill.

dragon, drăh-gong, *m* dragon; termagant; dragoon.

draguer, drăh-gheh, *v* to dredge.

drainer, dray-neh, *v* to drain.

dramaturge, drăh-măh-tEEsh, *mf* dramatist; playwright.

drame, drăhm, *m* drama; play; *fam* catastrophe.

drap, drăh, *m* cloth; sheet.

drapeau, drăh-poh, *m* flag; colours; **sous les – x,** soo lay –, in the army.

draper, drăh-peh, *v* to cover with cloth; **se –,** to drape; to wrap oneself up.

draperie, drăhp-ree, *f* drapery; cloth-trade.

drapier, drăh-pe-eh, *m* draper; clothier.

dressage, dress-ăhsh, *m* training; dressing; erection.

dresser, dress-eh, *v* to erect; to pitch; to lay out; to train; **se –,** to stand up.

dressoir, dress-o'ăhr, *m*

sideboard; dresser.

drogue, drog, *f* drug; *fam*
rubbish.

droguer, drogh-eh, *v* to
drug; **se –,** to take drugs.

droguiste, drogh-eesst, *m*
pharmacist.

droit, dro'ăh, *m* right;
authority; law;
title;duuty; tax;
franchise; **faire son –,**
fair *song* –, to read law;
qui de –, ke der –, those
whom it may concern.

droit, e, dro'ăh, *adv*
straight; directly; **tout –,**
too –, straight on; *a*
straight; right; erect;
straightforward;
righteous.

droite, dro'ăht, *f* right
hand; right side.

droiture, dro'ăh-tEEr, *f*
straightforwardness.

drôle, drohl, *m* rogue;
scamp; *a* funny; queer.

dru, e, drE, *adv* thick;
hard; *a* fledged; dense;
close; thick.

du, dE, contraction of **de
le.**

dû, dE, *pp & a* owed; been
obliged; owing.

duc, dEEk, *m* duke.

duché, dE-sheh, *m*
dukedom; duchy.

duchesse, dE-shess, *f*
duchess.

dudit, dE-de, *a* of or from
the said.

duel, dE-ell, *m* duel.

dûment, dE-mahng, *adv*
duly.

dune, dEEn, *f* dune.

duo, dE-o, *m* duet.

dupe, dEEp, *f* dupe.

duper, dE-peh, *v* to dupe.

duperie, dEp-ree, *f*
trickery.

duplicata, dE-ple-kăh-tăh,
m duplicate.

duplicité, dE-ple-se-teh, *f*
duplicity; double-
dealing.

duquel, dE-kell, *pron*
contraction of **de
lequel,** whose; from
whom; of which; from
which.

dur, dEEr, *m* hardness; *fam*
tough guy.

dur, e,* dEEr, *a* hard;
harsh; rough; stiff.

durable, dE-răh-bl, *a*
lasting.

durant, dE-rahng, *prep*
during.

durcir, dEEr-seer, *v* to
harden; to set.

durcissement, dEEr-siss-
mahng, *m* hardening.

durée, dE-reh, *f* duration.

durer, dEE-reh, *v* to last; to
hold out.

dureté, dEEr-teh, *f*
hardness; harshness.

duvet, dE-vay, *m* down.

dynamite, de-năh-meet, *f*
dynamite.

E

eau, oh, *f* water; rain; **– de vie,** –der vee, spirit; brandy; **– minérale,** –me-neh-rähl mineral water.

ébahir (s'), seh-bäh-eer, *v* to be amazed (**de,** at).

ébats, eh-bäh, *mpl* frolics.

ébattre (s'), seh-bäh-tr, *v* to frolic.

ébauche, eh-bohsh, *f* sketch; outline.

ébaucher, eh-boh-sheh, *v* to sketch; to roughcast.

ébène, eh-bain, *f* ebony.

ébéniste, eh-beh-neesst, *m* cabinet-maker.

éblouir, eh-bloo-eer, *v* to dazzle.

éblouissement, eh-bloo-iss-mahng, *m* dazzling; dizziness.

éboulement, eh-bool-mahng, *m* landslide.

ébouriffé, e, eh-boo-re-feh, *a* dishevelled; tousled (hair).

ébranlement, eh-brahngl-mahng, *m* shaking; commotion.

ébranler, eh-brahng-leh, *v* to shake; to disturb; to put in motion; **s' –,** to totter; to begin to move.

ébrécher, eh-breh-sheh, *v* to notch; to indent; to chip.

ébruiter, eh-brwe-teh, *v* to divulge; **s'–,** to become known.

ébullition, eh-bE-le-se-ong, *f* boiling.

écaille, eh-kah'e, *f* scale; tortoiseshell.

écailler, eh-kah'e-eh, *v* to scale; to open (of shell fish).

écarlate, eh-kähr-läht, *a* & *f* scarlet.

écarquiller, eh-kähr-kee-yeh, *v* to open wide (eyes); to straddle.

écart, eh-kähr, *m* step aside; separation; digression; discrepancy; error; *adv phr* à l'–, ah l'–, aside.

écarté, eh-kähr-teh, *a* remote; lonely.

écartement, eh-kähr-ter-mahng, spacing; putting aside.

écarter, eh-kähr-teh, *v* to separate; to keep off; **s'–,** to deviate; to move aside.

ecclésiastique, eh-kleh-ze-ähss-teeck, *m* clergyman; *a* ecclesiastical.

écervelé, e, eh-sair-ver-leh, *a* harebrained; crazy.

échafaud, eh-shäh-foh, *m* scaffolding; stage; scaffold.

échafaudage, eh-shäh-foh-dähsh, *m* scaffolding; building up.

échafauder, eh-shäh-foh-deh, *v* to erect scaffolding; to pile up.

échalote, eh-shäh-lot, *f* shallot.

échancrer, eh-shahng-

kreh, v to indent; to hollow out.

échange, eh-shahn**gsh**, m exchange; barter; **libre –** lee-br –, free trade.

échanger, eh-sahng-**sheh**, v to exchange.

échantillon, eh-shahng-tee-yong, m sample; pattern.

échappatoire, eh-shäh-pah-to'åhr, f evasion; loophole.

échappée, eh-shäh-peh, f escapade; vista.

échappement, eh-shähp-mahng, m escape; leakage; exhaust.

échapper, eh-shäh-peh, v to escape; to avoid; to slip; **s' –**, to steal away.

écharde, eh-shahrd, f splinter.

écharpe, eh-shährp, f scarf; sling; sash; **en –** ahng n'–, slanting.

écharper, eh-shähr-peh, v to cut to pieces.

échasse, eh-shähss, f stilt.

échassier, eh-shähss-e-eh, m wading-bird.

échauder, eh-shoh-deh, v to scald.

échauffement, eh-shohf-mahng, m heating; overheating; overexcitement.

échauffer, eh-shoh-feh, v to heat; to overheat; to excite; to provoke.

échauffourée, eh-shoh-foo-reh, f skirmish; affray.

échéance, eh-sheh-ahngss, f falling due; expiration; maturity.

échéant, eh-sheh-ahng, pp falling due; occurring; **le cas –**, ler kah z'–, should it so happen.

échec, eh-shayk, m check; failure; blow; pl chess; chessmen.

échelle, eh-shell, f ladder; steps; scale.

echelon, ehsh-long, m rung; step; degree.

échelonner, ehsh-lonn-eh, v to arrange by degrees; to space out; to stagger.

écheveau, ehsh-voh, m hank; skein.

échevelé, e, eh-sherv-leh, a dishevelled.

échine, eh-sheen, f spine; backbone; chine; loin (of pork).

échiner, eh-she-neh, v to work to death.

échiquier, eh-she-ke-eh, m exchequer; chessboard.

écho, eh-ko, m echo.

échoir, eh-sho'åhr, v to fall due; to fall to the lot of.

échoppe, eh-shop, f stall.

échouer, eh-shoo-eh, v to run aground; to fail.

échu, e, eh-shE, pp fallen due; outstanding.

éclabousser, eh-kläh-booss-eh, v to splash.

éclair, eh-klayr, m lightning; flash; éclair.

éclairage, eh-klay-rähsh, m lighting; illumination.

éclaircie, eh-klayr-see, f clearing; glade opening.

éclaircir, eh-klayr-seer, v to clear up; to elucidate.

éclairer, eh-klay-reh, v to light; to enlighten.

éclaireur, eh-klay-rer, m scout.

éclat, eh-kläh, m splinter; explosion; clap; splendour; uproar; scandal.

éclatant, e, eh-kläh-tahng, a bright; brilliant; resounding; flagrant; loud.

éclater, eh-kläh-teh, v to burst; to explode; to shine.

éclisse, eh-kleess, f wedge; splint.

éclopé, e, eh-klop-eh, a lame; cripple.

éclore, eh-klor, v to hatch; to dawn; to open.

éclosion, eh-kloh-ze-ong, f hatching; opening.

écluse, eh-klEEz, *f* lock; dam.

éccœurer, eh-ker-reh, *v* to sicken.

école, eh-kol, *f* school.

écoli-er, ère, eh-koll-e-eh, *mf* schoolboy; schoolgirl.

éconduire, eh-kong-dweer, *v* to show out; to deny.

économat, eh-konn-omm-äh, *m* bursar's office.

économe, eh-konn-omm, *m* steward; bursar; *a* economical; saving.

économie, eh-konn-omm-ee, *f* economy; saving; *pl* savings.

économique,* eh-konn-omm-eeck, *a* economic(al).

économiser, eh-konn-omm-e-zeh, *v* to economize; to save.

économiste, eh-konn-omm-eesst, *m* economist.

écorce, eh-korss, *f* bark; rind; peel; skin; outside.

écorcher, eh-kor-sheh, *v* to skin; to graze; to fleece.

écorchure, eh-kor-shEEr, *f* graze.

Écosse, eh-koss *f* Scotland.

écossais, e, eh-koss-say *a*

Scottish.

écosser, eh-koss-eh, *v* to shell; to hull.

écot, eh-ko, *m* share; quota; reckoning.

écoulement, eh-kool-mahng, *m* flow; drainage; turnover.

écouler, eh-koo-leh, *v* to flow out; to elapse; to sell off.

écoute, eh-koot, *f* listening place; (radio) listening time.

écouter, eh-koo-teh, *v* to listen; to pay attention to.

écouteu-r, se, eh-koo-ter, *mf* listener; *m* receiver (telephone), ear-phone.

écran, eh-krahng, *m* screen.

écrasant, e, eh-krăh-zahng, *a* crushing; overwhelming; humiliating.

écraser, eh-krăh-zeh, *v* to crush; to overwhelm; to run over.

écrémer, eh-kreh-meh, *v* to skim.

écrevisse, eh-krer-veess, *f* cray-fish.

écrier (s'), seh-kre-eh, *v* to exclaim.

écrin, eh-krang, *m* jewellery box; casket.

écrire, eh-kreer, *v* to

write.

écriteau, eh-kre-toh, *m* bill; board.

écriture, eh-kre-tEEr, *f* writing; hand-writing; Scripture; *pl* accounts.

écrivain, eh-kre-vang, *m* writer; author.

écrou, eh-kroo, *m* screw-nut.

écroulement, eh-krool-mahng, *m* falling down; collapse; ruin.

écrouler (s'), seh-kroo-leh, *v* to fall down; to collapse.

écru, e, eh-krE, *a* unbleached; raw.

écueil, eh-ker'e, *m* rock; reef; stumbling-block.

écuelle, eh-kE-ell, *f* bowl.

écume, eh-kEEm, *f* foam; froth; scum.

écumer, eh-kE-meh, *v* to skim; to foam.

écureuil, eh-kE-rer'e, *m* squirrel.

écurie, eh-kE-ree, *f* stable; stud.

écusson, eh-kEEss-ong, *m* badge; coat of arms.

écuyer, eh-kwee-yeh, *m* squire; riding-master; rider.

eczéma, eks-zeh-măh, *m* eczema.

édenté, e, eh-dahng-teh, *a* toothless.

édicter, eh-dick-teh, *v* to decree; to exact.

édification, eh-de-fe-käh-se-ong, *f* edification; building.

édifice, eh-de-feess, *m* building; structure.

édifier, eh-de-fe-eh, *v* to edify; to erect; to enlighten.

édit, eh-de, *m* edict; decree.

éditer, eh-de-teh, *v* to publish; to edit.

éditeur, eh-de-ter, *m* publisher.

édition, eh-de-se-ong, *f* edition; publishing.

édredon, eh-drer-dong, *m* eiderdown.

éducation, eh-dE-käh-se-ong, *f* education; breeding; upbringing; training.

éduquer, eh-dE-keh, *v* to educate; to bring up.

effacer, eh-fähss-eh, *v* to efface; to rub out; to wipe out; to eclipse.

effaré, e, eh-fäh-reh, *a* scared.

effaroucher, eh-fäh-roo-sheh, *v* to scare away; **s'–,** to take fright.

effectif, eh-fehck-teeff, *m* effective strength.

effecti-f, ve, eh-fehck-teeff, *a* effective; actual; number of pupils.

effectivement, eh-fehck-teev-mahng, *adv* effectively; actually; that is so.

effectuer, eh-fehck-tE-eh, *v* to effect; to carry out.

efféminé, e, eh-feh-me-neh, *a* effeminate.

effervescence, eh-fair-vayss-ahngss, *f* effervescence; excitement.

effet, eh-fay, *m* effect; impression; bill; – **secondaire** – ser-gong-dair, side effect; *pl* goods; effects; bills.

effeuiller, eh-fer'e-yeh, *v* to strip off leaves or petals.

efficace,* eh-fe-kähss, *a* efficacious; effective.

effilé, e, eh-fe-leh, *a* slender; slim; sharp; frayed.

efflanqué, e, eh-flahng-keh, *a* lean; thin; lank.

effleurer, eh-fler-reh, *v* to skim; to touch slightly; to glance over.

effluve, eh-flEEv, *m* effluvium.

effondrement, eh-fong-drer-mahng, *m* subsidence; collapse.

effondrer (s'), seh-fong-dreh, *v* to fall in; to collapse.

efforcer (s'), seh-for-seh, *v* to strive; to endeavour.

effort, eh-for, *m* effort; endeavour; strain; exertion.

effrayant, e, eh-fray-yahng, *a* frightening; dreadful; *fam* awful.

effrayé, e, eh-fray-yeh *a* frightened.

effrayer, eh-fray-yeh, *v* to frighten.

effréné, e, eh-freh-neh, *a* unbridled; unrestrained.

effriter (s'), seh-fre-teh, *v* to crumble away.

effroi, eh-fro'äh, *m* fright; terror.

effronté, e, eh-frong-teh, *a* impudent.

effrontément, eh-frong-teh-mahng, *adv* impudently.

effronterie, eh-frongt-ree, *f* impudence; insolence.

effroyable,* eh-fro'äh-yäh-bl, *a* frightful; *fam* tremendous.

effusion, eh-fE-ze-ong, *f* effusion; overflowing; shedding.

égal, e, eh-gähl, *a* equal; even; like; same; level; **cela m'est** –, släh may t' –, it is all the same to me.

également, eh-gähl-mahng, *adv* equally; alike; both; likewise; also.

égaler, eh-gäh-leh, *v* to equal; to match.

égaliser, eh-gäh-le-zeh, *v* to equalise; to level; to smooth.

égalitaire, eh-gäh-le-tair, *a* levelling.

égalité, eh-gäh-le-teh, *f* evenness; equality; uniformity; deuce (in tennis).

égard, eh-gähr, *m* regard; respect; consideration.

égaré, e, eh-gäh-reh, *a* stray; bewildered; out of the way; erring.

égarement, eh-gähr-mahng, *m* error; wandering; aberation; distraction.

égarer, eh-gäh-reh, *v* to mislead; to lead astray; to bewilder; **s'–,** to lose one's way.

égayer, eh-gay-yeh, *v* to enliven; to cheer up.

églantine, eh-glahng-teen, *f* sweetbriar; dog rose.

église, eh-gleez, *f* church.

egoïsme, eh-go-issm, *m* selfishness.

egoïste, eh-go-isst, *m* selfish person; *a* selfish; egoist.

égorger, eh-gor-sheh, *v* to cut the throat of; to kill.

égosiller (s'), seh-goz-ee-yeh, *v* to make oneself hoarse.

égout, eh-ghoo, *m* drain; sewer; drip.

égoutter, eh-ghoot-eh, *v* to drain; to drip.

égratigner, eh-gräh-teen-yeh, *v* to scratch.

égrener, eh-grer-neh, *v* to shell; to pick.

éjaculer, eh-shah-kEE-leh, *v* to ejaculate.

éjecter, eh-sheck-teh, *v* to eject; *fam* to chuck out.

élaborer, eh-läh-bor-eh, *v* to elaborate; to work out.

élaguer, eh-läh-gheh, *v* to lop; to prune.

élan, eh-lahng, *m* spring; start; dash; impetus; *v* **prendre de l'–,** prahngdr der l'–, to dash.

élancé, e, eh-lahngss-eh, *a* slender; slim; graceful.

élancer, eh-lahngss-eh, *v* to dart; **s'–,** to rush.

élargir, eh-lähr-sheer, *v* to widen; to extend; to release.

élastique, eh-lähss-teeck, *a* & *m* elastic; springy.

électeur, eh-leck-ter, *m* elector.

élection, eh-leck-se-ong, *f* election; polling.

électricien, eh-leck-tre-se-ang, *m* electrician.

électricité, eh-leck-tre-se-teh, *f* electricity.

électriser, eh-leck-tre-zeh, *v* to electrify.

électronique, eh-leck-tro-neeck, *a* electronic; **jeu –, sher –,** *m* computer game.

électrophone, eh-leck-tro-fon, *m* record player.

élégamment, eh-leh-gäh-mahng, *adv* elegantly.

élégance, eh-leh-gahngss, *f* elegance.

élégie, eh-leh-shee, *f* elegy.

élément, eh-leh-mahng, *m* element; unit (of furniture); **–s de base,** der-bähz, *mpl* the elements.

élémentaire, eh-leh-mahng-tair, *a* elementary; rudimentary.

éléphant, h-leh-fahng, *m* elephant.

élevage, ehl-vähsh, *m* cattle breeding.

élévation, eh-leh-väh-se-ong, *f* elevation; raising; rise.

élève eh-layv, *mf* pupil; scholar; student; *f* breeding (of cattle).

élevé, e, ehl-veh, *pp* & *a* raised; lofty; brought up; bred.

élever, ehl-veh, *v* to raise; to elevate; to build; to extol; to bring up (child); **s' –,** to rise; to amount (à, to).

élider, eh-le-deh, *v* to elide; to cut off; to omit.

éliminer, eh-le-me-neh, *v* to eliminate; to get rid of.

élire, eh-leer, *v* to elect; to choose.

élision, eh-le-ze-ong, *f* ellision; omission.

élite, eh-leet, *f* pick; élite.

elle, ell, *pron* she; her; it; **elles,** they; them.

ellipse, eh-lips, *f* ellipsis.

éloge, eh-losh, *m* praise; commendation.

élogieu-x, se,* eh-losh-e-er, *a* eulogistic.

éloigné, e, eh-lo'ăhn-yeh, *a* removed; distant; out of the way; disinclined.

éloignement, eh-lo'ăhn-yer-mahng, *m* distance; absence; aversion.

éloigner, eh-lo'ăhn-yeh, *v* to remove; to keep away; to delay; to estrange.

éloquemment, en-lock-ăh-mahng, *adv* eloquently.

éloquence, eh-lock-ahngss, *f* eloquence.

élu, e, eh-lE, *pp* & *a* elected.

éluder, eh lE deh, *v* to elude; to evade.

émail, eh-mah'e, *m* enamel; glaze.

émaner, eh-măh-neh, *v* to emanate.

émarger, eh-măhr-sheh, *v* to annotate; to draw a salary.

emballage, ah-ng-băh-lăhsh, *m* packing; wrapping.

emballer, ahng-băh-leh, *v* to pack; to pack up; to wrap; **s'–,** to bolt; to turn away; *fam* to get carried away (excitement, anger, etc).

embarcadère, ahng-băhr-kăh-dair, *m* (departure/landing) wharf; pier.

embarcation, ahng-băhr-kăh-se-ong, *f* small boat; craft.

embarquer, ahng-băhr-keh, *v* to embark; to ship; to board (a plane).

embarras, ahng-băh-răh, *m* encumbrance; hindrance; difficulty; perplexity; embarrassment; fuss.

embarrassant, ahng-băh-răhss-ahng, *a* cumbersome; awkward; embarrassing.

embarrasser, ahng-băh-răhss-eh, *v* to encumber; to perplex; to embarrass.

embaucher, ahng-boh-sheh, *v* to hire; to engage; to enlist; to entice away.

embaumer, ahng-boh-meh, *v* to perfume; to embalm.

embellir, ahng-bay-leer, *v* to embellish; to improve (in looks).

embêtant, e, ahng-bay-tahng *a fam* annoying; bothering.

embêter, ahng-bay-teh, *v fam* to bother; to bore; **s'–,** to be bored.

embêtement, ahng-bayt-mahng, *m* bother; trouble.

emblée (d'), dahng-bleh, *adv* at the first attempt; straight off.

emblème, ahng-blaym, *m* emblem; badge.

emboîter, ahng-bo'ah-teh, *v* to encase; to interlock.

embolie, ahng-bo-le, *f* embolism; blood clot.

embonpoint, ahng-bong-po'ang, *m* plumpness.

embouchure, ahng-boo-shEEr, *f* mouth;

mouthpiece.

embourber (s'), sahng-boohr-beh, *v* to get stuck in the mire; *fam* to become involved in.

embouteillage, ahng-boo-tay-yähsh, *m* bottling; *fam* traffic jam; bottle neck.

embranchement, ahng-brahngsh-mahng, *m* branching-off; branch-line.

embrancher (s'), sahng-brahng-sheh, *v* to branch off.

embrasé, e, ahng-bräh-zeh, *pp & a* in flames; burning.

embraser, ahng-bräh-zeh, *v* to set on fire; to kindle.

embrasser, ahng-brähss-eh, *v* to embrace; to kiss.

embrasure, ahng-bräh-zEer, *f* door fame; window frame; opening.

embrayage, ahng-bray-yash, *m* engaging of clutch; clutch.

embrayer, ahng-bray-yeh, *v* to engage the clutch.

embrouillé, e, ahng-broo'e-yeh, *pp & a* entangled; intricate.

embrouiller, ahng-broo'e-yeh, *v* to tangle; to confuse.

embrumé, e, ahng-brE-meh *a* foggy; misty.

embryon, ahng-bree-yong, *m* embryo.

embûche, ahng-bEEsh, *f* snare; trap.

embuscade, ahng-bEss-kähd, *f* ambush.

émeraude, ehm-rohd, *f* emerald.

émeri, ehm-re, *m* emery (board).

émerveiller, eh-mair-vay'e-yeh, *v* to astonish; to fill with wonder.

émétique, eh-meh-teeck, *m* emetic.

émet-teur, trice, *m* transmitter, *a* transmitting; broadcasting.

émettre, eh-met-tr, *v* to issue; to express; to broadcast.

émeute, eh-mert, *f* riot; disturbance; outbreak.

émietter, eh-me-ayt-eh, *v* to crumble.

émigrer, eh-me-greh, *v* to emigrate.

émincé, eh-mang-seh, *m* thin slices of meat.

éminemment, eh-me-näh-mahng, *adv* eminently.

éminence, eh-me-nahngss, *f* eminence.

émissaire, eh-miss-air, *m* emissary.

émission, eh-miss-e-ong, *f* issue; uttering; transmission; (radio) programme.

emmagasiner, ahng-mäh-gäh-ze-neh, *v* to store.

emmancher, ahng-mahng-sheh, *v* to put a handle on; to haft; to begin; **s'–,** to fit together.

emmêler, ahng-may-leh, *v* to entangle.

emménager, ahng-meh-näh-sheh, *v* to move in.

emmener, ahngm-neh, *v* to take away; to lead away.

emmitoufler, ahng-me-too-fleh, *v* to wrap up (warmly).

émoi, eh-mo'äh, *m* agitation; anxiety; flurry; emotion.

émolument, eh-moll-E-mahng, *m* emolument; gain; profit; *pl* salary; fees.

émotion, eh-mohss-e-ong, *f* emotion.

émousser, eh-mooss-eh, *v* to blunt; to dull.

émouvant, e, eh-moo-vahng, *a* touching; stirring.

émouvoir, eh-moo-vo'ähr, *v* to move; to stir up; to rouse; to affect.

empailler, ahng-pah'e-yeh,

v to pack in straw; to stuff (animals).

empaqueter, ahng-păhck-teh, *v* to pack up.

emparer (s'), sahng-păh-reh, *v* to take possession.

empêché, e, ahng-pay-sheh, *pp* & *a* prevented; embarrassed; in a difficulty.

empêchement, ahng-paysh-mahng, *m* impediment; hindrance; obstacle.

empêcher, ahng-pay-sheh, *v* to prevent; to hinder; to keep from.

empereur, ahngp-rer, *m* emperor.

empeser, ahng-per-zeh, *v* to starch.

empester, ahng-pess-teh, *v* to infect; to stink.

empêtrer, ahng-pay-treh, *v* to entangle.

emphase, ahng-fahz, *f* emphasis; bombast; pomposity.

emphatique,* ahng-făh-teeck, *a* emphatic; bombastic.

empierrer, ahng-pe-ay-reh, *v* to pave.

empiéter, ahng-pe-eh-teh, *v* to encroach; to trespass.

empiler, ahng-pe-leh, *v* to pile up; to stack.

empire, ahng-peer, *m* empire; *fig* rule; control.

empirer, ahng-pe-reh, *v* to make worse; to get worse.

emplacement, ahng-plăhss-mahng, *m* location; site; place.

emplâtre, ahng-plah-tr, *m* plaster; helpless person.

emplette, ahng-plett, *f* purchase; **faire des –s,** fayr dehz –, to do one's shopping.

emplir, ahng-pleer, *v* to fill up (**de,** with).

emploi, ahng-plo'ăh, *m* employment; use; occupation; situation.

employé, ahng-plo'ăh-yeh, *m* employee; clerk.

employer, ahng-plo'ăh-yeh, *v* to employ; to use.

employeur, ahng-plo'ăh-yer, *m* employer.

empocher, ahng-posh-eh, *v* to pocket.

empoigner, ahng-po'ăhn-yeh, *v* to grasp; to arrest.

empois, ahng-po'ăh, *m* starch.

empoisonner, ahng-po'ăh-zonn-eh, *v* to poison; to infect; *fam* to annoy; to irritate.

emporté, e, ahng-por-teh, *a* passionate; quick-tempered.

emportement, ahng-por-ter-mahng, *m* transport; outburst; fit.

emporter, ahng-por-teh, *v* to carry away; **s'–,** to fly into a rage.

empourprer (s'), sahng-poohr-preh, *v* to flush; to turn crimson.

empreinte, ahng-prangt, *f* impress; mark; stamp; – **digitale,** – de-she-tăhl, fingerprint.

empressé, e, ahng-press-eh, *a* eager; assiduous; obliging.

empressement, ahng-press-mahng, *m* earnestness; assiduous attention.

empresser (s'), sahng-press-eh, *v* to hasten (**de,** to).

emprisonner, ahng-pre-zonn-eh, *v* to imprison.

emprunt, ahng-prung, *m* loan; borrowing.

emprunté, e, ahng-prung-teh, *pp* & *a* borrowed; self-conscious.

emprunter, ahng-prung-teh, *v* to borrow.

ému, e, eh-mE, *pp* & *a* moved (by emotion).

émule, eh-mEEl, *m* imitator; rival; competitor.

en, ahng, *pron* some; any;

of it; of them; of, from or about him, her, it; there; *prep* in; into; within; at; in the; like a; by; while; – **-ligne**, – leen-yer *a, adv comput* on-line.

encadrer, ahng-kăh-dreh, *v* to frame; to encircle.

encaisse, ahng-kayss, *f* cash in hand; cash balance.

encaissé, ahng-kayss-eh, *a* embanked; with high banks; hollow.

encaissement, ahng-kayss-mahng, *m* packing; payment; cashing; encashment; embankment.

encaisser, ahng-kayss-eh, *v* to pack; to collect; to receive; to embank.

en-cas, ahng-kah, *m* (stand-by) snack.

encastrer, ahng-kăhss-treh, *v* to fit in; to embed.

encaustique, ahng-kohs-teeck, *f* wax polish; furniture polish.

encaver, ahng-kăh-veh, *v* to store in a cellar.

enceinte, ahng-sangt, *f* enclosure; precincts; *a* pregnant.

encens, ahng-sahng, *m* incense; *fam* praise;

flattery.

enchaînement, ahng-shain-mahng, *m* chaining up; train (of events).

enchaîner, ahng-shay-neh, *v* to chain up; to fetter; to connect.

enchanté, ahng-shahng-teh, *pp & a* enchanted; spellbound; delighted.

enchantement, ahng-shahngt-mahng, *m* enchantment; spell; delight.

enchanter, ahng-shahng-teh, *v* to enchant; to delight; to charm.

enchant-eur, eresse, ahng-shahng-ter, *mf* enchanter; *a* bewitching; enchanting.

enchâsser, ahng-shahss-eh, *v* to enshrine; to set.

enchère, ahng-shair, *f* bidding; auction.

enchérlr, ahng-sheh-reer, *v* to outbid; to get dear.

enchevêtrer, ahngsh-vay-treh, *v* to entangle.

enclaver, ahng-klăh-veh, *v* to enclose; to wedge in.

enclin, e, ahng-klang, *a* inclined; prone.

enclore, ahng-klor, *v* to enclose; to fence in.

enclos, ahng-kloh, *m* enclosure; paddock.

enclume, ahng-klEEm, *f* anvil.

encoche, ahng-kosh, *f* notch.

encoignure, ahng-konn-yEEr, *f* corner; corner-cupboard.

encolure, ahng-koll-EEr, *f* neckline.

encombrement, ahng-kong-brer-mahng, *m* obstruction; traffic jam.

encombrer, ahng-kong-breh, *v* to encumber; to obstruct; to crowd.

encontre (à l'– de), ăh lahng-kong-trer der, *prep* against; contrary to.

encore, ahng-kor, *adv* still; again; yet; **pas–,** păh z' –, not yet.

encourager, ahng-koo-răh-sheh, *v* to encourage.

encourir, ahng-koo-reer, *v* to incur.

encre, ahng-kr, *f* ink.

encrier, ahng-kre-eh, *m* inkstand.

encroûté, ahng-kroo-teh, *a* full of prejudices; set in one's ways.

encyclopédie, ahng-se-klop-eh-dee, *f* encyclopaedia.

endetter, ahng-day-teh, *v* to get into debt; **s'–,** to run into debt.

endiablé, ahng-de-ăh-bleh, *pp* & *a* furious; wicked; wild.

endiguer, ahng-de-gheh, *v* to dam in; to bank up.

endimancher (s'), sahng-de-mahng-sheh, *v* to put on one's Sunday best.

endoctriner, ahng-dock-tre-neh, *v* to instruct; to gain over.

endolori, e, ahng-doll-or-e, *a* aching; tender.

endommager, ahng-domm-ăh-sheh, *v* to damage.

endormi, e, ahng-dor-me, *pp* & *a* gone to sleep; sleeping; sleepy; sluggish; numb.

endormir, ahng-dor-meer, *v* to send to sleep; to lull; *fam* to deceive; **s'–,** to fall asleep; to lie idle.

endos, endossement, ahng-doh, ahng-dohss-mahng, *m* endorsement.

endosser, ahng-dohss-eh, *v* to put on; to endorse.

endroit, ahng-dro'ăh, *m* place; spot; part; right side.

enduire, ahng-dweer, *v* to coat.

enduit, ahng-dwe, *m* coat; layer.

endurant, e, ahng-dE-rahng, *a* enduring; patient; tolerant.

endurcir, ahng-dEEr-seer, *v* to harden; to inure.

endurcissement, ahng-dEEr-siss-mahng, *m* hardening; obduracy; toughness.

énergie, eh-nair-shee, *f* energy; force.

énergique,* eh-nair-sheeck; *a* energetic.

énergumène, eh-nair-ghE-main, *m* rowdy customer.

énervant, eh-nair-vahng, *a fam* aggravating; irritating.

énerver, eh-nair-veh, *v* to irritate.

enfance, ahng-fahngss, *f* childhood; infancy.

enfant, ahng-fahng, *mf* child; infant; **tout(e) petit(e) –,** too-per-te –, *mf* toddler.

enfanter, ahng-fahng-teh, *v* to give birth to.

enfantillage, ahng-fahng-tee-yăhsh, *m* childishness.

enfantin, e, ahng-fahng-tang, *a* childish.

enfariner, ahng-făh-re-neh, *v* to cover with flour.

enfer, ahng-fair, *m* hell.

enfermer, ahng-fair-meh, *v* to shut in; to lock up; to enclose.

enfilade, ahng-fe-lăhd, *f* row; line; long string.

enfiler, ahng-fe-leh, *v* to thread; to string; to run through.

enfin, ahng-fang, *adv* at last; finally; in short; on the whole; after all.

enflammer, ahng-flăh-meh, *v* to set on fire; to rouse.

enfler, ahng-fleh, *v* to swell; to inflate; to puff up.

enfoncé, ahng-fong-seh, *pp* & *a* smashed in; sunk; done for.

enfoncer, ahng-fong-seh, *v* to sink into; to drive in; to smash; to surpass.

enfouir, ahng-foo-eer, *v* to bury; to hide in the ground.

enfourcher, ahng-foohr-sheh, *v* to straddle; to mount.

enfreindre, ahng-frang-dr, *v* to infringe.

enfuir (s'), sahng-fweer, *v* to run away; to vanish; to leak.

enfumer, ang-fE-meh, *v* to smoke out.

engagement, ahng-gahsh-mahng *m* commitment; engagement; contract; agreement.

engager, ahng-găh-sheh, *v* to engage; to pawn; to invite; to advise; **s'–,** to enlist; to undertake.

engelure, ahngsh-lEEr, *f* chilblain.

engendrer, ahng-shahng-dreh, *v* to beget; to father; to engender.

engin, ahng-shang, *m* engine; machine; tackle; missile.

englober, ahng-glob-eh, *v* to lump together; to unite.

engloutir, ahng-gloo-teer, *v* to swallow up; to engulf.

engloutissement, ahng-gloo-tiss-mahng, *m* swallowing up; sinking.

engorger, ahng-gor-sheh, *v* to obstruct; to block up.

engouement, ahng-goo-mahng, *m* infatuation.

engouffrer, ahng-goo-freh, *v* to engulf; to devour; to swallow up.

engourdi, e, ahng-goohr-de, *pp* & *a* numbed; dull; torpid.

engrais, ahng-gray, *m* manure.

engraisser, ahng-grayss-eh, *v* to fatten; to manure.

engrener, ahng-grer-neh, *v* to throw into gear.

engueuler, ahng-gher-leh, *v fam* to scold; to blow up; to abuse.

enhardir, ahng-ǎhr-deer, *v* to embolden.

énigme, eh-neegm, *f* enigma; riddle.

enivrer, ahng-ne-vrehh, *v* to intoxicate; to enrapture; **s'–,** to get drunk.

enjamber, ahng-shahng-beh, *v* to stride over.

enjeu, ahng-sher, *m* stake.

enjoindre, ahng-sho'ang-dr, *v* to enjoin; to order.

enjôler, ahng-shoh-leh, *v* to wheedle.

enjoliver, ahng-sholl-e-veh, *v* to embellish.

enjoué, e, ahng-shoo-eh, *a* playful; lively; sprightly.

enlacer, ahng-lǎhss-eh, *v* to lace; to entwine; to interweave; to clasp.

enlaidir, ahng-lay-deer, *v* to disfigure; to grow ugly.

enlèvement, ahng-layv-mahng, *m* carrying away; removal; kidnapping.

enlever, ahngl-veh, *v* to lift; to take (away) to run away with; to kidnap; **s'–,** to rise; to come off; to be sold.

ennemi, ain-me, *m* enemy.

ennemi, e, ain-me, *a*

hostile; adverse; enemy.

ennoblir, ahng-nob-leer, *v* to ennoble.

ennui, ahng-nwe, *m* tediousness; boredom; annoyance; trouble.

ennuyer, ahng-nwee-yeh, *v* to tire; to annoy; to bore; **s'–,** to feel bored.

ennuyeu-x, se,* ahng-nwee-yer, *a* boring; annoying.

énoncer, eh-nong-seh, *v* to state; to articulate.

enorgueillir (s'), sahng-nor-gher-yeer, *v* to pride oneself (**de,** on).

énorme, eh-norm, *a* enormous; huge.

énormément, eh-nor-meh-mahng, *adv* enormously; *fam* tremendously.

enquérir (s'), sahng-keh-reer, *v* to enquire.

enquête, ahng-kayt, *f* inquiry; inquest.

enraciner, ahng-rǎhss-e-neh, *v* to root.

enragé, e, ahng-rǎh-sheh, *a* mad; enraged; furious; desperate.

enrager, ahng-rǎh-sheh, *v* to be mad; to be in a rage; **faire –,** fair **–,** to drive mad.

enrayer, ahng-ray-yeh, *v* to stop.

enregistrement, ahng-rer-shiss-trer-mahng, *m* check in; registration; entry; recording (record, etc).

enregistrer, ahng-rer-shiss-treh, *v* to register: to record.

enrhumer (s'), sahng-rE-meh, to catch a cold.

enrichi, e, ahng-re-she, *a* & *mf* upstart.

enrichir, ahng-re-sheer, *v* to enrich; to embellish.

enrôler, ahng-roh-leh, *v* to enrol; to enlist.

enroué, e, ahng-roo-eh, *a* hoarse.

enrouler, ahng-roo-leh, *v* to roll up.

ensanglanter, ahng-sahng-glahng-teh, *v* to stain with blood.

enseigne, ahng-sayn-yer, *m* ensign; midshipman; sub-lieutenant; *f* (neon) sign; *pl* colours.

enseignement, ahng-sayn-yer-mahng, *m* teaching; instruction; tuition; education.

enseigner, ahng-sayn-yeh, *v* to teach; to inform; to direct.

ensemble, ahng-sahng-bl, *m* whole; ensemble; mass; general appearance; harmony; *adv* together; at the same time.

ensevelir, ahng-serv-leer, *v* to shroud; to bury.

ensoleillé, ahng-soll-ay-yeh, *a* sunny.

ensorceler, ahng-sor-ser-leh, *v* to bewitch.

ensuite, ahng-sweet, *adv* afterwards; after; then; next.

ensuivre (s'), sahng-swee-vr, *v* to follow; to ensue.

entailler, ahng-tah'e-yeh, *v* to notch.

entamer, ahng-tăh-meh, *v* to begin; to make the first cut in.

entasser, ahng-tăhss-eh, *v* to heap up; to stack; to pile up.

entendement, ahng-tahngd-mahng *m* understanding; sense; judgment.

entendre, ahng-tahng-dr, *v* to hear; to understand; to mean; **bien entendu,** be-ang n'ahng-tahng-dE, of course.

entente, ahng-tahngt, *f* understanding; sense; meaning.

enterrement, ahng-tair-mahng, *m* burial; funeral.

enterrer, ahng-tay-reh, *v* to bury; *fam* to outlive.

en-tête, ahng-tayt, *m* heading.

entêté, e, ahng-tay-teh, *a* obstinate; stubborn.

entêter, ahng-tay-teh, *v* to make giddy; **s'–,** to be obstinate.

enthousiasme, ahng-too-ze-ăhssm, *m* enthusiasm.

entier, ahng-te-eh, *m* entirety; whole.

enti-er, ère,* ahng-te-eh, *a* whole; perfect; full.

entonner, ahng-tonn-eh, *v* to start singing.

entonnoir, ahng-tonn-o'ăhr, *m* funnel; *geog* crater.

entorse, ahng-torss, *f* sprain; strain; twist.

entortiller, ahng-tor-tee-yeh, *v* to twist; to wind; to entangle; to get round.

entourage, ahng-too-răhsh, *m* environment; setting; circle (of family and friends, etc).

entourer, ahng-too-reh, *v* to surround (**de,** with).

entracte, ahng-trăhckt, *m* interval between the acts.

entraider (s'), sahng-tray-deh, *v* to help one another.

entrailles, ahng-trah'e, *fpl* entrails; bowels;

feelings.

entrain, ahng-trang, *m* spirits; life; animation.

entraînant, e, ahng-tray-nahng, *a* captivating; winning.

entraînement, ahng-train-mahng, *m* force; impulse; sway; training; coaching.

entraîner, ahng-tray-neh, *v* to carry away; to involve; to bring about; to train.

entraîneur, ahng-tray-ner, *m* trainer; coach.

entrant, ahng-trahng, *a* coming in; entering.

entrave, ahng-trähv, *f* impediment; *pl* fetters.

entre, ahng-tr, *prep* between; among; into; in.

entrebâiller, ahng-trer-bah'e-yeh, *v* to half-open; to set ajar.

entrechoquer (s'), sahng-trer-shock-eh, *v* to clash.

entrecôte, ahng-trer-koht, *f* steak (from ribs).

entrecouper, ahng-trer-koo-peh, *v* to intercept; to

entrecroiser (s'), sahng-trer-kro'äh-zeh, *v* to intertwine.

entre-deux, ahng-trer-der,

m space between; insertion.

entrée, ahng-treh, *f* entrance; admission; beginning; entry; entrée.

entrefaites, ahng-trer-fayt, *fpl* **sur ces –**, SEEr say z' –, meanwhile; at that moment.

entrelacement, ahng-trer-lähss-mahng, *m* intertwining.

entrelardé, e, ahng-trer-lähr-deh, *a* streaky.

entremêler, ahng-trer-may-leh, *v* to intermingle; **s' –**, to interpose.

entremets ahng-trer-may, *m* sweet; dessert.

entremetteur, ahng-trer-met-er, *m* go-between.

entremettre (s'), sahng-trer-met-tr, *v* to intervene.

entrepont, ahng-trer-pong, *m* between decks.

entreposer, ahng-trer-poh-zeh, *v* to store; to put in bond.

entrepositaire, ahng-trer-poh-ze-tair, *m* bonder.

entrepôt, ahng-trer-poh, *m* warehouse; bonded store.

entreprenant, e, ahng-trer-prer-nahng, *a* enterprising; pushing;

bold; venturous.

entreprendre, ahng-trer-prahng-dr, *v* to undertake; to contract for; to attempt.

entrepreneur, ahng-trer-prer-ner, *m* contractor; manufacturer; builder; – **de pompes funèbres**, – der pongb fE-nay-br, undertaker.

entreprise, ahng-trer-preez, *f* enterprise; undertaking; contract; attempt.

entrer, ahng-treh, *v* to enter (**dans, en**, into); to begin; to bring in; **faire –**, fair –, to show in.

entresol, ahng-trer-sol, *m* mezzanine.

entretenir, ahng-trert-neer, *v* to keep up; to maintain; to cherish; **s'–**, to converse; to keep fit.

entretien, ahng-trer-te-ang, *m* upkeep; maintenance; conversation; interview.

entrevoir, ahng-trer-vo'ähr, *v* to have a glimpse of; to foresee.

entrevue, ahng-trer-vE, *f* interview.

entrouvert, e, ahng-troo-vair, *a* ajar; half open.

entrouvrir, ahng-troo-vreer, *v* to half open.

énumérer, eh-nE-meh-reh, *v* to enumerate.

envahir, ahng-väh-eer, *v* to invade; to encroach on; to overrun.

enveloppe, ahngv-lop, *f* envelope; wrapper; cover.

envelopper, ahngv-lop-eh, *v* to envelop; to wrap up; to cover.

envenimer, ahngv-ne-meh, *v* to embitter; s'–, to fester.

envergure, ahng-vair-ghEEr, *f* span; scope; width.

envers, ahng-vair, *prep* towards; to; *m* wrong side; à l' –, äh l'–, inside out.

envi (à l'), äh lahng-ve, *adv* in emulation (**de**, of).

envie, ahng-vee, *f* envy; inclination; wish.

envier, ahng-ve-eh, *v* to envy; to long for.

environ, ahng-ve-rong, *adv* about; *pl* environs surroundings; outskirts; vicinity.

environnement, ahng-ve-rong-mahng, *m* (ecological) environment.

environner, ahng-ve-ronn-eh, *v* to surround.

envisager, ahng-ve-zäh-sheh, *v* to look at; to face; to consider.

envoi, ahng-vo'äh, *m* sending; dispatch; consignment; goods; parcel; remittance.

envoler (s'), sahng-voll-eh, *v* to fly away.

envoyé, ahng-vo'äh-yeh, *m* messenger; envoy (newspaper) correspondant.

envoyer, ahng-vo'äh-yeh, *v* to send; to forward; to dispatch.

épagneul, eh-pähn-yerl, *m* spaniel.

épais, se, eh-pay, *a* thick.

épaisseur, eh-payss-er, *f* thickness.

épaissir, eh-payss-eer, *v* to thicken.

épanchement, eh-pahngsh-mahng, *m* outpouring; discharge.

épancher, eh-pahng-sheh, *v* to pour out; to vent; s' –, to overflow; to open one's heart.

épandre, eh-pahng-dr, *v* to spread; to scatter.

épanouir (s'), seh-päh-noo-eer, *v* to blossom; to open out; to beam.

épargne, eh-pährn-yer, *f*

economy; saving.

épargner, eh-pährn-yeh, *v* to save; to spare; to have mercy on.

éparpiller, eh-pähr-pee-yeh, *v* to scatter.

épars, e, eh-pähr, *a* scattered; dishevelled.

épatant, e, eh-päh-tahng, *a fam* wonderful; super; great.

épater, eh-päh-teh, *v fam* to amaze.

épaule, eh-pohl, *f* shoulder.

épave, eh-pähv, *f* wreck; waif; remnant; down and out.

épée, eh-peh, *f* sword.

épeler, eh-pleh, *v* to spell (word).

éperdu, e, * eh-pair-dE, *a* distracted; aghast; desperate.

éperon, eh-prong, *m* spur; buttress.

épervier, eh-pair-ve-eh, *m* hawk; sweep-net.

épi, eh-pe, *m* ear (of wheat); spike; cluster.

épice, eh-peess, *f* spice; **pain d'–**, pang d –, ginger-bread.

épicerie, eh-peess-ree, *f* grocery; grocer's shop.

épici-er, ère, eh-peess-e-eh, *mf* grocer.

épidémie, eh-pe-deh-mee,

f epidemic.

épiderme, eh-pe-dairm, *m* epidermis.

épier, eh-pe-eh, *v* to spy; to watch.

épiler, eh-pe-leh, *v* to depilate; to pluck (eyebrows).

épiloguer, eh-pe-logh-eh, *v* to hold forth.

épinards, eh-pe-năhr, *mpl* spinach.

épine, eh-peen, *f* thorn; spine.

épineu-x, se, eh-pe-ner, *a* thorny; prickly; ticklish.

épingle, eh-pang-gl, *f* pin; – de sûreté, – der sEEr-teh, safety pin.

épingler, eh-pang-gleh, *v* to pin; to fasten with a pin.

épisode, eh-pe-zod, *m* episode.

épître, eh-pee-tr, *f* epistle.

éploré, e, eh-plor-eh, *a* in tears; weeping.

éplucher, eh-plε-sheh, *v* to pick; to peel; (*fam*) to examine.

épointer, eh-po'ang-teh, *v* to blunt.

éponge, eh-pongsh, *f* sponge.

éponger, eh-pong-sheh, *v* to sponge up; to mop.

épopée, eh-pop-eh, *f* epic poem.

époque, eh-pock, *f* epoch; time; date; period.

épouse, eh-pooz, *f* wife; spouse.

épouser, eh-poo-zeh, *v* to marry; to espouse (a cause, etc).

épousseter, eh-pooss-teh, *v* to dust.

épouvantable, * eh-poo-vahng-tăh-bl, *a* frightful; terrible.

épouvantail, eh-poo-vahng-tah'e, *m* scarecrow.

épouvante, eh-poo-vahngt, *f* fright; terror.

epouvanter, eh-poo-vahng-teh, *v* to frighten; to terrify.

époux, eh-poo, *m* husband; spouse; *pl* married couple.

éprendre (s'), seh-prahng-dr, *v* to fall in love (de, with).

épreuve, eh-prerv, *f* trial; test; proof; print (photo).

épris, e, eh-pre, *pp* & *a* smitten.

éprouver, eh-proo-veh, *v* to try; to experience; to feel.

épuisement, eh-pweez-mahng, *m* draining; exhaustion.

épuisé, eh-pwee-zeh, *a* exhausted; tired out.

épuiser, eh-pwee-zeh, *v* to drain; to exhaust; to use up.

épurer, eh-pe-reh, *v* to purify; to refine.

équateur, eh-kwăh-ter, *m* equator.

équerre, eh-kair, *f* set-square.

équestre, eh-kess-tr, *a* equestrian.

équilibre, eh-ke-lee-br, *m* equilibrium; poise; balance.

équipage, eh-ke-păhsh, *m* equipage; equipment; carriage; crew.

équipe, eh-keep, *f* gang; team; set; crew.

équipée, eh-ke-peh, *f* prank; lark.

équiper, eh-ke-peh, *v* to equip; to fit out.

équipement, eh-keep-mahng, *m* equipment; facilities; outfit.

équitable, * eh-ke-tăh-bl, *a* equitable; fair.

équitation, eh-ke-tăh-se-ong, *f* riding.

équité, eh-ke-teh, *f* equity.

équivalent, e, eh-ke-văh-lahng, *a* & *m* equivalent.

équivoque, eh-ke-vock, *f* ambiguity; *a* equivocal; dubious.

érable, eh-răh-bl, *m*

maple.

éraflure, eh-răh-flEEr, *f* slight scratch.

éraillé, e, eh-rah'e-eh, *pp* & *a* frayed; bloodshot; hoarse.

ère, air, *f* era; epoch.

érection, eh-reck-se-ong, *f* erection; raising.

éreinté, e, eh-rang-teh, *a* worn out; harassed.

éreinter, eh-rang-teh, *v* to break the back of (horse); to exhaust; to criticise; s'–, to tire oneself out.

ergot, air-go, *m* spur (of cock, etc).

ermite, air-meet, *m* hermit.

érotique, eh-ro-teeck, *a* erotic.

errant, e, air-rahng, *a* wandering; roaming.

errer, air-reh, *v* to wander; to stray; to err.

erreur, air-rer, *f* error; mistake.

erroné, e, * air-ronn-eh, *a* erroneous.

éruption, eh-rEp-se-ong, *f* eruption; **entrer en –**, ahng-treh-ahng –, to erupt.

érythème, eh-re-taym, *m* nappy rash.

escabeau, ess-kăh-boh, *m* stepladder; stool; steps.

escadre, ess-kăh-dr, *f* squadron; fleet.

escadron, ess-kăh-drong, *m* squadron; **chef d'–**, shaif d–, major.

escalade, ess-kăh-lăhd, *f* scaling; climb.

escale, ess-kăhl, *f* port of call; stopover; touch down.

escalier, ess-kăh-le-eh, *m* stairs; staircase; steps; – **roulant**, –roo-lahng, escalator.

escalope, ess-kăh-lop, *f* thin slice of meat (usually veal); escalope.

escamoter, ess-kăh-mot-eh, *v* to make disappear.

escapade, ess-kăh-păhd, *f* prank; escapade.

escargot, ess-kăhr-go, *m* snail.

escarpé, e, ess-kăhr-peh, *a* steep; abrupt.

esclaffer (s'), sess-klăh-feh, *v* – **de rire**, – der reer, to burst out laughing; to shake with laughter.

esclandre, ess-klahng-dr, *m* scandal; scene.

esclavage, ess-klăh-văhsh, *m* slavery.

esclave, ess-klăhv, *mf* slave.

escompte, ess-kongt, *m* discount; rebate.

escompter, ess-kong-teh, *v* to discount; *fam* to expect.

escorter, ess-kor-teh, *v* to escort; to convoy; to accompany.

escouade, ess-koo-ăhd, *f* squad; gang.

escrime, ess-kreem, *f* fencing.

escrimer (s'), sess-kree-meh, *v* to endeavour; to try hard.

escroc, ess-kro, *m* swindler; crook.

escroquer, ess-krock-eh, *v* to swindle.

espace, ess-păhss, *m* space; room; infinity; vacancy.

espacer, ess-păhss-eh, *v* to space; to leave space between.

espadrille, ess-păh-dree-ye, *f* canvas shoe with rope sole.

espagnol, e, ess-păhn-yol, *a* & *mf* Spanish; Spaniard; *m* Spanish.

espèce, ess-payss, *f* species; kind; sort; case; *pl* specie.

espérance, ess-peh-rahngss, *f* hope; expectation.

espérer, ess-peh-reh, *v* to hope; to expect; to trust.

espiègle, ess-pe-ay-gl, *a* mischievous.

espion, ess-pe-ong, m spy.

espionnage, ess-pe-oh-nähsh, m espionage.

espoir, ess-po'ahr, m hope; expectation; **avec –,** ăh-veck –, a hopefully.

esprit, ess-pre, m spirit; soul; ghost; mind; intellect; wit; talent; feeling.

esquif, ess-keeff, m skiff.

esquimau, ess-ke-moh, mf & a Eskimo; ice lolly.

esquinter, ess-kang-teh, v fam to exhaust; to smash; to ruin; to spoil.

esquisse, ess-keess, f sketch; outline.

esquiver, ess-ke-veh, v to avoid; to elude; **s'–,** to slip away.

essai, eh-say, m trial; attempt; essay; try; **coup d'–,** koo d–, first attempt.

essaim, eh-sang, m swarm; host.

essayer, eh-say-yeh, v to try; to try on; to attempt; **s'–,** to try one's skill (à, dans, at).

essence, eh-sahngss, f petrol; essence.

essentiel, eh-sahng-se-ell, m main thing.

essentiel, le, * eh-sahng-se-ell, a essential.

essieu, eh-se-er, m axle.

essor, eh-sor, m com rapid expansion.

essorer, eh-sor-eh, v to wring (clothes); to squeeze; to soar.

essoreuse, eh-sor-erz, f spin-dryer.

essouffler, eh-soo-fleh, v to make breathless.

essuie-glace, eh-swee-glähss, m windscreen wiper.

essuie-mains, eh-swee-mang, m hand towel.

essuyer, eh-swee-yeh, v to wipe; to dry; to sustain; to go through.

est, esst, m east.

estampe, ess-tahngp, f print; engraving.

estampille, ess-tahng-pee-ye, f stamp; mark; trademark.

estimation, ess-tee-mäh-se-ong, f estimate; valuation.

estime, ess-teem, f esteem; regard.

estimer, ess-tee-meh, v to estimate; to consider.

estomac, ess-tomm-ăh, m stomach.

estrade, ess-trähd, f platform.

estragon, ess-träh-gong, m tarragon.

estropier, ess-trop-e-eh, v to cripple; to maim.

esturgeon, ess-tEEr-shong, m sturgeon.

et, eh, conj and.

étable, eh-tăh-bl, f stable; cattle-shed.

établi, e, eh-tăh-ble, pp & a established.

établir, eh-tăh-bleer, v to establish; to set; to institute; to prove.

établissement, eh-tăh-bliss-mahng, m establishment; institution; setting up.

étage, eh-tăhsh, m story; floor; step; layer.

étagère, eh-tăh-shair, f set of shelves; shelf.

étai, eh-tay, m stay; prop.

étain, eh-tang, m tin; pewter.

étalage, eh-tăh-lăhsh, m window display.

étaler, eh-tăh-leh, v to display; to spread out; **s'–,** to sprawl; to spread; fam to fall flat on one's face.

étalon, eh-tăh-long, m stallion; standard (of weights, etc).

étamine, eh-tăh-meen, f cheesecloth; sieve; stamen.

étanche, eh-tahngsh, a watertight.

étancher, eh-tahng-sheh, v to staunch; to make

watertight; to stop; to quench.

étang, eh-tahng, *m* pond; pool.

étape, eh-tăhp, *f* stop over; stage.

état, eh-tăh, *m* state; plight; profession; trade; list; statement; nation.

état-major, eh-tăh măh-**shor,** *m* staff; headquarters.

étau, eh-toh, *m* vice.

étayer, eh-tay-yeh, *v* to prop up.

été, eh-teh, *m* summer.

éteindre, eh-tang-dr, *v* to extinguish; to turn off (light, etc); to fade.; **s'–,** to die out.

éteint, e, eh-tang, *pp* & *a* put out; extinct; faint.

étendard, eh-tahng-dăhr, *m* standard; flag.

étendre, eh-tahng-dr, *v* to extend; to spread; to stretch; to expand; to lay down; **s'–,** to stretch out; to stretch (plain, etc).

étendu, e, eh-tahng-dE, *pp* & *a* extended; spread; extensive.

étendue, eh-tahng-dEE, *f* extent.

éternel, le, * eh-tair-nell, *a* eternal; unending.

éternuer, eh-tair-nE-eh, *v* to sneeze.

éther, eh-tair, *m* ether.

ethnique, ayt-neeck, *a* ethnic.

étinceler, eh-tangss-leh, *v* to sparkle; to gleam.

étincelle, eh-tang-sell, *f* spark.

étioler (s'), seh-te-oll-eh, to grow emaciated.

étiquette, eh-te-kett, *f* label; tag; etiquette.

étirer, eh-te-reh, *v* to stretch.

étoffe, eh-tof, *f* stuff; cloth; material.

étoile, eh-to'ăhl, *f* star; decoration; asterisk.

étole, eh-tol, *f* stole.

étonnant, eh-tonn-ahng, *a* astonishing; wonderful; surprising.

étonner, eh-tonn-eh, *v* to astonish; to astound; to surprise.

étouffer, eh-too-feh, *v* to suffocate; to stiffle; to smother; to choke; to hush up.

étourderie, eh-toohr-der-ree, *f* thoughtlessness; blunder.

étourdi, e, eh-toohr-de, *pp* & *a* stunned; heedless; scatterbrained; giddy.

étourdir, eh-toohr-deer, *v* to stun; to deafen; **s'–,**

to escape from oneself.

étourdissant, e, eh-toohr-diss-ahng, *a* deafening; dazzling.

étourdissement, eh-toohr-diss-mahng, *m* giddiness; dizziness.

étourneau, eh-toohr-noh, *m* starling; scatter-brain.

étrange, * eh-trahngsh, *a* strange; odd; queer.

étranger, eh-trahng-sheh, *m* stranger; foreigner; foreign countries; **à l'–,** ăh l'–, abroad.

étrang-er, ère, eh-trahng-sheh, *a* strange; foreign.

étranglé, eh-trahng-gleh, *pp* & *a* strangled; narrow; tight.

étrangler, eh-trahng-gleh, *v* to strangle.

être, ay-tr, *v* to be; to exist; to belong; *m* being; existence; individual.

étreindre, eh-trang-dr, *v* to bind; to clasp; to grasp.

étreinte, eh-trangt, *f* fastening; grasp; embrace.

étrenne, eh-trenn, *f* (usually *pl*) New Year's gifts.

étrier, eh-tre-yeh, *m* stirrup; **le coup de l'–,** ler koo der l'–, stirrup cup..

étrille, eh-tree-ye, *f* currycomb.

étriqué, e, eh-tre-keh, *a* tight; skimpy.

étroit, e, * eh-tro'ăh, *a* narrow; tight; close; strict; **à l'–**, ăh l–, cramped.

étroitesse, eh-tro'ăh-tess, *f* narrowness; tightness; closeness.

étude, eh-tEED, *f* study; chambers; practice; survey; **faire ses –s à**, fair seh zeh-tEED-ăh, to be educated at.

étudiant, eh-tE-de-ahng, *m* student.

étudier, eh-tE-de-eh, *v* to study; to observe; **s' –**, to endeavour (à, to).

étui, eh-twee, *m* case; box; needle-case; sheath.

étuvée, eh-tE-veh, *f* cooking by steam; **à l' –**, ăhl –, steamed.

eucharistie, er-kăh-riss-tee, *f* Eucharist.

euphonie, er-fon-ee, *f* euphony.

euh! er, *interj* hum! well!

Europe, er-rop, *f* Europe.

eux, er, *pron* them; they.

évacuer, eh-văh-kE-eh, *v* to evacuate; to vacate.

évader (s'), seh-văh-deh, *v* to escape; to get away.

évaluer, eh-văh-lE-eh, *v* to value; to estimate.

évangile, eh-vahng-sheel, *m* Gospel.

évanouir (s'), seh-văh-noo-eer, *v* to faint; to vanish.

évanouissement, eh-văh-noo-iss-mahng, *m* fainting; swoon.

évaporer (s'), seh-văh-por-eh, *v* to evaporate.

évasé, e, eh-vah-zeh, *pp & a* widened; flared.

évasi-f, ve, * eh-vah-zeeff, *a* evasive.

évasion, eh-vah-se-ong, *f* escape; flight.

éveil, eh-vay'e, awakening; *m* warning; **en –**, ahng n'–, on the alert.

éveillé, e, eh-vay'e-yeh, *pp & a* awakened; wide awake; vigilant; alert.

éveiller, eh-vay'e-yeh, *v* to awaken; to call.

événement, eh-venn-mahng, *m* event; occurrence; issue.

éventail, eh-vahng-tah'e, *m* fan; range (of choices).

éventer, eh-vahng-teh, *v* to fan; to air; to make flat; **s' –**, to spoil; to go flat.

éventrer, eh-vahng-treh, *v* to rip open; to disembowel.

éventualité, eh-vahng-tE-ăh-le-teh, *f* contingency; possibility.

éventuel, le, * eh-vahng-tE-ell, *a* contingent; possible; eventual.

évêque, eh-vayk, *m* bishop.

évertuer (s'), seh-vair-tE-eh, *v* to exert oneself; to do one's utmost.

évidemment, eh-ve-dăh-mahng, *adv* evidently; obviously.

évidence, eh-ve-dahngss, *f* evidence.

évident, e, eh-ve-dahng, *a* evident; clear.

évider, eh-ve-deh, *v* to scoop out.

évier, eh-ve-eh, *m* sink.

évincer, eh-vang-seh, *v* to turn out; to oust.

éviter, eh-ve-teh, *v* to avoid; to dodge.

évolué, eh-vol-E-eh, *a* advanced; developed.

évolution, eh-voll-E-se-ong, *f* evolution.

évoquer, eh-vock-eh, *v* to conjure up; to call up.

exact, e, * egg-zăhckt, *a* exact; accurate; true; punctual.

exaction, egg-zăhck-se-ong, *f* extortion.

exactitude, egg-zăhck-te-

tEEd, f exactness; accuracy; punctuality.

exagérer, egg-zăh-**sheh**-reh, v to exaggerate; to go too far.

exalté, e, egg-zăhl-teh, pp & a exalted; elated; enthusiastic; fanatic.

exalter, egg-zăhl-teh, v to extol; to praise.

examen, egg-zăh-mang, m examination; abbr exam; scrutiny.

examinateur, egg-zăh-me-năh-ter, m examiner.

examiner, egg-zăh-me-neh, v to examine; to inquire into.

exaspérer, egg-zăhss-peh-reh, v to exasperate; to provoke.

exaucer, egg-zoh-seh, v to hear; to grant.

excédent, eck-seh-dahng, m surplus; excess.

excéder, eck-seh-deh, v to exceed; to exasperate.

excellemment, eck-say-lăh-mahng, adv excellently.

excellence, eck-say-lahngss, f excellence.

excellent, e, eck-say-lahng, a excellent.

exceller, eck-say-leh, v to excel.

excentrique, * eck-sahng-treeck, a eccentric.

excepté, eck-sayp-teh, prep except.

excepter, eck-sayp-teh, v to except.

exception, eck-sayp-se-ong, f exception.

excès, eck-say, m excess.

excessi-f, ve, * eck-sayss-eeff, a excessive; exorbitant.

excitant, e, eck-se-tahng, a exciting; stimulating.

excitation, eck-se-tăh-se-ong, f excitement.

excité, e, eck-si-teh a randy.

exciter, eck-se-teh, v to excite; to rouse.

exclamer (s'), secks-klăh-meh, v to exclaim.

exclure, ecks-klEEr, v to exclude.

exclusi-f, ve, * ecks-klE-zeeff, a exclusive.

exclusivité, ecks-klE-ze-ve-teh, f exclusiveness; sole rights.

excommunier, ecks-komm-E-ne-eh, v to excommunicate.

excroissance, ecks-kro'ăh-sahngss, f excrescence; growth.

excursion, ecks-kEEr-se-ong, f excursion; tour; outing.

excuse, ecks-kEEz, f excuse; pl apology.

excuser, ecks-kE-zeh, v to excuse; **s'–,** to apologise; to decline (offer, etc).

exécrer, ecks-eh-kreh, v to execrate.

exécutant, egg-zeh-kE-tahng, m performer.

exécuter, egg-zeh-kE-teh, v to execute; to perform; to carry out; **s'–,** to make an effort; to yield.

exécution, egg-zeh-kE-se-ong, f execution; performance.

exemplaire, egg-zahng-plair, m copy; a exemplary.

exemple, egg-zahng-pl, m example; instance; copy; **par –,** păhr –, for instance; interj really!

exempt, e, egg-zahng, a exempt; exempted; free.

exempter, egg-zahng-teh, v to exempt; to dispense.

exercer, egg-zair-seh, v to exercise; to train up; to practise; to follow (a profession).

exercice, egg-zair-seess, m exercise; practice; financial year; drill.

exhaler, egg-zăh-leh, v to exhale; to vent.

exhausser, egg-zohss-eh, v to raise.

exhiber, egg-ze-beh, v to

exhibit; to show.

exhorter, egg-zor-teh, *v* to exhort.

exhumer, egg-zE-meh, *v* to exhume; to bring to light.

exigeant, e, egg-ze-shahng, *pp* & *a* exacting; hard to please.

exigence, egg-ze-shahngss, *f* exigency; demand.

exiger, egg-ze-sheh, *v* to exact; to demand; to insist upon.

exigu, ë, egg-ze-ghE, *a* scanty; small; slender.

exiguïté, egg-ze-ghE-e-teh, *f* scantiness.

exil, egg-zeel, *m* exile.

exiler, egg-ze-leh, *v* to exile; to banish.

existence, egg-ziss-tahngss, *f* existence; life.

exister, egg-ziss-teh, *v* to exist; to live.

exode, egg-zod, *m* exodus.

exonérer, egg-zonn-eh-reh, *v* to exonerate.

exorbitant, e, egg-zor-be-tahng, *a* exorbitant.

exorciser, egg-zor-se-zeh, *v* to exorcise.

exotique, egg-zo-teeck, *a* exotic.

expansi-f, ve, ecks-păhng-seeff, *a* expansive; exuberant; effusive.

expédient, ecks-peh-de-

ahng, *m* resource; *a* expedient; advisable.

expédier, ecks-peh-de-eh, *v* to post; to expedite; to despatch; to draw up.

expéditeur, ecks-peh-de-ter, *m* sender; shipper; forwarding agent.

expéditi-f, ve, ecks-peh-de-teeff, *a* expeditious.

expédition, ecks-peh-de-se-ong, *f* expedition; forwarding; consignment; copy.

expérience, ecks-peh-re-ahngss, *f* experience; experiment.

expérimenter, ecks-peh-re-mahng-teh, *v* to experiment; to try; to test.

expert, ecks-pair, *m* expert; specialist; valuer; surveyor; a skilled; — **comptable,** – kong-tăh-bl, *m* chartered accountant.

expertise, ecks-pair-teez, *f* valuation; survey.

expier, ecks-pe-eh, *v* to atone for.

expirer, ecks-pe-reh, *v* to expire; to breath out; to die.

explicati-f, ve, ecks-ple-kăh-teeff, *a* explanatory.

explication, ecks-ple-kăh-se-ong, *f* explanation.

expliquer, ecks-ple-keh, *v* to explain; to construe; to account for.

exploit, ecks-plo'ăh, *m* deed, feat.

exploitation, ecks-plo'ăh-tăh-se-ong, *f* working; cultivation; exploitation.

exploiter, ecks-plo'ăh-teh, *v* to work; to cultivate; to turn to account; to take advantage of.

exploiteur, ecks-plo'ăh-ter, *m* exploiter; *fam* swindler.

explorer, ecks-plor-eh, *v* to explore.

exploser, ecks-plo-zeh, *v* to explode; to blow up.

explosi-f, ve ecks-plo-zeef *a* & *n* explosive *m*.

explosion, ecks-plo-ze-ong, *f* explosion; outbreak.

exportation, ecks-por-tăh-se-ong, *f* export.

exporter, ecks-por-teh, *v* to export.

exposant, ecks-po-zahng, *m* exhibitor; petitioner.

exposé, ecks-po-zeh, *m* statement; account.

exposer, ecks-po-zeh, *v* to expose; to exhibit; to explain.

exposition, ecks-po-ze-se-ong, *f* exposure;

exhibition; statement.

exprès, ecks-pray, *adv* on purpose.

exprès, ecks-pray, *a* & *m* express (of letter).

expr-ès, esse, ecks-pray, *a* express; explicit.

express, ecks-press, *m* express train; *a* express.

expression, ecks-prayss-e-*ong*, *f* expression; utterance; expressiveness.

exprimer, ecks-pre-meh, *v* to squeeze out; to express; **s'** –, to express oneself.

expulser, ecks-pEEl-seh, *v* to expel; to turn out.

exquis, e,* ecks-ke, *a* exquisite.

extase, ecks-tahz, *f* ecstasy.

extasier (s'), secks-tah-ze-eh, *v* to be enraptured.

exténuer, ecks-teh-nE-eh, *v* to extenuate; to exhaust.

extérieur, ecks-teh-re-er, *m* exterior; outside.

extérieur, e,* ecks-teh-re-er, *a* external; outward; foreign.

exterminer, ecks-tair-me-neh, *v* to destroy.

externe, ecks-tairn, *m* day-pupil; resident medical student; *a* external.

extincteur, ecks-tangk-ter, *m* fire-extinguisher.

extinction, ecks-tangk-se-*ong*, *f* extinction; suppression; paying off.

extirper, ecks-teer-peh, *v* to root out.

extorquer, ecks-tor-keh, *v* to extort.

extra, ecks-träh, *m* extra; *a inv* first rate; wonderful.

extrader, ecks-träh-deh, *v* to extradite.

extraire, ecks-trair, *v* to extract.

extrait, ecks-tray, *m* extract; abstract; certificate.

extraordinaire,* ecks-träh-or-de-nair, *a* unusual; extraordinary.

extravagant, ecks-träh-väh-gah*ng*, *a* extravagant; eccentric.

extraverti, e, ecks-träh-vair-te *mf* & *a* extrovert.

extrême,* ecks-traym, *a* extreme; utmost; *m* extreme limit.

extrêmité, ecks-treh-me-teh, *f* extremity; end; last moments.

F

fable, făh-bl, *f* fable; story; byword.

fabricant, făh bre-kahng, *m* manufacturer.

fabrication, făh-bre-kăh-se-ong, *f* manufacture.

fabrique, făh-breeck, *f* factory.

fabriquer, făh-bre-keh, *v* to manufacture; to make; to forge.

fabuleu-x, se,* făh-bE-ler, *a* fabulous.

façade, făhss-ăhd, *f* front; facade.

face, făhss, *f* face (of sth); front; aspect; side; **en –,** ahng –, opposite.

facétie, făh-seh-see, *f* joke.

facétieu-x, se,* făh-seh-se-er, *a* jocular.

fâché, fah-sheh, *a* angry (**contre,** with); sorry (**de,** for); on bad terms (**avec,** with).

fâcher, fah-sheh, *v* to offend; to anger; **se –,** to take offence; to get angry.

fâcheu-x, se,* fah-sher, *a* annoying; unfortunate.

facile,* făh-seell, *a* easy.

facilité, făh-se-le-teh, *f* ease; ability; readiness; *pl* easy terms.

faciliter, făh-se-le-teh, *v* to facilitate.

façon, făh-song, *f* way; manner; *pl* affectation.

façonner, făh-sonn-eh, *v* to shape; to form; to turn (on lathe).

factage, făhck-tăhsh, *m* porterage; carriage.

facteur, făhck-ter, *m* postman; agent; factor;

maker (of musical instruments).

factice, făhck-teess, *a* factitious.

factieu-x, se,* făhck-se-er, *a* factious.

factionnaire, făhck-se-onn-air, *m* sentry.

facture, făhck-tEEr, *f* invoice; bill.

facultati-f, ve,* făh-kEEl-tah-teeff, *a* optional.

faculté, făh-kEEl-teh, *f* faculty; power.

fadaise, făh-dayz, *f* rubbish; nonsense.

fade, făhd, *a* insipid; flat; dull.

fagot, făh-go, *m* faggot; bundle.

fagoter, făh-got-eh, *v* to bundle up; to rig out.

faible, fay-bl, *m* weak side; partiality; *a** weak; feeble; poor.

faiblesse, fay-bless, *f* weakness; deficiency; indulgence; swoon.

faiblir, fay-bleer, *v* to weaken; to relax.

faïence, făh-yahngss, *f* earthenware; crockery.

failli, fah'e-yee, *pp* & *a* fallen; bankrupt; **j'ai – tomber,** shay – tong-beh, I nearly fell.

faillir, fah'e-yeer, *v* to err; to fail; to almost...

faillite, fah'e-yeet, f failure; bankruptcy; **faire – fair –**, to go bankrupt.

faim, fang, f hunger.

fainéant, e, fay-ney-ahng, mf & a idler; idle; slothful

faire, fair, v to make; to do; to be; to matter; to form; to arrange; **– de l'auto-stop, –** der-loh-toh-stop, hitch-hike; **– don de, –** dong der, to donate; **– du vélo, –** dE-veh-loh, fam ride a bike; **– la navette, –** lāh-nāh-vett, to commute.

faire-part, fair-par, m announcement card (death, wedding, etc).

faisable, fer-zāh-bl, a feasible.

faisan, fer-zahng, m pheasant.

faisandé, e, fer-zahng-deh, a (flavour) high; gamy.

faisceau, fayss-oh, m bundle; pile.

faiseur, fer-zer, m maker; doer; jobber; fussy person.

fait, fay, pp & a made; done; full-grown; accustomed; dressed up; **c'est bien –**, say be-ang –, serves (him, her, them, you, us, etc) right.

fait, fay, m fact; act; deed; doing; making; feat; **–s divers, –** de-vair, miscellaneous news.

faîte, fayt, m summit; ridge; pinacle.

faix, fay, m burden.

falaise, fāh-layz, f cliff.

fallacieu-x, se,* fāhl-lāh-se-er, a fallacious.

falloir, fāh-lo'āhr, v to be necessary; to be obliged; should; ought; to want; **il faut que je ...**, ill foh ker sher ..., I must; **il me faut**, ill mer foh, I want.

falot, fāh-lo, m lantern.

falot, e, fāh-lo, a wan; grey.

falsifier, fāhl-se-fe-eh, v to counterfeit; to adulterate.

famé, e, fāh-meh, a famed; **bien –**, be-ang –, of good repute.

famélique, fāh-meh-leeck, m starveling; a starving.

fameu-x, se,* fāh-mer, a famous; first-rate.

familiariser, fāh-me-le-āh-re-zeh, v to familiarize.

familier, fāh-me-le-eh, m intimate; conversant (with, avec).

famili-er, ère,* fāh-me-le-eh, a familiar.

famille, fāh-mee-ye, f family; kind.

famine, fāh-meen, f famine.

fanal, fāh-nǎhl, m lantern; beacon.

fanatisme, fāh-nǎh-tissm, m fanaticism.

faner, fāh-neh, v to make hay; to wither; **se –**, to fade away.

faneur, fāh-ner, m haymaker.

fanfare, fahng-fāhr, f flourish (of trumpets); brass band.

fanfaron, fahng-fāh-rong, m boaster; blusterer.

fange, fahngsh, f mire; mud; dirt.

fanion, fah-ne-ong, m flag.

fantaisie, fahng-tay-zee, f fancy; imagination.

fantasmagorie, fahng-tāhss-māh-gor-ee, f phantasmagoria.

fantasque, fahng-tāhsk, a odd; whimsical.

fantassin, fahng-tāhss-ang, m foot-soldier.

fantastique,* fahng-tass-teeck, a fantastic.

fantôme, fahng-tohm, m phantom; spectre; ghost.

faon, fahng, m fawn.

farce, fāhrss, f stuffing; farce; practical joke.

farcir, fāhr-seer, v to stuff; to cram.

fard, făhr, *m* make-up.

fardeau, făhr-doh, *m* burden; load.

farder, făhrdeh, *v* to paint; to make-up.

farfouiller, făhr-foo-yeh, *v* to rummage.

farine, făh-reen, *f* flour; meal.

farineu-x, se, făh-re-ner, *a* floury.

farouche, făh-roosh, *a* wild; fierce; sullen; shy.

fascicule, făhss-se-kEEl, *m* part; instalment; pamphlet.

fasciner, făhss-se-neh, *v* to fascinate.

fastidieu-x, se, * făhss-te-de-er, *a* tedious.

fastueu-x, se, * făhss-tE-er, *a* pompous; ostentatious.

fatal, e, * făh-tăhl, *a* fatal; inevitable.

fatalisme, făh-tăh-lissm, *m* fatalism.

fatigant, e, făh-te-gahng, *a* tiring; tedious.

fatigue, făh-teegh, *f* fatigue; stress; wear and tear.

fatiguer, făh-te-gheh, *v* to fatigue; to annoy.

fatras, făh-trah, *m* jumble; rubbish.

fatuité, făh-tE-e-teh, *f* conceit.

faubourg, foh-boohr, *m* outskirt; suburb; quarter.

fauché, foh-sheh, *a fam* stony broke.

faucher, foh-sheh, *v* to mow; to cut; to reap (field, corn etc); to mow down; *fam* to pinch.

faucille, foh-see-ye, *f* sickle.

faucon, foh-kong, *m* falcon.

faufiler, foh-fe-leh, *v* to tack; to baste; to insert; **se –,** to creep in.

faune, fohn, *f* fauna; wildlife.

faussaire, fohss-air, *m* forger.

fausser, fohss-eh, *v* to distort; to buckle; to be out of tune.

fausset, fohss-ay, *m* spigot; falsetto.

fausseté, fohss-teh, *f* falseness; falsehood; insincerity.

faute, foht, *f* fault; error; mistake; lack; **– de, –** der, for want of.

fauteuil, foh-ter'e, *m* armchair; **– roulant, –** roo-lahng wheelchair.

fauti-f, ve, * foh-teeff, *a* faulty; guilty.

fauve, fohv, *m* fawn colour; wild beast; *a* tawny, buff.

fauvette, foh-vett, *f* warbler.

faux, foh, *adv* falsely; *m* falsehood; imitation; forgery.

fau-x, sse, * foh, *a* false; sham; base; bad; imitated; out of tune.

faux, foh, *f* scythe.

faux-fuyant, foh-fwee-yahng, *m* evasion; subterfuge.

faveur, făh-ver, *f* favour; interest.

favorable, * făh-vor-ăh-bl, *a* favourable.

favori, te, făh-vor-e, *a* & *mf* favourite.

favoris, făh-vor-e, *mpl* sideburns.

favoriser, făh-vor-e-zeh, *v* to favour; to befriend; to aid.

fax, făhks, *m* fax.

faxer, făhks-eh, *v* to fax.

fébrile, feh-breell, *a* feverish.

fécond, e, feh-kong, *a* fruitful; productive; teeming.

féconder, feh-kong-deh, *v* to fertilize.

fédéré, feh-deh-reh, *a* federate; federated.

fée, feh, *f* fairy.

féerie, feh-ree, *f* magical spectacle; enchantment; pantomime.

féerique, feh-reeck, *a*
magical; enchanting.

feindre, fang-dr, *v* to feign;
to pretend.

feint, e, fang, *pp* & *a*
feigned; pretended;
mock; feint.

feinte, fangt, *f* pretence;
sham.

fêler, fay-leh, *v* to crack
(glass, etc).

félicitations, feh-le-se-
tăh-se-ong, *f*
congratulation.

félicité, feh-le-se-teh, *fpl*
happiness.

féliciter, feh-le-se-teh, *v*
to congratulate; **se –,** to
be pleased (**de,** with).

félin, e, feh-lang, *a* feline.

félon, feh-long, *m* traitor;
a felonious; traitorous.

félonie, feh-lonn-ee, *f*
treason.

félure, fay-lEEr, *f* crack;
split.

femelle, fer-mell, *f* & *a*
female.

féminin, feh-me-nang, *m*
feminine gender.

féminin, e, feh-me-nang, *a*
feminine; womanly.

femme, făhmm, *f* woman;
wife; **–agent, –** ăh-
shahng, policewoman; **–
d'affaires, –** dăh-fair,
businesswoman. **– de
chambre, –** der shahng-

br, chambermaid; **– de
charge, –** der shăhrsh,
housekeeper; **– de
ménage, –** der meh-
năhsh, charwoman;
cleaning woman.

fémur, feh-mEEr, *m*
thighbone.

fenaison, fer-nay-zong, *f*
haymaking.

fendre, fahng-dr, *v* to
cleave; to split; to crack;
to break through; **se –,**
to split; to lunge.

fendu, e, fahng-dE, *pp* & *a*
slit; cleft; cloven.

fenêtre, fer-nay-tr, *f*
window.

fente, fahngt, *f* split,
crack; slot.

fer, fair, *m* iron;
horseshoe; sword; *pl*
fetters.

fer-blanc, fair-blahng, *m*
tin plate.

ferblanterie, fair-blahngt-
ree, *f* plate making.

férié, e, feh-re-eh, *a:* **jour
–, shoohr –,** holiday
(general); bank holiday.

fermage, fair-măhsh, *m*
tenant farming.

ferme, fairm, *f* farm; farm-
house; farming.

ferme, fairm, *adv* firmly;
hard; *a** firm; steady;
strong; stiff.

ferment, fair-mahng, *m*

leaven; ferment.

fermenter, fair-mahng-
teh, *v* to ferment; to
rise.

fermer, fair-meh, *v* to
shut; to close; **– à clef, –**
ăh kleh, to lock.

fermeté, fair-mer-teh, *f*
firmness; steadfastness;
strength.

fermeture, fair-mer-tEEr, *f*
closing; shutting.

fermeture éclair, fair-mer-
tEEr eh-klayr, *f* zip.

fermi-er, ére, fair-me-eh,
mf farmer.

fermoir, fair-mo'ăhr, *m*
clasp.

féroce,* feh-ross, *a*
ferocious; wild; very
strict.

ferraille, fay-rah'e *f* scrap-
iron; old iron.

ferrailleur, fay-rah'e-yer,
m scrap merchant.

ferré, e, fay-reh, *pp* & *a*
iron-shod; versed;
skilled.

ferrer, fay-reh, *v* to bind
with iron; to shoe; to
metal.

ferrure, fay-rEEr, *f* iron-
work; horseshoeing.

ferry-boat, feh-re-boht, *m*
car ferry.

fertile, fayr-teel, *a* fertile;
productive.

fervent, e, fair-vahng, *a*

fervent.

ferveur, fair-ver, *f* fervour.

fesse, fayss, *f* buttock; bottom.

fessée, fayss-eh, *f* spanking.

fesser, fayss-eh, *v* to spank.

festin, fayss-tang, *m* feast; banquet.

feston, fayss-tong, *m* festoon.

fête, fayt, *f* feast; festivity; festival; celebration; saint's day; birthday; public holiday.

fêter, fay-teh, *v* to celebrate; to observe a holiday; to welcome.

fétide, feh-teed, *a* fetid.

feu, fer, *m* fire; fireplace; passion; dash; – **d'artifice,** – dăhr-te-fiss, fireworks; – **de circulation,** – der-ser-kE-lăh-se-ong, *mpl* traffic lights.

feu, e, fer, *a* late; deceased.

feuillage, fer'e-yăhsh, *m* foliage.

feuille, fer'e, *f* leaf; sheet; paper.

feuilleter, fer'e-yer-teh, *v* to leaf through; to run through; to make puff pastry.

feuilleton, fer'e-yer-tong,

m serial; literary or scientific article; instalment.

feutre, fer-tr, *m* felt; felt hat.

fève, fayv, *f* bean.

février, feh-vre-eh, *m* February.

fiacre, fe-ăh-kr, *m* hackney-coach.

fiançailles, fe-ahng-sah'e, *fpl* engagement; betrothal.

fiancé, e, fe-ahng-seh, *mf* fiancé; fiancée.

fiancer (se), ser fe-ahng-seh, *v* to become engaged.

fibre, fee-br, *f* fibre; feeling; constitution.

ficeler, fis-leh, *v* to tie up; to do up.

ficelle, fe-sell, *f* string; twine; trick; long thin loaf of bread.

fiche, feesh, *f* index card; form; peg.

ficher, fee-sheh, *v* to drive in; to fix; to put; to give; **se –,** *fam* not to care less (**de,** about).

fichu, fee-shE, *m* small shawl; scarf.

fichu, e, fee-shE, *a* (*pop*) wretched; got up; done for; off-colour.

ficti-f, ve,* fick-teeff, *a* fictitious.

fiction, fick-se-ong, *f* invention; fiction.

fidèle,* fe-dell, *a* faithful; true; exact; *m* believer.

fidélité, fe-deh-le-teh, *f* fidelity; loyalty.

fiel, fe-ell, *m* gall; bitterness; hatred.

fiente, fe-ahngt, *f* dung; droppings.

fier (se), ser fe-eh, *v* to trust; to count on.

fi-er, ère,* fe-air, *a* proud; haughty.

fierté, fe-air-teh, *f* pride; dignity.

fièvre, fe-ay-vr, *f* fever; restlessness; excitement; **avoir de la –,** ăh-vo'ăh der lăh –, to have a temperature.

fifre, fee-fr, *m* fife; fifer.

figer, fe-sheh, *v* to congeal; to curdle; to fix.

figue, feeg, *f* fig.

figuier, fe-ghe-eh, *m* figtree.

figurant, fe-ghE-rahng, *m* walk on actor; extra.

figure, fe-ghEEr, *f* figure; form; face; countenance.

figuré, e, fe-ghE-reh, *a* figurative.

figurer, fe-ghE-reh, *v* to figure; to represent; **se –,** to imagine.

fil, feel, *m* thread; yarn;

wire; edge; grain; current.

filament, fe-lăh-mahng, *m* filament; thread; string.

filandreu-x, se, fe-lahng-drer, *a* stringy; tough.

filant, e, fe-lahng, *a* shooting (stars).

file, feel, *f* file; row; rank; line.

filer, fe-leh, *v* to spin; to draw; to shadow; to run; to slip away; to ladder (stocking); – **à l'anglaise,** – ăh lahng-glayz, to take French leave.

filet, fe-lay, *m* thread; net; snare; fillet; trickle.

filial, e, fe-le-ăhl, *a* filial.

filiale, fe-le-ăhl, *f* subsidiary company.

filigrane, fe-le-grăhn, *m* filigree; watermark.

fille, fee-ye, *f* girl; maid; daughter; servant; **petite –,** per-teet –, granddaughter.

filleul, e fee-yerl, *mf* godson; goddaughter.

film, feelm, *m* film; movie.

filon, fe-long, *m* lode; vein.

filou, fe-loo, *m* pickpocket; crook; cheat.

filouter, fe-loo-teh, *v* to cheat.

fils, feess, *m* son; boy; **petit –,** per-te –, grandson.

filtre, feel-tr, *m* filter; percolator; **bout –,** boo –, filter-tip (cigarette).

filtrer, feel-treh, *v* to filter; to strain.

fin, fang, *f* end; close; aim; purpose.

fin, e,* fang, *a* fine; thin; refined; sly; sharp (financier).

final, e,* fe-năhl, *a* final.

finalement, fe-năhl-mahng, *a* finally; lastly; at last.

finance, fe-nahngss, *f* finance.

financer, fe-nahngss-eh, *v* to lay out money.

financier, fe-nahngss-e-eh, *m* financier.

financi-er, ère,* fe-nahngss-e-eh, *a* financial.

finaud, e, fe-noh, *a* cunning.

finesse, fe-ness, *f* fineness; nicety; delicacy; acuteness.

fini, fe-ne, *m* finish.

fini, e, fe-ne, *pp* & *a* finished; consummate; finite.

finir, fe-neer, *v* to finish; to put an end to.

fiole, fe-ol, *f* phial; flask.

firmament, feer-măh-mahng, *m* firmament.

fisc, feessk, *m* treasury; tax authorities; revenue.

fissure, feess-EEr, *f* fissure; crack; rent.

fixation, feek-săh-se-ong, *f* fixing; fixation.

fixe,* feeks, *a* steady; firm; regular; fixed.

fixer, feek-seh, *v* to fix; to determine; to set, finalize.

fixité, feek-se-teh, *f* fixedness; stability.

flacon, flăh-kong, *m* flagon; small bottle; perfume bottle.

flageoler, flăh-sholl-eh, *v* to shake; to tremble.

flageolet, flăh-sholl-ay, *m* flageolet; small kidney bean.

flagrant, e, flăh-grahng, *a* flagrant; **en – délit,** ahng – deh-le, in the very act.

flair, flayr, *m* scent; keenness; flair.

flamant, flăh-mahng, *m* flamingo.

flambeau, flahng-boh, *m* torch; light.

flamber, flahng-beh, *v* to flame; to singe; to blaze.

flamboyer, flahng-bo'ăh-e-eh, *v* to blaze; to glow.

flamme, flăhmm, *f* flame.

flammèche, flăh-maish, *f*

spark; flake.

flan, flahng, *m* custard tart.

flanc, flahng, *m* flank; side; loins.

flancher, flahng-sheh, *v* to flinch; to give in.

flâner, flah-neh, *v* to stroll.

flanquer, flahng-keh, *v* to flank; to throw; to hit.

flaque, flăhck, *f* puddle.

flasque, flăhssk, *a* flabby; weak.

flatter, flăh-teh, *v* to flatter; to pat; to fawn upon.

flatteu-r, se,* flăh-ter, *mf* flatterer; *a* flattering.

flatuosité, flăh-tE-o-ze-teh, *f* flatulency.

fléau, fleh-oh, *m* scourge; curse.

flèche, flaish, *f* arrow; beam; spire.

fléchir, fleh-sheer, *v* to bend; to give way; to bow; to appease; to fall.

fléchissement, fleh-shiss-mahng, *m* bending; giving way.

flegme, flegm, *m* phlegm; impassivity; composure.

flemme, flem, *f* laziness.

flétrir, fleh-treer, *v* to wither; to fade; to brand; to disgrace; **se –,** to fade.

flétrissure, fleh-triss-EEr, *f* withering; stigma.

fleur, fler, *f* flower; blossom; prime; **à –de,** ăh – der on the surface of.

fleurir, fler-reer, *v* to flower; to bloom; to thrive; to adorn with flowers.

fleuve, flerv, *m* river.

flexion, fleck-se-ong, *f* bending.

flirter, fleer-teh, *v* to flirt.

flocon, flock-ong, *m* flake; flock.

floraison, flor-ay-zong, *f* flowering; blooming.

florissant, e, flor-iss-ahng, *a* flourishing.

flot, flo, *m* wave; stream; crowd; floating.

flottant, e, flot-ahng, *a* floating; wavering.

flotte, flot, *f* fleet; float; (*fam*) water; rain.

flotter, flot-teh, *v* to float; to waft; to waver; (*fam*) to rain.

flou, e, floo, *a* soft; hazy.

fluctuer, flEEk-tE-eh, *v* to fluctuate.

fluet, te, flE-ay, *a* slender; thin.

fluide, flE-eed, *m & a* fluid.

flûte, flEEt, *f* flute; long loaf of bread; tall

champagne glass.

flux, flE, *m* flux; flow.

fluxion, flEEk-se-ong, *f* inflammation; swelling.

foi, fo'ăh, *f* faith; trust; belief.

foie, fo'ăh, *m* liver.

foin, fo'ang, *m* hay.

foire, fo'ăhr, *f* fair.

fois, fo'ăh, *f* time; occasion; **une –,** EEn –, once; **à la –,** ăh lăh –, at once; both.

foison, fo'ăh-zong, *f* plenty; **à –,** ăh –, abundantly.

foisonner, fo'ăh-zonn-eh, *v* to abound.

fol, fol, *a* (see **fou**).

folâtre, foll-ah-tr, *a* playful; frolicsome.

folâtrer, foll-ah-treh, *v* to frolic.

folie, foll-ee, *f* madness; extravagance; mania.

folio, foll-e-o, *m* folio.

folle, foll, *f* mad woman.

follet, foll-ay, *a* merry; **feu –,** fer –, will o' the wisp.

foncé, e, fong-seh, *a* (colour) dark.

foncer, fong-seh, *v* to deepen; to sink; to dash; to rush (**sur,** at).

fonci-er, ère, fong-se-eh, *a* real estate; thorough; fundamental; **crédit –,** kreh-de –, mortgage loan society.

foncièrement, fong-se-air-mahng, *adv* thoroughly; fundamentally.

fonction, fongk-se-ong, *f* function; *pl* office; duties.

fonctionnaire, fongk-se-onn-air, *m* official; civil servant.

fonctionner, fongk-se-onn-eh, *v* to work; to be going; to function.

fond, fong, *m* bottom; foundation; depth; ground; substance; amount; à –, ăh –, thoroughly.

fondamental, e,* fong-dăh-mahng-tăhl, *a* fundamental.

fondant, fong-dahng, *m* fondant sweet.

fondant, e, fong-dahng, *a* melting.

fonda-teur, trice, fong-dăh-ter, *mf* & *a* founder.

fondé, e, fong-deh, *pp* & *a* founded; justified; – de pouvoir, – der poo-vo'ăhr, proxy.

fondement, fongd-mahng, *m* foundation; ground.

fonder, fong-deh, *v* to found; to build; to establish; se –, to be based on; to rely.

fonderie, fongd-ree, *f* foundry.

fondeur, fong-der, *m* founder.

fondre, fong-dr, *v* to melt; to cast; to disappear; to pounce.

fondrière, fong-dree-air, *f* quagmire; bog.

fonds, fong, *m* land; property; fund; funds; cash; *pl* securities; – de commerce, – der komm-airss, business.

fontaine, fong-tain, *f* fountain; spring; cistern.

fonte, fongt, *f* melting; casting; cast-iron; holster.

fonts, fong, *mpl* font; – baptismaux, – băh-tiss-moh, christening font.

footballeur, foot-boll-er, *m* footballer.

for, for, *m* – intérieur, – ang-teh-re-er, conscience.

forain, e, for-ang, *a* foreign; travelling (of theatre, fair etc).

forban, for-bahng, *m* pirate.

forçat, for-săh, *m* convict.

force, forss, *a* plenty of; *f* strength; power; ability.

forcé, e, for-seh, *pp* & *a* forced; affected; travaux –s, trăh-voh –, penal servitude.

forcément, for-seh-mahng, *adv* forcibly; necessarily.

forcené, e, for-ser-neh, *mf* & *a* maniac; mad; furious.

forcer, for-seh, *v* to force; to break open; to compel.

forer, for-eh, *v* to bore; to drill.

forestier, for-ayss-te-eh, *m* forester.

foret, for-ay, *m* drill; borer.

forêt, for ay, *f* forest.

forfait, for-fay, *m* crime; fine; forfeit; contract; à –, ăh –, by contract.

forfanterie, for-fahngt-ree, *f* bragging.

forge, forsh, *f* forge; ironworks.

forger, for-sheh, *v* to forge; to hammer; to make up; to form; se –, to imagine; to build up.

forgeron, for-sher-rong, *m* blacksmith.

formaliser (se), ser for-măh-le-zeh, to take offence (de, at).

formalité, for-măh-le-teh, *f* formality; ceremony.

format, for-măh, *m* size.

formation, fo-măh-se-ong, *f* training; formation; structure.

forme, form, *f* form;

shape; method; mould;
structure; *pl* manners.

formel, le,* for-mell, *a*
formal; express.

former, for-meh, *v* to
form; to create; to train;
se –, to take form.

formidable, for-me-dǎhbl,
a fearsome; *fam*
tremendous; super.

formulaire, for-mE-lair, *m*
form.

formule, for-mEEl, *f*
formula; prescription;
form.

formuler, for-mE-leh, *v* to
draw up; to express; to
prescribe.

fort, for, *adv* very;
extremely; *m* strongest
part; thickest; height;
fort; forte.

fort, e,* for, *a* strong;
stout; great; clever;
thick; loud; severe; hard.

forteresse, for-rayss, *f*
fortress.

fortifiant, e, for-te-fe-
ahng, *a* strengthening;
tonic.

fortifier, for-te-fe-eh, *v* to
strengthen; to fortify.

fortuit, e,* for-twee, *a*
accidental; fortuitous.

fortune, for-tEEn, *f*
fortune; chance; luck.

fortuné, e, for-tE-neh, *a*
fortunate; well-off.

fosse, fohss, *f* pit; hole;
grave.

fossé, fohss-eh, *m* ditch;
fig gulf.

fossette, fohss-ett, *f*
dimple.

fossile, foss-eell, *m & a*
fossil.

fossoyeur, fohss-o'ǎh-yer,
m grave-digger.

fou, folle, foo, fol, *mf*
lunatic; fool; (chess)
bishop; *a* * mad; foolish;
in love. (Before a
masculine noun
beginning with a vowel
or **h** mute, the
masculine is **fol,** fol,
instead of **fou**).

foudre, foo-dr, *f* lightning;
thunderbolt; thunder;
coup de –, coo der –,
love at first sight.

foudroyant, e, foo-dro'ǎh-
yahng, *a* crushing;
startling; terrifying.

foudroyé, foo-dro'ǎh-yeh,
pp thunderstruck.

foudroyer, foo-dro'ǎh-yeh,
v to strike by lightning.

fouet, foo-ay, *m* whip;
flogging.

fouetter, foo-ay-teh, *v* to
whip; to flog; to lash; to
whisk.

fougère, foo-**shair,** *f* fern.

fougue, foogh, *f* fire;
impetuosity; spirit.

fouille, foo'e-ye, *f*
excavation; digging.

fouiller, foo'e-yeh, *v* to
excavate; to dig; to
search; to rummage.

fouillis, foo'e-yee, *m*
confusion; jumble.

fouine, foo-een, *f* marten.

foulant, e, foo-lahng, *a*
pressing; crushing.

foulard, foo-lǎhr, *m* silk
handkerchief; scarf.

foule, fool, *f* crowd;
throng; mob.

fouler, foo-leh, *v* to press;
to tread; to trample; to
sprain.

foulure, foo-lEEr, *f* sprain.

four, foohr, *m* oven; kiln;
furnace; *fig* failure.

four à micro-ondes,
foohrǎhme-kroh-ongd *m*
microwave oven.

fourbe, foohrb, *m* cheat; *a*
tricky; deceitful.

fourberie, foohr-ber-ree, *f*
cheat; trickery.

fourbir, foohr-beer, *v* to
furbish.

fourbu, e, foohr-bE, *a*
foundered; tired out.

fourche, foohrsh, *f* fork;
pitch fork.

fourcher, foohr-sheh, *v* to
branch off; to dig with
pitch fork.

fourchette, foohr-shett, *f*
(table) fork; wishbone.

fourchu, e, foohr-shE, *a* forked; split.

fourgon, foohr-gong, *m* waggon; good's van.

fourgonner, foohr-gonn-eh, *v* to poke; to rake.

fourmi, foohr-me, *f* ant; **avoir des –s,** ah-vo'ăhr deh –, to have pins and needles (sensation).

fourmilière, foohr-me-le-air, *f* ant-hill.

fourmiller, foohr-mee-yeh, *v* to teem; to swarm (**de,** with).

fourneau, foohr-noh, *m* stove; furnace; boiler.

fournée, foohr-neh, *f* ovenful; batch; lot.

fourni, e, foohr-ne, *pp* & *a* furnished; thick; supplied.

fournir, foohr-neer, *v* to supply; to provide; to stock.

fournisseur, foohr-niss-er, *m* supplier; tradesman.

fourniture, foohr-ne-tEEr, *f* supply; *pl* fittings; supplies.

fourrage, foo-răhsh, *m* fodder.

fourré, foo-reh, *m* thicket.

fourré, e, foo-reh, *a* lined; fur-lined; filled (of chocolates, etc).

fourreau, foo-roh, *m* sheath; scabbard; cover.

fourrer, foo-reh, *v* to stuff; to cram; to line with fur.

fourreur, foo-rer, *m* furrier.

fourrière, foo-re-air, *f* pound.

fourrure, foo-rEEr, *f* fur.

fourvoyer, foohr-vo'ăh-yeh, *v* to lead astray.

foyer, fo'ăh-yeh, *m* hearth; home; centre; theatre entrance hall; foyer.

fracas, frăh-kah, *m* noise; din; crash; roar; fuss.

fracasser, frăh-kăhss-eh, *v* to shatter; to smash.

fraction, frăhck-se-ong, *f* fraction.

fractionner, frăhck-se-onn-eh, *v* to divide into fractions.

fracture, frăhck-tEEr, *f* fracture; breaking.

fracturer, frăhck-tE-reh, *v* to fracture; to break.

fragile,* frăh-sheel, *a* fragile; brittle; frail.

fragilité, frăh-she-le-teh, *f* brittleness; frailty.

fragment, frăhg-mahng, *m* fragment; piece; scrap.

frai, fray, *m* spawn; spawning.

fraîcheur, fray-sher, *f* freshness.

fraîchir, fray-sheer, *v* to freshen.

frais, fray, *mpl* expenses; charges; efforts.

frais, fraîche,* fray; fraysh, *a* fresh; cool; new.

fraise, frayz, *f* strawberry.

framboise, frahng-bo'ăhz, *f* raspberry.

franc, frahng, *m* franc.

franc,-he* frahng, frahngsh, *a* free; open; frank; genuine.

français, e, frahng-sseh, *a* French; *mf* Frenchman; Frenchwoman; *m* French language.

franchir, frahng-sheer, *v* to clear (an obstacle); to leap over; to overcome.

franchise, frahng-sheez, *f* freedom; openness; exemption.

franciser, frahng-se-zeh, *v* to gallicize.

franco, frahng-ko, *adv* free of charge; paid.

francophone, frahng-ko-fonn, *a* French-speaking.

frange, frahngsh, *f* fringe.

franglais, frahng-gleh, *m* mixture of French and English.

franquette, frahng-kett, *f*; **à la bonne –,** ăh lăh bonn –, without ceremony.

frappant, e, frăh-pahng, *a*

striking.

frapper, frăh-peh, v to strike; to knock; to rap; to ice; **se –,** to get flustered.

fraternel, le,* frăh-tair-nell, a brotherly; fraternal.

fraterniser, frăh-tair-ne-zeh, v to fraternize.

fraternité, frăh-tair-ne-teh, f brotherhood; fraternity.

fraude, frohd, f fraud; deceit; smuggling.

frauder, froh-deh, v to defraud; to smuggle.

frauduleu-x, se,* froh-dE-ler, a fraudulent.

frayer, fray-yeh, v to open up; to clear a path; to spawn.

frayeur, fray-yer, f fright; dread; terror.

fredaine, frer-dayn, f prank; escapade.

fredonner, frer-donn-eh, v to hum.

frégate, freh-găht, f frigate; frigate-bird.

frein, frang, m bit; bridle; brake; check.

freiner, freh-neh, v to brake; to put on the brakes.

frelater, frer-lăh-teh, v to adulterate.

frêle, frehl, a weak; frail.

frelon, frer-long, m hornet; drone.

frémir, freh-meer, v to shudder; to tremble; to rustle; to simmer.

frémissement, freh-miss-mahng, m shuddering; quivering; rustling.

frêne, frain, m ash tree.

frénésie, freh-neh-zee, f frenzy.

frénétique,* freh-neh-teeck, a frantic.

fréquemment, freh-kăh-mahng, adv frequently.

fréquence, freh-kahngss, f frequency; quickness.

fréquent, e, freh-kahng, a frequent.

fréquenter, freh-kahng-teh, v to frequent; to associate with.

frère, frair, m brother; friar.

fresque, fressk, f fresco.

fret, fray, m freight; chartering.

fréter, freh-teh, v to charter; to freight.

frétiller, freh-tee-yeh, v to frisk; to wriggle; to quiver.

freux, frer, m rook.

friable, fre-ăh-bl, a friable; crumbly (rock).

friand, e, fre-ahng, a fond of (delicacies).

friandise, fre-ahng-deez, f

delicacy; titbit.

fricandeau, fre-kahng-doh, m larded veal.

fricassée, fre-kăhss-eh, f fricassée.

fricasser, fre-kăhss-eh, v to fricassee; pop to fritter away.

friche, freesh, f wasteland.

fricot, fre-ko, m pop stew, ragout.

fricoter fre-kot-eh, v pop to cook.

friction, frick-se-ong, f friction; rub-down.

frictionner, frick-se-onn-eh, v to rub.

frigidaire, fre-she-dair, m refrigerator.

frigide, fre-sheed, a frigid.

frigo, fre-go, m fam fridge.

frigorifier, fre-gor-e-fe-eh, v to chill; to refrigerate.

frileu-x, se,* fre-ler, a chilly; sensitive to cold.

frime, freem, f sham.

frimousse, fre-mooss, f fam (little) face.

fringale, frang-găhl, f sudden hunger.

fringant, e, frang-ghang, a smart; lively.

fripé, e, fre-peh, pp & a crumpled.

friper, fre-peh, v to crumple; to crease.

fripi-er, ère, fre-pe-eh, mf secondhand clothes

dealer.

fripon, ne, fre-pong, *mf* &
a rogue; rascal; roguish.

frire, freer, *v* to fry.

frise, freez, *f* frieze.

friser, free-zeh, *v* to curl;
to touch; to skim.

frisson, friss-ong, *m*
shiver; shudder; thrill.

frissonner, friss-onn-eh, *v*
to shiver; to quiver; to
shudder.

frit, e, free, *pp* & *a* fried;
pop done for;
squandered.

frites, freet, *f* chips.

friture, free-tEEr, *f* frying;
dripping; fried fish;
crackling noises
(telephone, etc).

frivole, free-vol, *a*
frivolous.

froc, frock, *m* frock (of
monk, etc).

froid, fro'ăh, *m* cold;
coldness.

froid, e,* fro'ăh, *a* cold;
cool; indifferent.

froideur, fro'ăh-der, *f*
coldness; coolness;
indifference.

froissement, fro'ăhss-
mahng, *m* bruising;
crumpling; offence.

froisser, fro'ăhss-eh, *v* to
rumple; to offend; **se –,**
to take offence (**de,** at).

frôlement, frohl-mahng, *m*

light rubbing or
touching.

frôler, froh-leh, *v* to touch
slightly; to graze.

fromage, from-ăhsh, *m*
cheese.

froment, from-ahng, *m*
wheat.

froncer, frongss-eh, *v* to
frown; to gather
(sewing).

fronde, frongd, *f* sling;
catapult; rebellion.

front, frong, *m* forehead;
brow; impudence; front;
faire –, fair–, to face it.

frontière, frong-te-air, *f*
frontier; border.

fronton, frong-tong, *m*
pediment.

frottement, frot-mahng, *m*
rubbing; friction.

frotter, frot-eh, *v* to rub;
to polish.

frottoir, frot-o'ăhr, *m*
rubbing cloth; scrubbing
brush.

frou-frou, froo-froo, *m*
rustling.

frousse, froos, *f fam* fear;
avoir la –, ăh-vo'ăhr-lăh
–, to be scared.

fructifier, frEEk-te-fe-eh, *v*
to bear fruit.

fructueu-x, se,* frEEk-tE-
er, *a* fruitful; profitable.

frugal, e,* frE-ghăl, *a*
frugal.

fruit, frwee, *m* fruit;
offspring; profit.

fruiti-er, ère, frwee-te-eh,
mf greengrocer; *a* fruit-
bearing.

frusques, frEEsk, *fpl fam*
clothes; effects; togs.

fruste, frEEst, *a* defaced;
uncultivated.

frustrer, frEEs-treh, *v* to
frustrate; to defraud.

fugiti-f, ve, fE- she-teeff, *a*
fugitive; transient.

fugue, fEEgh, *f* fugue;
spree.

fuir, fweer, *v* to flee; to
shun; to leak; to escape.

fuite, fweet, *f* flight;
escape; evasion; leakage.

fulgurant, e, fEEl-ghE-
rahng, *a* flashing.

fumée, fE-meh, *f* smoke;
fume; dream.

fumer, fE-meh, *v* to
smoke; to steam; to
manure; to fertilise.

fumet, fE-may, *m* pleasant
smell of cooking; scent;
bouquet.

fumier, fE-me-eh, *m*
manure; dung-hill;
manure heap.

fumiger, fE-me-sheh, *v* to
fumigate.

fumiste, fE-meesst, *m*
heating engineer;
shirker.

fumivore, fE-me-vor, *a*

smoke-consuming.

fumoir, fE-mo'ăhr, *m* smoke house.

funambule, fe-nahng-bEEl, *m* tightrope walker.

funèbre, fE-nay-br, *a* funeral; mournful; dismal; funereal.

funérailles, fE-neh-rah'e, *fpl* funeral.

funeste, fE-naysst *a* fatal; disastrous.

funiculaire, fE-ne-kE-lair, *m & a* funicular.

fur, fEEr, *m*; **au — et à mesure,** oh – eh ăh merzEEr, in proportion; gradually.

furet, fE-ray, *m* ferret.

fureter, fEEr-teh, *v* to ferret out; to rummage.

fureur, fE-rer, *f* fury; rage; mania; **faire –,** fair – to be all the rage.

furibond, e, fE-re-bong, *a* furious.

furie, fE-ree, *f* fury; rage.

furieu-x, se,* fE-re-er, *a* furious; mad; raging.

furoncle, fE-rong-kl, *m* boil.

furti-f, ve,* fEEr-teeff, *a* furtive; stealthy.

fusain, fE-zang, *m* charcoal pencil.

fuseau, fE-zoh, *m* spindle; taper; *pl* ski pants.

fusée, fE-zeh, *f* fuse; rocket; barrel; spindleful.

fuselage, fEEz-lăhsh, *m* fuselage; body.

fuselé, e, fEEz-leh, *a* tapering.

fusible, fE-zee-bl, *m* fuse; fuse wire.

fusil, fE-ze, *m* rifle; gun.

fusillade, fE-zee-yăhd, *f* rifle fire; shooting; execution.

fusiller, fe-zee-yeh, *v* to shoot.

fusion, fE-ze-ong, *f* fusion; melting; amalgamation.

fusionner, fE-ze-onn-eh, *v* to amalgamate.

fût, fE, *m* cask; stock; shaft.

futaille, fE-tah'e, *f* cask; barrel.

futé, e, fE-teh, *a* sly; cunning; crafty, streetwise.

futile,* fE-teel, *a* futile; frivolous.

futilité, fE-te-le-teh, *f* futility; frivolousness.

futur, e, fE-tEEr, *m* future; future tense; *fam mf* intended (husband, wife); *a* future; to come.

fuyant, e, fwee-yahng, *a* fleeting; fleeing; receding.

fuyard, e, fwee-yăhr *mf* runaway; *a* runaway; fugitive; shy.

gabarit, găh-băh-re, *m* template; gauge; *fig* size.

gâcher, gah-sheh, *v* to mix; to make a mess of; to spoil.

gâchis, gah-she, *m* slush; mess; confusion; waste.

gaffe, găhf, *f* boat-hook; *fam* blunder; **faire une –** fair EEn –, to put one's foot in it; *fam* **faire –**, to take care.

gage, găhsh, *m* pledge; pawn; forfeit; *pl* wages.

gager, găh-sheh, to bet.

gageure, găh-sh EEr, *f* wager.

gagne-pain, găhn-yer-pang, *m* livelihood; bread winner.

gagner, găhn-yeh, *v* to earn; to win; to persuade; **se –**, to be catching.

gai, e, gheh, *a* gay; lively; cheerful.

gaiement, gheh-mahng, *adv* gaily.

gaieté, gheh-teh, *f* gaiety; cheerfulness.

gaillard, e, gah'e-yăhr, *a* strong; free; *m* chap.

gain, ghang, *m* gain; profit; advantage.

gaine, ghain, *f* sheath; case; corset; girdle.

galamment, găh-lăh-mahng, *adv* courteously.

galant, găh-lahng, *m* lover; ladies' man.

galant, e, găh-lahng, *a* courteous; polite; worthy.

galanterie, găh-lahngt-ree, *f* love affair; politeness.

galbe, găhlb, *m* curve; contour.

gale, găhl, *f* mange; scabies.

galère, găh-lair, *f* galley; *pl* penal servitude; **quelle –, kell –**, what an ordeal!

galerie, găhl-ree, *f* gallery; spectators.

galet, găh-lay, *m* pebble; shingle.

galetas, găhl-tah, *m* garret.

galette, găh-lett, *f* flat cake; biscuit.

galeu-x, se, găh-ler, *a* scabby; mangy.

gallicisme, găhl-le-sissm, *m* French idiom.

galoche, găh-losh, *f* galosh; clog.

galon, găh-long, *m* braid; *pl* stripes.

galop, găh-lo, *m* gallop; great haste; scolding.

galoper, găh-lop-eh, *v* to gallop; to run on.

galopin, găh-lop-ang, *m* urchin; scamp.

gambader, gahng-băh-deh, *v* to gambol.

gamelle, găh-mell, *f* lunch box; mess-tin.

gamin, e, găh-mang, *mf* kid; urchin; youngster.

gamme, găhm, *f* gamut; scale.

ganglion, gahng-gle-ong, *m* ganglion; glands;

swelling.

ganse, ghahngss, *f* cord; braid.

gant, ghahng, *m* glove; – **de toilette**, – der to'ăhlett, face-flannel.

garage, găh-răhsh, *m* garage.

garant, e, găh-rahng, *mf* guarantor; surety; bail.

garantie, găh-rahng-tee, *f* guarantee; warranty; safeguard.

garantir, găh-rahng-teer, *v* to guarantee; to secure; to protect.

garce, găhrss, *f fam* bitch.

garçon, găhr-song, *m* boy; lad; bachelor; waiter.

garçonnière, găhr-sonn-e-air, *f* bachelor pad.

garde, găhrd, *m* guard (person); watchman; warden.

garde, găhrd, *f* guard (service); care; keeping; watch; protection; nurse.

garder, găhr deh, *v* to guard; to watch; to look after; to keep.

garderie, găhr-der-re, *f* creche.

gardien, ne, găhr-de-ang, *mf* guardian; keeper; trustee; – **de but**, – der-bEt, goalkeeper.

gare, găhr, *f* station;

terminus.

gare! găhr, *interj* look out!

garenne, găh-rain, *f* warren.

garer, găh-reh, *v* to park (car); to shunt; **se** –, to get out of the way.

gargarisme, găhr-găh-reessm, *m* gargle.

garnement, găhr-ner-mahng, *m* scamp; rascal.

garnir, găhr-neer, *v* to furnish (**de**, with); to adorn; to line; to decorate; to garnish.

garnison, găhr-ne-zong, *f* garrison.

garniture, găhr-ne-tEEr, *f* set; trimming; ornaments; garnishing.

garrot, găh-roh, *f* tourniquet.

garrotter, găh-rott-eh, *v* to tie down; to garotte.

gars, gah, *m* lad.

gaspiller, găhss-pee-yeh, *v* to squander; to waste.

gastronome, găhss-tronn-omm, *m* gourmet.

gâteau, gah-toh, *m* cake.

gâter, gah-teh, *v* to spoil; to damage; to spoil (person).

gauche, gohsh, *f* left side; *a* left; clumsy.

gauchement, gohsh-mahng, *adv* awkwardly.

gauch-er, ère, goh-sheh, *a*

left-handed.

gaucherie, gohsh-ree, *f* awkwardness.

gaufre, ghoh-fr, *f* wafer; waffle.

gaule, gohl, *f* long pole; switch.

gave, găhv, *m* stream; torrent.

gaver(se), gahv-eh(se), *v* to stuff oneself (with food).

gavroche, găh-vrosh, *m* street urchin.

gaz, gahz, *m* gas; gaslight.

gaze, gahz, *f* gauze.

gazeu-x, se, gah-zer, *a* sparkling; fizzy.

gazomètre, gah-zo-met-tr, *m* gasometer.

gazon, gah-zong, *m* grass; turf; green.

gazouiller, găh-zoo'e-yeh, *v* to warble; to chirp.

geai, shay, *m* jay; jackdaw.

géant, e, sheh-ahng, *mf* & *a* giant; giantess; gigantic.

geindre, shang-dr, *v* to whimper; to whine.

gel, shehl, *m* frost; freezing.

gelée, sher-leh, *f* frost; jelly.

geler, sher-leh, *v* to freeze.

gémir, sheh-meer, *v* to groan; to lament; to grieve.

gémissement, sheh-miss-mahng, m groan; lamentation.

gemme, shaym, f gem; a **sel –,** sell –, rock salt.

gênant, e, shay-nahng, a troublesome; awkward; embarrassing.

gencive, shahng-seev, f gum.

gendarme, shahng-dăhrm, m policeman.

gendre, shahng-dr, m son-in-law.

gêne, shayn, f hindrance; embarrassment; financial difficulties.

gêner, shay-neh, v to hinder; to inconvenience; **se –,** to put oneself out.

général, e,* sheh-neh-răhl, a & mf general.

généreu-x, se,* sheh-neh-rer, a generous.

générosité, sheh-neh-roz-e-teh, f generosity.

genèse, sher-nayz, f genesis; Genesis; birth; origin.

genêt, sher-nay, m broom; furze.

génial, e,* sheh-ne-ăhl, a inspired; full of genius.

génie, sheh-nee, m genius; spirit; engineers.

genièvre, sher-ne-ay-vr, m juniper; gin.

génisse, sheh-neess, f heifer.

génitif, sheh-ne-teeff, m genitive case.

genou, sher-noo, m knee.

genre, shahng r, m kind; species; gender; manner; form.

gens, shahng, mf pl people.

gent, shahng, f race; tribe.

gentil, le, shahng-tee, a nice; kind; good.

gentilhomme, shahng-tee-yomm, m nobleman; gentleman.

gentillesse, shahng-tee-yess, f kindness.

gentiment, shahng-te-mahng, adv nicely.

géographie, sheh-ogh-răh-fee, f geography.

geôli-er, ère, shoh-le-eh, mf jailer.

géologue, sheh-oll-ogh, m geologist.

géométrie, sheh-omm-eh-tree, f geometry.

gérance, sheh-rahngss, f management.

gérant, e, sheh-rahng, mf manager; manageress; director.

gerbe, shairb, f sheaf; bundle; bunch; spray.

gercé, e, shair-seh, a chapped.

gerçure, shair-sEEr, f crack; chap (of hands).

gérer, sheh-reh, v to manage; to run.

germain, e, shair-mang, a german; first cousin.

germe, shairm, m germ; shoot; seed.

gérondif, sheh-rong-deeff, m gerund.

gésier, sheh-ze-eh, m gizzard.

geste, shesst, m gesture; motion; sign.

gesticuler, shess-te-kE-leh, v to gesticulate.

gestion, shess-te-ong, f management; administration.

gibecière, sheeb-se-air, f shoulder bag.

gibelotte, sheeb-lot, f rabbit stewed in wine.

gibet, shee-bay, m gallows.

gibier, she-be-eh, m game (birds, animals).

giboulée, she-boo-leh, f shower (rain).

giboyeu-x, se, she-bo'ah-yer, a well stocked with game.

gicler, she-kleh, v to spurt out.

gifle, shee-fl, f slap in the face.

gigantesque, she-gahng-tayssk, a gigantic.

gigot, she-go, m leg of lamb.

gigoter, shе-got-eh, v to kick about.

gilet, shе-lay, m waistcoat.

gingembre, shang-shahng-br, m ginger.

girafe, shе-răhf, f giraffe.

girofle, shе-rofl, m clove.

giroflée, shе-rof-leh, f wall-flower.

girouette, shе-roo-ayt, f vane; weathercock.

gisant, shе-zahng, a lying.

gisement, shеez-mahng, m layer; deposit; stratum.

gît, shе, v lies; **ci –, se –,** here lies.

gîte, sheet, m holiday home; shelter; lair; deposit; leg of beef.

givre, shee-vr, m (hoar) frost.

glabre, glah-br, a clean-shaven.

glace, glăhss, f ice; ice-cream; mirror; car window.

glacé, e, glăhss-eh, pp & a frozen; icy; glazed; crystallized.

glacial, e, glăhss-e-ăhl, a icy; freezing.

glacière, glăhss-e-air, f ice-box; refrigerator.

glaçon, glăhss-ong, m icicle; ice cube.

glaieul, glăh-yerl, m gladiolus; iris.

glaise, glayz, f clay.

glaive, glayv, m sword.

gland, glahng, m acorn; tassel.

glaner, glăh-neh, v to glean.

glapir, glăh-peer, v to yelp; to yap.

glas, glah, m knell; toll bell.

glissant, e, gliss-ahng, a slippery; sliding.

glisser, gliss-eh, v to slip; to slide; to glide; to touch lightly; **se –,** to creep.

globe, glob, m globe; ball; orb.

gloire, glo'ăhr, f glory; pride; halo.

glorieu-x, se, * glor-e-er, a glorious; proud; vainglorious.

glorifier, glor-e-fe-eh, v to glorify; **se –,** to glory (**de,** in).

gloser, glohz-eh, v to gloss; to criticise.

glousser, glooss-eh, v to cluck.

glouton, ne, gloo-tong, mf glutton; a gluttonous.

glu, glE, f birdlime.

gluant, e, glE-ahng, a sticky.

glycine, glee-seen, f wisteria.

gober, gob-eh, v to gulp down; to swallow; fam

to believe anything; to adore (someone).

godet, god-ay, m saucer (for painters); bowl.

godiche, godichon, ne, god-eesh, god-e-shong, mf & a ninny; awkward.

goéland, gweh-lahng, m seagull.

goélette, gweh-lett, f schooner.

gogo, gogh-o, adv phr fam; **à –, ăh –,** in abundance.

goguenard, e, gog-năhr, mf & a jeering; mocking.

goinfre, gwang-fr, m fam greedy guts.

golf, golf, m golf; golf course.

golfe, golf, m gulf.

gomme, gomm, f gum; rubber.

gond, gong, m hinge.

gondole, gong-dol, f gondola.

gondoler, gong-do-leh, v to warp; to buckle.

gonfler, gong-fleh, v to swell; to inflate.

gorge, gorsh, f throat; breast; pass; groove.

gorgée, gor-sheh, f mouthful; gulp; sip.

gorger, gor-sheh, v to gorge; to cram.

gosier, goz-e-eh, m throat; gullet.

gosse, goss, m fam kid; youngster.

goudron, goo-drong, m tar.

gouffre, goo-fr, m gulf; abyss.

goujat, goo-shāh, m lout.

goulot, goo-lo, m neck (of a bottle).

goulu, e, goo-lE, mf & a glutton; greedy.

goulûment, goo-lEE-mahng, adv greedily.

gourd, e, goohr, a numb.

gourde, goohrd, f gourd; flask; fam fool.

gourdin, goohr-dang, m cudgel.

gourer (se), ser goohr-eh, v fam to be mistaken.

gourmand, e, goohr-mahng, mf & a greedy; glutton.

gourmandise, goohr-mahng-deez, f greediness; love of food; pl delicacies.

gourmé, e, goohr-meh, pp & a stiff; starched; formal.

gourmet, goohr-may, m epicure; gourmet.

gousse, gooss, f pod; husk; shell; clove.

goût, goo, m taste; flavour; liking; style.

goûter, goo-teh, v to taste; to relish; to try; m afternoon tea.

goutte, goot, f drop; dram; sip.

gouttière, goo-te-air, f gutter; drain-pipe.

gouvernail, goo-vair-nah'e, m rudder; helm.

gouvernant, goo-vair-nahng, m ruler.

gouvernante, goo-vair-nahngt, f governess; housekeeper; nanny.

gouverne, goo-vairn, f guidance; rule of conduct.

gouvernement, goo-vair-ner-mahng, m government; management; steering.

gouverneur, goo-vair-ner, m governor; tutor.

grabat, grāh-bāh, m pallet.

grâce, grahss, f grace; mercy; thanks; charm.

gracier, grāh-se-eh, v to pardon.

gracieu-x, se,* grāh-se-er, a gracious; kind; courteous; pleasant; grateful.

grade, grāhd, m grade; rank; degree.

gradé, grāh-deh, m non-commissioned officer.

gradin, grāh-dang, m tier; step.

gradué, grāh-dE-eh, m graduated; graded.

graduel, le,* grāh-dE-ell, a gradual.

grain, grang, m grain; seed; corn; squall.

graine, grayn, f seed; berry; grain, – **de soja,** – der-soh-shāh, soya bean.

graissage, grayss-āsh, m greasing; lubrication.

graisse, grayss, f grease; fat; dripping; suet.

graisser, grayss-eh, v to grease.

graisseu-x, se, grayss-er, a greasy.

grammaire, grāh-mair, f grammar.

grammatical, e,* grāh-māh-te-kāhl, a grammatical.

gramme, grāhm, m gram(me).

grand, grahng, m greatness; grown-up.

grand, e,* grahng, a great; big; tall; grown up; much.

grandeur, grahng-der, f greatness; size; magnitude; dignity.

grandiose, grahng-de-ohz, m grandeur; a grand.

grandir, grahng-deer, v to grow; to increase; to exaggerate.

grandmère, grahng-mair, f grandmother.

grand-oncle, grahng-t'ong-kl, m great-uncle.

grand-père, grahng-pair, *m* grandfather.

grandroute, grahng-root, *f* main road.

grandtante, grahng-tahngt, *f* great-aunt.

grange, grahngsh, *f* barn.

granit, grăh-neet, or grăh-nee, *m* granite.

granule, grăh-nEEl, *m* granule.

graphique, grăh-feeck, *m* graph; diagram; *a** graphic.

graphite, grăh-feet, *m* graphite.

grappe, grăhp, *f* bunch; cluster.

grappin, grăh-pang, *m* grappling iron.

gras, grah, *m* fat part; (legs) calf; fat (on meat).

gras, se, grah, *a* fat; plump; greasy; rich.

grassement, grahss-mahng, *adv* plentifully.

grasseyer, grăhss-ay-yeh, *v* to roll one's r's.

grassouillet, te, grăhss-oo'e-yay, *a* plump; chubby.

gratification, grăh-te-fe-kăh-se-ong, *f* bonus.

gratifier, grăh-te-fe-eh, *v* to favour; to confer; to bestow.

gratin, grăh-tang, **au –**, oh

–, (cooked) cheese topped.

gratis, grăh-tiss, *pop* free; *adv* gratis.

gratitude, grăh-te-tEEd, *f* gratitude.

gratte-ciel, grăht-se-ell, *m* skyscraper.

gratter, grăh-teh, *v* to scratch; to scrape.

grattoir, grăh-to'ăhr, *m* scraper.

gratuit, e,* grăh-twee, *a* gratuitous; free.

gratuité, grăh-twee-teh, *f* gratuitousness.

grave,* grăhv, *a* grave; serious; deep.

gravelle, grăh-vell, *f* stones (in bladder, etc).

gravelure, grăhv-lEEr, *f* obscenity smut.

graver, grăh-veh, *v* to engrave.

graveur, grăh-ver, *m* engraver; etcher.

gravier, grăh-ve-eh, *m* gravel; grit.

gravir, grăh-veer, *v* to climb.

gravité, grăh-ve-teh, *f* gravity; weight; sedateness; seriousness.

graviter, grăh-ve-teh, *v* to gravitate.

gravure, grăh-vEEr, *f* engraving; print.

gré, greh, *m* will; liking;

thankfulness.

gredin, e, grer-dang, *mf* villain; scoundrel.

gréer, greh-eh, *v* to rig.

greffe, grayf, *m* record-office; registrar's office.

greffe, grayf, *f* graft; grafting.

greffier, gray-fe-eh, *m* registrar.

grêle, grayl, *f* hail; *a* slender; slim.

grêlon, gray-long, *m* hailstone.

grelot, grer-lo, *m* small round bell.

grelotter, grer-lot-eh, *v* to shiver.

grenade, grer-năhd, *f* grenade; pomegranate.

grenadier, grer-năh-de-eh, *m* grenadier; pomegranate tree.

grenadine, grer-năh-deen, *f* pomegranate syrup; grenadine.

grenat, grer-năh, *m* garnet; a garnet; red.

grenier, grer-ne-eh, *m* garret; granary; lumber-room.

grenouille, grer-noo'e-ye, *f* frog.

grenu, e, grer-nE, *a* grainy; (oil) clotted.

grès, gray, *m* sandstone; stoneware.

grève, grayv, *f* strand;

beach; strike.

grever, grer-veh, *v* to burden.

gréviste, greh-veesst, *m* striker.

gribouiller, gre-boo'e-yeh, *v* to scrawl; to scribble.

grief, gree-eff, *m* grievance; cause of complaint.

grièvement, gree-ayv-mahng, *adv* severely; grievously.

griffe, greeff, *f* claw; clutch; signature; stamp.

griffer, greeff-eh, *v* to scratch.

griffonner, greeff-onn-eh, *v* to scribble.

grignoter, green-yot-eh, *v* to nibble.

grigou, gre-goo, *m* miser; skinflint.

gril, gree, *m* grid; grill.

grillade, gree-yähd, *f* grilling; grilled meat.

grillage, gree-yähsh, *m* grilling; iron-railing; grate.

grille, gree-ye, *f* iron bar; iron gate; railing.

griller, gree-yeh, *v* to grill; to toast; to rail in.

grillon, gree-yong, *m* cricket.

grimace, gree-mähss, *f* grimace; wry face.

grimper, grang-peh, *v* to climb; to creep up.

grincement, grangss-mahng, *m* gnashing; grating; grinding (of teeth).

grincer, grang-seh, *v* to grate; to gnash; to creak.

grincheu-x, se,* grang-sher, *a* grumpy; crabby.

gringalet, grang-gäh-lay, *m* skinny man.

grippe, greep, *f* influenza; flu.

gripper, greep-eh, *v* to gripe; to clutch; to snatch up.

grippe-sou, greep-soo, *m* skinflint; miser.

gris, gre, *m* grey.

gris, e, gre, *a* grey; dull.

grisâtre, gre-zah-tr, *a* greyish.

griser, gre-zeh, *v fam* to make tipsy; to excite.

grisonner, gre-zonn-eh, *v* to go grey.

grive, greev, *f* thrush.

grogner, gronn-yeh, *v* to grunt; to growl; to grumble.

grognon, gronn-yong, *a & mf f inv* grumpy; grumbler.

groin, grwang, *m* snout.

grommeler, gromm-leh, *v* to grumble; to mutter.

grondement, grongd-mahng, *m* growling; snarl; rumbling.

gronder, grong-deh, *v* to growl; to roar; to rumble; to scold.

gros, groh, *m* main part; bulk; wholesale.

gros, groh, *adv* much; a great deal; **en –,** wholesale.

gros, se,* groh, *a* big; large; fat; coarse; pregnant; **– lot, – lo** *m* jackpot.

groseille, groh-zay'e, *f* currant; **– à maquereau, – äh mähck-roh,** gooseberry.

grossesse, gross-ayss, *f* pregnancy.

grosseur, gross-er, *f* size; tumour.

grossi-er, ère,* gross-e-eh, *a* coarse; rough; vulgar.

grossièreté, gross-e-air-teh, *f* coarseness; rudeness; rude thing.

grossir, gross-eer, *v* to enlarge; to put on weight.

grossissant, e, gross-iss-ahng, *a* magnifying.

grotesque, grot-essk, *m* grotesque; *a** grotesque; absurd.

grotte, grot, *f* grotto.

grouiller, groo'e-yeh, *v* to stir; to swarm; to rumble.

groupe, groop, *m* group; clump; cluster.

groupement, groop-mahng, *m* group.

grouper, groo-peh, *v* to group.

gruau, grE-oh, *m* wheat flour; oatmeal; gruel.

grue, grE, *f* crane.

grumeau, grE-moh, *m* clot; lump; curd.

gruyère, grE-yair, *m* Gruyère cheese.

guenille, gher-nee-ye, *f* rag; tattered garment.

guêpe, ghayp, *f* wasp.

guêpier, ghay-pe-eh, *m* wasps' nest.

guère (ne...), ner ...ghair, *adv* hardly; not much.

guéret, gheh-ray, *m* fallow land.

guéridon, gheh-re-dong, *m* pedestal table.

guérir, gheh-reer, *v* to cure; to heal; to recover.

guérison, gheh-re-zong, *f* cure; recovery.

guerre, ghair, *f* war; strife.

guerri-er, ère, ghair-e-eh, *mf & a* warrior; warlike; martial.

guerroyer, ghair-o'ăh-yeh, *v* to wage war.

guet, gay, *m* watch; **au –**, oh –, on the watch.

guet-apens, gay t'ăh-pahng, *m* ambush; trap.

guetter, ghay-teh, *v* to watch for; to look for.

gueule, gherl, *f* mouth (of animal); jaws; *pop* mug; **– de bois, –** der-boo'ăh, hangover; **avoir la – de bois**, ăh-vo'ăhr lah – der bo'ăh, *v* to have a hangover.

gueuler, gher-leh, *v fam* to bawl.

gueu-x, se, gher, *a* beggarly; wretched; *mf* beggar; tramp.

gui, ghe, *m* mistletoe.

guichet, ghe-shay, *m* ticket office; box office; booking office; pay desk; wicket; turnstile.

guide, gheed, *m* guide; guide-book; *f* rein.

guider, ghe-deh, *v* to guide.

guidon, ghe-dong, *m* flag; handlebars.

guigne, gheen-yer, *f* black cherry; bad luck.

guignol, gheen-yol, *m* puppet show; Punch & Judy show.

guillemet, gheel-may, *m* inverted comma.

guillotine, ghee-yot-een, *f* guillotine.

guimauve, ghe-mohv, *f* marshmallow.

guindé, e, ghang-deh, *pp & a* hoisted; strained; stiff.

guinée, ghe-neh, *f* guinea.

guinguette, ghang-gayt, *f* open-air café; dance hall.

guirlande, gheer-lahngd, *f* garland; wreath.

guise, gheez, *f* way; humour; fancy; **à votre –**, ăh voh-tr –, as you wish.

guitare, ghe-tăhr, *f* guitar.

gymnase, sheem-nahz, *m* gymnasium; gym.

gynécologue, shee-nehck-o-log, gynaecologist.

There is no liaison with or elision before words marked thus; §

§**ha!** ăh, *interj* ha! ah!

habile,* ăh-beell, *a* skillful; clever; qualified.

habileté, ăh-beell-teh, *f* skillfulness; ability; cleverness.

habillement, ăh-bee-yer-mahng, *m* clothing; suit of clothes.

habiller, (s') săh-bee-yeh, *v* to get dressed.

habit, ăh-be, *m* coat; dress-coat; tails; *pl* clothes.

habitant, e, ăh-be-tahng, *mf* inhabitant; resident; occupant; inmate.

habitation, ăh-be-tăh-se-ong, *f* place of residence; dwelling; abode; house.

habiter, ăh-be-teh, *v* to inhabit; to live in; to reside.

habitude, ăh-be-tEEd, *f* habit; use; practice; **comme d', –,** komm d' –, as usual.

habitué, e, ăh-be-tE-eh, *mf* regular customer.

habituel, le,* ăh-be-tE-ell, *a* customary.

habituer, ăh-be-tE-eh, *v* to accustom; to inure.

§**hache,** ăhsh, *f* axe; hatchet.

§**hacher,** ăh-sheh, *v* to chop; to cut to pieces; to mince (meat, etc).

§**hachette,** ăh-shett, *f* hatchet.

§**hachis,** ăh-she, *m* hash; minced meat.

§**hagard, e,** ăh-găhr, *a* haggard.

§**haie,** ay, *f* hedge; fence; line; row.

§**haillon,** ah'e-yong, *m* rag; tatter.

§**haine,** ain, *f* hatred; hate; spite.

§**haineu-x, se,*** ay-ner, *a* hateful; spiteful.

§**haïr,** ăh'e-eer, *v* to hate.

§**haïssable,** ăh-eess-ăh-bl, *a* odious; hateful.

§**halage,** ah-lăhsh, *m* towing.

§**hâlé, e,** ah-leh, *a* tanned; sunburnt.

haleine, ăh-lain, *f* breath; wind.

§**haler,** ah-leh, *v* to tow; to brown; to tan.

§**haleter,** ăhl-teh, *v* to pant.

§**halle,** ăhl, *f* market; market-place.

§**hallebarde,** ăhl-băhrd, **il pleut des –,** ill pler day –, it rains cats and dogs.

§**hallier,** ăh-le-eh, *m* thicket.

hallucination, ăhl-lE-se-năh-se-ong, *f* hallucination.

§**halte,** ăhlt, *f* halt; stop; halting-place; **–là! –** lăh, stop!

§**haltère,** ăhl-tair, *f* dumb-bell.

§**haltèrophile,** ăhl-teh-rofe-lee, f weight-lifting.

§**hamac**, ăh-măhck, m hammock.

hamburger, ahng-boor-gair m hamburger.

§**hameau**, ăh-moh, m hamlet.

hameçon, ăhm-song, m fish-hook; fig bait.

§**hampe**, ahngp, f staff; handle.

§**hanche**, ahngsh, f hip; haunch.

§**handicapé, e,** ang-de-kăh-peh, disabled (person); handicapped; **les –s,** leh –, pl the handicapped; the disabled.

§**hangar**, ahng-găhr, m shed; outhouse; warehouse; hangar.

§**hanneton**, ăhn-tong, m may-bug.

§**hanter**, ahng-teh, v to frequent; to haunt.

§**happer**, ăh-peh, v to snap up; to snatch; to catch.

§**harangue**, ăh-rahng-gh, f harangue; address; speech.

§**haras**, ăh-rah, m stud farm.

§**harasser**, ăh-răhss-eh, v to tire out.

§**harceler**, ăhr-ser-leh, v to harass; to plague.

§**harde**, ăhrd, f leash; pl old clothes.

§**hardi, e,** ăhr-de, a bold; impudent.

§**hardiment**, ăhr-de-mahng, adv boldly.

§**hardiesse**, ăhr-de-ess, f boldness; assurance; impudence.

§**hareng**, ăh-rahng, m herring.

§**hargneu-x, se**, ăhrn-yer, a surly; peevish.

§**haricot**, ăh-re-ko, m kidney-bean; **–vert, –** vair, French bean.

harmonie, ăhr-monn-ee, f harmony; harmonics; agreement.

harmonieu-x, se,* ăhr-monn-e-er, a harmonious.

§**harnachement**, ăhr-năhsh-mahng, m harnessing; harness.

§**harnais**, ăhr-nay, m harness.

§**haro**, ăh-ro, m hue and cry; outcry.

§**harpagon**, ăhr-păh-gong, m fam miser.

§**harpe**, ăhrp, f harp.

§**harpon**, ăhr-pong, m harpoon.

§**hasard**, ăh-zăhr, m luck; chance; risk.

§**hasardeu-x, se,*** ăh-zăhr-der, a hazardous; unsafe.

§**hâte**, aht, f haste; hurry.

§**hâter**, ah-teh, v to hasten; to urge on; to expedite.

§**hâti-f, ve,*** ah-teeff, a forward; early; hasty.

§**hausse**, ohss, f block; rise.

§**hausser**, ohss-eh, v to arise; to lift; to increase; to advance; **– les épaules, –** leh zeh-pohl, to shrug one's shoulders.

§**haussier**, ohss-e-eh, m (Stock Exchange) bull.

§**haut**, oh, m height; summit.

§**haut**, oh, adv high up; far back; loudly.

§**haut, e,*** oh, a high; lofty; tall; erect; great.

§**hautain, e,*** oh-tang, a haughty.

§**hautbois**, oh-bo'ăh, m oboe.

§**hauteur**, oh-ter, f height; eminence; haughtiness.

§**haut-parleur**, oh-pahr-ler, m loudspeaker; amplifier.

§**havane**, ăh-văhn, m Havana cigar.

§**hâve**, ahv, a wan; emaciated.

§**havre**, ah-vr, m harbour.

§**havresac**, ah-vrer-săhck, m knapsack.

hayon, ăhy-yong, m auto

hatchback; tail-gate.

§**hé!** eh, *interj* hey! stop that!

hebdomadaire, ehb-domm-äh-dair, *a* weekly; *fam* weekly paper.

héberger, eh-bair-sheh, *v* to lodge; to offer a home to.

hébété, e, eh-beh-teh, *a* dazed; vacant.

hébreu, eh-brer, *m* & *a* Hebrew.

hectare, eck-tähr, *m* hectare (100 ares, 2.47 English acres).

§**hein!** ang, *interj* eh! what!

hélas! eh-lähss, *interj* alas!; *adv* sadly.

§**héler,** eh-leh, *v* to hail.

hélice, eh-leess, *f* propeller.

hélicoptère, eh-li-cop-tair, *m* helicopter.

hémisphère, eh-miss-fair, *m* hemisphere.

hémorragie, eh-mor-äh-shee, *f* haemorrhage.

hémorroïdes, eh-mor-o-eed, *fpl* piles.

§**hennir,** äh-neer or eh-neer, *v* to neigh.

herbage, air-bähsh, *m* grass; pasture.

herbe, airb, *f* grass; herb; weed.

herboriste, air-bor-eest, *m* herbalist.

§**hère,** air, *m* wretch; poor devil.

héréditaire, eh-reh de-tair, *a* hereditary.

hérédité, eh-reh-de-teh, *f* heredity.

hérésie, eh-reh-zee, *f* heresy.

§**hérisser,** eh-riss-eh, *v* to bristle (up); **se –,** to stand on end (of hair).

§**hérisson,** eh-riss-ong, *m* hedgehog.

héritage, eh-re-tähsh, *m* inheritance; heritage.

hériter, eh-re-teh, *v* to inherit; *fam* to get.

hériti-er, ère, eh-re-te-eh, *mf* heir; heiress.

hermétique,* air-meh-teeck, *a* hermetic.

hermine, air-meen, *f* ermine.

§**hernie,** air-nee, *f* hernia; rupture.

héroïne, eh-ro-een, *f* heroine; heroin.

héroïque,* eh-ro-eeck, *a* heroic.

§**héron,** eh-rong, *m* heron.

§**héros,** eh-ro, *m* hero.

hésiter, eh-ze-teh, *v* to hesitate.

hétéroclite, eh-teh-rock-leett, *a* heterogeneous.

hétérosexuel, le, eh-teh-ro-seck-sE-ell *a*, *mf* heterosexual.

§**hêtre,** ay-tr, *m* beech.

heure, er, *f* hour; time; moment; o'clock.

heureu-x, se,* er- rer, *a* happy; lucky; successful; favourable; blessed.

§**heurt,** er, *m* shock; blow; collision.

§**heurter,** er-teh, *v* to knock; to jostle; to offend.

hiberner, e-bair-neh, *v* to hibernate.

§**hibou,** e-boo, *m* owl.

§**hic,** eeck, *m fam* rub; difficulty.

§**hideu-x, se,*** e-der, *a* hideous.

hier, e-air, *adv* yesterday.

§**hi-fi,** e-fe *a* & *f* hi-fi.

hilarité, e-läh-re-teh, *f* hilarity; mirth.

hippique, ip-peeck, *a* of horses; racing.

hippocampe, ip-pock-ahngp, *m* sea horse.

hippodrome, ip-pod-romm, *m* hippodrome; circus; racecourse.

hirondelle, e-rong-dell, *f* swallow.

§**hisser,** iss-eh, *v* to hoist.

histoire, iss-to'ähr, *f* history; story; tale; fib; trifle; important matter; **faire des –s,** fair deh-z

–, to make a fuss.

historien, iss-tor-e-ang, *m* historian.

historique,* iss-tor-eeck, *a* historical.

§**hi-tech,** e-tek *a* & *m* hi-tech.

hiver, e-vair, *m* winter.

hiverner, e-vair-neh, *v* to winter; to go into winter quarters.

§**hocher,** osh-eh, *v* to shake; to toss; to nod.

§**hochet,** osh-eh, *m* child's rattle.

§**holà!** oll-ăh, *interj* hi!

holocauste, oll-o-kohst *m* holocaust.

§**homard,** omm-ăhr, *m* lobster.

homicide, omm-ee-seed, *m* murder; *mf* murderer; *a* murderous.

hommage, omm-ăhsh, *m* homage; token; *pl* respects.

homme, omm, *m* man; *fam* husband; – d'affaires, – dăh-fair, *m* businessman.

homosexuel, le, omm-o-secks-Eél, *a* & *m* gay; homosexual.

honnête, onn-ayt, *m* honesty; *a** honest; decent; respectable.

honnêteté, onn-ayt-teh, *f* honesty; decency.

honneur, onn-er, *m* honour; credit; respect.

honorable,* onn-or-ăh-bl, *a* honourable; respectable; proper; creditable.

honoraire, onn-or-air, *a* honorary.

honoraires, onn-or-air, *mpl* fee; fees.

honorer, onn-or-eh, *v* to honour (**de,** with).

honorifique, onn-or-e-feeck, *a* honorary.

§**honte,** ongt, *f* shame; disgrace; scandal.

§**honteu-x, se,*** ong-ter, *a* shameful; ashamed; bashful.

hôpital, op-e-tăhl, *m* hospital.

§**hoquet,** ock-ay, *m* hiccup; gasp.

§**horde,** ord, *f* horde.

horaire, or-air, *m* timetable (rail, etc).

horizon, or-e-zong, *m* horizon.

horizontal, e,* or-e-zong-tăhl, *a* horizontal.

horloge, or-losh, *f* clock.

horloger, or-losh-eh, *m* watchmaker, clock-maker.

horlogerie, or-losh-ree, *f* watchmaking; **mouvement d'–,** moov-mahng d –, clockwork.

§**hormis,** or-me, *adv* but; except.

hormone, or-monn *f* hormone.

horreur, or-rer, *f* horror; frightful thing; dread; awe; abhorrence.

horrible,* or-ree-bl, *a* horrible; awful; shocking.

horripilant, or-ree-pee-lahng, *a* hair-raising; *fam* exasperating.

§**hors,** or, *prep* out; beyond; past; except; – de combat, – der kong-băh, disabled.

§**hors-d'œuvre,** or der-vr, *m* hors d'oeuvre; starter.

horticulteur, or-te-kEEl-ter, *m* horticulturist.

hospice, oss-peess, *m* asylum, hospice.

hospitali-er, ère,* oss-pe-tăh-le-eh, *a* hospitable.

hospitalité, oss-pe-tăh-le-teh *f* hospitality.

hostie, oss-tee, *f* victim; host (holy bread).

hostile,* oss-steel, *a* hostile; adverse.

hôte, oht, *m* host; guest.

hôtel, oh-tell, *m* hotel; mansion; town house.

hôteli-er, ère, oh-ter-le-eh, *mf* hotelier; landlord.

hôtellerie, oh-tell-ree, *f*

inn; hostelry.

hôtesse, oh-tess, *f* hostess; landlady; guest; **– de l'air, –** der lair, air hostess.

§**hotte,** ott, *f* basket; hood (fireplace, etc).

§**houblon,** oo-blong, *m* hop; hops.

§**houille,** oo'e-ye, *f* coal.

§**houillère,** oo'e-yair, *f* coal-mine; colliery; *a* coalbearing.

§**houle,** ool, *f* surge; swell (of sea).

§**houleu-x, se,** oo-ler, *a* swelling; rough.

§**houppe,** oop, *f* tuft; powder-puff.

§**hourra!** oo-räh, *interj* hurrah!.

§**houspiller,** oos-pee-yeh, *v* to mob; to handle roughly; to abuse.

§**housse,** ooss, *f* dust-sheet.

§**houx,** oo, *m* holly.

§**hublot,** E-bloh, *m* porthole.

§**huer,** E-eh, *v* to hoot; to boo.

huile, weel, *f* oil.

huis, wee, m: **à – clos,** äh – kloh, behind closed doors; *jur* in camera.

huissier, weess-e-yeh, *m* usher; bailiff.

§**huit,** weet, *a* eight;

eighth.

§**huitaine,** weet-ain, *f* about eight; a week.

§**huitième,** weet-e-aym, *m* & *a* eighth.

huître, wee-tr, *f* oyster.

humain, e,* E-mang, *a* human; humane.

humains, E-mang, *mpl* mankind.

humanité, E-mäh-ne-teh, *f* humanity; human nature; *pl* humanities; humankind; mankind.

humble,* ung-bl, *a* humble; lowly.

humecter, E-meck-teh, *v* to moisten.

humer, E-meh, *v* to inhale; to sip up.

humeur, E-mer, *f* humour; temper; mood; fancy.

humide * E-meed, *a* humid; damp; moist.

humiliant, e, E-me-le-ahng, *a* humiliating.

humilier, E-me-le-eh, *v* to humble.

humoriste, E-mor-isst, *m* humorist.

§**huppé, e,** E-peh, *a* crested; *fam* best; well off.

§**hurler,** EEr-leh, *v* to howl; to yell.

hutte, EEt, *f* hut; shed.

hybride, e-breed, *a* hybrid.

hydravion, e-dräh-ve-ong,

m seaplane.

hydrogène, e-drosh-ain, *m* hydrogen.

hyène, e-ain, *f* hyena.

hygiène, e-she-ain, *f* hygiene.

hymne, eemn, *m* hymn; anthem.

hypermarché, e-pair-mähr-sheh *m* hypermarket.

hypertension, e-pair-tahng-se-ong, *f* hypertension; high blood pressure.

hypnotiser, ep-not-e-zeh, *v* to hypnotize.

hypocrisie, e-pock-re-zee, *f* hypocrisy.

hypocrite, e-pock-reet, *m* hypocrite; *a** hypocritical.

hypothécaire, e-pot-eh-kair, *a* mortgage.

hypothèque, e-pot-eck, *f* mortgage.

hypothèse, e-pot-ayz, *f* hypothesis.

hystérique, ees-teh-reeck, *a* hysterical.

ici, e-se, *adv* here; **par –**, păhr –, this way.

idéal, e-deh-ăhl, *m* ideal; *a** ideal.

idée, e-deh, *f* idea; notion; plan; outline; opinion.

identifier, e-dah*ng*-te-fe-eh, *v* to identify.

identique,* e-dah*ng*-teeck, *a* identical.

identité, e-dah*ng*-te-teh, *f* identity.

idiome, e-de-omm, *m* dialect; language.

idiot, e, e-de-o, *mf* idiot; *a* idiotic.

idiotie, e-de-oss-ee, *f* idiocy.

idiotisme, e-de-o-tissm, *m* idiom.

idolâtre, e-doll-ah-tr, *m* idolater; *a* idolatrous.

idolâtrer, e-doll-ah-treh, *v* to idolize.

idole, e-dol, *f* idol.

idylle, e-deel, *f* idyl.

if, eef, *m* yew.

ignare, een-yăhr, *mf* ignoramus.

ignoble, een-yob-l, *a* ignoble; base.

ignominie, een-yomm-e-nee, *f* ignominy.

ignominieu-x, se,* een-yomm-een-e-er, *a* ignominious.

ignorant, e, een-yor-ahng, *mf* ignorant person; *a* ignorant.

ignoré, e, een-yor-eh, *a* unknown; hidden; secret.

ignorer, een-yor-eh, *v* to be ignorant of; not to know.

il, ill, *pron* he; it; there; *pl*

they; – **y a**, – e ăh, there is; there are.

île, eel, *f* island.

illégal, e,* ill-leh-găhl, *a* illegal.

illégitime,* ill-leh-she-teem, *a* illegitimate; unlawful.

illettré, e, ill-lay-treh, *a* illiterate.

illicite,* ill-le-seet, *a* unlawful; illegal.

illimité, ill-le-me-teh, *a* unlimited.

illisible,* ill-le-zee-bl, *a* illegible.

illogique,* ill-losh-eeck, *a* illogical.

illumination, ill-lE-me-năh-se-ong, *f* illumination.

illuminé, e, ill-lE-me-neh, *mf* visionary; *a* illuminated; enlightened.

illusion, ill-lE-ze-ong, *f* illusion; delusion.

illusoire, ill-lE-zo'ăhr, *a* illusory; fallacious.

illustration, ill-lEs-trăh-se-ong, *f* illustration; celebrity.

illustre, ill-lEEs-tr, *a* illustrious.

illustré, e, ill-lEEs-treh, *a* illustrated; *m* magazine (with pictures).

illustrer, ill-lEs-treh, *v* to

illustrate.

îlot, ee-lo, *m* tiny island; plot; block (of houses).

image, e-măhsh, *f* image; picture; likeness.

imaginaire, e-măh-shenair *a* imaginary.

imaginati-f, ve, e-măhshe-năh-teef *a* imaginative.

imagination, e-măh-shenăh-se-ong, *f* imagination; **plein,e d'–, pland –,** *a* imaginative.

imaginer, e-măh-she-neh, *v* to imagine; to conceive; to contrive; **s' –,** to imagine.

imbécile, ang-beh-seell, *mf* idiot; fool; *a** imbecile; silly.

imberbe, ang-bairb, *a* beardless.

imbiber, ang-be-beh, *v* to soak; to imbibe.

imbroglio, ang-bro'e-lee-o, *m* confusion.

imbu, e, ang-bE, *a* imbued (**de,** with).

imbuvable, ang-bE-văh-bl, *a* undrinkable.

imiter, e-me-teh, *v* to imitate; to mimic.

immaculé, e, im-măh-kE-leh, *a* immaculate.

immanquable,* angmahng-kăh-bl, *a*

infallible.

immatériel, le, im-măhteh-re-ell, *a* immaterial; intangible.

immatriculer, im-măhtre-kE-leh, *v* to register (car, etc); to enrol.

immédiat, e,* im-meh-deăh, *a* immediate.

immensément, im-mahngseh-mahng, *adv* immensely.

immensité, im-mahng-seteh, *f* immensity.

immeuble, im-mer-bl, *m* real estate; building; block of flats.

immigration, im-me-grăhse-ong *f* immigration.

immiscer (s'), sim-misseh, *v* to meddle (**dans,** with, in).

immobile, im-mob-eell, *a* motionless; immovable.

immobili-er, ère, im-mobe-le-eh, *a* of real estate; **agence –ère,** ăh-shahngs –, estate agency.

immobiliser, im-mob-e-lezeh, *v* to realize; to fix.

immodéré, e, im-mod-ehreh, *a* immoderate.

immodérément, im-modeh-reh-mahng, *adv* immoderately.

immodeste, im-mod-esst, *a* immodest.

immonde, im-mongd, *a*

unclean; foul.

immoral, e,* im-mor-ăhl, *a* immoral.

immortel, le,* im-mortell, *a* immortal.

immuable,* im-mE-ăh-bl, *a* immutable.

immuniser, im-mE-ne-zeh, *v* to immunize.

immunité, im-mE-ne-teh, *f* immunity; exemption.

immutabilité, im-mE-tăhbe-le-teh, *f* immutability.

impair, e, ang-pair, *a* odd; uneven.

impardonnable, ang-păhrdonn-ăh-bl, *a* unforgivable.

imparfait, ang-păhr-fay, *m* imperfect tense; *a** imperfect.

impartial, e,* ang-păhr-seăhl, *a* impartial.

impasse, ang-pahss, *f* blind-alley; "no through road"; dead end; dilemma; fix.

impassible,* ang-păhss-eebl, *a* impassive; unmoved.

impatiemment, ang-păhsse-ăh-mahng, *a* impatiently; eagerly.

impatient, e, ang-păhss-eahng, *a* impatient; eager; fidgety.

impatienter, ang-păhss-e-

ahng-teh, v to make
impatient; to provoke; s'
–, to fret.

impayable, ang-pay-yăh-
bl, a invaluable; *fam*
very funny.

impénétrable,* ang-peh-
neh-trăh-bl, a
inscrutable;
impenetrable.

impératif, ang-peh-răh-
teeff, m imperative
mood.

impérati-f, ve,* ang-peh-
răh-teeff, a imperative.

impératrice, ang-peh-răh-
treess, f empress.

imperceptible,* ang-pair-
sep-tee-bl, a
imperceptible.

imperfection, ang-pair-
feck-se-ong, f
imperfection.

impérial, e,* ang-peh-re-
ăhl, a imperial.

impériale, ang-peh-re-ăhl,
f outside; top deck (of a
bus); a imperial.

impérieu-x, se,* ang-peh-
re-er, a imperious;
urgent.

impérissable,* ang-peh-
riss-ăh-bl, a
imperishable.

imperméable, ang-pair-
meh-ăh-bl, m
mackintosh; raincoat;
a* impervious;

waterproof.

impersonnel, le,* ang-
pair-sonn-ell, a
impersonal.

impertinemment, ang-
pair-te-năh-mahng, adv
impertinently.

impertinence, ang-pair-te-
nahngss, f impertinence;
insolence; rudeness.

impertinent, e, ang-pair-
te-nahng, mf
impertinent person; a
impertinent.

imperturbable,* ang-pair-
tEEr-băh-bl, a
imperturbable.

impétueu-x, se,* ang-peh-
tE-er, a impetuous.

impétuosité, ang-peh-tE-
oz-e-teh, f impetuosity;
vehemence.

impie, ang-pee, mf impious
person; a impious;
ungodly.

impiété, ang-pe-eh-teh, f
impiety.

impitoyable,* ang-pe-
to'ăh-yăh-bl, a pitiless.

implacable,* ang-plăh-
kăh-bl, a implacable.

implanter, ang-plahng-teh,
v to implant.

implicite,* ang-ple-seett, a
implicit.

impliquer, ang-ple-keh, v
to implicate; to involve;
to imply.

implorer, ang-plor-eh, v to
implore.

impoli,* e, ang-poll-e, a
uncivil; rude; impolite.

impolitesse, ang-poll-e-
tayss, f impoliteness;
rudeness; incivility.

impopulaire, ang-pop-E-
lair, a unpopular.

importance, ang-por-
tahngss, f importance.

important, ang-por-tahng,
m main point.

important, e, ang-por-
tahng, a important.

importa-teur, trice, ang-
por-tăh-ter, mf
importer.

importer, ang-por-teh, v
to import.

importer, ang-por-teh, v
to matter (only used in
3rd person, infinitive
and participles).

importun, e, ang-por-tung,
mf intruder; bore; a
importunate.

importuner, ang-por-tE-
neh, v to importune; to
pester; to dun.

imposable, ang-pohz-ăh-
bl, a taxable.

imposant, e, ang-pohz-
ahng, a imposing.

imposer, ang-pohz-eh, v to
impose; to tax; to
overwave.

imposition, ang-pohz-e-se-

ong, f imposition; tax;
assessment.

impossible, ang-poss-ee-bl,
m impossibility; a
impossible.

imposteur, ang-poss-ter, m
impostor; a deceitful.

impôt, ang-poh, m tax;
taxation; duty.

impotent, e, ang-pot-ahng,
mf & a disabled.

imprégner, ang-prehn-yeh,
v to impregnate.

imprenable, ang-prer-
năhl-bl, a impregnable.

impression, ang-press-e-
ong, f impression;
printing.

impressionner, ang-press-
e-onn-eh, v to impress;
to move (feelings).

imprévoyance, ang-preh-
vo'ăh-yahngss, f
improvidence.

imprévu, ang-preh-vE, m
the unexpected.

imprévu, e, ang-preh-vE, a
unforeseen; unexpected.

imprimé, ang-pre-meh, m
printed paper; pl printed
matter.

imprimer, ang-pre-meh, v
to impress; to print; to
stamp.

imprimerie, ang-preem-
ree, f printing; printing-
house.

imprimeur, ang-pre-mer,

m printer.

improbable, ang-prob-ăh-
bl, a unlikely.

improbe, ang-prob, a
dishonest.

improducti-f, ve,* ang-
prod-EEk-teeff, a
unproductive.

impromptu, ang-prongp-
tE, m & adv impromptu.

impropriété, ang-prop-re-
e-teh, f impropriety (of
language).

improvisa-teur, trice, ang-
prov-e-zăh-ter, mf & a
improviser.

improvisé, e, ang-prov-e-
zeh, pp & a improvised;
unprepared.

improviser, ang-prov-e-
zeh, v to improvise.

improviste (à l'), ăh lang-
prov-isst, adv unawares;
suddenly.

imprudemment, ang-prE-
dăh-mahng, adv
imprudently.

imprudence, ang-prE-
dahngss, f imprudence.

imprudent, e, ang-prE-
dahng, a imprudent.

impudemment, ang-pE-
dăh-mahng, adv
impudently.

impudence, ang-pE-
dahngss, f impudence.

impudent, e, ang-pE-
dahng, a impudent.

impudique, ang-pE-deeck,
a lewd; indecent.

impuissance, ang-pweess-
ahngss, f impotence;
powerlessness.

impuissant, e, ang-pweess-
ahng, a impotent;
ineffectual.

impulsi-f, ve,* ang-pEEl-
seeff, a impulsive.

impulsion, ang-pEEl-se-
ong, f impulse; impetus.

impunément, ang-pE-neh-
mahng, adv with
impunity.

impuni, e, ang-pE-ne, a
unpunished.

impur, e, ang-pEEr, a
impure.

impureté, ang-pEEr-teh, f
impurity.

imputer, ang-pE-teh, v to
impute; to ascribe; to
charge.

inabordable, e-năh-bor-
dăh-bl, a inaccessible.

inacceptable, e-năhck-
sep-tăh-bl, a
unacceptable.

inaccessible, e-năhck-sess-
ee-bl, a unapproachable.

inaccoutumé, e, e-năh-
koo-tE-meh, a
unaccustomed; unusual.

inachevé, e, e-năhsh-veh,
a unfinished.

inacti-f, ve,* e-năhck-
teeff, a inactive.

inadéquat, e, * e-năh-deh-kwăh, *a* inadequate.

inadmissible, e-năhd-me-se-bl, *a* inadmissible; unthinkable.

inadvertance, e-năhd-vair-tahngss, *f* inadvertence; oversight.

inaltérable, * e-năhl-teh-răh-bl, *a* unalterable.

inamovible, e-năh-mov-ee-bl, *a* irremovable.

inanité, e-năh-ne-teh, *f* inanity; futility.

inaperçu, e, e-năh-pair-sE, *a* unseen; unnoticed.

inappliqué, e, e-năh-ple-keh, *a* inattentive.

inappréciable, e-năh-preh-se-ăh-bl, *a* invaluable.

inattaquable, e-năh-tăh-kăh-bl, *a* unassailable.

inattendu, e, e-năh-tahng-dE, *a* unexpected.

inauguration, e-noh-ghE-răh-se-ong, *f* opening; unveiling.

incandescent, e, ang-kahng-dayss-sahng, *a* incandescent.

incapable, ang-kăh-păh-bl, *a* incapable; unfit; incompetent.

incapacité, ang-kăh-păh-se-teh, *f* incapacity; incompetence.

incarcérer, ang-kăhr-seh-reh, *v* to imprison.

incarnat, e, ang-kăhr-năh, *a* flesh-coloured; rosy.

incarné, e, ang-kăhr-neh, *a* incarnate.

incendie, ang-sahng-dee, *m* fire; conflagration.

incendier, ang-sahng-de-eh, *v* to set on fire.

incertain, e, ang-sair-tang, *a* uncertain; undecided; wavering.

incertitude, ang-sair-te-tEEd, *f* uncertainty; instability.

incessamment, ang-sayss-săh-mahng, *adv* immediately; directly.

incessant, e, ang-sayss-ahng, *a* incessant.

incidemment, ang-se-dăh-mahng, *adv* incidentally.

incident, ang-se-dahng, *m* incident; occurrence.

incident, e, ang-se-dahng, *a* incidental.

incinérer, ang-se-neh-reh, *v* to incinerate; to cremate.

incision, ang-se-ze-ong, *f* incision; lancing.

incitation, ang-se-tăh-se-ong, *f* incitement; instigation.

inciter, ang-se-teh, *v* to incite; to urge.

incivil, e, ang-se-veell, *a* uncivil; rude.

inclinaison, ang-kle-nay-zong, *f* tilting; incline.

inclination, ang-kle-năh-se-ong, *f* inclination; propensity; attachment.

incliner, ang-kle-neh, *v* to incline;to bend; s'–, to bow.

inclus, e, ang-klE, *a* enclosed; included; ci-–, se –, enclosed; herewith.

inclusi-f, ve, * ang-klE-zeeff, *a* inclusive.

incognito, ang-konn-yee-to, *m & adv* incognito.

incolore, ang-koll-or, *a* colourless.

incomber, ang-kong-beh, *v* to be incumbent (à, on).

incombustible, ang-kong-bEs-tee-bl, *a* incombustible; fire proof.

incommode, ang-komm-od, *a* inconvenient; troublesome.

incommoder, ang-komm-odd-eh, *v* to inconvenience; to annoy; to disturb.

incommodité, ang-komm-odd-e-teh, *f* inconvenience; discomfort.

incomparable, * ang-kong-păh-răh-bl, *a* matchless.

incompatible, * ang-kong-

păh-tee-bl, *a*
incompatible;
inconsistent.

incompétent, ang-kong-
peh-tahng, *a*
incompetent.

incompl-et, ète, * ang-
kong-play, *a* incomplete.

incompréhensible, ang-
kong-preh-ahng-see-bl,
incomprehensive.

incompris, e, ang-kong-
pre, *pp* & *a* not
understood;
unappreciated.

inconcevable, ang-kongss-
văh-bl, *a* inconceivable.

inconciliable, ang-kong-
se-le-ăh-bl, *a*
irreconcilable.

inconduite, ang-kong-
dweet, *f* misconduct.

incongru, e, ang-kong-grE,
a incongruous;
improper; rude.

inconnu, e, ang-konn-E,
mf unknown; stranger; *a*
unknown.

inconsciemment, ang-
kong-se-ăh-mahng, *adv*
unconsciously.

inconscience, ang-kong-
se-ahngss, *f*
unconsciousness.

inconscient, e, ang-kong-
se-ahng, *a* unconscious.

inconséquence, ang-kong-
seh-kahngss, *f*

inconsistency.

inconséquent, e, ang-
kong-seh-kahng, *a*
inconsistent.

inconstance, ang-kongss-
tahngss, *f* inconstancy;
fickleness.

inconstant, e, ang-kongss-
tahng, *a* inconstant;
unsteady; variable.

incontestable, * ang-kong-
tess-tăh-bl, *a*
unquestionable.

incontesté, e, ang-kong-
tess-teh, *a* undisputed.

incontinent, e, ang-kong-
te-nahng, *a* incontinent.

inconvenance, ang-kongv-
nahngss, *f* impropriety.

inconvenant, e, ang-
kongv-nahng, *a*
improper; unbecoming.

inconvénient, ang-kong-
veh-ne-ahng, *m*
inconvenience;
disadvantage.

incorporer, ang-kor-poh-
reh, *v* incorporate.

incorrect, e, * ang-kor-
reckt, *a* incorrect.

incrédule, ang-kreh-dEEl,
a incredulous.

incroyable, * ang-kro'ăh-
yăh-bl, *a* incredible;
unbelievable.

incruster, ang-krEEs-teh, *v*
to encrust (**de**, with); to
inlay.

inculper, ang-kEEl-peh, *v*
to charge; to accuse (**de**,
with; of).

inculquer, ang-kEEl-keh, *v*
to inculcate.

inculte, ang kEElt, *a*
uncultivated;
uneducated; rough.

incurable, ang-kE-răh-bl,
mf & *a* incurable.

indécemment, ang-deh-
săh-mahng, *adv*
indecently.

indécent, e, ang-deh-
sahng, *a* indecent.

indéchiffrable, ang-deh-
she-frăh-bl, *a* illegible;
incomprehensible.

indécis, e, ang-deh-se, *a*
undecided; wavering.

indéfendable, ang-deh-
fahng-dăh-bl, *a*
indefensible.

indéfini, e, ang-deh-fe-ne,
a indefinite.

indéfiniment, ang-deh-fe-
ne-mahng, *adv*
indefinitely.

indéfinissable, ang-deh-fe-
niss-ăh-bl, *a* indefinable.

indélébile, ang-deh-leh-
beell, *a* indelible.

indélicat, e, * ang-deh-le-
kăh, *a* indelicate;
unscrupulous.

indélicatesse, ang-deh-le-
kăh-tayss, *f* indelicacy.

indemne, ang-daymn, *a*

unhurt; without loss.

indemniser, ang-daym-ne-zeh, *v* to indemnify (**de,** for); to compensate.

indemnité, ang-daym-ne-teh, *f* indemnity; allowance.

indépendamment, ang-deh-pahng-dăh-mahng, *adv* independently.

indépendant, e, ang-deh-pahng-dahng, *a* independent.

indescriptible, ang-dess-kreep-tee-bl, *a* indescribable.

indéterminé, e, ang-deh-tair-me-neh, *a* indeterminate; unlimited; irresolute.

index, ang-dex, *m* index; forefinger.

indicateur, ang-de-kăh-ter, *m* indicator; timetable.

indica-teur, trice, ang-de-kăh-ter, *a* indicating; indicatory.

indicatif, ang-de-kăh-teeff, *a* indicative mood.

indicati-f, ve, ang-de-kăh-teeff, *a* indicative.

indice, ang-deess, *m* indication; sign; clue.

indicible, ang-deess-ee-bl, *a* inexpressible.

indifféremment, ang-de-feh-răh-mahng, *adv*

indifferently; indiscriminately.

indifférent, e, ang-de-feh-rahng, *a* indifferent; immaterial.

indigène, ang-de-shain, *mf* & *a* native; indigenous.

indigent, ang-de-shahng, *m* pauper.

indigent, e, ang-de-shahng, *a* indigent; needy.

indigeste, ang-de-shaysst, *a* indigestible.

indigne,* ang-deen-yer, *a* unworthy; undeserving.

indigné, e, ang-deen-yeh, *a* indignant.

indigner, ang-deen-yeh, *v* to make indignant.

indignité, ang-deen-yee-teh, *f* unworthiness; indignity.

indiquer, ang-de-keh, *v* to indicate.

indirect, e,* ang-de-reckt, *a* indirect.

indiscipliné, ang-diss-e-plee-neh, *a* unruly.

indiscr-et, éte,* ang-diss-kray, *a* indiscreet; tactless.

indispensable,* ang-diss-pahng-săh-bl, *a* indispensable.

indisponible, ang-diss-ponn-ee-bl, *a* unavailable.

indisposer, ang-diss-poz-eh, *v* to upset.

indistinct, e,* ang-diss-tangkt, *a* indistinct.

individu, ang-de-ve-dE, *m* individual, person.

individuel, le,* ang-de-ve-dE-ell, *a* individual.

indocile, ang-doss-eell, *a* untractable; disobedient.

indolemment, ang-doll-ăh-mahng, *adv* indolently.

indolent, e, ang-doll-ahng, *a* indolent; sluggish; lazy.

indolence, ang-doll-ahngss, *f* indolence.

indolore, ang-doll-or, *a* painless.

indomptable,* ang-dong-tăh-bl, *a* indomitable; ungovernable.

indompté, e, ang-dong-teh, *a* untamed; unsubdued.

indubitable,* ang-dE-be-tăh-bl, *a* indubitable.

induire, ang-dweer, *v* to induce; to lead; to infer.

indulgence, ang-dEEl-shahngss, *f* leniency.

indûment, ang-dEE-mahng, *adv* unduly.

industrie, ang-dEEs-tree, *f* industry; skill; trade.

industriel, ang-dEEs-tre-ell, *m* industrialist.

industriel, le,* ang-dEEs-tre-ell, *a* industrial.

industrieu-x, se,* ang-dEEs-tre-er, *a* industrious; skilful.

inébranlable,* e-neh-brahng-läh-bl, *a* immovable; resolute.

inédit, e, e-neh-dee, *a* unpublished; new.

ineffable,* e-neh-fäh-bl, *a* unspeakable.

ineffaçable, e-neh-fäh-säh-bl, *a* indelible.

inefficace,* e-neh-fe-kähss, *a* inefficient.

inégal, e,* e-neh-gähl, *a* unequal; irregular; uneven.

inélégant, e, e-neh-leh-gahng, *a* inelegant.

inénarrable, e-neh-nähr-räh-bl, *a* indescribable.

inepte, * e-nehpt, *a* inept; silly.

ineptie, e-nehp-see, *f* ineptitude; absurdity.

inépuisable,* e-neh-pwee-zäh-bl, *a* inexhaustible.

inerte, e-nairt, *a* inert; lifeless; sluggish; passive.

inertie, e-nair-see, *f* inertia; dullness.

inespéré, e, e-ness-peh-reh, *a* unhoped for.

inestimable, e-ness-te-mäh-bl, *a* invaluable.

inévitable,* e-neh-ve-täh-

bl, *a* unavoidable.

inexact, e,* e-negg-zäckt, *a* inaccurate; unpunctual.

inexcusable,* e-necks-kE-zäh-bl, *a* inexcusable.

inexécutable, e-negg-zeh-kE-täh-bl, *a* impracticable.

inexercé, e, e-negg-zair-seh, *a* unpractised; untrained.

inexigible, e-negg-ze-shee-bl, *a* non-recoverable.

inexorable,* e-negg-zor-äh-bl, *a* inexorable.

inexpérimenté, e, e-necks-peh-re-mahng-teh, *a* inexperienced; untried.

inexprimable,* e-necks-pre-mäh-bl, *a* inexpressible.

inextinguible, e-necks-tang-gwee-bl, *a* inextinguishable; uncontrollable.

infactus (du myocarde), ang-fähck-tEss dE me-oh-kährd, *m* coronary.

infaillible,* ang-fah'e-ee-bl, *a* infallible.

infaisable, ang-fer-zäh-bl, *a* impractical.

infamant, e, ang-fäh-mahng, *a* ignominious.

infame, ang-fahm, *mf* infamous person; *a*

infamous; vile; filthy.

infamie, ang-fäh-mee, *f* infamy; infamous thing.

infanterie, ang-fahngt-ree, *f* infantry.

infatigable, ang-fäh-te-gäh-bl, *a* indefatigable.

infatuer (s'), sang-fäh-tE-eh, *v* to become infatuated (**de,** with).

infécond, e, ang-feh-kong, *a* infertile; barren.

infect, e, ang-feckt, *a* stinking; foul.

infecter, ang-feck-teh, *v* to infect; to taint; to stink.

infection, ang-feck-se-ong, *f* infection.

inférer, ang-feh-reh, *v* to infer.

inférieur, e,* ang-feh-re-er, *a* inferior lower.

infernal, e,* ang-fair-nähl, *a* hellish.

infertile, ang-fair-teell, *a* unfruitful.

infester, ang-fess-teh, *v* to infest.

infidèle, ang-fe-dell, *mf* infidel; unbeliever.

infidèle, ang-fe-dell, *a* unfaithful; untrue; dishonest; unbelieving.

infiltrer (s'), sang-fill-treh, *v* to infiltrate.

infime, ang-feem, *a* lowest; tiny.

infini, e, ang-fe-ne, *a*

infinite; endless; boundless.

infiniment, ang-fe-ne-mahng, *adv* infinitely; extremely.

infirme, ang-feerm, *a* infirm; disabled.

infirmerie, ang-feerm-re, *f* infirmary; sick room; sick bay.

infirmi-er, ère, ang-feer-me-eh, *mf* nurse.

inflammable, ang-flăh-măh-bl, *a* inflammable.

inflammation, ang-flăh-măh-se-ong, *f* inflammation.

inflexible,* ang-fleck-see-bl, *a* inflexible.

infliger, ang-fle-sheh, *v* to inflict (**à,** on).

influent, e, ang-flE-ahng *a* influential.

influer, ang-flE-eh, *v* to exert an influence.

information, ang-for-măh-se-ong, *f* information; inquiry; *pl* news bulletin.

informe, ang-form, *a* shapeless.

informer, ang-for-meh, *v* to inform; to acquaint; **s'–,** to inquire.

infortune, ang-for-tEEn, *f* misfortune; adversity.

infortuné, e, ang-for-tE-neh, *mf* unfortunate person; *a* unfortunate.

infraction, ang-frăhck-se-ong, *f* infraction; breach.

infranchissable, ang-frahng-shiss-ăh-bl, *a* impassable; insuperable.

infructueu-x, se,* ang-frEEk-tE- er, *a* unfruitful.

infus, e, ang-fE, *a* innate.

infuser, ang-fE-zeh, *v* to infuse; to steep.

ingénier (s'), sang- sheh-ne-eh, *v* to strive.

ingénieur, ang- sheh-ne-er, *m* engineer.

ingénieu-x, se,* ang-sheh-ne-er, *a* ingenious.

ingénu, e, ang- sheh-nE, *mf* & *a* ingenuous person; ingenuous; candid.

ingénument, ang- sheh-nE-mahng, *adv* ingenuously.

ingérer (s'), sang- sheh-reh, *v* to meddle (**dans,** with).

ingrat, e, ang-grăh, *mf* & *a* ungrateful person; ungrateful; unprofitable; unpleasant.

ingrédient, ang-greh-de-ahng, *m* ingredient.

inguérissable, ang-greh-riss-ăh-bl, *a* incurable.

inhabile,* e-năh-beell, *a* unskilful; unfit.

inhabitable, e-năh-be-tăh-bl, *a* uninhabitable.

inhabité, e, e-năh-be-teh, *a* uninhabited.

inhaler, e-năh-leh, *v* to inhale.

inhérent, e, e-neh-rahng, *a* inherent.

inhumain, e,* e-nE-mang, *a* inhuman; cruel.

inhumation, e-nE-măh-se-ong, *f* interment; burial.

inhumer, e-nE-meh, *v* to bury; to inter.

inimitié, e-ne-me-te-eh, *f* enmity; antipathy.

inique,* e-neeck, *a* iniquitous; unfair.

iniquité, e-ne-ke-teh, *f* iniquity; injustice.

initial, e, e-ne-se-ăhl, *a* initial.

initiale, e-ne-se-ăhl, *f* initial.

initiative, e-ne-se-ăh-teev, *f* initiative.

initier, e-ne-se-eh, *v* to initiate; to instruct; to admit.

injecter, ang- shayk-teh, *v* to inject.

injure, ang- shEer, *f* injury; wrong; insult.

injurieu-x, se,* ang- shE-re-rr, *a* injurious; offensive.

injurier, ang- shE-re-eh, *v* to abuse; to swear at.

injuste,* ang- shEEst, *a* unjust; unfair; wrong.

inné, e, een-neh, *a* innate; inborn.

innocemment, e-noss-ăh-mahng, *adv* innocently.

innocent, e, e-noss-ahng, *mf* innocent person; *a* innocent; not guilty; harmless.

innombrable,* e-nong-brăh-bl, *a* innumerable.

inoccupé, e, e-nock-E-peh, *a* unoccupied.

inoculer, e-nock-E-leh, *v* to inoculate.

inoffensi-f, ve,* e-noff-ahng-seeff, *a* inoffensive.

inondation, e-nong-dăh-se-ong, *f* flood.

inonder, e-nong-deh, *v* to overflow; to flood.

inopiné, e, e-nop-e-neh, *a* unforeseen.

inopinément, e-nop-e-neh-mahng, *adv* unexpectedly.

inouï, e, e-noo-e, *a* unheard of; unprecedented.

inqui-et, ète, ang-ke-ay, *a* anxious; uneasy; worried.

inquiétant, e, ang-ke-eh-tahng, *a* alarming; worrying.

inquiéter, ang-ke-eh-teh, *v* to make uneasy; to alarm; to worry.

inquiétude, ang-ke-eh-tEEd, *f* anxiety; worry.

insalubre,* ang-săh-lEE-br, *a* unhealthy.

insatiable,* ang-săh-se-ăh-bl, *a* insatiable.

inscription, angss-krip-se-ong, *f* inscription; registration.

inscrire, angss-kreer, *v* to inscribe; to enter; to register.

insecte, ang-say-kt, *m* insect.

insensé, e, ang-sahng-seh, *mf & a* maniac; insane; senseless.

insensible,* ang-sahng-see-bl, *a* insensitive; unconscious; callous; imperceptible.

insérer, ang-seh-reh, *v* to insert; to put in.

insigne, ang-seen-yer, *a* notable.

insigne, ang-seen-yer, *m* badge; emblem; *pl* insignia.

insignifiant, e, ang-seen-yee-fe-ahng, *a* insignificant.

insinuant, e, ang-se-nE-ahng, *a* insinuating.

insinuer, ang-se-nE-eh, *v* to insinuate; to hint.

insipide, ang-se-peed, *a* insipid.

insistance, ang-sisstahngss, *f* insistence.

insociable, ang-soss-e-ăh-bl, *a* unsociable.

insolation, ang-sol-ăh-se-ong, *f* sunstroke; heatstroke.

insolemment, ang-soll-ăh-mahng, *adv* insolently.

insolence, ang-soll-ahngss, *f* insolence.

insolent, e, ang-soll-ahng, *mf & a* insolent person; insolent; cheeky.

insoluble, ang-soll-EE-bl, *a* insoluble.

insolvable, ang-soll-văh-bl, *a* insolvent.

insomnie, ang-somm-nee, *f* sleeplessness; insomnia.

insondable, ang-song-dăh-bl, *a* unfathomable.

insouciance, ang-soo-se-ahngss, *f* insouciance.

insouciant, e, ang-soo-se-ahng, *a* insouciant.

insoucieu-x, se, ang-soo-se-er, *a* heedless.

insoutenable, ang-soot-năh-bl, *a* indefensible; unbearable.

inspecter, angss-peck-teh, *v* to inspect; to examine.

inspec-teur, trice, angss-peck-ter, *mf* inspector; surveyor.

inspiration, angss-pe-rah-se-ong, *f* inspiration.

inspirer, angss-pe-reh, *v* to

inspire.

instable, angss-tăh-bl, *a* unstable.

installation, angss-tăh-lăh-se-ong, *f* installation; setting up; plant.

instamment, angss-tăh-mahng, *adv* earnestly; urgently.

instance, angss-tahngss, *f* entreaty; immediacy; degree of jurisdiction; suit.

instant, angss-tahng, *m* instant; **à l' –, ăh l –,** immediately; a moment ago.

instinct, angss-tang, *m* instinct.

instincti-f, ve,* angss-tangk-teeff, *a* instinctive.

instituer, angss-te-tE-eh, *v* to institute; to establish; to appoint.

institut, angss-te-tE, *m* institute; institution; school.

institu-teur, trice, angss-te-tE-ter, *mf* elementary school teacher; *f* governess.

institution, angss-te-tE-se-ong, *f* institution; school.

instruction, angss-trEEk-se-ong, *f* instruction;

judicial investigation.

instruire, angss-trweer, *v* to instruct; to investigate; to teach.

instruit, e, angss-trwee, *pp & a* instructed; learned.

instrument, angss-trE-mahng, *m* instrument; tool.

instrumenter, angss-trE-mahng-teh, *v* to draw (deeds, writs, etc).

instrumentiste, angss-trE-mahng-teesst, *m* instrumentalist.

insu (à l' – de), ăh lang-sE-der, *prep* unknown to.

insuffisamment, ang-sE-fe-zăh-mahng, *adv* insufficiently.

insuffisant, e, ang-sE-fe-zahng, *a* insufficient.

insulaire, ang-sE-lair, *mf & a* islander; insular.

insulte, ang-sEElt, *f* insult; abuse.

insulter, ang-sEEl-teh, *v* to insult; to abuse.

insupportable,* ang-sE-por-tăh-bl, *a* unbearable; badly behaved.

insurgé, e, ang-sEEr-sheh, *mf & a* insurgent.

insurger (s'), sang-sEEr-sheh, *v* to revolt; to rebel.

insurmontable, ang-sEEr-

mong-tăh-bl, *a* insurmountable.

insurrection, ang-sEEr-rayk-se-ong, *f* uprising.

intact, e, ang-tăhckt, *a* intact; whole; undamaged.

intarissable,* ang-tăh-riss-ăh-bl, *a* inexhaustible.

intègre,* ang-tay-gr, *a* upright; just; honest.

intellectuel, le,* ang-tell-leck-tE-ell, *a* intellectual.

intelligemment, ang-tell-le-shăh-mahng, *adv* intelligently.

intelligence, ang-tell-le-shahngss, *f* intelligence; knowledge; skill; harmony.

intelligent, e, ang-tell-le shahng, *a* intelligent; clever.

intempérie, ang-tahng-peh-ree, *f* inclemency.

intempesti-f, ve,* ang-tahng-pess-teeff, *a* untimely.

intendant, ang-tahng-dahng, *m* steward; bursar; quartermaster.

intense, ang-tahngss, *a* intense.

intensi-f, ve, ang-tahng-seeff, *a* intensive.

intenter, ang-tahng-teh, *v* to institute

(proceedings); to sue.

intention, ang-tahng-se-ong, f intention; purpose.

intentionné, e, ang-tahng-se-onn-eh, a; **bien** or **mal** –, be-ang, măhl –, well–, ill-disposed.

intercaler, ang-tair-kăh-leh, v to insert; to wedge in.

intercèder, ang-tair-seh-deh, v to intercede (**auprès de,** with).

intercepter, ang-tair-sep-teh, v to intercept.

interdire, ang-tair-deer, v to forbid; to ban; to suspend; fam to bewilder.

interdit, ang-tair-de, m interdict; person interdicted.

interdit, e, ang-tair-de, a speechless.

intéressant, e, ang-teh-rayss-ahng, a interesting.

intéressé, e, ang-teh-rayss-eh, pp & a interested; selfish.

intéresser, ang-teh-rayss-eh, v to interest; to concern.

intérêt, ang-teh-ray, m interest; profit; share; concern.

intérieur, ang-teh-re-er, m inside; home.

intérieur, e,* ang-teh-re-er, a interior; inner.

intérimaire, ang-teh-re-mair, a temporary.

interjeter, ang-tair-sher-teh, v to lodge an appeal.

interlocu-teur, trice, ang-tair-lock-E-ter, mf interlocutor.

interloquer, ang-tair-lock-eh, v to disconcert.

intermède, ang-tair-mayd, m interlude.

intermédiaire, ang-tair-meh-de-air, m & a medium; middleman; intermediate.

intermittence, ang-tair-mit-tahngss, f intermission.

internat, ang-tair-năh, m boarding-school.

international, e, ang-tair-năh-se-on-ăhl, a international.

interne, ang-tairn, mf & a boarder; house-surgeon; internal.

interner, ang-tair-neh, v to intern.

interpeller, ang-tair-pel-leh, v to put a question to; to call upon; to heckle.

interposer, ang-tair-poz-eh, v to interpose.

interprète, ang-tair-prayt,

m interpreter.

interroga-teur, trice, ang-tair-rogh-ăh-ter, mf & a examiner; enquiring.

interrogation, ang-tair-rogh-ăh-se-ong, f interrogation; question.

interrogatoire, ang-tair-rogh-ăh-to'ăhr, m examination; cross-examination.

interroger, ang-tair-rosh-eh, v to question; to examine.

interrompre, ang-tair-rong-pr, v to interrupt; to stop; **s'** –, to break off.

interrupteur, ang-tair-rEEp-ter, m switch.

intervalle, ang-tair-văhl, m interval.

intervenir, ang-tair-ver-neer, v to intervene; to interfere; to occur.

intervention, ang-tair-vahng-se-ong, f intervention.

intervertir, ang-tair-vair-teer, v to invert.

intestin, ang-tayss-tang, m intestine; bowel.

intimation, ang-te-măh-se-ong, f notification.

intime,* ang-teem, mf & a intimate friend; intimate; close; cosy.

intimer, ang-te-meh, v to

notify.

intimider, ang-te-me-deh, *v* to intimidate.

intimité, ang-te-me-teh, *f* intimacy.

intitulé, e, ang-te-tE-leh, *pp* & *a* entitled.

intolérable,* ang-toll-ehräh-bl, *a* insufferable.

intolérant, e, ang-toll-ehrahng, *a* intolerant.

intoxiqué, e, ang-tox-eekeh, *mf* addict.

intoxiquer, ang-tox-ickeh, *v* to poison (food, etc)

intraduisible, ang-trähdwe-zee-bl, *a* untranslatable.

intraitable, ang-tray-täh-bl, *a* intractable.

intransigeant, e, angtrahng-ze-shahng, *a* intransigent.

intrépide,* ang-treh-peed, *a* undaunted; fearless.

intrigant, e, ang-tregahng, *mf* & *a* schemer; intriguing.

intriguer, ang-tre-gheh, *v* to perplex; to plot; to intrigue.

intrinsèque,* ang-trangsayk, *a* intrinsic.

introduc-teur, trice, angtrod-EEk-ter, *mf* introducer.

introduire, ang-trod-weer,

v to introduce; **s'–,** to get into.

introuvable, ang-troovähl-bl, *a* not to be found.

intrus, e, ang-trE, *mf* intruder.

intuiti-f, ve,* ang-tE-eteeff, *a* intuitive.

inusable, e-nE-zäh-bl, *a* everlasting.

inutile,* e-nE-teel, *a* useless; unnecessary.

inutilité, e-nE-te-le-teh, *f* uselessness; *pl* useless things.

invalide, ang-väh-leed, *a* & *mf* invalid; infirm; army veteran; pensioner; disabled.

invalider, ang-väh-le-deh, *v* to invalidate.

invariable,* ang-väh-reäh-bl, *a* invariable.

invasion, ang-väh-se-ong, *f* invasion; irruption.

invectiver, ang-vayk-teveh, *v* to inveigh.

invendable, ang-vahngdäh-bl, *a* unsaleable.

invendu, e, ang-vahng-dE, *a* unsold.

inventaire, ang-vahngtair, *m* stocktaking; inventory.

inventer, ang-vahng-teh, *v* to invent.

inven-teur, trice, ang-

vahng-ter, *mf* inventor; discoverer; *a* inventive.

inventi-f, ve, ang-vahngteeff, *a* inventive.

inventorier, ang-vahngtor-e-eh, *v* to make an inventory of; to take stock.

inverse,* ang-vairss, *a* inverse; inverted.

investigation, ang-vaysste-gah-se-ong, *f* investigation; inquiry.

investir, ang-vayss-teer, *v* to invest.

invétéré, e, ang-veh-tehreh, *a* inveterate; compulsive (liar, smoker, etc).

invisible,* ang-vee-zee-bl, *a* invisible; unseen.

invité, e, ang-ve-teh, *mf* guest.

inviter, ang-ve-teh, *v* to invite; to urge; to request.

involontaire,* ang-vollong-tair, *a* involuntary.

invoquer, ang-vock-eh, *v* to invoke; to plead.

invraisemblable,* angvrayss-ahng-bläh-bl, *a* unlikely; unbelievable.

invraisemblance, angvrayss-ahng-blahngss, *f* unlikelihood.

invulnérable,* ang-vEElneh-räh-bl, *a*

invulnerable.

iode, e-od, *m* iodine.

irascible, e-răhss-ee-bl, *a* irritable.

irisé, e, e-re-zeh, *a* iridescent.

irlandais, e, eer-lahng-deh, *a* Irish; *mf* Irishman; Irishwoman; Irish.

ironie, e-ronn-ee, *f* irony.

ironique,* e-ronn-eeck, *a* ironic(al).

irréalisable, eer-reh-ăh-le-zăh-bl, *a* unrealisable.

irréductible, eer-reh-dEEk-tee-bl, *a* irreducible.

irréfléchi, e, eer-reh-fleh-she, *a* thoughtless.

irréflexion, eer-reh-fleck-se-ong, *f* thoughtlessness.

irréguli-er, ère,* eer-reh-ghE-le-eh, *a* irregular.

irrémissible,* eer-reh-miss-ce-bl, *a* unpardonable.

irrésolu, e,* eer-reh-zoll-E, *a* irresolute.

irrespectueu-x, se,* eer-ress-peck-tE- er, *a* disrespectful.

irresponsable,* eer-ress-pong-săh-bl, *a* irresponsible

irrévocable,* eer-eh-vock-ăh-bl, *a*

irrevocable.

irrigateur, eer-re-găh-ter, *m* (garden) hose.

irriguer, eer-re-gheh, *v* to irrigate.

irriter, eer-re-teh, *v* to irritate; to provoke.

isolé, e, e-zoll-eh, *a* isolated; lonely; detached.

isolement, e-zoll-mahng, *m* loneliness; seclusion.

issu, e, iss-E, *a* born; sprung from.

issue, iss-E, *f* issue; outlet; end.

isthme, issm, *m* isthmus.

Italie, e-tăh-lee *f* Italy.

italien-ne, e-tăhl-e-ang *a* & *mf* Italian.

itinéraire, e-te-neh-rair, *m* itinerary; route; guidebook.

ivoire, e-vo'ăhr, *m* ivory; whiteness.

ivre, e-vr, *a* drunk; intoxicated.

ivresse, e-vress, *f* drunkenness; rapture.

ivrogne, e-vronn-yer, *m* drunkard.

jabot, shăh-bo, *m* shirt-frill; crop (of a bird).

jacasser, shăh-kăhss-eh, *v* to chatter.

jacinthe, shăh-sangt, *f* hyacinth.

jadis, shăh-deess, *adv* formerly; of old.

jaillir, shah'e-eer, *v* to spout; to gush out; to spring forth.

jalon, shăh-long, *m* stake; pole; landmark.

jalouser, shăh-loo-zeh, *v* to envy.

jalousie, shăh-loo-zee, *f* jealousy; Venetian blind.

jalou-x, se, * shăh-loo, *a* jealous.

jamais, shăh-may, *adv* ever; never.

jambe, shahngb, *f* leg; shank.

jambon, shahng-bong, *m* ham.

jante, shahngt, *f* (wheel) rim.

janvier, shahng-ve-eh, *m* January.

japonais, e, shah-po-neh, *a* Japanese; *mf* Japanese.

japper, shăh-peh, *v* to yelp.

jaquette, shăh-kayt, *f* jacket.

jardin, shăhr-dang, *m* garden.

jardini-er, ère, shăhr-de-ne-eh, *mf* gardener.

jargon, shăhr-gong, *m* gibberish; jargon.

jarre, shăhr, *f* jar.

jarret, shăh-ray, *m* hamstring; hock; knuckle (veal); shin (beef).

jarretelle, shăhr-tell, *f* suspender; garter.

jaser, shah-zeh, *v* to chatter; to gossip.

jasmin, shăhss-mang, *m* jasmin.

jatte, shăht, *f* bowl.

jauge, shohsh, *f* gauge; tonnage.

jaunâtre, shoh-nah-tr, *a* yellowish.

jaune, shohn, *a* yellow.

jaunir, shoh-neer, *v* to make yellow; to turn yellow.

jaunisse, shoh-neess, *f* jaundice.

Javel (eau de), oh der shăh-vell, bleach.

javelot, shăhv-lo, *m* javelin.

jazz, dshăhz, *m* jazz.

je (j' before a vowel), sher, *pron* I.

jean, djeen, *m* jeans.

jésuite, sheh-zweet, *m* Jesuit.

Jésus, sheh-zE, *m* Jesus.

jet, shay, *m* throw; jet; ray.

jetable, sher-tăh-bl, *a*
disposable (pack, etc).

jetée, sher-teh, *f* pier;
jetty.

jeter, sher-teh, *v* to throw;
to fling; **à –, ăh –,**
disposable.

jeton, sher-tong, *m*
counter; token.

jeu, sher, *m* play; sport;
gambling; set; acting;–
concours, – kong-koohr
quiz; – **électronique, –**
eh-leck-tro-neeck,
computer game; **Jeux
olympiques, –** zoh-lang-
peek *mpl* Olympic
Games.

jeudi, sher-de, *m*
Thursday.

jeun (à), ăh-shung, *adv*
fasting; on an empty
stomach.

jeûne, shern, *m* fast;
fasting.

jeune, shern, *a* young;
junior; youthful; – **fille
au pair, –** fee-yoh-pair, *f*
au pair.

jeûner, sher-neh, *v* to fast.

jeunesse, sher-ness, *f*
youth; young people.

joaillerie, sho'ah'e-ree, *f*
jewellery; jewellery
trade.

joie, sho'ăh, *f* joy; delight;
gladness.

joignant, sho'ăhn-yahng,

pres part & *a* adjoining;
near to.

joindre, sho'ang-dr, *v* to
join; to adjoin; to clasp;
to get in touch.

joint, e, sho'ang, *a* joined;
united; **ci-joint,** se-sho'
ang, herewith; annexed.

joli, e, sholl-e, *a* pretty.

joliment, sholl-e-mahng,
adv nicely; *fam* very;
terribly.

jonc, shong, *m* rush; cane.

joncher, shong-sheh, *v* to
strew; to scatter.

jonction, shongk-se-ong, *f*
junction.

jongler, shong-gleh, *v* to
juggle.

joue, shoo, *f* cheek.

jouer, shoo-eh, *v* to play;
to gamble; to stake; to
act; to deceive.

jouet, shoo-ay, *m* toy.

joueu-r, se, shoo-er, *mf*
player; gambler.

joug, shoogh, *m* yoke.

jouir, shoo-eer, *v* to
enjoy; to possess; to use.

jouissance, shoo-iss-
ahngss, *f* enjoyment;
possession; use.

joujou, shoo-shoo, *m*
plaything; toy.

jour, shoohr, *m* day;
daylight; gap.

journal, shoohr-năhl, *m*
newspaper; journal;

diary; record book.

journali-er, ère, shoohr-
năh-le-eh, *a* daily.

journée, shoohr-neh, *f*
daytime; day's work;
day's pay.

journellement, shoohr-
nell-mahng, *adv* daily.

jovial, e,* shov-e-ăhl, *a*
jovial.

joyau, sho'ăh-yoh, *m*
jewel.

joyeu-x, se,* sho'ăh-yer, *a*
cheerful; merry; joyful.

jubilation, shE-be-lăh-se-
ong, *f* rejoicing.

jucher (se), ser shE-sheh,
v to roost; to perch.

judiciaire,* shE-de-se-air,
a judicial; legal.

judicieu-x, se,* shE-de-se-
er, *a* judicious.

juge, shEEsh, *m* judge;
magistrate.

jugement, shEEsh-mahng,
m judgment; trial;
sentence; opinion.

juger, shEE-sheh, *v* to
judge; to try; to
sentence; to believe.

jui-f, ve, shweef, *mf* & *a*
Jew, Jewess; Jewish.

juillet, shwe-yay, *m* July.

juin, shwang, *m* June.

jumeau, jumelle, shE-
moh, shE-mell, *mf* & *a*
twin.

jumelles, shE-mell, *fpl*

binoculars.

jument, shE-mah*ng*, *f*
mare.

jupe, sh*EE*p, *f* skirt.

jupon, shE-pong, *m*
petticoat.

juré, shE-reh, *m* juror.

jurer, shE-reh, *v* to swear;
to assure; to clash
(colours, etc).

juridique,* shE-re-deeck,
a judicial.

juron, shE-ro*ng*, *m* swear
word; curse.

jury, shE-re, *m* jury.

jus, shE, *m* juice; gravy.

jusque, sh*EE*s-ker, *prep* to;
as far as; until; up to;
down to; even.

juste, sh*EE*st, *m* upright
man; *a* just; correct; fair;
tight.

juste, sh*EE*st, *adv* just;
right; exactly.

justement, sh*EE*s-ter-
mah*ng*, *adv* just so;
exactly.

justesse, sh*EE*s-tess, *f*
accuracy; precision.

justice, sh*EE*s-teess, *f*
justice; fairness; law.

justifier, sh*EE*s-te-fe-eh, *v*
to justify; to prove.

jute, sh*EE*t, *m* jute.

juteu-x, se, sh*EE*-ter, *a*
juicy.

juvénile, shE-veh-neel, *a*
youthful.

juxtaposer, sh*EE*x-tăh-po-
zeh, *v* to place side by
side.

kaolin, kăh-oll-ang, *m*
china-clay; kaolin.

képi, keh-pe, *m* military
cap.

kermesse, kair-mess, *f*
bazaar; charity fête.

kilo(gramme), ke-loh-
grăhm; *m* kilo(gram).

kilomètre, ke-loh-met-tr,
m kilometre.

kiosque, ke-osk, *m* kiosk;
news stand.

klaxon, klacks-ong, *m*
horn.

klaxonner, klacks-on-eh,
v to hoot (horn).

krach, krăhck, *m* financial
disaster.

kyste, kee-st, *m* cyst.

la, lăh, *f art;* the; *pron* her;
it; *m* (music) A.

là, lăh, *adv* there; then.

labeur, lăh-ber, *m* labour;
toil; work.

labourieu-x, se,* lăh-bor-
e-er, *a* industrious;
laborious.

labourer, lăh-boo-reh, *v* to
till; to plough.

laboureur, lăh-boo-rer, *m*
ploughman; agricultural
labourer.

lac, lăhck, *m* lake.

lacer, lăh-seh, *v* to lace.

lacet, lăh-say, *m* (shoe)
lace; braid; snare.

lâche, lahsh, *m* coward; *a**
loose; cowardly.

lâcher, lah-shay, *v* to
slacken; to loosen; to
fork out; to release.

lâcheté, lahsh-teh, *f*
cowardice; meanness.

laconique,* lăh-konn-
eeck, *a* laconic.

lacs, lah, *m* snares.

lacté, e, lăhck-teh, *a*
milky; **voie –e,** vo'ăh –,
Milky Way.

lacune, lăh-kEEn, *f* gap;
blank.

lagune, lăh-ghEEn, *f*
lagoon.

laid, e,* lay, *a* ugly; plain.

laideron, layd-rong, *mf*
ugly creature.

laideur, lay-der, *f* ugliness.

lainage, lay-năhsh, *m*
woollen goods; woolly
garment.

laine, layn, *f* wool.

laisse, layss, *f* leash.

laisser, layss-eh, *v* to
leave; to bequeath; to
allow; to give up.

laissez-passer, layss-eh
păhss-eh, *m* pass.

lait, lay, *m* milk; **– écrémé,**
– eh-kreh-meh,
skimmed milk.

laitage, lay-tăhsh, *m* milk;
dairy produce.

laitance, lay-tahngss, *f* soft
roe.

laiterie, lay-tree, *f* dairy.

laiteu-x, se, lay-ter, *a*
milky.

laiti-er, ère, lay-te-eh, *mf*
milkman; milkwoman;
produits –s, prod-wee –,
dairy produce.

laiton, lay-tong, *m* brass.

laitue, lay-tE, *f* lettuce.

lambeau, lahng-boh, *m*
rag; shred; scrap.

lambris, lahng-bre, *m*
wainscot; panelling;
ceiling.

lame, lăhm, *f* blade; wave.

lamentable,* lăh-mahng-
tăh-bl, *a* pitiful;
deplorable.

lamentation, lăh-mahng-
tăh-se-ong, *f* lament;
bewailing.

lampadaire, lahng-păh-
dair, *m* floor lamp.

lampe, lahngp, *f* lamp.

lampion, lahng-pe-ong, *m*
chinese lantern.

lance, lahngss, *f* lance;
spear; staff.

lancer, lahng-seh, *v* to

throw; to fling; to issue; to launch.

lancinant, e, lahng-se-nahng, *a* (pain) shooting.

landau, lahng-do, *m* pram.

lande, lahngd, *f* heath; moor; waste land.

langage, lahng-gãhsh, *m* language; speech; expression.

lange, lahngsh, *f* nappy.

langoureu-x, se,* lahng-ghoo-rer, *a* pining; melancholy.

langouste, lahng-ghoost, *f* crayfish.

langue, lahng-gh, *f* tongue; language; (land) narrow strip.

languette, lahng-ghett, *f* small tongue; tab.

langueur, lahng-gher, *f* languor; weakness.

languir, lahng-gheer, *v* to languish; to pine away.

languissamment, lahng-ghiss-ãh-mahng, *adv* languishingly.

lanière, lãh-ne-air, *f* thong; lash.

lanterne, lahng-tairn, *f* lantern; lamp.

lapider, lãh-pe-deh, *v* to stone to death.

lapin, lãh-pang, *m* rabbit.

laps, lãhps, *m* lapse (of time).

laquais, lãh-kay, *m* lackey; footman; flunkey.

laque, lãhck, *m* lacquer.

laquelle, lãh-kell, *pron f* who; whom; which; that.

larcin, lãhr-sang, *m* larceny.

lard, lãhr, *m* bacon; lard.

larder, lãhr-deh, *v* to lard.

lardon, lãhr-dong, *m* chopped bacon; *fig* jibe.

large, lãhrsh, *m* breadth; width; open sea; *a* broad; generous.

largeur, lãhr-sher, *f* breadth; width.

larme, lãhrm, *f* tear: drop.

larmoyer, lãhr-mo'ãh-yeh, *v* to weep; to whine.

larron, lãh-rong, *m* thief.

larve, lãhrv, *f* larva; grub.

laryngite, lãh-rang-sheet, *f* laryngitis.

la-s, sse, lah, *a* tired; weary.

lasci-f, ve,* lãhss-eef, *a* lascivious; lewd.

laser, lãh-zair *m* laser.

lasser, lahss-eh, *v* to tire; to weary; to fatigue.

latent, e, lãh-tahng, *a* latent; concealed.

latte, lãht, *f* lath; slat.

lauréat, e lor-eh-ãh, *mf* laureate.

laurier, lor-e-eh, *m* laurel; bay.

lavabo, lãh-vãh-bo, *m* wash-basin; lavatory.

lavage, lãh-vãhsh, *m* washing; wash.

lavande, lãh-vahngd, *f* lavender.

lavement, lãhv-mahng, *m* enema.

laver, lãh-veh, *v* to wash.

laverie (automatique), lãhv-re-oh-toh-mãhteeck *f* launderette.

lave-vaisselle, lãhv-vayss-ell, *m* dishwasher.

lavoir, lãh-vo'ãhr, *m* wash house.

layette, lay-yett, *f* baby clothes.

le, ler, *m art* the; *m pron* him; it.

lécher, leh-sheh, *v* to lick.

leçon, ler-song, *f* lesson; lecture.

lec-teur, trice, leck-ter, *mf* reader; **lecteur de casettes, –** der-kãhss-ett, cassette player.

lecture, leck-tEEr, *f* reading.

ledit, ler-de, *a* the aformentioned; *f* **ladite,** lãh-deet.

légal, e,* leh-gãhl, *a* legal; lawful.

légaliser, leh-gãh-le-zeh, *v* to authenticate; to legalize.

légataire, leh-gãh-tair, *mf*

legatee.

légation, leh-găh-se-ong, f
legation.

légende, leh-shahngd, f
legend; references;
caption.

lég-er, ère,* leh-sheh, a
light; faint; fickle.

légèreté, leh-shair-teh, f
lightness; fickleness.

légion, leh-she-ong, f
legion.

législation, leh-shees-lăh-
se-ong, f legislation; set
of laws.

légiste, leh-sheesst, m
lawyer.

légitime,* leh-she-teem, a
legitimate; lawful.

legs, leh, m legacy.

léguer, leh-gheh, v to
bequeath.

légume, leh-ghEEm, m
vegetable.

lendemain, lahngd-mang,
m next day.

lent, e,* lahng, a slow;
sluggish.

lenteur, lahng-ter, f
slowness; delay.

lentille, lahng-tee-ye, f
lentil; lens; pl contact
lenses.

léopard, leh-op-ăhr, m
leopard.

lèpre, laypr, f leprosy.

lépreu-x, se, leh-prer, mf
& a leper; leprous.

lequel, ler-kell, m pron
who; whom; which;
that.

lesbien, ne, lays-be-ang a
lesbian.

lesbienne, layss-be-ayn f
lesbian.

lesdits, lay-de, a mpl the
aforementioned; f
lesdites, lay-deet.

léser, leh-zeh, v to wrong;
to injure.

lésine, leh-zeen, f
stinginess.

lésion, leh-ze-ong, f lesion;
injury; wrong.

lesquels, lay-kell, pl of
lequel; f **lesquelles,** lay-
kell, who; whom; which;
that.

lessive, layss-eev, f
laundry; wash;
detergent; washing
powder.

lest, lesst, m ballast.

leste,* lesst, a nimble.

lettre, lay-tr, f letter; note;
pl literature; letters.

lettré, e, lay-treh, a
learned; literary.

leur, ler, pers pron to
them.

leur, leurs, ler, poss a
their.

leurrer, ler-reh, v to lure;
to decoy.

levain, ler-vang, m yeast.

levant, ler-vahng, m East;

a rising.

levée, ler-veh, f raising;
removal; levy; post
collection.

lever, ler-veh, v to raise;
to collect; **se –,** to stand
up; to get up; m rising.

levier, ler-ve-eh, m lever;
crowbar.

lèvre, lay-vr, f lip.

lévrier, leh-vre-eh, m
greyhound.

levure, ler-vEEr, f yeast.

lézard, leh-zăhr, m lizard.

lézarde, leh-zăhrd, f
crevice; crack.

liaison, lee-ay-zong, f
joining; junction; affair;
liaison.

liant, e, lee-ahng, a pliant;
affable; sociable.

liasse, lee-ăhss, f bundle;
wad; file (of papers).

libellé, lee-bel-leh, m
wording.

libellule, lee-bel-lEEl, f
dragonfly.

libérer, lee-beh-reh, v to
liberate; to discharge.

liberté, lee-bair-teh, f
liberty; freedom; ease.

libraire, lee-brair, m
bookseller.

librairie, lee-bray-ree, f
bookshop; booktrade.

libre,* lee-br, a free; bold;
disengaged.

libre-échange, leebr-eh-shahng**sh**, *m* free trade.

libre-service, leebr-sair-
veess *m* self-service.

licence, lee-sahng**ss**, *f*
licence; degree;
licentiousness.

licencié, e le-sahng-se-eh,
a redundant.

licencier, lee-sahng-se-eh,
v to dismiss; to make
redundant.

licencieu-x, se,* lee-
sahng-se-er, *a* licentious.

licite,* lee-seett, *a* lawful;
licit.

lie, lee, *f* lees; dregs; *fig*
scum.

liège, lee-aysh, *m* cork;
cork-tree.

lien, lee-ang, *m* bond; tie;
band.

lier, lee-eh, *v* to bind; to
tie; to join; to thicken.

lierre, lee-air, *m* ivy.

lieu, lee-er, *m* place; spot.

lieutenant, lee-ert-nahng,
m lieutenant.

lièvre, lee-ay-vr, *m* hare.

ligne, leen-yer, *f* line; row;
rank; **en—,** ahng, *adv*
comput on-line.

ligoter, lee-got-eh, *v* to
bind; to tie up.

ligue, leegh, *f* league.

lilas, lee-läh, *m* lilac; *a*
lilac-coloured.

limace, lee-mähss, *f* slug.

limaçon, lee-mäh-song, *m*

snail.

limande, lee-mahng**d**, *f*
lemon sole.

lime, leem, *f* file.

limer, lee-meh, *v* to file;
to polish.

limier, lee-me-eh, *m*
bloodhound; detective.

limite, lee-meet, *f* limit;
boundary; landmark.

limitation de vitesse, le-
me-täh-se-ong-der-ve-
tess *f* speed limit.

limitrophe, lee-me-trof, *a*
bordering; adjacent.

limon, lee-mong, *m* slime;
mud; (vehicle) shaft.

limonade, lee-monn-ähd,
f lemonade.

lin, lang, *m* flax; linen.

linceul, lang-serl, *m*
shroud.

linge, langsh, *m* household
linen; cloth; rag.

lingerie, langsh-ree, *f*
underwear; lingerie;
linen closet.

lingot, lang-go, *m* ingot.

linon, lee-nong, *m* lawn
(fine linen).

linotte, lee-nott, *f* linnet;
tête de —, tayt der —,
scatter-brained person.

lion, ne, lee-ong, *mf* lion;
lioness.

liqueur, lee-ker, *f* liqueur.

liquidation, lee-ke-däh-se-
ong, *f* liquidation;

clearance.

liquide, lee-keed, *a & m*
liquid.

lire, leer, *v* to read.

lis, leess, *m* lily.

lis-eur, euse, lee-zer, *mf*
reader.

lisible,* lee-zee-bl, *a*
legible.

lisière, lee-ze-air, *f*
selvage; border.

lisse, leess, *a* smooth;
sleek; glossy.

liste, leest, *f* list; roll;
schedule; catalogue.

lit, lee, *m* bed; layer;
channel.

litanie, lee-täh-nee, *f* long
story; *pl* litany.

literie, leet-ree, *f* bedding.

litière, lee-te-air, *f* litter
(stable).

litige, lee-teesh, *m*
litigation.

litre, lee-tr *m* litre.

littéraire, lee-teh-rair, *a*
literary.

littéral, e,* lee-teh-rähl, *a*
literal.

littérateur, lee-teh-räh-
ter, *m* man of letters.

littérature, lee-teh-räh-
tEEr, *f* literature.

littoral, lee-tor-ähl, *m*
coastline; *a* of the coast.

livide, lee-veed, *a* livid.

livraison, lee-vray-zong, *f*
delivery.

livre, lee-vr, *m* book; *f* pound; pound sterling.

livrée, lee-vreh, *f* livery; servants.

livrer, lee-vreh, *v* to deliver; to betray.

livret, lee-vray, *m* booklet; savings book; bank book.

livreur, –euse, lee-vrer, *mf* delivery boy, girl, man, woman.

local, lock-ăhl, *m* place; premises.

local, e,* lock-ăhl, *a* local.

locataire, lock-ăh-tair, *m* tenant; lodger.

location, lock-ăh-se-ong, *f* letting; hiring; renting; – de voitures, – der vo'ăh-tEEr, car hire.

locomo-teur, trice, lock-omm-ot-er, *a* locomotive.

locomotive, lock-omm-ot-eev, *f* locomotive; engine.

locution, lock-E-se-ong, *f* locution; expression; idiom.

loge, losh, *f* lodge; hut; box.

logement, losh-mahng, *m* lodging; accommodation; quarters.

loger, losh-eh, *v* to lodge; to house; to dwell.

logiciel, lo-she-se-ell, *m comput* software.

logique, losh-eeck, *f* logic; *a** logical.

logis, losh-e, *m* dwelling; house; home.

loi, lo'ăh, *f* law; authority; act.

loin, lo'ang, *adv* far; distant.

lointain, e, lo'ang-tang, *a* remote; far off.

loisir, lo'ăh-zeer, *m* leisure; time.

Londres, long-dr *m* London.

long, ue,* long, *a* long; à long terme, ăh – tairm, long-term.

longer, long-sheh, *v* to pass along; to walk along; to coast.

longtemps, long-tahng, *adv* long; a long while.

longueur, long-gher, *f* length.

longue-vue, long-gh-vE, *f* telescope.

lopin, lop-ang, *m* patch of ground.

loque, lock, *f* rag; tatter.

loquet, lock-ay, *m* latch.

lorgner, lorn-yeh, *v* to ogle; to have an eye on.

lorgnette, lorn-yett, *f* opera-glasses.

lorgnon, lorn-yong, *m* eye-glass; pince-nez.

lors, lor, *adv* then; at the time; dès –, day –, ever since.

lorsque, lors-ker, *conj* when.

losange, loz-ahngsh, *m* lozenge; diamond.

lot, lo, *m* portion; share; prize; gros –, groh –, jackpot.

loterie, lot-ree, *f* raffle; lottery.

lotir, lot-eer, *v* to allot; to portion.

louable,* loo-ăh-bl, *a* laudable; praiseworthy.

louage, loo-ăhsh, *m* hire; letting out; renting.

louange, loo-ahngsh, *f* praise.

louche, loosh, *f* soup-ladle; *a* squint-eyed; suspicious.

louer, loo-eh, *v* to let; to rent; to hire; to praise.

loup, loo, *m* wolf.

loup-garou, loo-găh-roo, *m* bugbear.

loupe, loop, *f* magnifying glass.

lourd, e,* loor, *a* heavy; dull; clumsy.

lourdaud, loor-doh, *m* blockhead; *a* clumsy; lumpish.

lourdeur, loor-der, *f* heaviness; dullness.

louve, loov, *f* she-wolf.

loyal, e,* lo'ăh-yăhl, *a* honest; true; faithful.

loyauté, lo'ăh-yoh-teh, *f* honesty; fairness.

loyer, lo'ăh-yeh, *m* hire; rent.

lubie, lE-bee, *f* whim; fad.

lubrifiant, lE-bre-fe-ahng, *m* lubricant; *a* lubricating.

lubrifier, lE-bre-fe-eh, *v* to lubricate.

lucarne, lE-kăhrn, *f* skylight.

lucide,* lE-seedd, *a* lucid; clear.

lucrati-f, ve,* lE-krăh-teeff, *a* lucrative.

lueur, lE- er, *f* glimmer; gleam.

lugubre,* lE-ghE-br, *a* lugubrious.

lui, lwe, *pers pron* he; him; to him; her; to her; it; to it.

luire, lweer, *v* to shine; to glitter.

luisant, e, lwe-zahng, *a* shining; glossy.

lumière, lE-me-air, *f* light; *pl* knowledge.

lumineu-x, se,* lE-me-ner, *a* luminous.

lunaire, lE-nair, *a* lunar.

lundi, lung-de, *m* Monday.

lune, lEEn, *f* moon; – **de miel,** – der me-ell, honeymoon.

lunette, lE-nayt, *f* telescope; *pl* spectacles; –**s de soleil,** – der-soll-a'ye, sunglasses.

lustre, lEEs-tr, *m* lustre; gloss; chandelier.

luth, lEEt, *m* lute.

lutin, lE-tang, *m* goblin; imp (of child); *a* roguish.

lutiner, lE-te-neh, *v* to tease.

lutte, lEEt, *f* wrestling; struggle; contest; strife.

lutter, lE-teh, *v* to wrestle; to struggle.

luxe, lEEks, *m* luxury.

luxer, lEEk-seh, *v* to dislocate.

luxueu-x, se,* lEEk-sE- er, *a* luxurious.

luxure, lEEk-sEEr, *f* lust.

lycée, lee-seh, *m* secondary school.

lyre, leer, *f* lyre.

lyrique, lee-reeck, *a* lyrical.

lyrisme, lee-reessm, *m* lyricism.

ma, măh, *poss a f* my.

macabre, măh-kah-br, *a* macabre.

macédoine, măh-seh-do'ăhn, *f* mixed dish (of vegetables or fruit).

mâcher, mah-sheh, *v* to chew.

machinal, e,* măh-she-nähl, *a* mechanical.

machine, măh-sheen, *f* machine; engine; implement; **– à laver, –** ăh läh-veh, washing machine.

machiner, măh-she-neh, *v* to plot; to contrive.

mâchoire, mah-sho'ăhr, *f* jaw; jawbone.

mâchonner, mah-shonn-eh, *v* to munch.

maçon, măh-song, *m* mason; bricklayer; freemason.

madame, măh-dăhm, *f* madam; Mrs.

mademoiselle, măhd-mo'ăh-zell, *f* Miss; the young lady.

madone, măh-donn, *f* madonna.

madré, e, măh-dreh, *a* speckled; cunning.

magasin, măh-găh-zang, *m* shop; warehouse.

magasinage, măh-găh-ze-năhsh, *m* warehousing.

magazine, măh-găh-zeen, *m* magazine.

magie, măh-shee, *f* magic.

magique,* măh-sheeck, *a* magic; magical.

magistral, e,* măh-shees-trähl, *a* masterly; authoritative.

magistrat, măh-shees-träh, *m* magistrate.

magistrature, măh-shees-träh-tEEr, *f* magistracy; magistrates.

magnanime,* măhn-yăh-neem, *a* magnanimous.

magnétique, măhn-yeh-teeck, *a* magnetic.

magnétophone, măhn-yeh-toh-fonn, *m* tape recorder.

magnétoscope, măhn-yeh-toh-skop *f* video (recorder).

magnifique,* măhn-yee-feeck, *a* magnificent.

magot, mah-go, *m* nest egg.

mai, may, *m* May; maypole.

maigre,* may-gr, *a* lean; thin; scanty; barren.

maigrir, may-greer, *v* to become thin.

maille, mah'e, *f* mesh; stitch; (chain) mail.

maillot, mah'e-yo, *m* (sports) shirt; **– (de bain),** – (der-bang), swimsuit.

main, mang, *f* hand.

main-d'œuvre, mang-der-vr, *f* workmanship; labour.

main-forte, mang-fort, *f* assistance; help.

maint, e, mang, *a* many; several.

maintenant, mangt-nahng, *adv* now.

maintenir, mangt-neer, *v* to maintain; to secure; to keep up.

maintien, mang-te-ang, *m* maintenance; deportment; countenance.

maire, mair, *m* mayor.

mairie, may-ree, *f* townhall.

mais, may, *conj* but; – **oui,** – we, "why, yes".

maïs, măh-eess, *m* maize.

maison, may-zong, *f* house; home; firm.

maisonnette, may-zonn-ett, *f* cottage; small house.

maître, may-tr, *m* master; owner; teacher.

maîtresse, may-tress, *f* teacher; mistress.

maîtrise, may-treez, *f* mastery, self-control.

maîtriser, may-tre-zeh, *v* to master; to keep under control.

majesté, măh-shess-teh, *f* majesty.

majestueu-x, se,* măh-shess-tE-er, *a* majestic.

majeur, e, măh-sher, *a* greater; major; **force –e,** fors –, of necessity.

major, măh-shor, *m* major.

majorité, măh-shor-e-teh, *f* majority; coming of age.

majuscule, măh-**sh**EEs-kEEl, *f* capital (letter).

mal, măhl, *adv* ill; badly; amiss; on bad terms; *m* evil; mischief; misfortune; ache; sickness; – **de la route,** – der-lăh root, travel sickness.

malade, măh-lăhd, *mf* sick person; patient; *a* ill; sick.

maladie, măh-lăh-dee, *f* illness.

maladi-f, ve,* măh-lăh-deeff, *a* sickly.

maladresse, măh-lăh-dress, *f* awkwardness; blunder.

maladroit, e,* măh-lăh-dro'ăh, *a* clumsy.

malaise, măh-layz, *m* uneasiness; discomfort; dizziness.

malaisé, e, măh-lay-zeh, *a* difficult; incommodious.

malappris, e, măhl-ăh-pree, *mf* vulgar person; *a* illbred.

malavisé, e, măhl-ăh-ve-zeh, *a* ill-advised.

malaxer, măhl-acks-seh, *v* to knead; to mix; to massage.

malchance, măhl-shahngss, *f* bad luck.

mâle, mahl, *m* male; *a* male; manly; virile.

maléfice, măh-leh-feess, *m* witchcraft.

malencontreu-x, se,* măh-lahng-kong-trer *a* unlucky; unfortunate.

malentendu, măh-lahng-tahng-dE, *m* misunderstanding.

malfaisant, e, măhl-fer-zahng, *a* mischievous; noxious.

malfai-teur, trice, măhl-fay-ter, *mf* criminal.

malgré, măhl-greh, *prep* in spite of; despite.

malhabile,* măhl-ăh-beel, *a* unskillful.

malheur, măh-ler, *m* unhappiness; misfortune; bad luck.

malheureu-x, se,* măhl-er-rer, *mf* & *a* unhappy; wretched.

malhonnête,* măhl-onn-ayt, *a* dishonest.

malice, măh-leess, *f* malice; spite.

malicieu-x, se,* măh-le-se-er, *a* spiteful; mischievous.

malin, maligne,* măh-lang, măh-leen-yer *a* malignant; malicious; mischievous; sly; cunning.

malle, mähl, *f* trunk.

mallette, mäh-lett, *f* small suitcase.

malmener, mähl-mer-neh, *v* to handle roughly; to abuse.

malotru, e, mähl-ot-rE, *mf* ill-bred person; lout.

malpropre,* mähl-propr, *a* slovenly; dirty.

malsain, e, mähl-sang, *a* (things) unwholesome; (persons) unhealthy.

malséant, e, mähl-seh-ahng, *a* unbecoming.

malsonnant, e, mähl-sonn-ahng, *a* ill-sounding; offensive.

maltraiter, mähl-tray-teh, *v* to ill-treat; to injure.

malveillant, e, mähl-vay'e-ahng, *a* malevolent.

maman, mäh-mahng, *f* mummy.

mamelle, mäh-mell, *f* breast; udder.

mamelon, mäh-mer-long, *m* nipple; teat.

mammifère, mäh-me-fair, *m* mammal.

manche, mahngsh, *m* handle; *f* sleeve.

manchette, mahng-shett, *f* cuff.

manchon, mahng-shong, *m* muff.

manchot, e, mahng-sho, *a* & *mf* one-armed.

mandarine, mahng-däh-reen *f* satsuma.

mandat, mahng-däh, *m* mandate; money order; warrant.

mandataire, mahng-däh-tair, *m* proxy; agent.

mander, mahng-deh, *v* to send word; to order; to send for.

manège, mäh-naish *m* riding school; roundabout; *fam* trick.

manette, mäh-nett, *f* small handle.

mangeable, mahng-shäh-bl, *a* edible.

mangeaille, mahng-shäh'e, *f* feed; *fam* grub.

manger, mahng-sheh, *v* to eat; to squander; *m* food.

maniable, mäh-ne-äh-bl, *a* easy to handle.

maniaque, mäh-ne-ähck, *m* maniac; *a* eccentric.

manie, mäh-nee, *f* mania; craze.

maniement, mäh-ne-mahng, *m* handling; management.

manier, mäh-ne-eh, *v* to handle; to manage; to govern.

manière, mäh-ne-air, *f* manner; style; type; *pl* manners; airs.

maniéré, e, mäh-ne-eh-reh, *a* affected.

manifestation, mäh-ne-fes-tah-se-ong, *f* manifestation; political demonstration.

manifeste, mäh-ne-fest, *m* manifesto; manifest; *a** manifest; evident.

manifester, mäh-ne-fess-teh, *v* to manifest; to demonstrate.

manipuler, mäh-ne-pE-leh, *v* to manipulate; to handle.

manivelle, mäh-ne-vell, *f* handle; crank.

mannequin, mähn-kang, *m* dummy; fashion model.

manœuvre, mäh-ner-vr, *m* labourer; *f* move; drill.

manœuvrer, mäh-ner-vreh, *v* to handle; to work; to manœuvre.

manoir, mäh-no'ähr, *m* manor; mansion.

manque, mahngk, *m* lack; deficiency; failure.

manqué, é, mahng-keh, *a* missed; defective; failed.

manquement, mahngk-mahng, *m* omission; failure; oversight.

manquer, mahng-keh, *v* to fail; to want; to err; to miss; to be very near to (doing something).

mansarde, mahng-sährd, *f*

garret; attic.

manteau, mahng-toh, *m* coat; mantle.

manuel, măh-nE-ell, *m* textbook.

manuel, le,* măh-nE-ell, *a* manual.

manufacture, măh-nE-făhck-tEEr, *f* factory; making.

manuscrit, măh-nEEs-kree, *m* manuscript.

maquereau, măhck-roh, *m* mackerel.

maquette, măhck-ett, *f* model; dummy (book); mock-up

maquillage, măh-kee-yăhsh, *m* make-up.

maquiller, măh-kee-yeh, *v* to make up (face); to disguise.

maraîch-er, ère, măh-ray-sheh, *a* of market gardens.

marais, măh-ray, *m* marsh; swamp; bog.

marathon, măh-răh-tong *m* marathon.

marâtre, măh-rah-tr, *f* cruel stepmother.

marauder, măh-roh-deh, *v* maraud; to plunder.

marbre, măhr-br, *m* marble; marble slab.

marchand, e, măhr-shahng, *mf* tradesman; tradeswoman; dealer; *a*

saleable; merchant.

marchandage, măhr-shahng-dăhsh, *m* bargaining.

marchandise, măhr-shahng-deez, *f* goods; wares.

marche, măhrsh, *f* stair; walking; march; progress; running (trains, etc).

marché, măhr-sheh, *m* market; bargain; purchase; contract; **bon** –, bong –, cheap; **meilleur** –, may-yer – cheaper; **noir, –** no'ăhr, black market.

marchepied, măhr-sher-pe-eh, *m* stepping stone.

marcher, măhr-sheh, *v* to walk; to tread; to work; to move; to go (well, badly)

mardi, măhr-de, *m* Tuesday.

mare, măhr, *f* pool; pond.

marécage, măh-reh-kăhsh, *m* marsh; bog; swamp.

maréchal, măh-reh-shăhl, *m* marshal; **– ferrant,** – feh-rahng, blacksmith.

marée, măh-reh, *f* tide; fresh (sea) fish.

margarine, măhr-ghăh-reen, *f* margarine.

marge, măhrsh, *f* margin;

border; time.

marguerite, măhr-gher-reet, *f* daisy; marguerite.

mari, măh-re, *m* husband.

mariage, măh-re-ăhsh, *m* marriage; wedding; union.

marié, e, măh-re-eh, *mf* bridegroom; bride; *a* married.

marier, măh-ré-eh, *v* to marry; to unite; **se** –, to get married.

marin, măh-rang, *m* sailor; seaman.

marin, e, măh-rang, *a* marine; seagoing.

marinade, măh-re-năhd, *f* pickle; marinade.

marine, măh-reen, *f* navy; navigation; **bleu** –, bler –, navy blue.

marionnette, măh-re-onn-ett, *f* puppet; *pl* puppet show.

marmaille, măhr-mah'e, *f* crowd of kids.

marmite, măhr-meet, *f* stock-pot.

marmot, măhr-mo, *m* brat; child.

marmotter, măhr-mot-eh, *v* to mutter.

maroquin, măh-rock-ang, *m* morocco leather.

marquant, e, măhr-kahng, *a* prominent; striking.

marque, măhrk, *f* mark;

stamp; brand; token.

marquer, măhr–keh, *v* to mark; to be conspicuous.

marqueterie, măhr-kert-ree, *f* inlaid work.

marquis, e, măhr-ke, *mf* marquis; marchioness; marquee.

marraine, măh-rain, *f* godmother.

marrant, măh-rahng, *a fam* funny; amusing; odd.

marre, măhr, *adv* fed-up; **en avoir – (de),** ahng-ăh-vo'ăhr – der, *v* fed-up (with).

marron, măh-rong, *m* chestnut; *a* chestnut coloured; brown.

marronnier, măh-ronn-e-eh, *m* chestnut tree.

mars, măhrs, *m* March; Mars.

marseillaise, măhr-say'e-ayz, *f* Marseillaise.

marsouin, măhr-soo-ang *m* porpoise.

marteau, măhr-toh, *m* hammer; door knocker.

marteler, măhr-ter-leh, *v* to hammer; to torment.

martial, e,* măhr-se-ăhl, *a* martial.

martinet, măhr-te-nay, *m* swift; cat o'nine tails; whip.

martre, măhr-tr, *f* marten;

sable.

martyre, măhr-teer, *m* martyrdom.

masculin, e, măhss-kE-lang, *a & m* masculine; male.

masque, măhsk, *m* mask; pretence.

masquer, măhss-keh, *v* to mask; to disguise; to hide.

massacrer, măhss-ăh-kreh, *v* to slaughter; to spoil; to bungle.

masse, măhss, *f* mass; heap; bulk; lot; pool.

massif, măhss-eef, *m* thicket; clump of shrubs; chain of mountains.

massi-f, ve,* măhss-eef, *a* massive; heavy; solid.

massue, măhss-E, *f* club.

mastic, măhss-teeck, *m* putty.

mastiquer, măhss-te-keh, *v* to cement; to masticate.

mat, măht, *m* (chess) mate.

mat, e, măht, *a* mat; unpolished; dull; heavy.

mât, mah, *m* mast; pole.

matelas, măht-lăh, *m* mattress.

matelot, măht-lo, *m* sailor; seaman.

mater, măh-teh, *v* to checkmate; to mat; *fam*

to curb; to subdue.

matériaux, măh-te-re-oh, *mpl* materials.

matériel, măh-teh-re-ell, *m* stock; plant.

matériel, le,* măh-teh-re-ell, *a* a material.

maternel, le,* măh-tair-nell, *a* motherly; maternal; *f* nursery school.

maternité, măh-tair-ne-teh, *f* maternity; maternity ward.

math(s), măht *fpl* maths.

mathématiques, măh-teh-măh-teeck, *fpl* mathematics.

matiére, măh-te-air, *f* matter; material; subject; cause.

matin, măh-tang, *m* morning.

matinal, e, măh-te-năhl, *a* early.

matinée, măh-te-neh, *f* morning; matinee.

matois, e, măh-to´ăh, *mf* sly person; *a* cunning; artful.

matrice, măh-treess, *f* matrix; womb.

matricule, măh-tre-kEEl, *f* registration; roll.

maturité, măh-tE-re-teh, *f* maturity; ripeness.

maudire, moh-deer, *v* to curse.

maudit, e, moh-de, *a* cursed.

maugréer, moh-greh-eh, *v* to curse; to grumble.

maussade,* moh-săhd, *a* cross; sulky; dull.

mauvais, e, moh-vay, *a* evil; bad; ill; wrong.

mauve, mohv, *a & m* mauve.

mayonnaise, măh-yongn-nays *f* mayonnaise.

me, mer, *pron* me; to me; at me.

mécanicien, meh-kăh-ne-se-ang, *m* mechanic; engineer.

mécanique, meh-kăh-neeck, *f* mechanics; machinery; *a** mechanical.

mécanisme, meh-kăh-nissm, *m* mechanism; machinery.

méchamment, meh-shăh-mahng, *adv* wickedly; unkindly.

méchanceté, meh-shahngss-teh, *f* wickedness; unkindness.

méchant, e, meh-shahng, *mf* wicked person; naughty child; *a* wicked; ill-natured; naughty.

mèche, maysh, *f* wick; match; lock (of hair).

mécompte, meh-kongt, *m* miscalculation;

disappointment.

méconnaissable, meh-konn-ess-ăh-bl, *a* unrecognizable.

méconnaître, meh-konn-ay-tr, *v* to be unaware of.

méconnu, e, meh-konn-E, *pp & a* unacknowledged; unappreciated.

mécontent, e, meh-kong-tahng, *a* discontented; unhappy.

mécréant, meh-kreh-ahng, *m* unbeliever; wretch.

médaille, meh-dah´e, *f* medal; badge.

médaillon, meh-dah´e-yong, *m* medallion; locket.

médecin, mehd-sang, *m* physician; doctor.

médecine, mehd-seen, *f* medicine (art of).

média, meh-de-ăh *mpl* media.

médiat, e, meh-de-ăh, *a* mediate.

média-teur, trice, meh-de-ăh-ter, *mf* mediator.

médicament, meh-de-kăh-mahng, *m* medicine; *pl* medication.

médiocre,* meh-de-ockr, *a* mediocre.

médire, meh-deer, *v* to slander.

médisance, meh-de-zahngss, *f* slander.

méditer, meh-de-teh, *v* to meditate; to plan.

méditerranéen, ne, meh-de-tay-răh-neh-ahng *a* Mediterranean.

méduse, meh-dEEz, *f* jellyfish.

méfait, meh-fay, *m* misdeed.

méfiance, meh-fe-ahngss, *f* mistrust; caution.

méfiant, e, meh-fe-ahng, *a* mistrustful; suspicious.

méfier (se), ser meh-fe-eh, *v* to mistrust (de); to beware of.

mégarde (par), păhr meh-găhrd, *adv* inadvertently.

mégère, meh-shair, *f* shrew (of woman).

meilleur, e, may'e-er, *a* better; best.

mélancolique,* meh-lahng-koll-eeck, *a* melancholy; gloomy.

mélange, meh-lahngsh, *m* mixture; blending; medley.

mélanger, meh-lahng-sheh, *v* to mix; to blend.

mêlée, may-leh, *f* fray; scuffle; conflict; scrum.

mêler, may-leh, *v* to mix; to blend; to entangle.

mélodieu-x, se,* meh-lod-e-er, *a* melodious.

melon mer-long, *m* melon;

fam bowler hat.

membrane, mahng-brähn, *f* membrane; film.

membre, mahng-br, *f* penis; member; limb.

même, maym, *a* same; even; very; self.

mémoire, meh-mo'ähr, *m* memorandum; bill; *pl* memoirs *f* memory; fame.

menaçant, e, mer-näh-sahng, *a* threatening.

menace, mer-nähss, *f* menace; threat.

menacer, mer-nähss-eh, *v* to threaten.

ménage, meh-näsh, *m* housekeeping; cleaning; household; married couple.

ménagement, meh-näsh-mahng, *m* regard; caution; tact.

ménager, meh-näh-sheh, *v* to spare; to treat with tact.

ménag-er, ère, meh-näh-sheh, *a* domestic; of the household.

ménagère, meh-näh-**shair**, *f* housewife.

mendiant, e, mahng-de-ahng, *mf* & *a* beggar; begging.

mendicité, mahng-de-se-teh, *f* begging.

mendier, mahng-de-eh, *v* to beg.

mener, mer-neh, *v* to lead; to head; to convey.

meneur, mer-ner, *m* leader; ringleader.

méningite, meh-nang-**sheet,** *f* meningitis.

menotte, mer-not, *f* little hand; *pl* handcuffs.

mensonge, mahngss-ongsh, *m* lie.

menstruation, mahngss-trE-äh-se-ong *f* menstruation.

mensuel, le,* mahng-sE-ell, *a* monthly.

mental, e,* mahng-tähl, *a* mental.

mentalité, mahng-täh-le-teh, *f* frame of mind; mentality.

menteu-r, se, mahng-ter, *mf* liar; *a* lying.

menthe, mahngt, *f* mint.

mentionner, mahng-se-onn-eh, *v* to mention.

mentir, mahng-teer, *v* to lie; to fib.

menton, mahng-tong, *m* chin.

menu, mer-nE, *m* menu.

menu e, mer-nE, *a* thin; slender; fine; minor.

menuisier, mer-nwee-ze-eh, *m* joiner; carpenter.

méprendre (se), ser meh-prahng-dr, *v* to be mistaken.

mépris, meh-pree, *m* contempt; scorn.

méprisable, meh-pre-zäh-bl, *a* contemptible; despicable.

méprise, meh-preez, *f* mistake.

mépriser, meh-pre-zeh, *v* to despise; to scorn.

mer, mair, *f* sea; **mal de –,** mähl der –, seasickness.

mercernaire, mair-ser-nair, *m* & *a* mercenary; hireling.

mercerie, mair-ser-ree, *f* haberdashery.

merci, mair-se, *m* thanks; thank you; *f* mercy.

merci-er, ère, mair-se-eh, *mf* haberdasher.

mercredi, mair-krer-de, *m* Wednesday.

mère, mair, *f* mother; *a* principal.

méridien, ne, meh-re-de-ang, *a* meridian.

méridien, e, meh-re-de-ain, *f* meridian line; siesta.

méridional, e, meh-re-de-onn-ähl, *a* & *mf* southern; southerner.

mérite, meh-reet, *m* merit; worth; talent.

mériter, meh-re-teh, *v* to deserve; to be worth; to require.

méritoire,* meh-re-to'ähr,

a meritorious.

merlan, mair-lah*ng*, *m* whiting.

merle, mairl, *m* blackbird.

merveille, mair-vay'e, *f* marvel; wonder; *adv phr* à –, äh –, excellently.

merveilleu-x, se,* mair-vay'e-er, *a* wonderful.

mes, may, *poss a pl* my.

mésallier (se), ser meh-zäh-le-eh, *v* to marry beneath oneself.

mésange, meh-zah*ng*sh, *f* (bird) tit (mouse).

mésaventure, meh-zäh-vah*ng*-tEEr, *f* mischance; mishap.

mésestimer, meh-zess-te-meh, *v* to undervalue.

mesquin, e,* mess-ka*ng*, *a* mean; stingy.

mesquinerie, mess-keen-ree, *f* meanness; pettiness.

message, mess-ähsh, *m* message; errand.

messag-er, ère, mess-äh-sheh, *mf* messenger; courrier.

messagerie, mess-ähsh-ree, *f* mail service; shipping service.

messe, mayss, *f* mass.

mesure, mer-zEEr, *f* measure; measurement; proportion; step; propriety; (music) bar;

time.

mesuré, e, mer-zE-reh, *a* regular; guarded.

mesurer, mer-zE-reh, *v* to measure; to consider; to proportion.

mésuser, meh-zE-zeh, *v* to misuse.

métal, meh-tähl, *m* metal.

métamorphose, meh-täh-mor-fohz, *f* metamorphosis; transformation.

météore, meh-teh-or, *m* meteor.

météorologique, meh-teh-o-ro-lo-sheeck, *a* meteorological.

méthode, meh-tod, *f* method; way; system.

méthodique,* meh-tod-eeck, *a* methodical.

méticuleu-x, se,* meh-te-kE-ler, *a* meticulous; particular.

métier, meh-te–eh, *m* trade; profession; handicraft; loom.

métis, se, meh-tee, *mf & a* mixed-race; of multiracial/ multicultural origins.

métrage, meh-trähsh, *m* measuring; metric length; length of film.

mètre, met-tr, *m* metre; rule.

métrique, meh-treeck, *a*

metric.

métropole, meh-trop-ol, *f* metropolis; mother country.

métropolitain, meh-trop-oll-e-tang, *a* metropolitan.

Métro, meh-tro, *m* underground railway (Paris).

mets, may, *m* food; dish.

mettre, met-tr, *v* to put; to set; to wear; – **au point,** – ro-po'a*ng*, finalize.

meuble, mer-bl, *m* piece of furniture; *pl* furniture; *a* movable.

meubler, mer-bleh, *v* to furnish; to stock.

meule, merl, *f* grindstone; millstone.

meuni-er, ère, mer-ne-eh, *mf* miller.

meurtre, mer-tr, *m* murder.

meurtri-er, ère, mer-tre-eh, *mf* murderer; murderess; *a* deadly.

meurtrir, mer-treer, *v* to bruise.

meurtrissure, mer-triss-EEr, *f* bruise.

meute, mert, *f* pack of hounds; *fam* mob.

mi, me, *m* (music) Mi; E.

mi, me, half; mid; semi-.

miasme, me-ähssm, *m* miasma.

miauler, me-ohl-eh, *v* to mew.

microbe, me-krob, *m* microbe; *fam* germ.

microfilm, me-kroh-feelm, *m* microfilm.

microphone, me-kroh-fonn, *m* microphone.

microsillon, me-croh-se-yong, *m* L.P.

midi, me-de, *m* midday; noon; South (of France).

mie, me, *f* crumb (inside of a loaf).

miel, me-ell, *m* honey.

mielleu-x, se,* me-ell-er, *a* honeyed; bland; soft-spoken.

mien, ne, me-ang, *poss pron* mine.

miette, me-ett, *f* crumb; bit.

mieux, me-er, *adv* better; best; more; *m* best thing; *a* better.

mignon, ne, meen-yong, *a* cute; sweet.

migraine, me-grain, *f* migraine.

mijaurée, me-shohr-eh, *f* affected woman.

mijoter, me-shot-eh, *v* to simmer; *fig* to plot.

milieu, me-le-er, *m* middle; circle; environment; social class.

militaire, me-le-tair, *m* soldier; *a* military.

militant, e, me-le-tahng *a* militant.

mille, mill, *m* one thousand; mile; *a* thousand.

milliard, mill-e-ăhr, *m* one thousand millions.

millième, mill-e-aim, *m* & *a* thousandth.

million, mill-e-ong, *m* million.

millionième, mill-e-onn-e-emm, *m* & *a* millionth.

mime, meem, *m* mime.

minable, me-năh-bl, *a* shabby; pitiable.

minauder, me-nohd-eh, *v* to simper; to mince.

mince, mangss, *a* slender; slim; scanty.

mine, meen, *f* appearance; look; mine; lead (of pencil).

miner, me-neh, *v* to undermine; to wear away.

minerai, meen-ray, *m* ore.

minéral, e, me-neh-răhl, *a* mineral.

mineur, me-ner, *m* miner; *a* (music) minor; minor.

mineur, e, me-ner, *a* minor; under age.

miniature, me-ne-ăh-tEEr, *f* miniature.

mini-er, ère, me-ne-eh, *a* mining.

minime, me-neem, *a* very small; minimal; trifling.

minimum, me-ne-mom *m* minimum.

ministère, me-niss-tair, *m* ministry; services.

ministre, me-neestr, *m* minister; Secretary of State; clergyman.

minois, me-no'ăh, *m fam* pretty face.

minuit, me-nwe, *m* midnight.

minuscule, me-nEEs-kEEl, *f* small letter; *a* minute.

minute, me-nEEt, *f* minute; instant.

minutieu-x, se,* me-nEE-se-er, *a* particular; detailed.

miracle, me-răh-kl, *m* miracle; wonder.

miraculeu-x, se,* me-răh-kE-ler, *a* miraculous; wonderful.

mirage, me-răhsh, *m* mirage; delusion.

mirer, me-reh, *v* to aim at; **se –,** to look at (oneself).

miroir, me-ro'ăhr, *m* mirror; looking glass.

miroiter, me-ro'ăh-teh, *v* to flash; to glisten.

mise, meez, *f* placing; dress; stake.

misérable, me-zeh-răh-bl, *mf* wretch.

misère, me-zair, *f* misery; poverty; trifle.

miséricorde, me-zeh-re-kord, *f* mercy.

mission, miss-e-ong, *f* mission.

missionnaire, miss-e-onn-air, *n* missionary.

mitaine, me-tain, *f* mitten.

mite, meet, *f* clothes moth; mite.

mi-temps, me-tahng, *f* half-time; interval; part-time.

mitiger, me-te-sheh, *v* to mitigate.

mitraille, me-trah'e, *f* grapeshot.

mitrailleuse, me-trah'e-erz, *f* machine-gun.

mixte, meekst, *a* mixed; **école –,** eh-kol –, co-ed school.

mixtion, meeks-te-ong, *f* mixture; compounding; blending.

mobile, mob-eel, *m* moving body; motivé power; mobile; *a* movable; changing.

mobilier, mob-e-le-eh, *m* furniture.

mobili-er, ère, mob-e-le-eh, *a* movable; personal.

mobiliser, mob-e-le-zeh, *v* to mobilize.

mobilité, mob-e-le-teh, *f* mobility; instability.

mode, mod, *m* mood; mode; method.

mode, mod, *f* fashion; way; *pl* millinery.

modèle, mod-ell, *m* model; pattern; size.

modeler, mod-leh, *v* to model; to shape; to mould.

modération, mod-eh-răh-se-ong, *f* moderation.

modérer, mod-eh-reh, *v* to moderate; to quiet.

moderne, mod-airn, *mf* & *a* modern style; modern.

modeste, * mod-est, *a* modest; unassuming.

modestie, mod-ess-tee, *f* modesty.

modifier, mod-e-fe-eh, *v* to modify.

modique, * mod-eeck, *a* moderate; small.

modiste, mod-eest, *f* milliner.

moelle, mwähl, *f* marrow (bone); pith.

moelleu-x, se, * mwähller, *a* marrowy; soft; mellow.

mœurs, mers, *fpl* manners; customs; morals.

moi, mwäh, *pers pron* I; me; to me; *m* self; ego.

moindre, * mwang-dr, *a* less; **le –,** ler –, the least.

moine, mwähn, *m* monk; bed-warmer.

moineau, mwäh-noh, *m* sparrow.

moins, mwang, *adv* less; fewer; least; under; *prep* minus.

mois, mwäh, *m* month.

moisir, mwäh-zeer, *v* to go mouldy; *fam* to vegetate.

moisson, mwähss-ong, *f* harvest; crop.

moite, mwäht, *a* moist; damp; clammy.

moiteur, mwäh-ter, *f* moistness; dampness.

moiteé, mwäh-te-eh, *f* half; *adv* half; partly.

mol, le, * see **mou.**

molaire, moll-air, *f* molar tooth.

môle, mohl, *m* mole; pier.

molester, moll-ess-teh, *v* to molest; to vex.

mollasse, moll-ăhss, *a* flabby; spineless.

mollesse, moll-ess, *f* softness; indolence.

mollet, moll-ay, *m* calf (of the leg).

mollet, te, moll-ay, *a* soft; tender.

molletonné, moll-tonn-eh, *a* fleece-lined; with raised nap.

mollir, moll-eer, *v* to soften; to slacken; to

give way.

moment, mom-ahng, *m* moment; time; occasion.

momentané,* e, mom-ahng-tăh-neh, *a* momentary.

momie, mom-ee, *f* mummy.

mon, mong, *poss a m* my; *f* **ma,** măh, *pl* **mes,** may.

monarchie, monn-ăhr-shee, *f* monarchy.

monarque, monn-ăhrk, *m* monarch.

monastère, monn-ăhss-tair, *m* monastery.

monceau, mong,soh, *m* heap.

mondain, e, * mong-dang, *a* worldly; mundane; fashionable.

monde, mongd, *m* world; mankind; people; society.

mondial, e, mong-de-ăhl, *a* worldwide; global.

monétaire, monn-eh-tair, *a* monetary.

moniteur, monn-e-ter, *m* monitor; instructor; gazette.

monnaie, monn-ay, *f* money; coin; change.

monocle, monn-ockl, *m* eye-glass.

monomane, monn-omm-ăhn, *mf & a* monomaniac; obsessive.

monopole, monn-op-ol, *m* monopoly.

monotone, monn-ot-onn, *a* monotonous.

monseigneur, mong-sehn-yer, *m* my lord; your lordship; Ypur Grace; Your Royal Highness.

monsieur, mer-se-er, *m* gentleman; Mr; master; sir.

monstre, mongss-tr, *m* monster.

monstrueu-x, se, * mongss-trE-er, *a* monstrous; shocking.

mont, mong, *m* mount; mountain.

montage, mong-tăhsh, *m* raising; putting up.

montagnard, e, mong-tăhn-yăhr, *mf* mountaineer.

montagne, mong-tăhn-yer, *f* mountain.

montant, mong-tahng, *m* upright; rise; amount.

montant, e, mong-tahng, *a* rising; uphill; high-necked.

montée, mong-teh, *f* rise; ascent; step.

monter, mong-teh, *v* to ascend; to rise; to ride; to set up; to mount (jewel); **se –,** to amount.

monticule, mong-te-kEEl, *m* hillock.

montre, mong-tr, *f* (wrist) watch; show; display window.

montrer, mong-treh, *v* to show; to teach.

monture, mong-tEEr, *f* mount; frame; setting.

monument, monn-E-mahng, *m* monument.

moquer (se), ser mock-eh, *v* to mock; to make fun of.

moquerie, mock-ree, *f* mockery; derision.

moquette, mock-ett, *f* fitted carpet.

moqueu-r, se, mock-er, *a* mocking.

moral, mor-ăhl, *m* state of mind; morale; spirits.

moral, e, * mor-ăhl, *a* moral; mental.

morale, mor-ăhl, *f* morals; reprimand; moral (of story).

morceau, mor-soh, *m* piece; bit; morsel; extract.

morceler, mor-ser-leh, *v* to cut up into small pieces; to parcel out.

mordant, e, mor-dahng, *a* biting; sarcastic.

mordicus, mor-de-kEEss, *adv* stubbornly; doggedly.

mordre, mor-dr, *v* to bite; to gnaw; to eat away.

morfondre (se), ser mor-fong-dr, *v* to be chilled; to be bored stiff waiting.

morgue, morgh, *f* mortuary; arrogance.

moribond, e, mor-e-bong, *mf & a* dying person; dying.

morne, morn, *a* gloomy; sad; dull.

morose, mor-ohz, *a* morose.

morphine, mor-feen, *f* morphine.

mors, mor, *m* bit; **prendre le – aux dents,** prahng-dr ler – oh dahng, to bolt.

morsure, mor-sEEr, *f* bite; sting.

mort, mor, *f* death.

mort, e, mor, *mf* dead person; *a* dead; stagnant; spent.

mortalité, mor-täh-le-teh, *f* mortality; death-rate.

mortel, le, * mor-tell, *a* mortal; deadly; tedious; lethal.

mortier, mor-te-eh, *m* mortar.

mortifier, mor-te-fe-eh, *v* to mortify; to hang (game).

morue, mor-EE, *f* codfish.

morveu-x, se, mor-ver, *mf* dirty child; brat; *a* runny-nosed.

mot, moh, *m* word; saying; meaning; hint.

moteur, mot-er, *m* motor; engine; *fig* driving force.

mo-teur, trice, mot-er, *a* motive; moving.

motif, mot-eeff, *m* motive; reason.

motion, mo-se-ong, *f* motion; proposal.

motiver, mot-e-veh, *v* to state reason for; to motivate.

motocyclette, mot-oss-e-klett, *f* motor-cycle.

motocycliste, mot-oss-e-kleesst, *m* motor-cyclist.

motte, mot, *f* clod; peat; (butter) pat.

mou (mol before a word beginning with a vowel or **'h'** mute); *f* **molle,** moo, mol, *a* soft; indolent; (weather) muggy.

mouchard, moo-shähr, *m fam* sneak; informer.

mouche, moosh, *f* fly; beauty spot; bull's eye.

moucher, moo-sheh, *v* to wipe the nose of; **se –,** to blow one's nose.

moucheron, moosh-rong, *m* gnat; snuff (candle).

mouchoir, moo-sho'ähr, *m* handkerchief.

moudre, moodr, *v* to grind.

moue, moo, *f* pout.

mouette, moo-ett, *f* sea-gull.

mouillé, e, moo'e-yeh, *a* wet; soaked; anchored.

mouiller, moo'e-yeh, *v* to wet; to soak; to anchor.

moule, moo, *m* mould; cast; form; *f* mussel.

mouler, moo-leh, *v* to mould; to cast; to shape.

moulin, moo-lang, *m* mill; windmill; **– à paroles, –** äh päh-rol, chatter box.

moulu, e, moo-lE, *pp & a* ground.

mourant, e, moo-rahng, *mf & a* dying person; dying.

mourir, moo-reer, *v* to die; to die away; (fire, light) to go out.

mousquetaire, mooss-ker-tair, *m* musketeer.

mousse, mooss, *m f* moss; mousse; froth; lather; ship's-boy.

mousseline, mooss-leen, *f* muslin; chiffon.

mousser, mooss-eh, *v* to foam; to lather; to sparkle.

mousseu-x, se, mooss-er, *a* frothy; sparkling.

moustache, mooss-tähsh, *f* moustache; (animals) whiskers.

moustiquaire, mooss-te-kair, *m* mosquito-net.

moustique, mooss-teeck, *m* mosquito.

moutarde, moo-tăhrd, *f* mustard.

mouton, moo-tong, *m* sheep; mutton; sheepskin.

mouvant, e, moo-vahng, *a* moving; shifting.

mouvement, moov-mahng, *m* movement; motion; disturbance; traffic.

mouvementé, e, moov-mahng-teh, *a* agitated; lively; eventful; fluctuating.

mouvoir, moo-vo'ăhr, *v* to move; to stir; to start.

moyen, mo'ăh-yang, *m* means; medium; power.

moyen, ne, mo'ăh-yang, *a* middle; mean; average.

moyennant, mo'ăh-yay-nahng *prep* on condition, for a consideration.

moyenne, moăh-yain, *f* average; mean.

muer, mE-eh, *v* to moult; (voice) to break.

muet, te, mE-ay, *mf* dumb person; *a* dumb; taciturn.

mufle, mEE-fl, *m* muzzle; *fam* boor.

mugir, mE-sheer, *v* to low;

to bellow; to roar.

mugissement, mE-shiss-mahng, *m* lowing; bellowing; roaring.

muguet, mE-ghay, *m* lily of the valley.

mule, mEEl, *f* she-mule; slipper.

mulet, mE-lay, *m* mule; mullet.

multiplier, mEEl-te-ple-eh, *v* to multiply.

multitude, mEEl-te-tEEd, *f* multitude.

municipalité, mE-ne-se-păh-le-teh, *f* municipality; town-hall.

munificence, mE-ne-fe-sahngss, *f* munificence.

munir, mE-neer, *v* to provide; to supply; to arm (**de**, with).

munitions, mE-ne-se-ong, *fpl* ammunition; stores.

mur, mEEr, *m* wall; **au pied du** –, oh pe-eh dE –, in a corner.

mûr, e, * mEEr, *a* ripe; mature; mellow.

muraille, mE-rah'e, *f* wall; rampart.

mûre, mEEr, *f* mulberry; blackberry.

mûrir, mEE-reer, *v* to ripen; to mature.

murmure, mEEr-mEEr, *m* murmur; babbling; whisper.

murmurer, mEEr-me-reh, *v* to murmur; to grumble; to whisper.

muscade, mEEss-kăhd, *f* nutmeg.

muscat, mEEss-kăh, *m* muscatel.

muscle, mEEss-kl, *m* muscle.

musculeu-x, se, mEEss-kE-ler, *a* muscular.

museau, mE-zoh, *m* snout; muzzle; (*fam*) face.

musée, mE-zeh, *m* museum.

museler, mEEz-leh, *v* to muzzle.

muser, mE-zeh, *v* to loiter;.

musicien, ne, mE-ze-se-ang, *mf* musician; *a* musical; – **ambulant**, – ahng-bE-lahng, *n* busker.

musique, mE-zeeck, *f* music; band.

musulman, e, mE-zEl-mahng *a*, *mf* muslim.

mutation, mE-tăh-se-ong, *f* change; transfer.

mutiler, mE-te-leh, *v* to mutilate; to maim; to deface.

mutin, e, mE-tang, *mf* & *a* mutinous; unruly.

mutinerie, mE-teen-ree, *f* mutiny.

mutisme, mE-tissm, *m* silence; muteness.

mutuel, le, * mE-tE-ell, *a*
mutual.

myope, me-op, *a* myopic.

myosotis, me-oz-ot-iss, *m*
forget-me-not.

myrte, meert, *m* myrtle.

mystère, miss-tair, *m*
mystery.

mystérieu-x, se, * miss-
teh-re-er, *a* mysterious.

mystifier, miss-te-fe-eh, *v*
to mystify; to hoax.

mystique, * miss-teeck, *mf*
& *a* mystic; mystical.

nacelle, năh-sell, *f* small boat; basket (of balloon).

nacre, năh-kr, *f* mother-of-pearl.

nage, năhsh, *f* swimming.

nageoire, năh-sho'ăhr, *f* fin.

nager, năh-sheh, *v* to swim; to float.

nageu-r, se, năh-sher, *mf* swimmer.

naguère, năh-ghair, *adv* some time ago.

na-ïf, ïve,* năh-eeff, *a* naïve; unaffected.

nain, e, nang, *mf* & *a* dwarf.

naissance, ness-ahngss, *f* birth; descent; rise.

naissant, e, ness-ahng, *a* newborn; rising; budding.

naître, nay-tr, *v* to be born; to spring; to dawn.

naïveté, năh-eev-teh, *f* artlessness; simplicity.

nantir, nahng-teer, *v* to provide; to secure.

nantissement, nahng-tiss-mahng, *m* security; pledge.

nappe, năhpp, *f* tablecloth; sheet (of water).

narcisse, năhr-seess, *m* narcissus; daffodil.

narcotique, năhr-ko-teeck, *m* & *a* narcotic.

narguer, năhr-gheh, *v* to taunt.

narine, năh-reen, *f* nostril.

narration, năh-răh-se-ong, *f* narrative.

nasal, e,* năh-zăhl, *a* nasal.

nasiller, năh-zee-yeh, *v* to speak through one's nose.

natal, e, năh-tăhl, *a* natal; native.

natalité, năh-tăh-le-teh, *f* birthrate.

natation, năh-tăh-se-ong, *f* swimming.

nati-f, ve, năh-teeff, *a* native.

nation, năh-se-ong, *f* nation.

national, e, năh-se-onn-ăhl, *a* national.

nationalité, năh-se-onn-ăh-le-teh, *f* nationality.

nationaux, năh-se-onn-oh, *mpl* nationals.

natte, năht, *f* mat; matting; plait.

naturaliser, năh-tE-răh-le-zeh, *v* to naturalize.

naturaliste, năh-tE-răh-leesst, *m* naturalist; taxidermist.

nature, năh-tEEr, *f* nature; kind; constitution; *a* plain (of cooking).

naturel, năh-tE-rell, *m* nature; character; native.

naturel, le,* năh-tE-rell, *a* natural; unaffected; illegitimate.

naufrage, noh-frăhsh, *m* shipwreck.

nauséabond, e, noh-zehăh-bong, *a* nauseous.

nausée, noh-zeh, *f* nausea; disgust.

nautique, noh-teeck, *a* nautical; aquatic.

naval, e, năh-văhl, *a* naval.

navet, năh-vay, *m* turnip; *fam* bad film.

navette, năh-vett, *f* shuttle; **faire la –,** fair lăh –, to commute.

navigable, năh-ve-ghăh-bl, *a* navigable; seaworthy.

naviguer, năh-ve-gheh, *v* to navigate; to sail.

navire, năh-veer, *m* ship; vessel.

navrant, e, năh-vrahng, *a* heart-rending; distressing.

navrer, năh-vreh, *v* to break the heart of; to distress.

ne (n'), ner, *adv* not.

né, e, neh, *pp* & *a* born.

néanmoins, neh-ahng-mo'ang, *adv* nevertheless; for all that; however.

néant, neh-ahng, *m* naught; nothingness; worthlessness.

nébuleuse, neh-bE-lerz, *f* nebula.

nébuleu-x, se, neh-bE-ler, *a* nebulous; cloudy; obscure.

nécessaire, neh-sess-air, *m* the needful; necessaries; outfit; *a** necessary; needful.

nécessité, neh-sess-e-teh, *f* necessity; need; *pl* necessaries.

nécessiter, neh-sess-e-teh, *v* to necessitate; to compel.

nécessiteu-x, se, neh-sess-e-ter, *a* needy.

nef, neff, *f* nave; aisle.

néfaste, neh-făhsst, *a* ill-fated; unlucky; disastrous.

négati-f, ve,* neh-ghăh-teeff, *a* negative; *m* negative (photo).

négligé, neh-gle-sheh, *m* negligee.

négligé, e, neh-gle-sheh, *pp* & *a* neglected; careless; slovenly.

négligeable, neh-gle-shăh-bl, *a* negligible.

négligemment, neh-gle-shăh-mahng, *adv* carelessly.

négligence, neh-gle-shahngss, *f* neglect; needlessness; oversight.

négligent, e, neh-gle-shahng, *a* negligent; careless.

négliger, neh-gle-sheh, *v* to neglect; to omit; to

négoce, neh-goss, *m* trade; business; trafficking.

négociable, neh-goss-e-ăh-bl, *a* negotiable.

négociant, neh-goss-e-ahng, *m* merchant.

négocier, neh-goss-e-eh, *v* to negotiate; to deal; to trade.

nègre, négresse, nay-gr, neh-gress, *mf* Negro; Negress.

négrillon, ne, neh-gree-yong, *mf* Negro-boy, Negro-girl.

neige, naysh, *f* snow.

neiger, nay-sheh, *v* to snow.

neigeu-x, se, nay-sher, *a* snowy.

nénuphar, neh-nE-făhr, *m* water-lily.

néon, neh-ong *m* neon.

nerf, nair, *m* nerve; sinew; energy.

nerveu-x, se,* nair-ver, *a* nervous; vigorous; highly-strung.

nervure, nair-vEEr, *f* nerve; cording; rib.

net, nett, *m* fair copy; *adv* plainly; entirely; at once; flatly.

net, te,* nett, *a* neat; clean; net (prices); sharp.

netteté, nett-teh, *f*

cleanness; clearness;
distinctness.

nettoiement, nay-to'ăh-
mahng, *m* cleaning;
clearing.

nettoyage, nay- to'ăh-
yăhsh, *m* cleaning (at
dry cleaners).

nettoyer, nay-to'ăh-yeh, *v*
to clean; to wipe; to rid
of.

neuf, nerf, *a* nine; ninth.

neu-f, ve, nerf, *a* new;
fresh; raw;
inexperienced.

neutre, ner-tr, *m* & *a*
neuter; neutral.

neuvième, ner-ve-aym, *m*
& *a* ninth.

neveu, ner-ver, *m* nephew.

névralgie, neh-vrăhl-shee,
f neuralgia.

névrose, neh-vrohz, *f*
neurosis.

névrosé, é, neh-vro-zeh, *a*
& *n* neurotic.

nez, neh, *m* nose; face;
scent; – à –, – ăh –, face
to face.

ni, ne, *conj* neither; nor;
either; or.

niable, ne-ăh-bl, *a*
deniable.

niais, e,* ne-ay, *mf* & *a*
silly person; stupid.

niaiser, ne-ay-zeh, *v* to
play the fool; to trifle.

niaiserie, ne-ayz-ree, *f*

silliness; foolery.

niche, neesh, *f* nook;
kennel; trick.

nichée, ne-sheh, *f* nestful;
brood; lot.

nicher, ne-sheh, *v* to build
a nest; to lodge; **se –,** to
nestle.

nickelé, e, neek-leh, *pp* &
a nickelled; nickel-
plated.

nid, ne, *m* nest.

nièce, ne-ess, *f* niece.

nier, ne-eh, *v* to deny.

nigaud, e, ne-ghoh, *mf* &
a fool; foolish.

nimbe, nangb, *m* nimbus;
halo.

n'importe qui, nang-por-
ter-ke, *pron* anyone.

nipper, ne-peh, *v fam* to
rig out.

nitouche (sainte), sangt
ne-toosh, *f fam* little
hypocrite.

niveau, ne-voh, *m* level;
standard.

niveler, neev-leh, *v* to
level.

nivellement, ne-vell-
mahng, *m* levelling.

noble, nobl, *mf* & *a*
nobleman; noble.

noblesse, nob-less, *f*
nobility.

noce, noss, *f* wedding;
wedding-party; *pl*
usually: **voyage de –s,**

vo'ăh-yăhsh der –,
honeymoon.

noci-f, ve, noss-eeff, *a*
harmful.

nocturne, nock-tEErn, *m*
(music) nocturne; *a*
nocturnal; nightly; **vie**
–, ve –, *n* nightlife.

Noël, no-ell, *m*
Christmas.

nœud, ner, *m* knot; bow.

noir, no'ăhr, *m* black
(colour).

noir, e, no'ăhr, *mf* black
(person); Black; *a* black;
dark; gloomy; wicked.

noirâtre, no'ăh-rah-tr, *a*
blackish.

noiraud, e, no'ăh-roh, *mf*
& *a* swarthy-looking
person; swarthy.

noirceur, no'ăhr-ser, *f*
blackness.

noircir, no'ăhr-seer, *v* to
blacken.

noisette, no'ăh-zett, *f*
hazelnut; *a inv* nut-
brown.

noix, no'ăh, *f* walnut; nut;
kernel.

nom, nong, *m* name; fame;
noun; – **de famille,** – der
făh-mee-ye, surname.

nomade, nomm-ăhd, *mf* &
a nomad; nomadic.

nombre, nong-br, *m*
number; quantity.

nombreu-x, se, nong-brer,

a numerous; many.

nombril, nong-bre, *m* navel.

nomenclature, nomm-ahng-klăh-tEEr, *f* nomenclature.

nominal, e,* nomm-e-năhl, *a* nominal.

nominatif, nomm-e-năh-teeff, *m* nominative case.

nominati-f, ve, nomm-e-năh-teeff, *a* nominative; registered; personal.

nomination, nomm-e-năh-se-ong, *f* nomination; appointment.

nommément, nomm-eh-mahng, *adv* by name; particularly.

nommer, nomm-eh, *v* to call; to mention; to appoint; **se –,** to give one's name; to be called.

non, nong, *adv* no; not.

nonchalamment, nong-shăh-lăh-mahng, *adv* nonchalantly.

nonchalance, nong-shăh-lahngss, *f* nonchalance.

non-fumeur, nong-fE-mer *m* non-smoker.

nonne, nonn, *f* nun.

nonpareil, le, nong-păh-ray'e, *a* nonpareil; matchless.

non-sens, nong-sahngss, *m*

meaningless sentence.

nord, nor, *m* north; north wind; *a* north.

nord-est, nor-esst, *m* northeast.

nord-ouest, nor-wesst, *m* northwest.

normal, e,* nor-măhl, *a* normal; standard.

nos, noh, *poss a mfpl* our.

nostalgie, noss-tahl-shee, *f* nostalgia; homesickness.

notable,* not-ăh-bl, *a* notable; considerable; eminent.

notaire, not-air, *m* notary.

notamment, not-ăh-mahng, *adv* particularly.

note, not, *f* note; mark; bill; memorandum; memo.

noter, not-eh, *v* to note; to notice; to bear in mind.

notice, not-eess, *f* notice; instructions; account.

notifier, not-e-fe-eh, *v* to notify.

notion, noss-e-ong, *f* notion; idea.

notoire,* not-o'ăhr, *a* well-known; notorious.

notoriété, not-or-e-eh-teh, *f* notoriety.

notre, notr, *poss a m & f* our.

nôtre, noh-tr, *poss pron,*

ours.

nouer, noo-eh, *v* to tie; to knot; to engage in.

noueu-x, se, noo-er, *a* knotty; knotted.

nougat, noo-găh, *m* nougat.

nounou, noo-noo *f* nanny.

nourri, e, noo-re, *pp & a* fed; full; rich;

nourrice, noo-reess, *f* nurse; wet-nurse.

nourrir, noo-rEEr, *v* to feed; to nurse; to entertain (**de,** on; with).

nourrissant, e, noo-riss-ahng, *a* nourishing; nutritious.

nourrisson, noo-riss-ong, *m* newborn.

nourriture, noo-re-tEEr, *f* food; diet; sustenance.

nous, noo, *pers pron* we; us; to us; at us; ourselves; each other.

nouveau, noo-voh, *m* new thing; new person; *adv* newly.

nouveau (nouvel before a word beginning with a vowel or **h** mute), *f*

nouvelle,* noo-voh, noo-vell, *a* new; novel; recent; fresh; additional; another.

nouveau-né, e, noo-voh-neh, *a* newborn.

nouveauté, noo-voh-teh, *f*

newness; novelty; *pl* fancy articles.

nouvelle, noov-ell, *f* news; tidings; short story.

nova-teur, trice, nov-ăh-ter, *a* innovative.

novembre, nov-ahng-br, *m* November.

novice, nov-eess, *mf* novice; *a* inexperienced.

noyade, no'ăh-yăhd, *f* drowning.

noyau, no'ăh-yoh, *m* stone; kernel; nucleus; core.

noyer, no'ăh-yeh, *v* to drown; to swamp; to inundate; *m* walnut tree.

nu, nE, *m* nude; **à –,** ăh –, bare.

nu, e, nE, *a* naked; bare; plain.

nuage, nE-ăhsh, *m* cloud; mist; gloom.

nuageu-x, se, nE-ăh-sher, *a* cloudy.

nuance, nE-ahngss, *f* shade; tint; very small difference.

nuancer, nE-ahngss-eh, *v* to shade; to vary.

nubile, nE-beel, *a* marriageable.

nucléaire, nEE-cleh-air, *a* nuclear.

nudité, nE-de-teh, *f* nakedness; *pl* naked figures.

nuée, nE-eh, *f* cloud; swarm; shower of.

nuire (à), nweer ăh, *v* to hurt; to prejudice; to hinder.

nuisible,* nwee-zee-bl, *a* harmful; detrimental.

nuit, nwee, *f* night; **–** darkness; **– blanche, –** blahngsh, sleepless night; **la –,** lăh –, at night; **de –,** der –, at night.

nul, le, nEEl, *a* no; not any; of no force; void; worthless; *pron* nobody; no one.

nullement, nEEl-mahng, *adv* by no means.

nullité, nEEl-le-teh, *f* nullity; incapacity; nonentity.

numérateur, nE-meh-răh-ter, *m* numerator.

numérique,* nE-meh-reeck, *a* numerical.

numéro, nE-meh-ro, *m* number; size; ticket; item (on programme); issue (of magazines etc); **– de téléphone, –** der-teh-leh-fonn *m* telephone number.

numéroter, nE-meh-rot-eh, *v* to number.

nuptial, e, nEEp-se-ăhl, *a* nuptial.

nuque, nEEk, *f* nape of the neck.

nutriti-f, ve, nE-tre-teeff, *a* nourishing.

nylon, nee-long, *m* nylon.

nymphe, nangf, *f* nymph.

ô! o, *interj* oh!

obéir, ob-eh-eer, *v* to obey; to submit.

obéissance, ob-eh-iss-ahngss, *f* obedience; allegiance.

obéissant, e, ob-eh-iss-ahng, *a* obedient; dutiful.

obérer, ob-eh-reh, *v* to involve in debt.

obèse, ob-ayz, *a* obese; corpulent.

obésité, ob-eh-ze-teh, *f* obesity; corpulence.

objecter, ob-sheck-teh, *v* to object; to allege against.

objectif, ob-sheck-teeff, *m* objective; lens; aim; target.

objecti-f, ive,* ob-sheck-teeff, *a* objective.

objection, ob-sheck-se-ong, *f* objection.

objet, ob-shay, *m* object; subject; matter; thing.

oblation, ob-läh-se-ong, *f* offering.

obligataire, ob-le-gäh-tair, *m* debenture-holder.

obligation, ob-le-gäh-se-ong, *f* obligation; duty; debenture.

obligatoire,* ob-le-gäh-to'ähr, *a* obligatory; compulsory.

obligeamment, ob-le-shäh-mahng, *adv* obligingly.

obligeance, ob-le-shahngss, *f* obligingness; kindness.

obligeant, e, ob-le-shahng, *a* obliging; kind.

obliger, ob-le-sheh, *v* to oblige; to compel; to bind.

oblique,* ob-leeck, *a* oblique; slanting; underhand.

obliquité, ob-le-kwe-teh, *f* obliquity; insincerity.

oblitérer, ob-le-teh-reh, *v* to obliterate; to cancel.

obscène, ob-sain, *a* obscene.

obscur, e, ob-skEEr, *a* dark; obscure; hidden.

obscurcir, ob-skEEr-seer, *v* to darken; to cloud; *fig* to obscure.

obscurément, ob-skE-reh-mahng, *adv* obscurely.

obscurité, ob-skE-re-teh, *f* darkness; obscurity.

obséder, ob-seh-deh, *v* to obsess.

obsèques, ob-sayk, *fpl* funeral.

obséquieu-x, se,* ob-seh-ke-er, *a* obsequious.

observa-teur, trice, ob-sair-väh-ter, *mf* & *a* observer; observant.

observation, ob-sair-väh-se-ong, *f* observation; observance; remark; reprimand.

observatoire, ob-sair-väh-to'ähr, *m* observatory.

observer, ob-sair-veh, *v* to observe; to comply with.

obsession, ob-seh-se-ong, *f*

obsession.

obstacle, obs-tăh-kl, *m* obstacle; hindrance.

obstination, obs-te-năh-se-ong, *f* obstinacy; stubbornness.

obstiné, e, obs-te-neh, *mf & a* obstinate person; obstinate; stubborn.

obstinément, obs-te-neh-mahng, *adv* obstinately.

obstiner (s'), sobs-te-neh, *v* to be obstinate; to persist (à, in).

obstruer, obs-trE-eh, *v* to obstruct.

obtempérer (à), ob-tahng-peh-reh, *v* to obey (a summons, etc); to comply with.

obtenir, ob-ter-neer, *v* to obtain; to get; to procure.

obtus, e, ob-tE, *a* obtuse; dull.

obus, ob-EEz, or ob-E, *m* shell (artillery).

occasion, ock-ăh-ze-ong, *f* occasion; opportunity; bargain; **d'–,** second-hand.

occasionnel, le,* ock-ăh-ze-onn-ell, *a* occasional.

occasionner, ock-ăh-ze-onn-eh, *v* to occasion; to cause.

occident, ock-se-dahng, *m* West.

occidental, e, ock-se-dahng-tăhl, *a* western.

occulte, ock-EElt, *a* occult; secret.

occupant, e, ock-E-pahng, *mf & a* occupier; occupying.

occupation, ock-E-păh-se-ong, *f* occupation; work; profession; capture (of place).

occupé, e, ock-E-peh, *pp & a* occupied (place); engaged; busy.

occuper, ock-E-peh, *v* to occupy; to employ; to inhabit.

occurrence, ock-E-rahngss, *f* occurrence.

océan, oss-eh-ahng, *m* ocean; sea.

océanique, oss-eh-ăh-neeck, *a* oceanic.

ocre, ockr, *f* ochre.

octobre, ock-tobr, *m* October.

octogénaire, ock-tosh-eh-nair, *mf & a* octogenarian.

octogone, ock-to-gonn, *m* octagon.

octroyer, ock-tro'ăh-yeh, *v* to grant.

oculaire,* ock-E-lair, *a* ocular.

oculiste, ock-E-lisst, *m* oculist.

odeur, od-er, *f* odour; smell; fragrance; repute.

odieu-x, se,* od-e-er, *a* odious; hateful; obnoxious.

odorant, e, od-or-ahng, *a* odorous; fragrant.

odorat, od-or-ăh, *m* sense of smell.

œil, er-ye, *m* eye; look; bud; *pl* yeux, yer.

œillade, er'e-yăhd, *f* wink.

œillet, er'e-yay, *m* eyelet; pink; carnation.

œuf, erf, *m* egg; *pl* œufs, er.

œuvre, er-vr, *f* work; society; works.

offensant, e, off-ahng-sahng, *a* offensive.

offense, off-ahngss, *f* offence; trespass; contempt.

offensé, e, off-ahng-seh, *mf & a* offended party.

offenser, off-ahng-seh, *v* to offend; to injure; to shock.

offenseur, off-ahng-ser, *m* offender.

offensi-f, ve,* off-ahngss-eef, *a* offensive.

office, off-eess, *m* office; duty; worship; service; *f* pantry.

officiel, le,* off-eess-e-ell, *a* official.

officier, off-eess-e-eh, *v* to officiate; *m* officer.

officieu-x, se,* off-eess-e-eer, *a* officious; semiofficial.

offrande, off-rahngd, *f* offering.

offre, ofr, *f* offer; tender; bid.

offrir, off-reer, *v* to propose; to present; to bid.

offusquer, off-EEss-keh, *v* to obscure; to offend.

oh! o, *interj* oh!

oie, wăh, *f* goose.

oignon, onn-yong, *m* onion; bulb.

oindre, wang-dr, *v* to anoint.

oiseau, wăh-zoh, *m* bird.

oiseu-x, se,* wăh-zer, *a* idle; trifling; useless.

oisi-f, ve,* wăh-zeeff, *a* idle; unoccupied.

oisiveté, wăh-zeev-teh, *f* idleness.

oison, wăh-zong, *m* gosling; (*fig* & *fam*) fool.

olive, oll-eev, *f* olive; *a inv* olive-green.

olivier, oll-e-ve-eh, *m* olive-tree.

olympique, oll-ang-peeck, *a* Olympic.

ombrage, ong-brăhsh, *m* shade; umbrage.

ombrageu-x, se,* ong-brăh-sher, *a* touchy; easily offended.

ombre, ong-br, *f* shade; shadow; ghost.

ombrelle, ong-brell, *f* parasol.

ombreu-x, se, ong-brer, *a* shady.

omelette, omm-lett, *f* omelet.

omettre, omm-et-tr, *v* to omit; to leave out.

omission, omm-iss-e-ong, *f* omission.

omnibus, omm-ne-bEEss, *m* omnibus.

omoplate, omm-op-lăht, *f* shoulder-blade.

on, ong *indefinite pron m sing* one; someone; anyone; people; we; you; they.

once, ongss, *f* ounce; grain; bit.

oncle, ong-kl, *m* uncle.

onction, ongk-se-ong, *f* unction.

onctueu-x, se,* ongk-tE-er, *a* unctuous; oily.

onde, ongd, *f* wave; surge; water; sea.

ondée, ong-deh, *f* shower.

ondoyant, e, ong-do'ăh-yahng, *a* undulating; flowing.

ondoyer, ong-do'ăh-yeh, *v* to undulate; to baptize privately.

onduler, ong-dE-leh, *v* to undulate; to wave

(hair).

onéreu-x, se,* onn-eh-rer, *a* onerous.

ongle, ong-gl, *m* nail; claw.

onglée, ong-gleh, *f* numbness in fingertips (caused by cold).

onguent, ong-ghahng, *m* ointment; salve.

onze, ongz, *m* & *a* eleven; eleventh.

onzième, ong-ze-aym, *m* & *a* eleventh.

opacité, op-ăh-se-teh, *f* opacity.

opaque, op-ăhck, *a* opaque.

opéra-teur, trice, op-eh-răh-ter, *mf* operator.

opération, op-eh-răh-se-ong, *f* operation; transaction.

opératoire, op-eh-răh-to'ăhr, *a* operative.

opérer, op-eh-reh, *v* to operate; to operate on; to work.

opiner, op-e-neh, *v* to give one's opinion.

opiniâtre, op-e-ne-ah-tr, *a* stubborn.

opiniâtrément, op-e-ne-ah-treh-mahng, *adv* stubbornly.

opiniâtrer (s'), sop-e-ne-ah-treh, *v* to be obstinate.

opinion, op-e-ne-ong, *f*

opinion.

opportun, e, op-or-tung, *a* opportune; timely; seasonable.

opportunité, op-or-tE-ne-teh, *f* opportuneness; seasonableness; opportunity.

opposant, e, op-o-zahng, *mf* opponent; *a* adverse.

opposé, op-oz-eh, *m* opposite; reverse.

opposé, e, op-oz-eh, *a* & *pp* opposite; contrary; opposed.

opposer, op-oz-eh, *v* to oppose; **s'–,** to be opposed; to object (**à,** to).

opposition, op-oz-e-se-ong, *f* opposition; contrast.

oppresser, op-ress-eh, *v* to oppress.

oppression, op-ress-e-ong, *f* oppression.

opprimer, op-re-meh, *v* to oppress; to crush.

opprobre, op-robr, *m* disgrace; shame; opprobrium.

opter, op-teh, *v* to choose; to decide.

opticien, op-tiss-e-ang, *m* optician.

optimisme, op-te-mism, *m* optimism; **avec –,** ăh-veck –, *a* hopefully.

option, op-se-ong, *f* option.

optique, op-teeck, *f* optics; *a* optical; optic.

opulence, op-E-lahngss, *f* opulence; wealth.

opulent, e, op-E-lahng, *a* opulent; wealthy.

or, or, *conj* now; well.

or, or, *m* gold.

oracle, or-ăh-kl, *m* oracle.

orage, or-ăhsh, *m* storm.

orageu-x, se,* or-ăh-sher, *a* stormy.

oraison, or-ay-zong, *f* oration; orison.

oral, e,* or-ăhl, *a* oral; verbal; oral examination.

orange, or-ahngsh, *f* orange; *a inv* orange-coloured.

orangeade, or-ahng-shăhd, *f* orangeade.

oranger, or-ahng- sheh, *m* orange tree.

orateur, or-ăh-ter, *m* speaker; orator.

oratoire, or-ăh-to'ăhr, *m* oratory; *a* oratorial.

orbite, or-beet, *f* orbit; socket.

orchestre, or-kestr, *m* orchestra; band; stalls.

orchidée, or-ke-deh, *f* orchid.

ordinaire, or-de-nair, *m* the ordinary custom; *a**

ordinary; common; vulgar; **d'–, d–,** usually.

ordinateur, or-de-năh-ter, *m* computer; **– personnel,** – pair-sonn-ell, *m* personal computer.

ordonnance, or-donn-ahngss, *f* prescription.

ordonna-teur, trice, or-donn-ăh-ter, *mf* organizer; manager; *a* directing.

ordonné, or-donn-eh, *a* orderly; tidy.

ordonner, or-donn-eh, *v* to order; to prescribe; to ordain.

ordre, or-dr, *m* order; discipline; warrant; decoration; **– du jour, – dE-shoohr,** *m* agenda.

ordure, or-dEEr, *f* filth; filthy thing; *pl* rubbish.

orée, or-eh, *f* border; edge (of a wood etc).

oreille, or-ay'e, *f* ear.

oreiller, or-ay'e-yeh, *m* pillow; **taie d'–,** tay-d'–, *f* pillow slip.

oreillons, or-ay'e-yong, *mpl* mumps.

orfèvre, or-fay-vr, *m* goldsmith; silversmith.

organe, or-ghăhn, *m* organ; voice; agent; spokesman.

organique,* or-ghăhneeck, a organic.

organisa-teur, trice, or-ghäh-ne-zäh-ter, mf organizer.

organisation, or-ghäh-ne-zah-se-ong, f organizing; organization.

organiser, or-ghäh-ne-zeh, v to organize; to get up.

organisme, or-ghäh-nism, m organism; structure.

organiste, or-ghäh-neesst, m organist.

orgasme, or-gähz-m m orgasm.

orge, orsh, f barley.

orgelet, or-sher-lay, m sty (on eye).

orgie, or-shee, f revel; drinking-bout; orgy.

orgue, orgh, m organ.

orgueil, or-gher'e, m pride; haughtiness.

orgueilleu-x, se,* or-gher'e-yer, a proud; haughty.

orient, or-e-ahng, m Orient; East.

oriental, e, or-e-ahng-tähl, a Eastern; oriental.

orienter, or-e-ahng-teh, v to direct; to guide.

orifice, or-e-feess, m orifice; aperture.

originaire,* or-e-she-nair, a native; originating.

original, e, or-e-she-nähl, mf eccentric person;

original; a* original; novel; odd.

originalité, or-e-she-näh-le-teh, f originality; eccentricity.

origine, or-e-sheen, f origin; beginning; source; extraction.

orme, orm, m elm.

ornement, or-ner-mahng, m ornament.

orner, or-neh, v to adorn; to decorate; to deck.

ornière, or-ne-air, f rut; beaten track; groove.

orphelin, e, or-fer-lang, mf & a orphan.

orphelinat, or-fer-le-näh, m orphanage.

orteil, or-tay'e, m toe; **gros –,** grohz–, big toe.

orthographe, or-tog-rähf, f spelling.

ortie, or-tee, f nettle.

os, oss, m bone; pl os, oh.

osciller, oss-sil-leh, v to oscillate; fig to waver.

osé, e, o-zeh, a & pp daring; bold; cheeky; attempted.

oseille, oz-ay'e, f sorrel.

oser, o-zeh, v to dare; to venture.

osier, o-ze-eh, m wicker; osier.

osselet, oss-lay, m small bone.

osseu-x, se, oss-er, a bony.

ostensible,* oss-tahng-see-bl, a ostensible.

otage, ot-ähsh, m hostage.

ôter, oht-eh, v to take away; to relieve; to pull off.

ou, oo, conj or; either; else.

où, oo, adv where; when; in which; on which; at which.

ouate, oo-äht, f cotton-wool; wadding; padding.

oubli, oo-ble, m forgetfulness; forgetting; oblivion.

oublier, oo-blee-yeh, v to forget; to overlook; to neglect.

ouest, west, m West; a inv westerly; western.

oui, wee, adv yes.

ouï-dire, oo-e-deer, m inv hearsay.

ouïe, oo-ee, f hearing; pl gills.

ouïr, oo-eer, v to hear (not used very often).

ouragan, oo-räh-ghahng, m hurricane.

ourdir, oor-deer, v to warp; fam to plot.

ourlet, oor-lay, m hem.

ours, oors, m bear.

ourse, oors, f she-bear.

outil, oo-te, m tool; implement.

outillage, oo-tee-yähsh, m

tools; implements; plant.

outrage, oo-trăhsh, *m* outrage; insult.

outrager, oo-trăh-sheh, *v* to insult; to outrage.

outrageu-x, se,* oo-trăh-sher, *a* outrageous.

outrance, oo-trahngss, *f* excess; à –, ăh –, to excess.

outre, oo-tr, *f* leather-bottle.

outre, oo-tr, *prep* beyond; besides; *adv* beyond.

outré, e, oo-treh, *pp & a* exaggerated; extravagant; indignant.

outremer, oo-trer-mair, *m* overseas.

outrepasser, oo-trer-păhss-eh, *v* to go beyond; to exceed.

outrer, oo-treh, *v* to overdo; to exasperate.

ouvert, e,* oo-vair, *pp & a* opened; open; bare; frank.

ouverture, oo-vair-tEEr, *f* opening; overture; inauguration; *pl* proposals.

ouvrable, oo-vrăh-bl, *a* workable; **jour** –, shoor –, working day.

ouvrage, oo-vrăhsh, *m* work; workmanship; piece of work.

ouvré, e, oo-vreh, *a* diapered; wrought; worked.

ouvre-boîte, oo-vr-bo'ăht, *m inv* tin opener.

ouvri-er, ère, oo-vre-yeh, *mf* worker; labourer.

ouvrir, oo-vreer, *v* to open; to begin; to sharpen (appetite).

ovale, o-văhl, *a & m* oval; oviform; *m* oval.

ovation, o-văh-se-ong, *f* ovation.

ovipare, o-ve-păhr, *a* oviparous.

ovulation, o-vEE-lăh-se-ong, *f* ovulation.

oxyde, ox-eed, *m* oxide.

oxygène, ox-e-shenn, *m* oxygen.

ozone, oz-onn, *f* ozone.

pacifique,* păh-se-feeck, *a* peaceful; pacific.

pacte, păckt, *m* pact; covenant.

pagaie, pah'e-gay, *f* paddle.

page, păhsh, *m* (boy) page; *f* (book) page.

paie, pay, *f* pay; wages.

paiement, pay-mahng, *m* payment.

païen, ne, păh-e-ang, *mf* & *a* pagan; heathen.

paillasse, pah'e-yăhss, *f* straw-mattress.

paillasson, pah'e-yăhss-ong, *m* doormat.

paille, pah'e, *f* straw; chaff; flaw; mote; *a* strawcoloured.

pain, pang, *m* bread; loaf; livelihood; – **complet,** – kong-play, wholemeal bread; **petit** –, per-te –,

roll.

pair, e, pair, *a* even; equal.

paire, pair, *f* pair; couple; brace.

pairie, pay-ree, *f* peerage.

paisible,* pay-zee-bl, *a* peaceful; quiet; still.

paître, pay-tr, *v* to graze; to feed on; to pasture.

paix, pay, *f* peace; quiet; rest.

palais, păh-lay, *m* palace; palate.

pâle, pahl, *a* pale; wan; white.

palefrenier, păhl-frer-ne-eh, *m* groom; stable boy.

pâleur, pah-ler, *f* paleness.

palier, păh-le-eh, *m* (stair) landing; floor.

pâlir, pah-leer, *v* to turn pale; *fig* to wane.

palissade, păh-liss-ăhd, *f*

paling; fence.

pallier, păhl-le-eh, *v* to palliate.

palme, păhlm, *f* palm; triumph.

palmier, păhl-me-eh, *m* palm-tree.

pâlot, te, pah-loh, *a fam* palish; peaky.

palper, păhl-peh, *v* to feel; to finger.

palpiter, păhl-pe-teh, *v* to throb.

paludisme, păh-LEE-dism, *m* malaria.

pâmer (se), ser pah-meh, *v* to swoon; nearly to die (**de,** with).

pamplemousse, pang-pl-mooss, *m* grapefruit.

pan, pahng, *m* piece; part; (shirt) tail.

panache, păh-năhsh, *m* plume; tuft; *fam* flourish.

panaché, e, păh-năh-sheh, *m* shandy; *a* variegated; mixed.

panaris, păh-năh-re, *m* whitlow.

pancarte, pahng-kăhrt, *f* placard; sign; notice.

pané, e, păh-neh, *a* covered with breadcrumbs.

panier, păh-ne-eh, *m* basket; hamper.

panique, păh-neeck, *f* panic.

panne, păhn, *f*
breakdown.

panneau, păh-noh, *m*
sign; panel; board; trap;
snare.

panse, pahngss, *f fam*
paunch; belly.

panser, pahngss-eh, *v* to
dress (wound); to
groom.

pantalon, pahng-tăh-long,
m trousers.

pantin, pahng-tang, *m*
puppet.

pantoufle, pahng-too-fl, *f*
slipper.

paon, ne, pahng, *mf*
peacock; pea-hen.

papa, păh-păh, *m* daddy;
dad.

papauté, păh-poh-teh, *f*
papacy.

pape, păhp, *m* Pope.

paperasse, păh-răhss, *f*
bumph; old paper;
wastepaper.

papeterie, păhp-tree, *f*
paper mill; paper trade;
stationery; stationer's
shop.

papetier, păhp-te-eh, *m*
stationer.

papier, păh-pe-eh, *m*
paper; – **à lettres**, – ăh
let-tr, note-paper; –
d'emballage, – dahng-
băh-lăhsh, wrapping
paper; – **hygiénique**, –

e-she-eh-neeck, toilet
paper.

papillon, păh-pee-yong, *m*
butterfly; – **de nuit**, –
der nwee, moth.

papillote, păh-pee-yot, *f*
curl-paper.

paquebot, păhck-boh, *m*
liner; steamer; ship.

pâquerette, pahck-rett, *f*
daisy.

Pâques, pahk, *m* Easter.

paquet, păh-kay, *m* parcel;
packet.

par, păhr, *prep* by;
through; out of; per; a;
about; for; with; at; in;
into.

parachute, păh-răh-shEEt,
m parachute.

parade, păh-răhd, *f*
parade; display; show

parader, păh-răh-deh, *v* to
parade; to show off.

paradis, păh-răh-de, *m*
Paradise; heaven;
(theatre) the gods.

parafe, paraphe, păh-răhf,
m flourish; initials.

parage, păh-răhsh, *m*
extraction; birth; **aux –
s**, oh –, in the vicinity

paragraphe, păh-răh-grăf,
m paragraph.

paraître, păh-ray-tr, *v* to
appear; to look; to come
out; to show; **vient de –**,
ve-ang der –, just out.

paralyser, păh-răh-le-zeh,
v to paralyze.

paralysie, păh-răh-le-zee, *f*
paralysis.

parapet, păh-răh-pay, *m*
parapet.

parapluie, păh-răh-plwee,
m umbrella.

parasite, păh-răh-zeet, *m*
parasite; *a* parasitic.

paratonnerre, păh-răh-
tonn-air, *m* lightning
conductor.

paravent, păh-răh-vahng,
m screen; folding screen.

parc, păhrk, *m* park;
enclosure; playpen.

parcelle, păhr-sell, *f* small
part; particle; plot.

parce que, păhr-ser ker,
conj because.

parchemin, păhr-sher-
mang, *m* parchment; *pl*
diplomas.

parcimonieu-x, se,* păhr-
se-monn-e-er, *a*
parsimonious.

parcourir, păhr-koo-reer,
v to travel over; to go
through; to glance at.

parcours, păhr-koohr, *m*
distance; line; journey;
route.

pardessus, păhr-der-sE, *m*
overcoat.

pardon, păhr-dong, *m*
forgiveness; pardon.

pardonner, păhr-donn-eh,

v to forgive; to excuse.
pare-brise, păhr-breez, *m*
inv in pl windscreen.
pare-chocs, păhr-shock, *m*
inv in pl bumper.
pareil, le,* păh-ray'e, *a*
like; similar; such; to
match.
pareille, păh-ray'e, *f* the
like; the same.
parent, e, păh-rahng, *mf*
relative; kinsman;
kinswoman; parents
(father and mother);
relatives.
parenté, păh-rahng-teh, *f*
relationship;
consanguinity; kith and
kin; family.
parer, păh-reh, *v* to adorn;
to dress; to ward off
(evil).
paresse, păh-ress, *f*
idleness; sluggishness;
indolence.
paresseu-x, se, păh-ress-
er, *mf* idler; *a** idle; lazy;
slothful.
parfaire, păhr-fair, *v* to
perfect; to complete.
parfait, e,* păhr-fay, *a*
perfect; faultless.
parfois, păhr-fo'ăh, *adv*
sometimes; now and
then.
parfum, păhr-fung, *m*
perfume; scent.
parfumer, păhr-fE-meh, *v*

to perfume; to scent.
pari, păh-ree, *m* bet;
wager; stake.
parier, păh-re-eh, *v* to bet;
to wager; to stake.
parité, păh-re-teh, *f* parity;
equality.
parjure, păhr-shEEr, *m*
perjury; perjurer.
parjurer (se), ser păhr-
shE-reh, *v* to perjure
oneself.
parking, păhr-keeng *m*
car park.
parlant, e, păhr-lahng, *a*
speaking; talking.
parlement, păhr-ler-
mahng, *m* Parliament.
parlementer, păhr-ler-
mahng-teh, *v* to parley.
parler, păhr-leh, *v* to
speak; *m* way of
speaking.
parleu-r, se, păhr-ler, *mf*
talker.
parmi, păhr-me, *prep*
among; amongst; amid;
amidst.
parodie, păh-rod-ee, *f*
parody.
paroi, păh-ro'ăh, *f* wall;
side; partition.
paroisse, păh-ro'ăhss, *f*
parish; parishioners.
paroissien, ne, păh-
ro'ăhss-e-ang, *mf*
parishioner.
parole, păh-rol, *f* word;

speech; saying; right to
speak; promise.
parquer, păhr-keh, *v* to
park.
parquet, păhr-kay, *m*
inlaid floor; flooring.
parrain, păh-rang, *m*
godfather; sponsor.
parricide, păh-re-seed, *mf*
parricide.
parsemer, păhr-ser-meh, *v*
to strew (**de,** with).
part, păhr, *f* share;
portion; participation.
partage, păhr-tăhsh, *m*
sharing.
partance, păhr-tahngss, *f*
departure; **en –,** ahng –,
about to depart.
partant, păhr-tahng, *adv*
consequently.
partenaire, păhr-ter-nair,
mf (at cards or dancing)
partner.
parterre, păhr-tair, *m*
flowerbed; (theatre) pit.
parti, păhr-tee, *m* party;
side; decision; profit.
partial, e,* păhr-se-ăhl, *a*
partial; biased.
participation, păhr-te-se-
păh-se-ong, *f*
participation; share.
participe, păhr-te-seep, *m*
participle.
participer, păhr-te-se-peh,
v to share (**à,** in).
particularité, păhr-te-kE-

2 1 4

läh-re-teh, *f* peculiarity.

particule, păhr-te-kEEL, *f* particle.

particuli-er, ère, păhr-te-kE-le-eh, *mf* private person; individual; *a** particular; peculiar; odd; specific.

partie, păhr-tee, *f* part; party; match; outing; business; parcel; client; adversary.

partiel, le,* păhr-se-ell, *a* partial.

partir, păhr-teer, *v* to set out; to leave; to go off.

partition, păhr-te-se-ong, *f* partition; score (music).

partout, păhr-too, *adv* everywhere.

parure, păh-rEEr, *f* ornament; dress.

parvenir, păhr-ver-neer, *v* to reach; to succeed.

parvenu, e, păhr-ver-nE, *mf* upstart; self-made person.

parvis, păhr-ve, *m* parvis.

pas, pah, *m* step; gait; threshold.

pas, pah, *adv* not; not any; – **du tout,** – dE too, not at all.

passable,* păhss-ăh-bl, *a* passable; tolerable.

passag-er, ère, păhss-ăh-sheh, *mf* passenger; *a** transitory.

passant, e, păhss-ahng, *mf* passer-by.

passe, păhss, *f* pass; spell; situation; channel.

passé, păhss-eh, *prep* after; *m* the past.

passé, e, păhss-eh, *pp* & *a* past; last; faded.

passer, păhss-eh, *v* to pass; to exceed; to omit; to allow; to pass away; to fade; to cease; to spend (time).

passereau, păhss-roh, *m* sparrow.

passerelle, păhss-rell, *f* footbridge; gangway.

passible, păhss-ee-bl, *a* liable (de, to).

passif, păhss-eeff, *m* liabilities; passive voice.

passi-f, ve* păhss-eeff, *a* passive.

passion, păhss-e-ong, *f* passion.

passionnant, păhss-e-onn-ahng, *a* thrilling; fascinating.

passionné, e, păhss-e-onn-eh, *a* passionate; passionately fond (de, pour, of).

passionnément, păhss-e-onn-eh-mahng, *adv* passionately.

passoire, păhss-o'ăhr, *f* strainer; colander.

pastèque, păhss-teck, *f* watermelon.

pasteurisé, e, păhss-ter-e-zeh *a* pasteurized.

pastille, păhss-tee-ye, *f* pastille; lozenge.

patauger, păh-toh-sheh, *v* to dabble; to flounder; to make a mess of.

pâte, paht, *f* paste; dough; *pl* pasta; – **d'amandes,** – dăh-mahngd *f* marzipan .

pâté, păh-teh, *m* pie; pâté; blot of ink; block (of houses); savoury pie.

patelin, păht-lang, *m fam* native village; small village.

patente, păh-tahngt, *f* licence; patent.

patère, păh-tair, *f* peg; curtain-hook.

paternel, le,* păh-tair-nell, *a* fatherly; on the father's side.

pâteu-x, se,* pah-ter, *a* pasty; sticky; heavy (style, voice); dull.

patiemment, păh-se-ăh-mahng, *adv* patiently.

patience, păh-se-ahngss, *f* patience; puzzle.

patient, e, păh-se-ahng, *mf* sufferer; culprit; *a* patient.

patienter, păh-se-ahng-teh, *v* to have patience.

patinage (sur glace), păh-te-nähsh (sEEr-glähss) *f*

ice skating.

patiner, păh-te-neh, *v* to skate.

patinoire, păh-te-noăhr *f* ice rink.

patio, păh-te-oh *m* patio.

pâtisserie, pah-tiss-ree, *f* pastry; patisserie.

patois, păh-to'ăh, *m* dialect; patois.

pâtre, pah-tr, *m* herdsman; shepherd.

patrie, păh-tree, *f* native country; homeland; home.

patrimoine, păh-tre-mo'ăhn, *m* patrimony.

patriote, păh-tre-ot, *m* patriot; *a* patriotic.

patron, ne, păh-trong, *mf* employer; patroness; boss; skipper; pattern.

patronner, păh-tronn-eh, *v* to patronise; to stencil.

patrouille, păh-troo'ye, *f* patrol.

patte, păht, *f* paw; foot; leg; strap; flap.

pâturage, pah-tE-răhsh, *m* pasture; grazing.

paume, pohm, *f* palm (of the hands).

paupière, poh-pe-air, *f* eyelid.

pause, pohz, *f* pause; stop; rest.

pauvre, poh-vr, *m* poor

man; *a** poor; wretched.

pauvresse, poh-vress, *f* beggar woman.

pauvreté, poh-vrer-teh, *f* poverty; wretchedness.

pavaner (se), ser păh-văh-neh, *v* to strut.

pavé, păh-veh, *m* paving stone; pavement.

pavillon, păh-vee-yong, *m* pavilion; flag.

pavoiser, păh-vo'ăh-zeh, *v* to deck with flags.

pavot, păh-voh, *m* poppy.

payant, e, pay-yahng, *mf* payer; *a* paying; charged for.

paye, see **paie**.

payement, see **paiement**.

payer, pay-yeh, *v* to pay; to stand; to treat.

pays, pay-ee, *m* country; home; place.

paysage, pay-ee-zăhsh, *m* landscape; scenery.

paysan, ne, pay-ee-zahng, *mf* peasant; *a* rustic.

péage, peh-ăhsh, *m* toll.

peau, poh, *f* skin; hide; peel; *fig* life.

pêche, paysh, *f* fishing; fishery; angling; peach.

péché, peh-sheh, *m* sin.

pécher, peh-sheh, *v* to sin; to err.

pêcher, pay-sheh, *v* to fish; to angle; *m* peach tree.

pêcheu-r, se, pay-sher, *mf* fisherman; fisherwoman.

péch-eur, eresse, peh-sher, pehsh-ress, *mf* sinner.

pécuniaire,* peh-kE-ne-air, *a* pecuniary.

pédaler, peh-dăh-leh, *v* to pedal; to cycle.

pédant, e, peh-dahng, *mf* pedant; *a* pedantic.

pédestre,* peh-dess-tr, *a* pedestrian.

pédicure, peh-de-kEEr, *mf* chiropodist; pedicure.

pedigree, peh-de-greh, *m* pedigree.

peigne, payn-yer, *m* comb.

peigner, payn-yeh, *v* to comb; **se –,** to comb one's hair.

peignoir, payn-yo'ăhr, *m* dressing gown; bathrobe.

peindre, pang-dr, *v* to paint; to depict; to represent.

peine, payn, *f* pain; punishment; difficulty; sorrow.

peiner, pay-neh, *v* to grieve; to labour; to toil.

peintre, pang-tr, *m* painter; decorator.

peinture, pang-tEEr, *f* painting; picture; description; paint.

péjorati-f, ve, peh-shorăh-teef, *a* derogatory.

pêle-mêle, payl-mayl, *adv* pell-mell; *m* jumble.

peler, per-leh, *v* to peel; to pare.

pèlerin, payl-rang, *m* pilgrim.

pèlerinage, payl-re-năhsh, *m* pilgrimage.

pèlerine, payl-reen, *f* cape.

pelle, payl, *f* shovel; spade.

pelleterie, payl-tree, *f* fur trade; *pl* furs.

pellicule, payl-le-kEEl, *f* dandruff; film; roll (film).

pelote, plot, *f* pin cushion; ball (of wool, etc).

pelouse, plooz, *f* lawn; grass plot.

peluche, plEEsh, *f* plush.

pelure, plEEr, *f* paring; peel; rind.

pénalité, peh-năh-le-teh, *f* penal system; penalty.

penaud, e, per-noh, *a* abashed; shamefaced.

penchant, pahng-shahng, *m* declivity; inclination; partiality.

pencher, pahng-sheh, *v* to incline; to lean.

pendaison, pahng-day-zong, *f* hanging.

pendant, pahng-dahng, *prep* during; *m* counterpart; earring.

pendre, pahng-dr, *v* to hang; to hang up.

pendule, pahng-dEEl, *m* pendulum; *f* clock.

pêne, payn, *m* bolt (of a block).

pénétrant, e, peh-neh-trahng, *a* penetrating; piercing; keen.

pénétrer, peh-neh-treh, *v* to penetrate; to enter.

pénible,* peh-nee-bl, *a* painful; laborious.

péniche, peh-neesh, *f* barge.

pénicilline, peh-ne-se-leen *f* penicillin.

pénitence, peh-ne-tahngss, *f* penance; penitence; repentance; disgrace.

pénitent, e, peh-ne-tahng, *mf* penitent; *a* penitent.

pénombre, peh-nong-br, *f* semi darkness; dim light.

pensant, e, pahng-sahng, *a* thinking.

pensée, pahng-seh, *f* thought; opinion; pansy.

penser, pahng-seh, *v* to think; to deem.

penseu-r, se, pahng-ser, *mf* thinker.

pensi-f, ve,* pahng-seeff, *a* pensive; thoughtful.

pension, pahng-se-ong, *f* pension; guesthouse; boarding school.

pensionnaire, pahng-se-

onn-air, *mf* boarder; pensioner.

pente, pahngt, *f* slope; gradient; bent.

Pentecôte, pahngt-koht, *f* Whitsun.

pénurie, peh-nEE-ree, *f* scarcity; dearth; poverty.

pépier, peh-pe-eh, *v* to chirp.

pépin, peh-pang, *m* pip; kernel; hitch.

pépinière, peh-pe-ne-air, *f* nursery.

percale, pair-kăhl, *f* cotton cambric.

perçant, :, pair-sahng, *a* piercing; sharp; shrill.

percé, e, pair-seh, *pp* & *a* pierced; in holes.

percepteur, pair-sep-ter, *m* tax-collector.

percer, pair-seh, *v* to pierce; to bore.

percevoir, pair-ser-vo'ăhr, *v* to collect (taxes, etc); to perceive.

perche, pairsh, *f* pole; perch.

percher (se), pair-sheh, *v* to roost; to perch.

perdant, e, pair-dahng, *mf* loser; *a* losing.

perdre, pair-dr, *v* to lose; to waste; to ruin; to corrupt.

perdrix, pair-dree, *f* partridge.

perdu, e, pair-dE, *pp* & *a* lost; ruined; done for; spoilt.

père, pair, *m* father.

perfectionnement, pair-feck-se-onn-mahng, *m* improvement; perfecting.

perfectionner, pair-feck-se-onn-eh, *v* to improve; to perfect.

perfide, pair-feed, *mf* perfidious person; *a** perfidious.

perforer, pair-for-eh, *v* to bore; to punch.

péricliter, peh-re-kle-teh, *v* to be in jeopardy.

péril, peh-reel, *m* peril; danger.

périlleu-x, se,* peh-ree-yer, *a* perilous.

périmé, e, peh-re-meh, *a* out of date; lapsed.

période, peh-re-od, *m f* period.

périodique, peh-re-od-eeck, *a* periodical; *m* periodical (publication).

péripétie, peh-re-peh-see, *f* ups and downs; *pl* vicissitudes.

périphérique, peh-re-feh-reeck *m* ring road.

périr, peh-reer, *v* to perish; to die; to be lost.

périssable, peh-riss-ăh-bl, *a* perishable.

perle, pair, *f* pearl; bead.

permanent, e, pair-măh-nahng, *a* permanent; standing (committee); *f* permanent wave.

permanente, pair-măh-nahngt *f hair* perm.

permettre, pair-met-tr, *v* to allow; to enable.

permis, pair-mee, *m* permit; licence; pass.

permis, e, pair-mee, *pp* & *a* allowed; allowable.

permis de conduire, pair-me-der-kong-dweer *m* driving licence.

permission, pair-miss-e-ong, *f* permission; leave.

pernicieu-x, se,* pair-ne-se-er, *a* pernicious; hurtful.

perpétuel, le,* pair-peh-tE-ell, *a* perpetual.

perpétuer, pair-peh-tE-eh, *v* to perpetuate.

perpétuité, pair-peh-twe-teh, *f* endlessness; à –, ăh –, for life.

perplexe, pair-plex, *a* perplexed.

perron, pay-rong, *m* flight of steps to door of house.

perroquet, payr-ock-ay, *m* parrot.

perruche, pay-rEEsh, *f* budgerigar.

perruque, pay-rEEk, *f* wig.

persécuter, pair-seh-kE-teh, *v* to persecute; to importune.

persévérance, pair-seh-veh-rahngss, *f* perseverance.

persévérer, pair-seh-veh-reh, *v* to persevere; to persist.

persienne, pair-se-ain, *f* (outside) shutter.

persil, pair-see, *m* parsley.

persistant, e, pair-siss-tahng, *a* persistent.

persister, pair-siss-teh, *v* to persist (à, dans, in).

personnage, pair-sonn-ăhsh, *m* personage; somebody; character (in novel, etc.).

personnalité, pair-sonn-ăh-le-teh, *f* personality; person.

personne, pair-sonn, *pron* anybody; (ne) –, (ner) –, no one; nobody; *f* person; individual.

personnel, pair-sonn-ell, *m* staff.

personnel, le,* pair-sonn-ell, *a* personal.

personnifier, pair-sonn-e-fe-eh, *v* to personify; to impersonate.

perspective, pairs-peck-teev, *f* perspective; prospect.

perspicace, pairs-pe-kăhss,

a perspicacious.

persuader, pair-sE-ăh-deh, *v* to persuade; to convince; to prevail on.

persuasion, pair-sE-ăh-ze-ong, *f* persuasion.

perte, pairt, *f* loss; waste; ruin; *med* discharge; death.

pertinemment, pair-te-năh-mahng, *adv* pertinently.

perturba-teur, trice, pair-tEEr-băh-ter, *mf* disturber; *a* disturbing.

perturbation, pair-tEEr-băh-se-ong, *f* disturbance.

perturber, pair-tEEr-beh, *v* to disrupt; disturb; break up.

pervers, e, pair-vair, *mf* evil-doer; pervert; *a* perverse.

perversion, pair-vair-se-ong, *f* perversion.

pervertir, pair-vair, *v* to pervert; to corrupt.

pesamment, per-zăh-mahng, *adv* heavily.

pesant, e, per-zahng, *a* weighty; ponderous.

pesanteur, per-zahng-ter, *f* weight; gravity; dullness.

peser, per-zeh, *v* to weigh; to ponder; to be a burden.

peste, pesst, *f* plague; *fam*

pest; bore.

pester, pess-teh, *v* to rave (**contre,** at).

pétillant, e, peh-tee-yahng, *a* sparkling; crackling.

pétiller, peh-tee-yeh, *v* to crackle; to sparkle.

petit, e, per-te, *mf* young child; young animal; *a** little; small; **– ami, – ăh-me,** *m* boyfriend.

petite-fille, per-teet-fee-ye, *f* granddaughter.

petit-fils, per-te-feess, *m* grandson.

pétition, peh-te-se-ong, *f* petition.

pétitionnaire, peh-te-se-onn-air, *mf* petitioner.

petits-enfants, per-te-zahng-fahng, *mpl* grandchildren.

pétri, e, peh-tre, *pp* & *a* kneaded.

pétrin, peh-trang, *m* kneading-trough; *fam* **dans le –,** dahng ler –, in a mess.

pétrir, peh-treer, *v* to knead; to mould.

pétulant, e, peh-tE-lahng, *a* lively; full of spirits.

peu, per, *adv* little; not much; *m* little; few; bit.

peuplade, per-plăhd, *f* tribe.

peuple, per-pl, *m* people;

nation; the masses.

peupler, per-pleh, *v* to populate (**de,** with); to throng.

peuplier, per-ple-eh, *m* poplar.

peur, per, *f* fear; fright; dread.

peureu-x, se,* per-rer, *a* timid; fearful.

peut-être, per-t'ay-tr, *adv* perhaps.

phare, făhr, *m* lighthouse; beacon; headlight.

pharmacie, făhr-măh-see, *f* pharmacy; chemist's shop.

pharmacien, făhr-măh-se-ang, *m* chemist; pharmacist.

phase, fahz, *f* phase; stage; turn; **en – terminale,** ahng – tair-me-năhl, *a* *med* terminal (illness).

phénomène, feh-nomm-ain, *m* phenomenon; *fam* freak.

philatéliste, fe-lăh-teh-leesst, *m* stamp-collector.

philosophe, fe-loz-off, *m* philosopher; *a* philosophical.

philosophie, fe-loz-off-ee, *f* philosophy.

philtre, feel-tr, *m* love potion.

phonographe, fonn-og-rãhf, m phonograph.

phoque, fock, m seal.

phosphore, foss-for, m phosphorous.

photocopie, fot-o-ko-pee, f photocopy.

photographe, fot-og-rãhf, m photographer.

photographie, fot-og-rãh-fee, f photograph; photography.

phrase, frahz, f sentence.

phtisie, ftee-zee, f consumption.

physicien, fe-ze-se-ang, m physicist.

physiologie, fe-ze-oll-osh-ee, f physiology.

physionomie, fe-ze-onn-omm-ee, f physiognomy; look; expression.

physique, fe-zeeck, m constitution; f physics; a* physical.

piaffer, pe-ăh-feh, v to paw the ground.

piailler, pe-ah'e-yeh, v to squall.

piano, pe-ăh-no, adv softly; m piano (forte).

pic, peek, m pickaxe; peak; woodpecker; à –, ăh –, sheer (drop).

picoter, pe-kot-eh, v to prick; to tease; to peck.

pie, pee, f magpie.

pièce, pe-ess, f piece; bit; play; room; document.

pied, pe-eh, m foot; footing; leg; stalk.

piédestal, pe-eh-dess-tăhl, m pedestal.

piège, pe-aysh, m snare; trap.

pierre, pe-ayr, f stone; flint; gem.

pierreries, pe-ay-rer-ree, fpl gems; precious stones.

pierreu-x, se, pe-ay-rer, a stony.

piété, pe-eh-teh, f piety.

piétiner, pe-eh-te-neh, v to trample; to mark time.

piéton, pe-eh-tong, m pedestrian.

piètre,* pe-ay-tr, a paltry; wretched; worthless.

pieu, pe-er, m stake.

pieuvre, pe-ervr f octopus.

pieu-x, se,* pe-er, a pious; godly.

pigeon, pe-shong, m pigeon; dove.

pigeonnier, pe-shonn-e-eh, m pigeon-house; dovecot.

pigment, peeg-mahng, m pigment.

pignon, peen-yong, m gable.

pile, peel, f heap; pier; battery (of torch, radio); reverse (of coin); fam thrashing.

piler, pe-leh, v to pound; to crush.

pilier, pe-le-eh, m pillar; post.

pillage, pee-yăhsh, m plundering; pillage.

piller, pee-yeh, v to plunder; to pillage; to ransack; to pilfer.

pilon, pe-long, m pestle; pounder.

pilori, pe-lor-e, m pillory.

pilote, pe-lot, m pilot.

pilule, pe-lEEl, f pill.

pimbêche, pang-baish, f minx.

piment, pe-mahng, m pimento

pimpant, e, pang-pahng, a spruce; smart.

pin, pang, m pine; pine-tree.

pince, pangss, f pincers; pliers; crowbar; tongs.

pincé, e, pang-seh, a affected; stiff-necked.

pinceau, pang-soh, m brush.

pincée, pang-seh, f pinch (of salt etc).

pince-nez, pangss-neh, m pince-nez.

pincer, pang-seh, v to pluck (harp, guitar, etc); to play; to catch in the act.

pince-sans-rire, pangss-sahng-reer, m person of

dry humour.

pincettes, pang-sett, *fpl* tongs; tweezers.

ping-pong, pe-ng-pongg *f* table tennis.

pintade, pang-tähd, *f* guinea-fowl.

piocher, pe-osh-eh, *v* to dig; to work hard.

pion, pe-ong, *m* pawn.

pioncer, pe-ong-seh, *v pop* to snooze.

pionnier, pe-onn-e-eh, *m* pioneer.

pipe, peep, *f* tobacco-pipe; pipe.

piquant, e, pe-kahng, *a* pricking; pungent; stinging; sharp.

pique, peek, *m* (cards) spade.

picque-nique, peek-neek, *m* picnic.

piquer, pe-keh, *v* to prick; to sting; to bite; to goad; to spur; to rouse; to offend; to be pungent; *fam* to pinch (steal); – **à la machine**, – äh läh mäh-sheen, to machine sew.

piquet, pe-kay, *m* stake; peg.

piqûre, pe-kEEr, *f* sting; bite; injection.

pirate, pe-räht, *m* pirate.

pire, peer, *a* worse; *m* **le –**, ler –, the worst.

pirouetter, pe-roo-ett-eh, *v* to whirl round.

pis, pee, *adv* worse; *m* udder.

pis-aller, pe-z'äh-leh, *m* makeshift.

piscine, peess-seen, *f* swimming pool.

pissenlit, peess-ahng-lee, *m* dandelion.

piste, peesst, *f* track; trail; trace; scent; runway; – **de ski**, – der-ske, ski slope.

pistolet, peesst-toll-ay, *m* pistol.

piston, peess-tong, *m* piston; sucker; *fam* influence.

piteu-x, se,* pe-ter, *a* pitiful.

pitié, pe-te-eh, *f* pity; compassion.

pitoyable,* pe-to'äh-yäh-bl, *a* pitiful; pitiable; wretched.

pittoresque,* pit-tor-esk, *a* picturesque; graphic.

pivot, pe-voh, *m* pivot; *fig* basis; support.

placard, pläh-kähr, *m* cupboard; poster; bill.

place, plähss, *f* place; spot; square; space; seat; situation; fortress.

placement, plähss-mahng, *m* placing; sale; investment.

placer, plähss-eh, *v* to place; to sell; to invest.

placide,* plähss-eed, *a* placid.

plafond, pläh-fong, *m* ceiling.

plage, plähsh, *f* beach; shore.

plagiaire, pläh-she-air, *m* plagiarist.

plaider, play-deh, *v* to plead; to argue; to intercede.

plaideu-r, se, play-der, *mf* litigant.

plaidoirie, play-do'äh-ree, *f jur* pleading; address.

plaie, play, *f* wound; sore; plague.

plaignant, e, playn-yahng, *mf* plaintiff.

plaindre, plang-dr, *v* to pity; **se –**, to complain.

plaine, plain, *f* plain; flat open country.

plainte, plangt, *f* lamentation; complaint; charge.

plainti-f, ve,* plang-teeff, *a* plaintive; mournful.

plaire, plair, *v* to please; to be agreeable; to suit; **s'il vous plaît**, sill voo play, (if you) please.

plaisamment, play-zäh-mahng, *adv* pleasantly; humourously.

plaisant, e, play-zahng, *a*

pleasing; funny; droll.

plaisanter, play-zahng-teh, *v* to joke; to jest; to trifle (**avec,** with).

plaisanterie, play-zahngt-ree, *f* joke; jest; fun; humour; mockery.

plaisir, play-zeer, *m* pleasure; recreation.

plan, plahng, *m* plan; model; map; scheme; – (**des rues**), – deh-rE, *m* street plan.

plan, e, plahng, *a* level; even; flat.

planche, plahngsh, *f* plank; board; shelf; plate; garden bed.

planche de surf, plahngsh-der-sErf *f* surfboard.

plancher, plahng-sheh, *m* floor.

planer, plāh-neh, *v* to soar; to hover; to smooth.

planeur, plāh-ner, *m* glider.

plante, plahngt, *f* plant; sole of the foot.

planté, e, plahng-teh, *pp* & *a* planted; situated; **bien –,** be-ang –, firmly set.

planter, plahng-teh, *v* to plant; to set; to fix.

planton, plahng-tong, *m* orderly.

plaque, plãhck, *f* plate; slab; badge; (number) plate.

plastique, plãhss-teeck, *m* & *a* plastic.

plastron, plãhss-trong, *m* shirt front.

plat, e,* plãh, *a* flat; level; dull; straight (hair); *m* dish; course.

platane, plãh-tăhn, *m* plane-tree.

plateau, plãh-toh, *m* tray; disc; plateau.

plâtrage, plah-trăhsh, *m* plastering; plaster-work.

plâtras, plah-trăh, *m* rubbish (plaster).

plâtre, plah-tr, *m* plaster; plaster cast.

plâtrer, plah-treh, *v* to plaster; to patch up.

plausible,* ploh-zee-bl, *a* plausible.

plèbe, playb, *f* mob.

plein, e,* plang, *a* full; whole; broad; (animal) pregnant.

plénière, pleh-ne-air, *af* plenary; full.

plénitude, pleh-ne-tEEd, *f* plenitude; fullness.

pleurer, pler-reh, *v* to weep; to cry; to mourn.

pleureu-r, se, pler-rer, *a* weeping; *mf* mourner.

pleurnicher, pler-ne-sheh, *v* to whimper; to snivel.

pleurs, pler, *mpl* tears; weeping; lament.

pleuvoir, pler-vo'ăhr, *v* to rain.

pli, ple, *m* fold; pleat; wrinkle; crease; bend; letter.

pliable, ple-ăh-bl, *a* flexible; docile.

pliant, ple-ahng, *m* folding chair; *a* flexible; folding.

plier, plee-eh, *v* to fold; to bend; to give way.

plissé, e, pliss-eh, *pp* & *a* pleated; tucked.

plisser, pliss-eh, *v* to pleat; to crease; to corrugate.

plomb, plong, *m* lead; shot; sinker; plumb-line; seal; fuse.

plombage, plong-băhsh, *m* plumbing; sealing; (teeth) filling.

plomber, plong-beh, *v* to fill (tooth).

plombier, plong-be-eh, *m* plumber.

plonger, plong- sheh, *v* to dive.

pluie, plwee, *f* rain; –s **acides,** – ăh-seed, *pl* acid rain.

plume, plEEm, *f* feather; nib; quill.

plupart (la), lăh plE-păhr, *f* most; the greatest part; most people.

pluriel, le, plE-re-ell, *m* &

a plural.

plus, plE, *adv* more; **le –,** ler –, the most.

plusieurs, plE-ze-er, *pron* & *a* several.

plus-que-parfait, plEEs-ker-păhr-fay, *m* pluperfect.

plutôt, plE-toh, *adv* rather; sooner.

pluvieu-x, se, plE-ve-er, *a* rainy.

pneu, pner, *m* tyre.

pneumatique, pner-măh-teeck, *m* express letter sent by a tube (in Paris).

poche, posh, *f* pocket; bag; pouch; net.

pocher, posh-eh, *v* to poach (egg); to bruise (eye).

pochette, posh-ett, *f* small pocket; kit.

poêle, po'ăhl, *m* stove; pall; *f* frying pan.

poème, po-emm, *m* poem.

poésie, po-eh-zee, *f* poetry; poems.

poète, po-ett, *m* poet.

poétique, po-eh-teeck, *f* poetics; *a** poetical.

poids, po'ăh, *m* weight; burden.

poignant, e, po'ăhn-yahng, *a* poignant.

poignard, po'ăhn-yăhr, *m* dagger.

poigne, po'ăhn-yer, *f* grip; will; energy.

poignée, po'ăhn-yeh, *f* handful; handle.

poignet, po'ăhn-yay, *m* wrist; wristband; cuff.

poil, po'ăhl, *m* hair (animal); hair (on human body); bristle; *fam* mood; **au –,** great; hunkydory.

poilu, e, po'ăh-lE, *a* hairy; shaggy.

poinçon, po'ang-song, *m* bodkin; awl; punch; stamp; die.

poinçonner, po'ang-sonn-eh, *v* to punch (ticket, etc); to stamp.

poindre, po'ang-dr, *v* to dawn.

poing, po'ang, *m* fist; hand.

point, po'ang, *adv* no; not; none; never.

point, po'ang, *m* point; stop; stitch; dot; mark; full stop; degree.

pointe, po'angt, *f* point; tip; touch; dawn.

pointer, po'ang-teh, *v* to point; to prick; to aim; to soar.

pointillé, po'ang-tee-yeh, *m* stippling; dotted line.

pointilleu-x, se, po'ang-tee-yer, *a* fastidious.

pointu, e, po'ang-tE, *a* pointed; sharp.

pointure, po'ang-tEEr, *f* size (shoes, gloves, etc).

poire, po'ăhr, *f* pear; *slang* sucker.

poireau, po'ăh-roh, *m* leek; wart.

poirier, po'ăh-re-eh, *m* pear tree.

pois, po'ăh, *m* pea; **petits –,** per-te –, green peas.

poison, po'ăh-zong, *m* poison.

poisseu-x, se, po'ăhss-er, *a* sticky.

poisson, po'ăhss-ong, *m* fish.

poissonnerie, po'ăhss-onn-ree, *f* fish market or shop.

poitrine, po'ăh-treen, *f* chest; breast; lungs; bosom; brisket.

poivre, po'ăh-vr, *m* pepper.

poivrier, po'ăh-vree-eh, *f* pepperpot.

poivron po'ăh-vrong, *m* green or red sweet pepper.

poix, po'ăh, *f* pitch; shoemaker's wax.

pôle, pohl, *m* pole.

polémique, poll-eh-meeck, *f* polemics; controversy; *a* polemical.

poli, e, poll-ee, *a* polished; polite; civil; refined.

police, poll-eess, *f* police;
agent de –, ăh-shahng
der –, policeman.

polichinelle, poll-e-she-
nell, *m* Punch; buffoon.

polici-er, **ère**, poll-iss-e-
eh, *a* of the police; *m*
policeman; *f*
policewoman.

poliment, poll-e-mahng,
adv politely.

polir, poll-eer, *v* to polish;
to brighten; to improve.

polisson, **ne**, poll-iss-ong,
mf mischievous child;
scamp.

politesse, poll-e-tess, *f*
politeness; civility; good
breeding.

politique, poll-e-teeck, *f*
policy; politics; *a**
political; prudent;
politic.

pollen, poll-ang *m* pollen.

polluer, poll-lE-eh, *v* to
pollute.

pollution, poll-lE-se-ong *f*
pollution.

poltron, **ne**, poll-trong, *mf*
coward; *a* cowardly.

polythène, poll-e-tayn *m*
polythene.

pommade, pomm-ăhd, *f*
lip-salve; ointment.

pomme, pomm, *f* apple; –
de terre, – der tair,
potato.

pommé, **e**, pomm-eh, *a*

rounded; *fam* downright.

pommelé, **e**, pomm-leh, *a*
dappled; mottled.

pommette, pomm-ett, *f*
cheekbone.

pommier, pomm-e-eh, *m*
apple tree.

pompe, pongp, *f* pomp;
pump; – **à essence**, –
ăh-eh-sangss, petrol
pump.

pomper, pong-peh, *v* to
pump up; to imbibe.

pompeu-x, **se**,* pong-per,
a pompous; stately.

pompier, pong-pe-eh, *m*
fireman.

pomponner, pong-ponn-
eh, *v* to adorn; **se –**, to
smarten oneself.

ponce (pierre), pe-ayr
pongss, *f* pumice stone.

ponctuation, pongk-tE-ah-
se-ong, *f* punctuation.

ponctuel, **le**,* pongk-tE-
ell, *a* punctual.

pondre, pongdr, *v* to lay
eggs.

pont, pong, *m* bridge;
deck.

pontage, pong-tăsh, *m*
med bypass.

populace, pop-E-lăhss, *f*
the masses.

populaire,* pop-E-lair, *a*
popular.

population, pop-E-lăh-se-
ong, *f* population.

populeu-x, **se**, pop-E-ler, *a*
populous.

porc, por, *m* pig; swine;
hog; pork.

porcelaine, por-ser-lain, *f*
porcelain; chinaware.

porc-épic, por-keh-peeck,
m porcupine.

porche, porsh, *m* porch.

pore, por, *m* pore.

poreu-x, **se**, por-er, *a*
porous.

pornographie, por-nog-
răhf-ee, *f* pornography.

port, por, *m* port; harbour;
carriage; postage;
deportment.

portable, por-tăh-bl, *a*
wearable.

portail, por-tah'e, *m*
portal.

portant, **e**, por-tahng, *a*
bearing; **bien –**, be-ang
–, in good health; **mal –**,
măhl –, in bad health.

portati-f, **ve**, por-tăh-
teeff, *a* portable.

porte, port, *f* door; gate;
doorway; threshold;
pass.

porte-bagages, por-ter-
băh-găhsh, *m* luggage
rack.

porte-clefs, por-ter-kleh,
m inv key-ring.

portefeuille, por-ter-fer'e,
m portfolio; wallet.

porte-monnaie, por-termonn-ay, *m* purse.

porte-parapluies, por-ter-
păh-răh-plwee, *m*
umbrella-stand.

porte-plume, por-ter-
plEEm, *m* penholder.

porter, por-teh, *v* to bear;
to carry; to wear; to
induce; to tell; **comment
vous portez-vous?**
komm-ahng voo por-teh
voo? how are you?

porteu-r, se, por-ter, *mf*
porter; carrier; holder.

porti-er, ère, por-te-eh,
mf doorkeeper.

portière, por-te-air, *f* door
(of car, train, etc).

portion, por-se-ong, *f*
portion: allowance.

portrait, por-tray, *m*
portrait; likeness.

pose, pohz, *f* putting; pose;
affectation.

posé, e, poh-zeh, *pp & a*
placed; sedate.

posément, poh-zeh-
mahng, *adv* sedately;
slowly.

poser, poh-zeh, *v* to place;
to pose.

poseu-r, se, poh-zer, *mf*
affected person.

positi-f, ve,* poh ze-teeff,
a positive; matter-of-
fact.

position, poh-ze-se-ong, *f*
position; status; posture.

possédé, e, poss-eh-deh,
mf mad; *a* possessed.

posséder, poss-eh-deh, *v*
to possess; to enjoy.

possesseur, poss-ess-er, *m*
owner.

possession, poss-ess-e-ong,
f ownership; right;
possession.

possibilité, poss-e-be-le-
teh, *f* possibility.

possible, poss-ee-bl, *m*
utmost; *a* possible.

postal, e, poss-tăhl, *a*
postal.

poste, post, *m* post;
station; position; *f* post
office; – **de télévision,**
der-teh-leh-ve-se-ong,
television set.

poster, poss-teh, *v* to post;
to station.

postérieu-r, e,* poss-teh-
re-er, *a* subsequent;
later; hind.

postérité, poss-teh-re-teh,
f posterity; issue.

post-scriptum, post-skrip-
tom, *m* postscript.

postuler, poss-tEh-leh, *v* to
apply for.

posture, poss-tEEr, *f*
posture; position.

pot, po, *m* pot; jug;
tankard; jar; crock;
carton (of yoghurt).

potable, pot-ăh-bl, *a*
drinkable.

potage, pot-ăhsh, *m* soup;
pour tout –, poohr too
–, *fam* in all.

potager, pot-ăh-sheh, *m*
kitchen garden.

potasse, pot-ăhss, *f*
potash.

poteau, pot-oh, *m* post;
stake.

potelé, e, pot-leh, *a*
plump; fat.

potence, pot-ahngss, *f*
gallows; gibbet.

poterie, pot-ree, *f*
earthenware; pottery.

potier, pot-e-eh, *m* potter.

potin, pot-ang, *m* pewter;
fam gossip; clatter.

pou, poo, *m* louse.

poubelle, poo-bell, *f*
dustbin.

pouce, pooss, *m* thumb;
big toe; inch.

poudre, poo-dr, *f* powder;
dust; gunpowder.

poudrier, poo-dre-eh, *m*
powder compact.

pouffer, poo-feh, *v* – **de
rire,** – der reer, to burst
out laughing.

poulailler, poo-lah'e-yeh,
m coop.

poulain, poo-lang, *m* foal;
colt.

poule, pool, *f* hen.

poulet, poo-lay, *m*
chicken; *fam* detective.

poulie, poo-lee, *f* pulley;

block.

pouls, poo, *m* pulse.

poumon, poo-mong, *m* lung.

poupe, poop, *f* stern.

poupée, poo-peh, *f* doll; puppet.

pour, poohr, *prep* for; towards; to; in order to; as to.

pourboire, poohr-bo'ăhr, *m* gratuity; tip.

pourceau, poohr-soh, *m* hog; pig; swine.

pourcentage, poohr-sahng-tähsh, *m* percentage.

pourparler, poohr-pähr-leh, *m* usually *pl* parley; conference; negotiations.

pourpre, poohr-pr, *m* & *a* crimson; *f* purple dye.

pourquoi, poohr-kwäh, *adv* & *conj* why; wherefore; what for; *m* reason.

pourrir, poo-reer, *v* to rot.

pourriture, poo-re-tEEr, *f* decay; rot.

poursuite, poohr-sweet, *f* pursuit; *pl* proceedings.

poursuivre, poohr-swee-vr, *v* to pursue; to proceed against.

pourtant, poohr-tahng, *adv* yet; still; however.

pourtour, poohr-toohr, *m* circumference.

pourvoi, poohr-vo'äh, *m* appeal.

pourvoir, poohr-vo'ăhr, *v* to provide; to supply; to endow (à, for; de, with).

pourvoyeu-r, se, poohr-vo'äh-yer, *mf* purveyor.

pourvu que, poohr-vE, ker, *conj* provided that.

pousser, pooss-eh, *v* to push; to thrust; to urge on; to utter; to grow.

poussette, pooss-ett, *f* push-chair; buggy.

poussière, pooss-e-air, *f* dust; powder; spray.

poussin, pooss-ang, *m* chick.

poutre, pootr, *f* beam; rafter; girder.

pouvoir, poo-vo'ăhr, *v* to be able; to be allowed.

pouvoir, poo-vo'ăhr, *m* power; authority; power of attorney.

prairie, pray-ree, *f* meadow; prairie.

praline, präh-leen, *f* sugar-almond.

praticable, präh-te-käh-bl, *a* practicable; feasible.

praticien, ne, präh-te-se-ang, *mf* practitioner.

pratique, präh-teek, *f* practice; experience; *a** practical; useful.

pratiquer, präh-te-keh, *v*

to practise; to use; to make; to associate with.

pré, preh, *m* meadow.

préalable, preh-ăh-läh-bl, *a* previous; *adv phr* au –, first of all.

préavis, preh-ah-ve, *m* previous notice.

précaire, preh-kair, *a* precarious.

précaution, preh-koh-se-ong, *f* precaution; caution.

précédemment, preh-seh-däh-mahng, *adv* previously.

précédent, e, preh-seh-dahng, *a* preceding; *m* precedent.

précéder, preh-seh-deh, *v* to precede.

précepteur, preh-sep-ter, *m* tutor.

prêcher, pray-sheh, *v* to preach; to lecture.

précieu-x, se, preh-se-er, *a* precious; valuable; affected.

précipice, preh-se-peess, *m* precipice.

précipitamment, preh-se-pe-täh-mahng, *adv* hurriedly; headlong.

précipiter, preh-se-pe-teh, *v* to precipitate; to hurl headlong; to hasten.

précis, preh-se, *m* summary; précis.

précis, e, preh-se, *a* precise; exact; specific.

précisément, preh-se-zeh-mahng, *adv* precisely; just so.

préciser, preh-se-zeh, *v* to state precisely; to specify.

précité, e, preh-se-teh, *a* aforesaid.

précoce, preh-koss, *a* precocious; early.

préconiser, preh-konn-e-zeh, *v* to extol; to advocate.

prédicateur, preh-de-käh-ter, *m* preacher.

prédire, preh-deer, *v* to predict; to foretell.

préface, preh-fähss, *f* preface.

préférable,* preh-feh-räh-bl, *a* preferable; advisable.

préférer, preh-feh-reh, *v* to prefer; to like better.

préfet, preh-fay, *m* prefect; administrator (of French county).

préjudice, preh-shE-deess, *m* prejudice; wrong.

préjudiciable, preh-shE-de-se-äh-bl, *a* prejudicial.

préjugé, preh-shE-sheh, *m* prejudice; preconception.

prélasser (se), ser preh-lähss-eh, *v* to strut; to loll around.

prélever, prehl-veh, *v* to deduct beforehand; to levy.

préliminaire, preh-le-me-nair, *a* preliminary.

prélude, preh-lEEd, *m* prelude.

prématuré,* e, preh-mäh-tE-reh, *a* premature.

premier, prer-me-eh, *m* chief; leader; first.

premi-er, ère,* prer-me-eh, *a* first; former; early; next; leading.

prémunir, preh-mE-neer, *v* to forewarn; to caution.

prendre, prahngdr, *v* to take; to seize; to assume; to congeal; to set; to catch on; – **un bain de soleil,** – ung bang-der soll-a'ye, *v* sunbathe.

preneu-r, se, prer-ner, *mf* taker; buyer.

prénom, preh-nong, *m* first name; given name.

préoccuper, preh-ock-E-peh, *v* to preoccupy; to engross the mind; to disturb.

préparatif, preh-päh-räh-teeff, *m* preparation (used almost exclusively in the plural).

préparer, preh-päh-reh, *v* to prepare; to get ready.

prépondérance, preh-pong-deh-rahngss, *f* preponderance; sway.

préposé, preh-poh-zeh, *m* official in charge.

près, pray, *adv* & *prep* near; close by; – **de,** about to.

présage, preh-zähsh, *m* presage; omen.

présager, preh-zäh-sheh, *v* to forebode.

pré-salé, preh-säh-leh, *m* salt-meadow lamb.

presbyte, prez-beet, *mf* & *a* long-sighted; far-sighted.

presbytère, prez-be-tair, *m* vicarage.

prescience, preh-se-ahngss, *f* prescience.

prescrire, press-kreer, *v* to order; to prescribe.

préséance, preh-seh-ahngss, *f* precedence.

présence, preh-zahngss, *f* presence.

présent, e, preh-zahng, *a* present.

présenter, preh-zahng-teh, *v* to present; to offer; to introduce.

préservatif, preh-zair-väh-teef, *m* condom.

préservati-f, ve, preh-zair-väh-teeff, *a* preservative.

préserver, preh-zair-veh, *v*

to preserve (**de**, from).

président, preh-ze-dahng, *m* president; chairman.

présider, preh-ze-deh, *v* to preside.

présomption, preh-zongp-se-ong, *f* presumption; self-assurance.

présomptueu-x, se,* preh-zongp-tE- er, *a* presumptuous.

presque, press-ker, *adv* almost; nearly.

presqu'île, press-keel, *f* peninsula.

pressant, e, press-ahng, *a* pressing; urgent.

presse, press, *f* press; crowd; urgency; squeezer.

pressé, e, press-eh, *a* in a hurry; urgent; freshly squeezed (juice).

pressentiment, press-ahng-te-mahng, *m* presentiment.

pressentir, press-ahng-teer, *v* to have a presentiment of.

presser, press-eh, *v* to press; to crowd; to urge.

pression, press-e-ong, *f* pressure.

prestance, press-tahngss, *f* fine presence.

preste,* presst, *a* quick; nimble.

prestidigitateur, press-te-de-she-tăh-ter, *m* conjuror.

prestige, press-teesh, *m* prestige.

prestigieu-x, se, press-te-she-er *a* glamorous (job).

présumer, preh-zE-meh, *v* to presume.

prêt, pray, *m* loan.

prêt, e, pray, *a* ready; prepared; willing.

prétendant, e, preh-tahng-dahng, *mf* claimant; pretender; suitor.

prétendre, preh-tahng-dr, *v* to claim; to intend; to maintain.

prétendu, e, preh-tahng-dE, *mf* intended (husband or wife); *a* so-called.

prête-nom, prayt-nong, *m* figurehead.

prétentieu-x, se,* preh-tahng-se-er, *a* pretentious; concieted.

prétention, preh-tahng-se-ong, *f* pretension; affectation.

prêter, pray-teh, *v* to lend; to ascribe; to give rise.

prêteu-r, se, pray-ter, *mf* lender.

prétexte, preh-text, *m* pretext; pretence.

prêtre, pray-tr, *m* priest.

preuve, prerv, *f* proof;

evidence; token.

prévaloir, preh-văh-lo'ăhr, *v* to prevail.

prévenance, prehv-nahngss, *f* kind attention.

prévenant, e, prehv-nahng, *a* obliging; prepossessing.

prévenir, prehv-neer, *v* to advise; to inform.

prévention, preh-vahng-se-ong, *f* imprisonment on suspicion; prevention.

prévenu, e, prehv-nE, *mf* accused; *a* prejudiced.

prévision, preh-ve-ze-ong, *f* forecast; anticipation.

prévoir, preh-vo'ăhr, *v* to foresee; to provide for or against.

prévoyance, preh-vo'ăh-yahngss, *f* foresight; forethought.

prier, pre-eh, *v* to pray; to entreat; to invite.

prière, pre-air, *f* prayer; entreaty; request.

primaire, pre-mair, *a* primary (school, etc); elementary.

prime, preem, *f* premium; bonus; option; *a* prime.

primer, pre-meh, *v* to surpass; to take the lead; to award a prize to.

primeur, pre-mer, *f* early fruit or vegetable;

freshness.

primevère, preem-vair, *f* primrose.

primiti-f, ve, * pre-me-teeff, *a* primitive.

prince, sse, prangss, *mf* prince; princess.

princi-er, ère, * prang-se-eh, *a* princely.

principal, prang-se-păhl, *m* chief (chief); main point; *a* principal; main.

principauté, prang-se-poh-te, *f* principality.

principe, prang-seep, *m* principle.

printani-er, ère, prang-tăh-ne-eh, *a* spring.

printemps, prang-tahng, *m* spring; springtime.

priorité, pre-or-e-teh, *f* priority; right of way.

pris, e, pre, *pp* & *a* taken; occupied; busy.

prise, preez, *f* taking; hold; quarrel; catch.

priser, pre-zeh, *v* to value; to take snuff.

priseu-r, se, pre-zer, *mf* snuff-taker; appraiser.

prison, pre-zong, *f* prison.

prisonni-er, ère, pre-zonn-e-eh, *mf* & *a* prisoner.

privation, pre-văh-se-ong, *f* privation; loss.

privauté, pre-voh-teh, *f* familiarity.

privé, e, pre-veh, *a* private.

priver, pre-veh, *v* to deprive.

privilège, pre-ve-laysh, *m* privilege.

prix, pre, *m* price; value; reward; prize.

probabilité, prob-ăh-be-le-teh, *f* probability.

probable, * prob-ăh-bl, *a* probable; likely.

probant, e, prob-ahng, *a* conclusive; convincing.

probe, prob, *a* honest; upright.

probité, prob-e-teh, *f* honesty; uprightness.

problème, prob-laym, *m* problem.

procédé, pross-eh-deh, *m* proceeding; behaviour; method.

procéder, pross-eh-deh, *v* to proceed; to behave; to prosecute (**contre**).

procédure, pross-eh-dEEr, *f* proceedings; practice.

procès, pross-ay, *m* lawsuit; trial; litigation.

procès-verbal, pross-ay-vair-băhl, *m* report; minutes; record.

prochain, prosh-ang, *m* neighbour.

prochain, e, prosh-ang, *a* next; nearest.

prochainement, prosh-ain-mahng, *adv* shortly.

proche, prosh, *a* close; *mpl* relations; *adv* near.

proclamer, prock-lăh-meh, *v* to proclaim.

procuration, prock-E-răh-se-ong, *f* proxy.

procurer, prock-E-reh, *v* to procure.

procureur, prock-E-rer, *m* proxy; attorney.

prodigalité, prod-e-găh-le-teh, *f* prodigality; extravagance.

prodige, prod-eesh, *m* prodigy; wonder.

prodigieu-x, se, * prod-e-she-er, *a* prodigious; wonderful.

prodigue, prod-eeg, *m* spendthrift; *a* prodigal.

prodiguer, prod-e-gheh, *v* to lavish; to squander.

produc-teur, trice, prod-EEk-ter, *mf* producer; *a* productive.

production, prod-EEk-se-ong, *f* production; product; output.

produire, prod-weer, *v* to produce; to yield; to show.

produit, prod-wee, *m* produce; product; proceeds.

profane, prof-ăhn, *mf* & *a* outsider; profane; lay.

profaner, prof-ăh-neh, *v*

to profane.

proférer, prof-eh-reh, *v* to utter.

professer, prof-ess-eh, *v* to profess; to teach.

professeur, prof-ess-er, *m* professor; teacher.

profession, prof-ess-e-ong, *f* profession; business.

profil, prof-eel, *m* profile; section.

profit, prof-e, *m* profit; gain; utility.

profiter, prof-e-teh, *v* to profit (**de,** by); to take advantage (**de,** of).

profond, e, prof-ong, *a* deep; profound; sound.

profondément, prof-ong-deh-mahng, *adv* deeply.

profondeur, prof-ong-der, *f* depth; profoundness.

programme, prog-răhm, *m* programme; bill; platform.

progrès, prog-ray, *m* progress; improvement.

prohiber, pro-e-beh, *v* to prohibit.

proie, prwăh, *f* prey.

projecteur, pro-sheck-ter, *m* projector; headlight.

projectile, pro-sheck-teel, *m & a* missile.

projection, prosh-eck-se-ong, *f* projection.

projet, prosh-ay, *m* project; scheme; rough draft.

projeter, prosh-teh, *v* to project; to plan.

prolétaire, proll-eh-tair, *m & a* proletarian.

prolonger, proll-ong-sheh, *v* to prolong; to protract; to lengthen.

promenade, promm-năhd, *f* walk; drive; ride; excursion.

promener, promm-neh, *v* to take about; to walk; **se –,** to take a walk.

promeneu-r, se, promm-ner, *mf* walker.

promesse, promm-ayss, *f* promise.

promettre, promm-ay-tr, *v* to promise; to look promising.

promontoire, promm-ong-to'ăhr, *m* promontory.

promouvoir, promm-oo-vo'ăhr, *v* to promote.

prompt, e, prong, *a* prompt; sudden; hasty.

promptitude, prong-te-tEEd, *f* quickness.

promulguer, promm-EEl-gheh, *v* to promulgate.

pronom, pron-ong, *m* pronoun.

prononcé, e, pron-ong-seh, *pp & a* pronounced; decided.

prononcer, pron-ong-seh, *v* to pronounce; to utter.

propagande, prop-ăh-gahngd, *f* propaganda.

propager, prop-ăh-**sheh,** *v* to propagate; **se –,** to spread.

propension, prop-ahng-se-ong, *f* propensity.

prophétie, prof-eh-see, *f* prophecy.

propice, prop-eess, *a* propitious; favourable.

proportionnel, le,* prop-or-se-onn-ell, *a* proportional; commensurate.

propos, prop-oh, *m* purpose; talk.

proposer, prop-oh-zeh, *v* to propose; to move; **se –,** to intend; to mean.

proposition, prop-oh-ze-se-ong, *f* proposal; proposition; clause.

propre, propr, *m* own characteristic; *a** own; proper; clean.

propreté, prop-rer-teh, *f* neatness; cleanliness.

propriétaire, prop-re-eh-tair, *mf* proprietor; landlord.

propriété, prop-re-eh-teh, *f* property; ownership; propriety.

propulsion, prop-EEl-se-ong, *f* propelling.

prorata, pro-răh-tăh, *m* proportion.

prorogation, pror-ogh-äh-se-ong, *f* prorogation; adjournment.

proroger, pror-osh-eh, *v* to extend; to adjourn.

prosaïque, pro-zäh-eek, *a* prosaic.

prosateur, pro-zäh-ter, *m* prose writer.

proscrire, pross-kreer, *v* to proscribe; to banish.

proscrit, e, pross-kre, *mf* exile; outlaw.

prose, prohz, *f* prose.

prospectus, pross-peck-tEss, *m* brochure.

prospère, pross-pair, *a* prosperous.

prospérer, pross-peh-reh, *v* to prosper; to thrive.

prosterner (se), ser pross-tair-neh, *v* to prostrate oneself.

prostituée, pross-te-tE-eh, *f* prostitute.

protec-teur, trice, prot-eck-ter, *mf* & *a* protector; protective.

protectorat, prot-eck-tor-äh, *m* protectorate.

protégé, e, prot-eh-sheh, *mf* protégé; dependent.

protéger, prot-eh-sheh, *v* to protect; to shield.

protestant, e, prot-ess-tahng, *mf* & *a* Protestant.

protester, prot-ess-teh, *v* to protest.

prouesse, proo-ess, *f* prowess; exploit.

prouver, proo-veh, *v* to prove; to show.

provenance, prov-nahngss, *f* origin; source.

provenir, prov-neer, *v* to proceed; to originate.

proverbe, prov-airb, *m* proverb.

proverbial, e,* prov-air-be-ähl, *a* proverbial.

providence, prov-e-dahngss, *f* Providence.

province, prov-angss, *f* province; the country.

provincial, e, prov-ang-se-ähl, *mf* & *a* provincial.

proviseur, prov-e-zer, *m* head (teacher).

provision, prov-e-ze-ong, *f* provision; supply; retainer.

provisoire,* prov-e-zo'ähr, *a* provisional.

provocant, e, prov-ock-ahng, *a* provoking; alluring.

provoca-teur, trice, prov-ock-äh-ter, *mf* aggressor; provoking.

provoquer, prov-ock-eh, *v* to provoke; to challenge; to cause.

prudemment, prE-däh-mahng, *adv* prudently.

prudence, prE-dahngss, *f* prudence.

pruderie, prEEd-ree, *f* prudishness.

prune, prEEn, *f* plum.

pruneau, prE-noh, *m* prune.

prunelle, prE-nell, *f* sloe; pupil (eye).

prunier, prE-ne-eh, *m* plum tree.

psaume, psohm, *m* psalm.

pseudonyme, pser-donn-eem, *m* pseudonym.

psychanalyste, pse-kǎh-näh-leest *mf* psychoanalyst.

psychiatre, pse-ke-äh-tr, *mf* psychiatrist.

psychologique, pse-koll-o-sheeck *a* psychological.

psychologue, pse-koll-og, *m* psychologist.

psychopathe, pse-ko-pǎht *mf* psychopath.

puant, e, pE-ahng, *a* stinking.

puanteur, pE-ahng-ter, *f* stench.

pubère, pE-bair, *a* pubescent.

public, pE-bleeck, *m* public.

publi-c, que,* pE-bleeck, *a* public; common.

publication, pE-bli-cah-se-ong, *f* publication; publishing.

publicité, pE-ble-se-teh, *f*

publicity; advertising.

publier, pE-ble-eh, *v* to publish.

puce, pEEss, *f* flea.

pucelle, pE-sell, *f* virgin.

pudeur, pE-der, *f* bashfulness; modesty; reserve.

pudique,* pE-deeck, *a* chaste; modest.

puer, pE-eh, *v* to stink; to smell strongly of.

puéril, e,* pE-eh-reel, *a* childish.

pugilat, pE- she-lăh, *m* boxing.

puis, pwee, *adv* then; afterwards; next; besides.

puiser, pwee-zeh, *v* to draw (water); to derive.

puisque, pweess-ker, *conj* since.

puissamment, pweess-ăh-mahng, *adv* powerfully; mightily.

puissance, pweess-ahngss, *f* power; force; influence.

puissant, e, pweess-ahng, *a* powerful; mighty; *fam* stout.

puits, pwee, *m* well; shaft; pit.

pull(-over), pEl (lo-vair) *m* pullover.

pulluler, pEEl-lE-leh, *v* to swarm.

pulsation, pEEl-săh-se-ong, *f* beating; throbbing.

pulvériser, pEEl-veh-re-zeh, *v* to pulverize.

punaise, pE-nayz, *f* bedbug; drawing-pin.

punir, pE-neer, *v* to punish.

punition, pE-niss-e-ong, *f* punishment.

pupille, pE-peell, *mf* ward; *f* pupil (of eye).

pupitre, pE-pee-tr, *m* desk; music-stand.

pur, e,* pEEr, *a* pure; genuine; clean; mere.

purée, pE-reh, *f* mash; purée; mashed potato.

pureté, pEEr-teh, *f* purity; chastity.

purgati-f, ve, pEEr-găh-teeff, *a* purgative.

purgatoire, pEEr-găh-to'ăhr, *m* Purgatory.

purge, pEErsh, *f* purge; clearing.

purger, pEEr-sheh, *v* to purge; to cleanse; *jur* to serve (a sentence).

purifier, pE-re-fe-eh, *v* to purify.

pus, pE, *m* pus; matter.

pusillanime, pE-zill-lăh-neemm, *a* faint-hearted.

pustule, pEEs-tEEl, *f* pimple.

putréfier, pE-treh-fe-eh, *v* to putrefy; to rot.

pyramide, pe-răh-meedd, *f* pyramid.

quadragénaire, kwăh-drăh-sheh-nair, *mf* & *a* forty year old.

quadrillé, e, kăh-dree-yeh, *a* checkered.

quadruple, kwăh-drEE-pl, *m* & *a* quadruple.

quai, kay, *m* quay; wharf; platform.

qualification, kăh-le-fe-kăh-se-ong, *f* title; description.

qualifier, kăh-le-fe-eh, *v* to qualify; to call.

qualité, kăh-le-teh, *f* quality; property; rank; qualification.

quand, kahng, *adv* when (at what moment); *conj* when (at the time).

quant à, kahng t'ăh, *prep* as to; as for.

quantité, kahng-te-teh, *f* quantity.

quarantaine, kăh-rahng-tain, *f* about forty; quarantine.

quarante, kăh-rahngt, *m* & *a* forty.

quarantième, kăh-rahng-te-aym, *m* & *a* fortieth.

quart, kăhr, *m* quarter; *nau* watch; point (of compass).

quartier, kăhr-te-eh, *m* quarter; piece; neighbourhood; district; –s **défavorisés,** – deh-

făh-vor-e-zeh *pl* inner-city; – **des prostituées,** – deh-pross-te-tE-eh *m* red-light district.

quasi, kăh-ze, *adv* quasi; all but; almost.

quatorze, kăh-torz, *m* & *a* fourteen.

quatorzième, kăh-tor-ze-aym, *m* & *a* fourteenth.

quatre, kăh-tr, *m* & *a* four.

quatre-vingt-dix, kăh-trer-vang-deess, *m* & *a* ninety.

quatre-vingts, kăh-trer-vang, *a* eighty.

quatrième, kăh-tre-aym, *m* & *a* fourth.

quatuor, kwăh-tE-or, *m* quartet.

que, ker, *pron* whom; that; which; what.

que, ker, *adv* how; how much; how many; why.

que, ker, *conj* that; if; when; as; until; while; whether; lest; **ne...–,** ner...–, only.

quel, le, kell, *a* what; what a; which.

quelconque, kell-kongk, *a* whatever; any; *fam* commonplace.

quelque, kell-ker, *adv* some; about; *a* some; any; a few; – **chose,** – shohz, something; anything *interrog*; – **part,**

– păhr, somewhere, anywhere.

quelquefois, kell-ker-fo'ăh, *adv* sometimes.

quelqu'un, e, kell-kung, *pron* somebody; someone; anyone *interrog; pl* **quelques-uns, unes**, kell-ker-z'ung, some; a few; any.

querelle, ker-rell, *f* quarrel; row.

question, kess-te-*ong*, *f* question; matter.

questionnaire, kess-te-onn-air, *m* set of questions; questionnaire.

quête, kayt, *f* quest; collection.

quêter, kay-teh, *v* to search; to make a collection.

queue, ker, *f* tail; tailpiece; train; cue; queue.

qui, ke, *pron* who; whom; which; that; whoever; what.

quiconque, ke-kongk, *pron* whoever.

quille, kee-ye, *f* keel; skittle.

quincaillerie, kang-kah'e-ree, *f* ironmongery; hardware shop.

quinquagénaire, kwang-kwăh-sheh-nair, *mf & a*

fifty year old.

quinte, kangt, *f* fit of coughing; fifth.

quintuple, kwang-tEE-pl, *m & a* fivefold.

quinzaine, kang-zain, *f* about fifteen; fortnight.

quinze, kangz, *m & a* fifteen; fifteenth.

quinzième, kang-ze-aym, *m & a* fifteenth.

quittance, ke-tahngss, *f* receipt; discharge.

quitte, keet, *a* clear; quit; – à, – ăh, at the risk of.

quitter, ke-teh, *v* to leave; to forsake; to depart.

qui-vive, ke-veev, *m* alert.

quoi, kwăh, *pron* what; which; that; (exclamation) what! how!

quoique, kwăh-ker, *conj* although.

quolibet, koll-e-bay, *m* gibe.

quote-part, kot-păhr, *f* quota.

quotidien, ne, kot-e-de-ang, *a* daily.

R

rabâcher, răh-bah-sheh, v to repeat over and over again.

rabais, răh-bay, m abatement; rebate.

rabaisser, răh-bess-eh, v to lower; to humble.

rabattre, răh-băh-tr, v to lower; to bring down; to deduct.

rabbin, răh-bang, m rabbi.

râblé, e, rah-bleh, a broad-backed.

raboter, răh-bot-eh, v to plane.

raboteu-x, se, răh-bot-er, a rugged; harsh; jagged.

rabougri, e, răh-boo-gre, a stunted.

raccommoder, răh-komm-od-eh, v to mend; to patch; to darn; to reconcile.

raccorder, răh-kor-deh, v to join; to unite.

raccourcir, răh-koohr-seer, v to shorten; to curtail.

raccrocher, răh-krosh-eh, v to hang up; **se –**, to clutch.

race, răhss, f face; breed; family.

rachat, răh-shăh, m repurchase.

racheter, răhsh-teh, v to buy back; to atone for.

rachitique, răh-she-teeck, a rickety.

racine, răh-seen, f root; origin.

racisme, răh-sism, m racism.

raciste, răh-seest a & mf racist.

raclée, rah-kleh, f pop thrashing; licking.

racler, rah-kleh, v to scrape.

racoler, răh-koll-eh, v to recruit; to pick up.

racontar, răh-kong-tăhr, m gossip.

raconter, răh-kong-teh, v to relate; to tell.

radeau, răh-doh, m raft.

radiateur, răh-de-ăh-ter, m radiator.

radieu-x, se,* răh-de-er, a radiant.

radio, răh-de-o, f radio.

radioactif, răh-de-oh-ăhk-teef a radioactive.

radiodiffusion, răh-de-o-diff-E-ze-ong, f broadcasting.

radiographie, răh-de-o-grăh-fe, f X-ray photography; X-ray.

radis, răh-de, m radish.

radoter, răh-dot-eh, v to rave; to drivel.

radoucir, răh-doo-seer, v to soften; to calm.

rafale, răh-făhl, f squall.

raffermir, răh-fair-meer, v to strengthen; to make firm.

raffiné, e, răh-fe-neh, a refined; delicate.

raffinerie, răh-feen-ree, f sugar refinery.

raffoler, răh-foll-eh, v to dote (**de**, on); fam to be mad about.

rafler, rah-fleh, *v fam* to steal; to snaffle

rafraîchir, răh-fray-sheer, *v* to cool; to chill; to refresh.

rafraîchissement, răh-fray-shiss-mahng, *m* cool drink; *pl* refreshments.

rage, răhsh, *f* rabies; rage; violent pain.

rager, răh-sheh, *v* to fume; to be in a rage.

ragoût, răh-goo, *m* stew; casserole.

raide, rayd, *adv* sharply; *a* stiff; tight; steep; stubborn.

raideur, ray-der, *f* stiffness; tightness; sternness.

raidir, ray-deer, *v* to stiffen; to tighten.

raie, ray, *f* streak; stroke; parting (hair); skate (fish).

rail, rah'e, *m* (railways) rail.

railler, rah'e-yeh, *v* to scoff at; to mock.

raillerie, rah'e-ree, *f* banter; jeer.

rainure, ray-nEEr, *f* groove.

raisin, ray-zang, *m* grapes.

raison, ray-zong, *f* reason; cause; satisfaction; right; ratio.

raisonnable,* ray-zonn-äh-bl, *a* reasonable; sensible.

raisonnement, ray-zonn-mahng, *m* reasoning; argument.

raisonner, ray-zonn-eh, *v* to reason.

rajeunir, răh-sher-neer, *v* to rejuvenate.

rajouter, răh-shoo-teh, *v* to add.

rajuster, răh-shEs-teh, *v* to readjust; to repair.

râle, rahl, *m* death rattle.

ralentir, răh-lahng-teer, *v* to slacken; to slow down.

râler, rah-leh, *v* to rattle (in one's throat); *fam* to moan.

rallier, răh-le-eh, *v* to rally; to rejoin.

rallonger, rah-long-sheh, *v* to lengthen; to let down.

ramadan, răh-măh-dang, *m* Ramadan.

ramage, răh-măhsh, *m* warbling; floral design.

ramas, răh-mah, *m* heap; set.

ramasser, răh-măhss-eh, *v* to gather; to pick up.

rame, răhm, *f* oar; (paper) ream; prop.

rameau, răh-moh, *m* bough; branch.

ramener, răhm-neh, *v* to bring back; to restore.

ramer, răh-meh, *v* to row.

ramifier (se), ser răh-me-fe-eh, *v* to branch out.

ramollir, răh-moll-eer, *v* to soften; to weaken.

ramoner, răh-monn-eh, *v* to sweep (chimneys).

ramoneur, răh-monn-er, *m* chimney sweep.

rampant, e, rahng-pahng, *a* creeping; servile.

rampe, rahngp, *f* hand-rail; slope; footlights.

ramper, rahng-peh, *v* to crawl.

rance, rahngss, *a* rancid.

rançon, rahng-song, *f* ransom.

rançonner, rahng-sonn-eh, *v* to ransom; *fam* to fleece.

rancune, rahng-kEEn, *f* rancour; grudge.

rang, rahng, *m* row; line; rank; range; rate.

rangée, rahng-sheh, *f* row; line; tier.

ranger, rahng-sheh, *v* to arrange; to tidy; to put away.

ranimer, răh-ne-meh, *v* to revive.

rapace, răh-păhss, *a* rapacious; *m* bird of prey.

rapatrier, răh-păh-tre-eh,

v to repatriate.

râpé, e, rah-peh, *pp* & *a* grated; threadbare.

râper, rah-peh, *v* to grate.

rapetisser, răhp-tiss-eh, *v* to shorten; to shrink.

rapide, răh-peed, *m* fast train; *a** fast.

rapidité, răh-pe-de-teh, *f* swiftness; speed.

rappel, răh-pell, *m* recall; call to arms; repeal.

rappeler, răhp-leh, *v* to call again; to remind; **se –,** to remember.

rapport, răh-por, *m* report; *fin* yield; relation; bearing.

rapporter, răh-por-teh, *v* to bring back; to report; to yield; to tell tales; **se – à,** to relate to.

rapporteur, răh-por-ter, *m* sneak; tell-tale; reporter; protractor.

rapprocher, răh-prosh-eh, *v* to bring near; to reconcile; to compare.

raquette, răh-kett, *f* racket; **– de tennis, –** der-teh-neess tennis racket.

rare,* răhr, *a* rare; scarce; uncommon.

rareté, răhr-teh, *f* scarcity; rare object.

ras, e, rah, *a* shorn; flat; smooth.

rasade, răh-zăhd, *f* glassful.

raser, rah-zeh, *v* to shave; to graze; to skim; *fam* to bore.

rasoir, rah-zo'ăhr, *m* razor.

rassasier, răhss-ăh-ze-eh, *v* to satiate; to satisfy (hunger, etc).

rassemblement, răhss-ahng-bler-mahng, *m* gathering; crowd.

rassembler, răhss-ahng-bleh, *v* to reassemble; to gather; **se –,** to meet.

rasseoir, răhss-o'ăhr, *v* to reseat; to settle.

rasséréner, răhss-eh-reh-neh, *v* to clear up; to calm.

rassis, e, răhss-e, *a* stale.

rassurer, răhss-E-reh, *v* to reassure.

rat, răh, *m* rat.

ratatiné, e, răh-tăh-te-neh, *pp* & *a* shrivelled up.

rate, răht, *f* spleen.

râteau, rah-toh, *m* rake.

râtelier, rah-ter-le-eh, *m* rack; *fam* false teeth.

rater, răh-teh, *v* to fail; to miss (a train, a target).

ratifier, răh-te-fe-eh, *v* to ratify.

ration, răh-se-ong, *f* ration; allowance.

rationnel, le,* răh-se-onn-ell, *a* rational.

ratisser, răh-tiss-eh, *v* to scrape; to rake; *mil* to comb (an area).

rattacher, răh-tăh-sheh, *v* to fasten; **se –,** to be connected (à, with).

rattraper, răh-trăh-peh, *v* to catch up; to recover; **se –,** to recoup oneself.

rature, răh-tEEr, *f* erasure.

rauque, rohk, *a* hoarse.

ravage, răh-văhsh, *m* ravage; devastation; havoc.

ravaler, răh-văh-leh, *v* to swallow again; to disparage.

ravi, răh-vee, *a* entranced; delighted.

ravin, răh-vang, *m* ravine.

ravir, răh-veer, *v* to rob; to carry off; to enrapture.

raviser (se), ser răh-ve-zeh, *v* to change one's mind.

ravissant, e, răh-viss-ahng, *a* ravishing; charming.

ravissement, răh-viss-mahng, *m* ravishment; rapture.

ravoir, răh-vo'ăhr, *v* to get back (only in *inf*).

rayer, ray-yeh, *v* to erase; to scratch; to stripe.

rayon, ray-yong, *m* ray;

bookshelf; radius; spoke; department.

rayonnement, ray-ongn-mahng *m* radiation.

rayonner, ray-yonn-eh, *v* to radiate.

rayure, ray-yEEr, *f* stripe.

réaction, reh-ăhck-se-ong, *f* reaction.

réagir, reh-ăh-sheer, *v* to react.

réaliser, reh-ăh-le-zeh, *v* to realize.

realiste, reh-ăh-leest *a* realistic; streetwise.

réalité, reh-ăh-le-teh, *f* reality.

rébarbati-f, ve, reh-băhr-băh-teeff, *a* repulsive.

rebattu, e, rer-băh-tE, *a* trite; hackneyed.

rebelle, rer-bell, *mf* rebel; *a* rebellious.

rebondi, e, rer-bong-de, *a* plump; chubby.

rebondir, rer-bong-deer, *v* to rebound; to bounce.

rebord, rer-bor, *m* edge; brim.

rebours, rer-boohr, *m* wrong way; reverse.

rebrousse-poil (à), ăh rer-brooss-po'ăhl, *adv* the wrong way.

rebrousser, rer-brooss-eh, *v* to brush up; – **chemin,** – sher-mang, to retrace one's steps.

rebut, rer-bE, *m* rejection; scum; outcast.

rebuter, rer-bE-teh, *v* to repulse; to dishearten.

récalcitrant, e, reh-kăhl-se-trahng, *a* refractory.

recaler, rer-kăhl-eh, *v* to fail an exam.

recéler, rer-seh-leh, *v* to receive (stolen goods); to harbour.

récemment, reh-săh-mahng, *adv* recently.

recensement, rer-sahngss-mahng, *m* census.

récent, e, reh-sahng, *a* recent.

récépissé, reh-seh-piss-eh, *m* acknowledgment of receipt.

réception, reh-sep-se-ong, *f* reception; receipt.

recette, rer-sett, *f* receipt; returns; recipe.

receveu-r, se, rer-ser-ver, *mf* receiver; collector; conductor (bus, etc).

recevoir, rer-ser-vo'ăhr, *v* to receive; to admit.

rechange, rer-shahng-sh, *m* replacement; **de –,** der –, spare.

réchaud, reh-shoh, *m* chafing dish; small stove.

réchauffer, reh-shoh-feh, *v* to reheat; to stir up.

recherche, rer-shairsh, *f* search; refinement; research.

recherché, e, rer-shair-sheh, *a* in great request; choice.

rechercher, rer-shair-sheh, *v* to search; to seek.

rechute, rer-shEEt, *f* relapse.

récidive, reh-se-deev, *f* second offence.

récif, rer-seeff, *m* reef.

récipient, reh-se-pe-ahng, *m* container.

réciproque,* reh-se-prock, *a* reciprocal.

récit, reh-se, *m* account; narration.

réciter, reh-se-teh, *v* to recite; to relate.

réclamation, reh-klăh-măh-se-ong, *f* claim; complaint.

réclame, reh-klăhm, *f* advertisement.

réclamer, reh-klăh-meh, *v* to claim; to protest; to implore; to need.

reclus, e, rer-klE, *mf* recluse.

recoin, rer-ko'ang, *m* corner; nook.

récolte, reh-kollt, *f* harvest; crop.

recommandable, rer-komm-ahng-dăh-bl, *a* commendable;

advisable.

recommandation, rer-komm-ahng-dăh-se-ong, *f* recommendation; advice.

recommander, rer-komm-ahng-deh, *v* to recommend; to advise; (letter) to register.

recommencer, rer-komm-ahngss-eh, *v* to begin again; to do it again.

récompense, reh-kong-pahngss, *f* reward.

récompenser, reh-kong-pahngss-eh, *v* to reward.

réconcilier, reh-kong-se-le-eh, *v* to reconcile.

reconduire, rer-kong-dweer, *v* to lead back; to see home.

réconforter, reh-kong-for-teh, *v* to fortify; to cheer up.

reconnaissance, rer-konn-ess-ahngss, *f* recognition; gratitude.

reconnaissant, e, rer-konn-ess-ahng, *a* grateful.

reconnaître, rer-konn-ay-tr, *v* to recognize; to acknowledge.

recourir, rer-koo-reer, *v* to have recourse.

recours, rer-koohr, *m* recourse; resource; appeal.

recouvrement, rer-koo-vrer-mahng, *m* recovery; (debts) collection; covering.

recouvrer, rer-koo-vreh, *v* to regain; to collect.

recouvrir, rer-koo-vreer, *v* to recover; to cover.

récréation, reh-kreh-ăh-se-ong, *f* recreation; play-time.

recréer, rer-kreh-eh, *v* to create again.

récrier (se), ser reh-kre-eh, *v* to exclaim; to protest.

recrue, rer-krE, *f* recruit.

recruter, rer-krE-teh, *v* to recruit.

recteur, reck-ter, *m* rector.

rectifier, reck-te-fe-eh, *v* to rectify.

recto, reck-to, *m* right-hand page.

reçu, rer-sE, *m* receipt.

recueil, rer-ker'e, *m* collection.

recueillement, rer-ker'e-mahng, *m* meditation; composure; quietude.

recueillir, rer-ker'e-eer, *v* to gather; to collect; **se –,** to collect one's thoughts.

recul, rer-kEEl, *m* retreat; retirement; room to move back.

reculé, e, rer-kE-leh, *a*

distant; remote.

reculer, rer-kE-leh, *v* to move back; to defer.

reculons (à), ăh rer-kE-long, *adv* backwards.

récupérer, reh-kE-peh-reh, *v* to retrieve; to recover.

récurer, reh-kE-reh, *v* to scour; to clean.

récuser, reh-kE-seh, *v* to challenge; to object; **se –,** to decline.

rédac-teur, trice, reh-dăhck-ter, *mf* editor; journalist.

rédaction, reh-dăhck-se-ong, *f* wording; editing; editorial staff; editorial office; essay.

rédemption, reh-dahngp-se-ong, *f* redemption; redeeming.

redescendre, rer-deh-sahng-dr, *v* to come down again; to take down again.

redevable, rerd-văh-bl, *a* indebted.

redevance, rerd-vahngss, *f* rent; royalty; due.

rédiger, reh-de-sheh, *v* to draw up; to edit.

redire, rer-deer, *v* to say again; to find fault (à, with).

redite, rer-deet, *f* repetition.

redoubler, rer-doo-bleh, *v*
to redouble; to increase;
to stay down (in
school).

redoutable, rer-doo-tăh-
bl, *a* formidable.

redouter, rer-doo-teh, *v* to
dread.

redresser, rer-dress-eh, *v*
to straighten; to correct.

réduction, reh-dEEk-se-
ong, *f* reduction;
discount.

réduire, reh-dweer, *v* to
reduce; to subdue; to
compel.

réduit, reh-dwe, *m* nook.

réel, le,* reh-ayl, *a* real.

réfectoire, reh-fehck-
to'ăhr, *m* refectory.

référendum, reh-feh-
rahng-dom, *m*
referendum.

référer, reh-feh-reh, *v* to
refer.

réfléchir, reh-fleh-sheer, *v*
to reflect; to ponder.

reflet, rer-flay, *m*
reflection.

refléter, reh-fleh-teh, *v* to
reflect.

réflexion, reh-fleck-se-
ong, *f fam* reflection.

refluer, rer-flE-eh, *v* to
flow back.

reflux, rer-flE, *m* ebbing;
ebb.

réforme, reh-form, *f*
reform; reformation.

réformer, reh-for-meh, *v*
to reform; to discharge.

refouler, rer-foo-leh, *v* to
drive back; to repress
(instinct, etc).

réfractaire, reh-frăhck-
tair, *a* refractory.

refrain, rer-frang, *m*
(song) refrain; chorus.

refréner, rer-freh-neh, *v*
to restrain.

réfrigérateur, reh-fre-
sheh-răh-ter, *m*
refrigerator.

refroidir, rer-fro'ăh-deer,
v to cool; to chill.

refuge, rer-fEE sh, *m*
refuge; shelter.

réfugié, e, reh-fE-she-eh,
mf & a refugee.

réfugier (se), ser reh-fE-
she-eh, *v* to take shelter.

refus, rer-fE, *m* refusal;
denial.

refuser, rer-fE-zeh, *v* to
refuse; to decline.

réfuter, reh-fE-teh, *v* to
refute; to disprove.

régal, reh-găhl, *m* treat;
pleasure.

régaler, reh-găh-leh, *v* to
entertain; **se –**, to enjoy
oneself.

regard, rer-găhr, *m* look;
glance.

regarder, rer-găhr-deh, *v*
to look at; to concern.

régate, reh-găht, *f* boat-
race; regatta.

régénérer, reh-sheh-neh-
reh, *v* to regenerate.

régie, reh-shee, *f*
administration; excise.

régime, reh-sheem, *m*
rule; diet.

région, reh-she-ong, *f*
region.

régir, reh-sheer, *v* to
govern; to rule.

régisseur, reh-shiss-er, *m*
manager; steward.

registre, rer-shees-tr, *m*
register; account.

règle, ray-gl, *f* ruler; rule;
discipline; *pl*
(menstrual) periods.

réglé, e, reh-gleh, *a* & *pp*
regular; steady.

règlement, ray-gler-
mahng, *m* regulation;
regulations.

régler, reh-gleh, *v* to
regulate; to rule; to
adjust.

réglisse, reh-gleess, *f*
liquorice.

règne, rayn-yer, *m* reign;
prevalence.

régner, rehn-yeh, *v* to
reign; to rule; to prevail.

regorger, rer-gor-sheh, *v*
to overflow; to abound.

regret, rer-gray, *m* regret;
sorrow.

regretter, rer-gray-teh, *v*

to regret; to be sorry.

régularité, reh-ghE-läh-re-teh, f regularity.

régula-teur, trice, reh-ghE-läh-ter, a regulating; standard.

réguli-er, ère,* reh-ghE-le-eh, a regular.

réhabituer (se), ser reh-äh-be-tE-eh, v to become reaccustomed (à, to).

rehausser, rer-ohss-eh, v to raise; to enhance.

réimpression, reh-ang-press-e-ong, f reprint.

rein, rang, m kidney; pl back.

reine, rayn, f queen; – **claude,** – klohd, greengage (plum).

réinstaller, reh-angs-täh-leh, v to reinstall; se –, to settle down again.

réintégrer, reh-ang-teh-greh, v to reinstate.

réitérer, reh-e-teh-reh, v to reiterate.

rejet, rer-shay, m rejection.

rejeter, rer sh-teh, v to throw back; to reject.

rejeton, rer sh-tong, m shoot; offspring.

rejoindre, rer-sho'ang-dr, v to rejoin; to join; to overtake; se –, to meet.

réjoui, e, reh-shoo'e, pp &

a delighted; jolly.

réjouir, reh-shoo-eer, v to rejoice; to delight; se –, to be delighted (de, at, with).

réjouissance, reh-shoo-iss-ahngss, f rejoicing.

relâche, rer-lahsh, f respite; (theatre) no performance; port of call.

relâche, e, rer-lah-sheh, a slack; lax.

relâcher, rer-lah-sheh, v to loosen; to abate; to release.

relais, rer-lay, m relay; stage.

relater, rer-läh-teh, v to relate.

relati-f, ve,* rer-läh-teeff, a relative.

relation, rer-läh-se-ong, f relation; connection; pl intercourse; dealings.

relayer, rer-lay-yeh, v to relieve; to relay.

relevé, rerl-veh, m (bank) statement; abstract.

relevé, e, rerl-veh, a raised; high; noble; spicy.

relever, rerl-veh, v to raise up again; to relieve; to notice; to dismiss.

relief, rer-le-eff, m relief; raised.

relier, rer-le-eh, v to bind

again; to connect; (books) to bind.

relieur, rer-le-er, m bookbinder.

religieu-x, se, rer-le-she-er, mf monk; nun; a* religious.

religion, rer-le-she-ong, f religion.

reliquaire, rer-le-kair, m reliquary; shrine.

relire, rer-leer, v to read again.

reliure, rer-le-Er, f bookbinding; binding.

reluire, rer-lweer, v to shine; to glitter.

remanier, rer-mäh-ne-eh, v to handle again; to alter.

remarquable,* rer-mähr-käh-bl, a remarkable.

remarque, rer-mährk, f remark; observation.

remarquer, rer-mähr-keh, v to remark; to observe.

remblai, rahng-blay, m embankment.

rembourrer, rahng-boo-reh, v to stuff.

rembourser, rahng-boohr-seh, v to reimburse; to refund.

rembrunir, rahng-brE-neer, v to darken; to make sad.

remède, rer-mayd, m remedy.

remédier, rer-meh-de-eh, *v* to remedy (à).

remerciement, rer-mair-se-mahng, *m* thanks.

remercier, rer-mair-se-eh, *v* to thank (de, for).

remettre, rer-met-tr, *v* to put back again; to put off; to deliver; to restore; to hand; to recollect.

remise, rer-meez, *f* putting back; delivery; remittance; discount; putting off; shed; outhouse.

rémission, reh-miss-e-ong, *f* forgiveness; remission.

remonte-pente, rer-mongt-pahngt, *m* ski lift.

remonter, rer-mong-teh, *v* to go up again; to go back to; to wind up; to restock.

remontoir, rer-mong-to'ăhr, *m* winder (of watch).

remontrer, rer-mong-treh, *v* to show again; to remonstrate.

remords, rer-mor, *m* remorse.

remorque, rer-mork, *f* trailer.

remorquer, rer-mor-keh, *v* to tow.

rémouleur, reh-moo-ler, *m* grinder.

remous, rer-moo, *m* eddy.

rempailler, rahng-pah-yeh, *v* to recover; to restuff with straw.

rempart, rahng-păhr, *m* rampart.

remplaçant, e, rahng-plăhss-ahng, *mf* substitute.

remplacer, rahng-plăhss-eh, *v* to replace; to succeed.

remplir, rahng-pleer, *v* to fill up; to fulfil.

remporter, rahng-por-teh, *v* to take back; to carry away; to win.

remue-ménage, rer-mE-meh-năhsh, *m* bustle; confusion.

remuer, rer-mE-eh, *v* to move; to stir; to wag.

rémunéra-teur, trice, reh-mE-neh-răh-ter, *mf* remunerator; *a* remunerative.

rémunérer, reh-mE-neh-reh, *v* to reward; to pay.

renaissance, rer-ness-ahngss, *f* rebirth; revival.

renaître, rer-nay-tr, *v* to be born again; to revive.

renard, rer-năhr, *m* fox.

renchérir, rahng-sheh-reer, *v* to raise the price of; to become more expensive.

rencontre, rahng-kong-tr, *f* meeting; encounter.

rencontrer, rahng-kong-treh, *v* to meet; to come across; to hit upon.

rendement, rahngd-mahng, *m* yield; output.

rendez-vous, rahng-deh-voo, *m* appointment; meeting place.

rendre, rahng-dr, *v* to give back; to render; to yield; to surrender; to make; to express.

rêne, rayn, *f* usually *pl* rein.

renégat, rer-neh-găh, *m* renegade.

renfermé, rahng-fair-meh, *m* musty smell; *a* withdrawn (person).

renfermer, rahng-fair-meh, *v* to shut up; to contain.

renflement, rahng-fler-mahng, *m* bulge.

renfoncement, rahng-fongss-mahng, *m* hollow; recess.

renforcer, rahng-for-seh, *v* to strengthen; to reinforce.

renfort, rahng-for, *m* reinforcement; help.

renfrogné, e, rahng-fronn-yeh, *a* sullen; frowning.

rengaine, rahng-gain, *f fam* old story; (same) old tune.

rengorger (se), ser rahng-

gor-sheh, *v* to swagger.

reniement, rer-ne-mah*ng*, *m* denial; disowning.

renier, rer-ne-eh, *v* to deny; to disown.

renifler, rer-ne-fleh, *v* to sniff; to snivel.

renne, renn, *m* reindeer.

renom, rer-no*ng*, *m* renown.

renommé, e, rer-nomm-eh, *a* renowned.

renommée, rer-nomm-eh, *f* fame.

renoncer, rer-nong*ss*-eh, *v* to renounce; to give up.

renouer, rer-noo-eh, *v* to tie again; to renew.

renouveler, rer-noov-leh, *v* to renew; to revive.

renouvellement, rer-noo-vell-mah*ng*, *m* renewal; renovation; increase.

renseignement, rah*ng*-sain-yer-mah*ng*, *m* information; enquiry.

renseigner, rah*ng*-sain-yeh, *v* to inform; **se –**, to enquire.

rente, rah*ng*t, *f* yearly income; annuity; funds.

renti-er, ère, rah*ng*-te-eh, *mf* person of independent means.

rentrée, rah*ng*-treh, *f* return; re-opening; payment; start of school year.

rentrer, rah*ng*-treh, *v* to enter again; to return; to gather in; to go home; to be included in.

renversant, e, rah*ng*-vair-sah*ng*, *a* stunning.

renverser, rah*ng*-vair-seh, *v* to upset; to reverse.

renvoi, rah*ng*-vo'äh, *m* sending back; dismissal; adjournment; reference.

renvoyer, rah*ng*-vo'äh-yeh, *v* to send back; to dismiss; to postpone.

repaire, rer-pair, *m* den; lair.

répandre, reh-pah*ng*-dr, *v* to spill; to spread; **se –** to spread about.

répandu, reh-pah*ng*-dE, *a* widespread; widely-known.

reparaître, rer-päh-ray-tr, *v* to reappear.

répara-teur, trice, reh-päh-räh-ter, *a* refreshing; restorative.

réparation, reh-päh-räh-se-o*ng*, *f* repair; atonement.

réparer, reh-päh-reh, *v* to repair; to atone for.

repartie, rer-pähr-tee, *f* retort; repartee.

repartir, rer-pähr-teer, *v* to set out again; to retort.

répartir, reh-pähr-teer, *v*

to deal out; to distribute.

repas, rer-pah, *m* meal; repast; **– froid**, – fro'äh, packed lunch.

repasser, rer-pah*ss*-eh, *v* to pass again; to iron; to resist.

repêcher, rer-pay-sheh, *v* to fish up; *fam* to help out.

repentir (se), ser rer-pah*ng*-teer, *v* to repent.

repentir, rer-pah*ng*-teer, *m* repentance.

répercuter, reh-pair-kE-teh, *v* to reverberate.

repère, rer-pair, *m* reference; **point de –**, po'a*ng* der –, landmark.

repérer, rer-peh-reh, *v* to mark; to locate; **se –**, to take one's bearings.

répertoire, reh-pair-to'ähr, *m* repertoire; repertory.

répéter, reh-peh-teh, *v* to repeat; to rehearse.

répétition, reh-peh-te-se-o*ng*, *f* repetition; rehearsal.

répit, reh-pe, *m* respite.

repl-et, ète, rer-play, *a* fat; plump.

repli, rer-ple, *m* fold; winding; coil; retreat.

replier, rer-ple-eh, *v* to fold again; to coil.

réplique, reh-pleek, *f*
rejoinder; cue; replica.

répliquer, reh-ple-keh, *v*
to reply; to rejoin.

répondant, reh-pong-
dahng, *m* surety; bail.

répondeur automatique
or **téléphonique,** reh-
pong-der-oh-toh-mǎh-
teeck, *m* answering
machine.

répondre, reh-pong-dr, *v*
to answer; to reply; to be
security for.

réponse, reh-pongss, *f*
answer; reply.

report, rer-por, *m* amount
brought forward.

reportage, rer-por-tǎhsh,
m report (newspaper);
running commentary;
scoop.

reporter, rer-por-teh, *v* to
carry over; **se –,** to refer
(à, to).

repos, rer-poh, *m* rest.

reposer, rer-poh-zeh, *v* to
put back; to rest; **se –,** to
rest; to rely.

repoussant, e, rer-pooss-
ahng, *a* repulsive.

repousser, rer-pooss-eh, *v*
to push back; to repel;
to shoot out again.

reprendre, rer-prahng-dr,
v to take back; to return;
to resume.

représaille, rer-preh-zah'e,

fpl reprisals; retaliation.

représentant, rer-preh-
zahng-tahng, *m*
representative.

représentation, rer-preh-
zahng-tǎh-se-ong, *f*
representation;
performance.

représenter, rer-preh-
zahng-teh, *v* to
represent; to point out;
to perform; to show
well.

réprimande, reh-pre-
mahngd, *f* reprimand.

réprimer, reh-pre-meh, *v*
to repress; to curb.

reprise, rer-preez, *f*
resumption; repetition;
darning.

repriser, rer-pree-zeh, *v* to
mend; to darn.

reproche, rer-prosh, *m*
reproach.

reprocher, rer-prosh-eh, *v*
to reproach.

reproduire, rer-prod-weer,
v to reproduce; **se –,** to
happen again.

réprouver, reh-proo-veh,
v to reprobate; to
disallow.

reptile, rehp-teel, *m*
reptile.

repu, e, rer-pE, *a* satiated.

république, reh-pE-bleeck,
f republic.

répudier, reh-pE-de-eh, *v*

to repudiate.

répugnant, e, reh-pEEn-
yahng, *a* repugnant.

répulsi-f, ve, reh-pEEl-siff,
a repulsive.

réputation, reh-pE-tǎh-se-
ong, *f* reputation;
character; **de bonne –,**
der-bonn –, reputable.

réputer, reh-pE-teh, *v* to
repute; to deem.

requérant, e, rer-keh-
rahng, *a* applicant;
plaintiff.

requérir, rer-keh-reer, *v* to
require; to demand.

requête, rer-kayt, *f*
request; petition.

requin, rerkang, *m* shark.

requis, erer-ke, *a*
necessary; requisite.

réseau, reh-zoh, *m* net;
network; system.

réservation, reh-zair-vǎh-
se-ong *f* reservation
(ticket, etc).

réserve, reh-zairv, *f*
reservation(doubt);
reserve; store.

réserver, reh-zair-veh, *v*
to reserve.

réservoir, reh-zair-vo'ǎhr,
m reservoir; tank; pond.

résidence, reh-ze-dahngss,
f residence; abode.

résider, reh-ze-deh, *v* to
reside.

résidu, reh-ze-dE, *m*

residue.

résignation, reh-zeen-yăh-se-ong, f resignation.

résigner, reh-zeen-yeh, v to resign.

résine, reh-zeen, f resin.

résistant, e, reh-ziss-tahng, a resistant; tough.

résister, reh-ziss-teh, v to resist.

résolu,* e, reh-zoll-E, a resolute.

résolution, reh-zoll-E-se-ong, f resolution.

résonner, reh-zonn-eh, v to resound.

résoudre, reh-zoo-dr, v to resolve; to dissolve.

respect, ress-pay, m respect; regard.

respectueu-x, se,* ress-payk-tE-er, a respectful.

respirer, ress-pe-reh, v to breathe; to inhale.

resplendir, ress-plahng-deer v to be resplendent.

resplendissant, e, ress-plahng-diss-ahng, a resplendent.

responsabilité, ress-pong-săh-be-le-teh, f responsibility.

responsable, ress-pongss-ăh-bl, a responsible; answerable.

ressaisir, ress-say-zeer, v to seize again; **se-,** to recover oneself.

ressembler, rer-sahng-bleh, v to resemble.

ressemeler, rer-serm-leh, v to resole.

ressentiment, rer-sahng-te-mahng, m resentment.

ressentir, rer-sahng-teer, v to feel; to resent.

resserrer, rer-say-reh, v to tighten.

ressort, rer-sor, m spring; jurisdiction; department.

ressortir, rer-sor-teer, v to get out again; to stand out; to result from (**de**); to be in the jurisdiction of.

ressource, rer-soohrss, f resource.

ressusciter, reh-sE-se-teh, v to resuscitate.

restant, ress-tahng, m remainder.

restaurant, ress-toh-rahng, m restaurant.

restauration rapide, ress-toh-răh-se-ong-răh-peed, f fast food.

restaurer, ress-toh-reh, v to restore; to refresh.

reste, resst, m remainder; pl remnants scraps; **du -,** dE-, besides.

rester, ress-teh, v to remain; to be left; to stay.

restituer, ress-te-tE-eh, v to refund; to restore.

restreindre, ress-trang-dr, v to restrict.

résultat, reh-zEEl-tăh, m result.

résulter, reh-zEEl-teh, v to result.

résumé, reh-zE-meh, m summary; résumé.

résumer, reh-zE-meh, v to sum up; to summarize.

rétablir, reh-tăh-bleer, v to restore; to re-establish; **se -,** to recover (one's health).

rétablissement, reh-tăh-bliss-mahng, m restoration; recovery.

retard, rer-tăhr, m delay; **en** ahng-, late.

retardataire, rer-tăhr-dăh-tair, mf & a straggler; in arrears.

retarder, rer-tăhr-deh, v to delay; to postpone; to be too slow.

retenir, rert-neer, v to detain; to withhold; to book.

retentir, rer-tahng-teer, v to resound.

retentissant, e, rer-tahng-tiss-ahng, a resounding; noisy.

retentissement, rer-tahng-tiss-mahng, m resounding.

retenue, rert-nE, *f*
modesty; reserve;
stoppage; detention.

réti-f,ve, reh-teeff, *a*
restive.

retiré, e, rer-te-reh, *pp* &
a withdrawn; secluded;
retired.

retirer, rer-te-reh, *v* to
draw again; to withdraw;
to retract; to reap.

retombée, rer-tong-beh, *f*
fallout (radioactive);
consequences.

retomber, rer-tong-beh, *v*
to fall again; to fall
back; to hang down.

rétorquer, reh-tor-keh, *v*
to retort.

retoucher, rer-too-sheh, *v*
to touch up.

retour, rer-toohr, *m*
return; recurrence;
reciprocity.

retourner, rertoohr-neh, *v*
to turn; to return.

retracer, rer-trăhss-eh, *v*
to retrace; to recall.

rétracter, reh-trăhck-teh,
v to retract; to recant.

retrai-te, rer-trayt, *f*
retreat; retirement;
shelter.

retraiter, rer-tray-teh, *v* to
pension off.

rétrécir, reh-treh-seer, *v*
to narrow; to shrink.

rétribuer, reh-tre-bE-eh, *v*

to remunerate.

rétribution, reh-tre-bE-se-
ong, *f* reward; salary;
payment.

rétrograder, reh-trog-răh-
deh, *v* to move back;
demote.

retrousser, rer-trooss-eh, *v*
to tuck up; to turn up.

retrouver, rer-troo-veh, *v*
to find again.

rétroviseur, reh-tro-ve-
zer, *m* driving mirror.

réunion, reh-E-ne-ong, *f*
reunion; meeting;
gathering.

réunir, reh-E-neer, *v* to
reunite; to gather; se –,
to meet.

réussir, reh-EEss-eer, *v* to
succeed; to thrive.

réussite, reh-EEss-eet, *f*
success.

revanche, rer-vahngsh, *f*
retaliation; revenge;
return (games); en –,
ahng –, in return.

rêve, rayv, *m* dream.

revêche, rer-vaysh, *a*
peevish, cantankerous.

réveil, reh-vay'e, *m*
awakening; alarm clock.

réveiller, reh-vay'e-yeh, *v*
to awake; to rouse; to
revive; se –, to wake up.

réveillon, reh-vay'e-yong,
m midnight supper
(New Year and

Christmas).

révéler, reh-veh-leh, *v* to
reveal; to disclose.

revenant, rerv-nahng, *m*
ghost.

revendeu-r, se, rer-vahng-
der, *mf* retailer.

revendication, rer-vahng-
de-kăh-se-ong, *f* claim;
demand.

revendiquer, rer-vahng-
de-keh, *v* to claim; to
demand.

revendre, rer-vahng-dr, *v*
to sell again.

revenir, rerv-neer, *v* to
come back; to recur; to
grow again; to amount;
to please; to cost.

revenu, rerv-nE, *m*
income; revenue.

rêver, ray-veh, *v* to dream;
to muse.

reverbère, reh-vair-bair,
m streetlamp.

révérence, reh-veh-
rahngss, *f* reverence;
curtsey.

révérer, reh-veh-reh, *v* to
revere.

rêverie, rayv-ree, *f*
musing; dreaming.

revers, rer-vair, *m* back;
reverse; (coat) facing;
turnup.

revêtir, rer-vay-teer, *v* to
clothe.

rêveu-r, se, ray-ver, *mf*

dreamer; *a** dreaming; pensive.

revient, rer-ve-ang, *m* price including V.A.T.

revirement, rer-veer-mahng, *m* sudden change; transfer.

réviser, rer-ve-zeh, reh-ve-zeh, *v* to revise.

revivre, rer-vee-vr, *v* to live again.

révocation, reh-vock-ăh-se-ong, *f* repeal; dismissal.

revoir, rer-vo'ăhr, *v* to see again; **au –,** oh –, goodbye.

révolte, reh-vollt, *f* revolt.

révolter, reh-voll-teh, *v* to rouse; to shock.

révolu, e, reh-voll-E, *a* past (of time).

révolution, reh-voll-E-se-ong, *f* revolution.

revue, rer-vE, *f* review; survey; magazine.

rez-de-chaussée, reh-der-shohss-eh, *m* ground floor.

rhabiller (se) ser răh-bee-yeh, *v* to get dressed again.

rhum, romm, *m* rum.

rhumatisme, rE-măh-tissm, *m* rheumatism.

rhume, rEEm, *m* cold.

riant, e, re-ahng, *a* smiling; pleasant.

ricaner, re-kăh-neh, *v* to sneer; to laugh unpleasantly.

riche, reesh, *a** rich; copious; fertile; *mf* wealthy person.

richesse, re-shess, *f* riches; wealth; fertility.

ricin, re-sang, *m* castor-oil plant.

ricochet, re-kosh-ay, *m* rebound.

ride, reed, *f* wrinkle; ripple.

rideau, re-doh, *m* curtain; screen.

rider, re-deh, *v* to wrinkle; to ripple.

ridicule, re-de-kEEl, *m* ridiculousness; *a** ridiculous.

ridiculiser, re-de-kE-le-zeh, *v* to ridicule.

rien, re-ang, *m* nothing; anything; trifle; **– que,** – ker only; **cela ne fait –,** slăh n'fay –, that does not matter.

rieu-r, se, re-er, *n & a* laugher; laughing.

rigide,* re-sheed, *a* rigid; stern; strict.

rigole, re-gol, *f* trench; drain; gutter.

rigoler, re-goll-eh, *v pop* to have fun; to giggle.

rigolo,–ote, re-goll-o, *a pop* jolly; funny.

rigoureu-x, se,* re-goo-rer, *a* rigorous.

rigueur, re-gher, *f* rigour; **de –,** der –, indispensable.

rime, reem, *f* rhyme.

rincer, rang-seh, *v* to rinse.

ripaille, re-pah'e, *f fam* feasting.

riposte, re-post, *f* parry and thrust; repartee.

rire, reer, *v* to laugh; to scoff at; to joke; *m* laughter.

ris, re, *m* sweetbread.

risée, re-zeh, *f* laughing-stock.

risible,* re-zee-bl, *a* laughable; ludicrous.

risqué, e, riss-keh, *a* hazardous; improper.

risquer, riss-keh, *v* to risk; to venture.

rivage, re-văhsh, *m* shore; bank.

rival, e, re-văhl, *a* rival.

rivaliser, re-văh-le-zeh, *v* to rival; to vie; to compete.

rive, reev, *f* bank; shore; border.

river, re-veh, *v* to rivet.

rivière, re-ve-air, *f* river; stream.

riz, re, *m* rice.

robe, rob, *f* robe; gown; dress; **– de chambre,** – der shahng-br, dressing gown.

robinet, rob-e-nay, *m* tap; stopcock.

robuste, rob-EEst, *a* robust; sturdy; stalwart.

roc, rock, *m* rock.

rocailleu-x, se, rock-ah'e-er, *a* stony; rugged.

roche, rosh, *f* rock; boulder.

rocher, rosh-eh, *m* rock (mass of).

rock and roll, rock-eh-roll *m* rock and roll.

rôder, rohd-eh, *v* to prowl; to roam.

rogner, ronn-yeh, *v* to cut; to pare; to clip.

rognon, ronn-yong, *m* kidney (of edible animals).

roi, ro'ăh, *m* king.

rôle, rohl, *m* role; part; character.

roman, romm-ahng, *m* novel.

romance, romm-ahngss, *f* sentimental song.

romanci-er, ère, romm-ahngss-e-eh, *mf* novelist.

romanesque, romm-ăhn-esk, *a* romantic.

romarin, romm-ăh-rang, *m* rosemary.

rompre, rong-pr, *v* to break; to snap; to break in.

ronces, rongss, *fpl*

brambles.

rond, e,* rong, *a* round; plump; full; *fam* drunk.

rond, rong, *m* round; circle.

ronde, rongd, *f* patrol; (music) semibreve.

rondelle, rong-dell, *f* washer; disc; slice.

rondeur, rong-der, *f* roundness; plumpness; frankness.

ronflant, e, rong-flahng, *a* snoring; bombastic.

ronfler, rong-fleh, *v* to snore; to roar.

ronger, rong-sheh, *v* to nibble; to corrode; erode.

ronron, rong-rong, *m* purr.

rosaire, roz-air, *m* rosary.

rosbif, ross-beeff, *m* roast beef.

rose, rohz, *f* rose; *a* rose; rosy; pink; *m* pink (colour).

roseau, roz-oh, *m* reed.

rosée, roh-zeh, *f* dew.

rosier, roh-ze-eh, *m* rose-tree.

rosser, ross-eh, *v fam* to give someone a good hiding.

rossignol, ross-een-yol, *m* nightingale; *fam* picklock; unsaleable article.

rot, roh, *m fam* belch.

rôti, roh-te, *m* roast meat; joint.

rôtir, roh-teer, *v* to roast.

rotule, rot-EEl, *f* kneecap.

rouage, roo-ăhsh, *m* wheel-work; machinery.

roucouler, roo-koo-leh, *v* to coo.

roue, roo, *f* wheel; **faire la –,** fair lăh –, to strut; to turn cartwheels.

roué, e, roo-eh, *mf* rake; *a* sly; artful.

rouet, roo-ay, *m* spinning wheel.

rouge, roosh, *m* red colour; red paint; *a* red.

rougeaud, e, roo-shoh, *a fam* red-faced.

rouge-gorge, roosh-gorsh, *m* robin redbreast.

rougeole, roo-shol, *f* measles.

rougeur, roo-sher, *f* redness.

rougir, roo-sheer, *v* to redden; to blush.

rouille, roo'e-ye, *f* rust; blight.

rouillé, roo'e-yeh, *a* rusty; rusted.

rouleau, roo-loh, *m* roll; roller.

roulement, rool-mahng, *m* rolling; rumbling; rotation.

rouler, roo-leh, *v* to roll; to wheel; to revolve.

roulette, roo-lett, f castor; roulette.

roulis, roo-le, m rolling.

roulotte, roo-lot, f caravan.

rouspéter, rooss-peh-teh, v *pop* to protest; to complain.

rousseur, rooss-er, f redness; **tache de –,** tăhsh der –, freckle.

roussir, rooss-eer, v to redden; to singe; to scorch.

route, root, f road; route; course; journey; **– à quatre voies,** – ăh-kăh-tr-vo'ăh, dual carriageway; **– de ceinture,** – der-sang-tEEr ring road (motorway).

routine, roo-teen, f routine; rote.

rou-x, sse, roo, a reddish; red-haired; russet.

royal, e,* ro'ăh-yăhl, a royal; regal.

royaume, ro'ăh-yohm, m kingdom.

royauté, ro'ăh-yoh-teh, f kingship; royalty.

ruade, rE-ăhd, f (horse) kick.

ruban, rE-bahng, m ribbon.

rubéole, rE-beh-oll, f German measles.

rubis, rE-be, m ruby.

ruche, rEEsh, f beehive.

rude,* rEEd, a harsh; severe; uneven; rough.

rudesse, rE-dess, f harshness; roughness; severity;

rudoyer, rE-do'ăh-yeh, v to treat roughly; to bully.

rue, rE, f street; road; thoroughfare.

ruelle, rE-ell, f lane; alley.

ruer, rE-eh, v (horse) to kick; **se –,** to rush.

rugby, rEg-be m rugby.

rugir, rE-sheer, v to roar.

rugissement, rE-shiss-mahng, m roaring; howling.

rugueu-x, se, rE-gher, a rough; rugged; wrinkled.

ruine, rween, f ruin; decay; downfall.

ruineu-x, se,* rwee-ner, a ruinous.

ruisseau, rwees-oh, m stream; brook; gutter.

ruisseler, rwees-leh, v to stream; to trickle down.

rumeur, rE-mer, f rumour; noise; report.

ruminant, e, rE-me-nahng, m & a ruminant; ruminating.

rupture, rEEp-tEEr, f rupture; breaking.

rural, e, rE-răhl, a rural.

ruse, rEEz, f cunning; artfulness; dodge.

rusé, e, rEE-zeh, a cunning; sly; wily; artful.

ruser, rEE-zeh, v to use cunning; to dodge.

rustaud, e, rEEss-toh, a boorish.

rustique, rEEss-teeck, a rural; rough.

rustre, rEEss-tr, m & a boor; boorish.

rut, rEEt, m rut.

rythme, reetm, m rhythm.

sa, săh, *poss a* his; her; its.

sabbat, săh-băh, *m* Sabbath.

sable, săh-bl, *m* sand; gravel.

sablonneu-x, se, săh-blonn-er, *a* sandy.

sabot, săh-bo, *m* wooden clog; hoof; – **(de Denver),** – (der-dahng-vair *m aut* wheel clamp.

sabotage, săh-bot-ăhsh, *m* sabotage.

saboter, săh-bot-eh, *v to* sabotage; to bungle.

sabre, săh-br, *m* sabre; broadsword.

sac, săhck, *m* bag; knapsack; sack; – **à dos,** – ăhdoh, backpack; rucksack; – **de couchage,** –der-koo-shăsh sleeping bag.

saccade, săh-kăhd, *f* jerk.

saccager, săh-kăh-sheh, *v* to ransack.

sacerdoce, săh-sair-doss, *m* priesthood.

sachet, săh-shay, *m* plastic bag; sachet; packet; purse.

sacoche, săh-kosh, *f* saddlebag (bicycle).

sacre, săh-kr, *m* consecration; coronation.

sacré, e, săh-kreh, *pp & a* sacred; holy; *vulg* confounded.

sacrement, săh-krer-mahng, *m* sacrament.

sacrer, săh-kreh, *v* to consecrate; to crown; to curse.

sacrifier, săh-kre-fe-eh, *v* to sacrifice.

sacrilège, săh-kre-laysh, *m & a* sacrilege; sacrilegious.

sacristain, săh-kriss-tang, *m* sexton.

sacristie, săh-kriss-tee, *f* vestry.

sagace,* săh-găhss, *a* sagacious; shrewd.

sage, săhsh, *a** wise; discreet; well-behaved.

sage-femme, săhsh-făhm, *f* midwife.

sagesse, săh-shess, *f* wisdom; prudence; good behaviour.

saignant, e, sayn-yahng, *a* bleeding; (meat) under-done; rare.

saigner, sayn-yeh, *v* to bleed.

saillie, sah'e-yee, *f* projection; spurt; *fam* outburst.

saillir, sah'e-yeer, *v* to jut out; to stand out.

sain, e,* sang, *a* sound; healthy; wholesome.

saindoux, sang-doo, *m* lard.

saint, e, sang, *mf & a** saint; holy; sacred.

sainteté, sang-ter-teh, *f* saintliness; holiness; sanctity.

saisie, say-zee, *f* seizure; distraint.

saisir, say-zeer, *v* to seize;

to startle; to understand; to distrain.

saisissant, e, say-ziss-ahng, *a* startling; thrilling.

saisissement, say-ziss-mahng, *m* shock; chill.

saison, say-zong, *f* season; time.

salade, săh-lăhd, *f* salad.

saladier, săh-lăh-de-eh, *m* saladbowl.

salaire, săh-lair, *m* wages; salary; *fig* reward.

salarié, e, săh-lăh-re-eh, *pp* & *a* paid.

sale,* săhl, *a* dirty; messy.

salé, e, săh-leh, *pp* & *a* salted; salt; spicy (story); salty.

saler, săh-leh, *v* to salt; *fig* to fleece.

saleté, săhl-teh, *f* dirtiness; nastiness; obscenity; dirty trick.

salière, săh-le-air, *f* saltcellar.

salir, săh-leer, *v* to soil; to dirty; to taint.

salissant, săh-le-sahng, *a* soiling; messy; easily soiled.

salive, săh-leev, *f* saliva; spittle.

salle, săhl, *f* hall; room; – **à manger,** – ăh mahng-sheh, dining room; – **d'attente,** – dăh-tahngt, waiting-room.

salon, săh-long, *m* living-room; exhibition.

salopette, săh-lo-pet, *f* overalls; dungarees; skisuit.

salubre, săhl-EE-br, *a* healthy; salubrious.

saluer, săh-lE-eh, *v* to salute; to bow; to greet.

salut, săh-lE, *m* salute; greeting; safety; salvation.

salutaire,* săh-lE-tair, *a* salutary; beneficial.

salutation, săh-lE-tăh-se-ong, *f* salutation; greetings.

samedi, săhm-de, *m* Saturday.

sanction, sahngk-se-ong, *f* sanction; approbation; penalty.

sanctuaire, sahngk-tE-air, *m* sanctuary.

sandale, sahng-dăhl, *f* sandal.

sang, sahng, *m* blood; race; parentage.

sang-froid, sahng-fro'ăh, *m* coolness.

sanglant, e, sahng-glahng, *a* bloody; outrageous.

sangler, sahng-gleh, *v* to strap; to gird.

sanglier, sahng-gle-eh, *m* wild boar.

sangloter, sahng-glot-eh, *v* to sob.

sangsue, sahng-sE, fleech; *fig* extortioner.

sanguinaire, sahng-ghe-nair, *a* blood-thirsty.

sanitaire, săh-ne-tair, *a* sanitary.

sans, sahng, *prep* without; but for; ...less.

sans-façon, sahng-făh-song, *m* straightforwardness.

sans-gêne, sahng-shayn, *m* overfamiliarity.

sans plomb, sahng-plong *a* unleaded (petrol, fuel).

santé, sahng-teh, *f* health.

saper, săh-peh, *v* to undermine.

sapeur, săh-per, *m* sapper; – **pompier,** – pong-pe-eh, fireman.

sapin, săh-pang, *m* fir; firtree.

sarcasme, săhr-kăhssm, *m* sarcasm.

sarcler, săhr-kleh, *v* to weed.

sardine, săhr-deen, *f* sardine.

sarrau, săh-roh, *m* (artist's) smock.

satané, e, săh-tăh-neh, *a fam* confounded.

satellite, săh-teh-leet, *m* satellite.

satiné, e, săh-te-neh, *a* satin-like; glazed; smooth.

satire, săh-teer, f satire.

satisfaction, săh-tiss-făhck-se-ong, f satisfaction.

satisfaire, săh-tiss-fair, v to satisfy; to meet.

satisfaisant, e, săh-tiss-fer-zahng, a satisfactory.

satisfait, e, săh-tiss-fay, a satisfied.

saturer, săh-tE-reh, v to saturate (**de,** with).

sauce, sohss, f sauce; gravy.

saucer, sohss-eh, v to drench; fam to reprimand.

saucière, sohss-e-air, f gravy-boat.

saucisse, sohss-eess, f sausage.

saucisson, sohss-iss-ong, m big sausage.

sauf, sohff, prep save; except; but.

sau-f, ve, sohff, a safe; secure.

sauf-conduit, sohf-kong-dwee, m safe-conduct.

sauge, sohsh, f sage.

saugrenu, e, soh-grer-nE, a absurd; preposterous.

saule, sohl, m willow; – **pleureur,** – pler-rer, weeping willow.

saumâtre, soh-mah-tr, a brackish; briny.

saumon, soh-mong, m salmon.

sauna, soh-năh m sauna.

saupoudrer, soh-poo-dreh, v to sprinkle (**de,** with).

saur, sor, a salted and smoked.

saut, soh, m leap; jump.

sauter, soh-teh, v to leap; to jump; to blow up; to skip; to fry briskly.

sauterelle, soht-rell, f grasshopper.

sauteu-r, se, soh-ter, mf & a leaper; leaping.

sautiller, soh-tee-yeh, v to hop; to skip.

sauvage, soh-văhsh, m savage; a* wild; untamed; shy; unsociable.

sauvagerie, soh-văhsh-ree, f savagery; unsociability.

sauvegarde, sohv-găhrd, f safeguard.

sauve-qui-peut, sohv-ke-per, m stampede.

sauver, soh-veh, v to save; to rescue; **se –,** to escape; to run away.

sauvetage, sohv-tăhsh, m life-saving; rescue; salvage.

sauveur, soh-ver, m saver; deliverer; Saviour.

savamment, săh-văh-mahng, adv skilfully; knowingly.

savant, e, săh-vahng, n scientist; scholar; a learned; skilful.

savate, săh-văht, f worn-out shoe.

saveur, săh-ver, f taste; savour; relish; flavour.

savoir, săh-vo'ăhr, v to know; to understand; to be able to; m learning.

savoir-faire, săh-vo'ăhr-fair, m skill; ability.

savoir-vivre, săh-vo'ăhr-vee-vr, m good breeding.

savon, săh-vong, m soap.

savonner, săh-vonn-eh, v to soap; to lather.

savonnette, săh-vonn-ett, f bar of soap.

savourer, săh-voo-reh, v to relish.

scabreu-x, se, skăh-brer, a rugged; dangerous; ticklish.

scandaleu-x, se,* skahng-dăh-ler, a scandalous.

scarlatine, skăhr-lăh-teen, f scarlet fever.

sceau, soh, m (wax) seal.

scélérat, e, seh-leh-răh, mf & a scoundrel; villainous.

sceller, sell-eh, v to seal.

scénario, seh-năh-re-o, m scenario; filmscript; screenplay.

scène, sayn, f scene; stage; row.

scepticisme, sehp-tiss-eessm, *m* scepticism.

sceptre, sayp-tr, *m* sceptre.

schéma, sheh-măh, *m* diagram; sketch-plan.

scie, se, *f* saw.

sciemment, se-ăh-mahng, *adv* knowingly.

science, se-ahngss, *f* science; learning.

scientifique,* se-ahng-te-feeck, *a* scientific.

scier, se-eh, *v* to saw.

scierie, se-ree, *f* saw-mill.

scintiller, sang-tee-yeh, *v* to twinkle; to sparkle.

scission, siss-e-ong, *f* division; secession.

sciure, se-EEr, *f* saw-dust.

scolaire, skoll-air, *a* scholastic; school.

scorbut, skor-bE, *m* scurvy.

scrupule, skrE-pEEl, *m* scruple; scrupulousness.

scrupuleu-x, se,* skrE-pE-ler, *a* scrupulous; precise.

scruter, skrE-teh, *v* to scrutinize.

scrutin, skrE-tang, *m* ballot; poll.

sculpter, skEEl-teh, *v* to sculpture; to carve.

se, ser, *pers pron* oneself; himself; herself; itself; themselves; each other; one another.

séance, seh-ahngss, *f* sitting; meeting; performance.

seau, soh, *m* bucket; pail.

sec, sayk, **sèche,*** saysh, *a* dry; harsh; barren.

sécher, seh-sheh, *v* to dry.

sécheresse, sehsh-ress, *f* dryness; drought; barrenness.

second, ser-gong, *m* assistant; second floor.

second, e,* ser-gong, *a* second.

seconde, ser-gongd, *f* (time) second; (railway) second-class.

seconder, ser-gong-deh, *v* to support; to further.

secouer, ser-koo-eh, *v* to shake; to shock; to stir up.

secourable, ser-koo-răh-bl, *a* helpful.

secourir, ser-koo-reer, *v* to help; to relieve.

secours, ser-koohr, *m* help; relief.

secousse, ser-kooss, *f* shake; jolt; blow; shock.

secret, ser-kray, *m* secret; secrecy.

secr-et, ète,* ser-kray, *a* secret; private.

secrétaire, ser-kreh-tair, *mf* secretary; writing desk.

secrétariat, ser-kreh-tăh-re-ăh, *m* secretaryship; secretariat.

secréter, ser-kreh-teh, *v* to secrete.

sectaire, seck-tair, *m & a* sectarian.

secte, seckt, *f* sect.

secteur, seckt-er, *m* sector; district area (served by electricity, etc); the mains.

section, seck-se-ong, *f* section; zone (on bus route, etc).

séculaire, seh-kE-lair, *a* age old; time-honoured.

séculi-er, ère, seh-kE-le-eh, *a* secular.

sécurité, seh-kE-re-teh, *f* security.

sédentaire, seh-dahng-tair, *a* sedentary.

séditieu-x, se,* seh-de-se-er, *a* seditious.

séduc-teur, trice, seh-dEEk-ter, *mf & a* seducer; fascinating; seductive.

séduire, seh-dweer, *v* to seduce; to delude; to captivate.

séduisant, e, seh-dwee-zahng, *a* captivating; enticing; glamorous (job).

seigle, say-gl, *m* rye.

seigneur, sehn-yer, *m* lord.

sein, sang, m breast;
bosom; fig womb; **au –
de,** oh – der, in the
midst of, **aux –s nus,** oh
– nE a topless.

seize, sayz, m & a sixteen.

seizième, say-ze-aym, m &
a sixteenth.

séjour, seh-**shoohr,** m
stay; sojourn; abode.

séjourner, seh-**shoohr**-
neh, v to stay; to dwell.

sel, sell, m salt; fam wit.

selle, sell, f saddle; stool.

seller, sell-eh, v to saddle.

self-service, self-sair-veess
a self-service.

selon, ser-long, prep
according to; – **que,** –
ker, according; whether.

semailles, ser-mah'e, fpl
sowing; sowing-time.

semaine, ser-main, f week;
week's wages.

semblable, sahng-blǎh-bl,
m fellow-man, a* alike;
similar.

semblant, sahng-blahng, m
appearance; show; **faire
–,** fair –, to pretend.

sembler, sahng-bleh, v to
seem; to appear.

semelle, ser-mell, f (boots,
shoes) sole.

semence, ser-mahngss, f
seed.

semer, ser-meh, v to sow;
to scatter.

semestre, ser-mays-tr, m
half-year.

semeu-r, se, ser-mer, mf
sower.

semi, ser-me, prefix semi;
half.

séminaire, seh-me-nair, m
seminary.

semonce, ser-mongss, f
lecture; reprimand;
rebuke.

semoule, ser-mool, f
semolina.

sénat, seh-nǎh, m senate.

senilité, seh-ne-le-teh, f
senility.

sens, sahngss, m sense;
senses; opinion;
direction; à – **unique,**
ǎh – E-neeck, a one-way
(street).

sensation, sahng-sǎh-se-
ong, f sensation;
excitement.

sensé, e, sahng-seh, a
sensible; judicious.

sensibilité, sahng-se-be-le-
teh, f sensibility;
sensitivity.

sensible, sahng-see-bl, a
sensitive; obvious; sore.

sensiblement, sahng-se-
bler-mahng, adv
perceptibly; greatly.

sensuel, le,* sahng-sE-ell,
a sensual.

sentence, sahng-tahngss, f
sentence; maxim;
judgment.

senteur, sahng-ter, f scent;
fragrance.

senti, e, sahng-te, a felt;
vividly expressed.

sentier, sahng-te-eh, m
path.

sentiment, sahng-te-
mahng, m sentiment;
sense; feeling.

sentimental, e, sahng-te-
mahng-tǎhl a romantic.

sentinelle, sahng-te-nell, f
sentry.

sentir, sahng-teer, v to
feel; to smell; to taste of;
to see; to foresee.

séparation, seh-pǎh-rǎh-
se-ong, f separation.

séparer, seh-pǎh-reh, v to
separate; to divide.

sept, sett, m & a seven.

septembre, sayp-tahng-br,
m September.

septentrional, e, sayp-
tahng-tre-onn-ǎhl, a
northern.

septième, say-te-aym, m &
a seventh.

septuple, sayp-tE-pl, a
sevenfold.

sépulture, seh-pEEl-tEEr, f
tomb; burial.

séquestre, seh-kayss-tr, m
sequestration;
sequestrator.

serein, e, ser-rang, a
serene.

sérénade, seh-reh-nähd, *f* serenade.

sérénité, seh-reh-ne-teh, *f* serenity.

sergent, sair-**shahng**, *m* ;ergeant.

série, seh-re, *f* series; set.

sérieu-x, se, * seh-re-er, *a* serious; earnest; grave.

serin, ser-rang, *m* canary bird; *pop* idiot.

seringue, ser-rang-gh, *f* syringe.

serment, sair-mahng, *m* oath.

sermon, sair-mong, *m* sermon; lecture.

sermonner, sair-monn-eh, *v* to lecture.

serpe, sairp, *f* billhook.

serpent, sair-pahng, *m* serpent; snake.

serpenter, sair-pahng-teh, *v* to meander.

serpette, sair-pett, *f* pruningknife.

serpillière, sair-pe-yair, *f* dishcloth; floorcloth.

serre, sair, *f* greenhouse; pressing; talon.

serré, e, say-reh, *a* close; compact; precise; tight.

serrer, say-reh, *v* to squeeze; to tighten; *fig* close-fought (match).

serrure, say-rEEr, *f* lock.

serrurier, say-rE-re-eh, *m* locksmith.

servant, sair-vahng, *m* gunner; *a* serving.

servante, sair-vahngt, *f* servant.

serviable, sair-ve-äh-bl, *a* obliging.

service, sair-veess, *m* service; attendance; duty; set; divine service; **– des chambres,** – deh-chang-br *m* roomservice.

serviette, sair-ve-ett, *f* napkin; towel; brief case.

servile,* sair-veell, *a* servile.

servir, sair-veer, *v* to serve; to wait upon; **se – de,** to use.

serviteur, sair-ve-ter, *m* servant.

ses, say, *poss a pl* his; her; its; one's.

session, sess-e-ong, *f* session; sitting; *jur* term.

seuil, ser'e, *m* threshold; sill; beginning.

seul, e,* serl, *a* only; sole; alone; mere; single.

sève, sayv, *f* sap; *fig* vigour.

sévère,* seh-vair, *a* severe; stern; harsh.

sévir, seh-veer, *v* to punish severely; to rage.

sevrer, ser-vreh, *v* to wean.

sexagénaire, secks-äh-sheh-nair, *mf & a* sixty

year old.

sexe, secks, *m* sex.

sexiste, secks-eest *a* sexist.

sextuple, secks-tEE-pl, *m & a* sixfold.

sexuel, le, secks-E-ell, *a* sexual.

sexy, seck-se *a* sexy.

si, se, *adv* so; however; yes; *conj* if; whether.

SIDA; sida; Sida, see-däh, *m* AIDS.

siècle, se-ay-kl, *m* century; time; age.

siège, se-aysh, *m* seat; see; siege.

siéger, se-eh-sheh, *v* to sit; to hold sittings.

sien, ne (le, la), ler se-ang, läh se-enn, *poss pron* his; her; its.

sieste, se-esst, *f* siesta; afternoon nap.

siffler, se-fleh, *v* to whistle; to hiss.

sifflet, se-flay, *m* whistle; hiss.

signal, seen-yähl, *m* signal.

signalé, e, seen-yäh-leh, *a* signal.

signalement, seen-yähl-mahng, *m* description.

signaler, seen-yäh-leh, *v* to signal; to point out.

signataire, seen-yäh-tair, *m* signer.

signature, seen-yäh-tEEr, *f*

signature.

signe, seen-yer, *m* sign; mark; token.

signer, seen-yeh, *v* to sign; **se –,** to cross oneself.

signifier, seen-yee-fee-eh, *v* to mean; to notify.

silence, se-lahngss, *m* silence; stillness.

silencieu-x, se,* se-lahng-se-er, *a* silent; still.

sillon, see-yong, *m* furrow; trail; wake.

sillonner, see-yonn-eh, *v* to furrow; to plough.

simagrée, se-mäh-greh, *f* grimace; *pl* fuss.

similaire, se-me-lair, *a* similar.

simple, sang-pl, *m* idiot; *pl med* medicinal plants; *a** simple; single; plain; **ticket –,** te-kay, *m* one-way ticket.

simplicité, sang-ple-se-teh, *f* simplicity.

simulacre, se-mE-läh-kr, *m* image; sham.

simuler, se-mE-leh, *v* to simulate; to feign.

simultané, e, se-mEEl-tähneh, *a* simultaneous.

simultanément, se-mEEl-täh-neh-mahng, *adv* simultaneously.

sincère,* sang-sair, *a* sincere; candid; true.

sincérité, sang-seh-re-teh, *f* sincerity; honesty.

singe, sangsh, *m* ape; monkey.

singer, sang-sheh, *v* to mimic.

singularité, sang-ghE-läh-re-teh, *f* singularity.

singuli-er, ère,* sang-ghE-le-eh, *a* singular; peculiar; odd.

sinistre, se-neess-tr, *m* disaster; *a** sinister; gloomy.

sinon, se-nong, *conj* if not; otherwise; or else; except.

sinueu-x, se, se-nE-er, *a* winding.

sirène, se-rain, *f* mermaid; siren.

sirop, se-roh, *m* syrup.

sis, e, se, *a* situated.

site, seet, *m* site; landscape; scenery.

sitôt, se-toh, *adv* as soon; **– que,** – ker, as soon as.

situation, se-tE-äh-se-ong, *f* situation; position.

situé, e, se-tE-eh, *a* situated.

six, seess (before a consonant, see), *m & a* six.

sixième, se-ze-aym, *m & a* sixth.

skateboard, sket-bor *m* skateboard.

ski, ske, *m* ski; skiing;

piste de –, peest-der –, *f* ski slope; **– nautique,** – noh-teeck water-skiing.

skier, ske-eh, *v* to ski.

sobre,* sobr, *a* sober; temperate; sparing.

sobriété, sob-re-eh-teh, *f* sobriety.

sobriquet, sob-re-kay, *m* nickname.

soc, sock, *m* ploughshare.

sociable, soss-e-äh-bl, *a* sociable.

social, e,* soss-e-ähl, *a* social.

socialisme, soss-e-äh-leessm, *m* socialism.

sociétaire, soss-e-eh-tair, *mf & a* member; partner.

société, soss-e-eh-teh, *f* society; party; partnership; company.

sociologue, soss-e-o-log, *m* sociologist.

socle, soc-kl, *m* pedestal.

sœur, serf, *f* sister; nun.

sofa, soh-fäh *m* sofa.

software, soft-wair, *m comput* software.

soi, so'äh, *pron* oneself; itself; self; himself; herself.

soi-disant, so'äh-de-zahng, *a* would-be; so-called; *adv* supposedly.

soie, so'äh, *f* silk; bristle.

soierie, so'äh-ree, *f* silk goods; silk-trade.

soif, so'ăhf, *f* thirst; **avoir –**, ăh-vo'ăhr –, to be thirsty.

soigné, e, so'ăhn-yeh, *a* done with care; well-groomed.

soigner, so'ăhn-yeh, *v* to take care of; to nurse.

soigneu-x, se, so'ăhn-yer, *a* careful.

soin, so'ăng, *m* care; *pl* attentions.

soir, so'ăhr, *m* evening; night.

soirée, so'ăh-reh, *f* evening (duration of); evening party.

soit, so'ăh, *conj* either; whether; or; suppose.

soit! so'ăh, *interj* so be it! well and good!

soixantaine, so'ăhss-ahng-tain, *f* about sixty.

soixante, so'ăhss-ahngt, *m & a* sixty; **–dix**, – dess, seventy.

soixantième, so'ăhss-ahng-te-aym, *m & a* sixtieth.

sol, sol, *m* soil; ground; the note G.

solaire, soll-air, *a* solar.

soldat, soll-dăh, *m* soldier.

solde, solld, *m* balance; sale (of remnants); *f* soldiers' pay.

solder, soll-deh, *v* to settle; to sell off.

sole, sol, *f* (fish) sole.

soleil, soll-ay'e, *m* sun; sunshine; sunlight.

solennel, le, soll-ăh-nell, *a* solemn.

solennité, soll-ăh-ne-teh, *f* solemnity.

solidaire, soll-e-dair, *a* jointly liable; interdependent.

solide, soll-eed, *a* solid; strong; firm; sound.

solitaire, soll-e-tair, *a* solitary; lonely.

solitude, soll-e-tEEd, *f* solitude; loneliness.

solive, soll-eev, *f* joist; rafter.

solliciter, soll-e-se-teh, *v* to solicit; to urge; to petition.

soluble, soll-E-bl, *a* soluble; soluble.

solution, soll-E-se-ong, *f* solution; break.

solvable, soll-văh-bl, *a* solvent.

sombre, song-br, *a* dark; gloomy; dismal; dull.

sombrer, song-breh, *v* (boat) to sink; **– dans**, – dahng, to sink into (poverty).

sommaire, somm-air, *m & a* summary; abstract.

sommation, somm-ăh-se-ong, *f* summons.

somme, somm, *m* nap; *f* sum; burden; **en –**, ahng

–, on the whole; in short.

sommeil, somm-ay'e, *m* sleep.

sommeiller, somm-ay'e-yeh, *v* to doze.

sommelier, somm-er-le-eh, *m* wine-waiter.

sommer, somm-eh, *v* to summon; to call upon.

sommet, somm-ay, *m* summit; top; acme.

sommier, somm-e-eh, *m* bed spring; bed base.

somnifère, somm-ne-fair, *m* sleeping pill.

somnolent, e, somm-noll-ahng, *a* sleepy; drowsy.

somnoler, somm-no-leh, *v* to drowse; to doze.

somptueu-x, se, songpt-tE-er, *a* sumptuous.

son, song, *poss a m* his; her; its; one's.

son, song, *m* sound; bran.

sonate, sonn-ăht, *f* sonata.

sondage, song-dăhsh, *m* opinion poll.

sonde, songd, *f med* probe.

sonder, song-deh, *v* to sound; to fathom; to probe.

songe, songsh, *m* dream.

songer, song-sheh, *v* to dream; to think; to muse.

songerie, songsh-ree, *f* dreaming.

songeu-r, se, song-**sher,** *mf* & *a* dreamer; thoughtful.

sonnant, e, sonn-ahng, *a* sounding; striking.

sonner, sonn-eh, *v* to sound; to ring; to strike (the hour).

sonnerie, sonn-ree, *f* ringing; (sound of) bells.

sonnette, sonn-ett, *f* small bell; door-bell; buzzer.

sonore, sonn-or, *a* sonorous.

sorbet, sor-bay, *m* sorbet.

sorcellerie, sor-sell-ree, *f* witchcraft; sorcery.

sorci-er, ère, sor-se-eh, *mf* & *a* sorcerer; wizard; witch.

sordide,* sor-deed, *a* sordid; disgusting; mean.

sornettes, sor-nett, *fpl* idle talk.

sort, sor, *m* fate; lot; spell.

sorte, sort, *f* sort; kind; manner.

sortie, sor-tee, *f* going out; way out; outburst.

sortir, sor-teer, *v* to go out; to emerge; to take out.

sosie, soz-ee, *m* double; doppleganger.

sot, te,* soh, sott, *a* silly; stupid; fool.

sottise, sot-eez, *f* silliness; foolishness; abuse (with

words).

sou, soo, *m* old French coin; *fam* penny.

soubresaut, soo-brer-soh, *m* convulsive moment.

souche, soosh, *f* stump; counterfoil.

souci, sooss-e, *m* care; anxiety; marigold.

soucier (se), ser sooss-e-eh, *v* to care (**de,** about; for); to mind; to be concerned.

soucieu-x, se,* sooss-e-er, *a* anxious; careworn.

soucoupe, soo-koop, *f* saucer.

soudain, e,* soo-dang, *a* sudden; unexpected; *fig* overnight.

soudain, *adv* suddenly.

soudaineté, soo-dain-teh, *f* suddenness.

soude, sood, *f* soda.

souder, soo-deh, *v* to solder; to weld.

soudure, soo-deer, *f* solder; soldering.

souffle, soo-fl, *m* breath; puff.

souffler, soo-fleh, *v* to blow; to breathe; to whisper; to prompt.

soufflet, soo-flay, *m* bellows; *fam* slap in the face; insult.

souffleter, soo-fler-teh, *v* to slap in the face; *fig* to

insult.

souffrance, soo-frahngss, *f* suffering; pain; **en –,** ahng –, unsettled; in suspense.

souffrant, e, soo-frahng, *a* suffering; poorly.

souffrir, soo-freer, *v* to suffer; to allow; to be injured.

soufre, soo-fr, *m* sulphur.

souhait, soo-ay, *m* wish.

souhaiter, soo-ay-teh, *v* to wish; to desire.

souiller, soo'e-yeh, *v* to dirty; to soil.

soûl, soo, *m fam* tout son –, too song –, to one's heart's content.

soûl, e, soo, *a pop* drunk.

soulagement, soo-lähsh-mahng, *m* relief; alleviation.

soulager, soo-läh-sheh, *v* to relieve; to soothe.

soûler (se), ser soo-leh, *v* to get drunk.

soulèvement, soo-layv-mahng, *m* rising; upheaval; insurrection.

soulever, sool-veh, *v* to raise; to lift; to stir up; **se –,** to rise; to revolt.

soulier, soo-le-eh, *m* shoe.

souligner, soo-leen-yeh, *v* to underline; to emphasize.

soumettre, soo-met-tr, *v*

to subdue; to submit; to lay before.

soumis, e, soo-me, *a* submissive.

soumission, soo-miss-e-ong, *f* submission; compliance.

soupape, soo-păhp, *f* valve.

soupçon, soop-song, *m* suspicion; surmise; *fig* a hint (of).

soupçonner, soop-sonn-eh, *v* to suspect.

soupe, soop, *f* soup.

souper, soo-peh, *v* to have supper; *m* supper.

soupeser, soo-per-zeh, *v* to weigh by hand.

soupière, soo-pe-air, *f* soup-tureen.

soupir, soo-peer, *m* sigh.

soupirail, soo-pe-rah'e, *m* small basement window.

soupirer, soo-pe-reh, *v* to sigh.

souple,* soo-pl, *a* supple; flexible; compliant.

source, soohrss, *f* source; spring (water).

sourcil, soohr-se, *m* eyebrow.

sourciller, soohr-see-yeh, *v* to frown.

sourd, e, soohr, *mf* & *a** deaf person; deaf; dull; secret; mute.

sourdine, soohr-deen, *f*

damper; **à la –,** ăh lăh–, secretly.

souriant, e, soo-re-ahng, *a* smiling.

souricière, soo-riss-e-air, *f* mousetrap.

sourire, soo-reer, *v* to smile; *m* smile.

souris, soo-ree, *f* mouse.

sournois, e,* soohr-no'ăh, *a* sly; cunning; artful.

sous, soo, *prep* under; beneath; below.

souscripteur, sooss-krip-ter, *m* subscriber.

souscrire, sooss-kreer, *v* to subscribe; to sign.

sous-entendre, soo-z'ahng-tahng-dr, *v* to imply.

sous-entendu, soo-z'ahng-tahng-dE, *m* implication.

sous-marin, soo-măh-rang, *m* submarine; *a* deep-sea; underwater.

soussigné, e, sooss-een-yeh, *mf* & *a* the undersigned; undersigned.

sous-sol, sooss-ol, *m* basement.

sous-titre, soo-tee-tr, *m* subtitle (cinema).

soustraction, sooss-trăhck-se-ong, *f* subtraction.

soustraire, sooss-trair, *v* to subtract; to shelter; **se –,**

to get away (**à,** from).

soutane, soo-tăhn, *f* cassock.

souteneur, soot-ner, *m* upholder; procurer.

soutenir, soot-neer, *v* to sustain; to support; to assert; to stand.

soutenu, soot-nE, *pp* & *a* sustained; lofty.

souterrain, soo-tay-rang, *m* subway; vault.

souterrain, e, soo-tay-rang, *a* underground; underhand.

soutien, soo-te-ang, *m* support; prop; supporter.

soutien-gorge, soo-te-ang-gorsh, *m* bra.

soutirer, soo-te-reh, *v* to draw off; *fig* to extract.

souvenir (se), ser soov-neer, *v* to remember (**de**).

souvenir, soov-neer, *m* remembrance; keepsake.

souvent, soo-vahng, *adv* often.

souverain, e, soov-rang, *mf* & *a** sovereign.

souveraineté, soov-rain-teh, *f* sovereignty; dominion.

soyeu-x, se, so'ah'e-er, *a* silky.

spacieu-x, se,* spăh-se-er, *a* roomy; spacious.

sparadrap, spăh-răh-drăp,

m bandage.

spécial, e,* speh-se-ăhl, *a* special; particular.

spécialité, speh-se-ăhl-e-teh, *f* speciality; line of business; proprietary article.

spécifier, speh-se-fe-eh, *v* to specify.

spectacle, speck-tăh-kl, *m* spectacle; show; play.

specta-teur, trice, speck-tăh-ter, *mf* spectator; *pl* audience.

spectre, speck-tr, *m* spectre; ghost.

spéculer, speh-kE-leh, *v* to speculate.

sperme, spairm, *m* sperm; semen.

sphère, sfair, *f* sphere; globe.

spirale, spe-răhl, *f* spiral; *a* spiral.

spirituel, le,* spe-re-tE-ell, *a* spiritual; witty.

spiritueu-x, se, spe-re-tE-er, *a* (alcoholic) spirit.

splendeur, splahng-der, *f* splendour; magnificence.

splendide,* splahng-deed, *a* splendid; magnificent.

spongieu-x, se, spong-she-er, *a* spongy.

spontané, e, spong-tăh-neh, *a* spontaneous.

spontanément, spong-tăh-neh-mahng, *adv* spontaneously.

sport, spor, *m* sport; *a* casual (of clothes); **–s d'hiver,** --de-vair, *mpl* winter sports.

squelette, sker-lett, *m* skeleton.

stable, stăh-bl, *a* stable; steady; durable.

stade, stăhd *m* stadium.

stage, stăhsh, *m* period of probation; course.

stagnant, e, stăhgh-nahng, *a* stagnant; still.

stalle, stăhl, *f* stall.

stance, stahngss, *f* stanza.

station, stăh-se-ong, *f* station; taxi-rank; **–- service,** – sair-veess, petrol station.

stationner, stăh-se-onn-eh, *v* to stop; to park.

stationnement, stăh-se-onn-mahng, *m* parking.

statistique, stăh-tiss-teeck, *f* statistics; *a* statistical.

statue, stăh-tE, *f* statue.

statuer, stăh-tE-eh, *v* to decree; to rule.

stature, stăh-tEEr, *f* stature; height.

statut, stăh-tE, *m* statute; regulation; status.

sténodactylo(graphe), steh-no-dăhck-te-log-răhf, *mf* shorthand-

typist.

sténographe, steh-nog-răhf, *mf* stenographer.

sténographie, steh-nog-răh-fe, *f* shorthand.

stéréo, steh-reh-oh *f* stéréo.

stéréophonique, steh-reh-o-fo-neeck, *a* stereophonic.

stérile,* steh-reel, *a* sterile; barren.

stérilité, steh-re-le-teh, *f* barrenness.

stigmate, stigg-măht, *m* stigma; brand; stain.

stigmatiser, stigg-măh-te-zeh, *v* to stigmatize.

stimulant, e, ste-mE-lahng, *a* stimulating; *m* stimulant.

stimuler, ste-mE-leh, *v* to stimulate; to urge on.

stipuler, ste-pE-leh, *v* to stipulate.

stoïque,* sto-eeck, *a* stoical.

stomacal, e, stomm-ăh-kăhl, *a* stomach.

stoppage, stop-ăhsh, *m* invisible mending.

store, stor, *m* blind.

strapontin, străh-pong-tang, *m* pull-down seat (on Metro).

stratégie, străh-teh-she *f* strategy.

strict, e,* strikt; *a* strict;

severe; precise.

strident, e, stre-dahng, *a*
shrill.

strié, e, stre-eh, *a* striated;
streaked; scored.

structure, strEEk-tEEr, *f*
structure; frame; build.

studieu-x, se,* stE-de-er, *a*
studious.

stupéfait, e, stE-peh-fay, *a*
stupefied; amazed;
flabbergasted.

stupéfier, stE-peh-fe-eh, *v*
to stupefy; to amaze.

stupeur, stE-per, *f* stupor.

stupide,* stE-peed, *a*
stupid.

stupidité, stE-pe-de-teh, *f*
stupidity.

style, steel, *m* style.

stylo, stee-lo, *m* fountain
pen; – à bille, – ăh bee-
ye, ball-point pen.

suaire, sE-air, *m* shroud.

suave,* sE-ăhv, *a* sweet;
soft; suave.

subdiviser, sEEb-de-ve-
zeh, *v* to subdivide.

subir, sE-beer, *v* to
undergo; to suffer; to
endure; to submit.

subit, e,* sE-bee, *a*
sudden.

subjecti-f, ve,* sEEb-
sheck-teeff, *a* subjective.

subjonctif, sEEb-shongk-
teeff, *a* subjunctive.

subjuguer, sEEb-shE-gheh,

v to subjugate.

sublime,* sEEb-leem, *a*
sublime.

submerger, sEEb-mair-
sheh, *v* to submerge, to
swamp.

subordonner, sE-bor-
donn-eh, *v* to
subordinate.

subséquemment, sEEb-
seh-kăh-mahng, *adv*
subsequently.

subséquent, e, sEEb-seh-
kahng, *a* subsequent.

subside, sEEb-seed, *m*
subsidy; grant.

subsister, sEEb-ziss-teh, *v*
to subsist; to stand.

substance, sEEbs-tahngss, *f*
substance.

substantiel, le,* sEEbs-
tahngss-e-ell, *a*
substantial.

substituer, sEEbs-te-tE-eh,
v to substitute (à, for).

substitut, sEEbs-te-tE, *m*
substitute; deputy.

subterfuge, sEEb-tair-fEE
sh, *m* subterfuge.

subtil, e,* sEEb-teel, *a*
subtle; sharp; acute;
keen.

subtilité, sEEb-te-le-teh, *f*
subtlety, acuteness.

subvenir, sEEb-ver-neer, *v*
to provide (à, for); to
help; to relieve.

subventionner, sEEb-

vahng-se-onn-eh, *v* to
subsidize.

subversi-f, ve,* sEEb-vair-
seeff, *a* subversive.

suc, sEEk, *m* juice; essence;
substance.

succéder, sEEk-seh-deh, *v*
to succeed; to follow
after.

succès, sEEk-say, *m*
success.

successi-f, ve,* sEEk-sess-
eeff, *a* successive.

succession, sEEk-sess-e-
ong, *f* succession;
inheritance.

succinct, e,* sEEk-sang, *a*
succinct; concise.

succomber, sEE-kong-beh,
v to succumb; to sink; to
yield; to die.

succion, sEEk-se-ong, *f*
suction.

succulent, e, sE-kE-lahng,
a juicy, savoury.

succursale, sE-kEEr-săhl, *f*
branch (of bank, etc).

sucer, sEEss-eh, *v* to suck;
to suck in, to drain.

sucre, sEE-kr, *m* sugar; –
glace, – glăhss, icing
sugar.

sucrer, sE-kreh, *v* to
sweeten; to sugar.

sucrerie, sE-krer-ree, *f*
sugar refinery; *pl* sweets.

sucrier, sE-kre-eh, *m*
sugar-bowl.

sud, sEEd, *m* South; *a* south, southern.

suer, sE-eh, *v* to sweat; *fig* to toil.

sueur, sE-er, *f* sweat, perspiration; *fig* toil.

suffire, sE-feer, *v* to suffice; to do; **cela suffit,** ser-lăh sE-fe, that will do.

suffisamment, sE-fe-zăh-mahng, *adv* sufficiently.

suffisance, sE-fe-zahngss, *f* sufficiency; conceit.

suffisant, e, sE-fe-zahng, *a* sufficient; conceited.

suffocant, e, sE-fock-ahng, *a* stifling.

suffoquer, sE-fock-eh, *v* to suffocate; to stifle.

suffrage, sE-frăhsh, *m* suffrage; approbation.

suggérer, sEEgh-sheh-reh, *v* to suggest; to hint.

suicide, swee-seed, *m* suicide.

suicider (se), ser swee-see-deh, *v* to commit suicide.

suie, swee, *f* soot.

suif, sweef, *m* tallow.

suinter, swang-teh, *v* to ooze out; to leak.

suite, sweet, *f* rest; consequence; attendants; series; sequence; continuation. **tout de –,** too der –, at once.

suivant, swee-vahng, *prep* according to; **au –,** oh –, next!

suivant, e, swee-vahng, *mf* attendant; *a* following; next.

suivi, e, swee-ve, *pp* and *a* followed; consistent; sought after.

suivre, swee-vr, *v* to follow; to result; to study; **faire –,** fair –, to forward.

sujet, sE-shay, *m* subject; person; cause; topic.

sujet, te, sE-shay, *a* subject; liable; inclined.

sujétion, sE-sheh-se-ong, *f* subjection; constraint.

superbe,* sE-pairb, *a* superb; majestic; proud.

supercherie, sE-pair-sher-ree, *f* deceit; cheat; fraud.

superficie, sE-pair-feess-ee, *f* surface; area.

superficiel, le,* sE-pair-fe-se-ell, *a* superficial; shallow.

superflu, e, sE-pair-flE, *a* superfluous; redundant.

supérieur, e,* sE-peh-re-er, *a* upper; superior.

supermarché, soo-pair-măhr-sheh *m* supermarket.

superstitieu-x, se,* sE-pair-ste-se-er, *a* superstitious.

supplanter, sE-plahng-teh, *v* to oust.

suppléant, e, sE-pleh-ahng, *mf* & *a* substitute; deputy.

suppléer, sE-pleh-eh, *v* to make good; **– à,** to make up for.

supplément, sE-pleh-mahng, *m* supplement; extra charge.

supplémentaire, sE-pleh-mahng-tair, *a* additional.

suppliant, e, sE-ple-ahng, *mf* & *a* supplicant.

supplication, sE-ple-kăh-se-ong, *f* entreaty.

supplice, sE-pleess, *m* torture; *fig* torment.

supplier, sE-ple-eh, *v* to entreat; to beseech.

supplique, sE-pleek, *f* petition.

support, sE-por, *m* support; stand.

supportable, sE-por-tăh-bl, *a* bearable.

supporter, sE-por-teh, *v* to support; to bear.

supposer, sE-poh-zeh, *v* to suppose; *jur* to substitute.

supposition, sE-poh-ze-se-ong, *f* supposition; *jur* substitution; forgery.

supprimer, sE-pre-meh, *v*
to suppress; to abolish.

supputer, sE-pE-teh, *v* to
reckon; to calculate.

suprématie, sE-preh-
mähss-ee, *f* supremacy.

suprême,* sE-praym, *a*
supreme; crowning; last.

sur, sEEr, *prep* on; upon;
over; above; by; out of;
towards; concerning.

sur, e, sEEr, *a* sour.

sûr, e,* sEEr, *a* sure; safe;
trustworthy.

surcroît, sEEr-kro'äh, *m*
increase.

surdité, sEEr-de-teh, *f*
deafness.

sûreté, sEEr-teh, *f* safety;
security.

surexciter, sEEr-eck-se-
teh, *v* to overexcite.

surf, sErf, *m* surfing.

surface, sEEr-fähss, *f*
surface; outside; area.

surfaire, sEEr-fair, *v* to
overcharge; to overrate.

surfin, sEEr-fang, *a*
superfine.

surgeler, sEEr-sher-leh, *v*
to deepfreeze.

surgir, sEEr-sheer, *v* to
arise; *fam* to appear
suddenly.

surhumain, e, sEE -E-
mang, *a* superhuman.

surintendant, sEEr-ang-
tahng-dahng, *m*

superintendent.

surlendemain, sEEr-
lahngd-mang, *m* two
days later.

surmener, sEEr-mer-neh, *v*
to overwork.

surmonter, sEEr-mong-teh,
v to overcome; (of
liquids) to rise above.

surnager, sEEr-näh-sheh, *v*
to float; *fig* to survive.

surnaturel, le,* sEEr-näh-
tE-rell, *a* supernatural.

surnom, sEEr-nong, *m*
nickname.

surnuméraire, sEEr-nE-
meh-rair, *m* & *a*
supernumerary.

surpasser, sEEr-pähss-eh, *v*
to exceed; to excel.

surplomber, sEEr-plong-
beh, *v* to overhang.

surplus, sEEr-plE, *m*
surplus; au – , oh – ,
moreover.

surprenant, e, sEEr-prer-
nahng, *a* surprising.

surprendre, sEEr-prahng-
dr, *v* to surprise.

surprise, sEEr-preez, *f*
surprise.

sursaut, sEEr-soh, *m* start;
jump.

sursauter, sEEr-soh-teh, *v*
to start; to give a jump;
to be startled.

surseoir, sEEr-so'ähr, *v* to
put off (à).

sursis, sEEr-see, *m* delay;
suspension; reprieve.

surtaxe, sEEr-tähcks, *f*
extra tax; surcharge.

surtout, sEEr-too, *adv*
above all; particularly.

surveillance, sEEr-vay'e-
ahngss, *f*
superintendence;
supervision.

surveiller, sEEr-vay'e-yeh,
v to supervise; to keep
an eye on; to watch
over; to invigilate.

survenir, sEEr-ver-neer, *v*
to come unexpectedly.

survie, sEEr-vee, *f*
survival; after life.

survivance, sEEr-ve-
vahngss, *f* survival.

survivre, sEEr-vee-vr, *v* to
survive (à); to outlive.

sus, sEEss, *prep* on; en –
de, ahng – der, *prep* over
and above.

susceptibilité, sEEss-ep-te-
be-le-teh, *f* touchiness.

susciter, sEEss-e-teh, *v* to
raise up; to create.

susdit, e, sEEss-de, *a*
aforesaid.

suspect, e, sEEss-paykt, *m*
& *a* suspect.

suspecter, sEEss-payk-teh,
v to suspect.

suspendre, sEEss-pahng-dr,
v to suspend; to hang-
up.

suspens (en), ahng sEEss-pahng, *adv* in abeyance.

suture, SEE-tEEr, *f* suture; *med* **point de –,** po'ang der –, stitch.

svelte, svaylt, *a* slender; slim.

syllabe, seell-lähb, *f* syllable.

sylvestre, sill-vays-tr, *a* sylvan.

symbole, sang-bol, *m* symbol.

symétrique,* se-meh-treeck, *a* symmetrical.

sympathique,* sang-päh-teeck, *a* likeable.

symptôme, sangp-tohm, *m* symptom.

syncope, sang-kop, *f* fainting fit.

syndicat, sang-de-kah, *m* union; syndicate.

syndicat d'initiative, sang-de-käh-de-ne-se-äh-teev *m* tourist office.

système, siss-taym, *m* system.

ta, tăh, *poss a f sing*
familiar form of 'your'.

tabac, tăh-băh, *m* tobacco;
snuff.

tabatière, tăh-băh-te-air, *f*
snuffbox.

table, tăh-bl, *f* table;
board; index.

tableau, tăh-bloh, *m*
picture; painting;
blackboard; list.

tablette, tăh-blett, *f* shelf;
lozenge; slab.

tablier, tăh-blee-eh, *m*
apron; pinafore.

tabouret, tăh-boo-ray, *m*
stool.

tache, tăhsh, *f* spot; stain;
blemish.

tâche, tahsh, *f* task; job.

tâcher, tah-sheh, *v* to
endeavour; to strive.

tacheté, e, tăhsh-teh, *a*
spotted; speckled.

tacite,* tăh-seet, *a*
implied; tacit.

taciturne, tăh-se-tEErn, *a*
taciturn; quiet.

tact, tăhckt, *m* touch; *fig*
tact; *fig* discretion.

taie (d'oreiller), tay(-dor-
ay'e-yeh) *f* pillow case.

taille, tah'e, *f* cut; waist;
height; pruning.

tailler, tah'e-yeh, *v* to cut;
to prune; to sharpen.

tailleur, tah'e-yer, *m*
tailor.

taillis, tah'e-ye, *m* copse;
thicket.

taire, tair, *v* to conceal; **se
–,** to be silent.

talc, tăhlk *m* talcum
powder.

talent, tăh-lahng, *m*
talent; ability.

talon, tăh-long, *m* heel;
counterfoil.

talonner, tăh-lonn-eh, *v*
to urge; to follow
closely.

talus, tăh-lE, *m* slope;
embankment.

tambour, tahng-boohr, *m*
drum; barrel.

tamis, tăh-mee, *m* sieve.

tampon, tahng-pong, *m*
plug; tampon; buffer; –
hygiénique, – e-she-eh-
neeck, tampon.

tamponner, tahng-ponn-
eh, *v* to stop up; to
collide.

tancer, tahngss-eh, *v* to
scold.

tandis que, tahng-de ker,
conj while; whilst;
whereas.

tangage, tahng-găhsh, *m*
pitching (of ship).

tanière, tăh-ne-air, *f* den;
lair.

tanner, tăh-neh, *v* to tan.

tant, tahng, *adv* so much;
as much; so many; as
many; – **mieux,** – me-er,
so much the better; –
pis, – pee, so much the
worse.

tante, tahngt, *f* aunt.

tantôt, tahng-toh, *adv*
presently; shortly; now
... now.

tapage, tăh-păhsh, *m*

uproar; row.

tape, tăhp, *f* slap; pat; thump.

taper, tăh-peh, *v* to tap; to pat; to strike.

tapir (se), ser tăh-peer, *v* to squat; to crouch.

tapis, tăh-pe, *m* carpet; rug; cover.

tapisserie, tăh-piss-ree, *f* tapestry.

tapissier, tăh-piss-e-eh, *m* upholsterer.

tapoter, tăhp-ot-eh, *v* to tap; to strum.

taquiner, tăh-ke-neh, *v* to tease.

tard, tăhr, *adv* late.

tarder, tăhr-deh, *v* to delay; to be long.

tardi-f, ve,* tăhr-deeff, *a* late; tardy; backward.

tare, tăhr, *f fig* blemish; *fig* defect; tare.

taré, e, tăh-reh, *a* damaged; ill-famed.

tarif, tăh-reeff, *m* tariff; price-list; rate; quotation.

tarir, tăh-reer, *v* (river)to dry up.

tarte, tăhrt, *f* tart.

tartine, tăhr-teen, *f* slice of bread and butter or jam.

tas, tah, *m* heap; pile; lot.

tasse, tahss, *f* cup.

tasser, tahss-eh, *v* to heap

up; to press down; **se –,** to settle.

tâter, tah-teh, *v* to feel; to try; to taste.

tâtillon, ne, tah-tee-yong, *mf & a* meddler; meddlesome.

tâtonner, tah-tonn-eh, *v* to grope; to feel one's way.

tâtons (à), ăh tah-tong, *adv* gropingly.

taudis, toh-dee, *m* hovel.

taupe, tohp, *f* mole.

taupinière, toh-pinn-e-air, *f* molehill.

taureau, toh-roh, *m* bull.

taux, toh, *m* rate.

taverne, tăh-vairn, *f* tavern.

taxer, tăhx-eh, *v* to tax; to assess; to accuse.

te, ter, *pers pron mf sing* (familiar form) you; to you; yourself.

technique, teck-neeck, *a* technical; *f* technique.

tee-shirt, tee-shert, *m* T-shirt.

teigne, tayn-yer, *f* moth; ringworm.

teindre, tang-dr, *v* to dye; to tint.

teint, tang, *m* complexion; dye; colour.

teinte, tangt, *f* tint; shade; tinge.

teinture, tang-tEEr, *f* dye;

dyeing; tincture.

tel, le, tell, *a* such; like; many; **– que, –** ker, similar to; such as.

télé, teh-leh, *f abbr* TV; telly.

télécopie teh-leh-ko-pee *f* fax; **envoyer par –,** ahng-vo'ăh-yeh-păhr –, *v* fax.

télégramme, teh-leh-grăhm, *m* telegram.

télégraphier, teh-leh-grăh-fe-eh, *v* to wire.

téléphone, teh-leh-fon, *m* telephone; **coup de –,** koo-der –, *m* telephone call; **numéro de –,** nE-meh-ro-der –, telephone number; **– public, –** pE-bleeck *f* pay-phone.

téléphonique, teh-leh-fonn-eeck, *a* telephonic; **cabine –,** kăh-been –, call-box; pay-phone.

télescope, teh-less-kop, *m* telescope.

télévision, teh-leh-ve-ze-ong, *f* television; **– par câble, –** păhr-kah-bl, cable television; **poste de –,** post-der –, television set.

tellement, tell-mahng, *adv* so; so much; **– que, –** ker, so much so that.

téméraire,* teh-meh-rair, *a* rash; foolhardy.

témoignage, teh-mo'ǎhn-yǎhsh, *m jur* testimony; *jur* evidence.

témoigner, teh-mo'ǎhn-yeh, *v* to show gratitude; *jur* to testify.

témoin, teh-mo-ang, *m* witness.

tempe, tahngp, *f* temple.

tempérament, tahng-peh-rǎh-mahng, *m* temperament; constitution.

tempérant, e, tahng-peh-rahng, *a* temperate.

température, tahng-peh-rǎh-tEEr, *f* temperature.

tempérer, tahng-peh-reh, *v* to moderate; to allay.

tempête, tahng-payt, *f* tempest; storm.

tempêter, tahng-pay-teh, *v* to storm; to fume.

temple, tahng-pl, *m* temple.

temporaire,* tahng-por-air, *a* temporary.

temporel, le,* tahng-por-ell, *a* temporal.

temps, tahng, *m* time; while; period; season; weather; tense; beat; **à – partiel,** ǎh – pǎhr-se-ell *a, adv* part-time.

tenace, ter-nǎhss, *a* tenacious.

tenailles, ter-nah'e, *fpl* pincers.

tendance, tahng-dahngss, *f* tendency; leaning.

tendon, tahng-dong, *m* sinew.

tendre, tahng-dr, *v* to stretch; to strain; to hold out; to tend.

tendre,* tahng-dr, *a* tender; affectionate; new.

tendresse, tahng-dress, *f* tenderness.

tendu, e, tahng-dE, *a* tight; stretched; tense.

ténèbres, teh-nay-br, *fpl* darkness; gloom.

teneur, ter-ner, *f* terms; contents.

tenir, ter-neer, *v* to hold; to keep: to last; to deem; to depend on; **– à,** – ǎh, to value; to care about.

tension, tahng-se-ong, *f* tension; **– artérielle,** – ǎhr-teh-re-ell, blood pressure.

tentant, e, tahng-tahng, *a* tempting.

tentation, tahng-tǎh-se-ong, *f* temptation.

tentative, tahng-tǎh-teev, *f* attempt; endeavour.

tente, tahngt, *f* tent.

tenter, tahng-teh, *v* to attempt; to tempt.

tenture, tahng-tEEr, *f* hangings; wallpaper.

ténu, e, teh-nE, *a* slender; thin.

tenue, ter-nEE, *f* holding; behaviour; attitude; dress.

térébenthine, teh-reh-bahng-teen, *f* turpentine.

terme, tairm, *m* term; limit; *pl* conditions.

terminal, tair-me-nǎhl *m* terminal (computer, oil, etc).

terminale, tair-me-nǎhl *a* terminal; **en phase –,** ahng-fǎhz –, *a med* terminal illness.

terminaison, tair-me-nay-zong, *f* ending.

terminer, tair-me-neh, *v* to finish; to conclude.

terminus, tair-me-nEs *m* terminal *rail*.

terne, tairn, *a* dull; colourless.

ternir, tair-neer, *v* to tarnish; to dim.

terrain, tay-rang, *m* ground; soil; piece of land.

terrasse, tay-rǎhss, *f* terrace.

terrasser, tay-rǎhss-eh, *v* to bring to the ground (in fight); excavate.

terre, tair, *f* earth; ground; land; estate; the world.

terrestre, tay-ress-tr, *a* terrestrial.

terreur, tay-rer, *f* terror; dread; awe.

terrible,* tay-ree-bl, *a* terrible; dreadful; frightful.

terrifier, tay-re-fe-eh, *v* to terrify.

terrine, tay-reen, *f* earthen dish; paté.

territoire, tay-re-to'ăhr, *m* territory.

terroriste, teh-ro-rest *mf* terrorist.

tertre, tair-tr, *m* hillock.

tes, tay, *poss a mf pl* (familiar form) your.

test, tayst *m* quiz.

testament, tess-tăh-mahng, *m* testament; will.

têtard, teh-tahr, *m* tadpole.

tête, tayt, *f fig* head; *fig* top; *fig* wits; presence of mind.

téter, teh-teh, *v* to suck (at the breast).

tétine, teh-teen, *f* teat.

têtu, e, tay-tE, *a* stubborn; headstrong.

texte, text, *m* text; subject.

textile, tex-teell, *m* textile; *a* textile; material.

textuel, le,* tex-tE-ell, *a* textual.

thé, teh, *m* tea; tea-party.

théâtral, e, teh-ah-trăhl, *a* theatrical.

théâtre, teh-ah-tr, *m* theatre; stage; plays; **coup de –,** koo der–, unexpected event.

théière, teh-yair, *f* teapot.

thème, taym, *m* topic; theme; exercise (at school).

théorie, teh-or-ee, *f* theory; drill; procession.

théorique,* teh-or-eeck, *a* theoretical.

thérapie, teh-răh-pe *f* therapy.

thermomètre, tair-momm-ay-tr, *m* thermometer.

thèse, tayz, *f* thesis; argument.

thon, tong, *m* tuna.

thorax, to-racks, *m* thorax; chest.

thym, tang, *m* thyme.

tibia, te-be-ăh, *m* shin-bone.

tic, teek, *m* tic; habit; twitch.

ticket, te-kay, *m* (bus, etc) ticket.

tiède,* te-aid, *a* lukewarm; tepid; *fig* indifferent.

tiédir, te-eh-deer, *v* to grow lukewarm.

tien, ne, te-ang, *poss pron mf* (familiar form) yours.

tier-s, ce, te-air, *mf* third

person; *a* third.

tige, teesh, *f* stem; stalk; trunk; rod; shaft.

tigre, tigresse, tee-gr, tee-gress, *mf* tiger; tigress.

tilleul, tee-yerl, *m* lime tree; lime blossom tree.

timbale, tang-băhl, *f* kettle-drum; metal cup.

timbre, tang-br, *m* bell; tone; stamp (postage).

timbré, e, tang-breh, *a* stamped; sonorous; *fam* dotty; mad.

timide,* te-meed, *a* timid; shy; bashful.

timoré, e, te-mor-eh, *a* timorous.

tintamarre, tang-tăh-măhr, *m* uproar; hubbub; clatter.

tinter, tang-teh, *v* to ring; to tinkle; to toll.

tir, teer, *m* shooting; firing; rifle range.

tirage, te-răhsh, *m* drawing; draught; printing; (newspapers) circulation.

tiraillement, te-rah'e-mahng, *m* pulling; pain.

tire-bouchon, teer-boo-shong, *m* corkscrew.

tiré, e, te-reh, *a* (face) drawn; worn out.

tirelire, teer-leer, *f* money-box; piggy bank.

tirer, te-reh, *v* to draw; to

pull; to drag; to verge on; to shoot.

tiret, te-reh, *m* hyphen; dash.

tiroir, te-ro'ăhr, *m* drawer; slide.

tisane, te-zăhn, *f* infusion.

tison, te-zong, *m* firebrand.

tisonnier, te-zonn-e-eh, *m* poker.

tisser, teess-eh, *v* to weave.

tissu, teess-E, *m* material; fabric.

titre, tee-tr, *m* title; right; certificate.

tituber, tee-tE-beh, *v* to stagger; to lurch.

titulaire, tee-tE-lair, *mf* holder; titular.

tocsin, tock-sang, *m* alarm-bell.

tohu-bohu, toh-E-boh-E, *m* hurly-burly.

toi, to'ăh, *pers pron mf sing* (familiar form) you (subject or object).

toile, to'ăhl, *f* cloth; linen; canvas; picture.

toilette, to'ăh-lett, *f* wash; lavatory; dress; dressing-table.

toiser, to'ăh-zeh, *v* to measure; *fig* to eye (someone).

toison, to'ăh-zong, *f* fleece; *fam* mop of hair.

toit, to'ăh, *m* roof; *fam* home.

tôle, tohl, *f* sheet iron.

tolérable, toll-eh-răh-bl, *a* tolerable.

tolérance, toll-eh-rahngss, *f* toleration.

tolérer, toll-eh-reh, *v* to tolerate.

tomate, tomm-ăht, *f* tomato.

tombant, e, tong-bahng, *a* falling.

tombe, tongb, *f* tomb; grave.

tombeau, tong-boh, *m* tomb; grave; tombstone.

tomber, tong-beh, *v* to fall; to abate; (– **sur**) to come across.

tome, tohm, *m* tome; volume.

ton, tong, *poss a m sing* (familiar form) your; *m* tone; style; shade.

tondeuse, tong-derz, *f* lawnmower; shears.

tondre, tong-dr, *v* to shear; to mow; to clip.

tonne, tonn, *f* ton (20 cwt); tun.

tonneau, tonn-oh, *m* cask; barrel.

tonner, tonn-eh, *v* to thunder.

tonnerre, tonn-air, *m* thunder.

toque, took, *f* cap.

toqué, e, tock-eh, *a (fam)* crazy.

torche, torsh, *f* torch.

torchon, tor-shong, *m* dishcloth; duster.

tordre, tor-dr, *v* to wring; to twist; **se –,** to writhe.

torpeur, tor-per, *f* torpor; numbness.

torpille, tor-pee-ye, *f* torpedo.

torpilleur, tor-pee-yer, *m* torpedo boat.

torréfier, tor-reh-fe-eh, *v* to roast.

torrent, tor-rahng, *m* torrent.

torrentiel, le, tor-rahng-se-ell, *a* torrential.

torse, torss, *m* torso; trunk; chest.

tort, tor, *m* wrong; harm; injury; **avoir –,** ăh-vo'ăhr –, to be wrong.

tortiller, tor-tee-yeh, *v* to twist; to shuffle; **se –,** to wriggle

tortue, tor-tE, *f* tortoise; turtle.

tortueu-x, se,* tor-tE- er, *a* winding; crooked.

torture, tor-tEEr, *f* torture.

tôt, toh, *adv* soon; early.

total, tot-ăhl, *m* total.

total, e,* tot-ăhl, *a* total; whole.

touchant, too-shahng, *prep* concerning;

regarding.

touchant, e, too-shahng, *a* touching; affecting.

touche, toosh, *f* touch; stroke; key.

toucher, too-sheh, *v* to touch; to cash; to hit; to affect; to be contiguous to.

toucher, too-sheh, *m* touch; feeling.

touffe, toof, *f* tuft; bunch; clump.

touffu, e, too-fE, *a* tufted; bushy; thick.

toujours, too-shoohr, *adv* always; ever; nevertheless.

toupet, too-pay, *m* tuft; impudence; *fig* cheek.

toupie, too-pee, *f* top; spinning top.

tour, toohr, *m* turn; revolution; circumference; trick; trip; lathe.

tour, toohr, *f* tower.

tourbe, toohrb, *f* peat; turf; mob.

tourbillon, toohr-bee-yong, *m* whirlwind.

tourelle, too-rell, *f* turret.

touriste, too-risst, *mf* tourist; tripper.

tourment, toohr-mahng, *m* torment; anguish.

tourmente, toohr-mahngt, *f* tempest; *fig* turmoil.

tourmenté, e, toohr-mahng-teh, *a* stormy; worried; unnatural.

tourmenter, toohr-mahng-teh, *v* to torment.

tournant, toohr-nahng, *m* turning; bend; corner; turning-point.

tournée, toohr-neh, *f* round; walk.

tourner, toohr-neh, *v* to turn; to change.

tourneur, toohr-ner, *m* turner; thrower.

tournevis, toohr-ner-veess, *m* screwdriver.

tournoi, toohr-no'ăh, *m* tournament.

tournoyer, toohr-no'ăh-yeh, *v* to whirl round.

tournure, toohr-nEEr, *f* figure; appearance; turn; course.

tourte, toohrt, *f* tart; fruit-pie.

tourterelle, toohr-ter-rell, *f* turtle-dove.

toussaint (la), lăh-tooss-ang, *f* All Saints' Day.

tousser, tooss-eh, *v* to cough.

tout, too, *adv* wholly; quite; *m* all; the whole; chief point.

tout, e, too, *a* all; whole.

tout, too, *pron* all; everything.

tout-à-l'égout, toot-ăh-leh-ghoo, *m* main sewer.

toutefois, toot-fo'ăh, *adv* yet; however.

toute-puissance, toot-pweess-ahngss, *f* omnipotence.

tout-puissant, too-pweess-ahng, *m* Almighty; *a* all-powerful.

toux, too, *f* cough; coughing.

toxique, tox-eeck, *m* poison; *a* poisonous.

trac, trăhck, *m fam* fear; stage-fright.

tracas, trăh-kah, *m* worry.

tracasser, trăh-kăhss-eh, *v* to worry; to plague.

trace, trăhss, *f* trace; track; footstep.

tracé, trăhss-eh, *m* outline; planning; line.

tracer, trăhss-eh, *v* to trace; to draw out; to lay down.

tracteur, trăhk-ter *m* tractor.

traduc-teur, trice, *mf* translator.

traduction, trăh-dEEk-se-ong, *f* translation; translating.

traduire, trăh-dweer, *v* to translate.

trafic, trăh-feek, *m* traffic; trade.

trafiquer, trăh-fe-keh, *v* to

trade; to traffic.

tragique,* trăh-**sheeck**, *a*
tragic.

trahir, trăh-eer, *v* to
betray; to deceive.

trahison, trăh-e-zong, *f*
treachery; betrayal;
treason.

train, trang, *m* train; pace;
rate; speed; way; style;
retinue.

traînard, tray-năhr, *m*
straggler; slowcoach.

traîneau, tray-noh, *m*
sledge.

traînée, tray-neh, *f* train;
trail.

traîner, tray-neh, *v* to
drag; to drawl; to lag
behind; to lie about.

traire, trayr, *v* to milk.

trait, tray, *m* dart; arrow;
stroke; dash (of pen,
etc); touch; draught;
act; feature.

traitable, tray-tăh-bl, *a*
tractable.

traite, trayt, *f* journey; *mil*
draft; slave trade.

traité, tray-teh, *m* treatise;
treaty.

traitement, trayt-mahng,
m treatment; salary.

traiter, tray-teh, *v* to treat;
to handle; to negotiate.

traître, sse, tray-tr, *mf* & *a*
traitor; traitress;
treacherous.

traîtreusement, tray-trerz-
mahng, *adv*
treacherously.

traîtrise, tray-treez, *f*
treachery; betrayal.

trajet, trăh-shay, *m*
journey; passage;
distance.

trame, trăhm, *f* woof;
weft; network; plot;
progress.

tramer, trăh-meh, *v* to
weave; to plot.

tranchant, trahng-shahng,
m edge.

tranchant, e, trahng-
shahng, *a* sharp; cutting;
peremptory.

tranche, trahngsh, *f* slice.

tranchée, trahng-sheh, *f*
trench; *pl* gripes.

trancher, trahng-sheh, *v*
to cut off; to decide; to
solve; to contrast (**sur,**
with).

tranquille,* trahng-keel, *a*
quiet; peaceful; easy.

tranquillisant, trahng-ke-
le-zahng *m* tranquilizer.

tranquilliser, trahng-ke-
le-zeh, *v* to calm.

tranquillité, trahng-ke-le-
teh, *f* calm; stillness.

transatlantique, trahngss-
ăht-lahng-teeck, *m*
ocean liner; *a*
transatlantic.

transborder, trahngss-bor-

deh, *v* to transship.

transcrire, trahngss-kreer,
v to transcribe.

transe, trahngss, *f* fear;
apprehension; trance.

transférer, trahngss-feh-
reh, *v* to transfer.

transfert, trahngss-fair, *m*
transfer.

transformer, trahngss-for-
meh, *v* to transform; to
change into.

transfusion, trahngss-fe-
ze-ong *f* transfusion.

transi, e, trahng-ze, *pp* & *a*
chilled; benumbed.

transiger, trahng-ze-sheh,
v to compound.

transitoire,* trahng-ze-
to'ăhr, *a* transitory.

transmettre, trahngss-met-
tr, *v* to transmit; to
broadcast.

transparence, trahngss-
păh-rahngss, *f*
transparency.

transparent, trahngss-păh-
rahng, *a* transparent.

transpiration, trahngss-pe-
răh-se-ong, *f*
perspiration.

transpirer, trahngss-pe-
reh, *v* to perspire; to
transpire.

transport, trahngss-por, *m*
carriage; conveyance;
rapture.

transporter, trahngss-por-

teh, *v* to convey; to
enrapture.

transvaser, trahngss-vah-
zeh, *v* to decant.

trappe, trăhp, *f* trap-door;
trap; pitfall.

trapu, e, trăh-pE, *a* thick-
set; dumpy.

traquenard, trăhck-năhr,
m snare; trap.

traquer, trăh-keh, *v* to
hunt out; to surround.

travail, trăh-vah'e, *m*
work; labour; toil.

travailler, trăh-vah'e-yeh,
v to work; too work on;
to ferment (of wine,
etc).

travaux, trăh-voh *mpl*
roadworks.

travers, trăh-vair, *m*
breadth; defect; oddity;
à –, ăh –, through.

traversée, trăh-vair-seh, *f*
passage; crossing.

traverser, trăh-vair-seh, *v*
to cross; to travel over;
to thwart.

traversin, trăh-vair-sang,
m bolster.

travestir, trăh-vess-teer, *v*
to disguise; to travesty.

trébucher, treh-bE-sheh, *v*
to stumble.

trèfle, tray-fl, *m* clover;
(cards) clubs.

treille, tray'e, *f* vine-
arbour.

treize, trayz, *m & a*
thirteen.

treizième, tray-ze-aym, *m
& a* thirteenth.

tréma, treh-mah, *m*
diaeresis.

tremblement, trahng-bler-
mahng, *m* shake; tremor;
– de terre, – der tair,
earthquake.

trembler, trahng-bleh, *v* to
tremble; to quake; to
shake; to quaver; to fear.

trémousser (se), ser treh-
mooss-eh, *v* to bestir
oneself.

tremper, trahng-peh, *v* to
dip; to soak; to temper
(steel).

trentaine, trahng-tenn, *f*
about thirty.

trente, trahngt, *m & a*
thirty.

trentième, trahng-te-aym,
m & a thirtieth.

trépasser, treh-pahss-eh, *v*
to die.

trépied, treh-pe-eh, *m*
tripod.

trépigner, treh-peen-yeh,
v to stamp.

très, tray, *adv* very; very
much; most.

trésor, treh-zor, *m*
treasure; treasury.

trésori-er, ère, treh-zor-e-
eh, *mf* treasurer.

tressaillir, tress-sah'e-yeer,

v to start; to thrill; to
shudder.

tresse, trayss, *f* plait.

tréteau, treh-toh, *m*
trestle; *pl* stage.

treuil, trer-e, *m* windlass.

trêve, trayv, *f* truce; – de,
– der, no more.

tri, triage, tre, tre-ăhsh, *m*
sorting; picking.

tribu, tre-bE, *f* tribe.

tribunal, tre-bE-năhl, *m*
tribunal; bench; Court
of Justice.

tribune, tre-bEen, *f*
tribune; platform;
grandstand.

tribut, tre-bE, *m* tribute.

tricher, tre-sheh, *v* to
cheat.

tricot, tre-ko, *m* knitting;
sweater.

tricoter, tre-ko-teh, *v* to
knit.

tricycle, tre-see-kl, *m*
tricycle.

trier, tre-eh, *v* to sort; to
pick; to choose.

trimbaler, trang-băh-leh, *v*
fam to carry about; to
trail (children) about.

trimestre, tre-mess-tr, *m*
quarter; term.

tringle, trang-gl, *f* rod;
curtain rail.

trinquer, trang-keh, *v* to
touch glasses; *fam* to
drink together.

triompher, tre-ong-feh, *v*
to triumph.

tripe, treep, *f* tripe; *pl fam*
guts.

triple,* tre-pl, *a* treble;
triple.

tripoter, tre-pot-eh, *v* to
mess about; to fiddle
with.

triste,* trisst, *a* sad;
gloomy; dreary.

tristesse, triss-tess, *f*
sadness; gloom;
melancholy.

triturer, tre-tE-reh, *v* to
grind; to masticate.

troc, trock, *m* barter;
exchange.

trognon, tronn-yong, *m*
core (of fruit); stalk (of
vegetable).

trois, tro'ăh, *m & a* three.

troisième, tro'ăh-ze-aym,
m & a third.

trombe, trongb, *f*
waterspout.

trombone, trong-bonn, *f*
trombone; paper clip.

trompe, trongp, *f* horn;
trunk (of elephant).

tromper, trong-peh, *v* to
deceive; to cheat; **se –,**
to make a mistake.

trompette, trong-pett, *f*
trumpet.

trompeu-r, se, trong-per,
mf & a* deceiver;
betrayer; deceitful.

tronc, trong, *m* trunk;
collection box.

tronçon, trong-song, *m*
stump.

trône, trohn, *m* throne.

tronquer, trong-keh, *v* to
mutilate; to cut off; to
curtail.

trop, tro, *adv* too; too
much; too many.

troquer, trock-eh, *v* to
barter; to exchange.

trotter, trot-eh, *v* to trot;
to run.

trottinette, trot-e-nett, *f*
child's scooter.

trottoir, trot-o'ăhr, *m*
pavement.

trou, troo, *m* hole; gap;
mouth; hovel.

trouble, troo-bl, *m*
disturbance; perplexity;
a muddy; dull; confused.

troubler, troo-bleh, *v* to
disturb; to make muddy;
to put out.

trouer, troo-eh, *v* to hole;
to pierce.

troupe, troop, *f* troupe;
gang; set; crew; *pl*
troops.

troupeau, troo-poh, *m*
flock; herd.

troupier, troo-pe-eh, *m*
soldier; trooper.

trousse, trooss, *f* pencil
case; toilet bag.

trousseau, trooss-oh, *m*

bunch of (keys);
trousseau.

trouvaille, troo-vah'e, *f*
discovery.

trouver, troo-veh, *v* to
find; to think; to
consider.

truc, trEEk, *m fam* trick;
thing; what's his name.

truffe, trEEf, *f* truffle.

truie, trwee, *f* sow.

truite, trweet, *f* trout.

truquer, trE-keh, *v* to fake.

tu, tE, *pers pron sing*
(familiar form) you.

tube, tEEb, *m* tube; pipe;
snorkel.

tuer, tE-eh, *v* to kill; to
slaughter.

tuerie, tE-ree, *f* slaughter.

tue-tête (à), ăh tE-tayt,
adv at the top of one's
voice.

tuile, tweel, *f* tile.

tumeur, tE-mer, *f* tumour;
growth.

tumulte, tE-mEElt, *m*
tumult; turmoil.

turbot, tEEr-bo, *m* turbot.

turbulence, tEEr-bE-
lahngss, *m* turbulence.

turbulent, tEEr-bE-lahng, *a*
turbulent; boisterous.

tutelle, tE-tell, *f* tutelage;
protection;
guardianship.

tu-teur, trice, tE-ter, *mf*
guardian.

tutoyer, tE-to'ăh-yeh, *v* to address as **tu**.

tuyau, twee-yoh, *m* pipe; tube; funnel; *fam* tip; hint.

type, teep, *m* type; symbol; *fam* bloke.

typhon, te-fong, *m* typhoon.

typique, te-peeck, *a* typical.

tyran, te-rahng, *m* tyrant.

tyrannie, te-răhn-nee, *f* tyranny.

tzigane, tse-găhn, *mf* & *a* gipsy.

ulcère, EEl-sair, *m* ulcer; sore.

ulcéré, EEl-seh-reh, *pp* & *a* ulcerated; *fig* embittered.

ultérieur, e,* EEl-teh-re-er, *a* subsequent; ulterior.

un, e, ung, *num a* & *n* one; unit; first.

un, e, ung, *indef art* & *pron* an; one; any.

unanime,* E-năh-neem, *a* unanimous.

uni, e, E-ne, *a* united; close-knit (family, etc); smooth; even; level; plain (fabric).

unième, E-ne-aym, *a* first (used only in compounds: **vingt et unième,** twenty-first, etc).

unifier, E-ne-fe-eh, *v* to unify.

uniforme, E-ne-form, *a* & *m* uniform.

uniformément, E-ne-for-meh-mahng, *adv* uniformly.

uniment, E-ne-mahng, *adv* evenly; plainly.

union, E-ne-ong, *f* union; marriage; harmony.

unique,* E-neeck, *a* only; sole; unique; matchless.

unir, E-neer, *v* to unite; to smooth.

unisson, E-niss-ong, *m* unison.

unité, E-ne-teh, *f* unity; unit.

univers, E-ne-vair, *m* universe.

universel, le,* E-ne-vair-sell, *a* universal.

universitaire, E-ne-vair-se-tair, *mf* & *a* member of the university; belonging to the university.

université, E-ne-vair-se-teh, *f* university.

urbain, e, EEr-bang, *a* urban.

urbanité, EEr-băh-ne-teh, *f* urbanity.

urgence, EEr-shahngss, *f* urgency; emergency.

urgent, e, EEr-shahng, *a* urgent.

urine, E-reen, *f* urine.

uriner, E-reen-eh, *v* to urinate; to make water.

urinoir, E-re-no'ăhr, *m* urinal.

urne, EE rn, *f* urn.

usage, E-zăhsh, *m* use; custom; habit; wear.

usagé, e, E-zăh-sheh, *a* used.

usé, e, E-zeh, *pp* & *a* worn out; stale; hackneyed.

user, E-zeh, *v* to wear; to spend; – **de,** to make use of

usine, E-zeen, *f* factory; works.

usité, e, E-ze-teh, *a* in use; customary.

ustensile, EEss-tahng-seel, *m* utensil.

usuel, le,* E-zE-ell, *a* usual.

usure, E-zEEr, *f* wear;
  usury.
usurpa-teur, trice, E-zEEr-
  pǎh-ter, *mf* & *a* usurper;
  usurping.
usurper, E-zEEr-peh, *v* to
  usurp.
ut, EEt, *m* ut; do; C.
utérus, E-teh-rEss, *m*
  uterus; womb.
utile, E-teel, *m* & *a**
  utility; useful;
  serviceable.
utiliser, E-te-le-zeh, *v* to
  utilize; to make use of.
utilité, E-te-le-teh, *f*
  utility; usefulness.
utopique, E-top-eeck, *a*
  utopian.

vacance, văh-kahngss, *f* vacancy; *pl* holidays.

vacant, e, văh-kahng, *a* vacant; unoccupied.

vacarme, văh-kăhrm, *m* hubbub; uproar; din.

vaccination, văhck-seen-ăh-se-ong, *f* vaccination.

vaccin, văhck-seen, *f* vaccine.

vache, văhsh, *f* cow; cowhide.

vaciller, văh-sill-leh or văh-see-yeh, *v* to waver; to wobble.

va-et-vient, văh-eh-ve-ang, *m* coming and going.

vagabond, e, văh-găh-bong, *a* & *mf* vagabond; vagrant.

vague, văhg, *m* vagueness; empty space; *a** vague;

indistinct; vacant; waste (land).

vague, văhg, *f* wave; billow; generation; – **de chaleur,** – der-shăh-ler heatwave.

vaguer, văh-gheh, *v* to ramble; to rove; to wander.

vaillamment, vah'e-yăh-mahng, *adv* valiantly.

vaillance, vah'e-yahngss, *f* valour; bravery.

vaillant, e, vah'e-yahng, *a* valiant; brave; gallant.

vain, e,* vang, *a* vain; fruitless; vainglorious.

vaincre, vang-kr, *v* to vanquish; to conquer; to defeat.

vaincu, vang-kE, *m* conquered; vanquished.

vainqueur, vang-ker, *m*

victor; prize-winner; *a* victorious.

vaisseau, vayss-oh, *m* vessel; ship; structure.

vaisselle, vayss-ell, *f* crockery; washing-up; **faire la –,** fayr lăh –, to do the dishes.

val, văhl, *m* vale; valley; dale.

valable,* văh-lăh-bl, *a* valid.

valet, văh-lay, *m* footman; (cards) jack.

valeur, văh-ler, *f* value; worth; courage; *pl* securities.

valeureu-x, se,* văh-ler-rer, *a* valiant; brave.

valide,* văh-leed, *a* valid.

validité, văh-le-de-teh, *f* validity.

valise, văh-leez, *f* suitcase.

vallée, văh-leh, *f* valley; vale; dale.

vallon, văh-long, *m* dale; small valley.

valoir, văh-lo'ăhr, *v* to be worth; to yield.

valse, văhls, *f* waltz.

valve, văhlv, *f* valve.

vanille, văh-nee-ye, *f* vanilla.

vanité, văh-ne-teh, *f* vanity.

vaniteu-x, se,* văh-ne-ter, *a* vain; vainglorious.

vanne, văhn, *f* sluice;

water-gate.

vanner, văh-neh, *v* to winnow.

vannerie, văhn-ner-ree, *f* basket-making trade.

vantard, e, vahng-tăhr, *mf & a* boaster; boastful; boasting.

vanter, vahng-teh, *v* to praise; to extol; **se –,** to boast.

vapeur, văh-per, *m* steamer; *f* vapour; steam.

vaporeu-x, se,* văh-por-er, *a* vaporous; hazy.

vaporiser, văh-por-e-zeh, *v* to vaporize; to spray.

vaquer, văh-keh, *v* to be vacant; **– à,** – ăh, to attend to.

vareuse, văh-rerz, *f* jumper; tunic.

variable,* văh-re-ăh-bl, *a* variable; changeable.

variation, văh-re-ăh-se-ong, *f* variation.

varice, văh-reess, *f* varicose vein.

varicelle, văh-re-sell, *f* chickenpox.

varier, văh-re-eh, *v* to vary; to differ.

variété, văh-re-eh-teh, *f* variety.

variole, văh-re-ol, *f* smallpox.

vase, vahz, *m* vase; urn;

vessel; *f* mud; slime.

vaseu-x, se, vah-zer, *a* muddy.

vaste,* văhsst, *a* vast; spacious; wide; great.

va-tout, văh-too, *m* last stake.

vaurien, ne, voh-re-ang, *mf* worthless person.

vautour, voh-toohr, *m* vulture.

vautrer (se), ser voh-treh, *v* to wallow; to sprawl.

veau, voh, *m* calf; calf's leather; veal.

vedette,* văh-dett, *f* motorboat; (film) star.

végétal, e, veh-sheh-tăhl, *a* vegetable.

véhément, e,* veh-eh-mahng, *a* vehement.

véhicule, veh-e-kEEl, *m* vehicle.

veille, vay'e, *f* wakefulness; watch; eve.

veillée, vay'e-yeh, *f* vigil.

veiller, vay'e-yeh, *v* to sit up; to watch; to be awake; **– (à)** to see to.

veilleuse, vay'e-yerz, *f* night-light; pilot light.

veine, vayn, *f* vein; *fam* luck.

velléité, veh-leh-e-teh, *f* slight desire.

vélo, veh-lo, *m fam* bicycle; **– tout terrain, –** too-tay-rang, mountain

bike.

vélodrome, veh-lod-rohm, *m* cycling track.

velours, ver-loohr, *m* velvet.

velouté, e, ver-loo-teh, *a* velvety; soft; rich (soup, etc).

velu, e, ver-lE, *a* hairy; shaggy.

venaison, ver-nay-zong, *f* venison.

venant, e, ver-nahng, *a* coming; thriving; **à tout –,** ăh-too–, to all comers.

vendable, vahng-dăh-bl, *a* marketable.

vendange, vahng-dahng sh, *f* vintage; grape harvest.

vendeu-r, se, vahng-der, *mf* seller; salesman (-woman); shop assistant.

vendre, vahng-dr, *v* to sell; to betray.

vendredi, vahng-drer-de, *m* Friday.

vénéneu-x, se, veh-neh-ner, *a* poisonous.

vénérer, veh-neh-reh, *v* to venerate.

vénérien, ne, veh-neh-re-ang, *a* venereal.

vengeance, vahng-shahngss, *f* revenge.

venger, vahng- sheh, *v* to avenge; to revenge.

veng-eur, eresse, vahng-sher, *mf* & *a* avenger.

véniel, le, veh-ne-ell, *a* venial.

venimeu-x, se, ver-ne-mer, *a* venomous.

venin, ver-nang, *m* venom; *fig* spite; *fig* rancour.

venir, ver-neer, *v* to come; to arrive; to happen; to grow; – **de,** –der, to have just…

vent, vahng, *m* wind; scent; *fig* emptiness.

venter, vahngt, *f* sale.

vente, vahng-teh, *v* to be windy.

ventilateur, vahng-te-lăh-ter, *m* ventilator; fan.

ventouse, vahng-tooz, *f* suction pad.

ventre, vahng-tr, *m* abdomen; belly; stomach.

ventru, e, vahng-trE, *a* corpulent; big-bellied.

venu, e, ver-nE, *mf* comer.

venue, ver-nE, *f* coming; arrival; growth.

vêpres, vay-pr, *fpl* vespers.

ver, vair, *m* worm; maggot.

verbal, e, * vair-băhl, *a* verbal.

verbe, vairb, *m* verb.

verbeu-x, se, vair-ber, *a* verbose.

verbiage, vair-be-ăhsh, *m* verbiage; mere talk.

verdâtre, vair-dah-tr, *a* greenish.

verdeur, vair-der, *f* greenness; tartness.

verdir, vair-deer, *v* to grow green; to make green.

verdoyant, e, vair-do'aăh-yahng, *a* verdant.

verdure, vair-dEEr, *f* greenness; verdure; foliage.

véreu-x, se, veh-rer, *a* worm-eaten; *fam* suspicious; dishonest.

verge, vairsh, *f* penis; rod; birch rod.

verger, vair-sheh, *m* orchard.

verglas, vair-glah, *m* black ice.

vergogne (sans), sahng vair-gonn-yer, *f* shameless.

véridique, * veh-re-deeck, *a* veracious; truthful.

vérifier, veh-re-fe-eh, *v* to verify; to check.

véritable, * veh-re-tăh-bl, *a* true; genuine; downright.

vérité, veh-re-teh, *f* truth.

vermeil, le, vair-may'e, *a* & *m* ruby; red; rosy.

vermine, vair-meen, *f* vermin.

vermisseau, vair-miss-oh, *m* small worm.

vermoulu, e, vair-moo-lE, *a* worm-eaten.

vernir, vair-neer, *v* to varnish.

vernis, vair-ne, *m* varnish; gloss; japan; French polish.

vérole (petite), per-teet veh-rol, *f* smallpox.

verre, vair, *m* glass.

verrerie, vay-rer-ree, *f* glassworks.

verrou, vay-roo, *m* bolt.

verrouiller, vay-roo'e-yeh, *v* to bolt.

verrue, vay-rE, *f* wart; verucca.

vers, vair, *prep* towards; about.

vers, vair, *m* verse; line.

versant, vair-sahng, *m* slope; bank.

verse (à), ăh vairss, *adv* (rain) in torrents.

versé, e, vair-seh, *a* well versed; well up (**dans, en,** in).

versement, vair-ser-mahng, *m* payment; instalment.

verser, vair-seh, *v* to pour; to shed; to lodge; to pay in; to overturn.

verset, vair-say, *m* verse (in Bible).

verso, vair-so, *m* back;

reverse (of paper, etc).

vert, e, vair, *a* green; unripe; sharp; *m* colour green.

vertement, vair-ter-mahng, *adv* sharply; severely.

vertical, e,* vair-te-kăhl, *a* vertical.

vertige, vair-teesh, *m* giddiness; vertigo.

vertigineu-x, se, vair-te-she-ner, *a* giddy; dizzy.

vertu, vair-tE, *f* virtue; chastity; power; property.

vertueu-x, se,* vair-tE-er, *a* virtuous.

verve, vairv, *f* animation; zest; spirits.

vessie, vayss-ee, *f* bladder.

veste, vaysst, *f* jacket.

vestiaire, vayss-te-air, *m* cloakroom; changing-room (sport).

vestibule, vayss-te-bEEl, *m* vestibule.

vestige, vayss-teesh, *m* vestige; remains; track.

veston, vayss-tong, *m* jacket.

vêtement, vaytt-mahng, *m* garment; *pl* clothes.

vétérinaire, veh-teh-re-nair, *mf* & *a* vet; veterinary surgeon; veterinary.

vêtir, vay-teer, *v* to

clothe; to dress; to array.

veu-f, ve, verf, *mf* & *a* widower; widow; widowed.

veule, verl, *a* weak; soft.

veuvage, ver-văhsh, *m* widowhood.

vexatoire, veck-săh-to'ăhr, *a* vexatious.

vexer, veck-seh, *v* to vex; to annoy.

viable, ve-ăh-bl, *a* viable.

viag-er, ère, ve-ăh-sheh, *a* for life.

viande, ve-ahngd, *f* meat; flesh.

vibrant, e, ve-brahng, *a* vibrating.

vibrer, ve-breh, *v* to vibrate.

vicaire, ve-kair, *m* curate.

vice, veess, *m* vice; defect; blemish; flaw.

vice versa, veess-vair-sa, *adv* vice versa.

vicié, e, veess-e-eh, *a* vitiated; corrupt.

vicier, veess-e-eh, *v* to vitiate; to corrupt.

vicieu-x, se,* veess-e-er, *a* vicious; faulty; depraved.

vicomte, ve-kongt, *m* viscount.

vicomtesse, ve-kong-tess, *f* viscountless.

victime, vick-teem, *f* victim.

victoire, vick-to'ăhr, *f* victory.

victorieu-x, se,* vick-tor-e-er, *a* victorious.

victuaille, vick-tE-ah'e, *f* victuals; *pl* provisions.

vidange, ve-dahng sh, *f* clearing out; draining.

vide, veed, *m* empty space; vacuum; *a* empty.

vidéo, vee-deh-oh, *f* video (film).

vidéo-cassette, vee-deh-oh-kăh-sett, *f* video cassette.

vider, vee-deh, *v* to empty; to drain; to settle.

vie, vee, *f* life; living; existence.

vieillard, ve-ay'e-ăhr, *m* old man.

vieille, ve-ay'e, *f* old woman.

vieillerie, ve-ay'e-ree, *f* old things.

vieillesse, ve-ay'e-ess, *f* old age.

vieillir, ve-ay'e-eer, *v* to grow old; to age.

vierge, ve-airsh, *f* virgin.

vieux, ve-er, *m* old man; *pl* old folk.

vieux (before a vowel or h mute: **vieil**), *f* **vieille**, ve-er, ve-ay'e, *a* old.

vi-f, ve,* veef, *a* alive; sharp; quick tempered;

bright (colour); strong; running.

vif-argent, veef-ăhr-shahng, *m* mercury.

vigie, ve-shee, *f* lookout.

vigilamment, ve-she-lăh-mahng, *adv* vigilantly.

vigilance, ve-she-lahngss, *f* vigilance.

vigilant, e, ve-she-lăhng, *a* vigilant.

vigne, veen-yer, *f* vine; vineyard.

vigneron, veen-yer-rong, *m* wine-grower.

vignoble, veen-yo-bl, *m* vineyard.

vigoureu-x, se,* ve-goo-rer, *a* vigorous; sturdy; energetic.

vigueur, ve-gher, *f* vigour; strength.

vil, e,* veel, *a* vile; base; mean; despicable.

vilain, e,* ve-lang, *a* ugly; nasty; (child) naughty.

vilenie, ve-ler-nee, *f* meanness; dirty trick; *pl* abuse.

vilipender, ve-le-pahng-deh, *v* to vilify.

village, ve-lăhsh, *m* village.

villageois, e, ve-lăh-sho'ăh, *mf* & *a* villager; rustic.

ville, veel, *f* town; city.

vin, vang, *m* wine.

vinaigre, ve-nay-gr, *m* vinegar.

vinaigrette, ve-nay-grett, *f* salad dressing.

vindicati-f, ve, vang-de-kăh-teeff, *a* revengeful.

vingt, vang, *m* & *a* twenty; twentieth.

vingtaine, vang-tain, *f* about twenty.

vingtième, vang-te-aym, *m* & *a* twentieth.

viol, ve-ol, *m* rape.

violation, ve-oll-ăh-se-ong, *f* violation; infringement.

violemment, ve-oll-ăh-mahng, *adv* violently.

violence, ve-oll-ahngss, *f* violence.

violent, e, ve-oll-ahng, *a* violent.

violer, ve-oll-eh, *v* to violate; to infringe; to rape.

violet, te, ve-oll-ay, *a* violet-coloured; *m* (colour) violet.

violette, ve-oll-ett, *f* violet.

violon, ve-oll-ong, *m* violin; *pop* jail.

vipère, ve-pair, *f* viper.

virage, ve-răhsh, *m* turning; bend; (photography); toning; changing (of colour).

virement, veer-mahng, *m*

(finance) transfer.

virer, ve-reh, *v* to turn; to take a bend; *naut* to tack.

virgule, veer-ghEEl, *f* comma.

viril, e,* ve-reel, *a* manly; virile.

virilité, ve-re-le-teh, *m* manhood; virility; vigour.

virtuel, le,* veer-tE-ell, *a* virtual.

virulence, ve-rE-lahngss, *f* virulence.

virus, ve-rEEss, *m* virus.

vis, veess, *f* screw.

visa, ve-zăh, *m* signature; visa.

visage, ve-zăhsh, *m* face; visage; look.

vis-à-vis, ve-zăh-ve, *adv* in relation to.

viscère, veess-sair, *m* intestines; internal organs.

visée, ve-zeh, *f* aim; design; end.

viser, ve-zeh, *v* to aim at; to aspire to; to endorse.

visible,* ve-zee-bl, *a* visible.

visière, ve-ze-air, *f* visor; peak (of hat, etc).

vision, ve-ze-ong, *f* vision; sight; phantom.

visionnaire, ve-ze-onn-air, *a* visionary.

visite, ve-zeet, *f* visit; search; medical examination.

visiter, ve-ze-teh, *v* to visit; to inspect; to search.

visqueu-x, se, veess-ker, *a* viscous; sticky.

visser, veess-eh, *v* to screw.

visuel, le,* ve-zE-ell, *a* visual.

vital, e, ve-tăhl, *a* vital.

vitalité, ve-tăh-le-teh, *f* vitality.

vitamine, ve-tăh-meen, f vitamine.

vite, veet, *adv* quickly; fast; *a* quick; swift.

vitesse, ve-tess, *f* quickness; speed; – **maximale permise,** – măhks-e-măhl-pair-meez, speed limit.

viticulture, ve-te-kEEl-tEEr, *f* wine growing.

vitrail, ve-trah'e, *m* stained glass window.

vitre, vee-tr, *f* pane; window pane.

vitrier, ve-tre-eh, *m* glazier.

vitrine, ve-treen, *f* shop-window; display case.

vivace, ve-văhss, *a* long-lived; deep-rooted.

vivacité, ve-văhss-e-teh, *f* vivacity; hastiness (of temper).

vivant, ve-vahng, *m* living person; lifetime.

vivant, e, ve-vahng, *a* living; alive; lively.

vivier, ve-ve-eh, *m* fish pond; breeding ground.

vivre, vee-vr, *v* to live; to board.

vivres, vee-vr, *mpl* food; provisions.

vocable, vock-ăh-bl, *m* word; term.

vocabulaire, vock-ăh-bE-lair, *m* vocabulary; word list.

vocal, e, vock-ăhl, *a* vocal.

vocatif, vock-ăh-teeff, *m* vocative case.

vocation, vock-ăh-se-ong, *f* vocation; calling.

vociférer, voss-e-feh-reh, *v* to bawl; to cry out.

vœu, ver, *m* vow; wish.

vogue, vogh, *f* vogue; fashion.

voguer, vogh-eh, *v* to sail.

voici, vo'ăh-se, *adv* here is; here are.

voie, vo'ăh, *f* way; road; track; gauge; means.

voilà, vo'ăh-lăh, *adv* there is; there are.

voile, vo'ăhl, *m* veil; voile; *f* sail.

voiler, vo'ăh-leh, *v* to veil; to cloak; to conceal.

voilier, vo'ăh-le-eh, *m* sail-maker; sailing boat.

voir, vo'ăhr, *v* to see; to behold; to inspect; to visit; to meet.

voire, vo'ăhr, *adv* indeed; nay; even.

voisin, e, vo'ăh-zang, *mf* neighbour; *a* adjoining.

voisinage, vo'ăh-ze-năhsh, *m* neighbourhood.

voiture, vo'ăh-tEEr, *f* motor car; cart; carriage; – **d'enfant,** – dahng-fahng *f* pram.

voix, vo'ăh, *f* voice; tone; vote.

vol, vol, *m* flight; theft; – **à l'étalalge,** – ăh-leh-tăh-lăhsh, shoplifting; – **libre,** – lee-br, hang-gliding.

volage, voll-ăhsh, *a* fickle.

volaille, voll-ah'e, *f* poultry.

volant, voll-ahng, *m* shuttlecock; steering wheel.

volant, e, voll-ahng, *a* flying; loose.

volcan, voll-kahng, *m* volcano.

volée, voll-eh, *f* flight (of birds); flock; volley (of gunfire); shower; peal (of bells).

voler, voll-eh, *v* to fly; to soar; to steal; **il ne l'a**

pas volé, ill ner lăh păh voll-eh, it serves him right.

volet, voll-ay, *m* shutter.

voleu-r, se, voll-er, *mf* thief; robber.

volière, voll-e-air, *f* aviary.

volontaire, voll-*ong*-tair, *m* volunteer; *a** voluntary; headstrong.

volonté, voll-ong-teh, *f* will; *pl* whims; caprices.

volontiers, voll-ong-te-eh, *adv* willingly.

voltage, voll-tăhsh, *m* voltage.

volte-face, voll-ter-făhss, *f* turning round; about-face.

voltiger, voll-te-sheh, *v* to flutter; to perform on rope, trapeze, etc.

voltigeur, voll-te-sher, *m* performer on rope, trapeze, etc.

volubilité, voll-E-be-le-teh, *f* volubility.

volume, voll-EEm, *m* volume; bulk; mass; size.

volumineu-x, se, voll-E-me-ner, *a* voluminous.

volupté, voll-EEp-teh, *f* voluptuousness; luxury.

vomir, vomm-eer, *v* to vomit; to throw up.

vomissement, vomm-iss-mahng, *m* vomiting.

vomitif, vomm-e-teeff, *m* emetic.

vorace,* vor-ăhss, *a* voracious; ravenous.

voracité, vor-ăhss-e-teh, *f* voracity; ravenousness.

vote, vot, *m* vote; suffrage; poll; division.

voter, vot-eh, *v* to vote.

votre, votr, *poss a* your; *pl* **vos,** voh.

vôtre (le, la, les), ler, lăh, leh voh-tr, *poss pron* yours.

vouer, voo-eh, *v* to devote; to vow; to dedicate.

vouloir, voo-lo'ăhr, *v* to be willing; to want; to require; to order; to consent.

vouloir, voo-lo'ăhr, *m* will.

voulu, e, voo-lE, *pp & a* wanted; required; intentional.

vous, voo, *pers pron* you.

voûte, voot, *f* vault.

vouvoyer, voo-vo'ăh-yeh, *v* to address formally (using **vous**).

voyage, vo'ăh-yăhsh, *m* travel; journey; trip; – **organisé,** – or-ghăh-ne-zeh, package holiday.

voyager, vo'ăh-shah-sheh, *v* to travel; to journey.

voyageu-r, se, vo'ăh-yăh-sher, *mf & a* traveller;

passenger; travelling.

voyant, e, vo'ăh-yahng, *mf* fortune-teller; *a* showy; gaudy.

voyelle, vo'ăh-yell, *f* vowel.

voyou, vo'ăh-yoo, *m* hooligan; ruffian.

vrac (en), ahng vrăhck, *adv* in bulk.

vrai, vray, *adv* truly; *m* truth.

vrai, e, vray, *a* true; genuine; regular; errant.

vraiment, vray-mahng, *adv* truly; indeed.

vraisemblable,* vray-sahng-blăh-bl, *a* likely.

vraisemblance, vray-sahng-blahngss, *f* likelihood.

vrille, vree-ye, *f* gimlet.

vu, vE, *prep* seeing; considering; *m* sight; examination.

vu, e, vE, *pp & a* seen; examined.

vue, vE, *f* sight; view; prospect; design; purpose.

vulgaire, vEEl-ghair, *m* the common people; *a** vulgar; coarse.

W

wagon, văh-gong *m*
carriage; car; – **lit,** – lee,
sleeping car; – **couloir,** –
koo-lo'ăhr, corridor
train.
W.C., (doo-bl) veh-seh,
mpl toilet.

xénophobe, zeh-noh-fob,
  a xenophobic.
xérès, keh-rayss, *m* sherry.
xylophone, ze-loh-fon, *m*
  xylophone.

y, e, *pron* to it; at it; by it;
for it; from it; to them;
at them, etc.

y, e, *adv* there; within; –
compris, – kong-pree,
including.

yaourt, yah-oort, *m*
yoghurt; yogurt.

yacht, e-ăhck, *m* yacht.

yeuse, e-erz, *f* ilex; holly;
oak.

yeux, e-er, *mpl* eyes.

yole, ee-ol, *f* yawl.

youyou, yoo-yoo, *m* dingy.

zèbre, zay-br, m zebra.

zébré, e, zeh-breh, a striped.

zéla-teur, trice, zeh-läh-ter, mf zealot.

zèle, zayl, m zeal; ardour; earnestness.

zénith, zeh-neet, m zenith.

zéphir, zeh-feer, m zephyr; gentle breeze.

zeppelin, zehp-lang, m zeppelin.

zéro, zeh-ro, m nought; zero; cipher; nobody.

zeste, zaysst, m zest; zeal.

zézaiement, zeh-zay-mahng, m lisping; limp.

zézayer, zeh-zay-yeh, v to lisp.

zibeline, zeeb-leen, f sable.

zigzaguer, zeeg-zäh-gheh, v to stagger; to zigzag.

zinc, zangk, m zinc; bar (in a café, pub, etc).

zingueur, zang-gher, m zinc-worker.

zodiaque, zod-e-ähck, m zodiac.

zona, zoh-näh, m shingles.

zone, zohn, f zone.

zoo, zoh, m zoo.

zoologie, zo-oll-osh-ee, f zoology.

zoophyte, zo-off-eet, m zoophyte.

zouave, zoo-ähv, m zouave.

zut! zEEt, interj fam bother! hang it!

ENGLISH FRENCH
ANGLAIS FRANÇAIS

DICTIONNAIRE
ANGLAIS-FRANÇAIS
(ENGLISH-FRENCH
DICTIONARY)

(Pour l'explication de la
prononciation figurée,
lire avec soin les pages
vi. et viii.)

a, é, *art* un; une.

abandon, a-bănn´-d'n, *v*
abandonner; **–ed,** *a*
abandonné; (morally)
dissolu.

abase, a-béce´, *v* abaisser;
humilier.

abash, a-băche´, *v*
déconcerter.

abate, a-béte´, *v* diminuer.

abbot, ăb´-otte, *n* abbé m.

abbreviate, ab-bri´-vi-éte,
v abréger.

abbreviation, ab-bri-vi-é´-
ch'n, *n* abréviation f.

abdicate, ăb´-di-quéte, *v*
abdiquer.

abdomen, ăb-dau´-menn,
n abdomen m.

abduction, ăb-doc´-ch'n, *n*
enlèvement m.

abeyance, a-bé´-annce, *n*
suspension f.

abide, a-bâïde´, *v*
demeurer; **– by,** s'en
tenir à.

ability, a-bil´-i-ti, *n*
habileté f; capacité f.

ablaze, a-bléze´, *a* en
flammes; enflammé.

able, é´-b'l, *a* capable;
habile; **to be –,** pouvoir.

abnormal*, ăb-nôr´-m'l, *a*
anormal.

aboard, a-bôrde´, *adv* à
bord.

abode, a-bôde´, *n* demeure
f.

abolish, a-bol´-iche, *v*
abolir.

abominable, a-bomm´-
inn-a-b'l, *a* abominable.

aboriginal, ăb-ŏr-idj´-inn-
'l, *a* aborigène.

abortion, a-bôr´-ch'n, *n*
avortement m.

abound, a-bâ´´ounnde, *v*
abonder.

about, a-bâoute´, *adv*
environ; à peu près;
autour; *prep* auprès de;
autour de; au sujet de.

above, a-bove´, *adv* en
haut; au-dessus; ci-
dessus; *prep* au-dessus de;
plus de; sur.

abrasion, a-bré´-j'n, *n*
écorchure f.

abreast, a-breste´, *adv* de
front.

abroad, a-brôde´, *adv* à
l'étranger.

abrupt*, a-bropte´, *a*
brusque; (steep) escarpé.

abscess, ăb´-sesse, *n* abcès
m.

abscond, ăb-skonnde´, *v*
s'enfuir; se cacher.

absence, ăb´-sennce, *n*
absence f; éloignement
m.

absent, ăb´-sennte, *a*
absent; *v* (**– oneself**)
s'absenter; **–ee,** *n* absent
m absente f; **–minded,** *a*
distrait.

absolute*, ăb´-sŏ-lioute, *a* absolu.

absolve, ăb-zolve´, *v* absoudre.

absorb, ăb-sorb´, *v* absorber.

abstain, ab-sténe´, *v* s'abstenir de.

abstainer, ab-sténe´-'r, *n* abstinent *m*.

abstemious*, ab-sti´-mi-euce, *a* sobre.

abstinence, ăb´-sti-nennce, *n* abstinence *f*.

abstract, ăb-străcte´, *v* abstraire; résumer.

abstract, ăb´-străcte, *n* résumé *m*; *a* abstrait.

absurd*, ăb-seurde´, *a* absurde.

abundant, a-bonne´d'nt, *a* abondant.

abuse, a-biouze´, *v* abuser de; injurier.

abuse, a-biouce´, *n* abus *m*; injures *fpl*.

abusive*, a-biou´-cive, *a* injurieux; abusif.

abyss, a-bisse´, *n* abîme *m*.

academy, a-kăd´-é-mi, *n* académie *f*.

accede, ăx-îde´, *v* accéder; monter (sur).

accelerate, ăx-el´-é-réte, *v* accélérer.

accent, ăx-ennte´, *v* accentuer.

accent, ăx´-ennte, *n* accent *m*.

accentuate, ăx-ennte´-iou-éte, *v* accentuer.

accept, ăx-epte´, *v* accepter; –ance, *n* acceptation *f*.

access, ăx´-esse, *n* accès *m*.

accession, ăx-ech'n, *n* avènement *m*.

accessory, ăx´-ess-ŏ-ri, *n* complice *m*; accessoire *m*.

accident, ăx´-i-dennte, *n* accident *m*.

accidental*, ăx-i-denn´-t'l, *a* accidentel; accessoire.

acclaim, ac-cléme´, *v* acclamer.

accommodate, ac-comm´-mŏ-déte, *v* accommoder; loger; fournir.

accommodation, ac-comm-mŏ-dé´-ch'n, *n* logement *m*; arrangement *m*; aménagement *m*.

accompaniment, ac-comm´-pa-ni-m'nt, *n* accompagnement *m*; accessoire *m*.

accompanist, ac-comm´-pa-nisste, *n* accompagnateur *m*, accompagnatrice *f*.

accompany, ac-comm´-pa-ni, *v* accompagner.

accomplice, ac-comm´-plisse, *n* complice *m*.

accomplish, ac-comm´-pliche, *v* accomplir.

accomplishment, ac-comm´-pliche-m'nt, *n* accomplissement *m*; –s, talents *mpl*.

accord, ac-côrde´, *v* accorder; *n* accord *m*; **of one's own –**, de plein gré; **in –ance with**, d'accord avec; **–ing to**, *prep* selon; d'après; **–ingly**, *adv* en conséquence

accordion, ac-côr´-di-n, *n* accordéon *m*.

accost, ac-coste´, *v* accoster, aborder.

account, a-câ´'ounnte´, *n* (bill) compte *m*; **on –**, (payment) en acompte; **–able**, *a* responsable; **–ant**, *n* comptable *m*.

accrue, ac-croue´, *v* provenir (de); s'accumuler.

accumulate, ac-kiou´-miou-léte, *v* (s')accumuler.

accuracy, ă´-kiou-ra-ci, *n* exactitude *f*; précision *f*.

accurate*, ă´-kiou-réte, *a* exact; correct; juste.

accursed, a-keur´-st, *a* maudit.

accusation, ac-kiou-zé´-

ch'n, n accusation f.

accuse, a-kiouze', v
accuser.

accustom, a-coss'-t'm, v
accoutumer; habituer.

ace, éce, n (cards) as m.

ache, éque, n douleur f;
mal m; v faire mal.

achieve, a-tchîve', v
accomplir, exécuter;
–ment, n
accomplissement m;
exploit m.

acid, ă'-side, n & a acide
m.; **— rain**, n pluies
acides fpl.

acidity, a-side'-i-ti, n
acidité; med aigreurs fpl.

acknowledge, ăc-nol'-
èdje, v reconnaître;
accuser réception de.

acne, ăc'-nî, n acné m.

acorn, é'-côrne, n gland
m.

acoustics, a-couss'-tiks,
npl acoustique f.

acquaint, a-couénnte', v
informer; **–ance**, n
connaissance f.

acquiesce, ă-coui-esse', v
acquiescer (à).

acquire, a-couâîre', v
acquérir; apprendre.

acquisition, a-coui-zi'-
ch'n, n acquisition f.

acquit, a-couitte', v
acquitter.

acquittal, a-coui'-t'l, n

acquittement m;
absolution f.

acre, é'-keur, n acre m.

acrid, ăc'-ridde, a âcre.

acrobat, ă'-cro-bătte, n
acrobate m/f.

across, a-crosse', adv à
travers; de l'autre côté;
prep au travers de.

act, ăcte, n action f;
(deed) acte m; (of a
play) acte m; (law) loi f;
v agir; (in theatre)
jouer; **–or**, n acteur m;
–ress, actrice f.

action, ăk'-ch'n, n action
f; procès m.

active*, ăc'-tive, a actif;
alerte; agile.

actual*, ăc'-tiou-al, a réel;
actuel.

actuate, ăc'-tiou-éte, v
mettre en action;
animer; faire agir.

acumen, a-kiou'-mène, n
perspicacité f.

acute, a-kioute', a aigu.

acuteness, a-kioute'-
nesse, n acuité f; finesse
f.

adamant, ăd'-a-mannte, a
inflexible.

adapt, a-dăpt', v adapter;
– oneself, s'adapter.

adaptation, a-dăpp-té'-
ch'n, n adaptation f.

add, ădde, v additionner;
–to, ajouter à; **–ition**, n

addition f; **–itional**, a
supplémentaire.

adder, ăd'-eur, n
(snake)vipère f.

addict, ăd'-icte', n
intoxiqué m & f;
personne adonnée (à) f;
–ed, a adonné (à).

additive, ăd'-di-tive, n
additif m.

addle, ăd'-'l, a (egg)
couvi;
fig vide.

address, ad-dresse', n
adresse f; (speech)
discours m; (letters,
etc.) adresser; (a
meeting) prendre la
parole; **–ee**, n
destinataire m & f.

adequate, ăd'-i-couéte, a
proportionnel; suffisant.

adhere, ăd-hîre', v
adhérer; s'en tenir à;
–nt, a & n, adhérent m;
partisan m.

adhesive, ăd-hî'-cive, n
colle f. a adhésif.

adjacent, ad-jé-sennte, a
adjacent (à); avoisinant.

adjective, ă'-djèque-tive,
n adjectif m.

adjourn, ad-jeurne', v
ajourner; remettre;
remise f.

adjournment, ad-jeurne'-
m'nt, n ajournement m.

adjunct, ăd'-jonn-kt, n

accessoire *m*; *a* adjoint.

adjust, ad-joste´, *v* ajuster; régler.

adjustment, ad-joste´-m'nt, *n* ajustement *m*.

adjutant, ăd´-djou-t'nt, *n* adjudant-major *m*.

administer, ad-minn´-isse-*teur*, *v* administrer.

admirable, ăd´-mi-ra-b'l, *a* admirable.

admiral, ăd´-mi-ral, *n* amiral *m*; –**ty,** amirauté *f*.

admire, ad-mâïre´, *v* admirer.

admission, ad-mi´-ch'n, *n* admission *f*; entrée *f*.

admit, ad-mitte´, *v* admettre; laisser entrer.

admittance, ad-mit´-t'nce, *n* entrée *f*; entrée *f*; aveu *m*.

admonish, ad-monn´-iche, *v* exhorter.

adolescence, ăd-au-lesse´-sennce, *n* adolescence *f*.

adolescent, ăd-au-lesse´-sennte, *a*, *n* adolescent(e) *m* & *f*.

adopt, a-dopte´, *v* adopter.

adore, a-daure´, *v* adorer.

adorn, a-dôrne´, *v* parer; –**ment,** *n* parure *f*.

adrift, a-drifte´, *adv naut* à la dérive.

adroit*, a-drô´ïte´, *a* adroit, habile.

adult, a-dolte´, *n* adulte *m* & *f*. *a* adulte.

adulterate, a-dol´-té-réte, *v* falsifier; corrompre.

adultery, a-dol´-té-ri, *n* adultère *m*.

advance, ăd-vânnce´, *v* avancer; (price) hausser; faire avancer; (progress) progrès *m*; (money) avance *f*; (prices) hausse *f*; **in –,** d'avance; –**ment,** *n* avancement *m*; progrès *m*.

advantage, ăd-vănn´-tèdje, *n* avantage *m*.

advantageous*, ăd-vann-té´-djeusse, *a* avantageux.

advent, ăd´-vennte, *n* venue *f*; *eccl* Avent *m*.

adventure, ad-venn´-tioure, *n* aventure *f*.

adventurer, ad-venn´-tiou-r'r, *n* aventurier *m*.

adventurous, ad-venn´-tiou-reuce, *a* aventureux.

adverb, ăd´-veurbe, *n* adverbe *m*.

adversary, ăd´-veur-sa-ri, *n* adversaire *m* & *f*.

adverse*, ăd´-veursse, *a* défavorable, adverse, opposé.

advertise, ăd´-veur-tâïze, *v* annoncer; faire de la réclame.

advertisement, ad-veur´-tize-m'nt, *n* annonce *f*; réclame *f*.

advertising, ăd´-veur-tăï´-zinng, *n* publicité *f*.

advice, ad-văïsse´, *n* conseil *m*.

advisable, ad-vâï´-za-b'l, *a* prudent; préférable.

advise, ad-vâïze´, *v* conseiller; aviser.

adviser, ad-vâï´-z'r, *n* conseiller *m*.

advocate, ăd´-vŏ-kéte, *n* avocat *m*; *v* soutenir.

aerated, é´-eu-ré-tedde, – **water,** *n* eau gazeuse *f*.

aerial, é-i´-ri-al, *n* antenne *f*; *a* aérien.

aerobics, é-eu-rau´-bikce, *n* aérobic *m*.

aerodrome, é´-eu-ro-drôme, *n* aérodrome *m*.

aeroplane, é´-eu-ro-pléne, *n* avion *m*.

aerosol, é´-eu-reu-sol, *n* aérosol *m*.

afar, a-fare´, *adv* loin; de loin; au loin.

affable, ăf´-fa-b'l, *a* affable.

affair, a-faire´, *n* affaire *f*; (love) aventure *f*; liaison *f*.

affect, a-fecte´, *v* affecter; émouvoir; prétendre; –**ed,** *a* (manners, style) maniéré; (moved) affecté, ému; **–ing,** touchant; **–ion,** n affection f, tendresse f.

affectionate*, a-féque´-chŏ-néte, a affectueux.

affidavit, a-fi-dé´-vitte, n déposition sous serment f.

affiliate, a-fil´-i-éte, v affilier.

affinity, a-fine´-i-ti, n affinité f.

affirm, a-feurme´, v affirmer; **–ative*,** a affirmatif.

affirmation, ă-feur-mê´-ch'n, n affirmation f.

affix, a-fixe´, v apposer; attacher.

afflict, a-flicte´, v affliger; **–ion,** n affliction f.

affluence, ă-flou-ennce, n affluence f; opulence f.

afford, a-faurde´, v avoir les moyens de.

affray, a-fré´, n échauffourée f; rixe f.

affront, a-fronnte´, n affront m; v affronter; insulter.

aflame, a-fléme´, adv & a enflammé; en flammes.

afloat, a-flôte´, adv à flot.

afraid, a-fréde´, **to be –,** v avoir peur; être effrayé.

afresh, a-fréche´, adv de nouveau.

aft, ăfte, adv naut à l'arrière.

after, âf´-t'r, adv après; suivant; prep après; **–noon,** n après-midi m & f; **–wards,** adv ensuite.

again, a-guénne´, adv encore; de nouveau.

against, a-gué´-n'ste, prep contre.

age, é´-dje, n âge m; (period) siècle m; **to be of –,** v être majeur; **–d,** a âgé; vieux.

agency, é´-djenn-ci, n agence f, entremise f; agent m.

agenda, ă-djenn´-d'r, n ordre du jour m.

agent, é´-dj'nt, n agent m; représentant m.

aggravate, ăg´-gra-véte, v aggraver; empirer; fam agacer.

aggregate, ăg´-gri-guette, v rassembler; n total m.

aggression, a-grè´-ch'n, n agression f; attaque f.

aggressive*, a-gresse´-ive, a agressif.

aggrieve, a-grîve´, v chagriner.

aghast, a-gâsste´, a consterné; bouche bée.

agile, ă-djâil, a agile.

agitate, ă-dji-téte, v agiter.

agitation, a-dji-té´-ch'n, n agitation f.

ago, a-gau´, a passé; adv **long –,** il y a longtemps.

agonize, ăg´-o-nâïze, v agoniser; torturer.

agony, ăg´-o-ni, n agonie f; (mental) angoisse f.

agree, a-grî´, v s'accorder; être d'accord; consentir; **–able,** a agréable; **–ment,** n accord m; contrat m.

agricultural, ăg-gri-kol´-tiou-r'l, a agricole.

agriculture, ăg´-gri-kol-tioure, n agriculture f.

aground, a-grâ'ounnde´, adv naut échoué.

ague, é´-guioue, n fièvre intermittente f.

ahead, a-hêdde´, adv en avant; devant.

aid, éde, n aide f; secours m; v aider.

AIDS n édeze, n SIDA; sida; Sida m.

ail, éle, v avoir mal; **–ing,** a souffrant.

ailment, éle´-m'nt, n maladie f; mal m.

aim, éme, v viser; n but m; visée f; **–less,** a sans but.

air, aire, v aérer, n air m; **––conditioned,** a climatisé; **––hostess,** hôtesse de l'air f; **––port,** aéroport m; **––tight,** a hermétique.

aisle, âîle, n nef f.

ajar, a-djârre´, a entrouvert.

akin, a-quinne´, a apparenté; de même nature.

alabaster, ăl´-a-băss-t'r, n albâtre m.

alarm, a-lârme´, n alarme f; **–clock,** réveil m.

alarming*, a-lârme´-ing, a alarmant.

album, ăl´-bomme, n album m.

alcohol, ăl-cau-holl, n alcool m.

alcoholic, ăl-cau-holl´-lique, n alcoolique m & f.

alert, a-leurte´, a éveillé; **on the –,** sur ses gardes; **–ness,** n vigilance f; vivacité f.

alias, é-li-ăsse, adv autrement dit; n nom supposé m.

alibi, ăl´-i-bâï, n alibi m.

alien, é´-lienne, n étranger m; a étranger.

alight, a-lâïte´, v descendre de; se poser sur; (aero) atterrir; a allumé; en flammes.

alike, a-lâïke´, adv également; a semblable.

alive, a-lâïve´, a vivant; éveillé.

all, oale, adv entièrement.

a tout; **– right,** adv très bien; **not at –,** pas du tout.

allay, a-lé´, v adoucir; calmer.

allege, a-lèdje´, v alléguer; **–d,** a présumée.

allegiance, a-li´-dji-annce, n allégeance f.

allergic, a-leur´-djique, a allergique (à).

allergy, ă´-leur-dji, n allergie f.

alleviate, a-li´-vi-éte, v adoucir; soulager.

alley, ăl´-lie, n ruelle f; allée f; **blind –,** impasse f.

alliance, a-lâï´-annce, n alliance f.

allied, ăl´-lâïde, a allié.

allot, a-lotte´, v assigner; **–ment,** n part f.

allow, a-lâ'ou´, v allouer; permettre; admettre

allowance, a-lâ'ou´-annce, n concession f; (monetary) allocation f; (rebate) remisé f.

alloy, a-lôïe´, n alliage m; v allier.

allude, a-lioude´, v faire allusion (à).

allure, a-lioure´, v attirer; séduire.

alluring, a-liou´-rinng, a alléchant.

allusion, a-liou´-j'n, n

allusion f.

ally, a-lâï´, n allié m. v allier.

Almighty, oal-mâï´-ti, n Tout-Puissant m.

almond, â´-mönnde, n amande f.

almost, oale´-mauste, adv presque.

alms, âmze, n aumône f; **– house,** hospice m.

aloft, a-lofte´, adv en l'air.

alone, a-laune´, a seul; solitaire.

along, a-lonng´, prep le long de.

aloof, a-loufe´, adv & a distant; réservé.

aloud, a-lâ'oude´, adv à haute voix; tout haut.

alphabet, ăl´-făb-ette, n alphabet m.

already, oal-redd´-i, adv déjà.

also, oal´-sau, adv aussi; également.

altar, oal´-t'r, n autel m.

alter, oal´-t'r, v changer; modifier.

alteration, oal-teur-é´-ch'n, n modification f.

alternate*, oal-teur´-néte, a alternatif.

alternating, oal-teur-né´-tinng; a alternant.

alternative, oal-teur´-né-tive, n alternative f.

although, oal-dzau´, conj

quoique; bien que.

altitude, ăl´-ti-tioude, n altitude f; élévation f.

altogether, oal-tou-gué´-dzeur, adv tout à fait.

aluminium, a-lioue-mine´-i-omme, n aluminium m.

always, oal´-ouèze, adv toujours.

amass, a-măsse´, v amasser.

amateur, ămm´-a-tioure, n amateur m.

amaze, a-méze´, v étonner; stupéfier; ébahir.

amazement, a-méze´-m'nt, n stupéfaction f.

ambassador, am-băss´-a-deur, n ambassadeur m.

amber, ămm´-b'r, n ambre m.

ambiguous*, ămm-bi´-ghiou-eusse, a ambigu.

ambition, amm-bi´-ch'n, n ambition f.

ambitious*, ămm-bi´-cheusse, a ambitieux.

ambulance, ămm´-biou-l'nse, n ambulance f.

ambush, ămm´-bouche, n embuscade f.

ameliorate, a-mill´-ior-éte, v améliorer.

amenable, a-mî´-na-b'l, a disposé à; justiciable de.

amend, a-mennde´, v modifier; corriger;

réformer; –ment, n modification m; **make –s,** v dédommager (de).

amenity, a-mî-nit-ti, n agrément m; commodité f.

amethyst, ămm´-î-tsist, n améthyste f.

amiable, é´-mi-a-b'l, a aimable.

amicable, ămm´-i-ca-b'l, a amical.

amid, amidst, a-midde´, a-midste´, prep au milieu de; **–ships,** adv par le travers.

amiss, a-mice´, a de travers; adv mal; **take –,** prendre en mauvaise part.

ammonia, a-mau´-ni-a, n ammoniaque f.

ammunition, ămm-ioue-ni´-ch'n, n munitions fpl.

amnesty, ămm´-nesse-ti, n amnistie f.

among(st), a-monng´(ste), prep parmi.

amorous*, ămm´-o-reuce, a amoureux.

amount, a-mâ´ounnte, n montant m; nombre m; quantité f; v s'élever à.

ample, ămm´-p'l, a ample; abondant.

amplify, ămm´-pli-faî, v amplifier.

amputate, amm´-pioue-téte, v amputer.

amuse, a-miouze´, v amuser.

amusement, a-miouze´-m'nt, n amusement m.

an, ănne, art un, une.

anaemic, a-nî´-mique, a med anémique.

anaesthetize, a-nîce-tz-eur-tâîze, v anesthésier.

analogous, a-năl´-o-gueusse, a analogue.

analysis, a-nă´-li-sice, n analyse f.

analyse, ănn´-a-lâîze, v analyser.

anarchy, ănn´-ar-ki, n anarchie f.

ancestor, ănn´-cèsse-teur, n ancêtre m & f.

anchor, ain´-n'g-keur, n ancre f / v ancrer.

anchorage, ain´-n'g-keur-édje, n mouillage m.

anchovy, ănn-tchô´-vi, n anchois m.

ancient*, énn´-tchi-ennte, a ancien; âgé.

and, ănnde, conj et.

angel, enne´-dj'l, n ange m.

anger, ain´-n'gheur, n colère f; v mettre en colère.

angina, ănn-djâî´-na, n angine f.

angle, ain´-n'gl, n angle

m; *v* (fish) pêcher à la ligne; **–r,** *n* pêcheur à la ligne *m.*

angling, ain´-n'glinng, *n* pêche à la ligne *f.*

angry, ain´-n'gri, *a* en colère; (vexed) irrité.

anguish, ain´-n'gouiche, *n* angoisse *f.*

animal, ă´-ni-mal, *n & a* animal *m.*

animate, ănn´-i-méte, *v* animer; **–d,** *a* animé.

animosity, a-ni-mo´-zi-ti, *n* animosité *f.*

aniseed, ănn´-i-sîde, *n* anis *m.*

ankle, ain´-n'kl, *n* cheville *f.*

annals, ănn´-alz, *npl* annales *fpl.*

annex, a-nex´, *v* annexer; *n* annexe *f.*

annihilate, a-nâï´-hi-léte, *v* anéantir, annihiler.

anniversary, a-ni-veur´-seu-ri, *n* anniversaire de mariage *m.*

annotate, ănn´-nau-téte, *v* annoter.

announce, a-nâ˝ounnce, *v* annoncer.

annoy, a-noa˘ï´, *v* ennuyer; tourmenter.

annoyance, a-noa˘ï´-n'se, *n* désagrément *m.*

annual, ă´-niou-eul, *n* annuaire *m; a** annuel.

annuity, a-niou´-i-ti, *n* rente annuelle *f.*

annul, a-nol´, *v* annuler; **–ment,** *n* annulation *f.*

anoint, a-nô˘ïnnte´, *v* oindre.

anomalous, a-nom´-a-leuce, *a* anomal.

anonymous*, a-no´-ni-meuce, *a* anonyme.

anorak, ă´-neu-răque, *n* anorak *m.*

another, a-nodzr´, *a* un(e) autre.

answer, ănn´-s'r, *v* répondre; résoudre; *n* réponse *f.*

answering machine, ănn-s'r-inng-ma-chîne, *n* répondeur automatique or téléphonique *m.*

ant, ănnte, *n* fourmi *f.*

antagonist, ănn-tăgue´-au-nist, *n* antagoniste *m.*

antecedent, ănn-ti-ci´-dennte, *n & a* antécédent.

antedate, ănn´-ti-déte, *v* antidater; avancer.

antelope, ănn´-ti-laupe, *n* antilope *f.*

anterior, ănn-ti´-ri-eur, *a* antérieur.

anteroom, ănn´-ti-roume, *n* antichambre *f.*

anthem, ănn´-tzème, *n* hymne national *m.*

antibiotic, ănn-ti-bâï-o´-tique, *n* antibiotique *m.*

anticipate, ănn-ti´-ci-péte, *v* anticiper; s'attendre à.

anticipation, ănn-tice-i-pé´-ch'n, *n* anticipation *f;* attente *f.*

antics, ănn´-tikss, *npl* gambades *fpl;* singerie *f.*

antidote, ănn´-ti-daute, *n* antidote *m.*

antifreeze, ănn´-ti-frîze, *n* anti-gel *m inv.*

antihistamine, ănn-ti-hice´-ta-mîne, *n* antihistaminique *m.*

antipathy, ănn-ti´-pa-tsi, *n* antipathie *f.*

antipodes, ănn-ti´-pŏ-dize, *npl* antipodes *mpl.*

antiquarian, ănn-ti-coué´-ri-anne, *n* antiquaire *m.*

antiquated, ănn´-ti-coué-tedde, *a* vieilli; suranné.

antique, ănn-tique´, *n* antiquité *f; a* ancien.

antiseptic, ănn-ti-sepp´-tique, *n & a* antiseptique *m.*

antler, ănn´-t'leur, *n* (stag, etc) bois *mpl.*

anvil, ănn´-vil, *n* enclume *f.*

anxiety, aingue-zâï´-é-ti, *n* inquiétude *f.*

anxious, aink´-chieuce, *a* inquiet; désireux.

any, ènn´-i, *a* quelque; l'un ou l'autre; **–body,**

pron quelqu'un; **–how,**
adv de toute façon;
n'importe comment;
–one, *pron* quelqu'un
(someone); n'importe
qui; n'importe lequel;
–where, n'importe où.

apart, *a*-pârte´, *adv* à part;
en dehors.

apartheid, *a*-pâr´-téte, *n*
apartheid *m*.

apartment, *a*-pârte´-m'nt,
n appartement *m*.

apathy, ă´-pa-tsi, *n* apathie
f.

ape, épe, *n* singe sans
queue *m*.

apéritif, *a*-pè´-ri-tîfe, *n*
apéritif *m*.

aperture, ă´-peur-tioure, *n*
ouverture *f*; orifice *m*.

apologize, *a*-pol´-ŏ-djâïze,
v faire des excuses.

apology, *a*-pol´-ŏ-dji, *n*
excuses *fpl*.

apostle, *a*-po´-s'l, *n* apôtre
m.

appal, *a*-poal´, *v*
épouvanter; **–ling,** *a*
épouvantable.

apparatus, ă*p*-pa-ré´-
teuce, *n* appareil *m*.

apparent*, *a*-pă´-rennte, *a*
évident; apparent.

apparition, ă*p*-pa-ri´-ch'n,
n apparition *f*.

appeal, *a*-pîle, *v* faire
appel; attirer; *n* appel *m*.

appear, *a*-pîre´, *v* paraître;
sembler; (law)
comparaître.

appearance, *a*-pî´-r'ns, *n*
apparence *f*.

appease, *a*-pîze´, *v* apaiser;
–ment, *n* apaisement *m*.

append, *a*-pennde´, *v*
apposer; annexer;
attacher.

appendix, ă*p*-penne´-
dikse, *n* appendice *m*;
annexe *f*.

appertain, ă*p*-peu-téne´, *v*
appartenir.

appetite, ă*p*´-pi-tâïte, *n*
appétit *m*.

appetizing, ă*p*´-pi-tâï-zing,
a appétissant.

applaud, *a*-ploade´, *v*
applaudir.

applause, *a*-ploaze´, *n*
applaudissement *m*.

apple, ă*p*´-'l, *n* pomme *f*;
– tree, pommier *m*.

appliance, *a*-plâï´-annce,
n appareil *m*; instrument
m.

applicant, ă´-pli-k'nt, *n*
candidat *m*.

application, ă*p*-pli-ké´-
ch'n, *n* demande *f*;
application.

apply, *a*-plâï´, *v* appliquer;
–to, s'adresser à; **– for a
job,** poser sa
candidature.

appoint, *a*-pô´ïnnte´, *v*

nommer; **–ment,** *n*
rendez vous *m*;
nomination *f*; situation
f.

apportion, *a*-pôr´-ch'n, *v*
répartir.

appraise, *a*-préze´, *v*
évaluer; **–r,** *n*
commissaire-priseur *m*;
appraisal, évaluation *f*.

appreciable, ă*p*-pri´-chi-a-
b'l, *a* appréciable.

appreciate, *a*-pri´-chi-éte,
v apprécier.

appreciation, ă*p*-pri-chi-
é´-ch'n, *n* appréciation *f*.

apprehend, ă*p*-pri-
hennde´, *v* saisir;
craindre.

apprehension, ă*p*-pri-
henn´-ch'n, *n* crainte *f*;
arrestation *f*.

apprehensive*, ă*p*-pri-
henn´-cive, *a* craintif.

apprentice, *a*-prenn´-tice,
v mettre en
apprentissage; *n*
apprenti *m*; **–ship,**
apprentissage *m*.

approach, *a*-prautche´, *v*
(s')approcher (de).

appropriate*, *a*-prau´-pri-
éte, *a* convenable.

approval, *a*-prou´-v'l, *n*
approbation *f*.

approve, *a*-prouve´, *v*
approuver.

approximate*, *a*-prox´-i-méte, *a* approximatif.

apricot, é´-pri-cotte, *n* abricot *m*.

April, é´prile, *n* avril *m*.

apron, é´-preune, *n* tablier *m*.

apt, ăpte, *a* apte; propre à; enclin à.

aptitude, ăp´-ti-tioude, *n* aptitude *f*; disposition *f*.

aqueduct, ă´-coui-dokte, *n* aqueduc *m*.

aqueous, ă´-coui-*euce*, *a* aqueux.

aquiline, ă´-coui-linne, *a* aquilin.

arable, ăr´-*a*-b'l, *a* labourable.

arbitrary, ăr´-bi-tra-ri, *a* arbitraire.

arbitrate, âr´-bi-tréte, *v* arbitrer; juger.

arbitration, ăr´-bi-tré-ch'n, *n* arbitrage *m*.

arbitrator, âr´-bi-tré-teur, *n* arbitre *m*.

arbour, âr-beur, *n* tonnelle *f*.

arc, ărc, *n* arc *m*; **–lamp,** lampe à arc *f*.

arcade, ăr-kéde´, *n* arcade *f*, galerie *f*.

arch, ârtche, *n* arche *f*; **–way,** vôute *f*.

arch, ârtche, *a* archi–; **–dishop,** *n* archevêque *m*; **–deacon,** archidiacre *m*; **–duke,** archiduc *m*.

archaeology, âr-kî-oll´-leu-dji, *n* archaéologie *f*.

archer, ârtch´-eur, *n* archer *m*; **–y,** tir à l'arc *m*.

architect, ăr´-ki-tecte, *n* architecte *m*.

archives, âr´-kâïvz, *npl* archives *fpl*.

arctic, ărc´-tik, *a* arctique.

ardent, âr´-d'nt, *a* ardent; véhément.

ardour, âr´-deur, *n* ardeur *f*; zèle *m*.

arduous*, âr´-diou-*euce*, *a* ardu; difficile.

area, ai´-ri-*a*, *n* surface *f*; cour de sous-sol *f*; zone *f*; région *f*.

arena, ăr´-îna, *n* arène *f*.

argue, âr´-ghiou, *v* raisonner, discuter; se disputer.

argument, âr´-ghiou-m'nt, *n* argument *m*.

arise, *a*-râïze´, *v* s'élever; provenir de.

aristocracy, ă-rice-to´-cra-ci, *n* aristocratie *f*.

aristocratic, ă-rice´-to-cra´-tik, *a* aristocratique.

arithmetic *a*-rits´-mé-tique, *n* arithmétique *f*.

ark, ârque, *n* arche *f*; **Noah's –,** arche de Noé *f*.

arm, ărme, *n* bras *m*; **– chair,** fauteuil *m*; **–ful,**

brassée *f*; **–let,** brassard *m*; **–pit,** aisselle *f*.

arm, ârme, *v* armer; **–ament,** *n* armement *m*; **–our,** armure *f*; blindage *m*; **–oured,** *a* blindé; **–oury,** *n* armurerie *f*; **–s,** *mil* armes *fpl*; (heraldry) armoiries *fpl*.

army, âr-mie, *n* armée *f*.

aromatic, *a*-rau-mă´-tik, *a* aromatique *n*; aromate *m*.

around, *a*-ră´ounnde´, *prep* autour de; *adv* à l'entour.

arouse, *a*-râ´ouze´, *v* exciter; (awake) éveiller.

arrange, *a*-réné´-dje, *v* arranger; disposer.

array, *a*-ré´, *v* ranger; revêtir; *n* ordre *m*; parure *f*.

arrears, *a*-rirze´, *npl* arrérages *mpl*; **to be in –** être en retard.

arrest, *a*-reste´, *v* arrêter; *n* arrestation *f*.

arrival, *a*-râï-v'l, *n* arrivée *f*; (com) arrivage *m*.

arrive, *a*-râïve´, *v* arriver.

arrogant, ăr´-ro-gannte, *a* arrogant.

arrow, ăr´-rau, *n* flèche *f*.

arsenal, âr´-s'n-'l, *n* arsenal *m*.

arson, âr´-s'n, *n* incendie par malveillance *m*.

art, ărte, n art m; artifice m; habileté f.

artery, âr´-teur-i, n artère f.

artful, ârte´-foull, a (sly) rusé.

artichoke, âr´-ti-tchauke, n artichaut m; **Jerusalem –,** n topinambour m.

article, âr´-ti-k'l, n article m; clause f.

articulate, ăr-ti´-kiou-léte, v articuler; a articulé.

artifice, âr´-ti-fisse, n artifice m, ruse f.

artificial*, âr-ti-fi´-ch'l, a artificiel.

artillery, âr-til´-eur-i, n artillerie f.

artisan, âr´-ti-zănne, n artisan m.

artist, âr´-tisste, n artiste m & f.

artless*, ârte´-lesse, a simple, naïf.

as, ăze, conj comme; car; aussi; que; à mesure que; puisque; **– for, – to,** quant à; **– soon –,** aussitôt que; **– well,** aussi.

asbestos, ass-bess´-teuce, n amiante m.

ascend, a-cennde´, v monter.

ascendancy, a-cenn´-denn-ci, n ascendant m.

ascent, a-cennte´, n ascension f; montée f.

ascertain, a-seur-téne´, v s'assurer de; constater.

ascribe, ass-crâïbe´, v attribuer, imputer.

ash, ăche, n cendre f; (tree) frêne m.

ashamed, a-chémmde´, a honteux.

ashore, a-chaure´, adv à terre; naut échoué.

ashtray, âche´-tré, n cendrier m.

aside, a-sâïde, adv de côté; à l'écart; à part.

ask, ăske, v demander; inviter.

askew, ass-kiou´, adv de travers.

asleep, a-slîpe´, a endormi; **fall –,** v s'endormir.

asp, ăspe, n (snake) aspic m.

asparagus, ass-păr´-a-gheuce, n asperge f.

aspect, ăss´-pecte, n aspect m; point de vue m.

aspen, ăss´-p'n, n tremble m.

aspersion, ăss-peur´-ch'n, n calomnie f.

asphyxia, ăss-fik´-si-a, n asphyxie f.

aspirate, ăss´-pi-réte, v aspirer; a aspiré.

aspire, ass-pâïre´, v aspirer

(à).

aspirin, ăss´-peu-rinn, n aspirine f.

ass, ăsse, n âne m, ânesse f; fam bête f.

assail, a-céle´, v assaillir; **–ant,** n assaillant m.

assassinate, a-săss´-i-néte, v assassiner.

assault, a-soalte´, v attaquer; n attaque f.

assay, a-cé´, v (metals) essayer; n essai m.

assemble, a-cemm´-b'l, v assembler; se réunir.

assembly, a-cemm´-bli, n assemblée f; montage m.

assent, a-cennte´, n assentiment m; v consentir à.

assert, a-seurte´, v affirmer; revendiquer; **–ion,** n assertion f; revendication f.

assess, a-cesse´, v taxer; évaluer.

assessment, a-cesse´-m'nt, n évaluation f; cote f.

asset, ăs´-sèt, n possession f; avoir m; atout m.

assets, ăs-sètse, npl actif m.

assiduous, a-ci´-diou-euce, a appliqué; assidu.

assign, a-sâïne´, v assigner à; jur transférer; **–ee,** n cessionnaire m; **–ment,** transfert m.

assist, *a*-ciste´, *v* aider; secourir.

assistant, *a*-ciss´-t'nt, *n* aide m& *f*; commis m; *a* auxiliaire.

assizes *a*-sâïz´-iz, *npl* assises *fpl*.

associate, *a*-sau´-chi-éte, *v* associer; n associé m.

assort, *a*-sôrte´, *v* assortir.

assortment, *a*-sôrte´-m'nt, n assortiment m.

assuage, *a*-souédje, *v* calmer; adoucir.

assume, *a*-sioume´, *v* supposer; prendre sur soi.

assuming, *a*-siou´-minng, *a* prétentieux; arrogant.

assumption, *a*-sommp´-ch'n, n présomption *f*.

assurance, *a*-chou´-r'ns, n assurance *f*.

assure, *a*-choure´, *v* assurer.

asterisk, *ass´*-teu-risque, n astérisque *f*.

astern, *a*-steurne´, *adv* naut à l'arrière.

asthma, *ăss´*-ma, n asthme m.

astir, *a*-steur´, *a* en mouvement; (up) debout.

astonish, *ass*-tonn´-iche, *v* étonner.

astound, *ass*-tâ'ounnde´, *v* stupéfier; ébahir.

astray, *ass*-tré´, *a* égaré.

astride, *ass*-trâïde´, *adv* à califourchon.

astrology, *ass*-troll´-leu-dji, n astrologie *f*.

astronaut, *ăss´*-tro-noat, n astronaute m.

astronomy, *a*-stron´-*a*-mi, n astronomie *f*.

astute*, *ass*-tioute´, *a* fin; avisé.

asylum, *a*-sâï´-leume, n asile m.

at, *ătte,* prep à; chez.

atheist, *é´*-tsï-isste, n athée m& *f*.

athlete, *ă´*-tslite, n athlète m.

athletic, *ă*-tslè´-tique, *a* athlétique.

atlas, *ătte´*-leuce, n atlas m.

atmosphere, *ătte´*-moss-fire, n atmosphère *f*; *fam* ambiance *f*.

atom, *ă´*-tŏme, n atome m.

atomizer, *ă´*-to-mâï-z'r, n vaporisateur m; atomiseur m.

atone, *a*-taune´, *v* expier; **–ment,** n expiation *f*.

atrocious*, *a*-trau´-cheuce, *a* atroce.

atrophy, *ât´*-rau-fi, n atrophie *f*; *v* atrophier.

attach, *a*-tătche´, *v* attacher; joindre; (law) saisir.

attachment, *a*-tătch´-m'nt, n attachement m.

attack, *a*-tăque´, *v* attaquer; n attaque *f*.

attain, *a*-téne´, *v* atteindre; **–ment,** n talent m.

attempt, *a*-temmpte´, *v* tenter; essayer; n tentative *f*, essai m; (crime) attentat m.

attend, *a*-ntende´, *v* assister à; **– to,** s'occuper de.

attendance, *a*-tenn´d'ns, n service m; auditoire m; présence *f*.

attendant, *a*-tenn´-d'nt, n employé m & *f*; ouvreuse *f*.

attention, *a*-tenn´-ch'n, n attention *f*.

attest, *a*-teste´, *v* attester.

attic, *ăt´*-tique, n grenier m; mansarde *f*.

attire, *a*-tâïre´, *v* vêtir; parer; n vêtements *mpl*.

attitude, *ăt´*-ti-tioude, n attitude *f*; pose *f*.

attorney, *a*-teur´-ni avoué m; avocat m; notaire m; **power of –,** procuration *f*.

attract, *a*-trăcte´, *v* attirer; **–ion,** n attraction *f*; (personal) attrait m; **–ive,** *a* attirant.

attribute, *a*-tri´-bioute, *v*

attribuer; n attribut m.

aubergine, ô´-beur-djin, n aubergine f.

auburn, ô´-beurne, a châtain.

auction, ôque´-ch'n, n vente aux enchères f.

auctioneer, ôque´-ch'n-îre, n commissaire-priseur m.

audacious*, ô-dé´-cheuce, a audacieux.

audacity, ô-dăss´-i-ti, n audace f.

audible, ô´-di-b'l, a distinct; intelligible.

audience, ô´-di-ennce; n (assembly) auditoire m, spectateurs mpl.

audit, ô´-ditte, v apurer; –or, n censeur m.

augment, ôgue-mennte´, v augmenter.

augur, ô´-gueur, v augurer; n augure m.

August, ô´-gueusste, n août m.

august, ô-gueusste´, a auguste.

aunt, ânnte, n tante f.

au pair, au-père´, n jeune fille au pair f.

auspicious*, ôss-pi´-cheuce, a propice.

austere, ô-stîre´, a austère.

authentic, ô-tsenn´-tique, a authentique.

author, ô´-tseur, n auteur m.

authoritative, ô-tsor´-i-ta-tive, a autoritaire.

authority, ô-tsor´-i-ti, n autorité f.

authorize, ô-tsŏr-âï´ze, v autoriser.

autograph, ô´-teu-grâfe, n autographe m.

automatic, ô-tŏ-mätt´-ique, a automatique.

Autumn, ô´-teumme, n automne m.

auxiliary, ôg-zil´-i-a-ri, a auxiliaire.

avail, a-véle´, n avantage m; utilité f; v servir à; – **oneself of,** profiter de.

available, a-véle´-a-b'l, a valable; disponible.

avalanche, ă´-va-lanche, n avalanche f.

avarice, ă´-va-risse, n avarice f.

avaricious*, a-va-ri´-cheuce, a avare.

avenge, a-venndje´, v venger.

avenue, ă´-vi-ni'ou, n avenue f.

average, ă´-veu-rédje, n moyenne f; a moyen.

aversion, a-veur-ch'n, n aversion f; repugnance f.

avert, a-veurte´, v détourner; écarter.

aviary, é´-vi-a-ri, n volière f.

aviation, é-vi-é´-ch'n, n aviation f.

avidity, a-vid´-i-ti, n avidité f.

avocado, ă-veu-câ´-dau, n avocat m.

avoid, a-vô'ïde´, v éviter.

await, a-ouéte´, v attendre.

awake, a-ouéqué´, v s'éveiller; réveiller.

awakening, a-ouéqué´-ninng, n réveil m.

award, a-ouôrde´, v adjuger; accorder; (prize) décerner, n récompense f; prix m.

aware, a-ouère´, to be –,v savoir; être au courant.

away, a-oué´, adv absent; loin; **far –,** au loin.

awe, oa, n admiration; crainte f; **to be held in awe by someone,** en imposer à quelqu'un; **to stand in awe of someone,** avoir une crainte respectueuse de quelqu'un.

awful, oa´-foull, a terrible; imposant.

awhile, a-ou'âïle´, adv pour un instant.

awkward, a´-koueurde, a gêné; (clumsy) gauche; –ness, n gaucherie f.

awning, oann´-inng, n

poincon *m*; banne *f*.
awry, *a*-râï´, *adv* de
    travers.
axe, ăx, *n* hache *f*.
axis, ăk´-siss, *n* axe *m*.
axle, ăk´-s'l, *n* essieu *m*.
azure, ă´-jioure, *n* azur *m*.

B

babble, băb´-b'l, n babil m. v babiller.
baby, bé´-bi, n bébé m.
bachelor, bătch´-eul-eur, n célibataire m; bachelier m.
back, băque, n dos m; arrière m; v (support) soutenir; (bet) parier; (car) aller en arrière; adv (behind) en arrière; (return) de retour; **–bone**, n épine dorsale f; **–ground**, fond m;**–pack**, n sac à dos m; **–ward**, adv en arrière; a (mentally) arriéré.
bacon, bé´-k'n, n lard m.
bad, bădde, a mauvais; méchant; **–ly**, adv mal; gravement.
badminton, băd´-minn-t'n, n badminton m.

badge, bàdje, n marque f; insigne m; écusson m.
badger, băd´-jeur, n blaireau m; v harceler.
baffle, băf´-f'l, v déjouer; confondre; déconcerter.
bag, băgue, n sac m; v mettre en sac.
baggage, băgg´-idje, n bagage m.
bail, béle, v cautionner. n caution f; **out on –**, sous caution.
bailiff, bé´-liff, n huissier m.
bait, béte, n appât m. v amorcer; (molest) tourmenter.
bake, béque, v cuire au four; **–r**, n boulanger m; **–ry**, boulangerie f.
balance, băl´-n'ce, v équilibrer; balancer; n

équilibre m; com solde m; **–sheet**, bilan m.
balcony, băl´-kau-ni, n balcon m.
bald, boalde, a chauve; **–ness**, n calvitie f.
bale, béle, n balle f; ballot m. v emballotter; naut écoper.
balk, baulk, boak, v frustrer; contrarier.
ball, boale, n balle f; (hard) boule f; (foot) ballon m; (dance) bal m.
ballast, băl´-aste, n lest m; v (weight) lester.
ballet, băl´-lay, n ballet m.
balloon, bal-loune´, n ballon m.
ballot, băl´-lŏtte, v voter; n scrutin m.
ballpoint (pen), boale´poa'innte-(pène), n stylo à bille m.
balm, bâ´me, n baume m.
bamboo, bămm-bou´, n bambou m.
ban, bănne, n ban m, interdiction f; v interdir.
banana, ba-na´-na, n banane f.
band, bănnde, n bande f; (brass) fanfare f; (string) orchestre m; (ribbon) bandeau m; (gang) bande f. v se liguer; **–age**, n bandage m; **– leader**, chef de musique

m.

bandy, bănn´-di, *a* bancal.

bang, bain-nng, *v* claquer (door); frapper; cogner. *n* détonation *f*; claquement *m*.

banish, bănn´-iche, *v* bannir.

banister, bănn´-iss-t'r, *n* rampe *f*.

bank, bain´-nk, *n* banque *f*; (river) rive *f*; (mound) talus *m*; *v* (money) déposer dans une banque; **–er,** *n* banquier *m*; **– holiday,** jour férié *m*; **– account,** compte en banque *m*; **–note,** billet de banque *m*; **–rupt,** *a* insolvable; **–ruptcy,** *n* faillite *f*.

banner, bănn´-*eur*, *n* bannière *f*; étendard *m*.

banquet, bănn´-couette, *n* banquet *m*; festin *m*.

banter, bănn´-teur, *n* raillerie *f*; *v* railler.

baptism, băp´-tizme, *n* baptême *m*.

bar, bâre, *n* bar *m*, buffet *m*, (metal) barre *f*; *jur* barreau *m*; *v* barrer; défendre.

barb, bârbe, *n* barbe *f*; **–ed,** *a* barbelé.

barbarian, bâre-bé´-ri-ann, *n* & *a* barbare *mf*.

barbarity, bâre-băr´-i-ti, *n*

barbarie *f*.

barbecue, bâr´-*beu*-kioue, *n* barbecue *m*.

barber, bâre-*beur*, *n* barbier *m*; coiffeur *m*.

bare, bère, *v* mettre à nu. *a* nu; **–faced,** effronté; **–footed,** nu-pieds; **–ly,** *adv* à peine; **–ness,** *n* nudité *f*; dénuement *m*.

bargain, bâre´-guinne, *v* marchander; *n* occasion *f*; bonne affaire *f*.

barge, bârdje, *n* chaland *m*, péniche *f*.

bark, bârque, *v* aboyer; *n* aboiement *m*; (tree) écorce *f*.

barley, bâre-li, *n* orge *f*.

barman, bâr´-m'n, *n* barman *m*.

barn, bâre-'n, *n* grange *f*.

barometer, ba-ro´-mi-teur, *n* baromètre *m*.

baron, bă´-reune, *n* baron *m*; **–ess,** baronne *f*.

barracks, băr´-axe, *npl* caserne *f*.

barrel, băr´-el, *n* tonneau *m*; (gun) canon de fusil *m*.

barren, băr´-enne, *a* stérile; (land) aride.

barrier, băr´-i-eur, *n* barrière *f*.

barrister, băr´-isse-t'r, *n* avocat *m*.

barrow, bâr´-au, *n*

brouette *f*.

barter, bâre´-teur, *v* échanger; *n* échange *m*.

base, béce, *v* baser. *n* base *f*. *a** vil; **–less,** sans fondement; **–ment,** *n* sous-sol *m*; **–ness,** bassesse *f*.

baseball, béce´-boale, *n* base-ball *m*.

bash, băch, *v* défoncer; cogner; *n* coup *m*.

bashful*, bâche´-foull, *a* timide.

bashfulness, bâche´-foull-nesse, *n* timidité *f*.

basic, bé´-sique, *a* fondamental; élémentaire; **the -s** les éléments de base *mpl*.

basically, bé´-sic-li, *a* au fond.

basin, bé´-s'n, *n* (dish) bol *m*; (wash) lavabo *m*.

basil, bă´-zil, *n* basilic *m*.

basis, bé´-cisse, *n* base *f*; fondement *m*.

bask, bâsque, *v* se chauffer au soleil.

basket, bâsse´-kett, *n* panier *m*; corbeille *f*.

bass, béce, *n* basse *f*; (fish) bar *m*.

bassoon, băss´oun, *n* basson *m*.

bastard, băss-teurde, *n* bâtard *m*.

baste, béste, *v* (cooking)

arroser de graisse; (sewing) bâtir; faufiler.

bat, bătte, n bat m; (animal) chauve-souris f.

batch, bătche, n fournée f; (articles, etc.) nombre m.

bath, bâts, n bain m; (tub) baignoire f; **—chair**, chaise roulante f; **—room**, salle de bain f.

bathe, bé-dze, v se baigner; **—r**, n baigneur m; baigneuse f; **bathing costume**, n maillot de bain m.

batter, băt´-eur, n pâte à friture f. v démolir.

battery, băt´-trî, n (of torch, radio) pile f; batterie f.

battle, băt´-'l, n bataille f; **—ship**, cuirassé m.

bawl, boal, v brailler.

bay, bé, n geog baie f. a (colour) bai; v aboyer (à); **at —**, aux abois; **—tree**, laurier m.

bayonet, bé´-onn-ette, n baïonnette f.

be, bî, v être.

beach, bîtche, n plage f; rivage m; grève f.

beacon, bi´-k'n, n phare m; naut balise f.

bead, bîde, n perle f; (drop) goutte f.

beak, bîke, n bec m.

beam, bîme, n rayon m; (smile) sourire m; (wood) pourtre f.

bean, bîne, n haricot m; (broad) fève f.

bear, bère, n ours m; v donner naissance à; porter; endurer; **—able**, a supportable.

beard, birde, n barbe f; **—ed**, a barbu; **—less**, a imberbe.

beast, bîste, n bête f; **wild —**, fauve m.

beat, bîte, v battre. n coup m; (pulse, etc) battement m; secteur m.

beautiful*, bioue´-ti-foull, a beau; magnifique.

beautify, bioue´-ti-fâï, v embellir.

beauty, bioue´-ti, n beauté f; **—spot**, grain de beauté m.

beaver, bî´-veur, n castor m.

becalm, bi-câme´, v calmer; naut abriter du vent.

because, bi-coaze´e, conj parce que; **— of**, à cause de.

beckon, bekk´'n, v faire signe.

become, bi-komme´, v devenir.

becoming, bi-komm´-

inng, a convenable; (conduct) bienséant; (dress) qui va bien; seyant.

bed, bedde, n lit m; **flower— —**, plate-bande f; **—ding**, literie f; **—pan**, bassin de lit m; **—ridden**, a alité; **—room**, n chambre à coucher f.

bedeck, bi-dèque´, v parer; orner.

bee, bî, n abeille f; **—hive**, ruche f.

beech, bîtche, n hêtre m.

beef, bîfe, n boeuf m; **— steak**, bifteck m.

beer, bîre, n bière f.

beetle, bî´-t'l, n coléoptère m; **black —**, cafard m.

beetroot, bîte´-route, n betterave f.

befitting, bi-fitt´-inng, a convenable à.

before, bi-foare´, adv & prep (time) avant; (place) devant; **—hand**, adv d'avance; à l'avance.

befriend, bi-frennde´, v traiter en ami; aider.

beg, bègue, v (alms) mendier; (request, etc) prier; **—gar**, n mendiant m; **—ging**, mendicité f.

begin, bi-guinne´, v commencer; **—ner**, n débutant m; **—ning**, commencement m.

begrudge, bi-grodge´, *v*
donner à contre-cœur.

beguile, bi-gâïle´, *v*
tromper; séduire.

behalf, bi-hâfe´, **on – of,**
en faveur de; au nom de;
de la part de.

behave, bi-héve´, *v* se
conduire; se comporter.

behaviour, bi-hé´-vieur, *n*
conduite *f*; tenue *f*.

behead, bi-hédde´, *v*
décapiter.

behind, bi-hâïnnde´, *adv*
en arrière; *prep* derrière;
a en arrière; en retard; *n*
derrière *m*.

behold, bi-haulde´, *v*
contempler; *interj*
regardez!

being, bî´-inng, *n*
existence *f*; (human)
être *m*.

belch, beltche, *v* avoir un
renvoi; *pop* roter; *n*
renvoi *m*; *pop* rot *m*.

belfry, bel´-fri, *n* beffroi *m*;
clocher *m*.

belie, bi-lâï´, *v* démentir.

belief, bi-lîfe´, *n* croyance
f; foi *f*.

believable, bi-lîve´-*a*-b'l, *a*
croyable.

believe, bi-lîve´, *v* croire;
–r, *n* croyant *m*.

bell, bell, *n* cloche *f*;
sonnette *f*; grelot *m*.

belligerent, bel-lidj´-eur-

'nt, *a* & *n* belligérant *m*.

bellow, bél´-lô, *v* beugler;
mugir.

bellows, bél´-lôze, *npl*
soufflet *m*.

belly, bél´-li, *n* ventre *m*.

belong, bi-lonng´, *v*
appartenir.

belongings, bi-lonng´-
inngze, *npl* affaires *fpl*.

beloved, bi-lo´-vèdde, *n* &
a bien-aimé *m*.

below, bi-lau´, *adv* & *prep*
au-dessous; en bas.

belt, bellte, *n* ceinture *f*;
mech courroie *f*.

bemoan, bi-maune´, *v*
gémir sur; se lamenter.

bench, benntche, *n* banc
m; tribunal *m*; établi *m*.

bend, bennde, *v* courber;
plier; *n* courbure *f*;
(road, etc) coude *m*;
tournant *m*; virage *m*.

beneath, bi-nîts´, *adv* &
prep sous; au-dessous.

benediction, benn-i-dic´-
ch'n, *n* bénédiction *f*.

benefactor, benn-i-fâque´-
teur, *n* bienfaiteur *m*.

beneficial*, benn-i-fî´-
cheul, *a* salutaire;
avantageux.

beneficiary, benn-i-fî´-
chi-*eur*-i, *n* bénéficiaire
m & *f*.

benefit, benn´-i-fite, *v*
profiter. *n* bénéfice *m*.

benevolence, bi-nèv´-ŏ-
lennce, *n* bienveillance
f.

benevolent, bi-nèv´-ŏ-
lennte, *a* bienveillant;
charitable.

benign, bi-nâïne´, *a*
bénin; doux.

bent, bennte, *pp* courbé;
résolu; *n fig* penchant *m*.

bequeath, bi-kouîds´, *v*
léguer.

bequest, bi-koueste´, *n*
legs *m*.

bereave, bi-rîve´, *v* priver
de; **–ment,** *n* perte *f*.

berry, bê´-ri, *n* baie *f*.

berth, beurts, *n* couchette
f.

beseech, bi-cîtche´, *v*
supplier; implorer.

beside, bi-sâïde´, *prep* à
côté de; hors de.

besides, bi-sâïdze, *adv* en
outre; d'ailleurs; *prep* en
plus; excepté.

besiege, bi-cîdje´, *v*
assiéger.

besotted, bi-sotte´-èdde, *a*
abruti.

best, besste, *adv* le mieux;
a & *n* le meilleur.

bestial, bess´-ti'l, *a* bestial.

bestir, bi-steur´, *v* –
oneself, se remuer.

bestow, bi-stau´, *v*
accorder; conférer; **–al,**
n don *m*.

bet, bette, *v* parier. *n* pari *m*; **–ting** (odds) cote *f*.

betoken, bi-tau´-k'n, *v* indiquer; dénoter.

betray, bi-tré *v* trahir; **–al,** *n* trahison *f*.

betroth, bi-traudz´, *v* fiancer.

betrothal, bi-traudz´-'l, *n* fiançailles *fpl*.

better, bett´r, *v* améliorer; *adv* mieux; *a* meilleur.

betterment, bett´-eur-m'nt, *n* amélioration *f*.

between, bi-touîne´, *prep* entre.

bevel, bév´'l, *v* tailler en biseau; **bevelled,** *a* de biais; en biseau.

beverage, bèv´-eur-idj, *n* boisson *f*; breuvage *m*.

bewail, bi-ouélé´, *v* déplorer.

beware, bi-ouère´, *v* se méfier de; prendre garde à.

bewilder, bi-ouile´-deur, *v* ahurir; déconcerter.

bewilderment, bi-ouile´-deur-m'nt, *n* ahurissement *m*.

bewitch, bi-ouitche´, *v* ensorceler; enchanter.

beyond, bi-ionnde´, *adv* au delà; là-bas; *prep* au delà de.

bias, bâï´-asse, *n* biais *m*; préjugé *m*; **biased,** *a* partial.

Bible, bâï´-b'l, *n* bible *f*.

bicker, bik´eur, *v* se quereller; se chamailler.

bicycle, bâï´-ci-k'l, *n* bicyclette *f*.

bid, bide, *v* commander; prier; (auction) faire une offre; *n* offre *f*; enchère *f*; **–ding,** commandement *m*; enchère *f*.

bide, bâïde, *v* attendre; endurer.

bier, bîre, *n* corbillard *m*; bière *f*.

big, bigue, *a* gros; grand; vaste.

bigot, bigg-eute, *n* bigot *m*; **–ed,** *a* bigot.

bike, bâïque, *n fam* vélo *m*; *n* bicyclette *f*; *v fam* faire du vélo.

bikini, bi-kî´-nî, *n* bikini *m*.

bilberry, bil´-bê-ri, *n* myrtille *f*.

bile, bâïle, *n* bile *f*.

bilingual, bâï-linn´-gou´eul, *a* bilingue.

bilious, bî´-li-euce, *a* bilieux.

bill, bil, *n* note *f*, compte *m*; facture *f*; (restaurant) addition *f*; (bird) bec *m*; (poster) affiche *f*; **– of exchange,** lettre de change *f*;

(parliamentary) projet de loi *m*; **– of fare,** menu *m*; **– of lading'** connaissement *m*.

billet, bil´-ette, *v* loger; *n mil* logement *m*.

billiards, bil´-lieurdze, *npl* billard *m*.

billion, bill´-ieune, *n* billion *m*.

bin, bine, *n* huche *f*; (wine) porte-bouteilles *m*; (refuse) boîte à ordures *f*; poubelle *f*.

bind, bâïnnde, *v* lier; obliger; (books) relier; **–ing** *n* reliure *f*. *a* obligatoire; **– up,** *v* bander.

binocular(s), bi-nok´-ioue-leur(ze), *n* jumelle *f*.

biography, bâï-o´-grä-fi, *n* biographie *f*.

birch, beurtche, *n* (tree) bouleau *m*; (punitive) verge *f*.

bird, beurde, *n* oiseau *m*.

birth, beurts, *n* naissance *f*; **–day,** anniversaire *m*; **–-mark,** tache de naissance *f*; **–place,** lieu natal *m*; **–rate,** natalité *f*.

biscuit, biss´-kitte, *n* biscuit *m*.

bishop, bich´-eup, *n* évêque *m*.

bit, bitte, n morceau m; (horse) mors m.

bitch, bitche, n chienne f; *pop* garce f.

bite, bâïte, v mordre; n morsure f; piqûre f.

biting, bâît´-inng, a mordant.

bitter*, bitt´-eur, a amer; **–ness,** n amertume f.

black, blăque, v (shoes) cirer; noircir; a noir; n noir m; **–berry,** n mûre f; **–bird,** merle m; **–currant,** cassis m; **–en,** v noircir. **–mail,** chantage m; v faire chanter; **–mailer,** n maître chanteur m.; **–market,** n marché noir m; **–smith,** forgeron m.

bladder, blăd´-eur, n vessie f.

blade, bléde, n lame f; (grass) brin m; (oar) plat m.

blame, bléme, v blâmer; n blâme m; faute f.

blameless*, bléme´-lesse, a irréprochable.

blanch, blânntche, v blanchir; pâlir.

bland, blănnde, a doux; **–ishment,** n flatterie f.

blank, blain-n'k, n blanc m; a blanc; (mind) vide.

blanket, blaing´-kette, n couverture f.

blare, bláre, v retentir.

blaspheme, blass-fîme´, v blasphémer.

blasphemy, blass´-fé-mi, n blasphème m.

blast, blăsste, v (explode) faire sauter; (blight) flétrir; n (gust) rafale f; (trumpet) son m, coup m.

blatant, blé´-t'nt, a bruyant.

blaze, bléze, v flamber. n flamme f; éclat m.

bleach, blîtche, v blanchir; décolorer.

bleak, blîque, a froid; exposé aux vents; morne.

bleat, blîte, v bêler; n bêlement m.

bleed, blîde, v saigner; **–ing,** n saignement m.

blemish, blèm´-iche, n tache f. v tacher; abîmer.

blend, blennde, v mélanger; n mélange m.

bless, bless, v bénir; **–ed,** a béni.

blessing, bless´-inng, n bénédiction f.

blight, blâïte, n nielle f; rouille f; *fam* influence néfaste.

blind, blâïnnde, n (window) store m; (venetian) jalousie f; n & a (sight) aveugle m & f; v aveugler. **–fold,** bander les yeux; **–ness,** n aveuglement m; cécité f.

blink, blinng-k, v clignoter; n battement de paupière m; **–er,** n (horse) œillère f.

bliss, blisse, n bonheur m; béatitude f.

blissful, bliss´-foull, a bienheureux.

blister, bliss´-t'r, n ampoule f; cloque f.

blithe*, blâîdz, a gai; joyeux.

blizzard, bliz´-eurde, n tempête de neige f.

bloated, blau´-tedde, a boursouflé; bouffi; **bloater,** n hareng fumé m.

block, bloque, v bloquer. n bloc m; billot m; obstacle m; (of houses) pâté de maisons m; **–ade,** blocus m; **–head,** n imbécile m & f.

bloke, blauque, n *fam* type m.

blonde, blonnde, a & n blonde (woman) f.

blood, blodde, n sang m; **–hound,** limier m; **–shot,** a injecté de sang; **–thirsty,** sanguinaire; **–pressure,** n tension artérielle; **–y,** sanglant.

blossom, bloss-*eume,* v fleurir. n fleur f.

blot, blotte, v tacher; (dry) sécher; n tache f; (ink) pâté m; **–ting paper,** papier buvard m.

blotch, blotche, n tache f; eclaboussure f.

blouse, blâ´-ouze, n blouse f; (woman's shirt) chemisier m.

blow, blau, n coup m. v souffler; (trumpet) sonner; (nose) se moucher.

blubber, blob-*eur,* n (whale) graisse de baleine f.

bludgeon, blod´-*jeune,* n matraque f.

blue, bloue, a & n bleu; **–bell,** n jacinthe des bois f; clochette f.

bluff, bloffe, n bluff m. v bluffer.

bluish, bloue´-iche, a bleuâtre.

blunder, blonne´-deur, n maladresse f; v commettre une maladresse.

blunt, blonnt, v émousser. a* brusque; emoussé.

blur, bleure, v brouiller; n tache f.

blush, bloche, v rougir; m rougeur f.

bluster, bloce´-teur, v faire du vacarme; n fanfaronnade f; **–er,** fanfaron m; **–ing,** a tapageur; (wind) violent.

boar, baure, n (wild) sanglier m.

board, baurde, n planche f; (directors) conseil d'administration m; (food) pension f; v garnir de planches; **notice –,** n tableau d'annonces m; **–er,** pensionnaire m & f; **–ing house,** pension f; **–ing school,** pensionnat m; pension f.

boast, bauste, v se vanter.

boaster, baus´-t'r, n vantard m.

boat, baute, n bateau m; (rowing) bateau à rames m; **motor–,** canot à moteur m; **steam–,** vapeur m; **– hook,** gaffe f.

bob, bobbe, v ballotter; osciller; s'agiter.

bobbin, bob´-ine, n bobine f.

bodice, bod´-ice, n corsage m.

bodkin, bode´-kinne, n passe-lacet m; poincon m.

body, bod´-i, n corps m; (vehicle) carrosserie f.

bog, bogue, n marécage m; **–gy,** a marécageux.

bogey-man, bau´-gui-mănne, n croquemitaine m.

bogie, bau´-gui, n mech boggie m.

boil, boa´ïle, v faire bouillir; bouillir. n med furoncle m.

boiler, boa´il´-eur, n chaudière f.

boisterous*, boïce´-teur-euce, a bruyant; turbulent.

bold*, bôlde, a hardi; audacieux; effronté.

boldness, bôlde´-nesse, n hardiesse f; effronterie f.

bolster, bôle´-steur, n traversin m; v fig soutenir.

bolt, bôlte, v verrouiller; décamper; n verrou m.

bomb, bomme, n bombe f; **–ard,** v bombarder.

bond, bonnde, n (tie) lien m; (word) engagement m; bon m; **in –,** (customs) à l'entrepôt m.

bondage, bonnd´-idj, n esclavage m; servitude f.

bone, baune, n os m; (fish) arête f.

bonfire, bonn´-fâïre, n feu de joie m.

bonnet, bonn´-ette, n

chapeau m; bonnet; (car) capot m.

bonus, bau´-neuce, n prime f, gratification.

bony, bau´-ni, a osseux.

boob, boub, n pop gaffe f. v faire une gaffe.

book, bouk, n livre m. v inscrire; réserver; **–binder,** n relieur m; **–case,** bibliothèque f; **–ing office,** guichet m; **–keeper,** comptable m; **–seller,** libraire m; **–shop,** librairie f; **–stall,** kiosque à journaux m.

boom, boume, n com boom m; (noise) grondement m; (spar) bout-dehors m; v gronder; com faire hausser; être à la hausse.

boon, boune, n bienfait m.

boor, boure, n rustre m; **–ish,** a grossier.

boot, boute, n botte f; **–maker,** bottier m.

booth, boudz, n cabine f.

booty, boue´-ti, n butin m.

booze, bouze, v fam boire (beaucoup); n fam alcool m.

border, bôre´-d'r, n frontière f; bord m; bordure f; **–ing,** a (adjacent) contigu à; touchant.

bore, bôre, v percer; (ground) forer; (weary) ennuyer; n calibre m; (person) raseur m; raseuse f; (thing) corvée f; barbe f.

born, bôrne, pp né.

borrow, bor´-au, v emprunter.

bosom, bou´-zeume, n sein m.

boss, bosse, n fam patron m. v mener; diriger.

botanist, bott´-a-niste, n botaniste mf.

botany, bott´-a-ni, n botanique f.

both, bôts, a les deux; pron – (of them), les deux; tous les deux m, toutes les deux f.

bother, bô´-dz'r, v tracasser; n ennui m.

bottle, bott´-'l, v mettre en bouteilles; n bouteille f.

bottom, bott´-eume, n fond m; bas m; derrière n.

bottomless, bott´-eume-lesse, a sans fond.

boudoir, bou´-do'ar, n boudoir m.

bough, bâ´ou, n rameau m; branche f.

bounce, bâ´ounnce, v rebondir.

bound, bâ´ounn´-de, v borner; (jump) bondir; n (jump) bond m; **–ary,** borne f limites fpl; – **for,** à destination de.

bountiful*, bâ´ounn´-ti-foull, a généreux.

bounty, bâ´ounn´-ti, n libéralité f; prime f.

bouquet, bou-kay, n bouquet m.

bout, bâ´oute, n (fencing) assaut m; accès m.

bow, bâ´ou, v saluer; s'incline;. n salut m; révérence f; (ship) avant m.

bow, bau, n (archery) arc m; (tie, knot) nœud m; (violin) archet m.

bowels, bâ´ou´-elze, n boyaux mpl; intestins mpl.

bowl, baule, n bol m; (ball) boule f; v jouer aux boules; (cricket) lancer la balle.

box, boxe, v boxer; n boîte f; (theatre) loge f; (on the ears) gifle f; **–ing,** n boxe f.

boy, boa´ï, n garcon m; **–cott,** v boycotter; n boycottage m; – **friend,** n (petit) ami m **–hood,** enfance f.

bra, brâ, n soutien-gorge m.

brace, bréce, v lier; fortifie;. n mech

vilebrequin m; (two) couple m; appareil dentaire m; **–s,** bretelles fpl.

bracelet, bréce´-lette, n bracelet m.

bracing, bréce´-inng, a fortifiant; tonique.

bracken, brăk-´n, n fougère f.

bracket, brăk´-ette, n console f; parenthèse f.

brackish, brăk´-iche, a saumâtre.

brag, brăgue, v se vanter; **–gart,** n vantard m.

braid, bréde, v tresser; n tresse f; (dress) galon m.

brain, bréne, n (substance) cervelle f; (mind) cerveau m; **–y** a fam intelligent.

braise, bréze, v braiser.

brake, bréque, n frein m; v freiner.

bramble, brămm´-b'l, n ronce f.

bran, brănne, n son m.

branch, brănntche, n branche f; com succursale f.

brand, brănnde, n marque f; (fire) brandon m; v marquer; stigmatiser; **–ish,** brandir.

brandy, brănn´-di, n eau de vie f.

brass, brăce, n laiton m;

cuivre jaune m.

brassière (fam bra), brắ-ssi-aire (bră), n soutien-gorge m.

bravado, bra-vâ´-dô, n bravade f.

brave*, bréve, a brave; courageux; v braver; **–ry,** n bravoure f.

brawl, broale, v se chamailler.

brawn, broanne, n fromage de tête m; muscles mpl; **–y,** a musclé.

bray, bré, v braire.

brazen, bré´-z'n, a de laiton; (insolent) effronté.

brazil nut, bra-zile´-notte, n noix du Brésil f.

breach, brîtche, n fracture f; violation f; rupture f.

bread, brède, n pain m; pop argent.

breadth, brèdts, n largeur f.

break, bréque, v casser; (amity, etc) rompre; (law) violer; (smash) briser; n brisure f; (pause) pause f; (school) récréation f; **–age,** casse f; **–down,** rupture f; dépression; écroulement m; mech panne f; **–er,** naut grosse vague f; **–water,** brise-lames m.

breakfast, brèque´-fâste, n petit-déjeuner m.

bream, brîmme, n brème f.

breast, breste, n sein m; poitrine f.

breath, brè-ts, n haleine f; souffle m; **–less,** a essoufflé.

breathe, brî-dz, v respirer.

breech, brîtche, n (firearms) culasse f.

breeches, brî´-tchiz, npl culotte f.

breed, brîde, v élever; procréer; se reproduire; n race f; espèce f; **–er,** éleveur m; **–ing,** élevage m; éducation f.

breeze, brîze, n brise f.

brevity, brèv´-i-ti, n brièveté f.

brew, broue, v brasser; faire infuser; **–er,** n brasseur m.

brewery, broue´-eur-i, n brasserie f.

briar, brăï´-eur, n (bramble) ronce f; églantier m.

bribe, brăïbe, v corrompre; fam graisser la pâte; n paiement illicite m.

bribery, brăï´-beur-i, n corruption f.

brick, brique, n brique f; **–layer,** maçon m.

bridal, brăï-d'l, a nuptial.

bride, brăïde, n mariée f;

–groom, marié *m*;
–smaid, demoiselle
d'honneur *f*.
bridge, bridje, *n* pont *m*;
naut passerelle *f*.
bridle, brâï´-d'l, *n* bride *f*;
v brider.
brief, brîfe, *n* dossier *m*. *a**
bref; **–case,** *n* serviette *f*;
–ing, instruction *f*;
directives *f*.
brigade, bri-guéde´, *n*
brigade *f*.
bright*, brâïte, *a* luisant;
lumineux; intelligent;
–en, *v* faire briller;
(enliven) égayer;
(weather) s'éclaircir;
–ness, *n* éclat *m*;
vivacité *f*.
brilliancy, bril´-iann-ci, *n*
éclat *m*; lustre *m*.
brilliant, bril´-iannte, *a*
brillant; éclatant.
brim, brime, *n* bord *m*;
–over, *v* déborder.
brimstone, brime´-staune,
n soufre *m*.
brine, brâïne, *n* saumure *f*.
bring, brinng, *v* apporter;
conduire; **– forward,**
com reporter; **– in,** *com*
rapporter; **– up,** élever.
brink, brinng-k, *n* bord *m*.
brisk, brisque, *a* vif;
animé; **–ness,** *n* vivacité
f.
brisket, briss´-quette, *n*

poitrine de bœuf *f*.
bristle, briss´-'l, *n* poil
raide *m*; soie *f*; *v* se
hérisser.
bristly, briss´-li, *a* dur;
poilu; hérissé.
brittle, britt´-'l, *a* fragile;
cassant.
broad, broad, *a* large;
(accent) prononcé.
broadcast, broade´-câste, *v*
radiodiffuser.
broadcasting, broade´-
câste-inng, *n* émission *f*.
brocade, brô-quéde´, *n*
brocart *m*.
broccoli, broque´-o-li, *n*
brocoli *m*.
brochure, brau´-chioure,
n prospectus *m*.
brogue, braugue, *n* patois
m; chaussure *f*.
broil, broa'île, *n* querelle *f*.
broken, brau´-k'n a cassé;
brisé.
broker, brau´-keur, *n*
courtier *m*; **stock–,**
agent de change *m*;
–age, courtage *m*.
bronchitis, bronng-kâï´-
tice, *n* bronchite *f*.
bronze, bronnze, *n* bronze
m; *v* bronzer.
brooch, brautche, *n*
broche *f*.
brood, broude, *v* couver;
fam remâcher; ruminer
(une idée); *n* couvée *f*.

brook, brouque, *n* ruisseau
m.
broom, broume, *n* balai *m*;
(plant) genêt *m*.
broth, brots, *n* bouillon *m*.
brothel, brotz´-'l, *n*
maison de débauche *f*;
pop bordel *m*.
brother, brodz´-*eur*, *n* frère
m **–hood,** fraternité *f*;
eccl confrérie *f*; **–in-law,**
beau-frère *m*; **–ly,** *a*
fraternel.
brow, brâ'ou, *n* front *m*;
sourcil *m*; **–beat,** *v*
intimider.
brown, brâ'oune, *v* brunir;
a brun; marron; **–ish,**
brunâtre.
browse, brâ'ouze, *v*
brouter; regarder dans
acheter.
bruise, brouze, *n*
contusion *f*; bleu *m*; *v*
meurtrir.
brunette, brou-nette´, *n*
brunette *f*.
brunt, bronnte, *n* choc *m*;
violence *f*.
brush, broche, *n* brosse *f*;
v brosser; (sweep)
balayer.
brushwood, broche´-
ou'oude, *n* broussailles
*f*pl.
brusque, breuske, *a*
brusque.
Brussels sprouts, bross´-

lze-spr'outse, *npl* choux de Bruxelles *mpl*.

brutal*, broue´-t'l, *a* brutal; **–ity,** *n* brutalité *f*.

brutalize, broue´-t'l-âïze, *v* abrutir; brutaliser.

brute, broute, *n* brute *f*.

bubble, bo´-b'l, *n* bulle *f*; *v* bouillonner; (wine) pétiller.

buck, boque, *a* mâle; *n* (deer) daim *m*.

bucket, bok´-ette, *n* seau *m*; baquet *m*.

buckle, bo´-k'l, *n* boucle *f*; *v* boucler; attacher.

bud, bodde, *n* bourgeon *m*; (flower) bouton *m*; *v* bourgeonner; fleurir.

budge, bodje, *v* bouger.

budget, bodj´-ette, *n* budget *m*.

buff, boffe, *a* couleur chamois; *v* polir.

buffalo, boff´-a-lau, *n* buffle *m*.

buffer, boff´-eur, *n* tampon (de choc) *m*.

buffet, boff´-ette, *n* (bar) buffet *m*; *v* battre.

buffoon, beuf-foune´, *n* bouffon *m*.

bug, bogue, *n* punaise *f*; insecte *m*; **–bear,** *fam* bête noire *f*.

buggy, bogue´-i, *n* boghei (carriage) *m*; poussette (for baby) *f*; poussette-

canne *f*; *fam* bagnole (car) *f*.

bugle, bioue´-g'l, *n mil* clairon *m*.

build, bilde, *v* bâtir; *n* forme *f*; **–er,** constructeur *m*; **–ing,** bâtiment *m*.

bulb, bolbe, *n* bulbe *m*; (lamp) ampoule électrique *f*.

bulge, bol-dj, *v* bomber; gonfler.

bulk, bolke, *n* volume *m*; **in –,** en gros.

bulky, boll´-ki, *a* volumineux; encombrant.

bull, boull, *n* taureau *m*; (stock exchange) haussier *m*; **–dog,** bouledogue *m*; **–finch,** bouvreuil *m*; **–'s eye,** (target) mouche *f*.

bullet, boull´-ette, *n* balle *f*.

bulletin, boull´-i-tinne, *n* bulletin *m*.

bullion, boull´-ieune, *n* or en barres *m*.

bully, boull´-i, *v* malmener; *n* tyran *m*; brute *f*.

bulrush, boull´-roche, *n* jonc *m*.

bulwark, boull´-ou'eurque; *n* rempart *m*; *naut* pavois *m*.

bumble bee, bomm´-b'l-bî, *n* bourdon *m*.

bump, bommpe, *n* coup *m*; secousse *f* (swelling) bosse *f*. *v* heurter; cogner.

bumper, bomm´-peur, *n* (glass) rasade *f*; (of car) pare-chocs *m*.

bumptious, bommpe´-cheuce, *a* arrogant.

bunch, bonntche, *v* grouper; se tasser. *n* (vegetables) botte *f*; (flowers) bouquet *m*; (grapes) grappe de raisin *f*; (keys) trousseau de clefs *m*; (people) groupe *m*.

bundle, bonn´-d'l, *n* paquet *m*; ballot *m*; (of wood) fagot *m*.

bung, bonng, *n* bondon *m*; **–hole,** bonde *f*.

bungalow, bonng´-ga-lau, *n* bungalow *m*.

bungle, bonng-g'l, *v* gâcher; **–r,** *n* gâcheur *m*.

bunion, bonn´-ieune, *n* oignon aux pieds *m*.

bunker, bonng´-keur, *n* (coal) soute à charbon *f*.

bunting, bonn´-tinng, *n* étamine *f*; (flags) drapeaux *mpl*.

buoy, bôa´ï, *n* bouée *f*; **–ancy,** légèreté *f*; *fam* entrain *m*; **–ant,** *a* flottable; *fam* plein d'entrain.

burden, beur´-d'n, *v* charger; accabler; *n* fardeau *m*; charge *f*; **–some,** *a* lourd.

bureau, biou´-rau, *n* (furniture) bureau *m*; secrétaire *m*; (office) bureau *m*; office *m*.

bureaucracy, biou-rau-cra-si, *n* bureaucratie *f*.

burglar, beur´-gleur, *n* cambrioleur *m*.

burglary, beur´-gleur-i, *n* cambriolage *m*.

burial, bè´-ri-al, *n* enterrement *m*.

burial-ground, bè´-ri-al-grâ´ounnde, *n* cimetière *m*.

burlesque, beur-lesque´, *n* & *a* burlesque *m*.

burly, beur´-li, *a* corpulent.

burn, beurne, *v* brûler; (arson) incendier; *n* brûlure *f*; **–er,** (gas; lamp) bec *m*.

burr, beurre, *n* (botanical) carde *f*.

burrow, beurr´-au, *v* terrer; *n* terrier *m*.

bursar, beurr´-sar, *n* (school) économe *m*.

burst, beurste, *v* éclater; (crack) crever; sauter.

bury, bèr-i, *v* enterrer.

bus, boss, *n* autobus *m*; **— stop,** *n* arrêt d'autobus *m*.

bush, bouche, *n* buisson *m*, fourré *m*; **–y,** *a* touffu.

business, biz´-nesse, *n* affaires *fpl*; occupation *f*.

businessman, biz´-nesse-m'n, *n* homme d'affaires *m*.

businesswoman, biz´-nesse-ou'oum´-min, *n* femme d'affaires *f*.

busker, boss´-keur, *n* musicien ambulant *m*.

bust, bosste, *n* buste *m*; poitrine *f*.

bustle, boss˝l, *v* se remuer; *n* mouvement *m*; remue-ménage *m*.

bustling, boss´-linng, *a* affairé.

busy, biz´-i, *a* occupé; affairé.

but, botte, *conj* mais; *adv* seulement.

butcher, boutt´-cheur, *n* boucher *m*; *v* massacrer.

butler, bott´-leur, *n* maître d'hôtel *m*.

butt, bott, *n* bout *m*; (gun) crosse *f*; (cask) tonneau *m*. *v* buter.

butter, bott´-eur, *v* beurrer; *n* beurre *m*; **–cup,** bouton d'or *m*; **––dish,** beurrier *m*; **–fly,** papillon *m*.

buttock, bott´-ôque, *n* fesse *f*; culotte de bœuf *f*.

button, bott´-'n, *n* bouton *m*; *v* boutonner; **––hole,** *n* boutonnière *f*.

buxom, box´-eume, *a* (woman) grassouillette *f*; bien en chair.

buy, bâï, *v* acheter; **–er,** *n* acheteur *m*; acheteuse *f*.

buzz, bozze, *v* bourdonner.

buzzard, bozz´-eurde, *n* buse *f*.

buzzer, boz´-zeur, *n* sonnette *f*.

by, bâï, *prep* par; près de; **–gone,** *a* passé; **— stander,** *n* spectateur *m*; **––word,** *n* dicton *m*.

bye-law, bâï´-loa, *n* réglement *m*; arrêté *m*.

bypass, bâï´-pâsse, *v* contourner; éviter; *n* auto route qui contourne *f*; *med* pontage *m*; *v med* coutourner.

cab, căbbe, n taxi m.

cabbage, căb´-idj, n chou m.

cabin, căb´-inn, n cabine f; (hut) cabane f.

cabinet, căb´-inn-ett, n cabinet m; **--maker,** ébéniste m.

cable, ké´-b'l, n câble m; v câbler.

cablegram, ké´-b'l-grămme, n câblogramme m.

cable television, ké-bl-tell´-i-vijn, n télévision par câble f.

cackle, căk´-'l, v caqueter; n caquet m.

café, căf´-é, n café m.

cafeteria, că-fi-tî´-ri-a, n caféteria f.

cage, kédje, n cage f; v mettre en cage.

cajole, ca-djaule´, v cajoler.

cake, kéque, n gâteau m; v se coaguler.

calabash, căl´-a-băche, n calebasse f.

calamitous, ca-lămm´-i-teuce, a désastreux.

calamity, ca-lămm´-i-ti, n calamité f.

calculate, căl´-kiou-léte, v calculer.

calendar, căl´-ènn-deur, n calendrier m.

calf, câfe, n veau m; (leg) mollet m.

calico, căl´-i-kô, n calicot m.

call, coal, v appeler; (name) nommer; (visit) visiter; passer chez; n appel m; visite f.

callous, căl´-euce, a

(unfeeling) insensible; endurci.

calm, câme, v calme;. n & a* calme m.

calorie, căl´-or-ri, n calorie f.

cambric, kéme´-brique, n batiste f.

camcorder, cămm´-caure-deur, n camescope m

camel, cămm´-'l, n chameau n.

cameo, cămm´-î-ô, n camée m.

camera, cămm´-eur-a, n appareil photographique m; **in –,** à huis clos;

camera man, n cameraman m.

camomile, cămm´-ô-mâîle, n camomille f.

camouflage, cămm´-a-flâje, n camouflage m.

camp, cămmpe, v camper. n camp m; **–bed,** lit de camp m; **–site,** n camping m; **to go camping,** v faire du camping.

campaign, cămm-péne´, n campagne f.

camphor, cămm´-feur, n camphre m.

campus, cămm´-peuce, n campus m.

can, cănne, n bidon m; (of food) boîte; v (preserve) conserver en boîte; n –

opener ouvre-boîte m.

can, cănne, v pouvoir; savoir.

canal, cănn-ăl´, n canal m.

canary, că-né´-ri, n canari m; serin m.

cancel, cănn-s'l, v annuler.

cancer, cănn´-ceur, n cancer m.

candid*, cănn´-dide, a candide; franc.

candidate, cănn´-di-déte, n candidat m.

candle, cănn´-d'l, n bougie f; chandelle f; **–stick,** bougeoir m; chandelier m.

candour, cănn´-deur, n candeur f; franchise f.

candy, cănn´-di, n bonbons mpl; v cristalliser.

cane, quéne, n canne f.

canine, că-nâïnne´, a canin; n (tooth) canine f.

canister, cănn´-iss-teur, n boîte en fer blanc f.

canker, caing´-k'r, n chancre m.

cannabis, cănn´-a-biss, n cannabis m.

cannibal, cănn´-i-b'l, n & a cannibale m & f.

cannon, cănn´-eune, n canon m.

canoe, ca-noue´, n

périssoire f; (native) pirogue f.

canon, cănn´-eune, n (title) chanoine m; (law) canon m.

canopy, cănn´-ŏ-pi, n baldaquin m.

cant, cănnte, n hypocrisie f.

cantankerous, cănn-taing´-keur-euce, a revêche.

canteen, cănn-tîne, n cântine f.

canter, cănn´-teur, v aller au petit galop.

canvas, cănn´-vasse, n toile f; (sail) voile f.

canvass, cănn´-vasse, v solliciter.

cap, căppe, n casquette f; (of bottle) capsule f; (pen) capuchon m.

capable, qué´-pa-b'l, a capable; competent.

capacity, ca-păsse´-i-ti, n capacité f.

cape, quépe, n geog cap m; (cover) cape f.

caper, qué´-peur, n cambriole, gambade f; (cooking) câpre f.

capital, căp´-i-t'l, n (city) capitale f; (money) capital m; (letter) majuscule f.

capitulate, ca-pitte´-ioue-léte, v capituler.

capricious*, ca-prich´-euce, a capricieux.

capsize, căp-sâîze´, v chavirer.

capstan, căp´-stănne, n cabestan m.

capsule, căp´-sioulle, n capsule f.

captain, căp´-t'n, n capitaine m; (sport) chef d'équipe m.

caption, căp´-ch'n, n légende f.

captive, căp´-tive, n & a, captif m; captive f.

captivity, căp-tive´-i-ti, n captivité f.

capture, căp´-tioure, v capturer; n prise f.

car, câre, n automobile f; voiture f; aero nacelle f; **-- ferry,** ferry-boat m; **-- hire,** location de voitures f; **--park,** parking m; **--phone,** téléphone de voiture m.

caramel, căr´-a-m'l, n caramel m.

carat, căr´-atte, n carat m.

caravan, căr´-a-vănne, n caravane f; roulotte f.

caraway, căr´-a-oué, n (seed) carvi m.

carbide, căr´-bâïde, n carbure m.

carbolic, căr-bol´-ique, a phénique; **–acid,** n phénol m.

carbon, căr´-b'n, n carbone m; **–copy,** n double m; **–paper,** n papier carbone m.

carbuncle, căr´-bonng-k'l, n med anthrax m.

carburettor, căr-bi'oue-rett´-'r, n carburateur m.

carcase, carcass, căr´-casse, n carcasse f.

card, cârde, v carder; n carte f; **–board,** cartòn m.

cardigan, cărd´-i-g'n, n cardigan m.

cardinal, căr´-di-n'l, n cardinal m; a cardinal.

care, quére, n soin m, attention f; inquiétude f; v se soucier de; **take –!** interj attention!; **take – of,** v faire attention à; **– for,** aimer; **–ful*,** a soigneux; prudent; **–less,** a négligent; sans soin; **–lessness,** n négligence f; **c/o,** chez; aux bons soins de; **–taker,** n gardien m; concierge m & f.

career, ca-rîre´, n carrière f.

caress, ca-resse´, v caresser; n caresse f.

cargo, căr´-gau, n cargaison f.

caricature, căr´-i-ca-tioure´, n caricature f.

carmine, câr´-mine, n carmin m.

carnage, câr´-nidj, n carnage m.

carnal*, câr-n'l, a charnel.

carnation, câr-né´-ch'n, n œillet m.

carnival, câr´-ni-v'l, n carnaval m.

carol, căr´-ŏl, n cantique de Noël m.

carp, cârpe, n (fish) carpe f; v chicaner sur.

carpenter, căr´-penn-teur, n charpentier m.

carpet, câr´-pette, n tapis m; moquette f.

carriage, căr´-idj, n voiture f; (freight) port m; (deportment) maintien m; (rail) wagon m.

carrier, căr´-i-eur, n entrepreneur de transports m; (on car, cycle, etc) porte-bagages m; **–-pigeon,** pigeon voyageur m.

carrion, căr´-ri-eune, n charogne f.

carrot, câr´-ŏtte, n carotte f.

carry, căr´-i, v porter; transporter.

cart, cârte, v transporter; fam trimbaler; n charette f; **–age,** camionnage m.

carton, căr´-t'n, n carton m; pot (of yoghurt) m; cartouche f.

cartoon, câr-toune´, n caricature f; dessin animé m.

cartridge, câr´-tridj, n cartouche f.

carve, cârve, v (wood) sculpter; (meat) découper.

carving, câr´-vinng, n sculpture f; découpage m.

cascade, căsse-quéde´, n cascade f.

case, quéce, n (box) caisse f; (cigarette etc) étui m; (jewel) écrin m; cas m; affaire f; **in –,** au cas où.

casement, quéce´-m'nt, n croisée f; fenêtre f.

cash, căche, n (argent liquide) m; v encaisser; **–-book,** n livre de caisse m; **–-box,** caisse f; **– card,** carte de retrait f; **– desk,** caisse f; **– dispenser,** distributeur automatique de billets m.

cashier, căche-îre´, n caissier m; caissière f.

cashmere, căche´-mîre, n cachemire m.

casino, ca-sî´-nau, n casino m.

cask, câsque, n tonneau m; baril m; fût m.

casket, câsse´-quette, n cassette f; écrin m.

casserole, câss´-a-rol, n cocotte (container) f; ragoût (en cocotte) (food) m; casserole m.

cassette, câss-ètte,´ n cassette f.; --**player**, lecteur de cassettes m.

cassock, câss´-ôque, n soutane f.

cast, câste, n (throw) coup m; (theatre) distribution des rôles f; (metal) moule m; v (throw) jeter; lancer; (metal) couler; --**iron**, n fonte f.

castanet, câsse´-ta-nette, n castagnette f.

caste, câste, n caste f.

castigate, câsse´-ti-guéte, v châtier.

castle, câ´-s'l, n château m.

castor, câsse´-tŏr, n (wheel) roulette f.

castor-oil, câsse´-tŏr-oa´ile, n huile de ricin f.

casual, căj´-iou-eul, a fortuit; indifférent; détaché.

casualty, căj´iou-eul-ti, n accidenté m; mil perte f.

cat, câtte, n chat m.

catalogue, căt´-a-logue, n catalogue m.

catarrh, ca-târre´, n catarrhe m.

catastrophe, ca-tăce´-trŏ-fi, n catastrophe f.

catch, cătche, n prise f; v attraper; --**ing**, a contagieux; --**up**, v rattraper.

category, căt´-i-gŏr-i, n catégorie f.

cater, qué´-teur, v approvisionner; --**er**, n traiteur m.

caterpillar, căt´-eur-pil-eur, n chenille f.

cathedral, ca-tsi´-dralle, n cathédrale f.

catholic, că´-tsŏ-lique, n & a, catholique m & f.

cattle, căt´-t'l, n bétail m.

cauldron, côl-t´-dronne, n chaudron m; chaudière f.

cauliflower, col´-i-flâ´ou-eur, n chou-fleur m.

caulk, côke, v calfater.

cause, côze, n cause f; v causer; occasionner.

caustic, côce´-tique, n & a caustique m.

cauterize, cô´-teur-âïze, v cautériser.

caution, cô´-ch'n, n prudence f; (warning) avis m; v avertir.

cautious, cô´-cheuce, a prudent.

cavalier, căv-a-lîre´, n cavalier m.

cavalry, căv´-al-ri, n cavalerie f.

cave, quéve, n caverne f; (animals') antre m.

cavil, căv´-il, v chicaner.

cavity, căv´-i-ti, n cavité f carie f.

CD, sî-dî, abbr CD m.

CD ROM, sî-dî-rome, abbr CD ROM m.

cease, sîce, v cesser; --**less**, a incessant.

ceasefire, sîce-fâïre, n cessez-le-feu m.

cedar, sî-deur, n cèdre m.

cede, sîde, v céder.

ceiling, sîl´-inng, n plafond m.

celebrate, sell´-i-bréte, v célébrer; --**d**, a célèbre.

celebration, sell-a-bré´-ch'n, n fête f.

celery, sell´-eur-i, n céleri m.

celestial, si-lesse´-ti-´l, a céleste.

celibacy, sell´-i-ba-ci, n célibat m.

cell, selle, n cellule f.

cellar, sell´-eur, n cave f.

celluloid, sell´-ioue-lo-ide, n celluloïde m.

cement, sé-mennte´, n ciment m; v cimenter.

cemetery, sém´-i-teur-i, n cimetière m.

cenotaph, senn´-ô-tăffe, n

cénotaphe m.

censor, senn´-seur, n censeur m; **–ship,** censure f.

censure, senn´-chioure, v censurer; n censure f.

census, senn´-ceusse, n recensement m.

cent, sennte, n sou m; centime m; **per –,** pour cent; **–enary,** a centenaire; **–ury,** n siècle m.

central, senn´-tr'l, a central; **–heating,** n chauffage central m; **–ize,** v centraliser.

centre, senn´-t'r, n centre m; v placer au centre.

cereal, sî´-rî-'l, n céréale f.

ceremonious*, sair-i-mau´-ni-euce, a cérémonieux.

ceremony, sair´-i-mau-ni, n cérémonie f.

certain*, seur´-t'n, a certain.

certificate, seur-tif´-i-quéte, n certificat m; acte m.

certify, seur´-ti-fâï, v certifier; (law) attester.

cessation, saiss-sé´-ch'n, n cessation f; suspension f.

cesspool, saiss´-poule, n fosse d'aisances f.

chafe, tchéfe, v irriter; écorcher.

chaff, tchâffe, v taquiner; n (husk) menue paille f.

chaffinch, tchâf´-finntche, n pinson m.

chain, tchéne, n chaîne f; **– up,** v enchaîner.

chair, tchaire, n chaise f; **– person,** président, m & f.

chalice, tchâl´-isse, n calice m.

chalk, tchôque, n craie f; **-y,** a crayeux.

challenge, tchâl´-inndje, v défier; n défi m.

chamber, tchéme´-b'r, n chambre f; **-lain,** chambellan m; **--pot,** pot de chambre m; **barrister's –s,** cabinet d'avocat m.

chambermaid, tchéme´-b'r-méde, n femme de chambre f.

chamois, chăme´oï, n chamois m.

champion, tchâme´-pi-eune, n champion m; v soutenir.

chance, tchânnce, n hasard m; (opportunity) occasion f; a fortuit; v risquer.

chancel, tchânn´-s'l, n sanctuaire m.

chancellor, tchânn´-seul-eur, n chancelier m.

chancery, tchânn´-ceu-ri,

n chancellerie f.

chandelier, chănn-di-lîre´, n lustre m.

change, tchéne-dje, v changer; n changement m; (cash) monnaie f; **–able,** a variable; **–less,** immuable.

changing room, tchéne-djinng-roumme, n cabine d'essayage (shop) f; vestiaire (sport) m.

channel, tchânn´-'l, n creuser; n canal m; voie f; (TV) chaîne f; **the English –,** La Manche f.

chant, tchânnte, v chanter; n chant m.

chaos, qué´-oce, n chaos m.

chap, tchăpe, (hands, lips, etc.) v gercer; n gercure f; (person) type m.

chapel, tchăp´-'l, n chapelle f.

chaperon, chăpe´-eur-aune, v chaperonner; n chaperon m.

chaplain, tchăp´-l'n, n aumônier m.

chapter, tchăp´-teur, n chapitre m.

char, tchâre, v carboniser; (clean) faire le ménage; **–woman,** n femme de ménage f.

character, căr´-ac-teur, n caractère m; genre m;

personnage m.

charcoal, tchâr´-caule, n
charbon de bois m; (art)
fusain m.

charge, tchârdje, n
attaque f; accusation f;
(load) chargement m;
(price) prix m; v
attaquer; accuser;
charger; (price)
demander; **to take –**, se
charger de.

chariot, tchâr´-i-otte, n
char m.

charitable, tchâr´-i-ta-b'l,
a charitable.

charity, tchâr´-i-ti, n
charité f.

charm, tchârme, v
charmer; n charme m.

charming, tchârm´-inng, a
charmant.

chart, tchârte, n carte f;
carte marine f;
graphique m; tableau m.

charter, tchâr´-teur, n
charte f; v (hire)
affréter.

chary, tché´-ri, a
circonspect; économe.

chase, tchéce, v chasser; n
chasse f.

chasm, căz'm, n abîme m.

chaste*, tchéste, a chaste;
–n, v châtier; purifier.

chastise, tchàss-tâïze´, v
châtier.

chat, tchătte, v bavarder.

n causerie f; **–ter**, caquet
m; v jaser; (teeth)
claquer; **–terbox**, n
moulin à paroles m.

chattel, tchătt´-'l, n
mobilier m; effets mpl.

chauffeur, chau´-feur, n
chauffeur m.

chauvinist, chau´-vi-
niste, n chauvin m & f.

cheap*, tchîpe, a & adv
bon marché; **–en**, v
baisser les prix;
discréditer (réputation);
–er, a meilleur marché;
–ness, n bon marché m;
médiocrité f.

cheat, tchîte, v tricher; n
tricheur m; tricheuse f.

cheating, tchîte´-inng, n
tricherie f.

check, tchèque, n
(restraint; chess) échec
m; (verification)
contrôle m; (pattern) à
carreaux mpl; v (stop)
arrêter; (repress)
réprimer; (verify)
vérifier; **–mate**, n échec
et mat m; v mater.

check in, tchèque-inne, n
enregistrement m.

check out, tchèque-
â-outte, n caisse f.

cheek, tchîque, n joue f;
fam toupet m.

cheer, tchîre, n gaieté f;
(applause) acclamation

f; v acclamer; (brighten)
égayer; **to –** (someone)
up, remonter le moral
(de quelqu'un); **–ful**, a
joyeux; gai; **–less**, triste;
sombre.

cheese, tchîze, n fromage
m.

chef, chèf, n chef m.

chemical, quèm´-i-k'l, a
chimique.

chemist, quèm´-isste, n
pharmacien,-ne m & f;
chimiste m; (shop)
pharmacie f; **–ry**, chimie
f.

cheque, tchèque, n
chèque m; **–book**,
carnet de chèques m; **–
card**, tchèque-cârde,
carte bancaire f.

chequered, tchèque´-
ourde, a varié,
mouvementé.

cherish, tchèr´-iche, v
chérir.

cherry, tchèr´-i, n cerise f;
–tree, cerisier m.

cherub, tchèr´-eub, n
chèrubin m.

chess, tchèss, n échecs
mpl.

chest, tchèste, n coffre m;
boîte f; (box) caisse f;
(human) poitrine f; **– of
drawers**, commode f.

chestnut, tchèste´-notte, n
marron m; châtaigne f;

(tree) châtaignier m; a châtain; **horse –,** n marron d'Inde m; (tree) marronnier m.

chew, tchiou, v mâcher.

chewing gum, tchiou-inng-gomme, n chewing-gum m.

chicken, tchik-enne, n poulet m; **–pox,** varicelle f.

chide, tchâïde, v réprimander.

chief, tchîfe, n chef m; fam patron m; a* principal.

chilblain, tchil-bléne, n engelure f.

child, tchâïlde, n enfant m & f; **–hood,** enfance f; **–ish,** a enfantin.

chill, tchill, n coup de froid m; v refroidir; réfrigérer.

chilly, tchil-i, a un peu froid; frais.

chime, tchâïme, v carillonner; n carillon m.

chimney, tchime-ni, n cheminée f.

chimney-sweep, tchime-ni-souîpe, n ramoneur m.

chin, tchine, n menton m.

china, tchâï-na, n porcelaine f.

chintz, tchine'tse, n perse f.

chip, tchipe, v tailler par éclats; ébrécher; n fragment m; éclat m; pomme frite f.

chiropodist, câï-rop-'-o-diste, n pédicure m.

chirp, tcheurpe, v gazouiller.

chisel, tchiz-'l, n ciseau m; v ciseler.

chivalrous, chiv-al-reusse, a courtois.

chives, tchâïvze, npl ciboulette f.

chloride, clau-râïde, n chlorure m.

chlorine, clau-rine, n chlore m.

chloroform, clau-ro-forme, n chloroforme m.

chocolate, tchok-ŏ-léte, n chocolat m.

choice, tchoa-ïce, n choix m; a choisi, surfin.

choir, couaï'r, n chœur m.

choke, tchauque, v étouffer; (block up) boucher; (car) n starter m.

cholera, col-eur-a, n choléra m.

cholesterol, cau-less-teur-'l, n cholestérol m.

choose, tchouze, v choisir; **choosy,** a fam difficile.

chop, tchoppe, n côtelette f; v hacher; **– off,** couper; **–per,** n hachoir

m.

choral, co-r'l, a choral.

chord, côrde, n mus accord m.

chorister, cor-iss-teur, n choriste m.

chorus, cô-reusse, n chœur m; refrain m.

Christ, craïsste, n le Christ.

christen, criss-'n, v baptiser; **–ing,** n baptême m.

Christian, criss-ti-'n, n & a chrétien m; chrétienne f.

Christianity, criss-ti-ann-i-ti, n christianisme m.

Christmas, criss-meusse, n Noël m; **– tree,** arbre de Noël m.

chronic, cronn-ique, a chronique.

chronicle, cronn-i-k'l, n chronique f.

chrysanthemum, cri-sanne-tsi-meumme, n chrysanthème m.

chuck, tcho-k, v jeter; lancer; flanquer.

chuckle, tcho-k'l, v rire tout bas; glousser; n gloussement m.

church, tcheurtche, n église f; **–yard,** cimetière m.

churlish, cheur-liche, a revêche; maussade.

churn, tcheurne, *n* baratter; *n* baratte *f.*

cider, sâï´-d'r, *n* cidre *m.*

cigar, si-gâre´, *n* cigare *m.*

cigarette, sig-a-rette´, *n* cigarette *f;* – **end,** *fam* mégot *m.*

cinder, sinn´-d'r, *n* cendre *f.*

cinema, si´-ni-ma, *n* cinéma *m.*

cinnamon, sin´-na-meune, *n* cannelle *f.*

cipher, sâï´-f'r, *v* chiffrer; *n* chiffre *m;* zéro *m.*

circle, seur´-k'l, *v* entourer; tourner autour de; *n* cercle *m.*

circuit, seur´-kitte, *n* circuit *m;* tournée *f.*

circuitous, seur-kiou´-i-teusse, *a* détourné.

circular, seur´-kiou-l'r, *n* & *a* circulaire *f.*

circulate, seur´-kiou-léte, *v* circuler; faire circuler.

circulation, seur-kiou-lé´-ch'n, *n* circulation *f;* (newspaper, etc) tirage *m.*

circumference, seur-komm´-feur-'nce, *n* circonférence *f.*

circumflex, seur´-keume-flèxe, *a* circonflexe.

circumscribe, seur´-keume-scrâïbe, *v* circonscrire.

circumspect, seur´-keume-specte, *a* circonspect.

circumstance, seur´-keume-stânnce, *n* circonstance *f.*

circumstantial, seur-keume-stânn´-ch'l, *a* circonstanciel; – **evidence,** *n* preuve indirecte *f.*

circus, seur´-keusse, *n* cirque *m;* (place) rondpoint *m.*

cistern, siss´-teurne, *n* citerne *f;* (lavatory) réservoir de chasse d'eau *m.*

cite, sâïte, *v* citer.

citizen, sit´-i-z'n, *n* citoyen *m;* –**ship,** nationalité *f.*

city, sit´-i, *n* cité *f;* grande ville.

civil, sïv´-il, *a* civil; –**ian,** *n* civil *m;* –**isation,** civilisation *f;* –**ity,** politesse *f,* civilité *f.*

claim, cléme, *n* réclamation *f;* (inheritance) droit *m;* demande de remboursement *f; v* réclamer; prétendre; –**ant,** *n* prétendant *m.*

clammy, clâ´-mi, *a* (hands) moite; (weather) humide.

clamour, clâmm´-eur, *v*

vociférer; *n* clameur *f.*

clamp, clâmmpe, *n* crampon *m; v* cramponner.

clan, clânne, *n* clan *m;* tribu *f; fam* clique *f.*

clandestine, clânne-desse´-tinne, *a* clandestin.

clang, clainng, *n* bruit métallique *m;* résonnement *m; v* retentir.

clap, clâppe, *v* applaudir; *n* (thunder) coup *m.*

clapping, clâpp´-inng, *n* applaudissement *m.*

claret, clâr´-ette, *n* vin rouge de Bordeaux *m.*

clarify, clâr´-i-fâï, *v* clarifier; éclaircir.

clarinet, clâr´-i-nette, *n* clarinette *f.*

clash, clâche, *n* choc *m;* conflit *m; v* (se) heurter; (of colours) jurer.

clasp, clâsspe, *v* étreindre. *n* étreinte *f;* (catch) fermoir *m.*

class, clâss, *n* classe *f;* (school) classe *f;* cours *m; v* classer.

classify, clâss´-i-fâï, *v* classifier.

clatter, clâtt´-eur, *n* fracas *m; v* retentir.

clause, cloaze, *n* clause *f;* (grammar) proposition *f.*

claw, cloa, *v* griffer; *n* griffe *f*; (bird of prey) serre *f*; (crab, etc) pince *f*.

clay, clé, *n* argile *f*; **–ey,** *a* argileux.

clean, clîne, *v* nettoyer; *a* propre; *adv* absolument; **–ing,** *n* nettoyage *m*; **–liness,** propreté *f*.

cleanse, clènnz, *v* purifier.

clear, clîre, *a* clair; net. *v* éclaircir; évacuer; dégager; (table) desservir; **–ness,** *n* clarté *f*.

clearance, clîr´-annce, *n* dégagement *m*; (customs) dédouanement *m*; (sale) liquidation *f*.

cleave, clîve, *v* fendre; (cling) s'attacher à.

cleft, clefte, *n* fente *f*.

clemency, clémm´-enn-ci, *n* clémence *f*.

clench, clentche, *v* serrer.

clergy, cleur´-dji, *n* clergé *m*; **–man,** pasteur *m*; prêtre *m*.

clerical, clé´-ri-k'l, *a* clérical; de bureau; **–error,** *n* erreur de plume *f*.

clerk, clărque, *n* employé *m*; (law) clerc *m*.

clever*, clèv´-eur, *a* habile; intelligent;

–ness, *n* habileté *f*.

click, clique, *n* déclic *m*.

client, clâï´-ennte, *n* client, -ente *m* & *f*; **–ele,** clientèle *f*.

cliff, cliffe, *n* falaise *f*.

climate, clâï´-méte, *n* climat *m*.

climax, clâï´-măxe, *n* comble *m*; point culminant *m*.

climb, clâïmme, *v* monter; grimper; (mountain, etc) gravir.

clinch, *v* conclure.

cling, clinng, *v* se cramponner; adhérer.

clinic, clinn´-ik, *n* centre médical *m*; (private) clinique *f*; **–al,** *a* clinique.

clink, clinnque, *v* tinter; (glasses) trinquer.

clinker, clinng´-keur, *n* mâchefer *m*.

clip, clippe, *v* (cut) tondre; couper; agrafer.

cloak, clauque, *n* manteau *m*; cape *f*; *v fig* voiler; **–room,** vestiaire *m*; (station) consigne *f*.

clock, cloque, *n* horloge *f*; pendule *f*; **–maker,** horloger *m*; **–work,** mouvement d'horlogerie *m*.

clod, clodde, *n* motte de terre *f*.

clog, clogue, *n* entrave *f*; (shoe) sabot *m*; *v* obstruer.

cloister, cloa´ïss´-t'r, *n* cloître *m*.

close, clauze, *n* fin *f*. *v* fermer; terminer; *a* (weather) lourd. *adv* (near) près de.

closet, cloz´-ette, *n* cabinet *m*; placard *m*.

closure, clau´-jeure, *n* fermeture *f*; résolution *f*.

clot, clotte, *v* cailler; *n* caillot *m*.

cloth, clots, *n* drap *m*; tissu *m*; **table– –,** nappe *f*.

clothe, claudz, *v* habiller; vêtir.

clothes, claudz-z, *npl* vêtements *mpl*; **–brush,** borsse à habits *f*.

clothing, claudz´-innng, *n* vêtements *mpl*.

cloud, clâ´oude, *n* nuage *m*; *v* obscurcir; **–y,** *a* nuageux.

clout, clâ´oute, *n* claque *f*; gifle *f*; influence *f*.

clove, clauve, *n* clou de girofle *m*.

clover, clauv´-'r, *n* trèfle *m*; **to be in –,** être comme coq en pâte.

clown, clâ´oune, *n* clown *m*.

club, clobbe, *n* club *m*; (cards) trèfle *m*; (stick)

massue f; **golf** –, club m;
–foot, pied bot m.
cluck, cloque, v glousser; n
gloussement m.
clue, clioue, n indice m.
clump, clommpe, n (trees)
bosquet m; (flowers)
massif m; touffe f.
clumsiness, clomme´-zi-
nesse, n maladresse f.
clumsy, clomme´-zi, a
maladroit; gauche.
cluster, closs´-teur, n
groupe m; (fruit) grappe
f; (trees) bosquet m; v se
grouper.
clutch, clotche, n griffe f;
(motor) embrayage m; v
saisir.
coach, cautche, n (motor)
car m; (rail) wagon m;
(tutor) répétiteur m; v
donner des leçons
particulières; (sport)
entraîner.
coagulate, cau-âgue´-ioue-
léte, v coaguler.
coal, caule, n houille f;
charbon de terre m; –
cellar, cave à charbon f; –
mine, mine f; **–man,**
charbonnier m.
coalition, cau-ă-li´-ch'n, n
coalition f.
coarse*, causse, a grossier,
gros; **–ness,** n grossièreté
f; rudesse f.
coast, causste, n côte f;

littoral m; v côtoyer.
coast-guard, causste´-
gârde, n garde-côte m.
coat, caute, n manteau m;
pardessus m; (animal)
manteau m; pelage m;
(paint) couche f.
coax, cauxe, v enjôler;
encourager.
cob, cobbe, n (corn) épi
de maïs m; (horse) cob
m; bidet; (swan) cygne
mâle m; (nut) noisette f.
cobbler, cob´-bleur, n
cordonnier m.
cobweb, cob´-ouèbbe, n
toile d'araignée f.
cocaine, cau´-kéne, n
cocaïne f.
cochineal, cotch´-i-nîl, n
cochenille f.
cock, coque, n (bird) coq
m; (gun) chien m; (turn
valve) robinet m; **–ade,**
cocarde f; **–erel,** cochet
m; **–roach,** blatte f,
cafard m.
cockle, coque´-'l, n coque
f.
cocoa, cau´-cau, n cacao
m.
coconut, cau´-cau-notte, n
noix de coco f.
cocoon, co-coune´, n
cocon m.
cod, codde, n morue f;
–liver oil, huile de foie
de morue f.

coddle, cod´-d'l, v choyer;
dorloter.
code, caude, n code m.
codicil, codd´-i-sile, n
codicille m.
co-education, cau-èd-iou-
ké´-ch'n, n coéducation
f; enseignement mixte
m.
coerce, cau-eurce´, v
contraindre.
coffee, cof´-i, n café m; **–-
pot,** cafetière f.
coffer, cof´-eur, n coffre m,
caisse f.
coffin, cof´-inne, n
cercueil m.
cog, cogue, n dent de roue
f; **–wheel,** roue dentée
f.
coherent*, cau-hî´-r'nt, a
cohérent.
cohesion, cau-hî´-j'n, n
cohésion f.
coil, coa'ile, n rouleau m;
(electric) bobine f; v enrouler; (reptile)
s'enrouler.
coin, coa'inne, n pièce de
monnaie f.
coincide, cau-inn-çâïde´,
v coïncider.
coincidence, cau-inn´-si-
d'ns, n coïncidence f.
coke, cauque, n coke m.
cold, caulde, n froid m;
med rhume m; a* froid.
colic, col´-ique, n colique

f.

collaborate, cŏl-la´-bo-
réte, *v* collaborer.

collapse, cŏl-lăpse´, *v*
s'affaisser; *n*
effondrement *m.*

collar, col´-eur, *n* col *m;*
(dog) collier *m;* **--bone,**
clavicule *f.*

collate, col-léte´, *v*
collationner; assembler.

colleague, col´-ligue, *n*
collègue *f.*

collect, cŏl-lècte´, *v*
rassembler; (stamps, etc)
collectionner; (money)
encaisser; (charity)
quêter; **–ion,** *n*
collection *f;* (charity)
quête *f;* (postal) levée *f;*
–ive*, *a* collectif; **–or,** *n*
collectionneur *m;* (tax)
percepteur *m.*

college, col´-idj, *n* collège
m; école *f.*

collide, cŏl-lâïde´, *v* se
heurter; se tamponner.

collier, col´-i-eur, *n*
mineur *m;* **–y,** houillère
f.

collision, cŏl-li-j'n, *n*
collision *f;* rencontre *f;*
(railway)
tamponnement *m;*
(ships) abordage *m.*

colloquial*, cŏl-lau´-coui-
al, *a* familier.

collusion, cŏl-lioue´-j'n, *n*
collusion *f.*

colon, cau-´l'n, *n* deux
points *mpl; anat* côlon
m.

colonel, queur´-n'l, *n*
colonel *m.*

colonist, col´-ŏnn-iste, *n*
colon *m.*

colonnade, col-ŏnn-éde´,
n colonnade *f.*

colony, col´-ŏ-ni, *n*
colonie *f.*

colossal, cau-loss´-'l, *a*
colossal.

colour, col´-eur, *n* couleur
f; v colorier.

colouring, col´-eur-inng, *n*
coloris *m;* teint *m.*

colt, caulte, *n* poulain *m.*

column, col´-eume, *n*
colonne *f.*

coma, cau´-mă, *n med*
coma *m.*

comb, caume, *n* peigne *m;*
(bird) crête *f; v* peigner.

combat, comm´-batte, *n*
combat *m; v* combattre;
–ant, *n* combattant *m;*
–ive, *a* batailleur.

combination, comm-bi-
né´-ch'n, *n* combinaison
f.

combine, cŏmm-bâïne´, *v*
combiner.

combustion, cŏmm´-
bosse´-tch'n, *n*
combustion *f.*

come, comme, *v* venir;

arriver; **– down,**
descendre; **–in,** entrer; **–
off,** se détacher; **– out,**
sortir; **– up,** monter.

comedian, cŏ-mi´-di-
anne, *n* comédien *m.*

comedy, comm´-i-di, *n*
comédie *f.*

comet, comm´-ette, *n*
comète *f.*

comfort, comm´-feurte, *n*
confort *m;* consolation *f;*
(relief) soulagement *m;*
v consoler.

comfortable, comm´-feur-
ta-b'l, *a* confortable.

comic, comm´-ique, *a*
comique.

coming, comm´-inng, *a*
proche; futur; *n* venue *f.*

comma, comm´-ma, *n*
virgule *f.*

command, cŏmm-ânnde´,
v commander; domine;.
n ordre *m;* (knowledge)
facilité *f;* **–er,**
commandant *m;*
–ment(s),
commandement(s) *m*
(*pl*).

commence, cŏmm-ennce´,
v commencer; **–ment,** *n*
commencement *m.*

commend, cŏmm-ennde´,
v recommander; (praise)
louer; **–ation,** *n* éloge *m;*
louange *f.*

comment, comm´-ennte,

n commentaire *m*;
observation *f*; *v*
commenter;
commentary, *n*
commentaire *m*.

commerce, comm´-*eurce,*
n commerce *m*.

commercial, cŏmm-*eur*-
ch'l, *a* commercial.

commiserate, cŏmm-iz´-
eur-éte, *v* plaindre.

commission, cŏmm-ich´-
'n, *v* charger de; *n*
commission *f*; *mil* brevet
m.

commit, cŏmm-itte´, *v*
commettre; envoyer en
prison; (bind) engager.

commitment, cŏmm-it´-
m'nt *n* engagement *m*;
responsabilité *f*.

committee, cŏmm-it´-ti, *n*
comité *m*.

commodious, cŏmm-aud´-
i-*euce,* *a* spacieux.

commodity, cŏmm-od´-i-
ti, *n* produit *m*;
marchandise *f*.

common, comm´-'n, *a*
commun; ordinaire;
–place, banal.

Commons, comm´-*eunze,*
npl (House of –)
Chambre des
Communes *f*.

commotion, cŏmm-au´-
ch'n, *n* commotion *f*.

commune, cŏmm-ioune´,
n commune *f*; *v*
converser.

communicate, cŏmm-
ioue´-ni-quéte, *v*
communiquer.

communication, cŏmm-
ioue´-ni-qué´-ch'n, *n*
communication *f*.

Communion, cŏmm-
ioue´-ni*eu*ne, *n*
communion *f*.

communism, cŏmm´-
ioue-niz'm, *n*
communisme *m*.

communist, cŏmm´-ioue-
nisste, *a* & *n*
communiste *mf*.

community, cŏmm-ioue´-
ni-ti, *n* communauté *f*.

commute, cŏmm-mioute´,
v faire la navette; *jur*
commuer.

compact, comm´-păcte, *n*
pacte *m*; (powder)
poudrier *m*. *a* compact.

compact disc, comm´-
păcte-disque, *n* disque
compact *m*.

companion, cŏmm-pănn´-
i*eu*ne, *n* compagnon *m*;
–ship, *n* camaraderie *f*.

company, cŏmm´-pa-ni, *n*
compagnie *f*.

comparative*, cŏmm-
păr´-a-tive, *a*
comparatif.

compare, cŏmm-père´, *v*
comparer.

comparison, cŏmm-păr´-i-
s'n, *n* comparaison *f*.

compartment, cŏmm-
parte´-m'nt, *n*
compartiment *m*; case *f*.

compass, comm´-passe, *n*
(magnetic) boussole *f*;
(a pair of) **–es,** *pl*
compas *m*.

compassionate, cŏmm-
păch´-*eu*ne-éte, *a*
compatissant.

compatible, cŏmm-pă´-ti-
b'l, *a* compatible.

compel, cŏmm-pel´, *v*
contraindre; forcer.

compensate, comm´-
penn-séte, *v* compenser.

compensation, cŏmm-
penn-sé´-ch'n, *n*
compensation *f*.

compete, cŏmm-pîte´, *v*
concourir.

competence, comm´-pi-
t'nce, *n* compétence *f*.

competent*, comm´-pi-
t'nt, *a* capable;
compétent.

competition, cŏmm-pi-ti´-
ch'n, *n com* concurrence
f; (games, sport)
concours *m*.

competitive, cŏmm-pè´-ti-
tive, *a* (prices)
concurrentiel;
compétitif ;
(examination) concours
m.

competitor, cŏmm-pett´-i-teur, n com concurrent m; (sport, etc) compétiteur m.

compile, cŏmm-pâîle´, v compiler; composer.

complacent, cŏmm-plé´-cennte, a content de soi-même.

complain, cŏmm-pléne´, v se plaindre.

complaint, cŏmm-plénnte´, n plainte f; maladie f.

complement, comm´-plî-m'nt, n effectif m; complément.

complete, cŏmm-plîte´, v achever; a* complet.

completion, cŏmm-plîch'n, n achèvement m.

complex, comm´-plexe, a compliqué; complexe; n complexe m.

complexion, cŏmm-plèque´-ch'n, n (face) teint m.

compliance, cŏmm-plâï´-'nt, n conformité f.

compliant, cŏmm-plâï´-'nt, a complaisant.

complicate, comm´-pli-quéte, v compliquer.

compliment, comm´-pli-m'nt, n compliment m; v faire des compliments; **-s**, npl compliments mpl.

comply, cŏmm-plâï´, v –

with, se conformer à.

component, cŏmm-pau´-n'nt, n composant m.

compose, cŏmm-pauze´, v composer; clamer.

composer, cŏmm-pau´-zeur, n compositeur m.

composition, cŏmm-pau-si´-ch'n, n composition f.

compositor, cŏmm-po´-zi-t'r, n compositeur m.

composure, cŏmm-pau-jeure, n calme m.

compound, comm´-pâ'ounnde, v composer; n espace clos m; a composé; – **interest**, intérêt composé m.

comprehend, cŏmm-pri-hennde´, v comprendre.

comprehension, cŏmm-pri-henn´-ch'n, n compréhension f.

compress, cŏmm-presse´, v comprimer; n compresse f.

comprise, cŏmm-prâïze´, v contenir; comprendre.

compromise, comm´-prŏ-mâîze, n compromis m; v compromettre.

compulsion, cŏmm-pol´-ch'n, n contrainte f.

compulsive, cŏmm-pol´-cive, a psych compulsif ; (liar, smoker, etc) invétéré .

compulsory, cŏmm-pol´-sŏr-i, a obligatoire.

compunction, cŏmm-ponnk´-ch'n, n remords m.

computation comm-piou-té-ch'n, n calcul m, computation f.

compute, cŏmm-pioute´, v estimer; calculer.

computer, cŏmm-piou-´t'r, n ordinateur m.

computer game, cŏmm-piou-t'r-guème, n jeu électronique m.

comrade, comm´-réde, n camarade m & f; compagnon m.

concave, conn´-quéve, a concave.

conceal, cŏnn-cîle´, v cacher.

concede, cŏnn-cîde´, v concéder.

conceit, cŏnn-cîte´, n vanité f; **-ed**, a prétentieux.

conceive, cŏnn-cîve´, v concevoir; (s') imaginer.

concentrate, conn´-seune-tréte, v concentrer.

concept, conn´-septte, n concept m.

conception, cŏnn-seppe´-ch'n, n conception f.

concern, cŏnn-seurne´, n affaire f; (disquiet) souci m; v concerner; **to be**

–ed, s'inquiéter.

concert, cŏnn´-*seurte,* n concert m.

concession, cŏnn-sèch´-eune, n concession f.

conciliate, cŏnn-cil´-i-éte, v concilier.

concise, cŏnn-sâïce´, a concis.

conclude, cŏnn-cloude´, v conclure.

conclusion, cŏnn-cloue-j´n, n conclusion f.

conclusive, cŏnn-cloue´-cive, a concluant.

concoct, cŏnn-cocte´, v élaborer; préparer; combiner.

concord, cŏnn´-côrde, n concorde f; accord m.

concrete, cŏnn´-crîte, n béton m; a concret.

concur, cŏnn-queur´, v concourir; être d'accord.

concussion, cŏnn-coch´-n, n choc m; *med* commotion f.

condemn, cŏnn-demme´, v condamner.

condense, cŏnn-dennce´, v condenser.

condescend, cŏnn-di-cennde´, v condescendre.

condescension, cŏnn-di-cenn´-ch'n, n condescendance f.

condition, cŏnn-di-´-ch'n,

n condition f.

conditional*, cŏnn-dich´-eun-´l, a conditionnel.

condole, cŏnn-daule´, v exprimer ses condoléances.

condolence, cŏnn-daul´-'ns, n condoléance f.

condom, cŏnn´-d'm, n préservatif m.

condone, cŏnn-daune´, v pardonner; fermer les yeux.

conducive, cŏnn-dioue´-cive, a contribuant à.

conduct, cŏnn-docte´, v conduire; *mus* diriger; n conduite f.

conductor, cŏnn-doct´-'r, n conducteur m; chef d'orchestre m.

cone, caune, n cône m; (ice cream) cornet m.

confectioner, cŏnn-féque´-cheunn-eur, n confiseur m; (shop) confiserie f; –y, bonbons mpl, confiserie f.

confederate, cŏnn-féd´-eur-éte, n & a confédéré m; complice m.

confederation, cŏnn-féd´-eur-é-´ch'n, n confédération f.

confer, cŏnn-feur´, v conférer; accorder.

conference, cŏnn´-feur-ennce, n conférence f;

congrès m.

confess, cŏnn-fesse´, v avouer; *eccl* confesser.

confession, cŏnn-fé-´ch'n, n aveu m; *eccl* confession f.

confide, cŏnn-fâïde´, v confier; se confier à.

confidence, cŏnn´-fi-d'ns, n confiance f; (faith) confiance f.

confident, cŏnn´-fi-dennte, a confiant; assuré.

confidential*, cŏnn-fi-denn´-ch'l, a confidentiel.

confine, cŏnn-fâïne´, v limiter; enfermer; –ment, n emprisonnement m; (birth) accouchement m; (lying-in) couches fpl.

confirm, cŏnn-feurme´, v confirmer.

confirmation, cŏnn-feur-mé-´ch'n, n confirmation f.

confiscate, cŏnn´-fisse-quéte, v confisquer.

conflagration, cŏnn-fla-gré-´ch'n, n incendie m; conflagration f.

conflict, cŏnn´-flicte, n conflit m; (combat) lutte f; v être en conflit.

conflicting, cŏnn-flique´-

tinng, *a* contradictorie.

conform, cŏnn-foarme´, *v*
se conformer.

confound, cŏnn-
fâ'ounnde´, *v* confondre.

confront, cŏnn-fronnte´, *v*
confronter; affronter.

confuse, cŏnn-fiouze´, *v*
déconcerter;
embrouiller.

confusion, cŏnn-fioue´-
j'n, *n* confusion *f*.

congeal, cŏnn-djîle´, *v*
congeler; se congeler.

congenial, cŏnn-djî´-ni-al,
a sympathique.

congenital, cŏnn-djenn´-
i-t'l, *a med* congénital.

congest, cŏnn-djeste´, *v*
entasser; congestionner;
–ion, *n* (traffic)
embouteillage *m*; *med*
congestion *f*.

congratulate, cŏnn-grăt´-
iou-léte, *v* féliciter.

congratulation, cŏnn-
grăt-iou-lé´-ch'n, *n*
félicitation.

congregate, conng´-gri-
guéte, *v* se rassembler.

congregation, cŏnng-gri-
gué´-ch'n, *n* assemblée *f*.

congress, conng´-gresse, *n*
congrès *m*.

conjecture, cŏnn-djéque´-
tioure, *n* conjecture *f*; *v*
conjecturer.

conjugal, cŏnn-djoue-g'l,

a conjugal.

conjunction, cŏnn-
djonngk´-ch'n, *n*
conjonction *f*.

conjurer, conn´-djeur-eur,
n prestidigitateur *m*.

connect, cŏnn-necte´, *v*
unir; relier à.

connection, cŏnn-nec´-
ch'n, *n* rapport *m*; lien
m; (train, etc)
correspondance *f*.

connoisseur, cŏnn-oss-
eur´, *n* connaisseur *m*.

conquer, conng´-queur, *v*
conquérir; vaincre.

conqueror, conng´-queur-
eur, *n* conquérant *m*.

conquest, conng´-coueste,
n conquête *f*.

conscience, conn´-
chennce, *n* conscience *f*.

conscientious*, cŏnn-
chienn´-cheuce, *a*
consciencieux.

conscious, conn´-cheuce,
a conscient; **–ness,** *n*
conscience *f*; *med*
connaissance *f*.

conscript, conn´-scripte, *n*
conscrit *m*.

consecrate, conn´-ci-
créte, *v* consacrer; bénir.

consecutive*, cŏnn-sèk´-
iou-tive, *a* consécutif.

consent, cŏnn-cennte´, *v*
consentir; *n*
consentement *m*.

consequence, conn´-ci-
couènnce, *n*
conséquence *f*.

consequently, conn´-ci-
couènn-tli, *adv* par
conséquent.

conservative, cŏnn-seur´-
va-tive, *n* & *a*
conservateur, -trice *m* &
f.

conservatory, cŏnn-seur´-
va-teur-i, *n* serre *f*.

conserve, cŏnn-seurve´, *v*
conserver.

consider, cŏnn-cid´-eur, *v*
considérer; **–able,** *a*
considérable; **–ate,**
attentionné, **–ation,** *n*
considération *f*; **–ing,**
prep vu; étant donné.

consign, cŏnn-sâïne´, *v*
livrer; consigner; **–ee,** *n*
destinataire *m*; **–ment,**
envoi *m*; **–or,** expéditeur
m.

consist, cŏnn-cisste´, *v*
consister; **–ency,** *n*
consistance *f*; **–ent,** *a*
compatible; conforme;
logique.

consolation, cŏnn-saule-
é´-ch'n, *n* consolation *f*.

console, cŏnn-saule´, *v*
consoler.

consonant, conn´-so-
nennte, *n* consonne *f*.

conspicuous, cŏnn-spik´-
iou-*euce*, *a* apparent; en

évidence; **to make oneself –**, se faire remarquer.

conspiracy, cŏnn-spir´-*a*-ci, n complot m.

conspirator, cŏnn-spir´-é-*teur*, n conspirateur m.

conspire, cŏnn-spâire´, v conspirer.

constable, conn´-sta-b'l, n agent de police m.

constabulary, cŏnn-stăb´-iou-*la*-ri, n gendarmerie f; police f.

constancy, conn´-stann-ci, n constance f.

constant, conn´-stannte, a constant; continuel.

constipated, conn´-sti-pé-t'd, a constipé.

constipation, cŏnn-sti-pé´-ch'n, n constipation f.

constituency, cŏnn-sti´-tiou-enn-ci, n circonscription électorale f.

constituent, cŏnn-sti´-tiou-'nt, n électeur m.

constitute, conn´-sti-tioute, v constituer.

constitution, cŏnn-sti-tiou´-ch'n, n constitution f.

constrain, cŏnn-stréne´, v contraindre.

constraint, cŏnn-strénnte´, n contrainte f.

constriction, cŏnn-stric´-ch'n, n rétrécissement m; resserrement m.

construct, cŏnn-strocte´, v construire.

construction, cŏnn-stroc´-ch'n, n construction f.

construe, conn´-stroue, v construire; interpréter.

consul, conn´-seul, n consul m; **–ate**, consulat m.

consult, cŏnn-solte´, v consulter; **–ation**, n consultation f.

consume, cŏnn-sioume´, v consumer; (food) consommer.

consumer, cŏnn-sioue´-*meur*, n consommateur m.

consummate, conn´-somm-éte, v consommer.

consummation, cŏnn-somm-mé´-ch'n, n consommation f; accomplissement m.

consumption, cŏnn-sommp´-ch'n, n (use) consommation f; *med* comsomption pulmonaire f.

consumptive, cŏnn-sommp´-tive, a & n tuberculeux.

contact, conn´-tăcte, n contact m; **– lens**, lentilles (de contact) fpl.

contagious, cŏnn-té´-djeuce, a contagieux.

contain, cŏnn-téne´, v contenir; retenir.

contaminate, cŏnn-tămm´-i-néte, v contaminer.

contemplate, cŏnn´-temm-pléte, v contempler.

contemporary, cŏnn-temm´-pŏ-*ra*-ri, n & a contemporain, -aine.

contempt, cŏnn-temmp´-'t, n mépris m.

contemptible, cŏnn-temmp´-ti-b'l, a méprisable.

contend, cŏnn-tennde´, v contester; (maintain) soutenir.

content, cŏnn-tennte´, v contenter; a satisfait; **–ment**, n contentement m.

content, cŏnn´-tennte, n contenu m.

contention, cŏnn-tenn´-ch'n, n prétention f.

contentious, cŏnn-tenn´-cheuce, a discutable.

contents, conn´-tenn-ts, npl contenu m.

contest, cŏnn-tesste´, v contester; concours m; match m.

contiguous, cŏnn-tigue´-iou-*euce*, a contigu.

continent, cŏnn´-ti-
nennte, n continent m.

contingency, cŏnn-tinn´-
djenn-ci, n éventualité f.

contingent, cŏnn-tinn´-
djennte, a éventuel.

continual*, cŏnn-tinn´-
iou'l, a continuel.

continuation, cŏnn-tinn´-
iou-é´-ch'n, n
continuation f.

continue, cŏnn-tinn´-
ioue, v continuer.

continuous*, cŏnn-tinn´-
iou-euce, a continu.

contortion, cŏnn-toar´-
ch'n, n contorsion f.

contraband, cŏnn´-tra-
bănnde, n contrebande
f.

contraceptive, cŏnn-tra-
sepp´-tive, a
contraceptif
anticonceptionnel; n
contraceptif m.

contract, cŏnn´-trăcte, n
contrat m; v contracter;
–ion, n contraction f;
–or, fournisseur m;
(builder) entrepreneur
m.

contradict, cŏnn-tra-
dicte´, v contredire;
–ion, n contradiction f.

contrary, cŏnn´-tra-ri, n
& a contraire m.

contrast, cŏnn´-traste, n
contraste m.

contrast, cŏnn-traste´, v
contraster.

contravene, cŏnn-tra-
vîne´, v enfreindre.

contravention, cŏnn-tra-
venn´-ch'n, n
contravention f.

contribute, cŏnn-trib´-
ioute, v contribuer.

contribution, cŏnn-trib-
iou´-ch'n, n
contribution f; (literary)
article m.

contrite, cŏnn´-trăïte, a
contrit.

contrivance, cŏnn-trăï´-
v'nce, n invention f;
dispositif m; fam
manigance f.

contrive, cŏnn-trăïve´, v
inventer; trouver
moyen; fam machiner.

control, cŏnn-traule´, v
contrôler; (feelings) (se)
maîtriser; n contrôle m;
(feelings) maîtrise f;
(authority) direction f;
–ler, contrôleur m.

controversial, cŏnn-trŏ-
veur´-ch'l, a
controversable.

controversy, cŏnn´-trŏ-
veur-ci, n controverse f.

convalescent, cŏnn-va-
less´-'nt, a & n
convalescent.

convenience, cŏnn-vî´-
ennce, n convenance f.

convenient, cŏnn-vî´-ni-
ennte, a commode.

convent, cŏnn´-vennte, n
couvent m.

convention, cŏnn-venn´-
ch'n, n convention f.

converge, cŏnn-veurdje´,
v converger.

conversant, conn-veur´-
s'nt, a au courant de.

conversation, cŏnn-veur-
cé´-ch'n, n conversation
f.

converse, cŏnn-veurse´, v
s'entretenir.

conversion, cŏnn-veur´-
ch'n, n conversion f.

convert, cŏnn-veurte´, v
convertir; n converti m.

convex, cŏnn´-vexe, a
convexe.

convey, cŏnn-vé´, v
transporter; transmettre;
présenter; –ance, n
transport m; (law)
transfert m.

convict, cŏnn-victe´, v
condamner; –ion, n
condamnation f; (belief)
conviction f.

convict, cŏnn´-victe, n
forçat m; bagnard m.

convince, cŏnn-vinnce´, v
convaincre.

convivial, cŏnn-viv´-ial, a
jovial; sociable.

convoy, cŏnn-voa'i´, v
convoyer; escorter; n

convoi *m*.

convulse, cŏnn-vol´, *v* convulser.

convulsion, cŏnn-vol´-ch'n, *n* convulsion *f*.

coo, cou, *v* roucouler.

cook, couk, *v* faire cuire; faire la cuisine; cuire; *n* cuisinier, -ère *m* & *f*.

cooker, couk´-eur, *n* cuisinière *f*.

cookery, couk´-eur-i, *n* cuisine *f*.

cool, coule, *v* refroidir; *a* frais; froid; **–ness**, *n* fraîcheur *f*; (nerve) sang froid *m*.

coop, coupe, *n* cage à poulets *f*.

co-operate, cau-op´-eur-éte, *v* coopérer.

cope, caupe, *v* – **with**, se débrouiller de.

copious*, cau´-pi-euce, *a* copieux.

copper, cop´-eur, *n* cuivre *m*; *a* de cuivre.

coppice, copse, cop´-ice, copce, *n* taillis *m*.

copy, cop´-i, *v* copier; *n* copie *f*; (of book) exemplaire *m*; (newspaper, etc) numéro *m*; **–right**, droits d'auteur *m*.

coquetry, coque´-éte-ri, *n* coquetterie *f*.

coral, cor´-al, *n* corail *m*.

cord, côrde, *v* corder; *n* corde *f*.

cordial, côr´-di-al, *a* cordial.

corduroy, coar´-diou-roa'ï, *n* velours côtelé *m*.

core, caure, *n* cœur *m*; trognon *m*.

cork, corque, *v* boucher; *n* liège *m*; (stopper) bouchon *m*; **–screw**, tire-bouchon *m*.

corn, côrne, *n* blé *m*; (foot, etc) cor *m*.

corner, côr´-n'r, *n* coin *m*; (road bend) tournant *m*; virage *m*.

cornflower, côrne´-flâ'ou-eur, *n* bluet *m*.

cornice, cor´-nice, *n* corniche *f*.

coronary, cor´-ŏ-neu-ri, *n* infactus *m* (du myocarde); thrombose coronarienne *f*.

coronation, cor-ŏ-né´-ch'n, *n* couronnement *m*.

coroner, cor´-o-neur, *n* magistrat enquêteur *m*.

coronet, cor´-o-nette, *n* couronne *f*.

corporal, coar´-pŏ-r'l, *n* caporal *m*; (artillery and cavalry) brigadier *m*; *a* corporel.

corporation, coar´-pŏ-ré´-ch'n, *n* corporation *f*.

corps, core, *n* corps *m*.

corpse, coarpse, *n* cadavre *m*.

corpulence, cor´-piou-lenn-ce, *n* corpulence *f*.

corpulent, cor´-piou-l'nt, *a* corpulent.

corpuscle, cor´-peuss-'l, *n* corpuscule *m*.

correct*, cŏr-recte´, *a* correct. *v* corriger; **–ive**, *a* correctif; **–ness**, *n* exactitude *f*.

correspond, cŏr-i-sponnde´, *v* correspondre; **–ence**, *n* correspondance *f*.

corridor, cŏr´-i-doar, *n* corridor *m*; couloir *m*.

corroborate, cŏr-rŏb´-ŏ-réte, *v* corroborer.

corroboration, cŏr-rŏb-ŏ-ré´-ch'n, *n* corroboration *f*.

corrode, cŏr-raude´, *v* corroder.

corrosive, cŏr-rau´-sive, *n* & *a* corrosif *m*.

corrugated, cor´-rou-gué-tedde, **– paper**, *n* papier ondulé *m*; **– iron**, tôle ondulée *f*.

corrupt, cŏr-ropte´, *v* corrompre. *a* corrompu.

corruption, cŏr-rope´-ch'n, *n* corruption *f*.

corset, cor´-cette, *n* corset *m*.

cortege, cŏr-téjé´, n
cortège m.

cost, coste, n prix m;
(expense) frais mpl; v
coûter; **–ly**, a coûteux;
–s, npl jur dépens mpl.

cost-of-living, cosse-teuv-
liv-inng, n coût de la vie
m.

costume, cosse´-tioume, n
costume m.

cosy, cauz´-i, a
confortable; à l'aise.

cot, cotte, n lit d'enfant
m.

cottage, cot´-idj, n
(thatched) chaumière f;
cottage m.

cotton, cot´-t'n, n coton
m; **–-wool**, ouate f; med
coton hydrophile m.

couch, câ'outche, n
canapé m; divan m.

cough, coaf, v tousser; n
toux f.

council, câ'ounn´-cil, n
conseil m; **–lor**,
conseiller m.

counsel, câ'ounn-s'l, n
avocat conseil m; v
conseiller; **–lor**, n
conseiller m; (law)
conseil m.

count, câ'ounnte, v
compter. n compte m;
–ing house, la
comptabilité f; **–less**, a
innombrable.

count, câ'ounnte, n (title)
comte m; **–ess**,
comtesse f.

countenance, câ'ounn´-
teu-nannce, v
approuver; n
contenance f.

counter, câ'ounn´-teur, n
comptoir m; (games)
jeton m; adv contre;
–act, v contrarier;
neutraliser; (frustrate)
déjouer; **–balance**,
contrebalancer; **–feit**, v
contrefaire; a faux; n
faux m; **–foil**, talon m;
–mand, v contremander;
n contre-ordre m;
–pane, couvre-lit m;
–part, contre-partie f;
–sign, v contresigner; n
mot d'ordre m.

country, conn´-tri, n
(state) pays m; (rural)
campagne f.

county, câ'ounn´-ti, n
comté m.

couple, cop´-p'l, v
accoupler; n couple m.

courage, cor´-idj, n
courage m.

courageous*, keur-é´-
djeuce, a courageux.

courgette, core´-jette, n
courgette f.

courier, cour´-ri-eur, n
messager m.

course, corse, n (river,

tuition) cours m;
(direction) route f;
(race) champ de courses
m; (meals) plat m; **of –**,
adv naturellement.

court, côrte, n (royal)
cour f; (law) tribunal m;
(tennis) court m; v faire
la cour à; **–ier**, n
courtisan m; **– martial**,
conseil de guerre m;
–ship, cour f; **–yard**,
cour f.

courteous*, keur´-ti-euce,
a courtois.

courtesy, keur´-ti-ci, n
courtoisie f.

cousin, co´-z'n, n cousin
m; cousine f.

cove, cauve, n geog anse f;
petite baie f.

covenant, cov´-nannte, n
pacte m; contrat m. v
stipuler.

cover, cov´-eur, n
couverture f; (lid)
couvercle m; (shelter)
abri m; v couvrir; n **–
up**, tentative pour
étouffer une affaire f.

covet, cov´-ette, v
convoiter.

cow, câ'ou, n vache f. v
intimider: **–slip**, n
coucou m.

cowboy, câ'ou´-boa'ï, n
cow-boy m.

coward, câ'ou´-eurde, n

lâche *m* & *f*; **–ice,**
lâcheté *f*.

cower, câ'ou´-*eur*, *v* se
tapir.

cowl, câ'oule, *n* (hood,
chimney) capuchon *m*.

coy, côa'i, *a* réservé,
timide.

crab, crâbbe, *n* crabe *m*; **––**
apple, pomme sauvage *f*.

crack, crâque, *n* (small)
craquelure *f*; fente *f*;
(glass) fêlure *f*; (noise)
craquement *m*; (whip)
claquement *m*; *v*
craqueler; fendre; fêler;
craquer; claquer; (nuts)
casser; **–er,** *n* (firework)
pétard *m*; (nut)
cassenoisette *m*; **–le,** *v*
craquer; (fire) pétiller.

cradle, cré´-d'l, *n* (crib)
berceau *m*.

craft, crâfte, *n* (trade)
métier *m*; *naut*
embarcation *f*;
(cunning) ruse *f*; **–sman,**
artisan *m*; **–y,** *a* rusé.

crag, crâgue, *n* rocher à
pic *m*.

cram, crâmme, *v* bourrer.

cramp, crâmmpe, *n*
crampe *f*.

cranberry, crânne´-bê-ri,
n airelle *f*.

crane, créne, *n* grue *f*.

crank, crain-ngk, *n* mech
manivelle *f*.

crash, crâche, *v* (break)
briser; (aero) s'écraser;
(car) se tamponner; *n*
(car, train) accident *m*;
(noise) fracas *m*.

crate, créte, *n* caisse *f*,
cageot *m*.

crater, cré-*teur*, *n* cratère
m.

crave, créve *v* implorer;
désirer ardemment.

craving, créve´-inng, *n*
désir ardent *m*.

crawl, croal, *v* ramper.

crayfish, cré´-fiche, *n*
écrevisse *f*; (sea)
langouste *f*.

crayon, cré´-onn, *n* pastel
m.

craze, créze, *n* (mode)
manie *f*.

crazy, cré´-zi, *a* toqué; fou.

creak, crîque, *v* grincer; *n*
craquement *m*.

cream, crîme, *n* crème *f*;
–y, *a* crémeux.

crease, crîce, *n* (press) pli
m; (crush) faux pli *m*; *v*
se froisser.

create, cri-été´, *v* créer,
produire.

creature, crî´-tioure, *n*
créature *f*.

creche, crèche *n* garderie;
f; *n* crèche *f*.

credentials, cri-denn´-
ch'lz, *npl* lettres de
créance *fpl*; papiers

d'identité *mpl*.

credible, crèd´-i-b'l, *a*
croyable.

credit, crèd´-itte, *n* crédit
m; *v* créditer; **– card,** *n*
carte de crédit *f*; **–able,** *a*
estimable, honorable;
–or, *n* créancier *m*.

credulous, crèd´-iou-
leuce, *a* crédule.

creed, crîde, *n* croyance *f*.

creek, crîque, *n* crique *f*.

creep, crîpe, *v* se traîner;
(silently) se glisser;
(plants, animals, etc)
ramper.

creeper, crî´-peur, *n* plante
grimpante *f*.

cremate, cri-méte´, *v*
incinérer.

cremation, cri-mé´-ch'n, *n*
crémation *f*.

crematorium, crèmm-ă-
tôr´-i'oume, *n*
crématorium *m*.

creole, crî´-ôle, *n* & *a*
créole *m* & *f*.

crescent, cress´-'nt, *n*
croissant *m*.

cress, cresse, *n* cresson *m*.

crest, cresste, *n* (heraldry)
armes *fpl*; (seal, etc)
écusson; *m* (hill, bird's)
crête *f*;
– fallen, *a* penaud.

crevice, crév´-ice, *n*
crevasse *f*.

crew, croue, *n* naut

équipage m.

crick, crique, n crampe f;
(neck) torticolis m.

cricket, cri´-quette, n
(insect) grillon m;
(game) cricket m.

crime, crâïme, n crime m.

criminal, crimm´-i-n'l, n
& a criminel m & f.

crimson, crimm´-z'n, n &
a cramoisi m.

cringe, crinn´-dje, v faire
des courbettes; se blottir.

crinkle, crinn´-k'l, v
froisser; n froissement m.

cripple, crip´-p'l, n
estropié m. v estropier.

crisis, crâï´-cisse, n crise f.

crisp, crispe, a (food)
croustillant.

criterion, crâï-ti´-ri-eune,
n critère m.

critic, cri´-tique, n
critique m; **–al***, a
critique.

criticism, crit´-i-ci-z'm, n
critique f.

criticize, crit´-i-sâïze, v
critiquer.

croak, crauque v (bird)
croasser; (frog) coasser;
n croassement m;
coassement m.

crochet, cro´-ché, n
crochet m; v faire du
crochet.

crockery, crok´-eu-ri, n
vaisselle f.

crocodile, crok´-o-dâïle, n
crocodile m.

crocus, cro´-queuce, n
crocus m.

crook, crouk, n crochet m;
(person) escroc m.

crooked, crouk´-edde, a
tordu; de travers;
malhonnête.

crop, crope, n récolte f;
(haircut) coupe f; v
tondre.

cross, crosse, n croix f. a
fâché; oblique; v
(intersect) croiser; **—
examine**, interroger;
–ing, n traversée f; **–out**,
v rayer; **–over**, traverser;
–road, n carrefour m.

crotchet, crotch´-ette, n
(music) noire f.

crouch, crâ´outche, v se
tapir; s'accroupir.

crow, crau, n corbeau m; v
(cock) chanter.

crowbar, crau´-bâre, n
pince f.

crowd, crâ'oude, n foule f.
v encombrer; (s')
entasser.

crown, crâ'ounne, n
couronne f; (top)
sommet m; v couronner.

crucial, croue´-ch'l, a
crucial; décicif.

crucible, croue´-ci-b'l, n
creuset m.

crucifix, croue´-ci-fixe, n

crucifix m.

crucify, croue´-ci-fâï, v
crucifier.

crude*, croude, a (raw)
cru; (vulgar) grossier.

cruel*, croue´-eul, a cruel;
–ty, a cruauté f.

cruise, crouze, v faire une
croisière; n croisière f.

cruiser, croue´-zeur, n
croiseur m.

crumb, cromme, n mie f;
(particle) miette f.

crumble, cromm´-b'l, v
tomber en poussière.

crumple, cromm´-p'l, v
chiffonner.

crunch, cronntche, v
croquer.

crush, croche, v écraser;
(pound) broyer; n cohue
f.

crust, crosste, n croûte f;
–y, a croustillant.

crutch, crotche, n béquille
f.

cry, crâï, v crier; (weep)
pleurer; n cri m.

cryptic, cripe´-tic a
occulte.

crystal, criss´-t'l, n cristal
m.

cub, cobbe, n (bear)
ourson m; (lion)
lionceau m.

cube, kioube, n cube m.

cubicle, kiou´-bi-c'l, n box
(in hospital) m; cabine

(at pool) *f*.

cuckoo, cou´-coue, *n* coucou *m*.

cucumber, kiou´-comm-b'r, concombre *m*.

cud, code, *n* (**to chew the –**) ruminer.

cuddle, cod´-d'l, *v* caresser.

cudgel, codd´-j'l, *n* gourdin *m*.

cue, kioue, *n* (billiard) queue *f*; (acting) réplique *f*.

cuff, coffe, *n* manchette *f*.

culinary, kiou´-li-na-ri, *a* culinaire.

culminate, col´-mi-néte, *v* culminer.

culpability, col-pa-bile´-i-ti, *n* culpabilité *f*.

culpable, col´-pa-b'l, *a* coupable.

culprit, col´-pritte, *n* coupable *m* & *f*.

cult, colte, *n* culte *m*.

cultivate, col´-ti-véte, *v* cultiver.

culture, col´-tioure, *n* culture *f*.

cumbersome, comm´-beur-somme, *a* encombrant.

cunning*, conn´-inng, *n* ruse *f*; *a* rusé.

cup, coppe, *n* tasse *f*; (trophy) coupe *f*.

cupboard, cob´-eurde, *n* placard *m*; armoire *f*.

cupola, kiou´-po-la, *n* coupole *f*.

cur, keur, *n* cabot *m*; *fig* vil individu *m*.

curate, kiou´-réte, *n* vicaire *m*.

curb, keurbe, *n* frein *m*; rebord de trottoir *m*; *v fig* réprimer.

curd, keurde, *n* lait caillé *m*.

curdle, keur´-d'l, *v* se figer; (milk) se cailler.

cure, kioure, *n* traitement *m*; (remedy) remède *m*; *v* guérir; (meat, fish, etc) saler; fumer.

curiosity, kiou-ri-o´-si-ti, *n* curiosité *f*.

curious*, kiou´-ri-euce, *a* curieux.

curl, keurle, *v* (hair) friser; *n* boucle *f*; **–ly**, *a* bouclé.

currant, cor´-annte, *n* (dried) raisin sec *m*.

currency, cor´-enn-ci, *n* monnaie *f*; **foreign –**, *n* devises *fpl*.

current, cor´-ennte, *n* courant *m*; *a* courant.

curse, keurce, *n* malédiction *f*; *v* maudire.

cursory, keur´-so-ri, *a* rapide; superficiel.

curt, keurte, *a* bref; brusque.

curtail, keur-télé, *v* abréger; **–ment**, *n* raccourcissement *m*.

curtain, keur´-t'n, *n* rideau *m*.

curtsy, keurtt´-ci, *n* révérence *f*.

curve, keurve, *n* courbe *f*; *v* courber.

cushion, cou´-ch'n, *n* coussin *m*.

custard, cosse´-teurde, *n* flan *m*, crème cuite *f*.

custody, cosse´-tŏ-di, *n* garde *f*; détention *f*.

custom, cosse´-teume, *n* coutume *f*; (trade) clientèle *f*; **–ary**, *a* d'usage; **–er**, *n* client *m*; **––house**, douane *f*; **–s** *npl* douane *f*; **–s-duty**, *n* droits de douane *mpl*.

cut, cotte, *n* coupure *f*; (joint, etc) tranche *f*; *v* couper; (suit diamonds, etc) trailler; **–lery**, argenterie *f*; **–let**, *n* côtellete *f*; **–ter**, *n* (tailor) coupeur *m*.

cuticle, kiou´-ti-k'l, *n* cuticule *f*.

cuttle-fish, cott´-'l-fiche, *n* seiche *f*.

cyclamen, sique´-lă-menn, *n* cyclamen *m*.

cycle, sâï´-k'l, *n* cycle *m*; (vehicle) bicyclette *f*; *fam* vélo; *v* faire de la bicyclette.

cylinder, sill´-inn-d*eu*r, *n*
cylindre *m*.
cynical, sinn´-i-k'l, *a*
cynique.
cypress, săï´-presse, *n*
cyprès *m*.

dabble, dăbb-'l, *v*
s'occuper; barboter;
(shares) boursicoter.

daffodil, dăff´-o-dile, *n*
narcisse sauvage *m*;
jonquille *f.*

dagger, dăgg´-'r, *n*
poignard *m.*

dahlia, dél´-i-ă, *n* dahlia
m.

daily, dé-li, *a* quotidien.

dainty, dénne´-ti, *a*
délicat.

dairy, dé´-ri, *n* laiterie *f*;
(shop) crèmerie *f.*

daisy, dé´-zi, *n* (field)
pâquerette *f.*

dale, déle, *n* vallon *m.*

dam, dăme, *n* digue *f*;
barrage *m*; *v* endiguer.

damage, dămm´-idj, *n*
dommage *m*; dégât *m*;
avarie *f*; *v* endommager,

abîmer.

damask, dămm´-*a*sque, *n*
damas *m.*

damn, dămme, *v* damner;
interj zut!

damnation, dămm-né´-
ch'n, *n* damnation *f.*

damp, dămmpe, *v*
mouiller; *a* humide.

dampness, dămmpe´-
nesse, *n* humidité *f*;
moiteur *f.*

damson, dămm´-s'n, *n*
prune de Damas *f.*

dance, dânnce, *v* danser; *n*
danse *f.*

dancer, dânne´-ceur, *n*
danseur *m*; danseuse *f.*

dandelion, dănn´-di-lâï-
onn, *n* pissenlit *m.*

dandruff, dănnde´-rof, *n*
pellicules *fpl.*

danger, déne´-djeur, *n*

danger *m*; –**ous*,** *a*
dangereux.

dangle, dănn´-g'l, *v*
pendiller; se balancer.

dare, daire, *v* oser;
(challenge) défier.

daring, daire´-inng, *n*
audace *f*; *a** audacieux.

dark, dârque, *a* sombre;
(skin) brun; –**ness,** *n*
obscurité *f.*

darling, dâre´-linng, *n* & *a*
chéri, -ie *m* & *f.*

darn, dârne, *v* repriser; *n*
reprise *f.*

dart, dârte, *n* dard *m*;
(game) fléchette *f*;
(sewing) pince *f.*

dash, dăche, *n* (short line)
trait *m*; *v* lancer; (rush)
s'élancer.

data, dé´-*ta*, *npl* données
fpl; information *f.*

data-processing, dé´-*ta*-
prau´-cess-inng, *n*
informatique *f.*

date, déte, *n* date *f*; (fruit)
datte *f*; *v* dater; –**d,** *a*
démodé.

daughter, doa´-t'r, *n* fille *f*;
–**in-law,** belle-fille *f.*

dauntless, doannte´-lesse,
a intrépide.

dawdle, doa´-d'l, *v* flâner;
traîner.

dawn, doanne, *n* aurore *f*;
v faire jour.

day, dé, *n* jour *m*; journée

f; **–break,** point du jour m.

dazzle, dăz´-z'l, v éblouir.

deacon, dî´-k'n, n diacre m.

dead, dède, a mort; **–en,** v amortir; **–ly,** a mortel.

deaf, deffe, a sourd; **–en,** v assourdir.

deafness, deff´-nesse, n surdité f.

deal, dîle, n quantité f; (business) affaire f; (wood) bois de sapin m; v (trade) faire des affaires; (attend to) s'occuper de; (cards) donner.

dealer, dîl´-eur, n négociant m.

dean, dîne, n doyen m.

dear*, dîre, a cher.

dearth, deurts, n manque m; pénurie f.

death, dèts, n mort f.

debar, di-bâre´, v exclure; priver de.

debase, di-béce´, v avilir; dégrader.

debate, di-béte´, v discuter; n débat m.

debauch, di-boatch´, v débaucher.

debauchery, di-boatch´-eur-i, n débauche f.

debenture, di-benn´-tioure, n obligation f.

debility, di-bile´-i-ti, n

débilité f.

debit, dèb´-itte, n débit m; v débiter.

debt, dette, n dette f; **–or,** débiteur m.

decade, dèque´-éde, n décennie f; décade f.

decadence, dè´-ca-dennce, n décadence f.

decaffeinated, di-că´-finn-é-t'd, a décaféiné.

decant, di-kănnte´, v décanter; **–er,** n carafe f.

decapitate, di-căpe´-i-téte, v décapiter.

decay, di-qué´, n (decline) décadence f; (rot) délabrement m; v détériorer; pourrir; (teeth) carier.

decease, di-cîce´, n décès m; **–d,** a décédé.

deceit, di-cîte´, n tromperie f; **–ful*,** a trompeur.

deceive, di-cîve´, v décevoir; tromper.

December, di-semm´-b'r, n décembre m.

decency, dî´-cenn-ci, n (moral) décence f.

decent, dî´-cennte, a décent; (nice) convenable.

deception, di-cepp´-ch'n, n tromperie f.

deceptive, di-cepp´-tive, a trompeur.

decide, di-sâide´, v décider; **–d,** * a décidé.

decimal, dé´-ci-m'l, a décimal.

decipher, di-sâï´-f'r, v déchiffrer.

decision, di-ci´-j'n, n décision f.

decisive,* di-sâï´-cive, a décisif.

deck, dèque, n pont m; v orner.

declaim, di-cléme´, v déclamer.

declaration, di-cla-ré´-ch'n, n déclaration f.

declare, di-clére´, v déclarer; se déclarer.

declension, di-clenn´-ch'n, n déclinaison f.

decline, di-clâïne´, v baisse f; (slope) pente f; (decadence) déclin m; v refuser; (grammar) décliner.

decompose, di-cŏmm-pauze´, v décomposer.

decompress, di-cŏmm-presse´, v décomprimer.

decorate, dè´-cŏ-réte, v décorer.

decorous, dè-cô´-reuce, a décent; convenable.

decoy, di-coa'ï´, n piège m; (bird) appeau m; (bait) appât m; v leurrer.

decrease, di-crîce´, v décroître; (knitting)

diminuer; n diminution f.

decree, di-crî´, n décret m; v décréter.

decry, di-crâî´, v décrier.

dedicate, dè´-di-quéte, v dédier.

deduce, di-diouce´, v déduire.

deduct, di-docte´, v déduire.

deduction, di-doc´-ch'n, n déduction f; (com) remise f.

deed, dîde, n action f; (heroic) exploit m; (law) acte m; titre m.

deem, dîme, v juger; estimer.

deep, dîpe, a profond; **–en,** v approfondir.

deep-freeze, dîpe´-frîze, n congélateur m.

deer, dire, n daim m; (red) cerf m.

deface, di-féce´, v dégrader; mutiler.

defamation, dé-fa-mé´-ch'n, n diffamation f.

defame, di-féme´, v diffamer.

default, di-foalte´, n défaut de payement m; (law) contumace f; v faire défaut.

defeat, di-fîte´, n défaite f; v vaincre; déjouer.

defect, di-fecte´, n défaut

m; **–ive,** a défectueux.

defence, di-fennce´, n défense f.

defenceless, di-fennce´-lesse, a sans défense.

defend, di-fennde´, v défendre; **–ant,** n défendeur m; **–er,** n défenseur m.

defensive, di-fenn´-cive, n défensive f; a défensif.

defer, di-feur´, v différer; ajourner.

deference, dèf´-eur-ennce, n déférence f.

defiance, di-fâî-´nce, n défi m.

deficiency, di-fich´-enn-ci, n manque m; défaut m.

deficient, di-fich´-'nt, a défectueux.

deficit, dèf´-i-cite, n déficit m.

defile, di-fâîle´, v souiller.

define, di-fâîne´, v définir.

definite, dèf´-i-nitte, a déterminé; défini.

definition, dèf-i-ni´-ch'n, n définition f.

deflect, di-flecte´, v dévier.

deform, di-foarme´, v déformer; **–ed,** a difforme.

defraud, di-froade´, v frauder.

defray, di-fré´, v défrayer.

deft*, defte, a adroit.

(clever) habile; (quick) leste.

defunct, di-fonnkt´, a défunt.

defy, di-fâî´, v défier; provoquer.

degenerate, di-djènn´-eur-éte, v dégénérer; n & a dégénéré m.

degrade, di-gréde´, v dégrader.

degree, di-grî´, n degre´ m; (university) licence f.

dehydrate, di´-hâî-dréte, v déshydrater; **–d,** a déshydraté; (milk, eggs, etc) en poudre .

deign, déne, v daigner.

deject, di-djèque't´, v décourager; déprimer.

dejection, di-djèque´-ch'n, n abattement m.

delay, di-lé´, n retard m; délai m; v tarder; différer.

delegate, dèl´-i-guéte, n délégué m.

delete, di-lîte´, v effacer; rayer; supprimer.

deliberate, di-lib´-eur-éte, v délibérer; a* délibéré.

delicacy, dèl´-i-ca-ci, n délicatesse f.

delicate*, dèl´-i-quéte, a délicat.

delicious*, di-lich´-euce, a délicieux.

delight, di-lâîte, v

342

enchanter; n délices fpl;
joie f.

delightful*, di-lâïte´-foull,
a délicieux.

delineate, di-linn´-i-éte, v
tracer.

delinquent, di-linng´-
couente, n délinquant, -
e m & f.

delirious*, di-lir´-i-euce, a
en délire.

delirium, di-lir´-i-eume, n
délire m.

deliver, di-liv´-eur, v
(letters) distribuer;
(goods) livrer; (set free,
rid) délivrer; **–y,** n
délivrance f; (letters)
distribution f; (goods)
livraison f.

delude, di-lioude´, v
tromper.

delusion, di-liou´-j'n, n
illusion f.

demand, di-mânnde´, v
exiger; n demande f.

demeanour, di-mî´-neur, n
conduite f; tenue f.

demented, di-menn´-
tedde, n & a dément m.

democracy, di-mo´-crasse-
i, n démocratie f.

democrat, dè´-mau-crate,
n démocrate m & f.

democratic, dè-mo-crã´-
tique, a démocratique.

demolish, di-mol´-iche, v
démolir.

demon, dî´-mônne, n
démon m.

demonstrate, dè´-monn-
stréte, v démontrer;
donner une
démonstration.

demonstrative, di-monn´-
stra-tive, a démonstratif;
expansif.

demoralize, di-mô-ră-
lâïze, v démoraliser.

demote, di-maute´, v
rétrograder.

demur, di-meure´, v
hésiter; s'opposer.

demure, di-mioure´, a
modeste.

den, dènne, n repaire m;
cabinet de travail m.

denial, di-nâï´-'l, n
dénégation f.

denim, dè´-nimme, n jean
m.

denomination, di-nŏmm-
i-né´-ch'n, n
dénomination f.

denote, di-naute´, v
dénoter.

denounce, di-nâ´ounnce´,
v dénoncer.

dense, dènnce, a dense;
épais; (person) stupide.

dent, dènnte, n marque f;
creux m; v cabosser;
bosseler.

dentist, dènn´-tiste, n
dentiste m.

denude, di-nioude´, v

dénuder.

deny, di-nâï´, v nier.

deodorant, di-ô´-deur-'nt,
n déodorant m;
désodorisant m.

deodorize, di-ô´-deur-âïze,
v désodoriser.

depart, di-pârte´, v partir.

department, di-pârtte-
m'nt, n branche f;
service m; (shop) rayon
m; **– store,** grand
magasin m.

departure, di-pâr´-tioure,
n départ m.

depend (upon), di-
pennde´, v (contingent)
dépendre; (trust)
compter sur; **–ant,** n
personne à la charge de;
–ent, a dépendant; à
charge.

depict, di-picte´, v
dépeindre.

depletion, di-plî´-ch'n, n
épuisement m.

deplore, di-plaure´, v
déplorer.

deport, di-paurte´, v
déporter.

deportment, di-paurte´-
m'nt, n maintien m.

depose, di-pauze´, v
déposer.

deposit, di-pauz´-itte, n
(bank, sediment) dépôt
m; (on account)
acompte m; arrhes fpl; v

déposer; –**or,** n déposant m.

depot, depp´-au, n dépôt m.

deprave, di-préve´, v dépraver.

deprecate, dè´-pri-quéte, v désapprouver.

depreciate, di-prî´-chi-éte, v déprécier.

depress, di-press´, v déprimer; décourager; –**ion,** n (trade) crise f; (spirits) abattement m; dépression f; (hollow) affaissement m.

deprive, di-prâïve´, v priver.

depth, depts, n profondeur f.

deputation, dè-piou-té´-ch'n, n députation f.

deputy, dèp´-iou-ti, n représentant m; remplaçant m; vice-...

derailment, di-réle´-m'nt, n déraillement m.

derange, di-rénndje´, v déranger.

derangement, di-rénndje´-m'nt, n dérangement m.

derelict, dèr´-i-licte, a abandonné; n (ship) épave f.

deride, di-râïde´, v railler.

derision, di-rî´-jeune, n dérision f.

derisive*, di-râï´-cive, a

dérisoire.

derive, di-râïve´, v dériver; provenir.

derogatory, di-ro´-geu-tôr-i, a péjoratif(ive).

descend, di-cennde´, v descendre; –**ant,** n descendant, -ante m & f.

descent, di-cennte´, n descente f; origine f.

describe, diss-crâïbe´, v décrire.

description, diss-crippe´-ch'n, n description f.

desecrate, dèss´-si-créte, v profaner.

desert, dèz´-eurte, n désert m.

desert, diz-eurte´, v abandonner; mil déserter; –**er,** n déserteur m; –**ion,** désertion f; abandon m.

deserve, di-zeurve´, v mériter.

design, di-zâïne´, n (sketch) dessin m; (intention) dessein m; (pattern) modèle m; motif m; v dessiner; (plan) projeter; créer; –**ing,** a intrigant.

desirable, di-zâï´-ra-b'l, a désirable; souhaitable.

desire, di-zâïre´, v désirer; n désir m.

desirous, di-zâï´-reuce, a

désireux.

desist, di-zisst´, v cesser.

desk, dessque, n bureau m; (school) pupitre m.

desolate, dess´-ŏ-léte, a désole; déserté.

despair, diss-pair´, n désespoir m; v désespérer.

despatch, diss-pătche´, v expédier; n dépêche f; envoi m.

desperate*, dess´-peur-éte, a désespéré; forcené.

despicable, dess´-pi-ca-b'l, a méprisable.

despise, diss-pâïze´, v mépriser.

despite, diss-pâïte´, prep en dépit de; malgré.

despoil, diss-poa´île´, v dépouiller.

despondent, diss-ponn´-d'nt, a découragé; déprimé.

despot, dess´-pŏtte, n despote m.

dessert, di-zeurte´, n dessert m.

destination, dèss-ti-né´-ch'n, n destination f.

destiny, dess´-ti-ni, n sort m; destin m.

destitute, dess´-ti-tioute, a indigent; dénué.

destitution, dess-ti-tiou´-ch'n, n denuement m.

destroy, diss-troa´ï´, v

détruire.

destruction, diss-trok´-ch'n, n destruction f.

destructive, diss-trok´-tive, a destructif.

desultory, dé´-seul-to-ri, a irrégulier; décousu.

detach, di-tătche´, v détacher; **–able,** a détachable.

detail, di-téle´, v détailler; n détail m.

detain, di-téne´, v détenir; retenir.

detect, di-tecte´, v découvrir; surprendre.

detective, di-tèque´-tive, n détective m; **– novel,** roman policier m.

detention, di-tenn´-ch'n, n détention f; (school) retenue f.

deter, di-teur´, v dissuader; détourner; **–rent,** n préventif; (nuclear, etc) arme de dissuasion f.

detergent, di-teur´-djennte, n détergent m; détersif m.

deteriorate, di-tî´-ri-o-réte, v détériorer.

determine, di-teur´-minne, v déterminer; décider.

detest, di-tesste´, v détester.

dethrone, di-tsrône´, v détrôner.

detonation, di-to-né´-ch'n, n explosion f.

detour, di-tour´, n détour m.

detract, di-trăcte´, v enlever (à); dénigrer.

detrimental*, dèt-ri-menn´-t'l, a préjudiciable.

deuce, diouce, n (tennis) égalité f; (cards, etc) deux m.

devaluate, di-val´-iou-éte, v dévaluer; **–tion,** n dévaluation f.

devastate, dè´-vass-téte v dévaster.

develop, di-vèl´-ŏpe, v développer.

development, di-vèl´-ope-m'nt, n développement m; exploitation f; fait m.

deviate, dî´-vi-éte, v dévier.

device, di-vâïce´, n moyen m; dispositif m; appareil m; truc m.

devil, dév´-'l, n diable m; **–ry,** diablerie f.

devise, di-vâïze´, v inventer; tramer; (law) léguer.

devoid, di-voa´ïde´, a dénué; dépourvu.

devote, di-vaute´, v dévouer; **– oneself to,** se consacrer à.

devour, di-vâ´oure´, v

dévorer.

devout*, di-vâ´oute´, a dévot; pieux.

dew, dioue, n rosée f.

dexterous*, deks´-teur-euce, a adroit; habile.

diabetes, dâï-a-bî´-tize, n diabète m.

diabolical*, dâï-a-bol´-i-k'l, a diabolique.

diagnose, dâï-ăgue-nauze´, v diagnostiquer.

diagonal, dâï-ăgue´-o-n'l, a diagonal.

diagram, dâï´-a-grămme, n diagramme m; schéma m.

dial, dâï´-al, n cadran m; v composer un numéro (de téléphone).

dialect, dâï-a-lecte, n dialecte m.

dialogue, dâï-a-logue, n dialogue m.

diameter, dâï-ămm´-i-teur, n diamètre m.

diamond, dâï´-a-meunnde, n diamant m; (cards) carreau m.

diarrhoea, dâï-a-rî´-a, n diarrhée f.

diary, dâï´-a-ri, n journal m; (pocket) agenda m.

dice, dâïce, npl dés mpl.

dictaphone, dic´-ta-faune, n machine à dicter f.

dictate, dic-téte´, v dicter; faire la loi.

dictator, dic-tét´-'r, n
dictateur m.

dictionary, dic´-chŏnn-a-
ri, n dictionnaire m.

die, dâî, v mourir.

diesel, di´-zeul, n auto
diesel m.

diet, dâî-ette, v (to go on
a –) faire un régime; n
régime m.

differ, dif-eur, v différer;
–ence, n différence f;
–ent, a différent.

difficult, diff´-i-keulte, a
difficile; **–y,** n difficulté
f.

diffident, diff´-i-d'nt, a
défiant de soi-même.

diffuse, dif-fiouze´, v
répandre; a diffus.

dig, digue, v (garden)
bêcher; (excavate)
creuser; (archeology)
faire des fouilles.

digest, di-djeste´, v
digérer; **–ion,** n
digestion f.

dignified dig´-ni-fâïde, a
digne.

dignitary, dig´-ni-ta-ri, n
dignitaire m.

dignity, dig´-ni-ti, n
dignité f.

digression, di-grèch´-
eunne, n digression f.

dike, dâïke, n digue f.

dilapidated, di-lăpp´-i-dé-
tedde, a délabré.

dilapidation, di-lăpp´-i-
dé-ch'n, n délabrement
m.

dilate, di-léte´, v dilater;
se dilater.

dilatory, dil´-a-tŏ-ri, a
tardif; dilatoire.

dilemma, di-lemm´-ma, n
dilemme m.

diligence, dil´-i-djennce, n
diligence f.

diligent*, dil´-i-djennte, a
appliqué.

dilute, di-lioute´, v diluer;
(wine) couper.

dim, dime, v obscurcir; a
trouble; faible.

dimension, di-menn´-
ch'n, n dimension f.

diminish, di-minn´-iche, v
diminuer.

dimple, dime´-p'l, n
fossette f.

din, dinn, n vacarme m; v
assourdir.

dine, dâîne, v dîner.

dinghy, dinng´-î, n youyou
m.

dingy, dinn´-dji, a sombre;
sale; défraîchi.

dining, dâî´-ninng, **– car,**
n wagon restaurant m; **–
room,** salle à manger f.

dinner, dinn´-eur, n dîner
m.

dip, dippe, v plonger;
tremper; baisser
subitement; (slope)

incliner.

diphtheria, diff-tsî´-ri-a, n
diphtérie f.

diplomacy, di-plau´-ma-ci,
n diplomatie f.

diplomat, dippe´-lau-
mätte, n diplomate m.

dire, dâïre, a cruel;
terrible; affreux.

direct, di-recte´, v diriger;
indiquer; a direct; **–ion,**
n direction f; **–ly,** adv
tout de suite; **–or,** n
directeur m;
administrateur m; **–ory,**
annuaire m.

dirt, deurte, n saleté f;
ordure f.

dirty, deur´-ti, a sale; v
salir.

disability, diss-a-bile´-i-ti,
n incapacité f.

disable, diss-é-'b'l, v
mutiler; mech mettre
hors de service; **–d,** a
infirme; invalide; npl the
–d les handicapés mpl.

disadvantage, diss-ăd-
vânne´-tidj, n
désavantage m.

disagree, diss-a-grî´, v être
en désaccord.

disagreeable, diss-a-grî´-a-
b'l, a désagréable.

disallow, diss-a-la'ou´, v
refuser; désapprouver.

disappear, diss-a-pîre, v
disparaître.

disappearance, diss-ap-pïr´-'nce, n disparition f.

disappoint, diss-a-poa'innte´, v décevoir; **–ment,** n déception f.

disapprove, diss-a-prouve´, v désapprouver.

disarm, diss-ârme´, v désarmer; **–ament,** désarmement m.

disaster, diz-âsse´-teur, n désastre m; accident m.

disastrous*, diz-âsse´-treuce, a désastreux.

disc, disque, n disque m.

discard, diss-cârde´, v rejeter.

discern, diz-zeurne´, v discerner.

discharge, diss-tchârdje´, n (dismissal) congé m; (gun) décharge f; med suppuration f; perte f; v congédier; décharger; (fulfil) remplir; (acquit) acquitter; (release) libérer.

disciple, diss-sâï´-p'l, n disciple m.

discipline, diss´-si-plinne, n discipline f.

disclaim, diss-cléme´, v renier; répudier.

disclose, diss-clauze´, v révéler.

disclosure, diss-clau´-jioure, n révélation f.

disco, diss´-cau, n discothèque.

discolour, diss-col´-eur, v décolorer.

discomfort, diss-comm´-feurte, n incommodité f; manque de confort m; (uneasy) malaise m.

disconnect, diss-cŏnn-necte´, v disjoindre; couper.

discontent, diss-cŏnn-tennte´, n mécontentement m; **–ed,** a mécontent.

discontinue, diss-cŏnn-tinn´-ioue, v cesser.

discord, diss´-coarde, n discorde f.

discotheque, diss´-cau-tèque, n discothèque f.

discount, diss´-câ'ounnte, n com remise f; fin escompte m.

discourage, diss-cor´-idj, v décourager.

discourse, diss-caurse´, v discourir; n discours m.

discourteous, diss-keur´-ti-euce, a discourtois.

discover, diss-cov´-eur, v découvrir.

discovery, diss-cov´-eur-i, n découverte f.

discreet*, diss-crîte´, a discret.

discrepancy, diss-crèp´-ann-ci, n différence f.

discriminate, diss-crimm´-

discuss, diss-cosse´, v discuter.

discussion, diss-coch´-'n, n discussion f.

disdain, diss-déne´, v dédaigner; n dédain m.

disdainful*, diss-déne´-foull, a dédaigneux.

disease, di-zîze´, n maladie f; **–d,** a malade.

disembark, diss-emm-bârque´, v débarquer; **–ation** n débarquement m.

disengaged, diss-enn-guédje´, a libre.

disentangle, diss-enn-tain´-g'l, v démêler.

disfigure, diss-figue´-eur, v défigurer.

disgrace, diss-gréce´, n disgrâce f; (shame) honte f; v déshonorer; **–ful,** a honteux.

disguise, diss-gâïze´, v déguiser; n déguisement m.

disgust, diss-gosste´, v dégoûter; n dégoût m; **–ing,** a dégoûtant.

dish, diche, n plat m; (food) mets m; **– cloth,** torchon m; **– up,** v servir.

dishearten, diss-hâre´-t'n, v décourager.

dishevelled, di-chè´-

vellde, *a* échevelé.

dishonest, diss-onn´-este, *a* malhonnête.

dishonour, diss-onn´-*eur*, *v* déshonorer; *n* déshonneur *m*.

dishwasher, diche-ou´oache-'r, *n* lave-vaisselle *m*.

disillusion, diss-il-lioue´-j'n, *v* désillusionner.

disinclination, diss-inn-cli-né´-ch'n, *n* aversion *f*.

disinfect, diss-inn-fecte´, *v* désinfecter; –**ant** *n* désinfectant *m*.

disinherit, diss-inn-hèr´-itte, *v* déshériter.

disintegrate, diss-inn´-teur-gréte, *v* désintégrer.

disintegration, diss-inn-teur-gré´-ch'n, *n* désintégration.

disjointed, diss-djoa'inn´-tedde, *a* désarticulé.

disk, disque, *n computt* disque *m*.

dislike, diss-lâïque´, *v* ne pas aimer; *n* aversion *f*.

dislocate, diss´-lo-kéte, *v* disloquer.

disloyal, diss-lo´-ial, *a* déloyal.

dismal*, diz´-m'l, *a* triste; lugubre; sombre.

dismay, diss-mé´, *v* consterner; *n*

consternation *f*.

dismiss, diss-mice´, *v* congédier; (mentally) écarter.

dismount, diss-mâ'ounnté´, *v* descendre de.

disobedient, diss-o-bî´-di-ennte, *a* désobéissant.

disobey, diss-o-bé´, *v* désobéir.

disorder, diss-oar´-deur, *n* désordre *m*.

disorganization, diss-oar-ga-nâï-zé´-ch'n, *n* désorganisation *f*.

disorganize, diss-oar´-ga-nâïze, *v* désorganiser.

disorientated, diss-or-i-enn-t'd, *a* désorienté.

disown, diz-aune´, *v* renier.

disparage, diss-pär´-idj, *v* dénigrer.

dispatch, (see **despatch**).

dispel, diss-pelle´, *v* chasser; dissiper.

dispensary, diss-penn´-sa-ri, *n* dispensaire *m*.

disperse, diss-peurce´, *v* disperser.

display, diss-plé´, *v* exposer; *n com* étalage *m*.

displease, diss-plîze´, *v* déplaire.

displeasure, diss-plè´-jeure, *n*

mécontentement *m*.

disposable, diss-pau´zib-'l, *a* (pack, etc) jetable; à jeter *f*; (income) disponible *f*; – **nappy,** *n* couche à jeter *f*; couche-culotte *f*.

disposal, diss-pau-z'l, *n* disposition *f*.

dispose, diss-pauze´, *v* disposer; se debarrasser.

disprove, diss-prouve´, *v* réfuter.

disputable, diss-pioue´-ta-b'l, *a* contestable.

dispute, diss-pi'out´e, *v* se disputer; contester; *n* dispute *f*; contestation *f*.

disqualify, diss-couoll´-i-fâï, *v* disqualifier.

disquiet, diss-couâï´-ètte, *v* inquiéter; *n* inquiétude *f*.

disregard, diss-ri-gârde´, *v* négliger; ne pas observer. *n* mépris *m*; indifférence *f*.

disrepute, diss-ri-pioute´, *n* discrédit *m*.

disrespect, diss-ri-specte´, *n* manque de respect *m*; irrévérence *f*; –**ful,** *a* irrespectueux.

disrupt, diss-ropt´, *v* perturber (disturb, break up); déranger (plans).

dissatisfy, diss-sät´-is-fâï, *v* mécontenter.

dissect, diss-secte´, *v*
disséquer.

dissemble, diss-semm´-b'l,
v dissimuler.

dissent, diss-sennte´, *v*
différer d'opinion.

dissimilar, diss-simm´-i-l'r,
a dissemblable.

dissipate, diss´-si-péte, *v*
dissiper.

dissociate, diss-sau-chi-
éte, *v* dissocier; se
désintéresser

dissolute, diss´-sŏ-lioute, *a*
dissolu.

dissolve, diss-solv´, *v*
dissoudre.

dissuade, diss-souéde´, *v*
dissuader.

distance, diss´-tannce, *n*
distance f.

distant, diss´-tannte, *a*
èloigné; distant.

distasteful, diss-téste´-
foull, *a* répugnant.

distemper, diss-temm´-
peur, *n* (paint) détrempe
f; (veterinary) maladie
des chiens f.

distend, diss-tennde´, *v*
dilater; gonfler.

distil, diss-till´, *v* distiller.

distinct*, diss-tinng´-kt, *a*
distinct; clair.

distinction, diss-tinng´-
kch'n, *n* distinction f.

distinguish, diss-tinng´-
gouiche, *v* distinguer.

distort, diss-toarte´, *v*
défigurer; *fig* dénaturer.

distract, diss-trākt´, *v*
distraire; détourner;
affoler; **–ion,** *n*
distraction f.

distrain, diss-tréne´, *v*
saisir.

distress, diss-tresse´, *n*
détresse f; (poverty)
misère f; *v* affliger; **–ing,**
a affligeant; pénible.

distribute, diss-trib´-ioute,
v distribuer.

distributor, diss-trib´-iou-
t'r, *n* concessionnaire m;
(in car, etc) distributeur
m.

district, diss´-tricte, *n*
région f; arrondissement
m.

distrust, diss-trosste´, *v* se
mefier de; *n* méfiance f.

disturb, diss-teurbe´, *v*
déranger; **–ance,** *n*
dérangement m; (mob)
désordre m.

disuse, diss-iouce´, *n*
désuétude f.

ditch, ditche, *n* fossé m.

dive, dâïve, *v* plonger.

diver, dâï´-veur, *n*
plongeur m; (salvage,
etc) scaphandrier m.

diverge, di-veurdje´, *v*
diverger.

diverse, dâï-veurse´, *a*
divers; varié.

diversion, di-veur´-ch'n, *n*
diversion f;
divertissement m; (road)
déviation f.

divert, di-veurte´, *v*
détourner; distraire.

divest, di-veste´, *v*
dépouiller de; (clothes)
dévêtir.

divide, di-vâïde´, *v* diviser;
partager.

divine, di-vâïne´, *v*
deviner; *a** divin.

division, di-vi´-j'n, *n*
division f.

divorce, di-vaurce´, *v*
divorcer; *n* divorce m.

divulge, di-voldje´, *v*
divulguer.

dizzy, diz´-i, *a* étourdi;
vertigineux.

do, doue, *v* faire;
accomplir; suffire.

docile, do´-sâïle, *a* docile.

dock, doc, *n* bassin m;
(court) banc des accusés
m; **dry –,** cale sèche f;
–yard, chantier
maritime m; arsenal m.

doctor, doc´-t'r, *n* docteur
m.

doctrine, doc´-trine, *n*
doctrine f.

document, doc´-iou-m'nt,
n document m.

documentary, doc´-iou-
menn´-ta-ri, *n*
documentaire m.

dodge, dodje, v esquiver; éviter; n truc m.

dog, dogue, n chien m; **–ged*,** a tenace.

dole, daule, v distribuer; n allocation de chômage f.

doleful*, daule´-foull, a plaintif; triste.

doll, dolle, n poupée f.

dollar, doll´-eur, n dollar m.

domain, dau-méne´, n domaine m.

dome, daume, n dôme m.

domestic, do-mess´-tique, n & a domestique m & f.

domesticated, do-mess´-ti-qué-tedde, a bonne ménagère.

domicile, domm´-i-sâîle, n domicile m.

dominate, domm´-i-néte, v dominer.

domineer, domm-i-nîre´, v régenter.

donate, dau-nétte´, v faire don de.

donation, dau-né´-ch'n, n donation f.

donkey, donng´-qui, n âne m; baudet m.

donor, dau´-neur, n donateur m.

doom, doume, n (fate) sort m; v condamner.

doomsday, doumze´-dé, n jugement dernier m.

door, daur, n porte f;

(vehicle) portière f; **–keeper,** concierge m & f; **–mat,** paillasson m; **–step,** pas de la porte m.

dormitory, dor´-mi-to-ri, n dortoir m.

dose, dauce, n dose f; v doser.

dot, dotte, n point m; v mettre un point sur; (art) pointiller.

double, dob´-'l, v doubler; n & a double m.

doubt, dâ'oute, v douter. n doute m; **–ful,** a douteux; **–less,** adv sans doute.

douche, douche, n douche f; v doucher.

dough, dau, n pâte f.

dove, dove, n colombe f; **–cot,** colombier m.

dowager, dâ'ou-édj-eur, n douairière f.

down, dâ'ounn, adv & prep en bas; n (feathers) duvet m; **–cast,** a abattu; **–fall,** n chute f; ruine f; **–pour,** pluie torrentielle f; **–stairs,** adv en bas; **–wards,** vers le bas.

dowry, dâ'ou´-ri, n dot f.

doze, dauze, v somnoler; n somme m.

dozen, doz´-'n, n douzaine f.

drab, drâbbe, a terne.

draft, drâfte, n (money)

traite f; (sketch) esquisse f; (writing) brouillon m; project m; v rédiger.

drag, drâgue, v traîner; (water) draguer.

dragon, drâgue´eune, n dragon m; **–fly,** libellule f.

drain, dréne, v faire égoutter; faire écouler; (land) drainer; n égout m; **–age,** système d'égouts m; **–pipe,** n gouttière f.

drake, dréke, n canard m.

drama, drâm´-a, n drame m.

dramatic, dra-ma´-tique, a dramatique.

draper, dré´-peur, n marchand de nouveautés f.

drastic, drass´-tique, a énergique; drastique.

draught, drâfte, n courant d'air m; potion f; (drinking) coup m; naut tirant d'eau m; **–board,** damier m; **–s,** (jeu de) dames fpl.

draughtsman, drâfts´-männe, n dessinateur m.

draw, droa, n (lottery) tirage m; (game) partie nulle f; v (pull) tirer; (pull out) arracher; (attract) attirer;

(sketch) dessiner; (bill) tirer; (money) retirer; – **back,** n inconvénient m; (furniture) tiroir m; **–ing,** (sketch) dessin m; **–ing room,** salon m.

drawl, droal, v parler d'une voix trainante; n débit trainant m.

dread, drèdde, v redouter; n terreur f; **–ful*,** a terrible.

dream, drîme, n rêve m; v rêver.

dreary, drî´-ri, a triste; morne; monotone.

dredge, drèdje, v draguer; **–r,** n dragueur m.

dregs, drègze, npl lie f; sédiment m.

drench, drenntche, v tremper.

dress, dresse, n robe f; toilette f; costume m; v habiller, vêtir; (wounds) panser; **–ing,** n med pansement m; (culinary) assaisonnement m; **–ing gown,** robe de chambre f; peignoir m; **–ing-room,** cabinet de toilette m.

dressmaker, dresse´-mék´-eur, n couturière f.

dribble, drib´-'l, v baver; (of water) dégoutter.

drift, drifte, n naut dérive f; (snow, etc) monceau

m; (tendency) but m; v dériver.

drill, drile, n mil exercise m; (tool) foret m; v exercer; forer; percer.

drink, drinnque, n boisson f; v boire.

drip, drippe, v dégoutter; n goutte f.

dripping, dripp´-inng, n (fat) graisse de rôti f.

drive, drâïve, v conduire; n (approach) allée f; (outing) promenade en . . (auto) f; (of car) conduite f.

driver, drâï´-veur, n conducteur m; chauffeur m.

driving licence, drâï-vinng-lâï-cennce, n permis de conduire m.

drizzle, driz´-z'l, v pleuvasser; n bruine f.

droll, draule, a drôle.

drone, draune, n faux-bourdon m; v bourdonner.

droop, droupe, v languir; (plants) tomber.

drop, droppe, n chute f; (liquid) goutte f; (prices) baisse f; v tomber; (let fall) laisser tomber.

drought, drâ'oute, n sécheresse f.

drown, drâ'ounne, v

noyer; se noyer.

drowsy, drâ'au´-zi, a somnolent.

drudge, drodje, v trimer; **–ry,** n corvée f.

drug, drogue, v droguer; n drogue f.

drum, dromme, n tambour m; **–mer,** tambour m.

drunk, dronnque, a ivre; soûl; **–ard,** ivrogne m; **–enness,** ivresse f; ivrognerie f.

dry, drâï, v sécher; a* sec; – **cleaning,** nettoyage à sec m.

dryness, drâï´-ness, n sécheresse f.

dual carriageway, dioue'l-cǎr-idj-oué, n route à quatre voies f.

dubious*, dioue´-bi-euce, a douteux.

duchess, dotch´-esse, n duchesse f.

duck, doque, n canard m; cane f; v plonger; se baisser.

due, dioue, n dû m; (toll, rights, etc) droits mpl; a (owing) dû; (bill) échu.

duel, dioue´-'l, n duel m.

duet, diou-ette´, n duo m.

duke, diouque, n duc m.

dull, dolle, a (weather) gris; (tedious) ennuyeux; (mind) lent; (metal) terne.

duly, dioue´-li, *adv*
dûment; en temps
voulu.

dumb, domme, *a* muet;
fam bête; **–found,** *v*
confondre.

dummy, domm´-i, *n* dress
m; mannequin *m*;
(sham) simulacre *m*;
(cards) le mort *m*.

dump, dommpe, *v*
déposer; *n* dépôt *m*.

dung, donng, *n* (horse)
crottin *m*; (cow) bouse
de vache *f*; (manure)
fumier *m*.

dungeon, donn´-djeune, *n*
cachot *m*.

dupe, dioupe, *v* duper; *n*
dupe *f*.

duplicate, dioue´-pli-
quéte, *n* duplicata *m*; *a*
double; *v* faire le double;
tirer (des copies).

durable, dioue´-ra-b'l, *a*
durable.

duration, dioue-ré´-ch'n,
n durée *f*.

during, dioue´-rinng, *prep*
pendant.

dusk, dossque, *n*
crépuscule *m*.

dusky, doss´-ki, *a* sombre;
(colour) noirâtre.

dust, dosste, *n* poussière *f*;
v épousseter; **–er,** *n*
chiffon *m*; **–man,**
éboueur *m*.

dustbin, dosste´-bine, *n*
boîte à ordures *f*;
poubelle *f*.

dutiful*, dioue´-ti-foull, *a*
obéissant; dévoué.

duty, dioue´-ti, *n* devoir
m; (customs) droits *mpl*;
(task) fonction *f*.

duvet, doue´-vé, *n* couette
f.

dwarf, douoarfe, *n & a*
nain, -e *m & f*; *v*
rapetisser.

dwell, douelle, *v*;
demeurer, habiter; **–er,** *n*
habitant *m*; **–ing,**
demeure *f*.

dwindle, douinn´-d'l, *v*
diminuer; s'amoindrir.

dye, dâï, *n* teinture *f*; *v*
teindre.

dynamite, dâïn´-a-mâïte,
n dynamite *f*.

dynamo, dâï´-na-mau, *n*
dynamo *f*.

dysentery, diss´-'n-tri, *n*
dysenterie *f*.

E

each, îtche, *pron* chacun, -une; *a* chaque; **– other**, *pron* l'un l'autre; l'une l'autre.

eager, î´-gueur, *a* avide; ardent.

eagerness, î´-gueur-nesse, *n* avidité *f*; empressement *m*.

eagle, î´-g'l, *n* aigle *m* & *f*.

ear, îre, *n* oreille *f*; (corn) épi *m*.

earl, eurle, *n* comte *m*.

early, eur´-li, *adv* de bonne heure; tôt; *a* matinal; tôt.

earn, eurne, *v* gagner; mériter; **–ings**, *npl* salaire *m*.

earnest*, eur´-nesste, *a* sérieux; sincère.

earring, îre´-rinng, *n* boucle d'oreille *f*.

earth, eurts, *n* terre *f*; monde *m*; *v* (electricity) mettre à la terre; **–enware**, *n* faïence *f*; **–ly**, *a* terrestre; **–quake**, *n* tremblement de terre *m*.

earwig, îre´-ouigue, *n* perce-oreille *m*.

ease, îze, *n* aise *f*; repos *m*; (facility) facilité *f*; *v* soulager.

easel, î´-z'l, *n* chevalet *m*.

easily, î´-zi-li, *adv* facilement.

east, îsste, *n* est *m*; **–erly**, *a* d'est; **–ern**, oriental.

Easter, îss´-teur, *n* Pâques *m*.

easy, î´-zi, *a* facile; **–chair**, *n* fauteuil *m*.

eat, île, *v* manger; (worm; acid) ronger; **–able**, *a*

mangeable; **–ables**, *npl* comestibles *mpl*.

eavesdropper, îvz´-dropp-eur, *n* oreille indiscrète *f*.

ebb, èbe, *v* refluer; *n* reflux *m*.

ebony, èb´-ŏ-ni, *n* ébène *f*.

eccentric, èque-senn-´-trique, *a* excentrique.

echo, èk´-au, *n* écho *m*; *v* répéter.

eclipse, i-klipse´, *n* éclipse *f*; *v* éclipser.

economic, èque-*a*-nomm´-ique, *a* économique.

economize, i-konn´-ŏ-mâize, *v* économiser.

economy, i-konn´-ŏ-mi, *n* économie *f*.

ecstasy, ex´-ta-zi, *n* extase *f*.

eczema, ex´-mă *n* eczéma, *m*.

eddy, éd´-i, *n* tourbillon *m*; remous *m*.

edge, èdje, *n* bord *m*; (blade) tranchant *m*; *v* border.

edible, èd´-i-b'l, *n* & *a* comestible *m*.

edify, èd´-i-fâï, *v* édifier.

edit, èd´-itte, *v* éditer; **–ion**, *n* édition *f*; **–or**, rédacteur *m*; **–orial**, *a* éditorial.

educate, èd´-iou-quéte, *v* instruire; éduquer.

education, èd-iou-ké´-

ch'n, n éducation f;
enseignement m; études
fpl.

eel, île, n anguille f.

efface, ef-féce´, v effacer.

effect, ef-fecte´, v
effectuer; n effet m;
–ive*, a efficace;
effectif; **–ual*,** a efficace.

effeminate, ef-femm´-i-
néte, a efféminé.

effervescent, ef-feur-vess´-
'nt, a effervescent.

efficiency, ef-fich´-enn-ci,
n efficacité f; capacité f.

efficient, ef-fich´-ennt, a
(person) capable;
compétent.

effort, ef´-feurte, n effort
m.

effrontery, ef-fron´-teur-i,
n effronterie f.

effusive, ef-fioue´-cive, a
expansif.

egg, ègg, n œuf m; **– cup,**
coquetier m.

egotism, ègg´-au-tizme, n
égoïsme m.

eiderdown, aï´-deur-
dâ'ounne, n édredon m.

eight, éte, n & a huit m;
–een, dix-huit m;
–eenth, dix-huitième m;
–h, huitième m; **–ieth,**
quatrevingtième m; **–y,**
quatre-vingts m.

either, aï´-dzeur, pron l'un
ou l'autre; conj ou; soit.

eject, i-djecte´, v expulser.

elaborate, i-lâb´-ŏ-réte, a
soigné; raffiné; v
élaborer.

elapse, i-lâpse´, v
s'écouler.

elastic, i-lãss´-tique, n & a
élastique m.

elate, i-léte´, v exalter; **–d,**
a exalté.

elbow, el´-bau, n coude m;
v coudoyer.

elder, el´-deur, n & a aîné
m & f; (tree) sureau m.

elderly, el´-deur-li, a assez
âgé.

eldest, el´-deste, n & a
aîné m & f.

elect, i-lecte´, v élire;
nommer; n & a élu m.

election, i-léque´-ch'n, n
élection f.

electric(al)*, i-léque´-
trique('l), a électrique.

electrician, i-léquetri´-
ch'n, n électricien m.

electricity, i-léque-tri-ci-
ti, n électricité f.

electrify, i-lèque´-tri-fâï, v
électriser; électrifier.

electron, i-lèque´-tronne,
n électron m; **–ics,**
électronique f.

electronic, i-lèque-
tronne´-ique, a
électronique.

electro-plate, i-lèqu´-tro-
pléte, n plaqué m; v
plaquer.

elegance, el´-i-gannce, n
élégance f.

elegant*, el´-i-gannte, a
élégant.

element, el´-i-m'nt, n
élément m.

elementary, i-li-menn´-ta-
ri, a élémentaire.

elephant, el´-i-fannte, n
éléphant m.

elevate, el´-i-véte, v
élever; exalter.

eleven, i-lèv´-'n, n & a
onze m; **–th,** onzième m.

elicit, i-liss´-ite, v obtenir
(**from,** de); mettre au
jour.

eligible, el´-i-dji-b'l, a
éligible; n un bon parti
m.

eliminate, i-lime´-i-néte, v
éliminer.

elite, é-lîte´, n élite f.

elk, elk, n élan m.

elm, elme, n orme m.

elongate, î´-longue-éte, v
prolonger; allonger.

elope, i-laupe´, v s'enfuir.

elopement, i-laupe´-m'nt,
n fugue amoureux f.

eloquent, el´-ŏ-couennte,
a éloquent.

else, elce, a autre; adv
autrement; **–where,**
ailleurs.

elucidate, i-lioue´-ci-déte,
v eclaircir.

elude, i-lioude´, v éviter; éluder.

elusive, i-lioue´-sive, a évasif.

emaciate, i-mé-chi-éte, v amaigrir.

email, i´-mèle, n courrier électronique m.

emanate, emm´-a-néte, v émaner.

emancipate, i-männ´-ci-péte, v émanciper.

embalm, emm-bâme´, v embaumer.

embankment, emm-bainque´-m'nt, n terrassement m; (railway) remblai m; (river) quai m.

embark, emm-bârke´, v embarquer.

embarrass, emm-băr´-ass, v gêner.

embarrassment, emm-băr´-ass-m'nt, n gêne f & m.

embassy, emm´-băss-i, n ambassade f.

embellish, emm-bell´-iche, v embellir.

ember, emm´-beur, n braise f.

embezzle, emm-bez´-z'l, v détourner.

embitter, emm-bitt´-eur, v fig aigrir.

embody, emm-bod´-i, v incorporer.

embrace, emm-bréce´, n étreinte f; v étreindre.

embroider, emm-broa'i-d'r, v broder.

embroidery, emm-broa'i-deur-i, n broderie f.

embroil, emm-broa'il´, v embrouiller.

emerald, emm´-eur-alde, n émeraude f.

emerge, i-meurdje´, v surgir; émerger; **–ncy,** n circonstance imprévu f; cas d'urgence m.

emetic, i-mett´-ique, n émétique m.

emigrant, emm´-i-grannte, n émigrant, -e m & f.

emigrate, emm´-i-gréte, v émigrer.

eminence, emm´-i-nennce, n éminence f.

eminent, emm´-i-nennte, a éminent; célèbre.

emissary, emm´-is-sa-ri, n íssaire m.

emit, i-mitte´, v émettre; dégager; exhaler.

emotion, i-mau´-ch'n, n émotion f; **–al,** a émotif; ému.

emperor, emm´-peu-reu n empereur m.

emphasis, emm´-fa-cice, n insistance f.

emphasize, emm´-fa-sâïze, v appuyer sur; mettre en valeur.

emphatic, emm-făte´-ique, a emphatique.

empire, emm´-pâïre, n empire m.

employ, emm-ploa'i´, v employer; **–er,** n patron m; employeur m; **–ment,** n emploi m.

empower, emm-pâ'ou´-eur, v autoriser.

empress, emm´-presse, n impératrice f.

empty, emm´-pti, a vide; v vider.

emulate, emm´-iou-léte, v marcher de pair avec (quelqu'un).

enable, enn-é-b'l, v permettre de.

enact, enn-ăcte´, v décréter.

enamel, enn-ămm´-'l, n émail m; v émailler.

enamoured, enn-ămm´-eurde, a épris de.

encamp, enn-cămmpe´, v camper.

enchant, enn-tchănnte´, v enchanter; **–ment,** n enchantement m.

encircle, enn-seur´-k'l, v entourer.

enclose, enn-clauze´, v (field) clôturer; (in) enfermer, joindre.

enclosure, enn-clau´-jeure, n enclos m; com

piéce jointe f.

encore, an-coare´, v bisser; *interj* bis!

encounter, enn-câ´ounn-*teur*, v rencontrer; n recontre f.

encourage, enn-cor´-idj, v encourager; **–ment,** n encouragement m.

encroach, enn-crautche´, v empiéter; (time, etc) abuser de; **–ment,** n empiétement m; abus m.

encumber, enn-comm´-*beur*, v encombrer.

encumbrance, enn-comm´-brannce, n embarras m; (property) charges fpl.

encyclopedia, en-sâï´-clau-pî´-di-a, n encyclopédie f.

end, ènnde, n fin f, bout m; v finir.

endanger, enn-dénn´-djeur, v mettre en danger.

endear, enn-dîre´, v rendre cher.

endeavour, enn-dèv´-eur, v s'efforcer; n effort m.

endive, enn´-dive, n endive f.

endless, ènnde´-lesse, a sans fin.

endorse, enn-doarse´, v endosser; approuver; **–ment,** n endossement m; sanction f.

endow, enn-dâ´ou´, v doter; **– with,** douer de.

endurance, enn-dioue´-rannce, n résistance f.

endure, enn-dioure´, v endurer; supporter.

enema, enn´-i-ma, n lavement m.

enemy, enn´-i-mi, n ennemi m.

energetic, enn-eur-djett´-ique, a énergique.

energy, enn´-eur-dji, n énergie f; force f.

enervate, enn´-eur-véte, v affaiblir.

enforce, enn-faurce´, v faire observer; imposer.

engage, enn-guédje´, v engager; embaucher; **–d,** a finacé; (reserved) retenu, occupé; **–ment,** n fiancailles fpl; mil combat m; (obligation) engagement m; (appointment) rendez-vous m.

engaging, enn-guédj´-inng, a engageant; attirant.

engender, enn-djenn´-d'r, v engendrer.

engine, enn´-djinne, n machine f; (rail) locomotive f; (car) moteur m; **–er,** mécanicien m;

(profession) ingénieur m; **–ering,** génie m.

England, inng´-lande, n Angleterre f.

English, inng´-liche, a anglais; n (language) anglais m.

engrave, enn-gréve´, v graver; **–r,** n graveur m; **–ing,** n gravure f.

engross, enn-grausse´, v absorber.

engulf, enn-golf´, v engouffrer.

enhance, enn-hânnce´, v rehausser; mettre envaleur.

enjoy, enn-djoa'ï´, v jouir de; **–ment,** n jouissance f; plaisir m; **– oneself,** v s'amuser.

enlarge, enn-lârdje´, v agrandir; dilater.

enlargement, enn-lârdje´-m'nt, n agrandissement m.

enlighten, enn-lâï´-t'n, v éclairer.

enlist, enn-lisste´, v enrôler; s'engager.

enliven, enn-jâï´-v'n, v animer; égayer.

enmity, enn´-mi-ti, n inimitié f; hostilité f.

enormous, i-nôr´-meuce, a énorme.

enough, i-no´, adv & a assez.

enquire, s'informer de; se renseigner.

enrage, enn-rédje´, v exaspérer; faire enrager.

enrapture, enn-râp´-tioure, v ravir; transporter.

enrich, enn-ritche´, v enrichir.

enrol, enn-raule´, v enrôler; s'inscrire.

ensign, enn´-sâïne, n (flag) enseigne f; (naval flag) pavillon m; (rank) enseigne m.

enslave, enn-sléve´, v asservir; captiver.

ensnare, enn-snére´, v prendre au piège.

ensue, enn-sioue´, v s'ensuivre.

ensure, enn-choure´, v s'assurer de; rendre sûr.

entail, enn-télé´, v entraîner; (law) substituer.

entangle, enn-tänn´-g'l, v emmêler.

enter, enn´-teur, v entrer; – up, inscrire.

enterprise, enn´-teur-prâïze, n entreprise f; (boldness) esprit d'entreprise m.

entertain, enn-teur-téné´, v divertir; (guests) recevoir; (consider) admettre; –ment, n divertissement m.

enthusiasm, enn-tsioue´-zi-âzme, n enthousiasme m.

entice, enn-tâïce´, v tenter; séduire.

entire*, enn-tâïre´, a entier, complet.

entitle, enn-tâî´-t'l, v intituler; donner droit à.

entomb, enn-toum´, v ensevelir.

entrance, enn´-trannce, n entrée f.

entrance, enn-trânnce´, v hypnotiser; transporter.

entreat, enn-trîte´, v supplier; implorer.

entrench, enn-trenche´, v se retrancher.

entrust, enn-trosste´, v confier à.

entry, enn´-tri, n entrée f; (record) écriture f.

entwine, enn-tou´âïne´, v enrouler; enlacer.

enumerate, i-niou´-mé-réte, v énumérer.

envelop, enn-vel´-ŏpe, v envelopper.

envelope, enn´-vel-ôpe, n enveloppe f.

envious*, enn´-vî-euce, a envieux.

environment, enn-vâï´-reun-m'nt, n milieu m; (ecological) environnement m.

environs, enn-vâï´-ronnze, npl environs mpl.

envoy, enn´-voa´ï, n envoyé m.

envy, enn´-vi, n envie f; v envier.

epicure, èp´-i-kioure, n gourmet m.

epidemic, èp-i-demm´-ique, n épidémie f.

episode, èp´-i-saude, n épisode m.

epistle, è-piss´-'l, n épître f.

epoch, i´-poque, n époque f.

equal, î´-coual, n & a* égal, -e m & f; v égaler; –ity, n égalité f; –ize, v égaliser.

equator, i-coué´teur, n équateur m.

equilibrium, i-coui-lib´-ri-eume, n équilibre m.

equip, i-couipe´, v équiper; munir.

equitable, èk´-oui-ta-b'l, a équitable.

equity, èk´-oui-ti, n équité f; justice f.

equivalent, i-coui-va-lennte, n & a équivalent m.

era, i´-ra, n ére f.

eradicate, é-râd´-i-quéte, v extirper; déraciner.

erase, i-réze´, v (rub out)

effacer; (cross out) rayer.

eraser, i-ré´-zeŭr, n gomme
à effacer f; (metal)
grattoir m.

erect, i-recte´, v ériger;
bâtir; a droit; debout.

ermine, eur´-mine, n
hermine f.

erode, i-raude´, v ronger.

erosion, i-rau-j'n, n
érosion; usure f.

erotic, i-rotte´-ique, a
érotique.

err, eure, v errer;
(mistake) se tromper.

errand, èrr´-annde, n
commission f.

erratic, err-rǎt´-tique, a
changeant; irrégulier.

erroneous*, err-rau´-ni-
euce, a erroné.

error, èrr´-eur, n erreur f;
faute.

erupt, i-ropt´, v entrer en
éruption.

eruption, i-rope´-ch'n, n
éruption f.

escalate, ess´-qeu-léte, v
(s')intensifier.

escalator, ess´-qeu-lét´-'r, n
escalier roulant m.

escape, ess-képe´, n fuite f.
évasion f; v échapper.

escort, ess-kôrte´, n
escorte f; cavalier m; v
escorter.

especially, ess-péch´-al-li,
adv surtout.

espionage, ess´-pi-a-nâge,
n espionage m.

essay, ès-sé´, n essai m;
composition f.

essential*, ess-senn´-ch'l,
a essentiel.

establish, ess-tǎb´-liche, v
établir.

establishment, ess-tǎb´-
liche-m'nt, n
établissement m.

estate, ess-téte´, n
propriété f; biens mpl;
(status) rang m;
(possessions) succession
f.

esteem, ess-tîme´, v
estimer; n estime f.

estimate, ess´-ti-méte, n
évaluation f; (cost)
devis m; v évaluer;
estimer.

estrange, ess-tréne´-dje, v
aliéner.

etch, ètch, v graver.

etching, ètch´-inng, n
gravure à l'eau forte f.

eternal*, i-teur´-n'l, a
éternel.

eternity, i-teur´-ni-ti, n
éternité f.

ether, î´-tseur, n éther m.

ethical, é´-tsi-k'l, a moral.

ethics, é´-tsiks, npl morale
f.

ethnic, èts´-nique, a
ethnique.

Europe, i'oue´-reup, n

Europe f.

evacuate, i-vǎk´-iou-éte, v
évacuer.

evade, i-véde´, v éviter;
éluder.

evaporate, i-vǎp´-ŏ-réte, v
s'évaporer.

evasive*, i-vé´-cive, a
évasif.

eve, îve, n veille f.

even, î´-v'n, adv même; a
égal; pair; quitte;
(smooth) uni.

evening, ive´-ninng, n soir
m; soirée f; – dress,
tenue de soirée f; robe
du soir f.

evensong, i´-venn-sonng,
n service du soir m.

event, i-vennte´, n
événement m; cas m;
–ful, a accidenté;
mémorable; –ually, adv
finalement.

ever, èv´-'r, adv toujours;
(at any time) jamais.

everlasting*, èv´-eur-lâst-
inng, a éternel.

every, év´-ri, a chaque;
tous les; –body, n tout le
monde; –thing, tout m;
–where, adv partout.

evict, i-victe´, v expulser;
–ion, n expulsion f.

evidence, èv´-i-dennce, n
évidence f; preuve f;
déposition f; give –, v
déposer.

evident, èv´-i-dennte, *a* évident.

evil, î´-v'l, *n* mal *m*; *a* mauvais; méchant.

evince, i-vinnce´, *v* manifester.

evoke, i-vauque´, *v* évoquer.

evolution, î´-vau-lioue-ch'n, *n* évolution *f*.

evolve, i-volve´, *v* déployer; émettre; évoluer.

ewe, ioue, *n* brebis *f*.

exact, egg-zàct´, *a** exact; *v* exiger; **–ing,** *a* exigeant; **–itude,** *n* exactitude *f*.

exaggerate, egg-zàdj´-i-réte, *v* exagérer.

exaggeration, egg-zàdj-i-ré´-ch'n, *n* exagération *f*.

exalt, egg-zoalt´, *v* exalter.

exam, egg-zàmm´, *abbr n* examen *m*.

examination, egg-zàmm-inn-é´-ch'n, *n* examen *m*; inspection *f*; (legal) interrogatoire *m*.

examine, egg-zàmm´-inne, *v* examiner.

example, egg-zàmm´-p'l, *n* exemple *m*.

exasperate, egg-zàss´-peur-éte, *v* exaspérer.

excavate, èx´-ca-véte, *v* faire des fouilles.

exceed, ex-cîde´, *v*

exceder; dépasser.

exceedingly, ex-cîd´-inng-li, *adv* excessivement.

excel, ex-celle´, *v* exceller; **–lent,** *a* excellent.

except, èk-cepte´, *v* excepter. *prep* sauf; excepté; **–ion,** *n* exception *f*; **take –ion,** *v* s'offenser; **–ional** *a* exceptionnel.

excerpt, èk-seurpte´, *n* extrait *m*.

excess, èk-cesse´, *n* excès *m*; (surplus) excédent *m*.

excessive, èk-cess´-ive, *a* excessif.

exchange, ex-tchéne´-dje, *n* échange *m*; (money) change *m*; (telephone) central *m*; *v* échanger.

exchequer, ex-tchèk´-eur, *n* ministère des finances *m*.

excise, èk-sàïze´, *n* régie *f*; *v* retrancher; supprimer.

excitable, èk-sàï´-ta-b'l, *a* excitable; nerveux.

excite, èk-sàïte´, *v* exciter; agiter.

excitement, èk-sàïte´-m'nt, *n* émotion *f*; agitation *f*.

exciting, èk-sàï´-tinng, *a* passionnant.

exclaim, ex-cléme´, *v* s'écrier.

exclamation, ex-clà-mé´-

ch'n, *n* exclamation *f*.

exclude, ex-cloude´, *v* exclure.

exclusive*, ex-cloue´-cive, *a* exclusif.

excruciating, ex-croue´-chi-éte-inng, *a* atroce.

excursion, ex-kor-ch'n, *n* excursion *f*.

excuse, ex-kiouze´, *v* excuser; *n* excuse *f*.

execute, èx´-ci-kioute, *v* exécuter; accomplir.

executioner, ex-ci-kiou´-chönn-*eur*, *n* bourreau *m*.

executor, ex-cè´-kioue-teur, *n* exécuteur.

exempt, egg-zemmpte, *v* dispenser; *a* dispensé.

exemption, egg-zemmpte´-ch'n, *n* dispense *f*.

exercise, èx´-eur-sàïze, *n* exercice *m*; *v* exercer.

exert, egg-zeurte´, *v* s'efforcer; **–ion,** *n* effort *m*.

exhaust, egg-zôste´, *v* épuiser; *n mech* échappement *m*.

exhibit, egg-zib´-itte, *v* exposer; montrer; *n* article exposé *m*.

exhibition, egg-zi-bi´-ch'n, *n* exposition *f*.

exhilarate, egg-zil´-à-réte, *v* réjouir.

exhilarating, egg-zil´-aréte-inng, *a* vivifiant.

exigency, èk´-si-djenn-ci, *n* exigence *f.*

exile, èk´-sâile, *v* exiler; *n* exil *m;* (person) exilé *m.*

exist, egg-zisste´, *v* exister; –ence, *n* existence *f.*

exit, èk´-citte, *n* sortie *f.*

exonerate, egg-zonn´-eur-éte, *v* exonérer; disculper; innocenter.

exorbitant, èk-sôre´-bi-t'nt, *a* exorbitant.

exotic, egg-zotte´-ique, *a* exotique.

expand, ex-pănnde´, *v* dilater; –ing, *a* extensible.

expansion, ex-pănn-ch'n, *n* expansion *f.*

expect, ex-pecte´, *v* attendre; s'attendre à; –ation, *n* attente *f.*

expedient, ex-pî´-di-ennte, *n* expédient *m; a* convenable.

expedite, ex´-pi-dâîte, *v* accélérer.

expedition, ex-peu-di´-ch'n, *n* expédition *f.*

expel, ex-pelle´, *v* expulser; renvoyer.

expend, ex-pennde´, *v* dépenser.

expenditure, ex-penn´-di-tioure, *n* dépense *f.*

expense, ex-pennse´, *n* dépense *f;* frais *mpl.*

expensive*, ex-penn´-cive, *a* coûteux; cher.

experience, ex-pi´-ri-ennce, *n* expérience *f; v* éprouver, faire l'expérience de.

experiment, ex-pair´-i-mennte, *n* expérience *f; v* expérimenter.

expert, ex-peurte´, *n & a* expert *m.*

expire, ex-pâîre´, *v* expirer.

explain, ex-pléne´, *v* expliquer.

explanation, ex-pla-né´-ch'n, *n* explication *f.*

explicit, ex-pli´-site, *a* explicite; clair.

explode, ex-plaude´, *v* faire explosion.

exploit, ex-ploa'ite´, *n* exploit *m; v* exploiter.

explore, ex-plaure´, *v* explorer.

explorer, ex-plaur´-eur, *n* explorateur *m.*

explosion, ex-plau-j'n, *n* explosion *f.*

explosive, ex-plau´-cive, *a & n* explosif *m.*

export, ex-paurte´, *v* exporter; *n* exportation *f;* –er, *n* exportateur *m.*

expose, ex-pauze´, *v* exposer; (fraud) démasquer; (plot) dévoiler.

expostulate, ex-poss´-tiou-léte, *v* faire des remontrances.

exposure, ex-pau-jeure, *n* exposition *f;* scandale *m.*

expound, ex-pâ'ounnde´, *v* exposer; expliquer.

express, ex-presse´, *n* express *m,* rapide *m; a* exprés; *v* exprimer; –ion, *n* expression *f.*

expulsion, ex-pol-ch'n, *n* expulsion *f.*

exquisite*, ex´-coui-zite, *a* exquis.

extend, ex-tennde´, *v* étendre; s'étendre.

extensive, ex-tenn´-cive, *a* étendu; vaste.

extent, ex-tennte´, *n* étendue *f;* point *m;* degré *m.*

extenuating, ex-tenn´-iou-é´-tinng, *a* atténuant.

exterior, ex-ti´-ri-eur, *n & a* extérieur *m.*

exterminate, ex-teur´-mi-néte, *v* exterminer.

external*, ex-teur´-n'l, *a* externe; extérieur.

extinct, ex-tinng´-kt, *a* éteint; (race, etc) disparu.

extinguish, ex-tinng´-gouiche, *v* éteindre.

extort, ex-tôrte´, *v* extorquer.

extorsion, ex-tôr´-ch'n, *n*
extorsion *f*.

extra, ex´-tra, *a* en plus; *n*
supplément *m*;
–ordinary, *a*
extraordinaire.

extract, ex-trăcte´, *v*
extraire; *n* extrait *m*.

extravagant, ex-tră´-va-
gannte, *a* dépensier.

extreme, ex-trîme´, *n*
extrême *m*; *a** extrême.

extremity, ex-trè´-mi-ti, *n*
extrémité *f*.

extricate, ex´-tri-kéte, *v*
dégager de.

extrovert, ex´-tra-veurte,
n extraverti,e *m* & *f*.

eye, âï, *n* œil *m*; troi *m*;
–ball, globe *m* (de l'œil);
–brow, sourcil *m*; **–lash,**
cil *m*; **–let,** œillet *m*;
–lid, paupière *f*; **–sight,**
vue *f*; **–witness,** témoin
oculaire *m*.

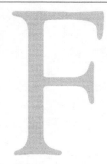

fable, fé´-b'l, n fable f.

fabric, făb´-rique, étoffe f; tissu m; structure f; **–ation,** fabrication f; invention f.

fabulous*, făb´-iou-leuce, a fabuleux.

façade, fă-sade´, n façade f.

face, féce, n figure f, visage m, face f; (clock) cadran m; v faire face à; **– cream,** n crème pour le visage f.

facilitate, fa-cil´-i-téte, v faciliter.

facilities, fă-si´-li-tîze, n équipement m.

facsimile, făk-simm´-i-li, n fac-similé m.

fact, făcte, n fait m.

factor, făk´-tŏr, n facteur m; élément m.

factory, făk´-teur-i, n fabrique f; usine f.

faculty, făk´-eul-ti, n faculté f; aptitude f.

fade, féde, v se faner; (colour) passer; (material) se déteindre.

fail, féle, v manquer; faillir; (exam, etc) échouer; n **without –,** sans faute; **–ing,** n défaut m; prep à défaut de; faute de; **–ure,** échec m; (insolvency) faillite f; (of person) raté, -ée m & f.

faint, fé-nnte, v s'évanouir; n évanouissement m; a* léger; faible.

fair, fère, a juste; beau; (hair) blond; n foire f; **–ness,** équité f; beauté f;

honnêteté f.

fairy, fé´-ri, n fée f.

faith, féts, n foi f; confiance f; **–ful*,** a fidéle.

fall, foal, n chute f; descente f; (prices) baisse f; v tomber; baisser.

fallacy, făl´-la-ci, n fausseté f; illusion f.

false*, foalse, a faux; artificiel.

falsehood, foalse´-houde, n mensonge m.

falsification, foal´-si-fi-qué´-ch'n, n falsification.

falsify, foal´-si-făï, v falsifier.

falter, foal´-teur, v hésiter; (speech) balbutier.

fame, féme, n renommée f; **–d,** a renommé.

familiar*, fa-mil´-i-eur, a familier; intime.

family, fămm´-i-li, n famille f.

famine, fămm´-inn, n famine f.

famish, fămm´-iche, v affamer.

famous, féme´-euce, a fameux; célèbre.

fan, fănne, n éventail m; ventilateur m; v éventer.

fanatic, fă-năt´-ique, n & a fanatique m & f.

fanaticism, fă-năt´-i-cizme, n fanatisme m.

fancy, fănn´-ci, n imagination f; (liking) goût m; (desire) envie f; v imaginer; avoir envie de.

fancy-dress, fănn´-ci-dresse, n déguisement m; travesti m.

fang, fainng, n (dog) croc m; (snake) crochet m.

fantastic, fănn-tăss´-tique, a fantastique.

fantasy, fănn´-ta-zi, n fantaisie f.

far, fâre, adv loin; a lointain; éloigné.

farce, fârce, n farce f.

fare, fère, n prix du parcours m; (food) chère f.

farewell, fère-ouel´, n adieu m.

farm, fârme, n ferme f; **–er,** fermier m.

farther, fâre´dzeur, adv plus loin; a plus éloigné.

fascinate, făss´-ci-néte, v fasciner.

fascinating, făss´-ci-né-tinng, a séduisant.

fashion, făche´-eune, n mode f; v façonner; **to be in –,** être à la mode; **–able,** a à la mode.

fast, fâste, a rapide; ferme; (colour) bon teint; n

jeûne m; v jeûner; **– food,** n restauration rapide f.

fasten, fâs´-s'n, v attacher; fixer; (close) fermer.

fastidious*, făss-tid´-i-euce, a difficile; exigeant.

fat, fătte, n graisse f; (meat) gras m; a (person) gros; (animal) gras; **–ten,** v engraisser; **–ty,** a graisseux, gras.

fatal*, fé´-t'l, a fatal; mortel.

fate, féte, n destin m; sort m; **–d,** a destiné.

father, fâ´dzeur, n père m; **–in-law,** beau-père m; **–ly,** a paternel.

fatigue, fa-tîgue´, n fatigue f; v fatiguer; n fatigue f.

fault, foalte, n faute f; (defect) défaut m; **–less*,** a impeccable; **–y,** défectueux.

favour, fé´-veur, n faveur f; grâce f; (com) honorée f; v favoriser; **to do** (someone) **a –,** rendre service; **–able,** a favorable; propice; **–ite,** n & a favori, -te m & f.

fawn, foanne, n faon m.

fax, făxe, n fax m; n télécopie f; v faxer; envoyer par télécopie.

fear, fîre, v craindre; n

crainte f, peur f; **–ful,** a effroyable; craintif; **–less,** intrépide.

feasible, fî´-zi-b'l, a praticable; faisable.

feast, fîsste, n fête f, festin m; v régaler.

feat, fîte, n exploit m; (skill) tour de force m.

feather, fé´-dzeur, n plume f; v emplumer.

feature, fît´-ieure, n trait m; particularité f.

February, fé´-brou-èr-i, n février m.

federation, fé´-deur-é´-ch'n, n fédération f.

fed-up, fèd-op-ouidz, (with) v en avoir marre (de).

fee, fî, n honoraires mpl; prix m.

feeble, fî´-b'l, a faible; débile; mou.

feed, fîde, v nourrir; (cattle) paître.

feel, fîle, v sentir; tâter; n toucher m; **–er,** n (insects) antenne f; **–ing,** toucher m; sensation f; sentiment m.

feign, féne, v feindre; simuler.

fell, fèle, v abattre; assommer.

fellow, fèl´-au, n membre m; collègue m; pop

garçon m; homme m;
–ship, camaraderie f.
felony, fèl´-au-ni, n crime
m.
felt, felte, n feutre m.
female, fî´-méle, n & a
femelle f; a & n féminin
m.
feminine, fème´-i-ninn, a
& n féminin m.
fence, fènnce, n clôture f;
v entourer;
(swordsmanship) faire
de l'escrime.
fender, fenn´-deur, n
garde-feu m.
ferment, feur-mennte´, v
fermenter; n ferment m.
fern, feurne, n fougère f.
ferocious*, fi-rau´-cheuce,
a féroce.
ferret, fèr´-ette, n furet m;
v fureter.
ferry, fèr´-i, n bac m; v
passer en bac.
fertile, feur´-tâîle, a
fertile.
fertilize, feur´-ti-lâïze, v
fertiliser.
fervent, feur´-vennte, a
fervent; ardent.
fester, fess´-teur, v
s'envenimer.
festival, fess´-ti-v'l, n fête
f; festival m; a de fête.
festive, fess´-tive, a
joyeux; de fête.
festoon, fess-toune´, n

feston m; v festonner.
fetch, fètche, v aller
chercher.
fetter, fèt´-teur, v
enchaîner; **–s,** npl fers
mpl.
feud, fioude, n inimitié f;
–al, a féodal.
fever, fî´-veur, n fièvre f;
–ish, a fiévreux.
few, fioue, a peu de; **a –,**
quelques.
fiancé, fi-onne´-sé, n
fiancé m.
fiancée, fi-onne´-sé, m
fiancée f.
fibre, fî´-beur, n fibre f.
fickle, fik´-'l, a volage;
inconstant.
fiction, fique´-ch'n, n
fiction f; roman m.
fictitious*, fique-tich´-
euce, a fictif; faux.
fidelity, fi-dél´-i-ti, n
fidélité f.
fidget, fid´-jette, v remuer;
–y, a remuant.
field, fîlde, n champ m;
pré m; (games) terrain
m.
fiend, fînnde, n démon m;
–ish, a diabolique.
fierce*, fîrce, a féroce;
farouche; furieux.
fiery, fâî´-eu-ri, a ardent;
fougueux.
fifteen, fiff´-tîne, n & a
quinze m; **–th,** n & a

quinzième m & f.
fifth, fifts, n & a
cinquième m & f.
fiftieth, fiff´-ti-its, n & a
cinquantième m & f.
fifty, fiff´-ti, n & a
cinquante m.
fig, figue, n figue f; **– tree,**
figuier m.
fight, fâîte, v se battre;
combattre; n combat m.
figure, figue´-ioure, n
figure f; forme f; ligne;
(number) chiffre m.
filch, filtche, v piquer,
voler.
file, fâïle, n (tool) lime f;
(office) classeur m;
dossier m; mil file f; v
limer; classer.
filigree, fil´-i-grî, n
filigrane m.
fill, file, v remplir; n
suffisance f.
filly, fil´-i, n pouliche f.
film, filme, n voile m;
(snapshots, etc)
pellicule f; (cinema)
film m; v filmer.
filter, fil´-teur, v filtrer; n
filtre m.
filth, filts, n saleté f; **–y,** a
sale.
fin, fine, n nageoire f.
final*, fâî´-n'l, a final;
décisif.
finalize, fâïn´-a-lâïze, v
mettre au point; fixer.

finally, fâïn´-a-li, *a* enfin; finalement (lastly, at last); définitivement (once and for all).

finance, fi-nãnnce´, *n* finance *f*; *v* commanditer.

financial*, fi-nãnn´-ch'l, *a* financier.

finch, finntche, *n* pinson *m*.

find, fâïnnde, *v* trouver.

fine, fâïne, *v* mettre à l'amende; *n* amende *f*; *a* fin; délicat; beau; subtil; excellent.

finery, fâï´-neur-i, *n* parure *f*.

finger, finng´-gueur, *n* doigt *m*; *v* toucher.

finish, finn´-iche, *v* finir; terminer; *n* fin *f*.

fir, feur, *n* sapin *m*; – **cone,** pomme de pin *f*.

fire, fâïre, *n* feu *m*; (conflagration) incendie *m*; *v* incendier; (gun, etc) tirer; – **alarm,** *n* avertisseur d'incendie *m*; – **brigade,** corps de pompiers *m*; – **engine,** pompe à incendie *f*; – **escape,** échelle de sauvetage *f*; –**man,** pompier *m*; –**place,** foyer *m*; –**proof,** *a* ininflammable; –**works,** *npl* feu d'artifice *m*.

firm, feurme, *n* maison (de commerce) *f*; *a** solide, ferme.

first, feurste, *n* & *a** premier, -ère *m* & *f*.

fish, fiche, *n* poisson *m*; *v* pêcher; –**bone,** *n* arête *f*; –**erman,** pêcheur *m*; – **hook,** hameçon *m*; –**monger,** poissonnier *m*.

fishing, fich´-inng, *n* pêche *f*; – **rod,** canne à pêche *f*.

fissure, fich´-ioure, *n* fissure *f*, fente *f*.

fist, fiste, *n* poing *m*.

fistula, fiss´-tioue-la, *n* fistule *f*.

fit, fite, *v* ajuster; correspondre; (clothes) aller; *n med* attaque *f*; *a* convenable; propre à; en forme.

fittings, fitt´-inngs, *npl* garnitures *fpl*, accessoires *mpl*.

five, fâïve, *n* & *a* cinq *m*.

fix, fixe, *v* fixer; arranger; *n* embarras *m*; impasse *f*.

fixture, fixé´-tioure, *n* objet fixé à demeure *m*.

fizzy, fi´-zi, *a* gazeux.

flabby, flăb´-i, *a* flasque; mollasse.

flag, flăgue, *n* drapeau *m*; *naut* pavillon *m*; –**ship,** vaisseau amiral *m*; –**staff,** hampe de drapeau *f*.

flagon, flăg´-ŏnn, *n* flacon *m*.

flagrant, flé´-grannte, *a* flagrant.

flake, fléke, *n* (metal) lame *f*; (snow, etc) flocon *m*.

flaky, flé´-ki, *a* (pastry) feuilleté.

flame, fléme, *n* flamme *f*; *v* flamber.

flange, flănndje, *n* rebord *m*; (wheel) boudin *m*.

flank, flain´-ngk, *v* flanquer; border; *n* flanc *m*.

flannel, flănn´-'l, *n* flanelle *f*; (face) gant de toilette *m*.

flap, flăppe, *n* battant *m*; (pocket) patte *f*; (wings) coup d'aile *m*; *v* battre; *fam* s'affoler.

flare, flère, *n* vive clarté *f*; flamme *f*; *v* flamboyer; (trousers, etc) évaser.

flash, flăche, *n* éclat *m*; (lightning) éclair *m*; (guns, etc) feu *m*.

flask, flăsske, *n* flacon *m*.

flat, flătte, *n* appartement *m*; *mus* bémol *m*; *a* plat.

flatten, flătt´-'n, *v* aplatir.

flatter, flătt´-eur, *v* flatter; –**ing*,** *a* flatteur; –**y,** *n* flatterie *f*.

flavour, flé´-veur, *n* saveur

f; goût m; (wine) bouquet m; v assaisonner.

flaw, floa, n défaut m; (metal) paille f.

flax, flåxe, n lin m.

flea, flî, n puce f.

flee, flî, v fuir; s'enfuir.

fleece, flîce, n toison f; v tondre; (rob) écorcher.

fleet, flîte, n flotte f; a* rapide; léger.

flesh, flèche, n chair f.

flexible, flè'-xi-b'l, a flexible; souple.

flicker, flik'-eur, v vaciller; clignoter; n battement m.

flight, flåïte, n (fleeing) fuite f; (birds, planes) vol m; (stairs) escalier m.

flimsy, flimm'-zi, a léger; fragile; (paper) papier pelure m.

flinch, flinntche, v broncher; fléchir.

fling, flinng, v lancer.

flint, flinnte, n silex m; (lighter) pierre f (à briquet).

flippant*, flipp'-annte, a léger; (person) désinvolte.

flirt, fleurte, v flirter; n flirt m & f.

float, flaute, n (angler's) flotteur m; v flotter; (on back) faire la planche; (a company) lancer.

flock, floque, n troupeau m; (birds) vol m; v s'attrouper.

flog, flogue, v fouetter.

flood, flodde, v inonder; n inondation f; (tide) marée f.

floor, flaure, n plancher m; (storey) étage m.

floppy disk, floppe-î-disque, n disquette f.

florid, flor'-ide, a fleuri; flamboyant.

florist, flor'-isste, n fleuriste m & f.

floss, flosse, n (dental) fil dentaire f; bourre de soie f.

flounce, flå'ounnce, n (dress) volant m; v se démener.

flour, flå'oueur, n farine f.

flourish, flor'-iche, n brandissement m; mus fanfare f; v prospérer; (brandish) brandir.

flout, flå'oute, v se moquer de.

flow, flau, n écoulement m; (river) cours m; v couler.

flower, flå'ou'-eur, n fleur f; v fleurir.

flu, floue, n grippe f.

fluctuate, floc'-tiou-éte, v fluctuer.

flue, floue, n tuyau de cheminée m.

fluency, floue'-enn-ci, n facilité f.

fluent, floue'-ennte, a facile; coulant.

fluff, floff, n duvet m; peluches fpl; –y, a pelucheux.

fluid, floue'-idd, n & a fluide m.

fluke, flouque, n (chance) coup de hasard m.

flurry, flor'-i, n émoi m; v agiter; troubler.

flush, floche, v (redden) rougir; (rinse) laver à grande eau; n rougeur f; a (level) au niveau de.

fluster, floce'-teur, v déconcerter; n agitation f.

flute, floute, n flûte f; –d, a cannelé.

flutter, flott'-eur, v palpiter; battre des ailes.

fly, flåï, n mouche f; (trouser) n braguette f; v voler; (flag) flotter.

foal, faule, n poulain m; v pouliner.

foam, faume, n écume f; v écumer.

focus, fau'-keuce, v mettre au point; régler; n foyer m.

fodder, fod'-r, n fourrage m.

foe, fau, n ennemi m.

foetus, fi´-teuce, n embryon m.

fog, fogue, n brouillard m; **–gy,** a brumeux; **–horn,** n sirène f.

foil, foa'ile, n (fencing) fleuret m; (metal) feuille f; v déjouer.

foist, foa'iste, v imposer; introduire; fourrer.

fold, faulde, n (clothes etc) pli m; (sheep) bercail m; v plier; (arms) croiser.

foliage, fau´-li-èdje, n feuillage m.

folk, fauke, n gens mpl & fpl.

follow, foll´-au, v suivre; fig s'ensuivre.

follower, foll´-au'r, n partisan m; disciple m.

folly, foll´-i, m folie f; (stupidity) sottise f.

foment, fo-mennte´, v fomenter.

fond, fonnde, a affectueux; **to be – of,** aimer.

fondle, fonn´-d'l, v choyer, caresser.

font, fonnte, n fonts baptismaux mpl.

food, foude, n nourriture f; (a food) aliment m.

fool, foull, n imbécile m & f; v duper; **–hardy,** a

téméraire; **–ish,** sot; imprudent.

foot, foutt, n pied m; **–ball,** football m; **–baller,** footballeur m; **–man,** valet de pied m; **–path,** sentier m; (pavement) trottoir m; **–print,** trace de pas f; **–step,** pas m.

for, fôr, prep pour; pendant. conj car.

forage, for´-idj, n fourrage m; v fourrage.

forbear, fôr-bére´, v supporter; s'abstenir.

forbearance, fôr-bèr´-annce, n indulgence f.

forbid, fôr-bide´, v défendre; **–ding,** a repoussant.

force, fôrce, v forcer; n force f; **–ful,** a vigoureux.

forceps, for´-seppse, n pince f; forceps m.

forcible, fôr´-ci-b'l, a énergique; par force.

ford, fôrde, v passer à gué; n gué m.

fore, fore, n avant m; a antérieur; **–arm,** n avantbras m; **–bode,** v présager; **–boding,** n présage m; **–cast,** prévision f; v prévoir; **–close,** v (law) forclore; **–fathers,** n aïeux mpl;

–finger, index m; **–going,** a précédent; **–gone,** préconcu; **–ground,** n premier plan m; **–head,** front m; **–man,** contremaître m; **–most,** a le plus avancé; principal; **–runner,** n précurseur m; **–see,** v prévoir; **–sight,** n prévoyance f; **–shall,** v devancer; **–taste,** n avant-goût m; **–tell,** v prédire; **–thought,** n préméditation f; **–warn,** v avertir.

foreign, for´-ine, a étranger; **–er,** n étranger, -éren m & f.

forest, for´-este, n forêt f.

forfeit, for´-fite, n gage m; (law) dédit m; v perdre; renoncer.

forge, fordje, v forger; (falsify) contrefaire; n forge f; **–ry,** contrefacon f; faux m.

forget, fôr-guètte´, v oublier; **–ful,** a oublieux; négligent; **–fulness,** n oubli m; **–-me-not,** (flower) myosotis m.

forgive, fôr-guive´, v pardonner.

forgiveness, fôr-guive´-nesse, n pardon m.

for(e)go, fore-gau´, v renoncer à; s'abstenir

de.

fork, forque, n fourchette f; (tool) fourche f; (road) bifurcation f; v bifurquer.

forlorn, fŏr-lôrne´, a abandonné; désespéré.

form, fôrme, n forme f; (a form to fill up) formule f; (seat) banc m; (class) classe f; v former; **–al*,** a de forme; formel; officiel; formalité f; **–ation,** n formation f; **–er,** a précédent; ancien; **–erly,** adv autrefois.

forsake, fôr-céque´, v délaisser; abandonner.

fort, fôrte, n fort m; **–ification,** fortification f; **–ify,** v fortifier; **–ress,** n forteresse f.

forth, fôrts, adv en avant; désormais; **–coming,** a prochain; **–with,** adv sur le champ.

fortieth, fôr´-ti-its, n & a quarantième m & f.

fortitude, fôr´-ti-tioude, n courage m.

fortnight, forte´-nâite, n quinzaine f; quinze jours.

fortunate*, fôr´-tiou-néte, a heureux.

fortune, fôr´-tioune, n fortune f; (fate) sort m.

forty, fôr´-ti, n & a

quarante m.

forward, fôr´-ouarde, v expédier; faire suivre; adv en avant; a avancé; affronté; **–ing-agent,** n agent de transport m; **–ness,** effronterie f.

fossil, foss´-il, n & a fossile m.

foster, fosse´-t'r, v élever; encourager; **–-parents,** npl parents adoptifs mpl.

foul, fâ'oule, v souiller; a* sale; impur; obscène; (unfair) déloyal; **– play,** nquelquechose de louche f.

found, fâ'ounnde, v fonder; (metal) fondre; **–ation,** n fondation f; fig fondement m; **–er,** v sombrer; n fondateur m; **–ling,** enfant trouvé m; **–ry,** fonderie f.

fountain, fâ'ounn´-tinne, n fontaine f; **– pen,** stylo m.

four, fôr, n & a quatre m; **–fold,** a quadruple; **–teen,** n & a quatorze m; **–th,** quatrième m & f.

fowl, fâ'oule, n volaille f.

fox, foxe, n renard m; **– terrier,** fox-terrier m.

foyer, foa'ï´-é, n foyer m.

fraction, frǎck´-ch'n, n fraction f.

fracture, frǎck´-tioure, v

fracturer; n fracture f.

fragile, frǎd´-jile, a fragile.

fragment, frǎgue´-m'nt, n fragment m.

fragrance, fré´-grannce, n perfum m.

fragrant, fré´-grannt, a parfumé.

frail, fréle, a frêle; **–ty,** n fragilité f.

frame, fréme, n forme f; cadre m; (car) chassis m; v former; (picture, etc) encadrer; **–s,** (glasses) n monture f.

franchise, frǎnn´-tchâïze, n franchise f.

frank*, frain-ngk, a franc; **–ness,** n franchise f.

frantic, frǎnn´-tique, a frénétique; furieux.

fraud, froade, n fraude f; **–ulent*,** a frauduleux.

fray, fré, n (scuffle) bagarre f; v (material) s'effiler.

freak, frîque, n phénomène m; **–ish,** a bizarre.

freckle, frèk´-'l, n tache de rousseur f.

free, frî, v libérer; délivrer; a libre; gratuit; **–dom,** n liberté f; **–mason,** franc-maçon m; **–trade,** libre échange m.

freeze, frîze, v geler; glacer; congeler.

freezer, frî´-*zeur, n*
congélateur *m.*

freezing, frîz´-inng, *n*
congélation *f; a* glacial.

freight, frête, *n* fret *m;*
cargaison *f; v* affréter.

frenzy, frenn´-zi, *n*
frénésie *f.*

frequency, fri´-couenn-ci,
n fréquence *f.*

frequent, fri´-couennte, *a*
fréquent; *v* fréquenter.

fresh*, frèche, *a* frais;
–ness, *n* fraîcheur *f.*

fret, frette, *v* se
tourmenter; **–ful,** *a*
irritable; **—saw,** *n* scie à
découper *f;* **–work,**
découpage *m.*

friar, fraï´-'r, *n* moine *m;*
–y, *n* monastère *m.*

friction, frique´-ch'n, *n*
friction *f;* frottement *m.*

Friday, fraï´-dé, *n*
vendredi *m;* **Good –,**
vendredi saint *m.*

fridge, fridje, *n* frigo *m.*

friend, frennde, *n* ami *m;*
–liness, bienveillance *f;*
a amical; **–ship,** *n* amitié
f.

fright, fraîte, *n* frayeur *f;*
peur *f;* **–en,** *v* effrayer;
–ened, *a* effrayé; **–ening,**
a effrayant; **–ful,** *a*
effroyable;
épouvantable.

frigid, fridj´-ide, *a* glacial;

frigide.

frill, frile, *n* volant *m;*
ruche *f;* (paper)
papillote *f.*

fringe, frinndje, *n* frange *f;*
bord *m; v* border.

frisk, frisque, *v* fouiller.

frisky, frisk´-i, *a* frétillant;
animé.

fritter, fritt´-'r, *n* beignet
m; v morceler; **– away,**
dissiper, gaspiller.

frivolous*, friv´-ŏ-leuce, *a*
frivole.

frock, froque, *n* (dress)
robe *f.*

frog, frogue, *n* grenouille *f.*

frolic, frol´-ique, *v*
folâtrer; *n* espièglerie *f.*

from, fromme, *prep* de;
depuis; de la part de;
d'après.

front, fronnte, *n* devant
m;
mil front *m; a* de face;
–age, *n* façade *f.*

frontier, fronnt´-i-*eur, n* &
a frontière *f.*

frost, froste, *v* glacer; *n*
gelée *f;* (hoar) givre *m;*
— bitten, *a* gelé; **–y,**
glacé.

froth, frôts, *n* écume *f;*
mousse *f; v* écumer;
mousser.

frown, frâ´oune, *v* froncer
les sourcils; *n*
froncement de sourcils

m.

frugal*, froue´-g'l, *a*
frugal.

fruit, froute, *n* fruit *m;*
–erer, fruitier *m;* **–ful,** *a*
fructueux; **–less,** stérile.

frustrate, fross-trête´, *v*
frustrer.

fry, fraï, *v* frire; faire frire.

fuchsia, fioue´-chi-*a, n*
fuchsia *m.*

fuel, fioue´-eul, *n*
combustible *m.*

fugitive, fioue´-dji-tive, *n*
& *a* fugitif, –ive *m* & *f.*

fugue, fiougue, *n* fugue *f.*

fulcrum, feul´-creum, *n*
point d'appui *m.*

fulfil, foull-fill´, *v*
accomplir; réaliser;
satisfaire; **–ment,** *n*
accomplissement *m;*
rélisation *f.*

full, foull, *a* plein;
complet.

fulness, foull´-nesse, *n*
plénitude *f;* abondance
f.

fulsome, foull´-seumme, *a*
vil; écœurant.

fume, fioume, *n* vapeur *f;*
v (rage) rager.

fun, fonne, *n* amusement
m; (joke) plaisanterie *f;*
–ny, *a* drôle; amusant.

function, fonnk´-ch'n, *n*
fonction *f; v*
fonctionner.

fund, fonnde, *n* fonds *mpl*; caisse *f.*

fundamental*, fonn-da-menn´-t'l, *a* fondamental *f.*

funeral, fioue´-neur-'l, *n* enterrement *m*; funérailles *fpl.*

funnel, fonn´-'l, *n* entonnoir *m*; (smoke) cheminée.

fur, feure, *n* fourrure *f*; (boiler) tartre *m*; *v* incruster; **–rier,** *n* fourreur *m.*

furious*, fioue´-ri-*euce*, *a* furieux.

furnace, feur´-nisse, *n* four *m*; fourneau *m*; (ship, etc) foyer *m.*

furnish, feur´-niche, *v* meubler; fournir.

furniture, feur´-ni-tioure, *n* meubles *mpl.*

furrow, for´-au, *v* sillonner; *n* sillon *m.*

further, feur´dzeur, *adv* en plus; loin; *a* supplémentaire; *v* avancer; seconder.

furtive*, feur´-tive, *a* furtif.

fury, fioue´-ri, *n* furie *f.*

fuse, fiouze, *n* (time) fusée *f*; (electric) plomb *m*; *v* fuser, sauter.

fuss, foce, *n* embarras *m*; cérémonies *fpl*; *fam* des histoires *fpl.*

fusty, foce´-ti, *a* sentant le renfermé; moisi.

futile, fioue´-tâîle, *a* futile; frivole.

future, fioue´-tioure, *n* avenir *m*; *a* futur.

gable, gué´-b'l, n pignon m.

gaff, găffe, n gaffe f.

gag, găgue, v bâillonner; n bâillon m; *fam* blague f.

gaiety, gué´-i-ti, n gaieté f.

gaily, gué´-li, adv gaiement.

gain, guéne, n gain m; v gagner; atteindre; (clock, etc) avancer.

gait, guéte, n démarche f; (horse) allure f.

gaiter, gué´-t'r, n guêtre f.

galaxy, găl´-ak-ci, n galaxie f.

gale, guéle, n tempête f.

gall, goal, n bile f; v irriter; – **stone**, n calcul biliaire m; – **bladder**, n vésicule biliaire f.

gallant, găl´-'nt, a brave; galant.

gallantry, găl´-ann-tri, n bravoure f; galanterie f.

gallery, găl´-eur-i, n galerie f; amphithéâtre m.

gallop, găl´-pe, v galoper; n galop m.

gallows, găl´-auze, n potence f; gibet m.

galvanism, găl´-vann-izme, n galvanisme m.

galvanize, găl´-vann-âïze, v galvaniser.

gamble, gămm´-b'l, v jouer de l'argent; miser; –**r**, n joueur m.

game, guéme, n jeu m; partie f; (birds, etc) gibier m; –**keeper**, garde-chasse m.

gammon, gămm´-eune, n cuisse de porc fumée f.

gander, gănn´-d'r, n jars m.

gang, gain´-ng, n équipe f; bande f; –**way**, passage m; (ship) passerelle f.

gaol, djéle, n prison f.

gap, găppe, n brèche f; ouverture f; trou m; écart m.

gape, guépe, v regarder bouche bée; s'ouvrir.

garage, ga-râdge´, n garage m.

garb, gârbe, n costume m, habit m.

garbage, gâr´-bidj, n ordures fpl.

garden, gâr´-d'n, n jardin m; (kitchen) (jardin) potager m; –**er**, jardinier m; –**ing**, jardinage m.

gargle, găr´-g'l, v se gargariser; n gargarisme m.

garland, gâr´-lannde, n guirlande f; v orner de guirlandes.

garlic, gâr´-lique, n ail m.

garment, gâr´-m'nt, n vêtement m.

garnish, gâr´-niche, v garnir; n garniture f.

garret, găr´-ette, n mansarde f.

garrison, găr´-i-s'n, n garnison f.

garrulous, găr´-ou-leuce, a bavard.

garter, gâr´-t'r, n jarretière f.

gas, găce, n gaz m; –**eous**,

a gazeux; – **cooker,** *n* cuisinière à gaz *f*; — **works,** usine à gaz *f*.

gash, gâche, *v* balafrer; *n* balafre *f*; coupure *f*.

gasp, gâsspe, *v* haleter; *n* soupir convulsif *m*.

gastric, gâss´-trique, *a* gastrique.

gate, guéte, *n* porte *f*; (iron) grille *f*; (wooden) barrière *f*.

gather, gădz´-eur, *v* rassembler; (pluck) cueillir; (conclude) comprendre; **–ing,** *n* réunion *f*; *med* abcès *m*.

gaudy, goa´-di, *a* voyant; criard.

gauge, guédje, *n* indicateur *m*; *n* (tool) calibre *m*; (railway) entre-rail *m*; (size) mesure *f*; *v* mesurer; estimer.

gaunt, goännte, *a* maigre; décharné.

gauze, goaze, *n* gaze *f*; (wire) toile métallique *f*.

gawky, goa´-ki, *a* dégingandé; gauche.

gay*, gué, *a* homosexuel; gai; joyeux; dissolu.

gaze, guéze, *v* regarder fixement; *n* regard fixe *m*.

gazelle, ga-zelle´, *n* gazelle *f*.

gazette, ga-zette´, *n* gazette *f*.

gear, guîeur, *n* équipment; (car) vitesse *f*; (car) boîte de vitesse *f*.

gelatine, djell´-a-tinn, *n* gélatine *f*.

gelding, guêl´-dinng, *n* cheval hongre *m*.

gem, djème, *n* pierre précieuse *f*.

gender, djenn´-d´r, *n* genre *m*.

general, djenn´-eu-ral, *n* général *m*; *a** général.

generalize, djenn´-eu-ra-lâîze, *v* généraliser.

generate, djenn´-eur-éte, *v* produire; engendrer.

generation, djenn-eur-é-ch´n, *n* génération *f*.

generosity, djenn-eur-o´-si-ti, *n* générosité *f*.

generous*, djenn´-eur-euce, *a* généreux.

genial, dji´-ni-al, *a* doux; cordial.

genetive, djenn´-i-tive, *n & a* génitif *m*.

genius, dji´-ni-euce, *n* génie *m*.

genteel, djenn-tîle´, *a* comme il faut.

gentle, djenn´-t'l, *a* doux; **–man,** *n* homme bien élevé *m*; monsieur *m*; **–ness,** douceur *f*.

gently, djenn´-tli, *adv* doucement.

gents, djennts *n* W.C. (pour hommes) *mpl*.

genuine*, djenn´-iou-ine, *a* authentique; sincère; **–ness,** *n* authenticité *f*; sincérité *f*.

geography, dji-og´-ră-fi, *n* géographie *f*.

geology, dji-ol´-o-dji, *n* géologie *f*.

geometry, dji-omm´-e-tri, *n* géométrie *f*.

geranium, dji-ré´-ni-omm, *n* géranium *m*.

germ, djeurme, *n* germe *m*; microbe *m*.

germinate, djeur´-mi-néte, *v* germer.

gesticulate, djesse-tik´-ioue-léte, *v* gesticuler.

gesture, djesse´-tioure, *n* geste *m*.

get, guette, *v* obtenir; (earn) gagner; (fetch) aller chercher; (attain) arriver; **– back,** recouvrer; **– down,** descendre; **– off,** descendre; **– on,** progresser; monter; s'entendre; **– out,** sortir; **– up,** se lever.

geyser, guî´-zeur, *n* geyser *m*; chauffe-bain *m*.

ghastly, gâce´-tli, *a* blême; (awful) épouvantable.

gherkin, gueur´-quine, *n*

cornichon *m*.

ghost, gôsste, *n* revenant
   m; fantôme *m*.

giant, djâï´-'nte, *n* géant
   m; **–ess,** géante *f*.

gibberish, guib´-*eur*-iche,
   n baragouin *m*.

gibbet, djib´-ette, *n* gibet
   m; potence *f*.

gibe, djâïbe, *v* se moquer
   de; *n* raillerie *f*.

giblets, djib´-letce, *npl*
   abatis *mpl*.

giddiness, guid´-i-ness, *n*
   vertige *m*.

giddy, guid´-i, *a* étourdi;
   vertigineux.

gift, guifte, *n* don *m*;
   cadeau *m*; talent *m*.

gifted, guif´-tédde, *a* doué.

gigantic, djâï-gânne´-
   tique, *a* gigantesque.

giggle, guig-'l, *v* rire
   nerveusement.

gild, guilde, *v* dorer.

gilding, gilt, guild´-inng,
   guilte; *n* dorure *f*.

gills, guilze, *npl* branchies
   fpl.

gimlet, guime´-lette, *n*
   vrille *f*.

gin, djine, *n* gin *m*.

ginger, djinn´-dj*eur*,
   gingembre *m*.

gipsy, djip´-ci, *n*
   bohémien *m*; tzigane *m*.

giraffe, dji-raffe´, *n* girafe
   f.

girder, gueur´-d'r, *n* poutre
   f; traverse *f*.

girdle, gueur´-d'l, *n* gaine
   f; *v* ceindre.

girl, gueurle, *n* fille *f*;
   jeune fille *f*; **–hood,**
   jeunesse *f*.

girth, gueurts, *n* contour
   m; (horse) sangle *f*.

gist, djisste, *n* substance *f*;
   essentiel *m*.

give, guive, *v* donner;
   remettre; **–in,** céder;
   –up, renoncer à.

gizzard, guiz´-*eur*de, *n*
   gésier *m*.

glacier, glé´-ci-*eur*, *n*
   glacier *m*.

glad, glädde, *a* heureux;
   content; **–den,** *v* réjouir;
   –ness, *n* joie *f*; plaisir *m*.

glade, gléde, *n* clairière *f*;
   percée *f*.

glamorous, *a* (person)
   séduisant; (job)
   prestigieux.

glance, glânnce, *n* coup
   d'œil *m*; *v* jeter un coup
   d'oeil; **– off,** dévier.

gland, glännde, *n* glande *f*.

glare, glère, *n* clarté *f*;
   (stare) regard fixe *m*; *v*
   éblouir; regarder
   fixement.

glaring, glèr´-inng, *a*
   éblouissant; voyant; (of
   fact etc) manifeste.

glass, glâce, *n* verre *m*;

miroir *m*; (pane) vitre *f*;
   –es, (spectacles) *n*
   lunettes *fpl*; **–ware,**
   verrerie *f*; **–y,** *a* vitreux;
   (smooth) lisse.

glaze, gléze, *v* vitrer;
   (cake, etc) glacer;
   (pottery) émailler; *n*
   (lustre) lustre *m*; émail
   m.

glazier, glé´-jeur, *n* vitrier
   m.

gleam, glîme, *n* lueur *f*;
   (ray) rayon *m*; *v* luire;
   briller.

glean, glîne, *v* glaner; **–er,**
   n glaneur, -euse *m* & *f*.

glee, glî, *n* joie *f*.

glen, glène, *n* vallon *m*.

glib, glibbe, *a* (of the
   tongue) bien déliée.

glide, glâïde, *v* glisser;
   planer; **–r,** *n* (aircraft)
   planeur *m*.

glimmer, glimm´-'r, *v* luire
   faiblement; *n* lueur *f*.

glimpse, glimmpse, *n* coup
   d'œil *m*; aperçu *m*.

glint, glinnte, *n* trait de
   lumière *m*; *v* luire.

glisten, gliss´-'n, *v*
   étinceler; reluire.

glitter, glitt´'r, *v* briller;
   étinceler; *n* éclat *m*.

gloat, glaute, *v* se réjouir
   de; couver des yeux.

global, glaub´-'l *a*
   mondial.

globe, glaube, n globe m;
sphère f.

globular, globb´-iou-l'r, a
sphérique.

gloom, gloume, n
obscurité f; (dismal)
tristesse f.

gloomy, gloumm´-i, a
obscur; (dismal) triste.

glorify, glau´-ri-faî, v
glorifier.

glorious*, glau´-ri-euce, a
glorieux; superbe.

glory, glau´-ri, n gloire f; v
– **in,** se glorifier de.

gloss, glsse, n lustre m; **–y,**
a luisant; brillant.

glove, glove, n gant m.

glow, glau, n éclat m;
rougeur f; v luire; rougir.

glue, gloue, n colle f; v
coller.

glum, gleumme, a morose.

glut, glotte, v (market)
inonder; (of food) (se)
gorger; n excès m.

glutton, glott´-'n, n
glouton, -onne m & f.

gnarled, nârlde, a noueux.

gnash, nâche, v grincer;
–ing, n grincement m.

gnat, nâtte, n cousin m,
moucheron m.

gnaw, noa, v ronger.

go, gau, v aller; partir;
mech marcher; – **away,**
s'en aller; partir; – **back,**
retourner; – **down,**

descendre; – **out,** sortir;
– **up,** monter; –
without, se passer de.

goad, gaude, n aiguillon m;
v aiguillonner; inciter.

goal, gaule, n but m.

goal, gaute, n chèvre f;
billy –, bouc m.

goalkeeper, gaule´-kîp-eur
n gardien de but m.

gobble, gob-'l, v avaler
avidement; dévorer.

goblin, gob´-linne, n lutin
m; farfadet m.

God, god, godde, m, Dieu
m; dieu m; **–child,**
filleul, -e m & f; **–dess,**
déesse f; **–father,** parrain
m; **–liness,** n piété f; **–ly,**
a pieux; dévot; **–mother,** n
marraine f.

goggles, gog´-g'lze, npl
grosses lunettes fpl.

goitre, goi´-teur, n goître
m.

gold, gaulde, n or m; **–en,**
a d'or; **–finch,** n
chardonneret m; **–fish,**
poisson rouge m; – **leaf,**
or en feuille m; **–smith,**
orfèvre m.

golf, golf, n golf m; –
course, terrain de golf
m.

gong, gon-ng, n gong m.

gonorrhœa, gonn-o-ri´-a,
n blennorragie f.

good, goudd, n bien m;

avantage m; a bon; sage;
–bye! interj adieu! au
revoir! **–morning,**
–afternoon, –day,
bonjour; **–night,**
bonsoir.

good-natured, goudd-
nét´-tiour'd, a d'un bon
naturel.

goodness, goudd´-nesse, n
bonté f.

goods, goudd´-ze, npl
marchandises fpl; effets
mpl.

goodwill, goudd-ouil´, n
bienveillance f;
(business) fonds m,
clientèle f.

goose, goûce, n oie f.

gooseberry, goûce´-beur-i,
n groseille à maquereau
f.

gore, gôre, n (blood) sang
m; v encorner.

gorge, gôrdje, n gorge f; v
se gorger de.

gorgeous*, gôr´-djeuce, a
somptueux; splendide.

gorilla, go-ril´-la, n gorille
m.

gorse, gôrse, n ajonc m.

gosling, goz´-linng, n
oison m.

gospel, goss´-p'l, n
évangile m.

gossip, goss´-ippe, v
bavarder; papoter; n
potin m; cancans mpl;

(person) commère f.

gouge, gâ'oudje, n gouge f.
v gouger; arracher.

gout, gâ'oute, n goutte f.

govern, gov'-eurne, v
gouverner; **–ess**, n
gouvernante f; **–ment**,
gouvernement m; **–or**,
gouverneur m; mech
régulateur m.

gown, gâ'oune, n robe f.

grab, grâbe, v empoigner;
saisir; n mech benne
preneuse f.

grace, gréce, n grâce f;
–ful*, a gracieux.

gracious*, gré'-cheuce, a
gracieux.

grade, gréde, n grade m;
degré m; rang m; v
classer; graduer.

gradient, gré'-di-ennte, n
pente f; rampe f.

gradual*, grâd'-iou-eul, a
progressif.

graduate, grâd'-iou-éte, n
diplômé, -e m & f; v
graduer; obtenir des
diplômes universitaires.

graft, grâfte, n greffe f; fig
corruption f. v greffer.

grain, gréne, n grain m; v
(paint) veiner.

gram(me), grâmme n
gramme m.

grammar, grâmm´-'r, n
grammaire f.

granary, grânn´-a-ri, n

grenier m.

grand*, grânnde, a
grandiose; magnifique;
–daughter, n petite-fille
f; **–father**, grand-père m;
–mother, grand'mère f;
–son, petit-fils m.

grant, grânnte, v accorder;
n subvention f; bourse f.

grape, grépe, n raisin m.

grape-fruit, grépe´-froute,
n pamplemousse m.

graph, grâffe n graphique
m.

grapple, grâp´-p'l, n
(hook) grappin m; v
lutter.

grasp, grâsspe, v
empoigner;
(understand)
comprendre; n étreinte
f; **–ing**, a avide.

grass, grâsse, n herbe f;
(lawn) gazon m;
–hopper, sauterelle f; **–y**,
a herbeux.

grate, gréte, n (fire) grille
f; v grincer; (cookery,
etc) râper.

grateful, gréte´-foull, a
reconnaissant.

gratification, grâ-ti-fi-
qué´-ch'n, n satisfaction
f.

gratify, grâ´-ti-fâî, v
satisfaire; **–ing**, a
agréable.

grating, gré´-tinng, n

grillage m; a grinçant.

gratis, gré´-tisse, adv
gratis.

gratitude, grâ´-ti-tioude, n
reconnaissance f.

gratuitous*, gra-tiou´-i-
teuce, a gratuit.

gratuity, gra-tiou´-i-ti, n
pourboire m.

grave, gréve, n tombe f; a*
grave; **–digger**, n
fossoyeur m; **–stone**,
pierre tombale f; **–yard**,
cimetière m.

gravel, grâv´-'l, n gravier
m.

gravitate, grâv´-i-téte, v
graviter.

gravity, grâv´-i-ti, n
gravité f.

gravy, gré´-vi, n jus m;
sauce f.

gray, grey, gré, a gris;
(complexion) blême.

graze, gréze, n écorchure f;
v effleurer; érafler;
(feed) paître.

grease, grîce, n graisse f; v
graisser.

greasy, grî´-zi, a graisseux;
(road surface) glissant.

great*, gréte, a grand;
–ness, n grandeur f.

greed, grîde, n
gourmandise f; avidité f;
–ily, adv goulûment; **–y**,
a gourmand; avide.

green, grîne, n & a vert m;

–gage, n reine-Claude f;
––grocer, fruitier m;
–house, serre f; **–ish**, a
verdâtre.

greet, grîte, v saluer; **–ing**,
n salutation f.

grenade, gre-néde´, n
grenade f.

grey, (see **gray**).

greyhound, gré´-
hâ'ounnde, n lévrier m.

grief, grîfe, n chagrin m,
douleur f; doléance f.

grievance, grî´-v'nce, n
grief m.

grieve, grîve, v s'affliger;
chagriner.

grievous, grî´-veuce, a
grave; accablant.

grill, grile, v griller; n gril
m.

grim*, grime, a sinistre;
menaçant.

grimace, gri-méce´, n
grimace f.

grime, grâime, n saleté f;
(dirt) crasse f.

grin, grinne, v grimacer;
. sourire à belles dents; n
large sourire m.

grind, grâinnde, v moudre;
(sharpen) aiguiser.

grinder, grâinn´-deur, n
rémouleur m; broyeur m;
(coffee, etc) moulin m.

grip, grippe, n (action)
étreinte f; (handle)
poignée f; v empoigner;

saisir.

gripe, grâipe, v (bowels)
donner la colique.

grisly, grize´-li, a affreux;
horrible.

grit, gritte, n gravier m;
sable m; **–ty**, a
graveleux.

groan, graune, v gémir; n
gémissement m.

grocer, grau´-ceur, n
épicier m; **–y**, épicerie f.

grog, grgue, n grog m.

groin, grô'ine, n aine f;
arch arête f.

groom, groume, n
palefrenier m.

groove, grouve, v rainer; n
rainure f.

grope, graupe, v tâtonner.

gross, grauce, n (12
dozen) grosse f; a
(coarse) grossier;
(obvious) flagrant;
–weight, n poids brut m.

ground, grâ'ounnde, v
naut échouer; n terrain
m; terre f; (reason) motif
m; base f; **––floor**, rez-
de- chaussée m; **–less**, a
sans fondement; **–work**,
n base f.

group, groupe, n groupe
m; v grouper.

grouse, grâ'ouce, n coq de
bruyère m; v grogner; se
plaindre.

grove, grauve, n bocage m,

bosquet m.

grovel, grov´-'l, v fig
ramper.

grow, grau, v pousser,
croître, grandir; cultiver;
–er, n cultivateur m; **–n
up**, adulte m & f; **–th**,
croissance f.

growl, grâ'oule, n
grognement m; v
grogner.

grub, grobbe, n larve f,
asticot m.

grudge, grodje, n rancune
f; v donner à regret;
envier à.

gruel, groue´-'l, n gruau m.

gruesome, groue´-somme,
a affreux, macabre.

gruff*, groffe; a brusque,
rude.

grumble, gromm´-b'l, v
grommeler; se plaindre;
–r, n grogneur m.

grunt, gronnte, v grogner;
n grognement m.

guarantee, ga-rann-tî´, v
garantir; n garantie f.

guard, gârde, n garde f; v
garder; **–ed**, a
circonspect.

guardian, gâr´-di-anne, n
gardien m; (trustee)
tuteur m.

guess, guesse, v deviner.

guest, guesste, n invité -ée
m & f; (hotel) client -e
m & f; **––house**, n

pension de famille *f*.

guidance, gâï´-d'nce, *n* direction *f*; conduite *f*; orientation *f*.

guide, gâïde, *v* guider; *n* guide *m*.

guild, guilde, *n* corps de métier *m*; corporation *f*.

guile, gâïle, *n* astuce *f*; artifice *m*; **–less,** *a* ingénu.

guilt, guilte, *n* culpabilité *f*; **–y,** *a* coupable.

guinea, gui´-ni, *n* guinée *f*; **– fowl,** pintade *f*; **– pig,** cochon d'Inde *m*.

guise, guâïze, *n* façon *f*; apparence *f*.

guitar, gui-târe´, *n* guitare *f*.

gulf, golfe, *n geog* golfe *m*; (abyss) gouffre *m*.

gull, golle, *n* mouette *f*; *v* duper.

gullet, goll´-ette, *n* gosier *m*.

gulp, golpe, *v* avaler; *n* gorgée *f*.

gum, gomme, *n* gomme *f*; (teeth) gencive *f*.

gun, gonne, *n* fusil *m*; (artillery) canon *m*; **–ner,** canonnier *m*; **–powder,** poudre à canon *f*; **–smith,** armurier *m*.

gurgle, gueur´-g'l, *v* gargouiller; *n*

gargouillement *m*.

gush, goche, *v* jaillir; *n* jaillissement *m*.

gust, gosste, *n* coup de vent *m*; rafale *f*.

gut, gotte, *n* boyau *m*; *v* vider.

gutter, gott´-'r, *n* gouttière *f*; (street) ruisseau *m*.

guy, gaille, *n* type *m*.

gym, djimme *abbr n* gymnase *m*.

gymnasium, djimm-né´-zi-mme, *n* gymnase *m*.

gymnastics, djimm-nǎss´-tikse, *npl* gymnastique *f*.

H

N.B. La lettre H doit
toujours s'aspirer
distinctement sauf dans
les quelques mots
marqués §.

haberdashery, hăb´-eur-
dăch-'ri, n mercerie f.

habit, hăb´-itte, n
habitude f; coutume f.

habitable, hăb´-i-ta-b'l, a
habitable.

habitual*, ha-bit´-iou-eul,
a habituel.

hack, hăque, v écharper;
hacher; couper.

hackneyed, hăque´-nidde,
a rebattu; banal.

haddock, hăd´-oque, n
aiglefin fumé m;
haddock m.

hæmorrhage, hém´-ridje,
n hémorragie f.

hag, hăgue, n mégère f;

–gard, a hagard.

haggle, hăgg´-'l, v
marchander.

hail, héle, n grêle f; v
grêler; (greet) saluer.

hair, hère, n poil m; (of
head only) cheveu m;
(horse) crin m; –brush,
brosse à cheveux f;
–dresser, coiffeur, -euse
m & f; –pin, épingle à
cheveux f; –y, a poilu;
chevelu.

hake, héke, n merluche f.

half, hâfe, n moitié f;
demi, -e m & f; a demi;
adv à moitié.

halibut, hăl´-i-botte, n
flétan m.

hall, hoal, n vestibule m;
entrée f; salle f; –-mark,
poinçon de contrôle m.

hallow, hal´-lau, v

sanctifier.

hallucination, hal-liou-ci-
né´-ch'n, n
hallucination f.

halo, hé´-lau, n auréole m;
(astronomy) halo m.

halt, hoalte, n arrêt m; v
arrêter; interj halte!

halter, hoal´-t'r, n licou m.

halve, hâve, v partager en
deux.

ham, hămme, n jambon
m.

hamburger, hămm´-beur-
gueur, n hamburger m.

hamlet, hămm´-lette, n
hameau m.

hammer, hămm´-'r, n
marteau m; v marteler.

hammock, hămm´-oque, n
hamac m.

hamper, hămm´-p'r, n
panier m; bourriche f; v
gêner.

hand, hănnde, n main f;
(clock) aiguille f; v
passer; donner; –-bag, n
sac à main m; –book,
manuel m; –cuffs,
menottes fpl; –ful,
poignée f; –kerchief,
mouchoir m; –le,
manche m; (door)
bouton m; v manier; –-
made, a fait à la main;
–rail, n rampe f; –y, a
utile; commode; à
portée.

handicapped, hănn-di-
căppe-'t, *v* (mentally)
handicapé
mentalement;
(physically) handicapé
physiquement.

handsome*, hănn'-
somme, *a* beau;
généreux.

hang, hain-ng, *v* pendre; –
up, *v* accrocher.

hangar, hain'-gueur, *n*
hangar *m*.

hanger, hain'-gueur, *n*
cintre *m*.

hang-gliding, haing-glăïd-
inng, *n* vol libre *m*.

hangover, haing-au'-v'r, *n*
gueule de bois *f*.

hanker, hain'-nkeur, *v*
désirer ardemment.

happen, hăp'-p'n, *v*
arriver; se passer.

happily, hăpp'-i-li, *adv*
heureusement.

happiness, hăpp'-i-nesse,
n bonheur *m*.

happy, hăpp'-i, *a* heureux.

harangue, hă-raingue, *n*
harangue *f*; *v* haranguer.

harass, hăr'-ăce, *v*
harceler.

harassment, hăr-ace-m'nt,
n harcelement *m*;
tracasseries *fpl*.

harbour, hâr'-b'r, *n* port
m; *v* héberger.

hard, hârde, *a* dur;

difficile; **–en,** *v* durcir;
refl
s'endurcir; **–ly,** *adv* à
peine; durement; **–ness,**
n dureté *f*; **–ship,** peine
f; privation *f*; **–ware,**
quincaillerie *f*; **–y,** *a*
robuste.

hare, hère, *n* lièvre *m*; **–
lip,** bec de lièvre *m*.

harm, hârm, *n* mal *m*; tort
m; *v* faire du mal; **–ful,** *a*
nuisible; **–less,**
inoffensif.

harmonious*, hâr-mô'-ni-
euce, *a* harmonieux.

harmonize, hăr'-mŏnn-
ăïze, *v* harmoniser.

harness, hăr'-nesse, *n*
équipment *m*; (horse)
harnais *m*; *v* harnacher;
(to a cart) atteler;
(forces) utiliser.

harp, hârpe, *n* harpe *f*; *v*
rabâcher.

harpoon, hâr-poune', *n*
harpon *m*.

harrow, hăr'-au, *n* herse *f*;
v fig tourmenter.

harsh, hârche, *a* (sound)
discordant; (severe) dur;
(colour) criard.

hart, hârte, *n* cerf *m*.

harvest, hăr'-veste, *n*
moisson *f*; récolte *f*; *v*
moissonner; récolter.

hash, hăche, *n* hachis *m*;
(*fig*) gâchis *m*; *v* hacher.

hassle, hasse-'l, *n fam*
difficulté(s) *f(pl)*.

hassock, hăs'-soque, *n*
carreau *m*, coussin *m*.

haste, héste, *n* hâte *f*; **–n,**
v hâter; se hâter.

hastily, héce'-ti-li, *adv* à la
hâte.

hat, hătte, *n* chapeau *m*;
–stand, porte-chapeaux
m.

hatch, hâtche, *n* trappe *f*;
naut écoutille *f*; *v* (eggs)
couver; (plot) tramer.

hatchback, hătche'-
băgue, *n* voiture avec
hayon arrière *f*.

hatchet, hâtch'-ette, *n*
hachette *f*.

hate, héte, *n* haine *f*; *v*
haïr; **–ful*,** *a* odieux.

hatred, hé'-tredde, *n*
haine *f*.

haughtiness, hoa'-ti-
nesse, *n* hauteur *f*;
arrogance *f*.

haughty, hoa'-ti, *a*
hautain; altier.

haul, hoale, *n* tirage *m*;
(catch) coup de filet *m*;
v tirer; (boat) haler;
(drag) traîner.

haunch, hoanntche, *n*
hanche *f*.

haunt, hoannte, *v* hanter;
fig fréquenter; *n*
rendezvous *m*; (animals)
repaire *m*.

have, hâve, *v* avoir;
posséder.

haversack, hăve´-eur-
săque, *n* havresac *m*.

havoc, hăv´-ŏque, *n* dégât
m; ravage *m*.

hawk, hoaque, *n* épervier
m; *v* colporter.

hawker, hoak´-'r, *n*
colporteur *m*.

hawthorn, hoa´-tsôrne, *n*
aubépine *f*.

hay, hé, *n* foin *m*; – **fever,**
rhume des foins *m*; –
loft, grange *f*; –**making,**
fenaison *f*; –**rick,** meule
de foin *f*.

hazard, hăz´-arde, *n*
hasard *m*; *v* hasarder.

hazardous, hăz´-ar-deuce,
a hasardeux.

haze, héze, *n* brume *f*.

hazel, hé´-z'l, *n* noisetier
m; –**nut,** noisette *f*.

hazy, hé´-zi, *a* brumeux

he, hî, *pron* il; lui.

head, hedde, *n* tête *f*; chef
m; principal *m*; directeur
m; –**ache,** mal de tête *m*;
–**ing,** entête *m*; titre *m*;
–**land,** promontoire *m*;
–**light,** phare *m*; –**long,**
adv tête baissée,
aveuglément; –**teacher,**
n directeur *m*; –
quarters, quartier
général *m*; –**strong,** *a*
entêté; opiniâtre; –**way,**

progrès *m*.

heady, hedd´-i, *a* capiteux.

heal, hîle, *v* guérir;
cicatriser; –**ing,** *n*
guérison *f*; *a* curatif.

health, hêlts, *n* santé *f*.

healthy, hêlts´-i, *a* sain;
(climate) salubre.

heap, hîpe, *n* tas *m*; *v*
entasser; amonceler.

hear, hîre, *v* entendre;
–**ing,** *n* (sense) ouïe *f*;
(judicial) audience *f*;
–**say,** ouï-dire *m*.

hearse, heurce, *n*
corbillard m.

heart, hârte, *n* cœur *m*;
courage *m*; –**attack,** *n*
crise cardiaque *f*;
–**broken,** *a* brisé de
douleur; –**burn,** *n*
aigreurs d'estomac *fpl*;
–**ily,** *adv* cordialement;
–**less,** *a* sans cœur.

hearth, hârts, *n* foyer *m*.

heat, hîte, *n* chaleur *f*; *v*
chauffer; –**er,** *n* réchaud
m; radiateur *m*.

heating, hîte´-inng, *n*
chauffage *m*.

heath, hîts, *n* lande *f*;
bruyère *f*.

heathen, hî´-dz'n, *n & a*
paien, -enne *m & f*.

heather, hèdz´-eur, *n*
bruyère *f*.

heatstroke, hîte´-strauke,
n insolation *f*.

heatwave, hîte´-ouéve, *n*
vague de chaleur *f*.

heave, hîve, *v* hisser;
(sigh) pousser un soupir.

heaven, hèv´-'n, *n* ciel *m*;
–**ly,** *a* céleste.

heaviness, hèv´-i-nesse, *n*
poids *m*; pesanteur *f*.

heavy, hèv´-i, *a* lourd;
pesant.

hectic, hèk´-tik, *a* agité;
mouvementé.

hedge, hèdje, *n* haie *f*;
–**hog,** hérisson *m*.

heed, hîde, *v* tenir compte
de; *n* attention *f*; –**ful***,
a attentif; –**less,**
inattentif; étourdi.

heel, hîle, *n* talon *m*.

heifer, hèf´-'r, *n* génisse *f*.

height, hâite, *n* hauteur *f*;
(person) taille *f*.

heighten, hâi´-t'n, *v*
rehausser; augmenter.

heinous*, hé´-neuce, *a*
atroce; abominable.

§heir, aire, *n* héritier *m*;
–**ess,** héritière *f*.

helicopter, he´-li-cop-t'r,
n hélicoptère *m*.

hell, hêle, *n* enfer *m*; –**ish,**
a infernal.

hello, hêle-au´ *int*, *n*
bonjour *m*; (on phone)
allô! ; (in surprise)
tiens!

helm, hêlme, *n* barre *f*;
(wheel) gouvernail *m*.

helmet, hêle´-mette, *n* casque *m*.

helmsman, hêlmze´-männe, *n* timonnier *m*.

help, helpe, *n* aide *f*; (in distress) secours *m*; *interj* au secours! *v* aider; secourir; **–er,** *n* aide *m*; **–ful,** *a* utile; serviable; **–less,** impuissant.

hem, hemme, *n* ourlet *m*; *v* faire un ourlet; **–in,** cerner.

hemisphere, hemm´-i-sfire, *n* hémisphère *m*.

hemlock, hemm´-loque, *n* cigue *f*.

hemp, hemmpe, *n* chanvre *m*.

hen, henne, *n* poule *f*; **— roost,** perchoir *m*.

hence, hennce, *adv* d'ici; **–forth,** désormais.

her, heur, *pron* elle; la; *poss a* son; sa; ses.

herb, heurbe, *n* herbe *f*; **–alist,** herboriste *m*.

herd, heurde, *n* troupe *f*; troupeau *m*; *v* s'attrouper; **–sman,** *n* pâtre *m*.

here, hîre, *adv* ici; **–about,** près d'ici; **–after,** ci-après; dorénavant; **–by,** par ceci; ici, là-dedans; ci-inclus; **–of,** de ceci; **–upon,** là-dessus; **–with,** avec ceci; ci-joint.

hereditary, he-redd´-i-ta-ri, *a* héréditaire.

heresy, hèr´-i-ci, *n* hérésie *f*.

heretic, hêr´-i-tique, *n* hérétique *m & f*.

hermit, heur´-mitte, *n* ermite *m*; **–age,** ermitage *m*.

hernia, hêr´-ni-a, *n* hernie *f*.

hero, hî´-rau, *n* héros *m*.

heroic, hi-rau´-ique, *a* héroïque.

heroin, hêr´-o-inn, *n* héroïne *f*.

heroine, hêr´-o-inn, *n* héroïne *f*.

heroism, hêr´-o-izme, *n* héroïsme *m*.

herring, hair´-inng, *n* hareng *m*.

hers, heurze, *poss pron* le sien; la sienne; les siens; les siennes.

herself, heur-self´, *pron* elle-même.

hesitate, hêz´-i-téte, *v* hésiter.

hesitation, hêz-i-té´-ch'n, *n* hésitation *f*.

heterosexual, hèt-ra-sexe´-siou-'l, *a, n* hétérosexuel, -le *m & f*.

hew, hioue, *v* couper; (stone) tailler.

hiccup, hik´-eupe, *n* hoquet *m*; *v* avoir le hoquet.

hide, hâïde, *v* cacher; *n* peau *f*; cuir *m*.

hideous*, hid´-i-euce, *a* hideux.

hiding, hâï´-dinng *n fig* raclée *f*.

hiding-place, hâï´-dinng-pléce, *n* cachette *f*.

hi-fi, hâï´-fâï, *abbr n* hi-fi *f*; *a* hi-fi.

high, hâï, *a* haut; élevé; (game) faisandé; **–est,** le plus élevé; le plus haut; **– fidelity,** haute fidélité; **–way,** grand-route *f*.

hijack, hâï-djăque, *n* détournement *m*; *v* détourner.

hilarious, hi-lère´-ri-euce, *a* désopilant.

hilarity, hil-ăr´-i-ti, *n* hilarité *f*.

hill, hile, *n* colline *f*; (road) côte *f*.

hilly, hil´-i, *a* accidenté; à pentes.

hilt, hilte, *n* garde *f*; (handle) poignée *f*.

him, himme, *pron* le; lui; **–self,** lui-même.

hind, hâïnnde, *n* biche *f*; *a* d'arrière.

hinder, hinn´-d'r, *v* empêcher; gêner.

hindermost, hinn´-d'r-mauste, *a* dernier.

hindrance, hinn´-

drannce, *n*
empêchement *m.*

hinge, hinndje, *n*
charnière *f;* (door) gond
m.

hint, hinnte, *n*
insinuation *f; v* insinuer.

hip, hippe, *n* hanche *f.*

hire, hâïre, *v* louer; *n*
location *f;* – **purchase,** *n*
vente à tempérament *f.*

his, hize, *poss pron* le sien;
la sienne; les siens; les
siennes; *poss a* son; sa;
ses.

hiss, hice, *v* siffler; *n*
sifflement *m.*

historian, hice-to´-ri-
anne, n historien *m.*

historical, hice-to´-ri-k'l,
a historique.

history, hice´-tŏr-i, *n*
histoire *f.*

hit, hitte, *v* frapper;
(target, etc) toucher; *n*
coup *m.*

hitch, hitch, *n* (obstacle)
anicroche *f; naut* amarre
f; v (pull up) remonter;
(hook on) attacher; --
hike, *v* faire de l'auto-
stop.

hi-tech, hǎï-tèque´ *abbr a*
& *n* hi-tech *m.*

hither, hidz´-'r, *adv* ici; par
ici; **-to,** *adv* jusqu'ici.

hive, hâïve, *n* ruche *f.*

hoard, haurde, *v* amasser;

(food, etc) accaparer; *n*
amas *m.*

hoarding, haurd´-inng, *n*
palissade *f.*

hoarse, haurse, *a* rauque;
enroué.

hoax, hauxe, *n*
mystification *f;* tour *m; v*
mystifier; jouer un tour.

hobble, hobb´-'l, *v*
clopiner; boitiller.

hobby, hobb´-i, *n* passe-
temps favori *m.*

hock, hoque, *n* vin du
Rhin *m;* (leg) jarret *m.*

hoe, hau, *n* binette *f,* houe
f; v biner.

hog, hogue, *n* cochon *m;*
porc *m.*

hogshead, hogz´-hédde, *n*
pièce *f;* tonneau *m.*

hoist, hoa'isste, *v* hisser.

hold, haulde, *v* tenir;
contenir; *n* prise *f;*
(ship) cale *f;* – **back,** *v*
retenir; **-er,** *n* possesseur
m, détenteur *m;* (shares,
etc) actionnaire *m & f;*
(receptacle) porte-. . . .
m; **-ing,** possession *f;*
com participation *f;* –
on, *v* tenir ferme; –
over, ajourner.

hole, haule, *n* trou *m.*

holiday, holl´-i-dé, *n* jour
de fête *m;* (leave) congé
m.

holidays, holl´-i-dèze, *npl*

vacances *fpl.*

holiness, hau´-li-nesse, *n*
sainteté *f.*

hollow, holl´-au, *n* cavité
f; (cheek) creux; *v* creuser.

holly, holl´-i, *n* houx *m.*

holocaust, holl´-au-cors't,
n holocauste *m.*

holy, hau´-li, *a* saint;
sacré; **-water,** *n* eau
bénite *f;* **-week,**
semaine sainte *f.*

homage, home´-idj, *n*
hommage *m.*

home, hôme, *n* maison *f;*
(circle) foyer *m,* chez soi
m; (homeland) patrie *f;*
at –, chez soi; **-less,** *a*
sans abri; **-ly,** intime;
(to be) **-sick,** (avoir) le
cafard; **-work,** *n* devoirs
mpl.

homosexual, hau-mau-
sexe´-sioue-'l, *a & n*
homosexuel, le *m & f.*

§**honest*,** onn´-este, *a*
honnête; **-y,** *n*
honnêteté *f.*

honey, honn´-i, *n* miel *m;*
-moon, lune de miel *f;*
-suckle, chèvrefeuille
m.

§**honorary,** onn´-eur-a-ri,
a honoraire.

§**honour,** onn´-eur, *n*
honneur *m; v* honorer.

§**honourable,** onn´-eur-a-
b'l, *a* honorable.

hood, houdd, n capuchon m; (vehicle) capote f.

hoodwink, houdd´-ouinnque, v tromper.

hoof, houff, n sabot m.

hook, houk, n crochet m; (large) croc m; (naut) gaffe f; (fish) hameçon m; v accrocher; – **and eye,** n agrafe f.

hooligan, hou´-li-g'n, n voyou m.

hoop, houpp, n cercle m; (toy) cerceau m.

hoot, houte, n (owl) hululement m; (derision) huée f; (motor) coup de klaxon m; v hululer; huer; (motor) klaxonner; **-er,** n klaxon m.

Hoover, hou´-veur, (TM) n aspirateur m.

hop, hoppe, v sautiller; n saut m; (plant) houblon m.

hope, hôpe, v espérer; n espoir m; **-ful,** a encourageant; plein d'espoir; **-fully,** avec espoir; avec optimisme; **-less,** sans espoir; inutile.

horizon, ho-raî´-zonne, n horizon m.

horizontal, hor-i-zonn´-t'l, a horizontal.

hormone, hoar´-maune, n hormone f.

horn, hoarne, n corne f; (motor) klaxon m; (hunt) cor de chasse m.

hornet, hoar´-nette n frelon m.

horrible, hor´-i-b'l, a horrible.

horrid*, hor´-ride, a horrible; affreux.

horrify, hor-ri-faï, v épouvanter; horrifier.

horror, hor´-rôr, n horreur f.

hors d'oeuvre, oar-deuve´, n hors d'oeuvre m.

horse, horce, n cheval m; **-back (on),** adv à cheval; **-hair,** n crin m; **-power,** puissance (f) en chevaux; **-radish,** n raifort m; **-shoe,** fer à cheval m.

hose, hauze, n tuyau d'arrosage m.

hospitable, hoss´-pi-ta-b'l, a hospitalier.

hospital, hoss´-pi-t'l, n hôpital m.

hospitality, hoss-pi-tă´-li-tî, n hospitalité f.

host, hauste, n (friend) hôte m; (army) armée f; (sacrament) hostie f; **-ess,** hôtesse f.

hostage, hoss´-tidj, n otage m.

hostel, hoss´-tell, n pension; **youth –,** n auberge de la jeunesse f.

hostile, hoss´-tâïle a hostile.

hot, hotte, a chaud; (food, sauces, etc) épicé; fort.

hotel, hô-tel´, n hôtel m.

hothouse, hott´-hâ´ouce, n serre f.

hound, hâ'ounnde, n chien de chasse m; v chasser; traquer.

§hour, âour, n heure f; **-ly,** adv d'heure en heure.

house, hâ'ouze, v loger.

house, hâ'ouce, n maison f; **-agent,** agent de location m; **-hold,** maison f; **-keeper,** femme de charge f; **– of Commons,** Chambre des Communes f; **-wife,** ménagère f; **-work,** ménage m.

hovel, hov´-'l, n taudis m; bouge m.

hover, hov´-'r, v voltiger; planer; hésiter.

hovercraft, hov´´r-crăfte, n aeroglisseur m.

how, hâ'ou, adv comment; **-ever,** cependant; **-much, many?** combien?

howl, hâ'oule, v hurler; n hurlement m.

hub, hobbe, n moyeu m.

huddle, hod´-d'l, v se

presser les uns contre les autres.

hue, hi'oue, n couleur f; (shade) nuance f.

hug, hogue, v étreindre; n étreinte f.

huge, hioudje, a immense; énorme, vaste.

hulk, holke, n *naut* ponton m.

hull, holle, n *naut* coque f.

hum, homme, v (insect) bourdonner; (engine) vrombir; (voice) fredonner; n bourdonnement m.

human*, hi'oue'-manne, a & n humain m.

humane, hi'oue-méne', a humain; compatissant.

humanity, hi'oue-mă'-ni-ti, n humanité f.

humble, homm'-b'l, a humble; v humilier.

humidity, hi'oue-mid'-i-ti, n humidité f.

humiliate, hi'oue-mil'-i-éte, v humilier.

humiliation, hi'oue-mil-i-ét'-ch'n, n humiliation f.

humorous*, hi'oue'-meur-euce, a comique.

humour, hi'oue'-meur, v complaire à; n (temper) humeur f; (wit) esprit m; humour m.

hunch, honntche, n bosse f; **–back,** bossu m.

hundred, honn'-dredde, n & a cent m; **–th,** a & n centième m & f.

hunger, honng'-gueur, v avoir faim; désirer; n faim f.

hungry, honng'-gri, a affamé; **to be –,** v avoir faim.

hunt, honnte, v chasser; n chasse f.

hurdle, heur'-d'l, n claie f; (sport) obstacle m.

hurl, heurle, v lancer; précipiter.

hurricane, hor'-i-cane, n ouragan m.

hurry, hor'-i, v se dépêcher; n hâte f.

hurt, heurte, v faire mal; (feeling) blesser.

hurtful, heurte'foull, a nuisible; blessant.

husband, hoze'-bănnde, n mari m; v ménager.

hush! hoche, *interj* chut! **– up,** v étouffer; n silence m.

husk, hossque, n (seeds) cosse f.

husky, hoss'-ki, a (voice) rauque; enroué.

hustle, hoss'-'l, v se presser; bousculer.

hut, hotte, n hutte f; baraque f.

hutch, hotche, n cabane à lapins f; clapier m.

hyacinth, hâï'-a-sinnts, n jacinthe f.

hydrant, hâï'-drannte, n bouche d'incendie f.

hydraulic, hâï-drau'-lique, a hydraulique.

hydro, hâï'-drau, **–gen,** n hydrogène m; **–phobia,** hydrophobie f; **–plane,** hydravion m.

hygiene, hâï'-djeen, n hygiène f.

hygienic, hâï-djeenn'-ique, a hygiénique.

hymn, himme, n hymne f.

hypermarket, hâï'-peu-mâr-kette, n hypermarché m.

hyphen, hâï'-fenne, n trait d'union m.

hypocrisy, hip-o'-cri-si, n hypocrisie f.

hypocrite, hip'-ŏ-crite, n hypocrite m & f.

hypodermic, hâï-po-deur'-mique, a hypodermique.

hypothetical, hâï-po-tsè'-ti-k'l, a hypothétique; supposé.

hysterical*, hice-tèr'-i-k'l, a hystérique.

I, âï, *pron* je, moi.

ice, âïce, *n* glace *f*; *v* glacer, frapper; **–berg,** *n* iceberg *m*; **––cream,** *n* glace *f*; **– rink,** patinoire *f*; **– skating,** patinage (sur glace) *f*.

icicle, âï´-ci-k'l, *n* glaçon *m*.

icing, âïce´-inng, *n* glace *f*; **– sugar** sucre glace *m*.

icy, âï´-ci, *a* glacial; glacé.

idea, âï-dî´-a, *n* idée *f*.

ideal, âï-dî´-eul, *n* & *a* idéal *m* **–ize,** *v* idéaliser.

identical*, âï-denn´-ti-k'l, *a* identique.

identify, âï-denn´-ti-fâï, *v* identifier.

identity, âï-denn´-ti-ti, *n* identité *f*.

idiom, i´-di-ŏmme, *n* idiome *m*.

idiot, i´-di-eute, *n* idiot, -e *m* & *f*; **–ic,** *a* idiot.

idle, âï´-d'l, *v* flâner; *a* oisif; paresseux; **–ness,** *n* oisiveté *f*; **–r,** flâneur *m*.

idol, âï´-dŏl, *n* idole *f*; **–ize,** *v* adorer.

idyll, âï´-dile, *n* idylle *f*.

if, if; *conj* si; **even –,** même si.

ignite, igue-nâïte´, *v* allumer; enflammer.

ignition, igue-ni´-ch'n, *n* (spark) allumage *m*; (car, etc) contact *m*.

ignoble, igue-nau´-b'l, *a* ignoble.

ignominious*, igue-nŏ-minn´-i-euce, *a* ignominieux.

ignominy, igue´-no-mi-ni, *n* ignominie *f*.

ignorance, igue´-nŏ-r'nce, *n* ignorance *f*.

ignorant, igue´-nau-r'nt, *a* ignorant; **to be ignorant of something,** ne rien connaître à.

ignore, igue-nore´, *v* ne pas tenir compte de; faire semblant de ne pas voir.

ill, il, *a* malade; **–ness,** *n* maladie *f*.

illegal*, il-lî´-gal, *a* illégal.

illegible, il-lèdj´-i-b'l, *a* illisible.

illegitimate*, il-li-djitt´-i-méte, *a* illégitime.

illiterate, il-li´-teur-éte, *n* & *a*, illettré, -e *m* & *f*.

illness, il´-nesse, *n* maladie *f*.

illogical*, il-lodj´-i-k'l, *a* illogique.

illuminate, il-lioue´-mi-néte, *v* éclairer; illuminer.

illumination, il-lioue-mi-né´-ch'n, *n* illumination *f*; éclairage *m*.

illusion, il-lioue´-j'n, *n* illusion *f*.

illusory, il-lioue´-so-ri, *a* illusoire.

illustrate, il´-leuce-tréte, *v* illustrer.

illustration, il-leuce-tré´-ch'n, *n* illustration *f*.

illustrious, il-loss´-tri-euce, *a* illustre; célèbre.

image, imm´-idj, n image f; portrait m.

imaginary, i-mădj´-inne-rî, a imaginaire.

imagination, i-mădj-i-né-ch'n, n imagination f.

imaginative, i-mădj´-inne-a-tive, a imaginatif; (person) plein, -e d'imagination.

imagine, i-mădj´-inne, v imaginer; s'imaginer.

imbecile, imm´-bi-sîle, n & a, imbécile m & f.

imbue, imm-bioue´, v imprégner; pénétrer.

imitate, imm´-i-téte, v imiter.

immaculate*, imm-măque´-iou-léte, a immaculé; impeccable.

immaterial, imm-ma-tî-ri-eul, a sans importance; indifférent.

immature, imm-ma-tioure´, a pas mûr.

immeasurable, imm-mèj-iou-ra-b'l, a incommensurable; infini.

immediate*, imm-mî´-di-éte, a immédiat.

immense, imm-mennce´, a immense.

immensity, imm-menn´-ci-ti, n immensité f.

immerge, imm-meurdje´, v immerger; plonger.

immigrant, imm´-mi-grannt, n & a immigrant, -e m & f.

immigrate, imm´-mi-gréte, v immigrer.

immigration, imm-i-gré´-ch'n, n immigration f.

imminent, imm´-mi-nennte, a imminent.

immoderate*, imm-mod´-eur-éte, a immodéré.

immodest*, imm-mod´-este, a immodeste.

immoral*, imm-mor´-'l, a immoral.

immortal*, imm-mor´-t'l, a immortel.

immortalize, imm-mor´-tal-âîze, v immortaliser.

immovable, imm-mouv´-a-b'l, a inébranlable.

immune, imm-mioune´, a immunisé.

immunity, imm-mioue´-ni-ti, n immunité f.

immunization, imm´-mioue-nâî-zé-ch'n, n immunisation f.

imp, immpe, n lutin m; fig petit diable m.

impact, imm´-păcte, n choc m; impact m.

impair, imm-paire´, v détériorer; abîmer.

impale, imm-péle´ v empaler.

impart, imm-pârte´, v communiquer.

impartial*, imm-pâr´-ch'l, a impartial.

impassable, imm-păss´-a-b'l, a impraticable.

impassive, imm-păss´-ive, a impassible.

impatience, imm-pé´-ch'nce, n impatience f.

impatient*, imm-pé´-ch'nt, a impatient.

impede, imm-pîde´, v empêcher; gêner.

impediment, imm-pèd´-i-m'nt, n empêchement m.

impel, imm-pelle´, v forcer; pousser.

impending, imm-penn´-dinng, a imminent.

imperative, imm-pair´-a-tive, n & a impératif m.

imperfect*, imm-peur´-fecte, n & a imparfait m.

imperfection, imm-peur-fèque´-ch'n, n imperfection f.

imperial, imm-pí´-ri-eul, a impérial.

imperil, imm-pair´-il, v mettre en danger.

imperishable, imm-pair´-i-cha-b'l, a impérissable.

impersonal, imm-peur´-sŏ-n'l, a impersonnel.

impersonate, imm-peur´-sŏ-néte, v personnifier.

impertinence, imm-peur´-ti-n'nce, n impertinence

f.

impertinent*, imm-peur´-ti-nennte, *a* impertinent.

impervious*, imm-peur´-vi-*euce*, *a* impénétrable.

impetuous*, imm-pett´-iou-*euce*, *a* impétueux.

impetus, imm-´pi-*teuce*, *n* impulsion *f*; élan *m*.

implant, imm-plânnte´, *v* implanter; inculquer.

implement, imm´-pli-m´nt, *n* instrument *m*; outil *m*.

implicate, imm´-pli-quéte, *v* impliquer.

implication, imm-pli-qué´-ch'n, *n* implication *f*; sous-entendu *m*.

implicit*, imm-pliss´-itte, *a* implicite.

implore, imm-plore´, *v* implorer.

imply, imm-plâï´, *v* impliquer; dénoter; insinuer.

impolite*, imm-po-lâïte´, *a* impoli.

import, imm´-porte, *v* importer; *n* importation *f*; **--duty**, droit d'entrée *m*; **--er**, importateur *m*.

importance, imm-por´-tannce, *n* importance *f*.

important, imm-por´-t'nt, *a* important.

impose, imm-pauze´, *v*

imposer; **-- upon**, abuser de.

imposing, imm-pauze´-inng, *a* imposant.

imposition, imm-po-zi´-ch'n, *n* abus *m*; (tax) impôt *m*.

impossibility, imm-poss´-i-bi´-li-ti, *n* impossibilité *f*.

impossible, imm-poss´-i-b'l, *a* impossible.

impostor, imm-poss´-t'r, *n* imposteur *m*.

impotent, imm´-po-tennte, *a* impuissant.

impound, imm-pâ'ounnde´, *v* (animals) mettre en fourrière; (law) déposer au greffe; saisir (des marchandises).

impoverish, imm-pov´-eur-iche, *v* appauvrir.

impracticable, imm-prăc´-ti-ca-b'l, *a* impraticable.

impregnable, imm-pregg´-na-b'l, *a* imprenable.

impregnate, imm-pregg´-néte, *v* imprégner; (fertilize) féconder.

impress, imm-presse´, *v* imprimer; (feelings) faire une impression; (make clear) faire bien comprendre; **-ion**, *n* impression *f*; (stamp) empreinte *f*; **-ive**, *a*

frappant; émouvant.

imprint, imm-prinnte´, *n* marque *f*; empreinte *f*; *v* empreindre; (mind) imprimer.

imprison, imm-prize´-onn, *v* emprisonner; **-ment**, *n* emprisonnement *m*.

improbable, imm-prob´-a-b'l, *a* improbable.

improper, imm-prop´-'r, *a* inconvenant.

improve, imm-prouve´, *v* améliorer; se perfectionner; **-ment**, *n* amélioration *f*.

improvident, imm-prove´-i-dennte, *a* imprévoyant.

improvise, imm´-pro-vâïze, *v* improviser.

imprudent*, imm-proue´-dennte, *a* imprudent.

impudence, imm´-pioue-dennce, *n* insolence *f*.

impudent*, imm´-pioue-dennte, *a* insolent.

impulse, imm´-polse, *n* impulsion *f*; elan *m*.

impure*, imm-pioure´, *a* impur.

impurity, imm-pioue´-ri-ti, *n* impureté *f*.

impute, imm-pioute´, *v* imputer.

in, inne, *prep* dans; en; à; *adv* dedans.

inability, inn-*a*-bil´-i-ti, *n*

impuissance *f*.

inaccessible, inn-ăc-sess´-i-b'l, *a* inaccessible.

inaccuracy, inn-ăc´-quiou-ra-ci, *n* inexactitude *f*.

inaccurate*, inn-ăc´-quiou-réte, *a* inexact.

inadequate, inn-ăd´-i-couéte, *a* insuffisant.

inadvertent*, inn-ăd-veur´-tennte, *a* inattentif.

inane, inn-éne´, *a* inepte; stupide.

inanimate, inn-ănn´-i-méte, *a* inanimé.

inapt, inn-ăpte´, *a* inapte; **–itude**, *n* inaptitude *f*.

inasmuch as, inn-*aze*-motche´ *ăze*, *conj* vu que.

inaudible, inn-oa-di-b'l, *a* inaudible.

inaugurate, inn-oa-guioue-réte, *v* inaugurer.

inborn, inn´-boarne, *a* inné.

incalculable, inn-cal´-kiou-*la*-b'l, *a* incalculable.

incapable, inn-qué´-pa-b'l, *a* incapable.

incapacitate, inn-ca-păss´-i-ti'ete, *v* rendre incapable.

incapacity, inn-ca-păss´-i-ti, *n* incapacité *f*.

incarnation, inn-câr-né´-ch'n, *n* incarnation *f*.

incautious*, inn-cô´-cheuce, *a* imprudent.

incense, inn-cennse´, *n* encens *m*; *v* provoquer.

incentive, inn-cenn´-tive, *n* motif *m*; stimulant *m*.

incessant, inn-cess´-annte, *a* incessant.

inch, inntche, *n* pouce anglais *m*.

incident, inn´-ci-dennt, *n* incident *m*; **–al**, *a* fortuit.

incision, inn-ci´-j'n, *n* incision *f*.

incite, inn-sâîte´, *v* inciter.

inclination, inn-cli-né´-ch'n, *n* inclination *f*; (disposition) penchant *m*.

incline, inn´-clâïne, *n* (slope) pente *f*; *v* incliner.

include, inn-cloude´, *v* comprendre; renfermer.

inclusive*, inn-cooue´-cive, *a* inclusif; compris.

incoherent*, inn-co-hî´-rennte, *a* incohérent.

income, inn´-comme, *n* revenu *m*, rentes *fpl*; **– tax**, impôt sur le revenu *m*.

incoming, inn´-comm-inng, *a* entrant;

nouveau.

incomparable, inn-comm´-pa-*ra*-b'l, *a* incomparable.

incompatible, inn-comm-patt´-i-b'l, *a* incompatible.

incompetent, inn-comm´-pi-tennte, *a* incompétent.

incomplete*, inn-comm-plîte´, *a* incomplet.

incomprehensible, inn-comm´-pré-henn´-si-b'l, *a* incompréhensible.

inconceivable, inn-cŏnn-cî´-va-b'l, *a* inconcevable.

inconclusive, inn-cŏnn-cloue´-cive, *a* inconcluant.

incongruous*, inn-conng´-grou-*euce*, *a* incongru.

inconsiderable, inn-cŏnn-si-*deur*-a-b'l, *a* insignifiant.

inconsiderate, inn-cŏnn-si´-*deur*-éte, *a* sans égards.

inconsistent*, inn-cŏnn-ciss´-tennte, *a* illogique.

inconsolable, inn-cŏnn-sol´-a-b'l, *a* inconsolable.

inconstant, inn-conn´-stannte, *a* inconstant.

inconvenience, inn-cŏnn-

vî´-ni-ennce, v
déranger; gêner; n
derangement m;
inconvénient m.

inconvenient, inn-cŏnn-
v´-ni-ennte, a
incommode.

incorporate, inn-kor´-po-
réte, v incorporer.

incorrect*, inn-cŏr-recte´,
a inexact; (behaviour)
incorrect.

incorrigible, inn-cor´-i-
dji-b'l, a incorrigible.

increase, inn-crîce´, v
augmenter; accroître; n
augmentation f;
accroissement m.

incredible, inn-crèd´-i-b'l,
a incroyable.

incredulous, inn-crèd´-
iou-leuce, a incrédule.

incriminate, inn-crimm´-
inn-éte, v incriminer.

incubate, inn´-kioue-béte,
v couver.

incubator, inn´-kioue-bé-
teur, n couveuse f.

inculcate, inn´-kol-quéte,
v inculquer.

incur, inn-queur´, v
encourir; (expenses)
faire.

incurable, inn-kiou´-ra-
b'l, a incurable.

indebted, inn-dett´-èdde,
a endetté; redevable.

indecent, inn-dî´-cennte,

a indécent.

indecision, inn-di-si-´j'n,
n indécision f.

indecisive, inn-di-sâï´-
cive, a indécis.

indeed, inn-dîde´, adv en
effet; vraiment.

indefatigable, inn-di-fătt´-
i-gă-b'l, a infatigable.

indefensible, inn-di-
fenn´-si-b'l, a
indéfendable.

indefinite*, inn-dèf´-i-
nitte, a indéfini.

indelible, inn-dèl´-i-b'l, a
indélébile; ineffacable.

indemnify, inn-demm´-ni-
fâï, v indemniser.

indemnity, inn-demm´-ni-
ti, n indemnité f.

independence, inn-di-
penn´-dennce, n
indépendance f.

independent*, inn-di-
penn´-dennte, a
indépendant.

indescribable, inn-di-
scrâï´-ba-b'l, a
indescriptible.

indestructible, inn-di-
strok´-ti-b'l, a
indestructible.

index, inn´-dexe, n table
des matières f; index m.

index-finger, inn´-dexe-
finng´-gueur, n index m.

indicate, inn´-di-quéte, v
indiquer.

indication, inn-di-qué´-
ch'n, n indication f.

indicator, inn´-di-qué-
teur, n indicateur m.

indict, inn-dâïte´, v
poursuivre.

indifference, inn-dif´-eur-
ennce, n indifférence f.

indifferent*, inn-dif´-eur-
ennte, a indifférent.

indigestible, inn-di-djess´-
ti-b'l, a indigeste.

indigestion, inn-di-djess´-
ti-'n, n indigestion f.

indignant, inn-dig´-
nannte, a indigné.

indignity, inn-dig´-ni-ti,
n indignité f.

indigo, inn´-di-go, n
indigo m.

indirect*, inn-di-recte´, a
indirect.

indiscreet*, inn-diss-
crîte´, a indiscret.

indiscriminate, inn-diss-
crimm´-i-néte, a sans
discernement; –ly, adv
indistinctement.

indispensable, inn-diss-
penn´-sa-b'l, a
indispensable.

indisposed, inn-diss-
pauz´d´, a indisposé.

indisputable, inn-diss-
piou´-ta-b'l, a
incontestable.

indistinct*, inn-diss-
tinng'kt´, a indistinct.

indistinguishable, inn-diss-tinng´-gouich-a-b'l, *a* imperceptible.

individual*, inn-di-vid´-iou-al, *a* individuel; *n* individu *m.*

indolent, inn´-dŏ-lennte, *a* indolent.

indoor, inn-daur´, *a* d'intérieur.

indoors, inn-daurze´, *adv* à l'intérieur; à la maison.

induce, inn-diouce´, *v* provoquer; causer; induire.

inducement, inn-diouce´-m'nt; *n* stimulant *m*; motif *m.*

indulge, inn-doldje´, *v* gâter; se livrer à; s'abandonner à.

indulgent*, inn-dol´-djennte, *a* indulgent.

industrial*, inn-doss´-tri-al, *a* industriel.

industrious*, inn-doss´-tri-euce, *a* laborieux.

industry, inn´-doss-tri, *n* industrie *f.*

inebriated, inn-i´-bri-é-tedde, *a* ivre.

ineffective*, inn-èf-fèque´-tive, *a* inefficace.

inefficient*, inn-èf-fich´-ennte, *a* inefficace; incapable.

inept, inn-epte´, *a* inepte; absurde.

inequality, inn-i-couol´-i-ti, *n* inégalité *f.*

inert, inn-eurte´, *a* inerte.

inestimable, inn-ess´-ti-ma-b'l, *a* inestimable.

inevitable, inn-èv´-i-ta-b'l, *a* inévitable.

inexcusable, inn-èks-kioue´-za-b'l, *a* inexcusable.

inexhaustible, inn-èks-hauss´-ti-b'l, *a* inépuisable.

inexpedient, inn-èks-pî´-di-ennte, *a* inopportun.

inexpensive, inn-èks-penn´-cive, *a* bon marché.

inexperienced, inn-èks-pî´-ri-enncd, *a* inexpérimenté; sans expérience.

inexplicable*, inn-èks´-pli-ka-b'l, *a* inexplicable.

inexpressible, inn-èks-press´-si-b'l, *a* inexprimable.

infallible, inn-fàll´-i-b'l, *a* infaillible.

infamous, inn´-fa-meuce, *a* infâme.

infancy, inn´-fann-ci, *n* enfance *f*; (law) minorité *f.*

infant, inn´-fannte, *n* enfant *m*; (law) mineur; -e *m & f.*

infantry, inn´-fann-tri, *n* infanterie *f.*

infatuation, inn-fàtt-iou-é´-ch'n, *n* engouement *m.*

infect, inn-fèkte´, *v* infecter; **–ious*,** *a* contagieux.

infer, inn-feur´, *v* inférer; déduire.

inference, inn´-feur-'nce, *n* déduction *f.*

inferior, inn-fî´-ri-*eur*, *n &* *a* inférieur *m.*

infernal*, inn-feur´-n'l, *a* infernal.

infest, inn-feste´, *v* infester.

infidel, inn´-fi-d'l, *n &* *a* infidèle *m & f.*

infiltrate, inn´-file-tréte, *v* infiltrer; imprégner.

infinite*, inn´-fi-nite, *a* infini.

infirm, inn-feurme´, *a* infirme; maladif.

infirmary, inn-feurm´-a-ri, *n* infirmerie *f.*

inflame, inn-fléme´, *v* enflammer.

inflammable, inn-flàmm´-a-b'l, *a* inflammable.

inflammation, inn-fla-mé´-ch'n, *n* inflammation *f.*

inflate, inn-fléte, *v* gonfler; (prices) hausser.

inflation, inn-flé´-ch'n, *n* inflation *f.*

inflexible, inn-flèk´-si-b'l,

a inflexible.

inflict, inn-flickte´, *v* infliger.

influence, inn´-flouennce, *n* influence *f*; *v* influencer.

influential, inn-flou-enn´-ch'l, *a* influent; **to be –,** avoir de l'influence.

influenza, inn-flou-enn´-za, *n* grippe *f*.

inform, inn-foarme´, *v* informer; **–al,** *a* sans cérémonie; **–ation,** *n* renseignements *mpl*.

infrequent, inn-frî´-couennte, *a* infréquent; rare.

infringe, inn-frinndje´, *v* empiéter; transgresser.

infringement, inn-frinndje´-m'nt, *n* infraction *f*.

infuriate, inn-fiou´-ri-éte, *v* rendre furieux.

infuse, inn-fiouze´, *v* inculquer; (tea, etc) infuser.

ingenious*, inn-djî´-ni-euce, *a* ingénieux.

ingenuity, inn-dji-niou´-i-ti, *n* ingéniosité *f*.

ingot, inng´-gôtte, *n* lingot *m*.

ingrained, inn-grénnde´, *a* enraciné; invétéré.

ingratiate, inn-gré´-chi-éte, *v* **– oneself with,** se faire bien voir de quelqu'un.

ingratitude, inn-grätt´-i-tioude, *n* ingratitude *f*.

ingredient, inn-grî´-di-ennte, *n* ingrédient *m*.

inhabit, inn-hãb´-itte, *v* habiter; **–able,** *a* habitable; **–ant,** *n* habitant *m*.

inhale, inn-héle´, *v* aspirer; (smoke) avaler.

inherent*, inn-hi´-r'nt, *a* inhérent.

inherit, inn-hér´-itte, *v* hériter; **–ance,** *n* succession *f*; héritage *m*.

inhibit, inn-hi´-bitte, *v* empêcher; inhiber; **–ion,** *n* inhibition *f*.

inhospitable, inn-hoss´-pit-a-b'l, *a* inhospitalier.

inhuman*, inn-hioue´-m'n, *a* inhumain.

iniquitous, inn-ik´-oui-teuce, *a* inique.

initial, inn-i´-ch'l, *n* initiale *f*; *a** initial; premier.

initiate, inn-i´-chi-éte, *v* initier; commencer.

initiative, inn-i´-cheutive, *n* initiative *f*.

inject, inn-djecte´, *v* injecter; **–ion,** *n* injection *f*; piqûre *f*.

injudicious*, inn-djioudich´-euce, *a* peu

judicieux.

injunction, inn-djonnk´-ch'n, *n* injonction *f*.

injure, inn´-djioure, *v* blesser; abîmer; nuire à.

injurious*, inn-djioue´-ri-euce, *a* nuisible.

injury, inn´-djeur-i, *n* blessure *f*; tort *m*.

injustice, inn-djoss´-tice, *n* injustice *f*.

ink, inng´-k, *n* encre *f*; **–stand,** encrier *m*.

inlaid, inn-léde´, *a* incrusté; (wood) marqueté.

inland, inn´-lännde, *n* & *a* intérieur *m*.

in-laws, inn´-loaz, *npl* beaux-parents *mpl*; belle famille *f*.

inlet, inn´-lette, *n* entrée *f*; *geog* bras de mer *m*.

inmate, inn´-méte, *n* pensionnaire *m* & *f*; interné *m*.

inmost, inn´-mauste, *a* le plus profond.

inn, inne, *n* auberge *f*; **–keeper,** aubergiste *m*.

inner, inn´-'r, *a* intérieur; secret; *n* **–city,** centre de zone urbaine *m*; quartiers défavorisés *mpl*.

innocent, inn´-o-cennte, *a* innocent.

innocuous*, inn-o´-kiou-

euce, a inoffensif.

innovation, inn-no-vé´-
ch'n, *n* innovation *f*.

innumerable, inn-nioue´-
meur-a-b'l, *a*
innombrable.

inoculate, inn-o´-kiou-
léte, *v* inoculer.

inoffensive, inn-o-fenn´-
cive, *a* inoffensif.

inopportune, inn-opp´-or-
tioune, *a* inopportun.

inquest, inn´-coueste, *n*
enquête *f*.

inquire, inn-couâïre, *v*
demander; s'informer.

inquiry, inn-couâ´ï-ri, *n*
demande *f*; enquête *f*; --
office, bureau de
renseignements *m*.

Inquisition, inn-couiz-i´-
ch'n, *n* Inquisition *f*.

inquisitive*, inn-couiz´-i-
tive, *a* curieux.

insane, inn-séne´, *a* fou;
dément.

insanity, inn-sann´-i-ti, *n*
folie *f*; démence *m*.

insatiable, inn-sé´-chi-a-
b'l, *a* insatiable.

inscription, inn-scripe´-
ch'n, *n* inscription *f*.

insect, inn´-secte, *n*
insecte *m*.

insecure, inn-ci-kioure´, *a*
peu sûr; hasardeux.

insensible, inn-senn´-si-
b'l, *a* insensible;

(unconscious) sans
connaissance.

inseparable, inn-sép´-a-ra-
b'l, *a* inséparable.

insert, inn-seurte´, *v*
insérer; introduire; --**ion,**
n insertion *f*;
(advertisement)
annonce *f*.

inside, inn-sâïde´, *n*
intérieur *m*; *a* intérieur;
adv en dedans.

insidious*, inn-si´-di-
euce, *a* insidieux.

insignificant, inn-sigg-
nif´-i-k'nt, *a*
insignifiant.

insincere*, inn-sinn-cire´,
a faux.

insinuate, inn-sinn´-iou-
éte, *v* insinuer.

insipid*, inn-sipp´-idde, *a*
insipide; fade.

insist, inn-sisste´, *v* exiger;
insister.

insolence, inn´-sŏ-lennce,
n insolence *f*.

insolent, inn´-sŏ-lennte, *a*
insolent.

insolvent, inn-soll´-
vennte, *a* insolvable.

inspect, inn-specte´, *v*
inspecter; --**ion,** *n*
inspection *f*; --**or,**
n inspecteur *m*.

inspiration, inn-spi-ré´-
ch'n, *n* inspiration *f*.

inspire, inn-spâïre, *v*

inspirer; --**d,** *a* inspiré.

install, inn-stoale´, *v*
installer; *mech* monter;
--**ation,** *n* installation *f*;
montage *m*.

instalment, inn-stoale´-
m'nt, *n* versement
partiel *m*; (of story, etc)
épisode *m*; **to pay by --s,**
v payer à tempérament.

instance, inn´-stannce, *n*
exemple *m*; cas *m*.

instant, inn´-stannte, *n*
instant *m*; *a* (date)
courant; --**aneous*,**
instantané; --**ly,** *adv* à
l'instant.

instead of, inn-stedde´
ove, *adv* au lieu de.

instep, inn´-steppe, *n* cou-
de-pied *m*.

instigate, inn´-sti-guéte, *v*
inciter.

instil, inn-stille´, *v*
instiller.

instinct, inn´-stinng-kt, *n*
instinct *m*.

institute, inn´-sti-tioute, *n*
institut *m*; *v* instituer.

institution, inn-sti-tiou´-
ch'n, *n* institution *f*;
établissement *m*.

instruct, inn-strocte´, *v*
instruire; charger de.

instruction, inn-stroc´-
ch'n, *n* instruction *f*.

instrument, inn´-strou-
m'nt, *n* instrument *m*.

insubordinate, inn-*seub*-oar´-din-nète, *a* insubordonné.

insufferable, inn-*sof*-*feur*-a-b'l, *a* insupportable.

insufficient, inn-sof-fi´-chennte, *a* insuffisant.

insulation, inn-siou-lé´-ch'n, *n* isolation *f*; (heat, pipes, etc) calorifugeage *m*.

insult, inn-sollté, *v* insulter; *n* insulte *f*.

insurance, inn-chou´-r'nce, *n* assurance *f*.

insure, inn-choure´, *v* assurer.

insurrection, inn-*seur*-rèque´-ch'n, *n* insurrection *f*.

intact, inn-tăcte, *a* intact.

integrate, inn´-*teur*-gréte, *v* rendre entier; intégrer.

intellect, inn´-*teur*-lecte, *n* intelligence *f*; intellect *m*; **–ual,** *a* intellectuel.

intelligence, inn-tel-´li-dj'nce, *n* intelligence *f*.

intelligent*, inn-tel´-li-dj'nt, *a* intelligent.

intemperate*, inn-temm´-peur-éte, *a* immodéré.

intend, inn-tennde´, *v* se proposer; avoir l'intention de.

intense*, inn-tennce´, *a* intense; vif.

intensive care, inn-tenne-cive-quère, *n* service de réanimation *m*.

intent, inn-teur´, *n* dessein *m*; *a* appliqué; **–ion,** *n* intention *f*; **–ionally,** *adv* exprès.

inter, inn-teur´, *v* enterrer; **–ment,** *n* enterrement *m*.

inter, inn´-*teur*, **–cept,** *v* intercepter; **–change,** échanger; **–course,** *n* commerce *m*; relations *fpl*; **–fere,** *v* se mêler de; **–ference,** *n* intervention *f*; (radio) bruit parasite *m*; **–lude,** intermède *m*; **mediate,** *a* intermédiaire; **–mingle,** *v* s'entremêler; **–mittent,** *a* intermittent; **–mix,** *v* entremêler; **–national,** *a* international; **–rupt,** *v* interrompre; **–val,** *n* intervalle *m*; (theatre) entracte *m*; **–vene,** *v* intervenir; **–vention,** *n* intervention *f*; **–view,** entrevue *f*; (for news) interview *f*; *v* interviewer.

interest, inn´-*teur*-reste, *n* intérêt *m*; *v* intéresser; **–ing,** *a* intéressant.

interior, inn-tî´-ri-eur, *n & a* intérieur *m*.

intern, inn-teurne´, *v* interner.

internal*, inn-teur´-n'l, *a* interne.

internet, inn´-*teur*-nett, *n* internet *m*.

interpret, inn-teur´-prette, *v* interpréter.

interpreter, inn-teur´-prett-'r, *n* interprète *m*.

interrogate, inn-terr´-ŏ-guéte, *v* interroger.

intestate, inn-tess´-téte, *a* intestat.

intestine, inn-tess´-tinne, *n* intestin *m*.

intimacy, inn´-ti-*ma*-ci; *n* intimité *f*.

intimate, inn´-ti-méte, *v* signaler; donner à entendre; *a** intime.

intimation, inn-ti-mé´-ch'n, *n* indice *m*; avis *m*.

intimidate, inn-ti´-mi-déte, *v* intimider.

into, inn´-tou, *prep* dans; en.

intolerable, inn-tol´-*eur*-a-b'l, *a* intolérable.

intoxicate, inn-toks´-i-quéte, *v* enivrer; griser.

intrepid*, inn-trepp´-ide, *a* intrépide.

intricate*, inn´-tri-quéte, *a* compliqué; embrouillé.

intrigue, inn-trîgue´, *n* intrigue *f*; *v* intriguer.

intriguing, inn-trî´-

guinng, *a* intrigant.

intrinsic, inn-trinn´-sique, *a* intrinsèque.

introduce, inn-trŏ-diouce´, *v* introduire; présenter.

introductory, inn-trŏ-doc´-tŏ-ri, *a* préliminaire.

intrude, inn-troude´, *v* s'imposer; déranger; être de trop.

intuition, inn-tiou-i´-ch'n, *n* intuition *f.*

inundate, inn´-ŏnn-déte, *v* inonder.

inundation, inn-ŏnn-dé´-ch'n, *n* inondation *f.*

inure, inn-ioure´, *v* endurcir; accoutumer.

invade, inn-véde´, *v* envahir; **–r,** *n* envahisseur *m.*

invalid, inn´-va-lide, *n* malade *m* & *f*; infirme *m* & *f* ; **–chair,** voiture d'infirme *f.*

invalid, inn-văl´-ide, *a* nul; non valable.

invaluable, inn-văl´-iou-a-b'l, *a* inestimable.

invariable, inn-vé´-ri-a-b'l, *a* invariable.

invasion, inn-vé´-j'n, *n* invasion *f.*

inveigle, inn-vî´-g'l, *v* séduire; attirer dans.

invent, inn-vennte´, *v* inventer; **–ion,** *n* invention *f;* **–or,** inventeur *m.*

inventory, inn´-venn-to-ri, *n* inventaire *m.*

invert, inn-veurte´, *v* intervertir; renverser.

invest, inn-veste´, *v* investir (money) placer; **–ment,** *n* placement *m;* **–or,** épargnant *m.*

investigate, inn-vess´-ti-guéte, *v* rechercher; faire une enquête.

investigation, inn-vesse-ti-gué´-ch'n, *n* enquête *f.*

inveterate, inn-vett´-eur-éte, *a* invétéré.

invigorate, inn-vig´-ŏr-éte, *v* fortifier.

invincible, inn-vinn´-ci-b'l, *a* invincible.

invisible, inn-viz´-i-b'l, *a* invisible.

invitation, inn-vi-té´-ch'n, *n* invitation *f.*

invite, inn-vâîte´, *v* inviter.

invoice, inn´-voa'ice, *n* facture *f.*

invoke, inn-vauke´, *v* invoquer.

involuntary, inn-vol´-onn-ta-ri, *a* involontaire.

involve, inn-volve´, *v*

impliquer; **–d,** *a* compliqué.

inward*, inn´-oueurde, *a* intérieur.

iodine, âï´-o-dine, *n* iode *m.*

ire, âïre, *n* courroux *m;* ire *f;* colère *f.*

iris, âï´-rice, *n* iris *m.*

irksome, eurk´-somme, *a* ennuyeux; pénible.

iron, âï´-eurne, *n* fer *m;* (flat) fer à repasser *m; a* de fer; *v* repasser; **–monger,** *n* quincaillier *m.*

ironic, âï-ronn-ik, *a* ironique.

irony, âï´-rŏnn-i, *n* ironie *f.*

irreconcilable, ir-rèk-ŏnn-sâï´-la-b'l, *a* irréconciliable; incompatible.

irregular*, ir-regg´-iou-l'r, *a* irrégulier.

irrelevant, ir-rèl´-i-v'nt, *a* hors de propos; déplacé.

irreproachable, ir-ri-prautch´-a-b'l, *a* irréprochable.

irresistible, ir-ri-ziss´-ti-b'l, *a* irrésistible.

irrespective, ir-ress-pèk´-tive, *adv* sans tenir compte de.

irresponsible, ir-ress-ponn´-ci-b'l, *a*

irresponsable.

irretrievable, ir-ri-trî´-va-b'l, *a* irréparable.

irrigate, ir´-ri-guéte, *v* irriguer; arroser.

irritable, ir´-ri-*ta*-b'l, *a* irritable; irascible.

irritate, ir´-ri-téte, *v* irriter; agacer.

island, aï´-lannde, *n* île *f*; –**er,** *n* insulaire *m* & *f*.

isle, âïlle, *n* île *f*; (islet) îlot *m*.

isolate, âï´-sŏ-léte, *v* isoler.

isolation, âï-sŏ-lé´-ch'n, *n* isolement *m*.

issue, i´-chiou, *n* progéniture *f*; (edition) numéro *m*; (result) issue *f*; résultat *m*; *v* émettre; publier; émaner; donner; délivrer.

isthmus, iss´-*me*uce, *n* isthme *m*.

it, itt, *pron* il; elle; le; la; lui; il; cela.

Italian, i-t*a*l-*ie*un, *a*, *n* Italien, -ne *m* & *f*.

italic, i-tal´-ique, *n* & *a* (type) italique *m*.

Italy, i´-t*a*-li, *n* Italie *f*.

itch, itch, *v* démanger; *n* démangeaison *f*.

item, âï´-temme, *n* article *m*; chose *f*; (news) article *m*.

its, itse, *poss pron* le sien; la sienne; les siens; les siennes. *poss a* son; sa; ses.

itself, itt-self´, *pron* lui-même; elle-même.

ivory, âï´-*veu*r-i, *n* ivoire *m*.

ivy, âï´-vi, *n* lierre *m*.

jabber, djăb´-'r, v jacasser. n baragouinage m.

jack, djăque, n mech cric m.

jackal, djăk´-oale, n chacal m.

jacket, djăk´-ette, n veston m; veste f; jaquette f.

jackpot, djăque´-potte, n gros lot m.

jade, djéde, n (stone) jade m.

jaded, djé´-dédde, a éreinté.

jag, djăgue, n brèche f. v ébrécher –ged, a entaillé; dentelé.

jail, djéle, n prison f; –er, geôlier m.

jam, djămme, n (conserve) confiture f; (traffic) embouteillage m. v (lock) coincer; (crowd) presser.

January, djănn´-iou-èr-i, n janvier m.

jar, djârre, n pot m; bocal m; (shock) secousse f; agacer.

jaundice, djoann´-dice, n jaunisse f.

jaw, djoa, n mâchoire f.

jay, djé, n geai m.

jazz, djăz, n jazz m; v – up animer.

jealous*, djèl´-euce, a jaloux; –y, n jalousie f.

jeans, djînnz, npl jean m.

jeer, djire, v railler. n raillerie f.

jelly, djèl´-i, n gelée f; –fish, méduse f.

jeopardize, djèp´-eur-dâïze, v compromettre.

jeopardy, djèp´-eur-di, n danger m; péril m.

jerk, djeurque, v donner une secousse; n secousse f.

jersey, djeur´-zi, n jersey m, tricot m.

jest, djesste, n plaisanterie f; v plaisanter.

jester, djess´-t'r, n farceur m; (court) bouffon m.

jet, djett, n (mineral) jais m; (liquid) jet m; (aircraft) avion à réaction m.

jettison, djett´-i-sonn, v jeter à la mer.

jetty, djett´-i, n jetée f.

Jew, djioue, n Juif m; –ess, Juive f; –ish, a juif, -ve.

jewel, djioue´-'l, n bijou m; joyau m; –ler, bijoutier m; –lery, bijouterie f.

jig, djigue, n gigue f.

jigsaw, djigue´-soa, n puzzle m.

jilt, djillte, v délaisser; plaquer.

jingle, djinng´-g'l, v tinter; n tintement m.

396

job, djobbe, n situation f;
emploi m; (task)
besogne f; travail m; job
m.

jockey, djok´-i, n jockey
m.

jocular, djok´-iou-l'r, a
jovial.

jog, djogue, v faire du
jogging.

join, djoa'ine, v joindre;
unir; (club) devenir
membre; – **in,** prendre
part à.

joiner, djoa'inn´-r, n
menuisier m.

joint, djoa'innte, n joint
m; (anatomy)
articulation f; (meat)
quartier m; (roast) rôti
m. a uni; collectif.

jointly, djoa'innt´-li, adv
conjointement.

joke, djauke, n
plaisanterie f; blague f. v
plaisanter.

joker, djauk´-'r, n farceur
m.

jolly, djoll´-i, a gai.

jolt, djault, n cahot m. v
cahoter; secouer.

jostle, djoss´-'l, v
coudoyer; bousculer.

journal, djeur-n'l, n
journal m; **–ism,**
journalisme m; **–ist,**
journaliste m & f.

journey, djeur´-ni, n

voyage m. v voyager.

jovial*, djau´-vi-al, a
jovial; joyeux.

joy, djoa'i, n joie f; **–ful*,**
a joyeux.

jubilant, djoue´-bi-l'nt, a
réjoui.

judge, djodje, n juge m;
connaisseur m; v juger.

judgment, djodje´-m'nt, n
jugement m.

judicial*, djoue-di´-ch'l, a
judiciaire.

judicious*, djoue-di´-
cheuce, a judicieux.

jug, djogue, n cruche f; pot
m; (large) broc m.

juggle, djogg´-g'l, v
jongler.

juggler, djogg´-l'r, n
jongleur m.

juice, djouce, n jus m;
(botanical) suc m.

juicy, djoue´-ci, a juteux;
succulent.

jukebox, djouke´-boxe, n
juke-box m.

July, djou-lâï´, n juillet m.

jumble, djomm´-b'l, n
fouillis m; v emmêler.

jump, djommpe, v sauter.
n saut m.

junction, djonngk´-ch'n, n
jonction f; (railway)
embranchement m;
(road) carrefour m.

juncture, djonngk´-tioure,
n conjoncture f.

June, djoune, n juin m.

jungle, djonng´-g'l, n
jungle f.

junior, djoue´-ni-eur, n &
a cadet m; a jeune.

juniper, djoue´-ni-p'r, n
genièvre m.

junk, djeunque, n
camelote (rubbish) f;
bric-à-brac m.

jurisdiction, djoue-rice-
dik´-ch'n, n juridiction
f.

juror, djoue´-reur, n juré
m.

jury, djoue´-ri, n jury m.

just, djosste, a & adv juste;
–ice, n justice f;
–ification, justification
f; **–ify,** v justifier; **–ly,**
adv justement.

jut, djotte, v faire saillie.

juvenile, djoue´-vi-nâïle,
a d'enfants; jeune.

kangaroo, kănng´-ga-roo, n kangourou m.

keel, kîle, n quille f.

keen*, kînne, a ardent; (blade) affilé.

keenness, kîn´-nesse, n acuité f; empressement m.

keep, kîpe, n entretien m; v garder; maintenir; tenir; rester; – **back,** retenir; – **off,** éviter; se tenir éloigné de; – **up,** maintenir; – **er,** n gardien m; –**sake,** souvenir m.

keg, quègue, n caque f, barillet m.

kennel, quènn´-'l, n chenil m.

kerb, queurb, n bord du trottoir m.

kernel, queur´-n'l, n noyau m; amande f.

kettle, quètt´-'l, n bouilloire f; –**drum,** timbale f.

key, kî, n clef f; (music) clef f; (piano) touche f; –**board,** clavier m; –**hole,** trou de serrure m.

kick, kique, v donner un coup de pied; ruer; n coup de pied m; (horse) ruade f.

kid, kidde, n chevreau m; fam gosse m & f.

kidnap, kidd´-năppe, v enlever; kidnapper.

kidney, kidd´-ni, n rein m; (cookery) rognon m.

kill, kille, v tuer.

kiln, kilne, n four m.

kilo, kî´-lau, n kilo m.

kin, kinne, n parenté f; a allié; –**dred,** de même

nature.

kind, kâïnnde, n espèce f, genre m, sorte f; a* bon; aimable; –**ness,** n bonté f.

kindergarten, kinn´-d'r-gar-t'n, n jardin d'enfants m; école maternelle f.

kindle, kinn´-d'l, v allumer; fig enflammer.

king, kinng, n roi m; –**dom,** royaume m.

kiosk, kî´-osque, n kiosque m.

kipper, kipp´-eur, n hareng fumé m.

kiss, kisse, n baiser m; v embrasser.

kit, kitte, n équipement m; trousse f.

kitchen, kitt´-chine, n cuisine f.

kite, kâïte, n cerf-volant m; (bird) milan m.

kitten, kit´-t'n, n chaton m.

knack, năcke, n don m; talent m; truc m.

knapsack, năpp´-săque, n havresac m.

knave, néve, n coquin m; (cards) valet m.

knead, nîde, v pétrir.

knee, nî, n genou m; –**cap,** rotule f.

kneel, nîle, v s'agenouiller; se mettre à

genoux.

knell, nêle, *n* glas *m*.

knickers, nick´-*eu*rse, *n* culotte (de femme) *f*.

knife, nâîfe, *n* couteau *m*; **pen–,** canif *m*.

knight, nâïte, *n* chevalier *m*; (chess) cavalier *m*.

knit, nitte, *v* tricoter; **–ting,** *n* tricot *m*.

knob, nobbe, *n* bouton *m*; (stick) pomme *f*.

knock, noque, *n* coup *m*; *v* frapper; **– against,** heurter; **– down,** renverser; **–er,** *n* (door) marteau *m*.

knot, not, *n* nœud *m*; *v* nouer.

knotty, nott´-i, *a* noueux; *fig* embrouillé.

know, nau, *v* savoir; connaître.

knowledge, noll´-idj, *n* connaissance *f*; savoir *m*.

knuckle, nok´-'l, *n* articulation *f*; jointure *f*.

label, lé´-b'l, n étiquette f;
v mettre une étiquette.

laboratory, lăb´-o-ra-to-ri,
n laboratoire m.

laborious*, la-bau´-ri-
euce, a laborieux;
pénible.

labour, lé´-beur, v
travailler; peiner; n
travail m; labeur m; **-er,**
travailleur m.

lace, léce, n dentelle f;
(shoe, etc) lacet m; v
lacer.

lacerate, lăss´-eur-éte, v
lacérer.

lack, lăque, v manquer de;
n manque m.

lacquer, lăk´-'r, n laque f;
v laquer.

lad, lădde, n garçon m,
jeune homme m.

ladder, lădd´-'r, n échelle
f.

ladle, lé´-d'l, n louche f; v
servir.

lady, lé´-di, n dame f;
-bird, coccinelle f; fam
bête à bon Dieu f.

lag, lăgue, v traîner; rester
en arrière; (boiler etc)
calorifuger.

lagoon, la-goune´, n
lagune f.

lair, lère, n repaire m.

lake, léque, n lac m.

lamb, lămme, n agneau m.

lame, léme, a boiteux; v
estropier.

lament, la-mennte´, v se
lamenter; n plainte f.

lamp, lămmpe, n lampe f;
(street lamp) réverbère
m; (electric bulb)
ampoule électrique f.

lance, lânnce, n lance f;

med bistouri m; v med
ouvrir au bistouri.

land, lânnde, n terre f;
(home) pays m; v
débarquer; (aircraft)
atterir; **-ing,**
débarquement m; (quay)
débarcadère m; (stairs)
palier m; **-lady,**
patronne f; **-lord,**
propriétaire m; **-mark,**
point de repère m;
-scape, paysage m;
-slide, éboulement m.

lane, léne, n (country)
chemin m; (town) ruelle
f; (traffic) file f;
(motorway) voie f.

language, lănng´-gouidje,
n langage m; langue f.

languid, lănng´-gouide, a
languissant.

languish, lănng´-gouiche,
v languir.

lanky, lain´-nki, a grand
et maigre.

lantern, lănn´-teurne, n
lanterne f.

lap, lăppe, n genoux mpl;
(sport) tour m; v
(drink) laper.

lapel, lă-pèl´, n revers
d'habit m.

lapse, lăpse, v s'écouler;
retomber; n cours m;
erreur f.

larceny, lăr´-ci-ni, n larcin
m.

lard, lârde, n saindoux m;
  –er, garde-manger m.

large*, lârdje, a grand;
  gros; fort; considérable.

lark, lârque, n alouette f.

laser, lé´-zeur, n laser m.

lash, lăche, n (whip) fouet
  m; (stroke) coup de
  fouet m; (eye) cil m; v
  fouetter; (bind)
  attacher.

lassitude, lăss´-i-tioude, n
  lassitude f.

last, lâsste, v durer; a
  dernier; **–ing,** durable.

latch, lătche, n loquet m;
  v fermer au loquet.

late, léte, adv tard; a en
  retard; tard; récent;
  tardif; (deceased) feu; **to
  be –,** v être en retard.

lately, léte´-li; adv
  dernièrement.

latent, lé´-tennte, a caché;
  latent.

lathe, lédz, n tour m.

lather, lădz´-´r, n mousse
  de savon f; v savonner.

latitude, lăt´-i-tioude, n
  latitude f.

latter*, lătt´-´r, a dernier
  (des deux).

lattice, lătt´-ice, n treillis
  m.

laudable, loa´-da-b'l, a
  louable.

laugh, lâfe, v rire; n rire m;
  –able, a risible; **–ter,**

rires mpl; hilarité f.

launch, loanntche, n
  (boat) chaloupe f; v
  lancer; **–ing,** n
  lancement m.

launderette, loann´-deur-
  rète, n laverie
  automatique f.

laundress, loann´-dresse,
  n blanchisseuse f.

laundry, loann´-dri, n
  blanchisserie f.

laurel, lau´-r'l, n laurier m.

lavatory, lăv´-a-tŏ-ri, n
  lavabo m; toilette f.

lavender, lăv´-enn-d'r, n
  lavande f.

lavish, lăv´-iche, a*
  prodigue; somptueux; v
  prodiguer.

law, loa, n loi f;
  (jurisprudence) droit m;
  –ful*, a légal; licite;
  légitime; **–suit,** n procès
  m; **–yer,** avocat m;
  (solicitor) avoué m.

lawn, loanne, n pelouse f.

lax, lăxe, a lâche; relâché;
  mou.

laxative, lăx´-a-tive, n & a
  laxatif m.

lay, lé, v coucher; placer;
  mettre; (hen) pondre.

layer, lé´-eur, n couche f.

layman, lé´-mănne, n
  laïque m.

laziness, lé´-zi-nesse, n
  paresse f.

lazy, lé´-zi, a paresseux.

lead, lèdde, n plomb m;
  (pencil) mine f; naut
  sonde f; v plomber.

lead, lîde, v conduire;
  guider; n (dog) laisse f;
  –ing, a premier;
  principal; **– singer,** n (in
  pop group) chanteur m;
  vedette f.

leader, lîde´-'r, n guide m;
  conducteur m; chef m;
  –ship, direction f;
  conduite f.

leaf, lîfe, n feuille f;
  (table) rallonge f.

leaflet, lîfe´-lett, n
  prospectus m.

league, lîgue, n ligue f;
  (measurement) lieue f.

leak, lîque, v fuir; (boats,
  etc) faire eau; n fuite f.

lean, lîne, n & a maigre m;
  – against, – on, v
  s'appuyer; **– out,** se
  pencher.

leap, lîpe, v sauter; bondir;
  n saut m.

leap-year, lîpe´-i´îre, n
  année bissextile f.

learn, leurne, v apprendre;
  –ed, a savant; **–er,** n
  étudiant m; apprenti m;
  –ing, (study) étude f;
  (knowledge) savoir m;
  érudition f.

lease, lîce, v louer; n bail
  m.

leash, lîche, n laisse f; v tenir en laisse.

least, lîste, adv le moins; a le moindre.

leather, lèdz´-'r, n cuir m; (patent) cuir verni m.

leave, lîve, n permission f; v partir, s'en aller; quitter; abandonner; laisser; (bequeath) léguer; –out, omettre; exclure.

lecture, lèque´tioure, n conférence f; réprimande f; v faire une conférence; réprimander.

lecturer, lèque´-tiour-'r, n conférencier m.

ledge, lèdje, n rebord m.

leech, lîtche, n sangsue f.

leek, lîque, n poireau m.

leer, lîre, v lorgner.

left, lefte, a & n gauche f; --handed, gaucher.

leg, lègue, n jambe f; (animal) patte f; (mutton, lamb) gigot m; (fowl) cuisse f; (furniture) pied m.

legacy, lègg´-a-ci, n legs m; héritage.

legal,* lî´-g'l, a légal; licite; –ize, v légaliser.

legation, li-gé´-ch'n, n légation f.

legend, lèdj´-ennde, n légende f.

legible, lèdj´-i-b'l, a lisible.

legion, lî´-dj'n, n légion f.

legislate, lèdj´-iss-léte, v légiférer.

legislation, lèdj-iss-lé´-ch'n, n législation f.

legitimacy, lidj-itt´-i-ma-ci, n légitimité f.

legitimate*, lidj-itt´-i-méte, a légitime.

leisure, lè´-jeure, n loisir m; convenance f.

leisurely, lè´-jeur-li, adv à loisir.

lemon, lèmm´-'n, n citron m; –ade, limonade f.

lend, lennde, v prêter.

length, lenng´-ts, n longueur f; (time) durée f; –en, v allonger; prolonger; –ways, adv en longueur; –y, a long; prolongé.

leniency, lî´-ni-enn-ci, n indulgence f.

lenient, lî´-ni-ennte, a indulgent.

lens, lennze, n lentille f; verre m.

Lent, lennte, n carême m.

lentil, lenn´-t'l, n lentille f.

leopard, lèp´-eurde, n léopard m.

leper, lèp´-'r, n lépreux m, -euse m & f.

leprosy, lèp´-rŏ-si, n lèpre f.

lesbian, lèz´-bî-eun, n lesbienne f; a lesbien.

less, lesse, adv moins; n & a moindre m.

lessee, less-î´, n locataire m.

lessen, less´-'n, v diminuer; (pain) alléger.

lesson, less´-'n, n lecon f.

let, lette, v laisser; permettre; (lease) louer.

lethal, lî´-ts'l, a mortel.

letter, lett´-'r, n lettre f; –box, boîte aux lettres f.

lettuce, lett´-ice, n laitue f.

level, lèv´-'l, n niveau m; a de niveau; uni; v niveler; (plane) aplanir; –crossing, n passage à niveau m.

lever, lî´-v'r, n levier m.

levity, lèv´-i-ti, n légèreté f.

levy, lèv´-i, v (taxes) imposer; n impôt m; (troops) levée f.

lewd*, lioude, a impudique.

lewdness, lioude´-nesse, n impudicité f.

liabilities, lâî-a-bil´-i-tèze, npl com passif m.

liability, lâî-a-bil´-i-ti, n responsabilité f.

liable, lâî´-a-b'l, a responsable; – to,

exposé à.

liaison, lî-é-′z'n, n liaison
f.

liar, lâï-′eur, n menteur, -
euse m & f.

libel, lâï-′-b'l, n
diffamation f; v
diffamer.

libellous, lâï-bel-′euce, a
diffamatoire.

liberal, lib-′eur'l, n & a*
libéral m.

liberate, lib-′eur-éte, v
délivrer; libérer.

liberty, lib-′eur-ti, n
liberté f.

librarian, lâï-′brè-′ri-
anne, n bibliothécaire
m.

library, lâï-′bré-ri, n
bibliothèque f.

licence, lâï-′cennce, n
permis m; autorisation f.

license, lâï-′cennce, v
autoriser.

licentious, lâï-cenn-′-
cheuce, a licencieux;
libertin.

lichen, lâï-′k'n n lichen
m.

lick, lique, v lécher; – up,
laper.

lid, lidde, n couvercle m;
(eye) paupière f.

lie, lâï, n (untruth)
mensonge m; v mentir;
(in a place, situation) se
trouver; –down,

(repose) se coucher.

lieutenant, lèf-′tenn-
annte, n lieutenant m.

life, lâïfe, n vie f;
(vivacity) vivacité f;
–**belt,** ceinture de
sauvetage f; –**boat,**
canot de sauvetage m; –
insurance, assurance sur
la vie f; –**less,** a
inanimé; sans vie; –**like,**
naturel; –**long,** de toute
la vie; –**size,** grandeur
naturelle; –**time,** n cours
de la vie m.

lift, lifte, n ascenseur m; v
lever; soulever.

light, lâïte, n lumière f;
clarté f; a* léger; clair v.
allumer; éclairer; –**en,**
alléger; –**bulb,**
ampoule f; –**er,**
(cigarette) briquet m;
(boat) allège f; –**house,**
phare m; –**ing,** éclairage
m; –**ness,** légèreté f.

lightning, lâïte-′ninng, n
(flash) éclair m; (strike)
foudre f; – **conductor,**
paratonnerre m.

like, lâïque, v aimer; a
pareil; égal; –**lihood,** n
probabilité f; –**ly,** a
probable; –**ness,** n
ressemblance f; –**wise,**
adv de même.

liking, lâïque-′inng, n
goût m; penchant m.

lilac, lâï-′laque, n lilas m.

lily, lil-′i, n lis m; – **of the
valley,** muguet m.

limb, limm, n (anatomy)
membre m.

lime, lâïme, n chaux f;
(bird lime) glu f; (fruit)
limette f; (tree) tilleul
m.

limit, limm-′itte, n limite
f; v limiter; **Ltd. Co.,** n
société anonyme f.

limp, limmpe, v boiter; a
(soft) mou; flasque.

limpet, limm-′pette, n
patelle f.

line, lâïne, n ligne f;
(business) partie f;
(rope) corde f; v
(garment) doubler.

lineage, linn-′i-idj, n
lignée f.

linen, linn-′enne, n toile
f; (laundry) linge m.

liner, lâï-′neur, n paquebot
m.

linger, linn-′gueur, v
tarder; languir.

lingerie, lin-′je-rî, n
lingerie f.

linguist, linn-′gouiste, n
linguiste m & f.

lining, lâïnn-′inng, n
doublure f.

link, linnque, v
enchaîner; unir; n
chaînon m; (cuff links)
boutons de manchettes

mpl.

linnet, linn´-ette, *n* linot *m.*

linseed, linn´-cîde, *n* graine de lin *f.*

lion, lâî´-*e*une, *n* lion*m;* –**ess,** lionne *f.*

lip, lippe, *n* lèvre *f;* –**stick,** rouge à lèvres *m.*

liquefy, lik´-oui-fâî, *v* liquéfier.

liqueur, li-kioure´, *n* liqueur *f.*

liquid, lik´-ouide, *n* & *a* liquide *m.*

liquidate, lik´-oui-déte, *v* liquider; (debts) acquitter.

liquidation, lik-oui-dé´-ch'n, *n* liquidation *f.*

liquor, lik´-*e*ur, *n* alcool *m.*

liquorice, lik´-*e*ur-ice, *n* réglisse *f.*

lisp, lispe, *v* zézayer; *n* zézaiement *m.*

list, lisste, *n* liste *f; naut* bande *f; v naut* donner de la bande.

listen, liss´-'n, *v* écouter.

listener, liss´-neur, *n* auditeur, -euse *m* & *f.*

literal*, litt´-*e*ur-al, *a* littéral.

literary, litt´-*e*ur-a-ri, *a* littéraire.

literature, litt´-*e*ur-a-tioure, *n* littérature *f.*

lithograph, lits´-o-grâfe, *n*

lithographie *f; v* lithographier.

litigate, litt´i-guéte, *v* plaider.

litigation, litt-i-gué´-ch'n, *n* litige *m.*

litre, lit´-'r, *n* litre *m.*

litter, litt´-'r, *n* (stretcher, stable) litière *f;* (untidiness) fouillis *m;* (bedding) paillasse *f;* (young) portée *f; v* (scatter) éparpiller.

little, lit´-t'l, *a* (quantity, time) peu de; (size) petit; *adv* peu.

live, live, *v* vivre; habiter; (dwell) demeurer.

live, lâïve, *a* vivant; vif; –**ly,** animé.

liver, liv´-eur, *n* foie *m.*

livid, liv´-ide, *a* livide.

living, liv´-inng, *n* vie *f; eccl* bénéfice *m; a* vivant; – **room,** *n* salle de séjour *m.*

lizard, liz´-eurde, *n* lézard *m.*

load, laude, *v* charger; *n* charge *f.*

loaf, laufe, *n* pain *m.*

loafer, lau´-feur, *n* (idler) fainéant *m.*

loam, laume, *n* terre glaise *f;* –**y,** *a* glaiseux.

loan, laune, *n* prêt *m;* emprunt *m.*

loathe, laudz, *v* détester,

abhorrer.

loathing, laudz´-inng, *n* aversion *f* dégoût *m.*

loathsome, laudze´-seume, *a* répugnant; odieux.

lobby, lob´-i, *n* antichambre *f;* couloir *m.*

lobe, laube, *n* lobe *m.*

lobster, lob´-st'r, *n* homard *m.*

local*, lau´-k'l, *a* local du pays; régional; –**ity,** *n* localité *f.*

locate, lau´-kéte, *v* situer; déterminer la position.

location, lau-qué´-ch'n, *n* emplacement *m.*

lock, loque, *n* serrure *f;* (hair) mèche *f;* (canal, etc) écluse *f; v* fermer à clef; –**et,** *n* médaillon *m;* – **in** (or **up**), *v* enfermer; –**jaw,** *n* tétanos *m;* – **out,** *v* laisser dehors; –**smith,** *n* serrurier *m.*

locomotive, lau´-ko-mau-tive, *n* locomotive *f.*

locust, lau´-keusste, *n* criquet *m,* locuste *f.*

lodge, lodje, *n* loge *f; v* loger.

lodger, lodj´-'r, *n* locataire *m* & *f.*

lodging, lodj´-inng, *n* logement *m.*

loft, lofte, *n* grenier *m;* –**y,** *a* haut; *fig* hautain.

log, logue, n bûche f; **–book**, (ship) journal de bord m.

logic, lodj´-ique, n logique f; **–al***, a logique.

loin, lô´ine, n (mutton) filet m; (veal) longe f.

loiter, loa´i´-t'r, v flâner; **–behind**, traîner.

loll, lolle, v se prélasser; (tongue) pendre la langue.

lollipop, loll´-i-poppe, n sucette f.

London, lonn´-d'n, n Londres m.

loneliness, laune´-li-nesse, n solitude f.

lone(ly), laune´(-li), a solitaire; isolé.

long, lonng, a long; adv longtemps; **– for**, v désirer ardemment; **–ing**, n désir ardent m; **—term**, a à long terme.

longitude, lonn´-dji-tioude, n longitude f.

loo, lou, n fam toilettes fpl.

look, louk, n regard m; v regarder; (seem) avoir l'air; **– after**, (take care of) s'occuper de; **– at**, regarder; **–er on**, n spectateur m; **– for**, v chercher; **–ing-glass**, n miroir m; (large) glace f; **–out**, v regarder par; n

naut vigie f; interj gare!

loom, loume, n métier m; v paraître au loin.

loop, loupe, n boucle f; **–hole**, (fort, etc) meurtrière f; **–the loop**, v boucler la boucle.

loose, louce, a lâche; (tooth) branlante; (morals) relâché; **–n**, v relâcher; desserer.

loot, loute, n butin m; v piller.

lop, loppe, v (prune) élaguer; **– off**, couper.

loquacious, lo-coué´-cheuce, a loquace.

Lord, lôrde, n (Deity) le Seigneur m; Dieu m.

Lord's Prayer, lôrdze prè´-eur, n Pater m.

lord, lôrde, n lord m.

lorry, lor´-ri, n camion m.

lose, louze, v perdre; (clock) retarder; **–r**, n perdant m.

loss, losse, n perte f.

Lost Property Office, loste prop´eur-ti of´-ice, n bureau des objets trouvés m.

lot, lotte, n (auction) lot m; (fate) sort m; (many) beaucoup.

lotion, lau´-ch'n, n lotion f.

lottery, lott´-eur-i, n loterie f.

loud*, lâ'oude, a fort; haut; (colours) voyant; **– speaker**, n (radio) haut-parleur m.

lounge, lâ-ounndje, n grand vestibule m; salon m; v flâner.

louse, lâ'ouce, n pou m.

lout, lâ'oute, n rustre m; (clumsy) lourdaud m.

love, love, v aimer; n amour m; affection f; **–liness**, beauté f; **–ly**, a charmant; **–r**, n amoureux m; (illicit) amant m.

low, lau, v mugir; a bas; vulgaire; **–er**, v baisser; humilier; **–land**, n pays plat m.

loyal*, lo´-ial, a loyal; fidèle; **–ty**, n loyauté f.

lozenge, loz´-enndje, n losange m; pastille f.

lubricate, lioue´-bri-quéte, v lubrifier; graisser.

lucid*, lioue-cide, a lucide.

luck, loque, n chance f; fortune f **–y**, a fortuné; veinard.

ludicrous*, lioue´-di-creuce, a risible; ridicule.

luggage, logg´-idj, n bagages mpl **left – office**, consigne m.

lukewarm, liouke´-

ouârme, *a* tiède.

lull, lolle, *v* endormir; (child) bercer; *n* calme *m*.

lullaby, loll´-*a*-bâï, *n* berceuse *f*.

lumbago, lomm-bé´-go, *n* lumbago *m*.

lumber, lomm´-b'r, *n* (timber) bois de charpente *m*. (old things) vieilleries *fpl*.

luminous*, loue´-minn-*euce*, *a* lumineux.

lump, lommpe, *n* morceau *m*; *med* grosseur *f*; **–y,** *a* grumeleux.

lunacy, loue´-na-ci, *n* aliénation mentale *f*; folie *f*.

lunar, loue´-n'r, *a* lunaire.

lunatic, loue´na-tique, *n* fou *m*, folle *f*.

lunch, lonntche, *n* déjeuner *m*; *v* déjeuner.

lung, lonng, *n* poumon *m*.

lurch, leurtche, *n* secousse *f*; (ship) coup de roulis *m*; **to leave in the –,** laisser dans l'embarras.

lure, lioure, *n* leurre *m*; *v* leurrer; attirer.

lurid, lioue´-ride, *a* (colour) blafard.

lurk, leurque, *v* (hide) se cacher.

luscious, loch´-*euce*, *a* succulent.

lust, losste, *n* luxure *f*; (greed) convoitise *f*; *v* convoiter; **–ful,** *a* sensuel.

lustre, loss´-teur, *n* lustre *m*.

lute, lioute, *n* luth *m*.

luxurious*, lok-siou´-ri-*euce*, *a* luxueux.

luxury, lok´-*seur*-i, *n* luxe *m*; somptuosité *f*.

lymph, limmfe, *n* lymphe *f*.

lynch, lintche, *v* lyncher.

lyrics, li´-riquece, *npl* paroles *fpl*.

macaroon, măc-*a*-rounne´, n macaron m.

mace, méce, n (staff) masse f.

machine, m*a*-chîne´, n machine f; **–ry,** mécanisme m; **–gun,** mitrailleuse f; **sewing––,** machine à coudre f.

machinist, m*a*-chînn´-iste, n mécanicien m.

mackerel, măc´-r'l, n maquereau m.

mackintosh, măc´-inn-toche, n imperméable m.

mad, mădde, a fou; (dog) enragé; **–man,** n aliéné m; **–ness,** folie f.

madam, măd´-*a*me, n madame f.

magazine, mă-g*a*-zine´, n (periodical) magazine m; (gun) magasin m;

(powder) poudrière f.

maggot, mägg´-*eute*, n ver m; larve f; asticot m.

magic, mădj´-ique, n magie f; a magique.

magistrate, mădj´-iss-tréte, n magistrat m.

magnanimity, măg´-nă-nimm´-i-ti, n magnanimité f.

magnanimous*, măg-nănn´-i-m*euce*, a magnanime.

magnet, măg´-néte, n aimant m; **–ic,** a magnétique. **–ism,** n magnétisme m; **–ize,** v magnétiser; aimanter.

magneto, măg-nî´-tau, n magnéto f.

magnificent*, măg-nif´-i-cennte, a magnifique.

magnify, măg´-ni-făï, v

grossir; **–ingglass,** n loupe f.

magnitude, măg´-ni-tioude, n grandeur f; importance f.

magpie, măg´-pâï, n pie f.

mahogany, m*a*-hog´-*a*-ni, n acajou m.

Mahometan, m*a*-homm´-è-tănne, n mahométan m.

maid, méde, n (young girl) jeune fille f; (servant) bonne f; **–en,** vierge f; **old –,** vieille fille f.

mail, méle, n (post) courrier m, poste f; (armour) cotte de mailles f; v expédier par la poste; **–bag,** n sac de poste m.

maim, méme, v mutiler.

main, méne, a* principal; essentiel; n (pipe, cable) conduit principal m; **–land,** terre ferme f.

maintain, méne-téne´, v maintenir; soutenir.

maintenance, méne´-teu-nannce, n maintien m; soutien m.

maize, méze, n mais m.

majestic, m*a*-djess´-tique, a majestueux.

majesty, mădj´-ess-ti, n majesté f.

major, mé´-djeur, n mil commandant m; a

majeur; **–ity,** n majorité f.

make, méque, v faire; fabriquer; n façon f; marque f; **–believe,** faire semblant; **–r,** n fabricant m; **–shift,** expédient m; **– up,** (face) maquillage m; v maquiller.

malady, măl´-a-di, n maladie f.

malaria, ma-lé´-ri-a, n paludisme m.

male, méle, n & a mâle m.

malediction, ma-lè-dique´-ch'n, n malédiction f.

malevolent*, ma-lèv´-ŏl-ennte, a malveillant.

malice, măl´-ice, n malice f; malveillance f.

malicious*, ma-li´-cheuce, a méchant; malveillant.

malign, ma-läïne´, v diffamer; calomnier.

malignant, ma-ligue´-nannte, a malfaisant; med malin.

malinger, ma-linng´-gueur, v faire le malade.

mallet, măl´-ette, n maillet m.

mallow, măl´-au, n mauve f.

malt, moalte, n malt m.

maltreat, măl-trîte´, v maltraiter.

mammal, mămm´-'l, n

mammifère m.

man, mănne, v armer; n homme m; **–hood,** virilité f; **–ly,** a viril; **–slaughter,** homicide m.

manacle, mănn´-a-k'l, v mettre les menottes.

manage, mănn´-idj, v (business) diriger; (accomplish, control) parvenir à; arriver à; **–ment,** n administration f; gestion f; direction f; **–r,** directeur m, gérant m.

mandate, mănn´-déte, n ordre m; (law) mandat m.

mandoline, mănn´-daulinne, n mandoline f.

mane, méne, n (of a horse, lion) crinière f.

mangle, main´-ng'l, v mutiler; écraser; (laundry) essoreuse f; v essorer.

mania, mé´-ni-a, n manie f; folie f.

maniac, mé´-ni-âque, n fou furieux m.

manicure, mănn´-ikioure, v faire les ongles.

manifest, mănn´-i-feste, a* manifeste; v manifester.

manifesto, mănn-i-feste´-au, n manifeste m.

manifold, mănn´-i-faulde,

a multiple; divers.

manipulate, ma-nipp´-iou-léte, v manipuler.

mankind, mănn-kâïnnde´, n humanité f.

manner, mănn´-'r, n manière f; façon f.

manners, mănn´-eurze, npl manières fpl.

manœuvre, ma-noue´-v'r, v manœuvrer; n manœuvre f.

manor, mănn´-ŏr, n manoir m.

mansion, mănn´-ch'n, n (country) château m.

manslaughter, mănn´-sloa-t'r, n homicide m.

mantelpiece, mănn´-t'l-pîce, n cheminée f.

manual*, mănn´-iou-'l, n & a manuel m.

manufacture, mănn-iou-făc´-tioure, v fabriquer; n fabrication f; **–r,** fabricant m.

manure, ma-nioure´, v fumer; n fumier m; engrais m.

manuscript, mănn´-iou-scripte, n manuscrit m.

many, menn´-i, a beaucoup.

map, măppe, n carte f; (town) plan m.

maple, mé´-p'l, n érable m.

mar, mâre, v gâter; défigurer.

marathon, mă´-ră-tsonne, n marathon m.

marble, mâr´-b'l, n marbre m; (toy) bille f.

march, mârtche, v marcher; n marche f.

March, mârtche, v mars m.

marchioness, mâr´-cheunn-esse, n marquise f.

mare, mère, n jument f.

margarine, mâr´-ga-rinne, m margarine f.

margin, mâr´-djinne, n marge f.

marginal*, mâr´-djinn-'l, a marginal.

marigold, mar´-i-gaulde, n souci m.

marine, ma-rîne´, a marin; n fusilier marin m.

mariner, mar´-i-neur, n marin m.

maritime, mar´-i-tâïmme, a maritime.

mark, mârque, v marquer; n marque f; **book–,** signet m; **trade–,** marque de fabrique f.

market, mâr´-kette, n marché m.

marmalade, mâr´-meu-léde, n confiture d'oranges f.

marmot, mâr´-motte, n marmotte f.

maroon, ma-rouneé, n &

a maroon; pourpré m; v abandonner.

marquee, mâr-ki´, n (tent) marquise f.

marquess, mâr´-couesse, n marquis m.

marriage, mâr´-idj, n mariage m.

married, măr´-idde, a marié; conjugal; – **couple,** n ménage m.

marrow, măr´-au, n moelle f; (vegetable) courge f.

marry, măr´-i, v marier; se marier; épouser.

marsh, mârche, n marais m.

marshal, mâr´-ch'l, n maréchal m.

mart, mârte, n marché m; (auction) salle de ventes f.

marten, mâr´-tenne, n martre f.

martial*, mâr´-ch'l, a martial; **court–,** n conseil de guerre m; – **law,** état de siège m.

martyr, mâr´-teur, n martyr m; v martyriser.

martyrdom, mâr´-teur-deume, n martyre m.

marvel, mâr´-v'l, n merveille f; v s'émerveiller.

marvellous*, mâr´-veul-euce, a merveilleux.

marzipan, mărre-´zi-pănne, n pâte d'amandes f.

masculine, măss´-kiou-line, n & a masculin m.

mash, mâche, n purée f; v écraser.

mask, mâssque, n masque m; v masquer.

mason, mé´-s'n, n maçon m; **–ry,** n maçonnerie f.

masquerade, măss-keur-éde´, v se déguiser.

mass, măsse, n masse f; eccl messe f; v masser.

massacre, măss´-a-k'r, n massacre m; v massacrer.

massage, mass-âge´, n massage m; v masser.

massive*, măss´-ive, a massif.

mast, mâste, n mât m.

master, măss´-t'r, v maîtriser; surmonter; n maître m; patron m; professeur m; **–ful*,** impérieux; **–ly,** a magistral; **–piece,** n chef-d'œuvre m.

masticate, măss´-ti-quéte, v mastiquer.

mastiff, măss´-tif, n mâtin m.

mat, mătte, n natte f; (door) paillasson m.

match, mâtche, n allumette f; (contest) match m; v assortir;

(contest) matcher; **–less**, *a* incomparable.

mate, méte, *n* camarade *m* & *f*; *v* accoupler.

material, ma-ti´-ri-al, *n* matière *f*; (building etc) matériaux *mpl*; (cloth) tissu *m*.

materialize, ma-ti´-ri-al-âîze, *v* matérialiser.

maternal*, ma-teur-n'l, *a* maternel.

maternity, ma-teur´-ni-ti, *n* maternité *f*.

mathematics, mă-tsi-măt´-ikse, *n* mathématiques *fpl*.

maths, mătsce, *n abbr* math(s) *fpl*.

matrimony, măt´-ri-mŏn-i, *n* mariage *m*.

matrix, mé´-trikse, *n* matrice *f*.

matron, mé´-tr'n, *n* infirmière en chef *f*.

matter, mătt´-'r, *n* matière *f*; (pus) pus *m*; (business, subject) affaire *f*; *v* avoir de l'importance.

matting, mătt´-inng, *n* natte *f*; (straw) paillasson *m*.

mattress, măt´-tress, *n* matelas *m*.

mature, ma-tioure´, *v* mûrir; (bill) échoir; *a* mûr.

maturity, ma-tiou´-ri-ti, *n*

maturité *f*; échéance *f*.

maul, moale, *v* déchirer à coups de griffes.

mauve, mauve, *n* & *a* mauve *m*.

maxim, măx´-simm, *n* maxime *f*.

maximum, măx´-si-momm, *n* & *a* maximum *m*.

may, mé, *v* pouvoir.

May, mé, *n* mai *m*; **–flower**, aubépine *f*.

maybe, mé´-bî, *a* pêut-etre.

mayonnaise, mé-i'au-néze´, *n* mayonnaise *f*.

mayor, mè´-*eur*, *n* maire *m*.

maze, méze, *n* labyrinthe *m*.

me, mie, *pron* moi; me.

meadow, mèd´-au, *n* pré *m*; prairie *f*.

meagre, mî´-gueur, *a* maigre.

meal, mîle, *n* farine *f*; (repast) repas *m*.

mean, mîne, *a* avare; (action) bas; *v* avoir l'intention de; vouloir dire; **–ing**, *n* signification *f*; **–ingless**, *a* dénué de sens.

means, minn´ze, *npl* moyens *mpl*.

meanwhile, mine´-houâîle, *adv* en

attendant.

measles, mîz´-'lz, *n* rougeole *f*.

measure, mèj´-eur, *n* mesure *f*; (tape) mètre (à ruban) *m*; *v* mesurer; **–ments**, *n* les mesures *fpl*.

meat, mîte, *n* viande *f*.

mechanic, mi-cănn´-ique, *n* ouvrier mécanicien *m*; **–al**, *a* mécanique; **–s**, *n* mécanique *f*.

mechanism, mè´-cănn-izme, *n* mécanisme *m*.

medal, mèd´-'l, *n* médaille *f*.

meddle, mèd´-'l, *v* se mêler de.

media, mî´-di-a, *npl* media *mpl*.

medieval, mèd-i-î´-v'l, *a* du moyen âge.

mediate, mî´-di-éte, *v* intervenir (en faveur de).

medical*, mèd´-i-k'l, *a* médical.

medication, mèd-i-qué´-ch'n *n* médicaments *mpl*.

medicine, mèd´-cine, *n* médecine *f*.

mediocre, mî´-di-ô-keur, *a* médiocre.

meditate, mèd´-i-téte, *v* méditer.

mediterranean, mè-i-teu-

ré-ni-*eun*, *a*
méditerranéen.

medium, mî´-di-ŏmme, *n*
moyen *m*; (person)
entremise *f*; (spiritualist)
médium *m*.

meek*, mîque, *a* doux;
humble.

meet, mîte, *v* rencontrer;
(obligations) remplir.

meeting, mî´-tinng, *n*
rencontre *f*; réunion *f*.

melancholy, mèl´-ann-
cŏl-i, *n* mélancolie *f*.

mellow, mèl-au, *a* doux;
moelleux.

melodious*, mèl-au´-di-
euce, *a* mélodieux.

melody, mèl´-o-di, *n*
mélodie *f*.

melon, mèl´-*eu*ne, *n*
melon *m*.

melt, melte, *v* to fondre.

member, memm´-b'r, *n*
membre *m*; (parliament)
député *m*; **–ship,**
adhésion *f*; cotisation *f*.

memento, mi-menn´-to, *n*
mémento *m*.

memo, mè´-mau, *n* note *f*.

memoir, memm´-ouâre, *n*
mémoire *m*.

memorable, memm´-ŏ-ra-
b'l, *a* mémorable.

memorandum, memm-ŏ-
rănn´-d'm, *n* note *f*;
memorandum *m*; **–
book,** carnet de notes *m*.

memorial, mi-mau´-ri-al,
n monument
commémoratif *m*.

memory, memm´-ŏ-ri, *n*
mémoire *f*.

menace, menn´-ace, *v*
menacer; *n* menace *f*.

menagerie, mi-nădj´-*eur*-i,
n ménagerie *f*.

mend, mennde, *v* réparer;
(sew) raccommoder.

menial, mî´-ni-al, *a*
servile; *n* domestique *m*
& *f*; subalterne *m* & *f*.

menstruation, menn-
stroue-é´-ch'n, *n*
menstruation *f*.

mental*, menn´-t'l, *a*
mental.

mention, menn´-ch'n, *v*
mentionner; *n* mention
f.

menu, menn´-iou, *n* menu
m; carte *f*.

mercantile, meur´-kann-
tâïle, *a* mercantile.

merchandise, meur´-
tchann-dâïze, *n*
marchandise *f*.

merchant, meur´-tch'nt, *n*
négociant *m*; marchand
m; *a* commercial; (fleet)
marchand.

merciful*, meur´-ci-foull,
a clément;
miséricordieux.

mercury, meur´-kiou-ri, *n*
mercure *m*.

mercy, meur´-ci, *n* grâce *f*;
indulgence *f*.

mere, mîre, *a** pur;
simple; seul; *n* lac *m*.

merge, meurdje, *v* fondre;
absorber; **–r,** *n* fusion *f*.

meridian, mi-ri´-di-anne,
n méridien *m*; *a*
méridien.

merit, mair´-itte, *n* mérite
m; *v* mériter.

meritorious*, mair-i-tau´-
ri-*euce*, *a* méritoire.

mermaid, meur´-méde, *n*
sirène *f*.

merriment, mair´-i-m'nt,
n gaieté *f*; joie *f*.

merry, mair´-i, *a* joyeux.

mesh, maiche, *n* maille *f*.

mesmerize, mez´-meur-
âïze, *v* hypnotiser.

mess, messe, *n* mess *m*;
(dirt) saleté *f*; (spoil)
gâchis *m*; *v* salir.

message, mess´-sédje, *n*
message *m*.

messenger, mess´-enn-dj'r,
n coursier, -ère *m* & *f*;
(restaurant, hotel, etc)
chasseur *m*.

messy, messe´-î, *a* sale; en
désordre.

metal, mett´-'l, *n* métal *m*;
–lic, *a* métallique.

meteor, mî´-ti-ŏre, *n*
météore *m*.

meter, mî-*teur*, *n*
compteur *m*.

method, maits´-ŏde, n
méthode f.

methylated spirit, mets´-i-
lé-tedd spir´-itte, n
alcool à brûler.

metre, mî´-teur, n mètre
m.

metric, mett´-rique, a
métrique.

metropolis, mi-trop´-ŏ-
lice, n métropole f.

mica, mâï´-ka, n mica m.

Michaelmas, mik´-el-
mass, n la Saint Michel
f.

microphone, mî´-crau-
faune, n microphone m.

microscope, mâï´-cross-
kaupe, n microscope m.

microwave (oven), mî´-
crau-ouève, n four à
micro-ondes m.

middle, midd´-'l, n centre
m; milieu m; a moyen;
–aged, a d'un certain
âge; –class (es), n
(people) classe moyenne
f; –man, intermédiaire
m.

midge, midje, n cousin m;
moucheron m.

midget, midj´-ette, n nain,
-e m & f.

midnight, midd´-nâïte, n
minuit m.

midshipman, midd´-
chipp-mănne, n aspirant
de marine m.

midwife, midd´-ouâïfe, n
sage-femme f.

mien, mîne, n mine f; air
m.

might, mâïte, n force f;
puissance f.

mighty, mâï´-ti, a
puissant; fort.

migraine, mî´-gréne, n
migraine f.

migrate, mâï´-gréte, v
émigrer.

mild*, mâïlde, a doux;
léger; tempéré.

mildew, mill´-dioue, n
moisissare f.

mile, mâïle, n mille m;
–stone, borne f.

militant, mi´-li-t'nt, a
militant.

military, mil´-i-ta-ri, n &
a militaire f.

milk, milque, n lait m; v
traire; –y, a laiteux; –y-
way, n voie lactée f.

mill, mill, n moulin m;
–er, meunier m.

milliner, mill´-i-n'r, n
modiste f; –y, modes fpl.

million, mill´ieune, n
million m.

millionaire, mill´ionn-air,
n millionnaire m.

mime, mâïme, n mime m.

mimic, mimm´-ique, v
mimer; n mime m.

mince, minnce, v hacher;
(words) mâcher.

mind, mâïnnde, n esprit
m; opinion f; v faire
attenti on à; (nurse)
soigner; –ful, a attentif.

mine, mâïne, poss pron le
mien; la mienne; les
miens; les miennes; à
moi.

mine, mâïne, n mine f; v
miner; –r, n mineur m.

mineral, minn´-eur-al, n
& a minéral m; – water,
n eau minérale f.

mingle, minng´-g'l, v
mélanger; se mêler.

miniature, minn´-i-a-
tioure, n miniature f.

minimize, minn´-i-mâïze,
v réduire; diminuer.

minimum, mi´-ni-momm,
a & n minimum m.

minister, minn´-iss-t'r, n
pasteur m;
(government) ministre
m; v pourvoir à;
administrer.

ministry, minn´-iss-tri, n
ministère m.

mink, minque, n vison m.

minor, mâï´-neur, n
mineur, -e m & f; a
mineur.

minority, minn-or´-i-ti, n
minorité f.

minstrel, minn´-str'l, n
ménestrel m.

mint, minnte, n la
Monnaie f; (plant)

menthe *f*; *v* frapper de la monnaie.

minuet, minn´-iou-ette, *n* menuet *m*.

minus, mâï´-neuce, *a* & *adv* moins; *prep* sans.

minute, minn´-itte, *n* minute *f*.

minute, mâïn-ioute´, *a* menu; (exact) minutieux.

miracle, mir´-*a*-k'l, *n* miracle *m*.

miraculous*, mi-răk´-iou-leuce, *a* miraculeux.

mirage, mi-râge´, *n* mirage *m*.

mire, mâïre, *n* fange *f*; boue *f*; bourbe *f*.

mirror, mir´-eur, *n* miroir *m*; *v* refléter.

mirth, meurts, *n* gaieté *f*; hilarité *f*.

mis, mîs, –**adventure,** *n* mésaventure *f*; –**apprehension,** malentendu *m*; –**appropriate,** *v* détourner; –**behave,** se conduire mal; –**carriage,** *n med* fausse couche *f*; –**carry,** *v* échouer; *med* faire une fausse couche *f*; –**conduct,** *n* mauvaise conduite *f*; –**construction,** mésinterprétation *f*; –**count,** *v* mal compter;

–**demeanour,** (law) délit *m*; –**direct,** *v* mal diriger; –**fortune,** malheur *m*; calamité *f*; –**giving,** crainte *f*; –**govern,** *v* mal gouverner; –**guide,** égarer; *fig* mal conseiller; –**hap,** *n* contretemps *m*; accident *m*; –**inform,** *v* mal renseigner; –**judge,** mal juger; –**lay,** égarer; –**lead,** tromper; –**manage,** mal gérer; –**place,** mal placer; –**print,** *n* faute d'impression *f*; –**pronounce,** *v* mal prononcer; –**represent,** fausser; –**statement,** *n* rapport inexact *m*; –**take,** *v* se tromper; *n* erreur *f*; –**taken,** *a* erroné; –**trust,** *v* se méfier de; *n* méfiance *f*; –**understand,** *v* mal comprendre; –**understanding,** *n* malentendu *m*; –**use,** *v* abuser de.

miscellaneous, miss-s'l-lé´-ni-euce, *a* varié; divers.

mischief, miss´-tchife, *n* mal *m*; dommage *m*; (of child) bêtise *f*.

mischievous*, miss´-tchi-veuce, *a* malicieux.

miser, mâï´-z'r, *n* avare *m*

& *f*; –**ly,** *a* mesquin.

miserable, miz´-eur-*a*-b'l, *a* misérable; triste.

misery, miz´-eur-i, *n* misère *f*; tourment *m*.

Miss, mice, *n* mademoiselle *f*.

miss, mice, *v* manquer; (someone's absence) regretter; –**ing,** *a* absent; perdu; manquant.

missile, miss´-âïl, *n* projectile *m*.

mission, mich´-eune, *n* mission *f*.

missionary, mich´-eune-ri, *n eccl* missionnaire *m* & *f*.

mist, miste, *n* brume *f*; –**y,** *a* brumeux.

Mister, (Mr) miss´teur, *n* monsieur *m*.

mistletoe, miss´-s'l-tau, *n* gui *m*.

mistress, miss´-tresse, *n* madame *f*; (school) maîtresse *f*; (kept) maîtresse *f*.

mitigate, mit´-i-guéte, *v* adoucir; mitiger.

mitre, mâï´-teur, *n* mitre *f*.

mix, mixe, *v* mêler; mélanger; (salad) tourner; –**ed,** *a* mixte; –**ture,** *n* mélange *m*.

moan, maune, *v* gémir; grogner; *n* gémissement *m*.

moat, maute, *n* fossé *m*.

mob, mobbe, n foule f;
bande f; v houspiller;
(enthusiasm) presser par
la foule.

mobile, mô´-bâîle, a & n
mobile m.

mobilize, môb´-il-âîze, v
mobiliser.

mock, moque, v se
moquer; a simulé; faux;
–ery, n moquerie f;
–ingly, adv en se
moquant.

mode, maude, n manière f;
(fashion) mode f.

model, modd´-´l n modèle
m, (fashion) mannequin
m; v modeler.

moderate, modd´-eur-éte,
v modérer; a* modéré;
passable.

moderation, modd-eur-é´-
ch'n, n modération f.

modern, modd´eurne, a
moderne.

modest*, modd´este, a
modeste.

modify, modd´-i-fâî, v
modifier.

moist, moa´isste, a moite;
humide; **–en,** v
humecter; **–ure,** n
humidité f.

mole, maule, n taupe f;
(mark) grain de beauté
m; (jetty) môle m; **–hill,**
taupinière f.

molest, mo-leste´, v

molester.

mollify, moll´-i-fâî, v
adoucir.

molten, maule´-t'n, a
fondu; en fusion.

moment, mau´-m'nt, n
moment m; **–ous,** a
important; mémorable.

momentum, mau-menn´-
tomme, n (impetus)
impulsion f.

monarch, monn´eurque,
n monarque m.

monarchy, monn´-eur-ki,
n monarchie f.

monastery, monn´-ass-tri,
n monastère m.

Monday, monn´-dé, n
lundi m.

monetary, monn´-eu-ta-ri,
a monétaire.

money, monn´-i, n argent
m; (coin) monnaie f;
–lender, prêteur
d'argent m; **–order,**
mandat- poste m.

mongrel, monng´-gr'l, n &
a bâtard, -e m & f.

monk, monng´-k, n moine
m.

monkey, monng´-ki, n
singe m.

monocle, monn´-o-k'l, n
monocle m.

monogram, monn´-ô-
grämme, n
monogramme m.

monopolize, monn-op´-ô-

lâîze, v monopoliser.

monopoly, mŏnn-op´-ŏ-li,
n monopole m.

monotonous*, mŏnn-ot´-
nŏ-neuce, a monotone.

monster, monn´-st'r, n
monstre m.

monstrous*, monn´-
streuce, a monstrueux.

month, monnts, n mois m;
–ly, a mensuel.

monument, monn´-iou-
m'nt, n monument m.

mood, moude, n humeur f;
(grammar) mode m.

moody, moud´-i, a
d'humeur changeante.

moon, moune, n lune f;
–light, clair de lune m.

moor, mou'r, n (heath)
lande f; v (ship) amarrer.

Moor, mou'r, n Maure m;
–ish, a mauresque.

mop, moppe, n balai à
laver m; v éponger.

mope, maupe, v s'attrister;
s'ennuyer.

moral, mor´al, n morale f;
a* moral; **–ity,** n
moralité f; **–s,** mœurs
fpl; moralité f.

morale, mo-râle´, n moral
m.

morass, mo-răce´, n
marécage m.

moratorium, môr-a-tô´-ri-
omme, n moratorium m.

morbid*, môr´-bidde, a

morbide.

more, môre, *adv* plus; plus de; davantage; encore.

moreover, môr-au´-v'r, *adv* en outre, de plus.

morning, môr´-ninng, *n* matin *m*; (period) matinée *f*; **good –**, bonjour.

morocco, mo-rok´-au, *n* (leather) maroquin *m*.

morose*, mŏ-rauce´, *a* morose.

morsel, môr´s'l, *n* morceau *m*.

mortal, môr´-t'l, *n* & *a**
mortel, -elle *m* & *f*; **–ity**, mortalité *f*.

mortar, môr´-t'r, *n* mortier *m*.

mortgage, môr´-guédje, *n* hypothèque *f*; *v* hypothéquer; **–e**, *n* créancier hypothécaire *m*; **–r**, débiteur hypothécaire *m*.

mortification, môr´-ti-fi-qué´-ch'n, *n* mortification *f*.

mortify, môr´-ti-fâï, *v* mortifier.

mortuary, môr´-tiou-a-ri, *n* morgue *f*.

mosaic, mô-zé´-ique, *n* & *a* mosaïque *f*.

mosque, mosske, *n* mosquée *f*.

mosquito, moss-kî´-tau, *n*

moustique *m*.

moss, moss, *n* mousse *f*.

most, mauste, *adv* extrêmement; le plus; *n* la plupart *f*; **–ly**, *adv* principalement.

moth, mot*z*, *n* papillon de nuit *m*; (clothes) mite *f*.

mother, mod*z*´-eur, *n* mère *f*; **–hood**, maternité *f*; **– in-law**, belle-mère *f*; **– of-pearl**, nacre *f*; **–ly**, *a* maternel.

motion, mau´-ch'n, *n* mouvement *m*.

motionless, mau´-ch'n-lesse, *a* immobile.

motive, mau´-tive, *n* motif *m*; *a* moteur.

motor, mau´-t'r, *n* moteur *m*; **–car**, automobile *f*; **–cycle**, motocyclette *f*; **–ing**, automobilisme *m*; **–ist**, automobiliste *m* & *f*; **–way**, *n* autoroute *f*.

mottled, mot´-t'ld, *a* bigarré.

motto, mot´-tau, *n* devise *f*.

mould, maulde, *v* mouler; *n* moule *m*; (mildew) moisissure *f*; (earth) terreau *m*; **–er**, mouleur *m*; **–ing**, moulure *f*; **–y**, *a* moisi.

mound, mâ´ounnde, *n* monticule *m*.

mount, mâ´ounnte, *n*

mont *m*; (horse, jewels) monture *f*; (picture) cadre *m*; *v* monter.

mountain, mâ´ounn´-tinne, *n* montagne *f*; **– bike**, (vélo) tout terrain *m*; **–eer**, montagnard, -e *m* & *f*; **–eering**, alpinisme *m*; **–ous**, *a* montagneux.

mourn, môrne, *v* se lamenter; pleurer; **–ful***, *a* triste; lugubre; **–ing**, *n* deuil *m*.

mouse, mâ´ouce, *n* souris *f*; **–trap**, souricière *f*.

mousse, mousse, *n* mousse *f*.

moustache, mousse-tache´, *n* moustache *f*.

mouth, mâ´out*s*, *n* bouche *f*; gueule *f*; (river) embouchure *f*; **–ful**, bouchée *f*; **–piece**, embouchure *f*; *fig* porte-parole *m*.

movable, moue´-va-b'l, *a* mobile.

move, mouve, *v* mouvoir; (house) déménager; (fidget) se remuer; (stir) bouger; *n* mouvement *m*; *fig* coup *m*.

movie, mou´-vî, *n* film *m*.

mow, mau, *v* faucher; (lawn) tondre.

mower, mau´-eur, *n* tondeuse *f*.

much, motche, *adv*
beaucoup; **how –?**
combien?

mud, modde, *n* boue *f*;
–dy, *a* boueux; **–guard,** *n*
garde-boue *m*.

muddle, modd´-'l, *n*
confusion *f*; fouillis *m*; *v*
embrouiller.

muff, moffe, *n* manchon
m; **–le,** *v* (sound)
étouffer; (cover)
emmitoufler; **–ler,** *n*
écharpe *f*.

mug, mogue, *n* gobelet *m*;
pot *m*.

mulberry, moll´-bèr-î, *n*
mûre *f*; **– tree,** mûrier *m*.

mule, mioule, *n* mulet *m*;
mule *f*.

mullet, mol´-ette, *n* mulet
m; **red –,** rouget *m*.

multiplication, mole´-ti-
pli-qué´-ch'n, *n*
multiplication *f*.

multiply, moll´-ti-plâî, *v*
multiplier.

multitude, moll´-ti-tioude,
n multitude *f*.

mummy, momm´-i, *n*
momie *f*.

mumps, mommpse, *npl*
oreillons *mpl*.

munch, monntche, *v*
mâcher; (crunch)
croquer.

municipal, miou-niss´-i-p'l
a municipal.

munition, miou-ni´-ch'n,
n munition *f*.

murder, meur-d'r, *v*
assassiner; *n* assassinat
m; **–er,** assassin *m*; **–ous,**
a meurtrier.

murky, meur-ki, *a* obscur;
ténébreux.

murmur, meur´-m'r, *v*
murmurer; *n* murmure
m.

muscle, moss´-'l, *n* muscle
m.

muse, miouze, *v* musarder;
méditer; *n* muse *f*.

museum, mioue-zî´-omme,
n musée *m*.

mushroom, moche´-
roumme, *n* champignon
m.

music, mi´oue´-zique, *n*
musique *f*; **–al,** *a*
musical.

musician, mi´oue-zi-ch'n,
n musicien, -enne *m* & *f*.

musk, mossque, *n* musc *m*.

muslim, moz´-limm, *a* & *n*
musulman, -e, *m* .

muslin, moze´-linne, *n*
mousseline *f*.

mussel, moss´-'l, *n* moule
f.

must, moste, *v* devoir;
falloir.

mustard, moss´-t'rd, *n*
moutarde *f*.

muster, moss´-t'r, *v*
rassembler; **mil** faire
l'appel.

musty, moss´-ti, *a* moisi.

mute, mioute, *n* & *a* muet,
-ette *m* & *f*.

mutilate, mioue´-ti-léte, *v*
mutiler.

mutineer, mioue-ti-nîre´,
n mutin *m*, révolté *m*.

mutinous, mioue´-ti-
neuce, *a* en révolte.

mutiny, mioue´-ti-ni, *n*
mutinerie *f*; *v* se mutiner
m.

mutter, mott´-'r, *v*
marmotter.

mutton, mott´-'n, *n*
mouton *m*; **leg of –,**
gigot *m*.

mutual*, mioue´-tiou-al, *a*
mutuel.

muzzle, mozz´-'l, *n* (for
dogs, etc) muselière *f*;
(snout) museau *m*; (gun)
bouche *f*; *v* museler.

my, mâï, *poss a* mon; ma;
mes; **–self,** *pron* moi-
même.

myrrh, meure, *n* myrrhe *f*.

myrtle, meur´-t'l, *n* myrte
f.

mysterious*, miss-tî´-ri-
euce, *a* mystérieux.

mystery, miss´-teur-i, *n*
mystère *m*.

mystify, miss´-ti-fâï, *v*
mystifier.

myth, mits, *n* mythe *m*;
–ology, mythologie *f*.

nag, năgue, v gronder; harceler; n (horse) bidet m.

nail, néle, n (metal) clou m; (human) ongle m; v clouer; **–brush,** n brosse à ongles f; **–file,** lime à ongles f.

naïve*, nâ-íve´, a naïf.

naked, né´-kedde, a nu; (trees, etc) dépouillé.

name, néme, v appeler; (specify) nommer; n nom m; **Christian/First –,** prénom m; **sur–,** nom de famille m; **–less,** a anonyme; **–ly,** adv à savoir; **–sake,** n homonyme m.

nanny, na´-nî, n nounou f.

nap, năppe, n (sleep) somme m; (cloth) poil m.

nape, népe, n nuque f.

naphtha, năph´-tsa, n naphte m.

napkin, năpp´-kinne, n serviette f.

nappy, na-pî, n couche f; **– rash,** n érythème m.

narcissus, năr-siss´-euce, n narcisse m.

narcotic, năr-cott´-ique, n & a narcotique m.

narrative, năr´-ra-tive, n narration f.

narrow, năr´-au, v rétrécir. a* étroit; **–minded,** étroit d'esprit; **–ness,** n étroitesse f.

nasal*, né´-z'l, a nasal.

nasturtium, nass-teur´-ch'm, n capucine f.

nasty, năsse´-ti, a méchant; mauvais; (dirty) sale.

nation, né´-ch'n, n nation f; pays m.

national, năch´-eunn-'l, a national.

nationality, năch-eunn-al´-i-ti, n nationalité f.

native, né´-tive, n & a natif, -ive m & f, indigène m & f; a natal (**my – country,** mon pays natal).

natural*, năt´-tiou-r'l, a naturel.

naturalization, năt´-tiou-ral-âï-zé´-ch'n, n naturalisation f.

nature, nét´-tioure, n nature f.

naught, noate, n rien m; zéro m.

naughty, noa´-ti, a vilain; pas sage.

nausea, nôr´-zî-a, n nausée f.

nauseous, nô´-si-euce, a nauséabond; écœurant.

nautical, nô´-ti-k'l, a nautique.

naval, né´-v'l, a naval; maritime; **– officer,** officier de marine m.

navel, né´-v'l, n nombril m.

navigate, nă-vi-guéte, v naviguer.

navigation, nă-vi-gué´-ch'n, n navigation f.

navigator, năv´-i-gué-teur,

n navigateur *m.*

navvy, năv´-i, *n* terrassier *m*; ouvrier *m.*

navy, né´-vi, *n* marine *f*; – **blue,** *a* bleu marine.

near, nîre, *a* proche. *prep* près de. *adv* près; *v* s'approcher de; **–ly,** *adv* presque; **–ness,** *n* proximité *f*; **––sighted,** *n & a* myope *m & f.*

neat, nîte, *a* (spruce) soigné; (dainty) délicat; (tidy) rangé; (not diluted) pur.

neatness, nîte´-ness, *n* netteté *f*; (clean) propreté *f.*

necessarily, nèss´-ess-a-ri-li, *adv* nécessairement.

necessary, nèss´-ess-a-ri, *a* nécessaire.

necessitate, ni-sess´-i-téte, *v* nécessiter.

necessity, ni-sess´-i-ti, *n* nécessité *f.*

neck, nèque, *n* cou *m*; (bottle) goulot *m*; **–lace,** collier *m*; **––tie,** cravate *f.*

need, nîde, *v* avoir besoin de; *n* besoin *m*; **–ful*,** *a* nécessaire; **–less*,** inutile; **–y,** nécessiteux.

needle, nî´-d'l, *n* aiguille *f.*

negation, ni-gué´-ch'n, *n* négation *f.*

negative, negg´-a-tive, *n*

négative *f. a** négatif.

neglect, nig-lecte´, *v* négliger; *n* négligence *f.*

negligence, negg´-li-djennce, *n* négligence *f.*

negligent, negg´-li-dj'nt, *a* négligent.

negotiate, ni-gau´-chi-éte, *v* négocier.

negotiation, ni-gau´-chi-é´-ch'n, *n* négociation *f.*

negress, nî´-gresse, *n* négresse *f.*

negro, nî-grau, *n* nègre *m.*

neigh, né, *v* hennir; *n* hennissement *m.*

neighbour, nè´-b'r, *n* voisin *m*; **–hood,** voisinage *m*; **–ly,** *a* bon voisin.

neither, naî´-dz'r, *pron & a* ni l'un ni l'autre. *adv* non plus;**–**... **nor,** *conj* ni...ni.

neon, nî´-onne, *n* néon *m.*

nephew, név´-iou, *n* neveu *m.*

nerve, neurve, *n* nerf *m*; (pluck, etc) sang froid *m*; (cheek) audace *f.*

nervous*, neur´-veuce, *c* nerveux; timide; excitable.

nest, nesste, *n* nid *m*; *v* nicher.

nestle, ness´-'l, *v* se nicher; se blottir.

net, nett, *n* filet *m*; *a*

(weight, etc) net.

nettle, nett´-'l, *n* ortie *f.*

network, nett´-oueurque, *n* réseau *m.*

neurotic, nioue-rotte´-ique *a & n* névrosé *m.*

neuralgia, nioue-rall´-dji-a, *n* névralgie *f.*

neuter, nioue´-teur, *n & a* neutre *m.*

neutral, nioue´-tr'l, *a* neutre.

never, nèv´-'r, *adv* (ne)...jamais; **–more,** plus jamais; **–theless,** *adv* néanmoins.

new, nioue, *a* neuf; nouveau; frais; **New year,** *n* nouvel an *m*; **New Year's Day,** jour de l'an *m.*

news, niouze, *npl* nouvelles *fpl*; (radio, TV) informations *fpl*; **–agent,** marchand de journaux *m*; **–paper,** journal *m.*

next, nexte, *a* prochain; suivant; (beside) à côté; voisin; *adv* ensuite.

nib, nibbe, *n* plume *f.*

nibble, nib-b'l, *v* grignoter; (rats, etc) ronger.

nice*, naïce, *a* agréable; sympathique; aimable; (subtle) scrupuleux.

nickel, nique´-'l, *n* nickel *m.*

nickname, nique´-néme, *n* surnom *m*.

nicotine, nique´-ô-tinne, *n* nicotine *f*.

niece, nîce, *n* nièce *f*.

night, nâïte, *n* nuit *f*; --**dress,** chemise de nuit *f*; --**fall,** tombée de la nuit *f*; --**ingale,** rossignol *m*; --**life,** vie nocturne *f*; --**ly,** *adv* tous les soirs; --**mare,** *n* cauchemar *m*.

nimble, nimm´-b'l, *a* leste; agile; vif.

nine, nâïne, *n* & *a* neuf *m*; --**teen,** dix-neuf *m*; --**teenth,** dix-neuvième *m* & *f*; --**tieth,** quatrevingt-dixième *m* & *f*; --**ty,** quatre-vingt-dix *m*.

ninth, nâïnnts, *n* & *a* neuvième *m* & *f*.

nip, nippe, *v* pincer; -- **off,** couper; filer.

nipple, nip´-p'l, *n* mamelon *m*.

nitrate, nâï´-tréte, *n* nitrate *m*.

nitrogen, nâï´-trô-dj'n, *n* azote *m*, nitrogène *m*.

no, nau, *adv* non; pas; ne ... pas; *a* aucun.

nobility, no-bil´-i-ti, *n* noblesse *f*.

noble, nau´-b'l, *n* noble *m*; *a* noble; généreux.

nobody, nau´-bŏdd-i, *n* un

rien *m*; *pron* personne *f*.

nod, nodde, *v* faire un signe de tête; *n* signe de tête *m*.

noise, noa´ize, *n* bruit *m*; --**less*,** *a* silencieux.

noisily, noa´iz´-i-li, *adv* bruyamment.

noisy, noa´-i-zi, *a* bruyant; tapageur.

nominal*, nomm´-i-n'l, *a* nominal.

nominate, nomm´-i-néte, *v* nommer; proposer.

nominee, nomm-i-ni´, *n* personne désignée *f*.

non, nonne, -- **commissioned officer,** *n* sous- officier *m*; --**plussed,** *a* confus; dérouté; --**sense,** *n* absurdité *f*; --**smoker,** non-fumeur *m*; --**stop,** *a* continu; (train, etc) direct.

nook, nouk, *n* coin *m*.

noon, noune, *n* midi *m*.

no one, *pron* (ne personne).

noose, nouce, *n* nœud coulant *m*.

normal*, nôr´-m'l, *a* normal.

north, nôrts, *n* nord *m*; --**erly,** *adv* au nord; *a* du nord.

nose, nauze, *n* nez *m*.

nostril, noss´-tr'l, *n* narine

f; naseau *m*.

not, notte, *adv* ne ... pas; ne ... point; pas.

notable, naute´-a-b'l, *a* notable; insigne.

notary, naute´-a-ri, *n* notaire *m*.

notch, notche, *v* entailler; *n* entaille *f*; coche *f*.

note, naute, *v* noter; remarquer; *n* note *f*; (currency) billet de banque *m*; --**book,** carnet *m*; --**d,** *a* fameux; célèbre; --**paper,** *n* papier à lettres *m*; --**worthy,** *a* digne de remarque.

nothing, no´-tsinng, rien *m*; **for** --, en vain.

notice, nau´-tice, *v* remarquer; faire attention; observer; *n* avis *m*; affiche *f*; (to quit) congé *m*; --**able,** *a* perceptible.

notify, nau´-ti-fâï, *v* notifier; signaler.

notion, nau´-ch'n, *n* notion *f*; idée *f*.

notoriety, nau-tŏ-râï´-è-ti, *n* notoriété *f*.

notorious, nau-tau´-ri-euce, *a* notoire; insigne.

notwithstanding, nott-ouidz-stǎnnd´-inng, *prep* & *conj* néanmoins; malgré.

noun, na'oune, *n* nom *m*,

substantif *m.*

nourish, nor´-iche, *v* nourrir; **-ing,** *a* nourrissant; **-ment,** *n* nourriture *f.*

novel, nov´-'l, *n* roman *m*; *a* nouveau; **-ist,** *n* romancier *m*; **-ty,** nouveauté *f*; innovation *f.*

November, no-vemm´-b'r, *n* novembre *m.*

novice, nov´-ice, *n* novice *m* & *f.*

now, nâ'ou, *adv* maintenant; **-adays,** de nos jours; **- and then,** de temps en temps.

nowhere, nau´-houère, *adv* nulle part.

noxious, noque´-cheuce, *a* nuisible; pernicieux.

nozzle, noz´-z'l, *n* bout *m*; lance *f*; jet *m.*

nuclear, nioue´-kli-îr, *a* nucléaire.

nucleus, nioue´-kli-*euce*, *n* noyau *m.*

nude, nioude, *n* & *a* nu *m.*

nudge, nodje, *n* coup de coude *m.*

nugget, nogg´-itte, *n* pépite *f.*

nuisance, nioue´-s'nce, *n* (annoyance) plaie *f*; (bother) ennui *m.*

null, nolle, *a* nul; **-ify,** *v* rendre nul.

numb, nomme, *a* engourdi; *v* engourdir; **-ness,** *n* engourdissement *m.*

number, nomm´-b'r, *n* nombre *m*; (of a series) numéro *m*; *v* numéroter; **-less,** *a* innombrable.

numerous, nioue´-*meur-euce,* *a* nombreux.

nun, nonne, *n* nonne *f*; religieuse *f.*

nuptial, nopp´-ch'l, *a* nuptial; **-s,** *npl* noces *fpl.*

nurse, neurce, *n* infirmière *f*; (male) infirmier *m*; *v* soigner; (suckle) nourrir; **-ry school,** *n* maternelle *f*; (plants, etc) pépinière *f*; **-ry-rhyme,** conte de nourrice *m.*

nut, notte, *n* noix *f*; (hazel) noisette *f*; (peanut) cacahuète *f*; *mech* écrou *m*; **-cracker,** casse-noisettes *m*; **-meg,** muscade *f*; **-shell,** coquille de noix *f.*

nutriment, nioue´-tri-m'nt, *n* nourriture *f.*

nutritious, nioue-tri´-cheuce, *a* nutritif.

nylon, nâï´-lonn, *n* nylon *m.*

oak, auque, n chêne m.

oar, ore, n rame f, aviron m; **–sman,** rameur de point m.

oasis, au-é´-cisse, n oasis f.

oat, aute, n avoine f; **–meal,** farine d'avoine m.

oath, auts, n serment m; (profane) juron m.

obdurate*, ob´-diou-réte, a endurci; obstiné.

obedience, o-bî´-di-ennce, n obéissance f.

obedient*, o-bî´-di-ennte, a obéissant.

obese, au-bîce´, a obèse.

obesity, au-bîs´-i-ti, n obésité f.

obey, o-bé´, v obéir.

obituary, o-bit´-iou-a-ri, n nécrologie f; a nécrologique.

object, ob-djete´, v protester; s'opposer à.

object, ob´-djcte, n objet m; (aim) but m; (grammar) complément m; **–ion,** objection f; **–ionable,** a répréhensible; **–ive,** n & a objectif m.

obligation, o-bli-gé´-ch'n, n obligation f.

obligatory, ob´-lî-ga-to-ri, a obligatoire.

oblige, o-blâïdje´, v obliger; (favour) rendre service.

obliging*, o-blâïdj´-inng, a obligeant.

obliterate, ob-litt´-eur-éte, v effacer.

oblivion, ob-liv´-i-eune, n oubli m.

oblivious, ob-liv´-i-euce, a oublieux.

oblong, ob´-lonng, a oblong; n rectangle m.

obnoxious*, ob-noque´-cheuce, a repoussant.

obscene*, ob-cîne´, a obscène.

obscure, ob-skioure´, v obscurcir; a* obscur.

observant, ob-zeur´-v'nt, n & a observateur m.

observation, ob-zeur-vé´-ch'n, n observation f.

observatory, ob-zeur´-va-tŏ-ri, n observatoire m.

observe, ob-zeurve´, v observer; remarquer.

obsolete, ob´-sôlîte, a suranné; hors d'usage.

obstacle, ob´-stă-k'l, n obstacle m.

obstinacy, ob´-sti-na-ci, n obstination f; opiniâtreté f.

obstinate, ob´-sti-néte, a entêté; obstiné.

obstruct, ob-strocte´, v encombrer; (hinder) empêcher; **–ion,** n encombrement m.

obtain, ob-téne´, v obtenir; se procurer.

obtrude, ob-troude´, v s'imposer.

obtrusive*, ob-trouce´-cive, a importun.

obviate, ob´-vi-éte, v obvier à.

obvious*, ob´-vi-*euce, a* évident; clair.

occasion, o-qué´-j'n, *n* occasion *f;* –**al,** *a* occasionnel; –**ally,** *adv* de temps en temps.

occult, ok´-kolte, *a* occulte, secret.

occupation, ok-kiou-pé´-ch'n *n* occupation *f.*

occupier, ok´-kiou-pâï-*eur,* *n* occupant *m;* (tenant) locataire *m* & *f.*

occupy, ok´-kiou-pâï, *v* occuper; s'occuper de.

occur, ok-keure´, *v* (to the mind) venir à l'esprit; (happen) arriver; (opportunity) se présenter.

occurrence, ok-keur´-ennse, *n* événement *m.*

ocean, au´-ch'n, *n* océan *m.*

ochre, ô´-keur, *n* ocre *f.*

octagon, ok´-ta-gonne, *n* & *a* octogone *m.*

octagonal, ok-ta´-gonn-al, *a* octogonal.

octave, ok´-téve, *n* octave *f.*

October, ok-tau´-b'r, *n* octobre *m.*

octopus, ok´-ta-*peuce, n* pieuvre *f.*

oculist, ok´-iou-liste, *n* oculiste *m.*

odd, odde, *a* (number)

impair; (single) dépareillé; (strange) étrange; –**ly,** *adv* singulièrement; –**s,** *npl* (betting) chances *fpl;* –**s and ends,** bricoles *fpl.*

odious*, au´-di-*euce, a* odieux; détestable.

odium, au´-di-*eume, n* odieux *m;* (hatred) haine *f.*

odour, o´-d'r, *n* odeur *f;* (sweet) parfum *m.*

of, ove, *prep* de; – **the,** du *m;* de la *f;* des *mpl* & *fpl.*

off, of, *adv* loin; à distance; *prep* de.

off-peak, of-pîque, *a* (rate) creux; *n* – **hours,** des heures creuses *fpl.*

offal, of´-f'l, *n* abats *mpl;* (refuse) rebut *m.*

offence, of-fennce´, *n* offense *f;* (law) délit *m.*

offend, of-fennde´, *v* offenser.

offensive, of-fenn´-cive, *a** offensif; *n* offensive *f.*

offer, of´-f'r, *v* offrir; *n* offre *f;* –**ing,** offrande *f.*

office, of´-ice, *n* bureau *m;* fonctions *fpl.*

officer, of´-iss-'r, *n* mil officier *m.*

official, of-ich´-'l, *n* fonctionnaire *m; a** officiel.

officious*, of-ich´-*euce, a*

officieux.

offspring, of´-sprinng, *n* descendant *m.*

oft, often, ofte, of´-'n, *adv* souvent; fréquemment.

ogle, au´-g'l, *v* lorgner.

oil, oa'ile, *n* huile *f; v* lubrifier; –**cloth,** *n* toile cirée *f.*

ointment, ô'innte´-m'nt, *n* pommade *f.*

okay, au-ké´, *a, adv* bien.

old, aulde, *a* vieux; âgé; antique; ancien**›**

old-fashioned, aulde-fâch´-*eun'd, a* démodé.

olive, ol´-ive, *n* olive *f;* –**oil,** huile d'olive *f.*

Olympic Games, au-limm-pique-guéme-'z, *n* Jeux olympiques *mpl.*

omelette, omm´-lette, *n* omelette *f.*

omen, au´-menne, *n* augure *m;* présage *m.*

ominous*, o´-mi-*neuce, a* de mauvais augure.

omission, o-mîch´-'n, *n* omission *f;* oubli *m.*

omit, o-mitte´, *v* omettre.

omnipotent, omm-nip´-o-tennte, *a* tout-puissant.

on, onne, *prep* en; à; sur. *adv* (upon) dessus; (onward) en avant; (date) sur; – **foot,** à pied.

once, ou'onnce, *adv* une fois; (formerly)

autrefois; **all at –**, tout d'un coup; **at –**, tout de suite; **– more**, encore une fois.

one, ou'onne, *n & a* un *m*; une *f*; *pron* un *m*; une *f*; *pron* (impersonal) on; **– way**, *a* (street) à sens unique; (ticket) simple.

onerous*, onn´-*eur-euce*, *a* onéreux.

oneself, ou'onne´-selfe, *pron* soi-même.

ongoing, onne-gau´-inng, *a* qui continue à évoluer.

onion, onn´-ieune, *n* oignon *m*.

on-line, onne-lâîne, *a*, *adv* en-ligne.

only, aune´-li, *adv* seulement; *a* unique; seul.

onslaught, onn´-sloate, *n* assaut *m*.

onward, onn´-oueurde, *adv* en avant.

onyx, onn´-ix, *n* onyx *m*.

ooze, ouze, *v* suinter; dégouliner; *n* vase *f*; fange *f*.

opal, au´-pal, *n* opale *f*.

opaque, ŏ-péque´, *a* opaque.

open, ŏp´-'n, *v* ouvrir. *a** ouvert; **–air**, en plein air; **–er**, **–ing**, ouverture *f*; occasion *f*.

opera, op´-*eur-a*, *n* opéra

m.

operate, op´-*eur*-éte, *v* faire marcher; *med* opérer.

operation, op-eur-é´-ch'n, *n* opération *f*.

operator, op´-*eur*-é-teur, *n* opérateur *m*.

opinion, ŏ-pinn´-ieune, *n* opinion *f*.

opium, au´-pi-omme, *n* opium *m*.

opponent, ŏ-pau´-nennte, *n* adversaire *m*.

opportune, op´-ŏr-tioune, *a* opportun; à propos.

opportunity, ŏ-por-tioue´-ni-ti, *n* occasion *f*.

oppose, ŏp-auze´, *v* opposer; s'opposer.

opposite, op´-ŏ-zitte, *adv* en face de; *a* opposé; *n* opposé *m*.

opposition, ŏp-pô-zi´-ch'n, *n* opposition *f*; *com* concurrence *f*.

oppress, ŏp-presse´, *v* opprimer; **–ion**, *n* oppression *f*; **–ive**, *a* tyrannique; (atmosphere) accablant.

optician, ŏp-tich´-'n, *n* opticien *m*.

option, op´-ch'n, *n* option *f*; **–al**, *a* facultatif.

opulent, op´-iou-lennte, *a* opulent.

or, aur, *conj* ou; **–else**, ou

bien.

oral*, au´-r'l, *a* oral.

orange, or´-inndje, *n* orange *f*.

orator, or´-*a*-t'r, *n* orateur *m*.

oratory, or´-*a*-tŏ-ri, *n* éloquence *f*; *eccl* oratoire *m*.

orb, oarbe, *n* (sphere) globe *m*; orbe *m*; sphère *f*.

orbit, oar´-bitte, *n* orbite *f*.

orchard, oar´-tcheurde, *n* verger *m*.

orchestra, oar´kess-tra, *n* orchestre *m*.

orchid, or´-kidde, *n* orchidée *f*.

ordain, oar-déné´, *v* ordonner.

ordeal, oar´-dîle, *n* épreuve *f*.

order, oar´-deur, *n* ordre *m*; (goods) commande *f*; *v* commander; **–ly**, *a* ordonné; (quiet) calme; *n* planton *m*.

ordinary, oar´-di-na-ri, *a* ordinaire.

ordnance, oard´-nannce, *n* artillerie *f*.

ore, aure, *n* minerai *m*.

organ, oar´-guenne, *n* orgue *m*; *med* organe *m*.

organic, oar-gănn´-ique, *a* organique.

organization, oar´-ga-nâi-zé´-ch'n, n organisation f.

organize, oar´-ga-nâize, v organiser.

orgasm, oar´-gă-zm, n orgasme m.

orgy, oar´-dji, n orgie f.

orient, oar´-ri-ennte, n orient m; **–al,** a oriental.

origin, or´-i-djinne, n origine f; **–al*,** a original.

originate, ŏr-idj´-i-néte, v provenir de.

ornament, oar´-na-mennte, n ornement m.

ornamental, oar´-na-menn´-t'l, a ornemental.

orphan, oar´-f'n, n orphelin, -e m & f; **–age,** orphelinat m.

orthodox, or´-tsŏ-dŏxe, n & a orthodoxe m & f.

orthography, oar-tsog´-ra-fi, n orthographe f.

oscillate, os´-sil-léte, v osciller.

ostentatious*, oss-tenn-té´-cheuce, a fastueux.

ostrich, oss´-tritche, n autruche f.

other, o´-dz'r, a autre; **the –one,** pron l'autre.

otherwise, o´-dz'r-ou'âïze, adv autrement.

otter, ot´-t'r, n loutre f.

ought, oate, v devoir;

falloir.

our, â'our, poss a notre; nos.

ours, â'ourze, poss pron le nôtre; la nôtre; les nôtres.

ourselves, â'our-celves´, pron nous-mêmes.

out, â'oute, adv hors, dehors; (extinguished) éteint; (issued) paru; **–bid,** v surenchérir; **–break,** n insurrection f; épidémie f; **–burst,** explosion f; **–cast,** proscrit m; **–cry,** clameur f; **–do,** v surpasser; **–fit,** n équipement m; **–fitter,** confectionneur m; (ships) armateur m; **–grow,** v devenir trop grand pour; **–last,** survivre à; dépasser...; **–law,** n proscrit m; v proscrire; **–lay,** n dépenses fpl; **–let,** débouché m; issue f; **–line,** v esquisser; **–live,** survivre à; **–look,** n perspective f; aspect m; **–lying,** a éloigné; **–number,** v surpasser en nombre; **–post,** n avantposte m; **–put,** rendement m; **–rage,** outrage m; **–rageous,** a outrageux, exorbitant;

–right, adv entièrement; **–run,** v dépasser en vitesse; **–side,** adv en dehors; n extérieur m; dehors m; **–size,** grande taille f; **–skirts,** confins mpl; **–standing,** a saillant; (debts) impayé; **–ward,** adv à l'extérieur; a extérieur m; **–ward bound,** naut à destination de l'étranger; **–wit,** v surpasser en finesse.

oval, au´-v'l, n & a ovale m.

ovary, au´-va-ri, n ovaire m.

oven, o´-v'n, n four m.

over, au´-v'r, adv par-dessus; prep sur; au-dessus de; **–alls,** n salopette f; **–bearing,** a arrogant; **–board,** adv par-dessus bord; **–cast,** a couvert; **–charge,** n surcharge f; **–coat,** (woman) manteau m; (man) pardessus m; **–come,** v vaincre; triompher de; **–do,** surmener; exagérer; **–dose,** n dose trop forte f; **–draw,** v excéder son crédit; **–due,** a en retard; (debt) arriéré m; **–flow,** v déborder; **–grow,** trop grandir; (botanical)

recouvrir; **–hang,**
surplomber; **–haul,** *mech*
examiner; mettre en
état; **–hear,** surprendre
une conversation;
–joyed, *pp* transporté de
joie; **–land,** *adv* par voie
de terre; **–lap,** *v*
chevaucher; **–load,**
surcharger; **–look,** avoir
vue sur; (forget) oublier;
(pardon) laisser passer;
–night, *adv* (pendant) la
nuit; (a train) de nuit;
(stay) d'une nuit; *fig*
soudain; **–power,**
(vanquish) maîtriser;
(heat, fumes, etc)
accabler; **–rate,**
surestimer; **–rule,** (set
aside) rejeter; **–run,**
envahir; infester; **–seas,**
a d'outremer; **–see,** *v*
surveiller; **–seer,** *n*
surveillant *m*; **–sight,**
inadvertance *f*; **–sleep,** *v*
dormir trop longtemps;
–take, rattraper; (car,
etc) doubler; **–throw,**
renverser; **–time,** *n*
(work) travail
supplémentaire *m*;
–turn, *v* renverser; se
renverser; **–weight,** *n*
excédent de poids *m*;
–whelm, *v* accabler;
écraser; **–work,** *v*
surmener; *n* surmenage

m.

owe, au, *v* devoir.

owing, au´-inng, dû; **– to,**
prep à cause de.

owl, â'oule, *n* hibou *m*.

own, aune, *v* posséder;
(admit) avouer; *a*
propre.

owner, aune´-'r, *n*
propriétaire *m*.

ox, oxe, *n* boeuf *m*.

oxygen, ok´-si-dj'n, *n*
oxygène *m*.

oyster, oa'iss´-t'r, *n* huître
f; **–bed,** parc à huîtres *m*.

ozone, au´-zaune, *n* ozone
f.

pace, péce, *n* pas *m*; (speed) allure *f*; *v* mesurer.

pacify, păss´-i-faï, *v* pacifier; calmer.

pack, păque, *v* emballer; empaqueter; (a case) faire les valises; *n* paquet *m*; (load) charge *f*; (cards) jeu *m*; (gang) bande *f*; (animals) troupeau *m*; (hounds) meute *f*; –**age**, colis *m*; –**age holiday**, voyage organisé *m*; –**ed lunch**, repas froid *m*; –**et**, paquet *m*; –**ing**, emballage *m*; *mech* garniture *f*.

pact, păcte, *n* pacte *m*.

pad, pădde, *v* (stuff) rembourrer; *n* (stamp pad) tampon *m*; (writing) bloc-notes *m*.

padding, pădd´-inng, *n* rembourrage *m*.

paddle, pădd´-d'l, *v* pagayer; (feet, hands) patauger; *n* pagaie *f*; –**steamer**, vapeur à roues *m*; –**wheel**, roue à aubes *f*.

paddock, pădd´-ŏque, *n* (meadow) enclos *m*.

padlock, pădd´-lŏque, *n* cadenas *m*; *v* cadenasser.

pagan, pé´-ganne, *n* & *a* païen *m*.

page, pédje, *n* page *f*; –**boy**, chasseur *m*.

pageant, pă´-djannte, *n* cortège *m*; spectacle *m*.

pail, péle, *n* seau *m*.

pain, péne, *v* faire mal; *n* douleur *f*; –**ful**, *a** douloureux; –**less**, sans douleur.

paint, péne-te, *v* peindre; *n* peinture *f*; (art) couleur *f*; –**brush**, pinceau *m*; –**er**, peintre *m*; –**ing**, (picture) tableau *m*.

pair, père, *n* paire *f*; couple (married people, etc) *m*.

palace, păl´-ace, *n* palais *m*.

palatable, păl´-a-ta-b'l, *a* agréable au goût.

palate, păl´-ate, *n* palais *m*.

pale, péle, *a* pâle; *v* pâlir; –**ness**, *n* pâleur *f*.

palette, păl´-ette, *n* palette *f*.

paling, péle´-inng, *n* palissade *f*.

palm, pâme, *n* palmier (tree) *m*; (hand) paume *f*; –**ist**, chiromancien *m*; –**istry**, chiromancie *f*; –**Sunday**, dimanche des Rameaux *m*.

palpitation, păl-pi-té´-ch'n, *n* palpitation *f*.

pamper, pămm´-p'r, *v* choyer.

pamphlet, pămm´-flitte, *n* brochure *f*.

pan, pănne, *n* (frying) poêle *f*; –**cake**, crêpe *f*.

pane, péne, *n* vitre *f*; carreau *m*.

panel, pănn´-'l, *n* panneau *m*; (persons) liste *f*.

pang, pain-ng, n angoisse f.

panic, pănn´-ique, n panique f.

pansy, pănn´-zi, n pensée f.

pant, pănnte, v haleter.

panther, pănn´-tseur, n panthère f.

pantomime, pănn´-tau-mâîme, n (Christmas) féerie f.

pantry, pănn´-tri, n (food) garde-manger m.

pants, pănntse, npl caleçon m.

papal, pé´-pal, a papal.

paper, pé´-p'r, v tapisser; n papier m; **news–,** journal m; **wall– –,** papier peint m.

par, pâre, n pair m; egalité f.

parable, păr´-a-b'l, n parabole f.

parachute, pă´-ra-choute, n parachute m.

parade, pa-réde´, v parader; n parade f.

paradise, pă´-ra-dâîce, n paradis m.

paraffin, pă´-ra-finne, n paraffine f; **– lamp,** lampe à pétrole f.

paragraph, pă´-ra-grăfe, n paragraphe m.

parallel, pă´-ral-lelle, a parallèle; (similar) semblable.

paralyse, pă´-ra-lâîze, v paralyser.

paralysis, pa-ral´-i-sisse, n paralysie f.

parasite, pă´-ra-sâîte, n parasite m.

parcel, pâr´-s'l, n paquet m; colis m.

parched, pârtch´-'t, a desséché; aride.

parchment, pârtch´-m'nt, n parchemin m.

pardon, pâr´-d'n, v pardonner; excuser; n pardon m; (official) grâce f.

parents, pè´-rennse, npl parents mpl.

parish, pă´-riche, n commune f; eccl paroisse f.

park, pârque, n parc m; **–ing,** (motors) stationnement m; **–ing meter,** n parcomètre m; **car –,** n parking m.

parley, pâr´-li, v parlementer; n pourparlers mpl.

parliament, pâr´-li-mennte, n parlement m.

parlour, pâr´-l'r, n petit salon m.

parochial, pa-rau´-ki-al, a communal; paroissial.

parrot, păr´-ŏtte, n perroquet m.

parry, păr´-i, v parer; n parade f.

parsimonious*, pâr-ci-mau´-ni-euce, a parcimonieux.

parsley, pârce´-li, n persil m.

parsnip, pârce´-nippe, n panais m.

parson, pâr´-s'n, n pasteur (Protestant) m; (Catholic) prêtre m.

parsonage, pâr´-sŏnn-idj, n presbytère m.

part, pârte, v séparer; (hair) faire la raie; n (share) (actor's) rôle m; (district) partie f; **– time,** a, adv à temps partiel.

partake, pâr-téque´, v participer à.

partial*, pâr-ch'l, a partial; **–ity,** n prédilection f.

participate, pâr-tiss´-i-péte, v participer à or de.

participle, pâr´-ti-ci-p'l, n (grammar) participe m.

particle, pâr´-ti-c'l, n particule f.

particular, par-tik´-iou-l'r, a spécial; exigeant; (exact) minutieux; **–s,** npl détails mpl.

parting, pârt´-inng, n séparation f; (hair) raie f.

partition, pâr-ti´-ch'n, n (wall) cloison f.

partner, pârte´n'r, n (business) associé m; (games) partenaire m & f; (dance) danseur m.

partnership, pârte´-n'r-chippe, n association f.

partridge, pârte´-ridje, n perdrix f.

party, pâr´-ti, n (political) parti m; fête f; (evening) soirée f.

pass, pâsse, v passer; (overtake) dépasser; (meet) rencontrer; (exam) réussir, n permis m; (mountain) passe f; **—book**, carnet de banque m; **–port**, passeport m.

passage, pâss´-idj, n passage m; (house) corridor m; (sea) traversée f.

passenger, pâss-inn-dj'r, n voyageur, -euse m & f; naut passager, -ère m & f.

passer-by, pâsse´-'r-bâï, n passant, -e m & f.

passion, pǎch´-ŏnne, n passion f; (anger) colère f.

passionate*, pǎch´-ŏnn-éte, a passionné.

past, pâsst, n & a passé m; prep au-delà de.

paste, péste, n pâte f; (adhesive) colle f; v coller.

pasteurized, passe´-tioure-âïz'd, a pasteurisé.

pastime, pâsse´-tâïme, n passe-temps m.

pastries, péss´-trize, npl pâtisserie f; gâteaux mpl.

pastry, péss´-tri, pâte f.

pasture, pâsse´-tioure, n pâturage m.

pat, pǎte, v caresser de la main; n caresse f.

patch, pǎtche, v rapiécer; n pièce f.

pâté, pâ´-té, n pâté m.

patent, pé´-tennte, v breveter; n brevet d'invention m; a breveté; **–leather**, n cuir verni m.

paternal*, pa-teur´-n'l, a paternel.

path, pâts, n sentier m; (garden) allée f.

pathetic, pâ-tsé´-tique, a pathétique.

patience, pé´-ch'nce, n patience f.

patient, pé´-ch'nt, n malade m & f. a* patient.

patio, pǎ´-ti-au, n patio m.

patriot, pé´-tri-ŏtte, n patriote m & f; **–ic**, a (person) patriote; (thing) patriotique.

patrol, pa-traule´, n patrouille f; v faire une ronde.

patronize, pǎ´-trŏnn-âïse, v favoriser; fig faire l'important.

pattern, pǎtt´-eurne, n modèle m; (sample) échantillon m; (paper, etc) patron m.

paunch, poanche, n panse f; ventre m.

pauper, poa´-p'r, n pauvre m & f.

pause, poaze, v faire une pause; s'arrêter; n pause f.

pave, péve, v paver; **–ment**, n trottoir m.

pavilion, pǎ-vil´-ieunne, n pavilion m.

paw, poa, n patte f; v (as a horse) piaffer.

pawn, poanne, n gage m; (chess) pion m; v mettre en gage; **– broker's shop**, n mont-de-piété m.

pay, pé, v payer; n (military) solde f; (workman's) salaire m; **–able**, a payable; **–er**, n payeur m; **–ment**, n paiement m; **–phone**, cabine téléphonique f; téléphone public.

pea, pî, n pois m; **–nut**, cacahuète f.

peace, pîce, n paix f;
–ful*, a paisible.

peach, pîtche, n pêche f;
–tree, pêcher m.

peacock, pî´-coque, n
paon m.

peak, pique, n (mountain)
pic m; fig sommet m.

peal, pîle, n (bells)
carillon m; (thunder)
coup de tonnerre m.

pear, père, n poire f; –tree,
poirier m.

pearl, peurle, n perle f.

peasant, pĕz´-'nt, n
paysan, -anne m & f;
–ry, les paysans mpl.

peat, pîte, n tourbe f.

pebble, pèb´-b'l, n galet m.

peck, pèque, v picoter; n
coup de bec m.

peculiar*, pi-kiou´-li-eur,
a singulier.

peculiarity, pi-kiou´-li-ăr´-
i-ti, n singularité f.

pedal, pède´-'l, n pédale f;
v pédaler.

pedantic, pé-dănn´-tique,
a (person) pédant;
(thing) pédantesque.

pedestal, pèd´-ess-t'l, n
piédestal m.

pedestrian, pi-dess´-tri-
anne, n piéton m.

pedigree, pèd´-i-grî, n
généalogie f; (dog)
pedigree m.

pedlar, pèd´-l'r, n

colporteur m.

peel, pîle, n pelure f; v
peler; éplucher.

peep, pîpe, v jeter un coup
d'œil; n coup d'œil m.

peer, pîre, n pair m; –age,
pairie f.

peevish*, pî´-viche, a
grincheux; maussade.

peg, pègue, n cheville f;
(for hats, etc) patère f;
clothes–, pince à linge
f.

pellet, pel´-lite, n boulette
f; (shot) grain de plomb
m.

pelt, pelte, n peau f; v
assaillir à coups de ...

pen, pène, n stylo m;
(cattle, etc) pare m;
–friend, correspondant
m; –holder, porte-plume
m; –knife, canif m;
–nib, plume f.

penal, pî-n'l, a pénal; –
servitude, n travaux
forcés mpl.

penalty, penn´-al-ti, n
peine f; (fine) amende f.

penance, penn´-nce, n
pénitence f.

pence, pènnce, n penny
m.

pencil, penn´-s'l, n crayon
m.

pendant, penn´-dennte, n
(jewel) pendentif m.

pending, penn´-dinng,

prep en suspens.

pendulum, penn´-diou-
leume, n pendule m.

penetrate, penn´-i-tréte, v
pénétrer.

penguin, penn´-gouinne,
n pingouin m.

penicillin, penn-i-ci-l´-
inne, n pénicilline f.

peninsula, penn-inn´-
siou-la, n péninsule f.

penis, pî-nisse, n pénis m.

penitent, penn´-i-tennte,
n & a pénitent, -e m &
f.

penniless, penn´-i-less, a
sans le sou.

pension, penn´-ch'n n
pension f; v mettre à la
retraite; –er, n retraité, -
e m & f; (of mil. or
naval homes) invalide
m.

pensive*, penn´-cive, a
pensif.

penurious, pi-niou´-ri-
euce, a indigent.

people, pî-p'l, n gens m &
fpl; (community) peuple
m.

pepper, pèp´-'r, n poivre
m; –mint, menthe
poivrée (plant) f;
bonbon à la menthe
(sweet) m.

per, peure, prep par; –cent,
pour cent; –centage, n
pourcentage m.

perceive, peur-cîve´, v
aparcevoir; s'apercevoir.

perception, peur-sèpp´-ch'n, n perception f.

perch, peurtche, n
perchoir (for birds) m;
(fish) perche f.

peremptory, pair´-emmptō-ri, a péremptoire.

perfect, peur´-fècte, a*
parfait; v perfectionner.

perfection, peur-fèque´-ch'n, n perfection f.

perfidious*, peur-fid´-i-euce, a perfide.

perforate, peur´-fo-réte, v
perforer.

perform, peur-foarme´, v
exécuter; (stage)
représenter; **–ance,** n
exécution f;
représentation f.

perfume, peur´-fioume, n
parfum m; v parfumer.

perhaps, peur-hăpse´, adv
peut-être.

peril, pèr´-ile, n péril m;
–ous, a périlleux.

period, pi´-ri-ode, n
période f; **menstrual –s,**.
règles fpl; **–ical,** a
périodique.

periscope, pèr´-iss-kôpe, n
périscope m.

perish, pèr´-iche, v périr;
(spoil) avarier.

perishable, pèr´-iche-a-b'l,
périssable.

perjury, peur´-djiou-ri, n
parjure m.

perk, peurque, n avantage
m; à-côtés mpl.

perm, peurme, n
permanente f.

permanent*, peur´-manennte, a permanent.

permeate, peur´-mi-éte, v
pénétrer.

permission, peur-mich´'n,
n permission f.

permit, peur´-mitte, n
permis m; v permettre.

pernicious*, peur-nich´-euce, a pernicieux.

perpendicular, peur-penndi´-kiou-lar, n & a
perpendiculaire f.

perpetrate, peur´-pi-tréte,
v commettre.

perpetual*, peur-pett´-iou-al, a perpétuel.

perplex, peur-plexe´, v
embarrasser.

persecute, peur´-si-kioute,
v persécuter.

persecution, peur-si-kiou´-ch'n, n persécution f.

perseverance, peur-si-vir´-'nce, n persévérance f.

persevere, peur-si-vire´, v
persévérer.

persist, peur-sisste´, v
persister.

person, peur´-s'n, n
personne f; **–al,** a*
personnel; **–al**

computer, n ordinateur
personnel m; **–ality,** n
personnalité f.

personify, peur-sonn´-i-fâï, v personnifier.

personnel, peur´-sŏ-nèl, n
personnel m.

perspective, peur-spève´-tive, n perspective f.

perspicacity, peur-spi-kă´-ci-ti, n perspicacité f.

perspiration, peur-spi-ré´-ch'n, n transpiration f.

perspire, peur-spâïre´, v
transpirer; suer.

persuade, peur-souéde´, v
persuader.

persuasion, peur-soué´-j'n,
n persuasion f.

pert, peurte, a éveillé;
impertinent.

pertinent, peur´-ti-nennte, a à propos.

perturb, peur-teurbe´, v
troubler; agiter.

perusal, peur-ouze´-'l, n
examen m; lecture f.

peruse, peur-ouze´, v lire
attentivement.

perverse, peur-veurce´, a
pervers; dépravé.

pervert, peur-veurte´, v
pervertir; dénaturer.

pest, peste, n peste f;
pestilence f.

pester, pess´-t'r, v
tourmenter; importuner.

pet, pette, n favori m;

(child) chéri m; v choyer; (spoil) gâter.

petal, pett´-'l, n pétale m.

petition, pi-ti´-ch'n, n requête f; v présenter une requête; –**er**, n pétitionnaire m & f.

petrify, pett´-ri-faï, v pétrifier.

petrol, pett´-rôlle, n essence f; – **pump**, pompe à essence f; – **station**, station-service f.

petroleum, pè-trau´-li-eume, n pétrole m.

petticoat, pett´-i-caute, n jupon m.

petty, pett´-i, a mesquin; –**cash**, n petite caisse f.

petulance, pett´-ioul-'nce, n pétulance f.

pew, pioue, n banc d'église m.

pewter, pioue´-t'r, n étaih m.

phantom, fănn´-teume, n fantôme m; spectre m.

pharmacy, fâr´-mă-sî, n pharmacie f.

phase, féze, n phase f.

pheasant, fèz´-'nt, n faisan m.

phenomenon, fi-nomm´-i-nŏnne, n phénomène m.

philosopher, fi-loss´-ŏf-'r, n philosophe m.

phlegm, flemme, n flegme

m.

phone, faune, n abbr téléphone m.

phosphate, fosse´-féte, n phosphate m.

phosphorus, fosse´-fo-reuce, n phosphore m.

photograph, fau´-to-grăfe, n photographie f.

photographer, fau-tog´-răf-'r, n photographe m.

phrase, fréze, n phrase f; locution f.

physical, fiz´-zi-k'l, a physique.

physician, fi-zi´-ch'n, n médecin m.

physics, fiz´-zix, npl la physique f.

piano, pi-ă´-nau, n piano m; **grand** –, piano à queue m.

pick, pique, n pic m; (–axe) pioche f; v choisir; (gather) cueillir; (bones) ronger; – **up**, ramasser; –**pocket**, n pickpocket m.

pickle, pik´-'l, v conserver au vinaigre.

pickles, pik´-'lze, npl conserves au vinaigre fpl.

picnic, pik´-nique, n pique-nique m.

picture, pik´-tioure, n tableau m; illustration f; portrait m; film m.

pie, pâï, n (meat) pâté m; (fruit-open) tourte f.

piece, pîce, n pièce f; (fragment, portion) morceau m; –**meal**, adv par morceaux; –**work**, n travail à pièces m.

pier, pire, n jetée f.

pierce, pîrce, v percer.

piercing, pire´-cinng, a percant.

piety, pâï´-i-ti, n piété f.

pig, pigue, n cochon m, porc m; –**iron**, fonte en gueuse f; –**sty**, porcherie f.

pigeon, pid´-jinne, n pigeon m.

pigeonhole, pid´-jinne-haule, n (papers) case f.

pike, pâïque, n pique f; (fish) brochet m.

pilchard, pill´-chârde, n pilchard m, sardine f.

pile, pâïle, n (heap) tas m; pieu m; (carpet, etc) poil m; v empiler; – **up**, n auto carambolage m; v s'entasser.

piles, pâïlze, npl med hémorroïdes fpl.

pilfer, pill´-f'r, v chiper.

pilgrim, pill´-grimme, n pèlerin, -e m & f.

pilgrimage, pill´-grimm-idj, n pèlerinage m.

pill, pile, n pilule f.

pillage, pill´-idj, n pillag~

m; v piller.

pillar, pill´-'r, *n* pilier *m;*
  --box, boîte aux lettres
  f.

pillow, pill´-au, *n* oreiller
  m; – **case,** taie d'oreiller
  f.

pilot, pâï´-leutte, *n* pilote
  m; v piloter.

pimple, pimm´-p'l, *n*
  bouton *m;* pustule *f.*

pin, pinne, *n* épingle *f;*
  (safety) épingle de
  sûreté *f; v* épingler.

pinafore, pinn´-a-faure, *n*
  tablier *m.*

pincers, pinn´-ceurze, *npl,*
  pince *f;* tenailles *fpl.*

pinch, pinntche, *v* pincer;
  (press) gêner; *n* pincée *f.*

pine, pâïne, *n* pin *m.*

pineapple, pâïne´-äpp-'l, *n*
  ananas *m.*

pinion, pinn´-ieune, *n*
  pignon *m; v* lier les bras.

pink, pinng-k, *a* rose; *n*
  œillet *m.*

pinnacle, pinn´-a-k'l, *n*
  pinacle *m.*

pint, pâïnnte, *n* pinte *f.*

pioneer, pâï-o-nîr´, *n*
  pionnier *m.*

pious*, pâï´-euce, *a* pieux.

pip, pippe, *n* pépin *m.*

  e, pâïpe, *n* tuyau *m;*
  nduit *m;* (tobacco)

  ´e *f.*
    pâï´-réte, *n* pirate

---

m.

pistol, piss´-t'll, *n* pistolet
  m.

piston, piss´-t'n, *n* piston
  m.

pit, pitte, *n* fosse *f;* (mine)
  mine *f;* (theatre)
  parterre *m.*

pitch, pitche, *n* poix *f;*
  mus ton *m; v naut*
  tanguer; (throw) lancer.

pitcher, pitch´-'r, *n* (jug)
  cruche *f.*

pitchfork, pitche´-
  foarque, *n* fourche *f.*

pitfall, pit´-foale, *n* piège
  m.

pith, pits, *n* moelle *f.*

pitiful*, pitt´-i-foull, *a*
  pitoyable.

pitiless*, pitt´-i-lesse, *a*
  impitoyable.

pity, pitt´-i, *n* pitié *f; v*
  avoir pitié de; plaindre;
  what a –! *interj* quel
  dommage!

pivot, piv´-eute, *n* pivot
  m.

placard, plä-kârde, *n*
  affiche *f; v* placarder.

place, pléce, *n* place *f;*
  (locality) lieu *m;* endroit
  m; v mettre.

placid*, pläss´-ide, *a*
  placide; calme.

plagiarism, plé´-dji-a-
  rizme, *n* plagiat *m.*

plague, plégue, *n* peste *f; v*

---

tourmenter.

plaice, pléce, *n* carrelet *m.*

plain, pléne, *n* plaine *f; a*
  simple; clair; (looks,
  etc) ordinaire.

plaint, pléne-te, *n* plainte
  f; lamentation *f;* **–iff,**
  plaignant, -e *m & f;*
  –ive*, *a* plaintif.

plait, pläte, *n* natte *f; v*
  tresser; (fold) plisser.

plan, plänne, *a* plan *m;*
  projet *m; v* projeter.

plane, pléne, *v* raboter; *n*
  rabot *m;* **–tree,** platane
  m.

planet, plänn´-ette, *n*
  planète *f.*

plank, plain-nk, *n* planche
  f.

plant, plännte, *v* planter;
  n plante *f; mech*
  outillage *m;* **–ation,**
  plantation *f.*

plaster, plâsse´-t'r, *v*
  plâtrer; *n* plâtre *m; med*
  emplâtre *m.*

plastic, plässe´-tique, *n*
  plastique *m.*

plate, pléte, *v* argenter;
  dorer; nickeler; *n*
  assiette *f;* (silver)
  argenterie *f;* (photo)
  plaque *f.*

plate-glass, pléte´-glâce, *n*
  glace *f.*

platform, plätt´-fôrme, *n*
  estrade *f;* (station) quai

m.

platinum, plătt´-i-nomme, n platine m.

play, plé, v jouer; n jeu m; (theatre) pièce f; **–er,** musicien, -ienne m & f; acteur m; actrice f; joueur, -euse m & f; **–ful*,** a enjoué; **–ground,** n terrain de jeux m; (school) cour f; **–ing-cards,** cartes à jouer fpl.

plea, plî, n procès m; prétexte m; défense f.

plead, plîde, v alléguer; (law) plaider.

pleasant*, plè´-z'nt, a plaisant; agréable.

please, plîze, v plaire; contenter; interj s'il vous plaît!

pleasing, plî´-zinng, a agréable; aimable.

pleasure, plè´-jeure, n plaisir m.

pleat, plîte, n pli m; **–ed,** a plissé.

pledge, plèdje, n gage m; (surety) garantie f; v (pawn) mettre en gage.

plenty, plenn´-ti, n abondance f.

pleurisy, plioue´-ri-si, n pleurésie f.

pliable, plâï´-a-b'l, a flexible.

pliers, plâï´-eurze, npl

pinces fpl.

plight, plâïte, n état m, situation f.

plod, plodde, v (work) bûcher; **–along,** (walk) marcher péniblement.

plodder, plodde´-'r, n bûcheur, -euse m & f.

plot, plotte, v tramer; n complot m; (land) parcelle f; (story, etc) sujet m; **–ter,** conspirateur m.

plough, plâ'ou, n charrue f; v labourer.

ploughman, plâ'ou´-manne, n laboureur m.

plover, plov´-'r, n pluvier m.

pluck, ploque, v plumer (bird); cueillir (fruit); n courage m.

plug, plogue, v boucher; n bouchon m; tampon m; **spark –,** bougie d'allumage f; **wall –,** prise de courant.

plum, plomme, n prune f; **–tree,** prunier m.

plumage, ploue´-midj, n plumage m.

plumb, plomme, v sonder; n plomb m; **–ing,** plombage m.

plumber, plomm´-eur, n plombier m.

plump, plommpe, a gras; (person) potelé.

plunder, plonn´-d'r, v piller; n pillage m.

plunderer, plonn´-deur-eur, n pillard m.

plunge, plonndje, v plonger; n plongeon m.

plural, ploue´-r'l, n & a pluriel m.

plus, plosse, prep plus.

plush, ploche, n peluche f.

ply, plâï, v (trade) exercer; (3-ply wool) laine à trois fils f; **– between,** v faire le service entre. . .

pneumatic, niou-mätt´-ique, a pneumatique.

pneumonia, niou-mau´-ni-a & n pneumonie f.

poach, pautche, v braconner; (eggs) pocher.

poacher, pautch´-'r, n braconnier m.

pocket, pok´-ette, v empocher; n poche f.

pod, pode, n cosse f; (garlic) gousse f.

poem, pau´-emme, n poème m.

poet, pau´-ette, n poète m; **–ry,** poésie f.

point, poa´-innte, v indiquer; (finger) montrer; (sharpen) tailler; n (tip) pointe f; (punctuation, position) point m; **–ed,** a pointu; fig direct; **–er,** n (rod) baguette f; (dog) chien d'arrêt m.

poise, poa´ize, n équilibre m; (person) maintien m.

poison, poa´i´-z'n, n poison m; v empoisonner; **–ous**, a (plant) vénéneux; (animal) venimeux.

poke, pauke, v pousser; (fire) attiser.

poker, pau´-keur, n tisonnier m; (cards) poker m.

pole, paule, n perche f; (arctic) pôle m.

police, pŏ-lîce´, n police f; **–man**, agent m; **– station**, commissariat de police m; **–woman**, femme-agent f.

policy, pol´-i-ci, n politique f; (insurance) police f.

polish, pol´-iche, n (gloss) luisant m; (shoes) cirage m; (furniture, etc) cire f; v polir; cirer; **French –**, vernir.

polite*, pŏ-lä̈ite´, a poli; **–ness**, n politesse f.

political, pŏ-lite´-i-k'l, a politique.

politician, pŏl-i-tiche´-ann, n homme politique m.

politics, pol´-i-tikse, n politique f.

poll, paule, n élection f; scrutin m; v voter.

pollen, pol´-enne, n pollen m.

pollute, pŏl-lioute´, v polluer.

pollution, pŏl-liou-ch'n, n pollution f.

polyester, pol-î-ès´-t'r, n polyester m.

polythene, pol-î-tsîne, n polythène f.

pomade, pau-méde´, n pommade f.

pomegranate, pomm´-gränn-éte, n grenade f.

pomp, pommpe, n pompe f; **–ous***, a pompeux.

pond, ponnde, n étang m.

ponder, ponn´-d'r, v réfléchir; méditer.

ponderous*, ponn´-deur-euce, a lourd; pesant.

pony, pau´-ni, n poney m.

poodle, poue´-d'l, n caniche m.

pool, poule, n (water) mare f; (swimming) piscine f; (cards) cagnotte f; poule f; v mettre en commun.

poop, poue´pe, n poupe f.

poor, pou´eur, a pauvre; n les pauvres mpl.

pop, poppe, v sauter; n (of a cork) bruit d'un bouchon qui saute m.

Pope, paupe, n pape m.

poplar, pop´-l'r, n peuplier m.

poplin, pop´-linne, n popeline f.

poppy, pop´-i, n coquelicot m.

populace, pop´-iou-léce, n peuple m; foule f.

popular*, pop´-iou-l'r, a populaire.

populate, pop´-iou-léte, v peupler.

population, pop-iou-lé´-ch'n, n population f.

populous, pop´-iou-leuce, a populeux.

porcelain, por´-ce-linne, n porcelaine f.

porch, paurtche, n porche m; portique m.

porcupine, poar´-kiou-pâine, n porc-épic m.

pore, paure, n pore m; **– over**, v étudier assidûment.

pork, paurque, n porc m; **–-butcher**, charcutier m.

porous, pau´-reuce, a poreux.

porpoise, poar´-peuce, n marsouin m.

porridge, por´-idj, n bouillie de gruau d'avoine f.

port, poar´te, n (wine) porto m; (harbour) port m; naut bâbord m; **– hole**, hublot m.

portable, paur´-ta-b'l, *a*
portatif.

portend, poar-tennde´, *v*
présager.

porter, paur´-t'r, *n*
(luggage) porteur *m*;
(door) portier *m*; **–age,**
factage *m*.

portfolio, paurt-fau´-li-au,
n serviette *f*.

portion, paur´-ch'n, *n*
portion *f*; (share) part *f*.

portly, paurt´-li, *a*
corpulent; majestueux.

portmanteau, paurt-
mănn´-tau, *n* valise *f*.

portrait, paur´-tréte, *n*
portrait *m*.

portray, paur-tré´, *v*
peindre; (describe)
décrire.

pose, pause, *n* pose *f*; *v*
poser; **– as,** se faire
passer pour.

position, po-zi´-ch'n, *n*
position *f*; situation *f*.

positive*, poz´-i-tive, *a*
positif; certain.

possess, pô-zesse´, *v*
posséder; **–ion,** *n*
possession *f*.

possessor, pô-zess´-eur, *n*
possesseur *m*.

possibility, poss-i-bil´-i-ti,
n possibilité *f*.

possible, poss´-i-b'l, *a*
possible.

possibly, poss´-i-bli, *adv*

peut-être.

post, pauste, *n* poste *f*;
courrier *m*; (wood, etc)
poteau *m*; (job) emploi
m, place *f*; *v* mettre à la
poste; **–age,** *n* port *m*;
–card, carte postale *f*;
–date, *v* postedater; **–er,**
n affiche *f*; (go) franco;
franco; **–man,** *n* facteur
m; **–master,** receveur des
postes *m*; **– mortem,**
autopsie *f*; **–office,**
bureau de poste *m*;
–pone, *v* remettre;
–script, *n* postscriptum
m.

posterior, poss-ti´-ri-eur,
& *a* postérieur *m*.

posterity, poss-tèr´-i-ti, *n*
postérité *f*.

posture, poss´-tioure, *n*
posture *f*.

pot, potte, *n* pot *m*;
(cooking) marmite *f*.

potash, pot´-ăche, *n*
potasse *f*.

potato, po-té´-tau, *n*
pomme de terre *f*.

potent, pau´-tennte, *a*
puissant; *fig* efficace.

potion, pau´-ch'n, *n*
potion *f*.

pottery, pot´-eur-i, *n*
poterie *f*.

pouch, pâ'outche, *n* poche
f; (tobacco) blague *f*.

poulterer, paule´-teur-eur,

n marchand de volaille
m.

poultice, paule´-tice, *n*
cataplasme *m*.

poultry, paule´-tri, *n*
volaille *f*.

pounce, pâ'ounce, *v* (on,
upon) fondre sur.

pound, pâ'ounde, *n* livre
sterling *f*; (weight) livre
f; (animals) fourrière *f*; *v*
(pulverise) broyer.

pour, paure, *v* verser;
(rain) pleuvoir à verse.

pour out, paure â'oute, *v*
verser; (serve) servir.

pout, pâ'oute, *v* faire la
moue.

poverty, pov´-eur-ti, *n*
pauvreté *f*.

powder, pâ'ou´-d'r, *n*
poudre *f*; *v* pulvériser;
(face) poudrer.

power, pâ'ou´-eur, *n*
pouvoir *m*; *mech* force *f*;
(state) puissance *f*;
–ful*, *a* puissant; **–less,**
impuissant.

pox, poxe, **small– –,** *n*
variole *f*; **chicken– –,**
varicelle *f*.

practicable, prăque´-ti-ca-
b'l, *a* praticable.

practical*, prăque´-ti-c'l, *a*
pratique.

practice, prăque´-tice, *n*
pratique *f*; (custom)
coutume *f*;

(professional) clientèle f; (exercise) exercise m.

practise, prăque´-tice, v s'exercer; (profession) exercer.

practitioner, prăque-tiche´-onn-*eur*, n praticien m.

praise, préze, v louer; n louange f; éloge m.

praiseworthy, préze´-oueur-*dzi*, a louable.

pram, prămme, n voiture d'enfant f; landau m.

prance, prănnce, v se cabrer; *fig* se pavaner.

prank, praïn-nk, n escapade f; farce f.

prawn, proanne, n bouquet m.

pray, pré, v prier.

prayer, prére, n prière f; –book, livre de prières m; **Lord's Prayer**, pater m.

preach, prîtche, v prêcher; –er, n prédicateur m.

precarious*, pri-ké´-ri-*euce*, a précaire.

precaution, pri-koa´-ch'n n précaution f.

precede, pri-cîde´, v précéder.

precedence, prè´-sid-ennce, n préséance f.

precedent, prè´-sid-ennte, n (example) précédent m.

precept, prî´-cèpte, n précepte m.

precinct, prî´-cinng-kt, n enceinte f.

precious*, prè´-cheuce, a précieux.

precipice, prèce´-i-pice, n précipice m.

precise*, pri-sâïce´, a précis; exact.

preclude, pri-cloude´, v exclure; empêcher.

precocious*, pri-kau´-cheuce, a précoce.

predecessor, pri-di-sess´-eur, n prédécesseur m.

predicament, pri-dik´-a-mennte, a mauvaise passe f; situation difficile f.

predicate, predd´-i-quéte, n (grammar) attribut m.

predict, pri-dicte´, v prédire; –ion, n prédiction f.

predominant, pri-domm´-i-nannte, a prédominant.

preface, preff´-ace, n préface f.

prefect, pri´-fecte, n préfet m.

prefer, pri-feur´, v préférer.

preferable, preff´-eur-a-b'l, a préférable.

preference, preff´-eur-ennce, n préférence f.

prefix, prè´-fixe, n préfixe

m; v mettre en tête.

pregnant, pregg´-nannte, a enceinte; (animals) pleine.

prejudice, prédj´-iou-dice, n préjugé m; préjudice m; v préjudicier; **–d**, a prévenu contre; **without** –, sans préjudice de.

prejudicial*, prédj-iou-dich´-'l, a préjudiciable.

prelate, prél´-éte, n prélat m.

preliminary, pri-limm´-i-na-ri, a préliminaire.

prelude, pré´-lioude, n prélude m.

premature*, pré´-ma-tioure, a prématuré.

premeditate, pri-medd´-i-téte, v préméditer.

premier, prî´-mi-eur, n président du conseil des ministres m; a premier.

premises, premm´-i-cize, npl locaux mpl.

premium, prî´-mi-eume, n prime f.

preparation, prip-a-ré´-ch'n, n préparation f.

prepare, pri-pére´, v préparer.

prepossessing, pri-pŏ-zess´-inng, a avenant.

preposterous*, pri-poss´-teur-euce, a absurde.

prerogative, pri-rog´-a-tive, n prérogative f.

prescription, pri-skrip´-ch'n, n med ordonnance f.

presence, préz´-ennce, n présence f; **– of mind,** présence d'esprit f.

present, pri-zennte´, v présenter; (gift) offrir (à, to).

present, préz´-ennte, n cadeau m; a présent; **–ation,** n présentation f; **–ly,** adv tout à l'heure.

presentiment, pri-zenn´-ti-mennte, n pressentiment m.

preservation, prèz-eur-vé´-ch'n, n protection f; (state, condition) conservation f.

preserve, pri-zeurve´, v préserver; conserver; (candied) confire; **–s,** npl conserves fpl.

preside, pri-zâïde´, v présider.

president, préz´-i-dennte, n président m.

press, presse, n presse f; v presser; appuyer; (clothes) repasser; **–ing,** a urgent; **–man,** n journaliste m.

pressure, préch´-eur, n pression f; urgence f.

presume, pri-zioume´, v présumer; (dare) oser.

presumption, pri-zomm´-ch'n, n présomption f.

pretence, pri-tennce´, n simulation f; prétexte m.

pretend, pri-tennde´, v prétendre; (sham) feindre; faire semblant.

pretentious*, pri-tenn´-cheuce, a prétentieux.

pretext, prî´-texte, n prétexte m.

pretty, pritt´-i, a joli.

prevail, pri-véle´, v prévaloir; **– upon,** persuader.

prevalent, prév´-a-lennte, a dominant; général.

prevent, pri-vennte´, v empêcher; **–ion,** n prévention f; **–ive,** a* préventif.

preview, prî´-vioue, n avant-première f.

previous, prî´-vi-euce, a précédent; préalable.

prey, pré, n proie f; v faire sa proie de.

price, prâïce, n prix m; **–less,** a hors de prix.

prick, prique, v piquer; n piqûre f; **–le,** épine f; **–ly,** a épineux.

pride, prâïde, n orgueil m; v (to **– oneself on**) s'enorgueillir de.

priest, prîste, n prêtre m.

prig, prigue, n pédant m; fat m; **–gish,** a suffisant.

prim, prime, a collet monté; (dress) soigneux.

primary, prâï´-ma-ri, a fondamental; **– school,** n école primaire f.

primate, prâï´-méte, n primat m.

prime, prâïme, n (of life) fleur de l'âge f; a premier; de première qualité; v préparer; **– minister,** n président du conseil m.

primer, prâï´-meur, n (school) livre élémentaire m.

primitive, primm´-i-tive, a primitif.

primrose, primm´-rauze, n primevère f.

prince, prinnce, n prince m; **–ly,** a princier; **–ss,** princesse f.

principal, prinn´-ci-p'l, n directeur m; chef m; (funds) principal m; a* principal.

principle, prinn´-ci-p'l, n principe m.

print, prinnte, v imprimer; n impression f; (photo) épreuve f; **–er,** imprimeur m; **–ing,** impression f; **–ing-works,** imprimerie f.

prior, prâï´-eur, n prieur m; a antérieur; adv avant de; **–ity,** n priorité f; **–y,** prieuré m.

prism, prizme, n prisme m;
–**atic,** a prismatique.

prison, priz´-'n, n prison f;
–**er,** prisonnier, -ère m &
f.

privacy, prâï´-va-ci, n
retraite f; intimité f.

private, prâï´-véte, a*
privé; personnel;
particulier; n (soldier)
simple soldat m.

privation, prâï-vé´-ch'n, n
privation f.

privilege, priv´-i-lidje, n
privilège m; v privilégier.

privy, priv´-i, a privé;
secret.

prize, prâïze, n prix m;
(ship) prise f; v évaluer.

probable, prob´-a-b'l, a
probable.

probate, pro´béte, n
vérification d'un
testament f.

probation, pro-bé´-ch'n, n
épreuve f, essai m; –**er,**
stagiaire m & f; eccl
novice m & f.

probe, praube, v sonder;
explorer; n sonde f.

problem, prob´-lemme, n
problème m.

procedure, prö-cîd´-ioure,
n procédé m; (law)
procédure f.

proceed, prö-cîde´, v
procéder; continuer;
–**ings,** npl mesures fpl;

(law) poursuites fpl.

proceeds, prau´-cîdze, npl
produit m; bénéfices
mpl.

process, prau´-cesse, n
cours m; (manufacture)
procédé m.

procession, prö-cé´-ch'n,
n procession f.

proclaim, prö-cléme´, v
proclamer; publier.

proclamation, prôc-là-
mé´-ch'n, n
proclamation f.

procure, prö-kioure´, v se
procurer; procurer.

prod, prôde, v piquer;
pousser.

prodigal*, prod´-i-g'l, a
prodigue.

prodigious*, prö-di´-
djeuce, a prodigieux.

prodigy, prod´-i-dji, n
prodige m.

produce, prö-diouce´, v
produire; n produit m;
denrées fpl; –**r,**
producteur, -trice m & f;
(stage) metteur en scène
m.

product, prod´-eucte, n
produit m; –**ion,**
production f; (stage)
représentation f.

profane, prö-féne´, v
profaner; a* profane.

profess, prö-fesse´, v
professer; déclarer; –**ion,**

n profession f; carrière f;
–**ional*,** a professionnel.

professor, prö-fess´-'r, n
professeur m.

proficiency, prö-fi´-
chenn-ci, n capacité f;
compétence f.

proficient, prö-fi´-ch'nt, a
avancé; verse.

profile, prau´-fâïle, n
profil m.

profit, prof´-itte, n
bénéfice m; v profiter;
–**able,** a avantageux;
–**eer,** n profiteur, -euse m
& f.

profound*, prö-
fâ´ounnde´, a profond.

profuse, prö-fiouce´, a
prodigue; abondant.

programme, prau´-
grämme, n programme
m.

progress, prau-gresse´, v
faire des progrès;
avancer.

progress, prau´-gresse, n
progrès m.

prohibit, prau-hib´-itte, v
interdire; défendre à.

project, prôd-jecte´, v
projeter; dépasser;
déborder; n projet m;
–**ile,** projectile m; –**ion,**
saillie f; –**or,** projecteur
m.

proletarian, prau-lè-té´-ri-
anne, n & a prolétaire

m.

prologue, prau´-logue, n prologue m.

prolong, prau-lonng´, v prolonger.

promenade, promm-eu-nâde´, v se promener; n promenade f.

prominent, promm´-i-nennte, a proéminent.

promise, promm´-iss, n promesse f; v promettre.

promissory note, promm´-iss-o-ri naute, n billet à ordre m.

promote, prŏ-maute´, v promouvoir; (business) lancer; **–r,** n promoteur m; **company –r,** lanceur d'affaires m.

promotion, prau-mau´-ch'n, n avancement m; promotion f.

prompt, prommpte, a* prompt; v suggérer; (stage) souffler; **–er,** n souffleur m.

prone, praune, a étendu; enclin à; (bent) courbé.

prong, pronng, n dent f; pointe f.

pronoun, prau-nâ'ounne, n pronom m.

pronounce, prŏ-nâ'ounnce´, v prononcer.

pronunciation, prŏ-nonn-ci-é´-ch'n, n

prononciation f.

proof, proufe, n preuve f; a à l'épreuve de.

prop, proppe, n soutien m; support m; v étayer; supporter.

propaganda, prop-a-gänn´-da, n propagande f.

propagate, prop´-a-guéte, v propager.

propel, prŏ-pelle´, v faire mouvoir.

propeller, prŏ-pell´-eur, n hélice f.

proper*, prop´-r, a propre; (fit) convenable.

property, prop´-eur-ti, n propriété f, biens mpl.

prophecy, prof´-i-si, n prophétie f.

prophesy, prof´-i-sâï, v prédire.

prophet, prof´-ette, n prophète m.

propitious*, pro-pich´-euce, a propice.

proportion, pro-paur´-ch'n, n proportion f.

proposal, pro-pauz´-'l, n proposition f.

propose, pro-pauze´, v proposer; offrir.

proposition, pro-pau-zich´-'n, n proposition f.

proprietor, pro-prâï´-è-teur, n propriétaire m.

proprietress, pro-prâï´-è-

tresse, n propriétaire f.

propriety, pro-prâï´-è-ti, n convenances fpl.

prose, prauze, n prose f.

prosecute, pross´-i-kioute, v (law) poursuivre.

prosecution, pross-i-kioue´-ch'n, n poursuites fpl.

prosecutor, pross´-i-kioue-teur, n plaignant m.

prospect, pross´-pecte, n vue f; (future) avenir m; v explorer; **–ive,** a futur.

prospectus, pross-pec´-teuce, n prospectus m.

prosper, pross´-p'r, v prospérer; **–ity,** n prospérité f; **–ous*,** a prospère.

prostitute, pross´-ti-tioute, n prostituée f.

prostrate, pross-tréte, v se prosterner; a abattu.

prostration, pross-tré´-ch'n, n prostration f.

protect, pro-tecte´, v protéger.

protection, pro-tec´-ch'n, n protection f.

protest, pro-tesste´, v protester; n protestation f.

protract, pro-tracte´, v prolonger.

protrude, pro-troude´, v faire saillie; déborder.

proud*, prâ'oude, a fier;

orgueilleux.

prove, prouve, *v* prouver; vérifier.

proverb, prov´-*eur*be, *n* proverbe *m*.

provide, prŏ-vâide´, *v* pourvoir; fournir.

Providence, prov´-i-dennce, *n* Providence *f*.

provident, prov´-i-dennte, *a* prévoyant.

province, prov´-innce, *n* province *f*.

provision, prŏ-vi´-j'n, *n* provision *f*; stipulation *f*; **–al*,** *a* provisoire; **–s,** *npl* comestibles *mpl*.

provocation, prŏv-ŏ-qué´-ch'n, *n* provocation *f*.

provoke, prŏ-vauke´, *v* provoquer; irriter.

prowl, prâ'oule, *v* rôder.

proximity, prok-simm´-i-ti, *n* proximité *f*.

proxy, prok´-ci, *n* fondé de pouvoir *m*; **by –,** par procuration.

prude, proude, *n* prude *f*; **–nce,** prudence *f*; **–nt*,** *a* prudent; **–ry,** *n* pruderie *f*.

prudish, prou´-diche, *a* prude.

prune, proune, *n* pruneau *m*; *v* (trees, etc) tailler.

pry, prâï, *v* fureter; fourrer son nez dans . . .

psalm, sâme, *n* psaume *m*.

pseudonym, sioue´-dô-nimme, *n* pseudonyme *m*.

psychiatrist, sâï-kâï´-a-trisst, *n* psychiatre.

psychiatry, sâï-kâï´-a-trî, *n* psychiatrie *f*.

psychoanalyst, sâï-cau-ă´-nă-lisste, *n* psychanalyste.

psychological, sâï-cau-lodj´-i-*q*uel, *a* psychologique.

psychology, sâï-col´-ŏdj-î, *n* psychologie *f*.

psychopath, sâï´-kau-păts, *n* psychopathe.

public, pobb´-lique, *n & a* public *m*; **–an,** *n* aubergiste *m*; **– house,** auberge *f*.

publication, pobb-li-qué´-ch'n, *n* publication *f*.

publicity, pobb-li´-si-tî, *n,* publicité *f*.

publish, pobb´-liche, *v* publier; (books, etc) éditer.

publisher, pobb´-lich-*eur,* *n* éditeur *m*.

pucker, pok´-'r, *v* rider; plisser; froncer (brows, etc).

pudding, poudd´-inng, *n* pudding *m*.

puddle, podd´-'l, *n* flaque *f*.

puerile, pioue´-*eur*-âïl, *a*

puéril.

puff, poffe, *v* souffler; (swell) boursoufler; *n* (breath) souffle *m*; (wind, etc) bouffée *f*; **powder –,** houppe *f*; **–y,** *a* boursouflé.

pug, pogg, *n* (dog) carlin *m*; **–nacious,** *a* batailleur; **–-nosed,** qui *a* le nez épaté.

pugilist, pioue´-djil-ist, *n* pugiliste *m*.

pull, poull, *n* coup *m*; *v* tirer; **– down,** abattre; démolir; (lower) baisser; **– out,** (draw) arracher; **–up,** remonter, hisser; **–over,** *n* pull *m*.

pullet, poull´ette, *n* poulette *f*.

pulley, poull´-i, *n* poulie *f*.

pulp, polpe, *n* pulpe *m*; **wood –,** pâte de bois *f*.

pulpit, poull´-pitte, *n* chaire *f*.

pulse, pollse, *n* pouls *m*.

pulverize, poll´-veur-âïze, *v* pulvériser.

pumice-stone, pomm´-ice staune, *n* pierre ponce *f*.

pump, pommpe, *n* pompe *f*; *v* pomper.

pun, ponne, *n* jeu de mots *m*.

punch, ponntche, *n* coup de poing *m*; (tool) poinçon *m*; (drink) punch *m*; (Punch and Judy) Guignol *m*; *v* donner un coup de poing; percer.

punctilious*, ponngk-til´-i-*euce*, *a* pointilleux.

punctual*, ponngk´-tiou-*eul*, *a* ponctuel.

punctuate, ponngk´-tiou-éte, *v* ponctuer.

punctuation, ponngk-tiou-é´-ch'n, *n* ponctuation.

puncture, ponngk´tioure, *n med* ponction *f*; (tyre) crevaison *f*; *v* crever.

pungency, ponn´-djenn-si, *n* âcreté *f*; aigreur *f*.

pungent, ponn´-djennte, *a* âcre; piquant.

punish, ponn´-iche, *v* punir; **–able**, *a* punissable.

punishment, ponn´-iche-mennte, *n* punition *f*.

punitive, pioue´-ni-tive, *a* punitif.

punt, ponnte, *n* bateau plat *m*.

puny, pioue´-ni, *a* chétif; faible.

pupil, pioue´-pile, *n* élève *m* & *f*; (eye) pupille *f*.

puppet, popp´-ette, *n* marionnette *f*; poupée *f*.

puppy, popp´-i, *n* jeune chien *m*.

purchase, por´-tchiss, *v* acheter; *n* achat *m*.

purchaser, por´-tché-seur, *n* acheteur, -euse *m* & *f*.

pure*, pioure, *a* pur; vierge.

purgative, peur´-ga-tive, *n* & *a* purgatif *m*.

purgatory, peur´-ga-tŏ-ri, *n* purgatoire *m*.

purge, peurdje, *v* purger; *n* purge *f*.

purify, pioue´-ri-fâï, *v* purifier.

purity, pioue´-ri-ti, *n* pureté *f*.

purloin, peur´-lô'ine, *v* dérober.

purple, peur´-p'l, *n* & *a* pourpre *m*.

purpose, peur´-*peuce*, *n* but *m*; **–ly**, *adv* exprès.

purr, peur, *v* ronronner.

purse, peurce, *n* porte-monnaie *m*; (prize) bourse *f*.

purser, peur´-ceur, *n* (ship's) commissaire *m*.

pursue, peur-sioue´, *v* poursuivre.

pursuit, peur-sioute´, *n* poursuite *f*.

purveyor, peur-vé´-eur, *n* fournisseur *m*.

pus, poss, *n* pus *m*; humeur *f*.

push, pouche, *v* pousser; *n* poussée *f*; **–chair**, *n* poussette *f*.

pushing, pouch´-inng, *a* (keen) entreprenant.

put, poutt, *v* mettre; placer; poser; **– off**, remettre; **– on**, mettre.

putrefy, pioue´-tri-fâï, *v* se putréfier; pourrir.

putrid, pioue´-tride, *a* putride.

putty, pott´-i, *n* mastic *m*.

puzzle, pozz-z'l, *v* embarrasser; intriguer; *n* embarras *m*; (toy) casse-tête *m*; puzzle *m*; **cross word –**, mots croisés *mpl*.

pyjamas, pi-djâ´-*maze*, *npl* pyjama *m*.

pyramid, pir´-*a*-mide, *n* pyramide *f*.

python, pâï´-tsonn, *n* python *m*.

quack, couăque, *v* cancaner; *n* charlatan *m*; **–ery,** charlatanisme *m*.

quadrille, couodd´rile, *n* quadrille *m*.

quadruped, couodd´-roupedde, *n* quadrupède *m*.

quadruple, couodd´-roup'l, *a* quadruple.

quagmire, couăgue´-mâïre, *n* marécage *m*.

quail, couéle, *n* caille *f*; *v* trembler.

quaint*, couénnte, *a* bizarre; pittoresque.

quaintness, couénnte´-nesse, *n* bizarrerie *f*; pittoresque *m*.

quake, couéque, *v* trembler; **earth–,** *n* tremblement de terre *m*.

quaker, coué´-keur, *n* (sect) quaker *m*.

qualification, couoll-i-fi-qué´-ch'n, *n* aptitude *f*.

qualified, couoll´-î-fâïd, *a* diplômé *m*.

qualify, couoll´-i-fâï, *v* qualifier; acquérir les qualités requises.

quality, couoll´i-ti, *n* qualité *f*.

quandary, couonn´-da-ri, *n* perplexité *f*.

quantity, couonn´-ti-ti, *n* quantité *f*.

quarantine, couor´-ann-tîne, *n* quarantaine *f*.

quarrel, couor´-elle, *n* dispute *f*; *v* se disputer.

quarrelsome, couor´-ell-seume, *a* querelleur.

quarry, couor´-i, *n* carrière *f*; (prey) proie *f*.

quarter, couôr´-t'r, *v* (to lodge) loger; diviser en quatre; *n* quart *m*; (period) trimestre *m*; (district) quartier *m*; **–day,** terme *m*; **–ly,** *a* trimestriel.

quartet, couôr-tette´, *n* quatuor *m*.

quartz, couortze, *n* quartz *m*.

quash, couoche, *v* subjuguer; réprimer; annuler.

quaver, coué´-v'r, *v* chevroter; *n mus* croche *f*.

quay, quî, *n* quai *m*.

queen, couîne, *n* reine *f*.

queer*, couire, *a* bizarre; étrange, drôle.

quell, couelle, *v* réprimer; dompter.

quench, couenntche, *v* éteindre; (thirst) apaiser sa soif.

querulous*, couèr´-ou-leuce, *a* plaintif.

query, coui´ri, *v* mettre en doute; *n* question *f*.

quest, coueste, *n* recherche *f*; enquête *f*.

question, couess´-tieune, *v* questionner; douter; *n*

question f; **–able,** a
contestable; **–mark,** n
point d'interrogation m.
queue, kioue, n queue f.
quibble, couib´-b'l, v
ergoter; n chicane f.
quick*, couique, a rapide;
(hurry) vite; (wit, etc)
vif; **–en,** v accélérer;
animer; **–lime,** n chaux
vive f; **–ness,** vitesse f;
vivacité f; **–sands,** sables
mouvants mpl; **–silver,**
mercure m.
quiet, couâï´-ette, v
calmer. a* tranquille.
quill, couille, n (pen)
plume d'oie f.
quilt, couillte, n couvre-
pieds m; édredon m.
quince, couinnce, n coing
m.
quinine, couinn´-âïne, n
quinine f.
quit, couitte, v quitter; **–s,**
a quitte.
quite, couâïte, adv tout à
fait; entièrement; assez.
quiver, couiv´-'r, n
carquois m; v trembler; n
tremblement m.
quiz, couiz, n test m;
(game) jeu-concours m.
quoit, coa'itte´, n palet m.
quota, cou'au´ta, n quote-
part f.
quotation, cou'au-té´-
ch'n, n citation f;

(price) devis m; (shares,
etc) cote f.
quote, cou'aute, v citer;
coter; faire un prix.

R

rabbi, răb´-bâï, n rabbin
m.
rabbit, răb´-itte, n lapin
m.
rabble, răbb´-'l, n
populace f; (riffraff)
canaille f.
rabid, răb´-ide, a enragé.
rabies, ré´-bi-ize, n rage f;
hydrophobie f.
race, réce, v courir; courir
vite; faire la course; n
(breed) race f; (contest)
course f; **–course,**
champ de courses m;
–horse, cheval de course
m; **–s,** courses fpl.
racism, ré´-si-z'm, n
racisme m.
racist, ré´-ssiste, a & n
raciste m f.
rack, răque, n (torture)
roue f; (luggage) filet m.

racket, răque´-ette, n
(sports) raquette f.
radar, ré-dâre, n radar m.
radiant*, ré´-di-annte, a
rayonnant; fig radieux.
radiate, ré´-di-éte, v
ravonner; (heat)
émettre des rayons.
radiation, ré-di-é-ch'n, n
rayonnement m.
radiator, ré´-di-é-teur, n
radiateur m.
radio, ré´-di-o, n radio f; –
station, station de radio
f.
radioactive, ré-di-o-ăc´-
tive, a radioactif.
radish, răd´-iche, n radis
m; **horse –,** raifort m.
radium, ré´-di-omme, n
radium m.
radius, ré´-di-euce, n
rayon m.

raffle, răff´-'l, n loterie f; v
mettre en loterie.
raft, râfte, n radeau n.
rafter, râf´-t'r, n chevron
m, poutre f.
rag, răgue, n chiffon m;
–ged, a en loques.
rage, rédje, n rage f; v être
furieux.
raid, réde, n incursion f;
(**air- –**) raid m; (**police**
–) descente de police f.
rail, réle, v railler; n
(railway) rail m; (stair)
barreau m; **–lery,**
raillerie f; **–way,** chemin
de fer m.
rain, réne, v pleuvoir; n
pluie f; **–bow,** arc-en-
ciel m; **–coat,**
imperméable m; **–fall,**
précipitation f; **–water,**
eau de pluie f; **–y,** a
pluvieux.
raise, réze, v lever;
(courage) relever; (to
lift) soulever; (increase)
augmenter; (heighten)
rehausser; (crops)
cultiver.
raisin, ré´-z'n, n raisin sec
m.
rake, réque, n râteau m;
(person) roué m; v mech
râtisser; (fire) secouer.
rally, răl´-i, v rallier;
rassembler; n rallye m.
ram, rămme, n bélier m; v

444

enfoncer; (ship) aborder.

rampant, rămm´-pannte, *a* rampant; exubérant.

rampart, rămm´-pârte, *n* rempart *m*.

rancid, rănn´-cide, *a* rance.

rancour, răng´-keur, *n* rancune *f*.

random, rănn´-d'm, at –, *adv* au hasard.

randy, rănn´-di, *a* excité; en chaleur.

range, réne´-dje, *n* série *f*; (kitchen) fourneau *m*; (extent) étendu *f*; (mountain) chaîne *f*; (practice) champ de tir *m*; (projectile) portée *f*; *v* ranger.

ranger, réne´-djeur, *n* garde forestier *m*.

rank, rain-nk, *a* (taste, smell) rance; *n* rang *m*; *mil* grade *m*; (row) rangée *f*.

ransack, rănn´-săque, *v* saccager; fouiller.

ransom, rănn´-seume, *n* rançon *f*; *v* rançonner.

rap, răppe, *n* coup *m*; *v* frapper.

rape, répe, *v* violer; enlever; *n* viol *m*.

rapid*, răp´-ide, *a* rapide; **–s,** *npl* rapides *mpl*.

rapture, răp´-tioure, *n* ravissement *m*.

rare*, raire, *a* rare; **–fy,** *v* raréfier.

rarity, ré´-ri-ti, *n* rareté *f*.

rascal, râsse´-c'l, *n* coquin *m*, fripon *m*.

rash*, râche, *n* (skin) éruption *f*. *a** téméraire; **–er,** *n* tranche de lard *f*; **–ness,** témérité *f*.

rasp, râsspe, *n* râpe *f*; *v* râper.

raspberry, râze´-beur-i, *n* framboise *f*.

rat, rătte, *n* rat *m*; **–-trap,** ratière *f*.

rate, réte, *n* proportion *f*; (tax; exchange; charge) taux *m*; (speed) vitesse *f*; *v* évaluer.

rather, râdz´-'r, *adv* plutôt; (somewhat) assez.

ratify, răt´-i-fâî, *v* ratifier.

ratio, ré´-chi-au, *n* proportion *f*.

ration, ră´-ch'n, *n* ration *f*; *v* rationner.

rational*, răch´-eunn-'l, *a* rationnel; raisonnable.

rattle, răt´-t'l, *n* (instrument) crécelle *f*; (toy) hochet *m*; (noise) tapage *m*; (death) râle *m*.

rattlesnake, răt´-t'l-snéke, *n* serpent à sonnettes *m*.

ravage, răv´-idj, *v* ravager; *n* ravage *m*.

rave, réve, *v* délirer; **– about,** s'extasier sur.

raven, ré´-v'n, *n* corbeau *m*.

ravenous, răv´-'n-euce, *a* vorace.

ravine, ră-vine´, *n* ravin *m*.

raving, ré´-vinng, *a* en délire; *fig* furieux.

ravish, ră´-viche, *v* ravir; **–ing,** *a* ravissant.

raw, roa, *a* cru; (wound) à vif.

ray, ré, *n* rayon *m*.

raze, réze, *v* raser; abattre.

razor, ré´-z'r, *n* rasoir *m*; **safety–,** rasoir mécanique *m*; **–-blade,** lame de rasoir *f*.

reach, rîtche, *v* atteindre; (arrive) parvenir à.

react, ri-acte´, réagir; **–ion,** *n* réaction *f*.

read, rîde, *v* lire; (for exam) étudier; **–er,** *n* lecteur *m*; correcteur *m*; **–ing,** lecture *f*.

readily, redd´-i-li, *adv* promptement; volontiers.

ready, redd´-i, *a* prêt; **– made,** tout fait; (clothes) le prêt à porter.

real*, rî´-'l, *a* réel; véritable.

reality, rî-ă´-li-tî, *n* réalité

f.

realize, ri´-al-âïze, v se rendre compte de; (sell) réaliser.

realm, relme, n royaume n.

reap, rîpe, v moissonner, récolter; **–er,** n moissonneur m; **–ing-machine,** moissonneuse f.

rear, rire, v élever; (prance) se cabrer; n mil arrière-garde f; (back) arrière m.

reason, rî´-z'n, v raisonner; n raison f.

reasonable, rî´-z'n-a-b'l, a raisonnable.

reassure, ri´-a-choure´, v rassurer.

rebate, ri-béte´, n rabais m; v rabattre.

rebel, rebb´-'l, n & a rebelle m & f.

rebel, ri-bel´, v se révolter; **–lion,** n rébellion f.

rebound, ri-bâ´ounnde´, v rebondir.

rebuff, ri-boffe´, v rebuter; n rebuffade f.

rebuke, ri-biouke´, v réprimander; n réprimande f.

recall, ri-coale´, v rappeler; (retract) retirer.

recapitulate, ri-ca-pit´-iou-léte, v récapituler.

recede, ri-cîde´, v reculer.

receipt, ri-cîte´, n reçu m; v acquitter.

receipts, ri-cîtse´, npl com recettes fpl.

receive, ri-cîve´, v recevoir; **–r,** n receveur m; (bankruptcy) syndic de faillite m.

recent*, rî´-cennte, a récent.

receptacle, ri-sèpe´-ta-k'l, n réceptacle m.

reception, ri-sèpe´-ch'n, n réception f.

recess, ri-cesse´, n (space) renfoncement m; alcôve f.

recipe, ress´-i-pi, n recette f.

reciprocate, ri-cip´-rô-quéte, v rendre la pareille.

recital, ri-sâï´-t'l, n récit m; récitation f; mus récital m.

recite, ri-sâïte´, v réciter.

reckless*, rèque´-lesse, a imprudent.

reckon, rèque´-'n, v compter, calculer.

reclaim, ri-cléme´, v réclamer; (land) défricher.

recline, ri-clâïne´, v se pencher; s'appuyer.

recluse, ri-clouce´, n & a

reclus, -e m & f.

recognition, rèk-ŏgue-niche´-'n, n reconnaissance f.

recognize, rèk´-ŏgue-nâïze, v reconnaître.

recoil, ri-coa'ile´, v reculer; n recul m.

recollect, rèk-ŏl-lecte´, v se rappeler; se souvenir de.

recollection, rèk-ŏl-lèque´-ch'n, n souvenir m.

recommence, ri-cŏmm-ennce´, v recommencer.

recommend, rè-cŏmm-ennde´, v recommander; **–ation,** n recommandation f.

recompense, rèk´-ŏmm-pennce, v récompenser; n récompense f.

reconcile, rèk´-ŏnn-sâïle, v réconcilier; concilier.

reconnoitre, rèk-ŏnn-no'i´-tr, v faire une reconnaissance.

reconsider, ri-cŏnn-cid´-'r, v considérer de nouveau.

record, ri-coarde´, v enregistrer; mentionner.

record, rèk´-oarde, n registre m; archives fpl; (gramophone) disque m; **–player,** n électrophone m.

recoup, ri-coupe´, v
dédommager.

recourse, ri-caurse´, n
recours m.

recover, rî-cov´-'r, v
recouvrer; (health) se
rétablir; **–y**, n
recouvrement m;
rétablissement m.

re-cover, ri-cov´-'r, v
recouvrir.

recreation, rèk-ri-é´-ch'n,
n divertissement m; **–
ground**, cour de
récréation f.

recruit, ri-croute´, n
recrue f; v recruter.

rectangular, rèk-tänng´-
guiou-l'r, a
rectangulaire.

rectify, rèk´-ti-fâî, v
rectifier.

rector, rèk´-t'r, n recteur
m; **–y**, presbytère m.

recumbent, ri-comm´-
bennte, a étendu;
couché.

recuperate, ri-kiou´-peur-
éte, v se remettre.

recur, ri-keur´, v se
reproduire; se répéter.

red, red, n & a rouge m;
–breast, n rougegorge m;
–den, v rougir; **–dish**, a
rougeâtre; **–hot**, chauffé
au rouge; **–light
district**, n quartier des
prostituées m; **–ness**, n
rougeur.

redeem, ri-dîme´, v
(promise) accomplir;
(bonds, etc) rembourser;
(pledge) dégager; (soul)
délivrer.

redemption, ri-demmp´-
ch'n, n com rachat m.

redouble, ri-dob´-'l, v
redoubler.

redress, ri-dresse´, v
réparer; n réparation f.

reduce, ri-diouce´, v
réduire; (disgrace)
rétrograder.

reduction, ri-doque´-ch'n,
n réduction f; rabais m.

redundant, ri-donn´-
deunt, a licencié;
superflu.

reed, rîde, n roseau m.

reef, rîfe, n récif m; (sail)
ris m; v prendre un ris.

reek, rîque, v fumer;
exhaler; empester; n
odeur forte f.

reel, rîle, n (cotton; film)
bobine f; (angling)
moulinet, m; v
chanceler.

refer, ri-feur´, v se référer;
(apply) s'adresser à; (to
a book) consulter.

referee, rèf´-eur-î´, n
arbitre m.

reference, rèf´-eur-'nce, n
allusion f; (testimonial)
référence f; **with – to**,

concernant.

referendum, rèf-eur-èn´-
deum, n référendum m.

refine, ri-fâïne´, v (sugar)
raffiner; (liquid) épurer;
–d, a raffiné; **–ment**, n
raffinement m.

reflect, ri-flecte´, v
réfléchir; (lights, etc)
refléter; **–ion**, n
réflexion f; **–or**,
réflecteur m.

reform, ri-fôrme´, v
réformer; se réformer; n
réforme f; **–ation**,
réformation f.

refrain, ri-fréne´, v
s'abstenir de.

refresh, ri-frèche´, v
rafraîchir; se rafraîchir.

refreshment, ri-frèche´-
m'nt, n rafraîchissement
m.

refrigerator, ri-fridje´-eur-
é-teur, n frigidaire m.

refuge, rèf´-ioudje, n
refuge m; (shelter) abri
m.

refugee, rèf-iou-djî´, n
réfugié, -ée m & f.

refund, ri-fonnde´, v
rembourser; n
remboursement m.

refusal, ri-fiou´-z'l, n refus
m.

refuse, ri-fiouze, v refuser.

refuse, rèf´-iouce, n rebut
m; (garbage) ordures fpl.

refute, ri-fioute´, v réfuter.

regain, ri-guéne´, v regagner; (health) récupérer.

regal*, rî´-g'l, a royal.

regale, ri-guéle, v régaler.

regard, ri-gârde´, v regarder; considérer; n regard m; (heed) égard m; **–less,** a sans égard; **–s,** npl amitiés fpl.

regatta, ri-găt´-ta, n régate f.

regenerate, ri-djenn´-eur-éte, v régénérer.

regent, rî´-djennte, n régent, -e m & f.

regiment, rèdj´-i-m'nt, n régiment m.

region, rî´-djeune, n région f.

register, rèdje´-iss-teur, v enregistrer; (letter) recommander; n registre m.

registrar, rèdge-iss-trâre, n (births, etc) officier de l'état civil m; (court) greffier m.

registration, rèdge-iss-tré´-ch'n n enregistrement m; inscription f.

registry, rèdge´-iss-tri, n bureau d'enregistrement m.

regret, ri-grette´, v regretter; n regret m.

regrettable, ri-grett´-a-b'l, a regrettable.

regular*, regg´-iou-l'r, a régulier.

regulate, regg´-iou-léte, v régler.

regulation, regg-iou-lé´-ch'n, n règlement m.

rehearsal, ri-heur´-s'l, n répétition f.

rehearse, ri-heurce´, v répéter.

reign, réne, n règne m; v régner.

reimburse, ri-imm-beurce´, v rembourser.

rein, réne, n rêne f.

reindeer, réne´-dire, n renne m.

reinforce, ri-inn-faurce´, v renforcer.

reinstate, ri-inn-stéte´, v réintégrer.

reject, ri-djecte´, v rejeter.

rejoice, ri-djoa'ice´, v réjouir.

rejoicings, ri-djoa'ice´-inngse, npl réjouissances fpl.

rejoin, ri-djô'ine´, v rejoindre.

rejuvenate, ri-djiou´-venn-éte, v rajeunir.

relapse, ri-lăpse´, n rechute f; v retomber.

relate, ri-léte´, v raconter; **–d,** a apparenté à.

relation, ri-lé´-ch'n, n

(relative) parent, -e m & f; com rapport m.

relative, rèl´-a-tive, n (person) parent, -e m & f; a* relatif.

relax, ri-lăxe´, v se détendre; **–ation,** n détente; relaxation f.

relay, réne, n (radio) relais m; v relayer.

release, ri-lice´, v relâcher; libérer; n décharge f.

relent, ri-lennte´, v se laisser fléchir.

relentless*, ri-lennte´-lesse, a implacable.

relevant, rèl´-i-vannte, a applicable; relatif.

reliable, ri-lâï´-a-b'l, a digne de confiance; sûr.

reliance, ri-lâï´-annce, n confiance f.

relic, rèl´-ique, n (of saint, martyr) relique f; **–s,** pl restes mpl.

relief, ri-lîfe´, n (anxiety; pain) soulagement m; (help) secours m; (raised) relief m.

relieve, ri-lîve´, v soulager; secourir.

religion, ri-lidj´-onn, n religion f.

religious*, ri-lidj´-euce, a religieux.

relinquish, ri-linng´-couiche, v abandonner.

relish, rèl´-iche, v

savourer; n saveur f.

reluctance, ri-loque´-t'nce, n répugnance f.

reluctant, ri-loque´-tannte, a peu disposé à.

rely, ri-lâï, v compter sur.

remain, ri-méne´, v rester; **–der,** n reste m.

remand, ri-mânnde; v (law) renvoyer à une autre audience.

remark, ri-mârque´, n remarque f; v remarquer.

remarkable, ri-mâr´-ka-b'l, a remarquable.

remedy, remm´-i-di, n remède m; v remédier á.

remember, ri-memm´-b'r, v se souvenir de.

remembrance, ri-memm´-brannce, n souvenir m.

remind, ri-mâïnnde, v rappeler.

remit, ri-mitte´, v remettre; **–tance,** n remise f.

remnant, remm´-nannte, n reste m; **–s,** pl (fabrics) coupons mpl.

remonstrate, ri-monn´-stréte, v faire des remontrances à.

remorse, ri-moarce´, n remords m.

remote, ri-maute´, a éloigné; reculé; lointain.

removal, ri-moue´-v'l, n déménagement m.

remove, ri-mouve´, v déménager; (shift) déplacer.

remunerate, ri-mioue´-neur-éte, v rémunérer.

remunerative, ri-mioue´-neur-a-tive, a rémunérateur; avantageux.

rend, rennde, v déchirer; **–er,** rendre; (account) présenter; **–ering,** n traduction f.

renegade, renn´-i-guéde, n renégat, -e m & f.

renew, ri-nioue´, v renouveler; **–al,** n renouvellement m.

renounce, ri-nâ'ounce´, v renoncer.

renovate, renn´-ŏ-véte, v renouveler.

renown, ri-nâ'oune´, n renommée f; renom m.

rent, rennte, n loyer m; (tear) déchirure f; v louer.

renunciation, ri-nonn-ci-é´-ch'n, n renonciation f.

repair, ri-paire´, v réparer; (sewing) raccommoder; n réparation f.

reparation, rèp-a-ré´-ch'n, n réparation f.

repartee, rèp-ar-tî´, n repartie f.

repay, ri-pé´, v

rembourser.

repeal, ri-pîle´, v révoquer; n révocation f.

repeat, ri-pîte´, v répéter.

repel, ri-pelle´, v repousser; **–lent,** a répulsif.

repent, ri-pennte´, v se repentir (de).

repetition, rèp-i-tiche´-'n, n répétition f.

replace, ri-pléce´, v (substitute) remplacer; (put back) replacer.

replenish, ri-plenn´-iche, v remplir.

reply, ri-plâï´, v répondre; n réponse f.

report, ri-paurte´, n rapport m; compte rendu m; (news) nouvelles fpl; (school) bulletin m; (noise) détonation f; v informer; signaler.

reporter, ri-paur´-t'r, n reporter m.

repose, ri-pauze´, n repos m; v (se) reposer.

repository, ri-poz´-i-tŏ-ri, n dépôt m.

represent, rèp-ri-zennte´, v représenter; **–ation,** n représentation f; **–ative,** représentant m.

reprieve, ri-prîve´, v commuer; remettre.

reprimand, rèp-ri-mânnde´, v réprimander.

reprimand, rép´-mânnde, n réprimande f.

reprint, ri-prinnte´, v réimprimer; n réimpression f; nouveau tirage m.

reprisal, ri-prâï´-z'l, n représaille f.

reproach, ri-prautche´, v reprocher à; n reproche m.

reprobate, rèp´-ro-béte, n vaurien m.

reproduce, ri-prŏ-diouce´, v reproduire.

reproduction, ri-prŏ-dock´-ch'n, n reproduction f.

reproof, ri-proufe´, n réprimande f.

reprove, ri-prouve´, v blâmer; censurer.

reptile, rèp´-tâïle, n reptile m.

republic, ri-pobb´-lique, n république f.

repudiate, ri-pioue´-di-éte, v répudier.

repugnant, ri-pog´-nannte, a répugnant.

repulse, ri-pollce´, v repousser; n échec m.

repulsive, ri-poll´-cive, a repoussant.

reputable, rèp´-ieu-tă-b'l, a de bonne réputation.

reputation, rèp´-iou-té-ch'n, n réputation f.

repute, ri-pioute´, n renom m.

request, ri-couesste´, n demande f; v demander.

require, ri-couâïre´, v avoir besoin de; exiger; –ment, n besoin m; exigence f.

requisite, rèk´-oui-zitte, a requis; nécessaire.

rescue, ress´-kioue, v sauver; n sauvetage m.

research, ri-seurtche´, n recherche f.

resemble, ri-zemm´-b'l, v ressembler (à).

resent, ri-zennte´, v garder rancune; **–ful***, a vindicatif; –ment, n ressentiment m.

reservation, rèz-eur-vé´-ch'n, n réservation f; (doubt) réserve f.

reserve, ri-zeurve´, v réserver; n réserve f.

reservoir, rèz´-eur-vo'ar, n réservoir m.

reside, ri-zâïde´, v résider; habiter; demeurer.

residence, rèz´-i-dennce, n résidence f; (stay) séjour m.

resident, rèz´-i-dennt, n habitant, -e m & f; pensionnaire m & f; a résidant.

resign, ri-zâïne´, v

abandonner; (a post) démissionner; (oneself to) se résigner à.

resin, rèz´-inn, n résine f.

resist, ri-zisste´, v résister à; **–ance,** n résistance f.

resolute*, rèz´-o-lioute, a résolu; déterminé.

resolution, rèz´-o-lioue´-ch'n, n résolution f.

resolve, ri-zolve´, v résoudre; décider.

resort, ri-zoarte´, **– to,** v recourir à.

resound, ri-zâ´ounnde´, v retentir; résonner.

resource, ri-soarce´, n ressource f.

respect, riss-pecte´, v respecter; n respect m, égard m; **–ability,** respectabilité f; **–able,** respectable; **–ful***, respectueux; **–ive***, respectif.

respite, ress´-pâïte, n répit m.

respond, riss-ponnde´, v répondre.

respondent, riss-ponn´-dennt, n défendeur m.

response, riss-ponnce´, n réponse f.

responsible, riss-ponn´-ci-b'l, a responsable.

rest, reste, n repos m; (sleep) somme m; (remainder) reste; v se reposer; **–ful**, *a* tranquille; **–ive**, rétif; **–less**, agité.

restaurant, ress´-to-rannte, *n* restaurant *m*; **– car**, wagon-restaurant *m*.

restore, ri-staure´, *v* restituer; (health) rétablir.

restrain, ri-stréne´, *v* retenir; réprimer.

restraint, ri-strénnte, *n* contrainte *f*.

restrict, ri-stricte´, *v* restreindre.

restriction, ri-strick´-ch´n, *n* restriction *f*.

result, ri-zollte´, *v* résulter; *n* résultat *m*.

resume, ri-zioumme´, *v* reprendre; continuer.

resumption, ri-zomm´-ch´n, *n* reprise *f*.

resurrection, rèz-eur-rèque´-ch´n, *n* résurrection *f*.

retail, rî´-téle, *v* vendre au détail; *n* vente au détail *f*; **–er**, détaillant *m*.

retain, ri-téne´, *v* retenir; (keep) garder.

retaliate, ri-tăl´-i-éte, *v* user de représailles.

retard, ri-târde´, *v* retarder.

reticent, rètt´-i-sennte, *a* réservé; taciturne.

retinue, rètt´-i-nioue, *n* suite *f*; cortège *m*.

retire, ri-tâïre´, *v* se retirer; **–ment**, *n* retraite *f*.

retort, ri-toarte´, *v* riposter; *n* réplique *f*.

retract, ri-trăcte´, *v* rétracter.

retreat, ri-trîte´, *v* se retirer; *n* retraite *f*.

retrench, ri-trenntche´, *v* retrancher.

retrieve, ri-trîve´, *v* recouvrer; réparer.

return, ri-teurne´, *v* (come back) revenir; (go back) retourner; (give back) rendre; *n* retour *m*; **–s**, rendement *m*; **– ticket**, billet d'aller et retour *m*.

reveal, ri-vîle´, *v* révéler.

revel, rèv´-'l, *v* faire bombance; *n* réjouissances *fpl*.

revenge, ri-venndje´, *v* se venger; *n* vengeance *f*.

revenue, rèv´-i-nioue, *n* revenu *m*; (state) fisc *m*.

reverse, ri-veurce´, *v* renverser; (engine) faire marche arrière; *n* revers *m*; (contraire *m*; *a* inverse.

revert, ri-veurte´, *v* revenir; retourner.

review, ri-vioue´, *v* examiner; (inspect) passer en revue; (books, etc) analyser; *n* revue *f*; (books) critique *f*.

revile, ri-vâïle´, *v* injurier.

revise, ri-vâïze´, *v* réviser.

revision, ri-vije´-'n, *n* révision *f*.

revive, ri-vâïve´, *v* ranimer; se ranimer.

revoke, ri-vauque´, *v* révoquer; *n* (cards) renonce *f*.

revolt, ri-volte´, *n* révolte *f*; *v* se révolter.

revolve, ri-volve´, *v* tourner.

revolver, ri-vole´-*veur*, *n* révolver *m*.

reward, ri-ouôrde´, *n* récompense *f*; *v* récompenser.

rheumatism, roue´-mă-tizme, *n* rhumatisme *m*.

rhinoceros, râï-noce´-i-rôsse, *n* rhinocéros *m*.

rhubarb, rou´-bârbe, *n* rhubarbe *f*.

rhyme, râïme, *n* rime *f*; *v* rimer.

rib, ribbe, *n* côte *f*.

ribbon, ribb´-'n, *n* ruban *m*.

rice, râïce, *n* riz *m*.

rich*, ritche, *a* riche; **–es**, *n* richesse *f*.

rick, rique, *n* meule *f*.

rickets, rik´-ètse, *n* rachitisme *m*.

rickety, rik´-ett-i, *a* branlant; *med* rachitique.

rid, ridde, *v* débarrasser; délivrer.

riddle, ridd´-'l, *n* énigme *f*; *v* cribler de.

ride, râïde, *v* monter à cheval; aller en auto; aller à bicyclette; *n* promenade à cheval.

ridge, ridje, *n* (mountain) crête *f*.

ridicule, ridd´-i-kioule, *v* ridiculiser; *n* ridicule *m*.

ridiculous*, ri-dik´-iou-leuce, *a* ridicule.

rifle, râï´-f'l, *v* piller; *n* fusil *m*.

rift, rifte, *n* fente *f*; fissure *f*.

rig, rigue, *v naut* gréer; (ship) gréement *m*.

right, râïte, *n* droite *f*; *v* rétablir; *a* droit; juste; en règle.

rigid*, rid´-jide, *a* rigide; raide.

rigorous*, rigg´-ŏr-euce, *a* rigoureux.

rigour, rigg´-eur, *n* rigueur *f*.

rim, rimme, *n* bord *m*; (brim) rebord *m*; (wheel) jante *f*.

rind, râïnnde, *n* (fruit) pelure *f*; (bacon) couenne *f*; (cheese) croûte *f*.

ring, rinng, *n* anneau *m*; (finger) bague *f*; (wedding) alliance *f*; (napkin) rond *m*; (circus) arène *f*; (of bell) coup de sonnette *m*; *v* sonner; tinter, – **road,** *n* (*Brit*) route de ceinture; (motorway) périphique *m*.

ringleader, rinng´-lî-d'r, *n* meneur *m*.

rinse, rinnse, *v* rincer.

riot, râï´-ŏte, *n* émeute *f*; *v* faire une émeute.

rip, rippe, *v* fendre; (cloth) déchirer.

ripe, râïpe, *a* mûr; **–n,** *v* mûrir.

ripple, rip´-p'l, *n* ride *f*.

rise, râïze, *v* se lever; (revolt) se soulever; (river) monter; (prices) hausser; (wages) augmentation *f*.

risk, risque, *v* risquer; *n* risque *m*.

rite, râïte, *n* rite *m*.

rival, râï´-v'l, *n* rival, -e *m* & *f*; *com* concurrent, -e *m* & *f*.

rivalry, râï´-val-ri, *n* rivalité *f*.

river, riv´-'r, *n* fleuve *m*; (small) rivière *f*.

rivet, riv´-ette, *v* river; *n* rivet *m*.

road, raude, *n* chemin *m*; route *f*; (street) rue *f*; **–map,** carte routière *m*, **–works,** *npl* travaux) *mpl*.

roam, raume, *v* rôder; errer.

roar, raure, *v* rugir; *n* rugissement *m*.

roast, rauste, *v* rôtir; *n* & *a* rôti *m*.

rob, robbe, *v* voler; dépouiller; **–ber,** *n* voleur, -euse *m* & *f*.

robbery, robb´-eur-i, *n* vol *m*.

robe, raube, *n* robe *f*; *eccl* vêtements *mpl*.

robin, robb´-inn, *n* rouge-gorge *m*.

robust*, ro-bosste´, *a* robuste; vigoureux.

rock, roque, *n* rocher *m*; *v* (quake) secouer; (roll) rouler; (cradle) bercer; **–y,** *a* rocailleux; (sea) plein de rochers.

rock and roll, roque´-eun-raule´ *n* rock and roll *m*.

rocket, rok´-ette, *n* fusée *f*.

rod, rodde, *n* baguette *f*; (fishing) canne à pêche *f*; (curtain) triangle *f*.

roe, rau, *n* chevreuil *m*; biche *f*; (fish) laitance *f*.

rogue, raugue, *n* fripon *m*; **–ry,** friponnerie *f*.

roll, raule, *v* rouler; (– up)

enrouler; n rouleau m;
(bread) petit pain m;
–call, appel m; –er,
roulette f; (garden,
steam) rouleau m;
–erskate, patin à
roulettes m.

romance, rau-mânnce´, n
roman m; mus romance
f.

romantic, rau-mânne´-
tique, a romantique;
sentimental.

romp, rommpe, v jouer
bruyamment.

roof, roufe, n toit m;
(mouth) palais m.

rook, rouque, n corneille
f.

room, roumme, n pièce f;
(bedroom) chambre f;
(public) salle f; (space)
place f, –service, service
des chambres m.

roost, rouste, v percher; n
perchoir m.

root, route, n racine f; v
s'enraciner.

rope, raupe, n corde f;
naut cordage m.

rosary, rau´-za-ri, n rosaire
m.

rose, rauze, n rose f; –
bush, rosier m.

rosemary, rauze´-mé-ri, n
romarin m.

rosin, roz´-inne, n
colophane f.

rosy, rauz´-i, a rosé;
vermeil.

rot, rotte, n pourriture f; v
pourrir.

rotate, rau´-téte, v
tourner.

rouge, rouge, n rouge m.

rough*, roffe, a (manners)
grossier; rude; (coarse)
rugueux; rude; (sea)
houleuse; (wind)
tempêteux; (bumpy)
cahoteux.

roughness, roffe´-nesse, n
rudesse f; grossièreté f.

round, râ´ounnde, a rond;
v arrondir; – about, a
détourné n manège m;
–ness, rondeur f.

rouse, râ´ouze, v exciter;
(awaken) éveiller.

rout, râ´oute, v mettre en
déroute; n déroute f.

route, route, n route f;
itinéraire m.

routine, rou-tîne´, n
routine f.

rove, rauve, v rôder; fig
errer.

row, rau, n rangée f;
(persons) file f;
(boating) canotage m; v
(scull) ramer.

row, râ´ou, n querelle f;
(noise) vacarme m.

royal*, roa´i´-al, a royal;
–ty, n royauté f;
(payment) droits

d'auteur mpl.

rub, robbe, v frotter; –ber,
n caoutchouc m;
(eraser) gomme à effacer
f; – off, v effacer.

rubbish, robb´-iche, n
ordures fpl; (junk)
camelot f.

ruby, roue´-bi, n rubis m; a
vermeil.

rucksack, roque´-săque, n
sac à dos m.

rudder, rodd´-'r, n
gouvernail m.

rude*, roude, a impoli;
(coarse) grossier.

rudiment, roue´-di-m'nt,
n rudiment f.

rue, roue, v déplorer;
–ful*, a lamentable.

ruffian, roffe´-iane, n
chenapan m.

ruffle, rof´-f'l, v déranger;
troubler.

rug, rogue, n couverture f;
(mat) tapis m.

rugby, rogg´-bî, n rugby m.

rugged, rogg´-ide, a
(scenery) accidenté.

ruin, roue´-inne, v ruiner;
n ruine f.

rule, roule, v gouverner;
(lines) régler; n
gouvernement m;
(regulation, etc) règle f.

ruler, roul´-'r, n (drawing)
règle f.

rum, romme, n rhum m.

rumble, romm´-b'l, *n*
grondement sourd *m*.

rummage, romm´-idj, *v*
fouiller; *n* fouillis *m*.

rumour, roue´-m'r, *n*
rumeur *f*.

run, ronne, *v* courir;
(colours) déteindre; –
away, fuir; *n* (horse)
cheval emballe *m*.

runway, ronn´-oué, *n* piste
f.

rupture, ropp´-tioure, *n*
rupture *f*; *med* hernie *f*.

rural, rou´-r'l, *a*
champêtre; rural.

rush, roche, *n* ruée *f*;
(water) torrent *m*;
(reed) jonc *m*; *v* se ruer;
se précipiter.

rust, rosste, *n* rouille *f*; *v*
rouiller; –**y,** *a* rouillé.

rustic, ross´-tique, *a*
rustique.

rustle, ross´-'l, *v* bruire; *n*
bruissement *m*; (silk)
frou frou *m*.

rusty, ross´-tî, *a* rouillé.

rut, rotte, *n* ornière *f*.

rye, râï, *n* seigle *m*.

S

sable, sé´-b'l, n (fur) zibeline f.

sachet, să´-ché, n sachet m.

sack, săque, n sac m; v piller.

sacrament, săc´-ră-m'nt, n sacrement m.

sacred, sé´-cridde, a sacré; consacré.

sacrifice, săc´-ri-făïce, n sacrifice m; v sacrifier.

sacrilege, săc´-ri-lédje, n sacrilége m.

sad*, sădde, a triste; **–ness,** n tristesse f.

saddle, săd´-d'l, n selle f; **–r,** sellier m.

safe, séfe, a sauf; sûr; n coffre-fort m; **–guard** sauvegarde f; v protéger; **–ty,** n sûreté f; **–ty pin,** épingle de sûreté; **–ty-**

razor, rasoir mécanique m.

sag, săgue, v s'affaisser.

sagacious*, sa-gué´-cheuce, a sagace.

sage, sédje, n sage m; (herb) sauge f; a* sage.

sail, séle, n voile f; v naviguer.

sailor, sé´-l'r, n matelot m; marin m.

saint, sénnte, n saint, -e m & f.

sake, séque, n cause f; égard m; amour m.

salad, săl´-ade, n salade f; **–dressing,** vinaigrette f.

salary, săl´-a-ri, n salaire m.

sale, séle, n vente f; (shop) solde m; **–able,** a vendable; **–sman,** n vendeur m **–swoman,**

vendeuse f.

salient, sé´-li-ennte, n & a saillant m.

saliva, sa-lăï´-va, n salive f.

sallow, săl´-au, a jaunâtre.

salmon, sămm´-'n, n saumon m.

saloon, sa-loune´, n salon m; **dining–,** salle à manger f.

salt, soalte, n sel m; a salé; **–cellar,** n salière f.

salty, soal´-tî a salé.

salute, sa-lioute´, v saluer; n salut m.

salvage, săl´-védje, n sauvetage m; v sauver.

salvation, săl-vé-ch'n, n salut m; **– army,** Armée du Salut f.

salver, sal´-v'r, n plateau m.

same, séme, a même.

sample, sâmme´-p'l, n échantillon m.

sanctify, sainnk´-ti-făï, v sanctifier.

sanction, sainnk´-ch'n, v sanctionner; n sanction f.

sanctuary, sainnk´-tiou-a-ri, n sanctuaire m.

sand, sănnde, n sable m; **–y,** a sablonneux.

sandal, sănn´-d'l, n sandale f.

sandwich, sănnde´-

houitche, n sandwich m.

sane, séne, a sain d'esprit.

sanguine, saing´-gouine, a
sanguin; confiant.

sanitary, sänn´-i-ta-ri, a
sanitaire; – towel, n
serviette hygiénique f.

sanity, sänn´-i-ti, n bon
sens m.

sap, säppe, n sève f; v
saper.

sapper, säpp´-eur, n mil
sapeur m.

sapphire, säf´-fäïre, n
saphir m.

sarcasm, sâr´-câzme, n
sarcasme m.

sarcastic, sâr-câs´-tique, a
sarcastique.

sardine, sâr-dîne´, n
sardine f.

sash, säche, n (belt)
écharpe f.

satchel, sätt´-ch'l, n
sacoche f; (school)
cartable m.

satellite, satt´-i-lâïte, n
satellite m.

satiate, sé´-chi-éte, v
rassasier.

satin, sätt´-inne, n satin
m; a de satin.

satire, sätt´-âïre, n satire f.

satisfaction, sätt-iss-fäk´-
ch'n, n satisfaction f.

satisfactory, sätt-iss-fäk´-
teur-i, a satisfaisant.

satisfy, sätt´-iss-fâï, v

satisfaire.

satsuma, sät-sou´-mä, n
mandarine f.

saturate, sätt´-iou-réte, v
saturer.

Saturday, sätt´-or-di, n
samedi m.

satyr, sätt´-eur, n satyre m.

sauce, soace, n sauce f;
–pan, casserole f.

saucer, soa´-seur, n
soucoupe f.

sauna, soa´-nä, n sauna m.

saunter, soann´-t'r, v
marcher en flânant.

sausage, soss´-idj, n
saucisse f; (preserved)
saucisson m.

savage, säv´-idj, a*
sauvage; féroce; n
sauvage m & f.

save, séve, v sauver;
(economize) épargner;
(keep) garder.

saving, sé´-vinng, a
économe; frugal;
(things) économique; n
économie f; –s, épargne
f.

Saviour, sé´-v'eur, n
Sauveur m; sauveur m.

savour, sé´-v'r, v avoir le
goût de; avoir l'odeur
de; n saveur f; –y, a
savoureux.

saw, soa, n scie f; v scier.

say, sé, v dire; –ing, n
dicton m.

scabbard, scäbb´-'rd, n
fourreau m.

scaffold, scäff´-ôlde, n
échafaud m.

scaffolding, scäff´-ôldd-
inng, n échafaudage m.

scald, scoalde, v échauder.

scale, skéle, n (fish)
écaille f; (measure)
échelle f; mus gamme f;
v ecailler; (climb)
escalader.

scales, skélze, npl balance
f.

scallop, scäll´-oppe, n
coquille Saint Jacques f.

scalp, scälpe, n cuir
chevelu m.

scamper, scämm´-p'r, v
déguerpir.

scan, scänne, v scruter;
(verse) scander.

scandal, scänn´-d'l, n
scandale m.

scandalous*, scänn´-däl-
euce, a scandaleux.

scanty, scänn´-ti, a
insuffisant; (tight)
étriqué.

scapegoat, sképe´-gaute, n
bouc émissaire m.

scar, scâre, n cicatrice f; v
cicatriser.

scarce*, skairce, a rare.

scarcity, skair´-ci-ti, n
rareté f; disette f.

scare, skaire, n panique f;
v effrayer; – away,

épouvanter; **–crow**, n
épouvantail m.

scarf, scärfe, n écharpe f;
foulard m.

scarlet, scâre-lette, n & a
écarlate f.

scarlet-fever, scâre´-lette-
fî´-veur, n scarlatine f.

scathing*, ské´-tsinng, a
cinglant.

scatter, scätt´-r, v
disperser; éparpiller.

scavenger, scäv´-enn-dj'r,
n boueur m.

scene, sîne, n scène f; **–ry**,
vue f; paysage m;
(theatre) décors mpl.

scent, sennte, n parfum m;
(trail) piste f; v
parfumer.

sceptical*, skepp´-ti-c'l, a
sceptique.

sceptre, sepp´-t'r, n
sceptre m

schedule, chedd´-ioule, n
inventaire m; liste f.

scheme, skîme, n plan m,
projet m; v projeter.

scholar, skol´-'r, n lettré, -
e m & f; (pupil) élève m
& f.

scholarship, skol´-'r-
chippe, n (prize) bourse
f.

school, skoul, n école f;
(male) **–teacher**, maître
d'école m; (female)
–teacher, maîtresse

d'école f.

schooner, skoue´-n'r, n
schooner.

sciatica, sâï-ätt´-i-ca, n
sciatique f.

science, sâï´-ennce, n
science f.

scientific, sâï-en-tiff´-
ique, a scientifique.

scissors, siz´-eurze, npl
ciseaux mpl.

scoff, skoffe, v se moquer
de; railler.

scold, skaulde, v gronder.

scoop, skoupe, n (shovel)
pelle à main f; v creuser.

scope, skaupe, n portée f;
étendue f; place f.

scorch, skoartche, v
roussir.

score, skaure, n (number)
vingtaine f; (games)
points mpl; v (win)
gagner; (cut) faire des
entailles; (keeping
count) marquer.

scorn, skoarne, n dédain
m; v dédaigner.

scornful*, skoarne´-foulle,
a dédaigneux.

Scotland, skott-land, n
Ecosse f.

Scottish, skott´-tiche, a
écossais.

scoundrel, skâ'ounn´-dr'l,
n coquin m; gredin m.

scour, skâ'oure, v recurer.

scourge, skeurdje, v

fouetter; n fouet m; fléau
m.

scout, skâ'oute, v aller en
éclaireur; n éclaireur m;
boy– –, boy-scout m.

scowl, skâ'oule, v froncer
les sourcils; n regard
menaçant m.

scraggy, skrägg´-'i, a
(thin) décharné.

scramble, skramm´-b'l, n
(struggle) lutte f; v
(climb) grimper; **– for**,
se bousculer pour.

scrap, skräppe, n fragment
m; (cloth) morceau m.

scrape, skrépe, v gratter;
(– mud off) décrotter.

scraper, skrépe´-'r, n
grattoir m; décrottoir m.

scratch, skrätche, n
égratinure f; (sport)
ligne de départ f; v
égratinger; (rub) gratter;
(sports) retirer; (glass)
rayer.

scream, skrîme, v crier;
hurler; n cri m.

screen, skrîne, n (fire;
cinema) écran m;
wind–, pare-brise m;
(partition) paravent m;
v protéger.

screw, skroue, n vis f; v
visser.

screwdriver, skroue-drâï´-
veur, n tournevis m.

scribble, skribb´-'l v

457

griffonner; n griffonnage m.

Scripture, skripp´-tioure, n Ecriture Sainte f.

scroll, skraule, n rouleau m.

scrounge, skrâ´oundje, v (sponge) écornifler; (steal) chiper; – **off**, vivre aux crochets de.

scrub, skrobbe, v laver à la brosse; n (bush) broussailles fpl.

scruple, scroue´-p´l, n scrupule m.

scrupulous*, scroue´-piou-leuce, a scrupuleux.

scrutinize, scroue´-ti-nâîze, v scruter.

scuffle, scoff´-´l, n bagarre f; v se battre.

scull, scolle, n godille f; v godiller.

scullery, scoll´-eur-i, n laverie f.

sculptor, scolp´teur, n sculpteur m.

sculpture, scolp´-tioure, v sculpter; n sculpture f.

scum, scomme, v écumer; n écume f; fig lie f.

scurf, skeurfe, n pellicules fpl.

scurrilous*, skorr´-i-leuce, a grossier; injurieux.

scuttle, skott´-´l, n (coal) seau à charbon m; v naut saborder.

scythe, sâîdze, n faux f.

sea, sî, n mer f; –**man**, marin m; –**sickness**, mal de mer m; –**side**, bord de la mer m; –**weed**, algue f; –**worthy**, a navigable.

seal, sîle, n cachet m; (official) sceau m; (animal) phoque m; v cacheter; –**ing-wax**, n cire à cacheter f; –**skin**, peau de phoque f.

seam, sîme, n couture f; (mine) veine f.

seamstress, sîme´-stresse, n couturière f.

sear, sîre, v (burn) brûler; (brand) marquer au fer.

search, seurtche, v (look for) chercher; (people; luggage) fouiller; n recherche f.

searchlight, seurtche´-lâîte, n projecteur m.

season, sî´-z´n, v assaisonner; (timber) sécher. n maison f; –**able**, a de saison; –**ing**, n assaisonnement m; –**ticket**, carte d'abonnement f.

seat, sîte, n siège m, place f; (bench) banc m; (country estate) propriété f; v asseoir; placer.

secluded, si-cloue´-dedde,

a retiré.

seclusion, si-cloue´-j'n, n retraite f.

second, sèk´-ŏnnde, v (support) seconder; n (time) seconde f; (duel) témoin m; n & a* deuxième m & f; –**ary**, a secondaire; –**hand**, d'occasion.

secrecy, sî´-cri-ci, n secret m.

secret, sî´-crète, n secret m; a* secret.

secretary, sèk´-ri-ta-ri, n secrétaire m & f.

secrete, si-crîte´, v cacher; (gland) sécréter.

secretion, si-crî´-ch'n, n sécrétion f.

sect, secte, n secte f.

section, sèk´-ch'n, n section f; (cross) coupe f.

secular, sèk´-iou-l'r, a (old) séculaire; (music) profane; (school) laïque.

secure, si-kioure´, v mettre en sûreté; s'assurer; a sûr; à l'abri.

securities, si-kiour´-i-tize, npl valeurs fpl.

security, si-kiour´-i-ti, n sûreté f; garantie f.

sedate*, si-déte´, a posé; calme.

sedative, sedd´-a-tive, n & a sédatif m; calmant m.

sedentary, sedd´-enn-*ta*-ri, *a* sédentaire.

sediment, sedd´-i-mennte, *n* sédiment *m*.

sedition, si-diche´-'n, *n* sédition *f*.

seditious*, si-diche´-*euce*, *a* séditieux.

seduce, si-diouce´, *v* séduire.

see, sî, *v* voir; – **through**, voir à travers; *fig* pénétrer; – **to**, veiller à.

seed, sîde, *n* graine *f*; semence *f*.

seek, sîque, *v* chercher; (strive) s'efforcer de.

seem, sîme, *v* sembler; paraître; –**ly**, *a* convenable.

seethe, sîdz, *v* bouillonner; *fig* grouiller.

seize, sîze, *v* saisir; (take possession) s'emparer de.

seizure, sî´-j'r, *n* prise *f*, capture *f*; (stroke) attaque *f*; (law) saisie *f*.

seldom, sell´-d'm, *adv* rarement.

select, si-lecte´, *v* choisir; *a* choisi; d'élite.

selection, si-lec´-ch'n, *n* choix *m*.

self, selfe, **one–**, *pron* soi-même; se . . . ; –**ish**, *a* égoïste; –**ishness**, *n* égoïsme *m*; –**catering**, *a*

(Brit) avec cuisine; – **service**, libre-service; self-service; –**starter**, *n* (motor) démarreur *m*.

sell, selle, *v* vendre; –**er**, *n* vendeur, -euse *m & f*.

Sellotape, sell´-au-tépe, *(TM)* *n* papier collant.

semblance, semm´-blannce, *n* semblant *m*.

semi, semm´-i, semi; demi; –**circle**, *n* demi-cercle *m*; –**colon**, point et virgule *m*.

seminary, semm´-i-na-ri, *n* séminaire *m*.

semolina, semm-ô-lî´-na, *n* semoule *f*.

senate, senn´-été, *n* sénat *m*.

send, sennde, *v* envoyer; expédier; – **away**, – **back**, renvoyer; –**er**, *n* expéditeur, -trice *m & f*; – **for**, *v* envoyer chercher; – **in advance**, envoyer à l'avance; – **on**, faire suivre.

senile, sî´-nâîle, *a* sénile.

senior, sî´-ni-*eur*, *a* aîné; (rank) plus ancien; – **partner**, *n* associé principal *m*.

sensation, senn-sé´-ch'n, *n* sensation *f*.

sense, sennce, *n* sens *m*; –**less**, *a* dénué de sens.

sensible, senn´-si-b'l, *a*

sensé.

sensitive*, senn´-si-tive, *a* sensible.

sensual*, senn´-chou-'l, *a* sensuel.

sentence, senn´-t'nce, *n* phrase *f*; (law) sentence *f*; *v* condamner.

sentiment, senn´-ti-m'nt, *n* sentiment *m*.

sentry, senn´-tri, *n* sentinelle *f*; –**box**, guérite *f*.

separate, sepp´-*a*-réte, *v* séparer; *a** séparé.

separation, sepp-*a*-ré´-ch'n, *n* séparation *f*.

September, sepp-temm´-b'r, *n* septembre *m*.

septic, sepp´-tique, *a* septique.

sequel, sî´-couelle, *n* suite *f*; conséquence *f*.

sequence, sî´-couennce, *n* série *f*; succession *f*.

serene*, si-rîne´, *a* calme; serein.

serge, seurdje, *n* serge *f*.

sergeant, sâr´-dj'nt, *n* sergent *m*.

serial, sî´-ri-al, *a* consécutif; *n* feuilleton *m*.

series, si´-rîze, *n* série *f*.

serious*, si´-ri-*euce*, *a* sérieux.

sermon, seur´-m'n, *n* sermon *m*.

serpent, seur´-pennte, n
serpent m.

servant, seur´-vannte, n
domestique m & f.

serve, seurve, v servir.

service, seur´-vice, n
service m; eccl office m.

serviceable, seur´-viss-a-
b'l, a utile.

servile, seur´-vâïle, a
servile.

servitude, seur´-vi-tioude,
n servitude f; (penal)
travaux forcés mpl.

session, sèch´-eune, n
session f; (sitting)
séance f.

set, sette, v (type)
composer; (to music)
mettre en ...; (fowls)
couver; (clock) régler;
(trap) tendre; (task)
imposer; (question)
poser; (example)
donner; (tools) affûter;
(plants) planter;
(fracture) réduire;
(solidify) cailler;
(jewels) monter; n
collection f; série f;
(china) service m;
(buttons, etc) garniture
f; – on fire, mettre le feu
à.

settee, sett´-ie, n canapé
m, divan m.

settle, sett´-l, v
(accounts) régler;

(finish) mettre fin à;
(decide) résoudre;
(assign) assigner;
(domicile) s'établir;
–ment, n colonie f;
(dowry) dot f;
(accounts) règlement m;
(agreement) solution f;
(foundation) tassement
m.

seven, sèv´-'n, n & a sept
m; **–teen,** dix-sept m;
–th, septième m & f;
–ty, soixante-dix m.

sever, sèv´-'r, v séparer;
(cut) couper net.

several, sèv´-eur-'l, a
plusieurs; divers.

severe*, si-vire´, a sévère;
rigoureux; violent.

severity, si-vèr´-i-ti, n
sévérité f.

sew, sau, v coudre; **–ing,** n
couture f; **–ing-cotton,**
fil à coudre m; **–ing-
machine,** machine à
coudre f.

sewage, sioue´-idj, n eaux
d'égout fpl.

sewer, sioue´-'r, n égout m.

sex, sexe, n sexe m; **–ual,** a
sexuel.

sexist, sexe´-iste, a sexiste.

sexy, sexe´-î, a sexy.

shabby, chàbb´-i, a râpé;
usé; (action) mesquin.

shackle, chàk´-'l, n
chaînes fpl; v enchaîner.

shade, chéde, n ombre f;
(colour) nuance f;
(lamp) abat-jour m;
(eyes) visière f; v
protéger; (art) ombrer.

shadow, chàd´-au, n
ombre f; v (follow) filer.

shady, ché´-di, a ombragé;
fig louche.

shaft, châfte, n (arrow)
flèche f; mech arbre m;
(mine) puits m; **–s,**
(vehicle) brancards mpl.

shaggy, chàgg´-i, a poilu;
velu.

shake, chéque, v secouer;
(nerves, etc) trembler;
(sway) ébranler; –
hands, serrer la main.

shaky, ché´-ki, a branlant;
tremblotant.

shall, châle, v aux I s. do
je ferai. we s. do nous
ferons.

shallow, chàl´-au, a peu
profond.

sham, chàmme, n feinte f;
a simulé; v feindre.

shame, chéme, n honte f;
v faire honte à; **–ful*,** a
honteux; **–less,** éhonté.

shampoo, chàmm´-poue,
n shampooing m.

shamrock, chàmm´-roque,
n trèfle m.

shandy, chànn´-dî, n
panaché m.

shape, chépe, n forme f; v

former; modeler.

share, chère, n part f;
(stock) action f; v
partager; participer à;
–**holder,** n actionnaire m
& f.

shark, chârque, n requin
m.

sharp, chârpe, a (blade)
tranchant; (point)
pointu; (edge) coupant;
(taste) piquant; (mind)
dégourdi; n (music)
dièse m; –**en,** v aiguiser;
–**ness,** n acuité f.

shatter, chătt´-'r, v briser;
fracasser; renverser.

shave, chéve, v raser; se
raser.

shaving, ché´-vinng, –
brush, n blaireau m.

shavings, ché´-vinngze,
npl copeaux mpl.

shawl, choale, n châle m.

she, chî, pron elle.

sheaf, chîfe, n (corn, etc)
gerbe f; (papers) liasse f.

shear, chîre, v tondre; –**s,**
npl cisailles fpl.

sheath, chîts, n (scabbard)
fourreau m.

shed, chedde, n hangar m;
v (tears, blood) verser;
(hair, leaves, feathers)
perdre.

sheen, chîne, n lustre m.

sheep, chîpe, n mouton m.

sheer, chîre, a pur; (steep)

perpendiculaire.

sheet, chîte, n drap m;
(paper, metal) feuille f;
–**lightning,** éclair de
chaleur m.

shelf, chelfe, n planche f,
rayon m; (a set) étagère
f.

shell, chelle, n (hard)
coquille f; (soft) cosse f;
(projectile) obus m; v
écosser; bombarder; –
fish n mollusque m;
crustacé m.

shelter, chel´-t'r, n abri m;
v abriter; protéger.

shepherd, chepp´-eurde, n
berger m, pâtre m.

sheriff, chè´-rife, n shérif
m.

sherry, chèr´-i, n Xérès m.

shield, childe, n bouclier
m; v protéger.

shift, chifte, n (working)
équipe f; v changer de
place.

shin, chine, n tibia m.

shine, châïne, v luire;
briller; n lustre m; éclat
m.

shingle, chinng´-g'l, n
galet m.

shingles, chinng´-g'lz, n
med zona m.

ship, chippe, n vaisseau m,
navire m, bateau m; v
embarquer; expédier; –
broker, n courtier

maritime m; –**ment,**
(cargo) chargement m;
–**owner,** armateur m;
–**wreck,** naufrage m.

shirk, cheurque, v éviter;
éluder.

shirker, cheur´-keur, n
flémard m.

shirt, cheurte, n chemise
f.

shiver, chiv´-'r, v
frissonner; n frisson m.

shoal, choale, n
(multitude) foule f;
(fish) banc m; (shallow)
haut fond m.

shock, choque, n secousse
f; (fright) choc m; v
(disgust) choquer; –
absorber, n amortisseur
m; –**ing,** a révoltant;
choquant.

shoddy, chodd´-i, a
(goods) camelote;
(persons) râpé.

shoe, choue, n chaussure f;
soulier m; (horse) fer à.
cheval m; v (horse)
ferrer; –**horn,** chausse-
pied m; –**lace,** lacet m;
–**maker,** cordonnier m;
–**polish,** cirage m.

shoot, choutte, v tirer;
(kill) tuer d'un coup de
feu; (execute) fusiller;
(grow) pousser; n chasse
f; (growth) pousse f;
–**ing,** tir m; –**ing-star,**

étoile filante *f*.

shop, choppe, *n* boutique *f*; (stores) magasin *m*; *v* faire des achats; – **assistant,** *n* vendeur, -se *m* & *f*; –**keeper,** marchand, -e *m* & *f*; –**lifting,** vol à l'étalage *m*.

shore, chaure, *n* côte *f*; (beach) rivage *m*; (land) terre *f*; (support) étai *m*; *v* étayer.

shorn, chorne, *a* tondu.

short, choarte, *a* court; (persons) petit; (need) dénué de; –**age,** *n* insuffisance *f*; –**circuit,** courtcircuit *m*; –**en,** *v* raccourcir; abréger; –**hand,** *n* sténographie *f*; –**ly,** *adv* sous peu; –**sighted,** *a* myope.

shot, chotte, *n* (noise) coup de feu *m*; (score, etc) coup *m*; (marksman) tireur *m*; (pellet) plomb de chasse *m*.

should, choude, *v* devoir.

shoulder, chaule´-d'r, *n* épaule *f*; *v* porter sur l'épaule.

shout, châ'oute, *n* cri *m*; *v* crier.

shovel, chov´-'l, *n* pelle *f*; *v* ramasser à la pelle.

show, chau, *n* spectacle *m*;

exposition *f*; *v* montrer; (teach) enseigner; –**room,** *n* salle d'exposition *f*; **prize–,** concours *m*; –**y,** *a* voyant.

shower, châ'ou´-*eur*, *n* (rain) averse *f*; –**bath,** (abblutions) douche *f*; –**y,** *a* pluvieux.

shred, chredde, *n* (tatter) lambeau *m*; *v* déchiqueter.

shrew, chroue, *n* mégère *f*.

shrewd, chroude, *a* malin; (cunning) rusé; sagace.

shriek, chrîque, *v* pousser des cris; *n* cri perçant *m*.

shrill, chrille, *a* perçant.

shrimp, chrimmpe, *n* crevette *f*.

shrine, chrâîne, *n* châsse *f*; sanctuaire *m*.

shrink, chrinnque, *v* rétrécir.

shrivel, chriv´-'l, *v* ratatiner.

shroud, chrâ'oude, *n* linceul *m*.

Shrove Tuesday, chrôve-tiouze´-dé, *n* mardi gras *m*.

shrub, chrobbe, *n* arbuste *m*.

shrug, chrogue, *v* hausser les épaules.

shudder, chodd´-'r, *n* frémissement *m*; *v*

frémir.

shuffle, choff´-'l, *v* (gait) traîner les pieds; (cards) battre.

shun, chonne, *v* éviter.

shunt, chonnte, *v* changer de voie; faire la manœuvre.

shut, chotte, *v* fermer.

shutter, chott´-'r, *n* volet *m*; (camera) obturateur *m*.

shuttle, chott´-'l, *n* navette *f*.

shy, châï, *a* timide; réservé; *v* se jeter de côté.

shyness, châï´-nesse, *n* timidité *f*.

sick, sique, *a* malade; –**en,** *v* (fig) dégoûter; –**ly,** *a* maladif; –**ness,** *n* maladie *f*; **to be –,** vomir.

sickle, sik´-'l, *n* faucille *f*.

side, sâïde, *n* côté *m*; (mountain) versant *m*; (river) bord *m*; (of record) face *f*; *v* prendre parti; –**board,** *n* buffet *m*; –**car,** side-car *m*; –**effect,** effet secondaire *m*; –**ways,** *adv* de côté.

siege, sîdje, *n* siège *m*.

sieve, sive, *n* (fine) tamis *m*; (coarse) crible *m*.

sift, sifte, *v* tamiser; cribler.

sigh, sâï, n soupir m; v
soupirer.

sight, sâite, v apercevoir; n
(eye) vue f; (spectacle)
spectacle m; (gun)
guidon m; **at –,** adv à
vue; **by –,** de vue.

sign, sâïne, v signer; n
signe m; (board)
enseigne f; **–post,**
poteau indicateur m.

signal, sigue´-n'l, n signal
m; v signaler.

signature, sigue´-na-
tioure, n signature f.

significant*, sigue-nif´-i-
cannte, a significatif.

signify, sigue´-ni-fâï, v
signifier.

silence, sâï´-lennce, n
silence m; v faire taire.

silencer, sâï´-lenn-ceur, n
(engine) silencieux m.

silent*, sâï´-lennt, a
silencieux.

silk, silque, n soie f; **–en,** a
de soie; **–worm,** n ver à
soie m; **–y,** a soyeux.

sill, sile, n (door) seuil m;
(window) rebord m.

silly, sill´-i, a sot; niais.

silver, sill´-v'r, n argent m;
a d'argent; v argenter.

silversmith, sill´-v'r-smits,
n orfèvre m.

similar*, simm´-i-l'r, a
semblable.

similarity, simm-i-lar´-i-ti,
n similitude f.

simile, simm´-i-li, n
comparaison f.

simmer, simm´-'r, v
mijoter.

simple, simm´-p'l, a
simple; **–ton,** n nigaud, -
e m & f.

simplicity, simm-pliss´-i-
ti, n simplicité f.

simplify, simm´-pli-fâï, v
simplifier.

simultaneous*, simm-eul-
té´-ni-euce, a simultané.

sin, sine, v pécher; n
péché m; **–ner,** pécheur
m, pécheresse f.

since, sinnce, prep depuis.
adv depuis lors; conj
(cause) puisque; (time)
depuis que.

sincere*, sinn-cire´, a
sincère.

sinew, sinn´-ioue, n
tendon m; fig nerf m.

sing, sinng, v chanter; **–er,**
n chanteur m; chanteuse
f; (star) cantatrice f;
–ing, chant m.

singe, sinndje, v roussir;
(hair) brûler.

single, sinng´-g'l, a seul;
célibataire; (ticket)
simple; **–handed,** seul;
– room, n chambre à un
lit f; chambre pour une
personne f.

singly, sinngue´-li, adv un
à un.

singular*, sinng´-guiou-l'r,
a singulier; unique.

sinister, sinn´-iss-teur, a
sinistre.

sink, sinnque, n évier m; v
enfoncer; couler; (ship)
sombrer; (scuttle)
saborder; (shaft) creuser.

sip, sipe, n gorgée f; v
boire à petites gorgées.

siphon, sâï´-f'n, n siphon
m.

siren, sâï-renn, n sirène f.

sirloin, seur-lô'ïne, n
aloyau m.

sister, siss´-t'r, n sœur f; **–
in-law,** belle-sœur f.

sit, sitte, v s'asseoir;
(incubate) couver;
–ting, a assis; n séance f;
–ting-room, salon m.

site, sâïte, n site m;
(building) emplacement
m.

situated, sit´-iou-é-tedde,
a situé.

situation, sit-iou-é´-ch'n,
n situation f.

six, sixe, n & a six m;
–teen, seize m; **–teenth,**
seizième m & f; **–th,**
sixième m & f; **–tieth,**
soixantième m & f; **–ty,**
soixante m.

size, sâïze, n dimension f;
(shoe) pointure f;
(persons) taille f; (glue)

colle f; v coller.

skate, skéte, v patiner; n patin m; (fish) raie f.

skateboard, skétt´-baurde, n skateboard m.

skating, skétt´-inng, n patinage m.

skating rink, skétt-inng-rinque, n patinoire m.

skeleton, skell´-eu-t'n, n squelette m.

sketch, sketche, v esquisser; n esquisse f; croquis m.

skewer, skioue´-eur, n brochette f; broche f.

ski, skî, n ski m; v skier; faire du ski; – **lift,** n remonte-pente m; – **slope,** piste de ski f.

skid, skidde, v déraper; n dérapage m.

skiff, skiffe, n esquif m; skiff m.

skiing, skî´-inng, n ski m.

skilful*, skill´-foull, a adroit; habile.

skill, skille, n habileté f, adresse f; (natural) talent m.

skim, skimme, v effleurer; écrémer; (scum) écumer; –**med milk,** n lait écrémé m.

skin, skinne, n peau f; (hide) cuir m; (peel) écorce f; (thin peel) pelure f.

skip, skippe, v sauter; sauter à la corde; manquer.

skipper, skipp´-'r, n patron de bateau m.

skirmish, skeur´-miche, n escarmouche f.

skirt, skeurte, n (dress) jupe f; v border.

skittles, skitt´-'lze, npl quilles fpl.

skull, skolle, n crâne m.

skunk, skonngk, n mouffette f; (fur) putois m.

sky, skâî, n ciel m; –**light,** lucarne f; –**scraper,** gratte-ciel m.

slab, slàbbe, n dalle f; plaque f.

slack, slàque, a (loose) lâche; n menu charbon m.

slacken, slàque´-'n, v relâcher; (pace) ralentir.

slander, slânne´-d'r, v calomnier; n calomnie f; (law) diffamation f; –**er,** calomniateur m.

slang, slain-ngue, n argot m.

slant, slânnte, v être en pente; incliner; n pente f; –**ing,** a oblique.

slap, slàppe, n gifle f; v gifler.

slash, slàche, v taillader; (gash) balafrer.

slate, sléte, n ardoise f; v couvrir d'ardoises.

slaughter, sloa´-t'r, v abattre; massacrer; n tuerie f; –**er,** tueur m; –**house,** abattoir m.

slave, sléve, n esclave m & f; –**ry,** esclavage m.

slay, slé, v tuer; massacrer.

sledge, slèdje, n traîneau m; –**hammer,** marteau de forgeron m.

sleek, slîque, a lisse; (manners) mielleux.

sleep, slîpe, v dormir; n sommeil m; –**ing-car,** wagon-lit m; – **bag,** sac de couchage m; – **ing pill,** somnifère m; –**less,** a sans sommeil; –**lessness,** n insomnie f; –**y,** a qui a sommeil.

sleet, slîte, n grésil m.

sleeve, slîve, n manche f.

sleigh, slé, n traîneau m.

sleight, slâîte, n tour d'adresse m; – **of hand,** prestidigitation f.

slender, slenn´-d'r, a mince; (figure) svelte; (means) modeste.

slice, slâîce, n tranche f; v couper en tranches.

slide, slâîde, n glissade f; (microscopic) porte-objet m; (photo) diapositif m; (lantern) verre m; v glisser.

slight, slâîte, n marque de mépris f; v traiter sans égards; a* mince; (mistake, etc) léger.

slim, slimme, a élancé; v se faire maigrir.

slime, slâïme, n vase f; limon m.

slimy, slâï'-mi, a vaseux, visqueux.

sling, slinng, n med écharpe f; v (throw) lancer. ·

slink, slinng-k, v s'esquiver.

slip, slippe, v glisser; –pery, a glissant.

slipper, slipp'-'r, n pantoufle f.

slit, slitte, v fendre; n fente f.

sloe, slau, n prunelle f.

slope, slaupe, v aller en pente; n pente f.

slot, slotte, n fente f; (box; machine) ouverture f.

sloth, slauts, n paresse f; indolence f.

slouch, slâ'outche, v marcher lourdement.

slovenly, slov'-'n-li, a sans soin.

slow*, slau, a lent; **to be** –, v (clock, etc) retarder.

slug, slogg, n limace f; (missile) lingot m.

sluggish*, slogg'-iche, a lent; (liver) paresseux.

sluice, slouce, n écluse f; –**gate**, vanne f.

slum, slomme, n bas quartier m; taudis m.

slumber, slomm'-b'r, v sommeiller; n sommeil m.

slump, slommpe, n fin effondrement des cours m.

slur, sleur, n tache f; v tacher; déprécier.

slush, sloche, n boue f, fange f.

slut, slotte, n souillon m & f.

sly, slâï, a sournois, rusé.

smack, smâque, v (hand) donner une claque; (lips) faire claquer; n claque f; (boat) smack m.

small, smoal, a petit; –**ness**, n petitesse f.

small-pox, smoal'-poxe, n petite vérole f.

smart, smârte, a vif; (clever) spirituel; habile; (spruce) pimpant; chic; v (pain) cuire.

smash, smâche, n collision f; com krach m; v briser en morceaux; briser.

smattering, smatt'-eur-inng, n connaissance superficielle f.

smear, smire, v barbouiller; n barbouillage m.

smell, smelle, v sentir; n odeur f.

smelt, smelte, v fondre; n (fish) éperlan m.

smile, smâïle, v sourire; n sourire m.

smite, smâïte, v frapper; affliger.

smith, smits, n forgeron m; –**y**, forge f.

smoke, smauke, v fumer; n fumée f; –**less**, a sans fumée; –**r**, n fumeur m.

smoky, smau'-ki, a enfumé.

smooth, smoudz, a* lisse; v lisser; (temper) apaiser.

smother, smodz'-'r, v étouffer; suffoquer.

smoulder, smaul'-d'r, v brûler sans flammes.

smudge, smodje, v tacher; n tache f.

smuggle, smog'-g'l, v passer en contrebande.

smuggler, smog'-gleur, n contrebandier m.

snack, snâque, n snack m.

snail, snéle, n colimaçon m; (edible) escargot m.

snake, snéque, n serpent m.

snap, snâppe, n (noise) claquement m; (bite)

coup de dent *m*; *v*
fermer bien; (break)
briser net; (fingers)
claquer les doigts;
(animal) happer; – **shut**,
v fermer bien.

snapshot, snăppe´-chotte,
n instantané *m*.

snare, snère, *n* piège *m*; *v*
prendre au piège.

snarl, snârle, *v* grogner; *n*
grognement *m*.

snatch, snătche, *v* saisir; –
at, *v* chercher à saisir; –
from, arracher à.

sneak, snîque, *n* cafard *m*;
v (steal) chiper; – **away**,
v s'esquiver furtivement.

sneer, snîre, *v* ricaner; *n*
ricanement *m*.

sneeze, snîze, *v* éternuer; *n*
éternuement *m*.

sniff, sniffe, *v* renifler.

snip, snipe, *n* coup de
ciseaux *m*; *v* couper avec
des ciseaux.

snipe, snâipe, *n* bécassine
f; –**r**, tireur d'élite *m*.

snob, snobbe, *n* snob *m*;
–**bish**, *a* poseur.

snore, snaure, *v* ronfler; *n*
ronflement *m*.

snorkel, snoar´-k'l, *n* tuba
m.

snort, snoarte, *v* renâcler;
n renâclement *m*.

snout, snâ'oute, *n* museau
m; (pig) groin *m*.

snow, snau, *v* neiger; *n*
neige *f*; –**drop**, perce-
neige *m*; –**storm**,
tempête de neige *f*.

snub, snobbe, *v* dédaigner;
n rebuffade *f*.

snub-nose, snobbe´-nauze,
n nez camus *m*.

snuff, snoffe, *n* tabac à
priser *m*; –**box**, tabatière
f.

so, sau, *adv* aussi; ainsi;
comme cela; si.

soak, sauque, *v* tremper.

soap, saupe, *n* savon *m*.

soar, saure, *v* s'élever;
planer.

sob, sobbe, *v* sangloter; *n*
sanglot *m*.

sober*, sau´-b'r, *a* sobre;
modéré.

sociable, sau´-cha-b'l, *a*
sociable.

social, sau´-ch'l, *a** social;
–**ism**, *n* socialisme *m*;
–**ist**, socialiste *m* & *f*.

society, sŏ-sâï´-i-ti, *n*
société *f*; compagnie *f*;
grand monde *m*.

sock, soque, *n* chaussette
f.

socket, sok´-ette, *n*
emboîture *f*; (eyes)
orbite *f*; (teeth) alvéole
m.

sod, sode, *n* motte de
gazon *f*.

soda, sau´-da, *n* soude *f*; –

water, eau de Seltz *f*.

soft*, softe, *a* mou; doux;
tendre; – **drink**, *n*
boisson non alcoolisé *f*;
–**en**, *v* adoucir; *fig*
attendrir; –**ness**, *n*
douceur *f*.

software, softe´-ouère, *n*
(comput) logiciel *m*;
software *m*.

soil, soa'ile, *v* souiller;
abîmer; *n* sol *m*; terre *f*.

sojourn, sô´-djeurne, *v*
séjourner; *n* séjour *m*.

solace, sol´-ace, *n*
consolation *f*; *v*
consoler.

solder, saule´-d'r, *n*
soudure *f*; *v* souder.

soldier, saule´-dj'r, *n*
soldat *m*.

sole, saule, *n* (shoes, etc)
semelle *f*; (fish) sole *f*; *v*
ressemeler; *a** seul;
unique.

solemn*, sol´-emme, *a*
solennel.

solicit, sŏ-liss´-itte, *v*
solliciter.

solicitor, sŏ-liss´-itt-r, *n*
avoué *m*; notaire *m*.

solicitude, sol-i´-ci-tioude,
n sollicitude *f*.

solid*, sol´-ide, *a* solide;
massif; –**ify**, *v* solidifier.

solitary, sol´-i-ta-ri, *a*
solitaire; seul.

solitude, sol´-i-tioude, *n*

solitude *f*.

soluble, sol´-iou-b'l, *a* soluble.

solution, so-lioue´-ch'n, *n* solution *f*.

solve, solve, *v* résoudre.

solvency, sol´-venn-ci, *n* solvabilité *f*.

solvent, sol´-vennte, *a* dissolvant; *com* solvable.

sombre, somme´-beur, *a* sombre.

some, somme, *art*, *a* & *pron* du *m*; de la *f*; des *mpl* & *fpl*; quelques; en; **–body,** *n* quelqu'un *m*; **–how,** *adv* de façon ou d'autre; **–one,** *pron* quelqu'un *m*; **–thing,** quelque chose *m*; **–times,** *adv* quelquefois; **–what,** quelque peu; **–where,** quelque part.

somersault, somm´-eur-solte, *n* saut périlleux *m*; culbute *f*.

somnambulist, somme-nämm´-bioue-liste, *n* somnambule *m* & *f*.

son, sonne, *n* fils *m*; **––in-law,** gendre *m*.

sonata, sŏ-nâ´-ta, *n* sonate *f*.

song, sonng, *n* chanson *f*; chant *m*.

soon, soune, *adv* bientôt; **as – as,** aussitôt que; **how –?** quand?

soot, soute, *n* suie *f*.

soothe, soudz, *v* adoucir; (pacify) calmer.

sophisticated, sau-fis´-tî-qué-téde, *a* sophistiqué.

sorcerer, saur´-ceur-eur, *n* sorcier *m*.

sorcery, saur´-ceur-i, *n* sorcellerie *f*.

sordid*, sôr´-dide, *a* sordide; vil.

sore, saure, *n* plaie *f*; mal *m*; *a** mal; douloureux.

sorrel, sorr´-'l, *n* oseille *f*.

sorrow, sor´-au, *n* chagrin *m*; affliction *f*; *v* s'affliger; **–ful,** *a* affligeant; triste.

sorry, sor´-i, *a* fâche; désolé; **I am –,** je regrette; pardon!

sort, sôrte, *n* espèce *f*; genre *m*, sorte *f*; *v* trier.

soul, saule, *n* âme *f*.

sound, sâ'ounnde, *v* sonner; *naut* sonder; *a* (health) robuste; (character) droit; (sleep) profond; *n* son *m*; (bells) son *m*; (channel) détroit *m*; **–proof,** *a* insonore; **–track,** *n* bande sonore *f*; **–ing,** *naut* sondage *m*.

soup, soupe, *n* potage *m*; soupe *f*.

soup-tureen, soupe-tioue-rîne´, *n* soupière *f*.

sour*, sâ'oueur, *a* sur; aigre.

source, saurce, *n* source *f*.

south, sâ'outs, *n* sud *m*; **– of France,** le midi *m*.

southerly, seudz´-eur-li, *a* du sud; méridional.

souvenir, sou-vi-nîre´, *n* souvenir *m*.

sovereign, sov´-eur-ine, *n* & *a* souverain *m*.

sow, sau, *v* semer; **–er,** *n* semeur *m*.

sow, sâ'ou, *n* truie *f*.

soya bean, soa'ï-a-bîne, *n* graine de soja *f*.

space, spéce, *n* espace *m*; (time) période *f*.

spacious*, spé´-cheuce, *a* spacieux.

spade, spéde, *n* bêche *f*; (cards) pique *m*.

span, spänne, *n* empan *m*; envergure *f*; (architecture) ouverture *f*; *fig* durée *f*; *v* traverser.

spangle, spain´-g'l, *v* pailleter; *n* paillette *f*.

spaniel, spänn´-ieule, *n* épagneul *m*.

spanner, spänn´-eur, *n* (tool) clef anglaise *f*.

spar, spâre, *v* s'exercer à la boxe; *n* *naut* espar *m*.

spare, spére, *a* de rechange; *v* (forbear) épargner; **can you – this?** pouvez-vous vous en passer?

sparing*, spére´-inng, a
frugal; économe.

spark, spârke, n étincelle
f; v étinceler.

sparkle, spär´-k'l, v
étinceler; (wine)
pétiller.

sparrow, spär´-au, n
moineau m.

spasm, späzme, n spasme
m.

spasmodic, späz-mod´-
ique, a spasmodique.

spats, spättse, npl guêtres
fpl.

spatter, spätt´-'r, v
éclabousser.

spawn, spoanne, n frai m;
v frayer.

speak, spîke, v parler; **–er,**
n orateur m.

spear, spîre, v percer d'un
coup de lance; n lance f.

special*, spè´-ch'l, a
spécial; particulier.

speciality, spèch-i-al´-i-ti,
n spécialité f.

specie, spî´-chî, n
numéraire m.

species, spî´-chîze, n
espèce f; sorte f.

specific, speu-si´-fique, a
précis; particulier; chem
spécifique.

specification, spess-i-fi-
qué´-ch'n, n description
f; (schedule) devis m.

specify, spess´-i-fâï, v
spécifier.

specimen, spess´-i-menn,
n spécimen m; modèle
m.

specious*, spî-cheuce, a
spécieux; plausible.

speck, spèque, n petite
tache f.

spectacle, spèk´-ta-k'l, n
spectacle m.

spectacles, spèk´-ta-k'lse,
npl lunettes fpl.

spectator, spèk-té´-t'r, n
spectateur, -trice m & f.

spectre, spèk´-t'r, n
spectre m.

speculate, spèk´-iou-léte,
v spéculer; méditer.

speech, spîtche, n parole f;
(discourse) discours m;
–less, a muet; fig
interdit.

speed, spîde, n vitesse f; **–
limit,** limitation de
vitesse; vitesse
maximale permise f; **–y,**
a prompt; rapide.

speedometer, spî-domm´-
it'r, n indicateur de
vitesse m.

spell, spelle, v épeler; n
charme m.

spend, spennde, v
dépenser; **–thrift,** n
dépensier, -ère m & f.

sphere, sfîre, n sphère f.

spice, spâïce, n épice f; v

épicer.

spicy, spâï´-ci, a épicé; fig
piquant.

spider, spâï´-d'r, n
araignée f.

spike, spâïke, n piquant m;
pointe f; v clouer.

spill, spille, v répandre;
renverser.

spin, spinne, v filer; faire
tourner; **–ning,** n filage
m.

spinach, spinn´-idj, n
épinards mpl.

spinal, spâïne´-'l, a spinal;
vertébral.

spindle, spinn-d'l, n fuseau
m; axe m.

spine, spâïne, n épine
dorsale f.

spinster, spinn´-st'r, n
femme non mariée f.

spiral, spâï-r'l, a spiral; n
spirale f.

spire, spâïre, n flèche f.

spirit, spir´-itte, n esprit
m; (alcohol) alcool m; s
(animation) entrain m;
–ed, a animé; **–ual,**
spirituel; **–ualist,** n
spiritualiste m.

spit, spitte; v cracher;
crachat m; (roasting)
broche f; **–toon,**
crachoir m.

spite, spâïte, v dépiter; n
dépit m; **–ful,** a
vindicatif; **in – of,** prep

468

malgré.

splash, splâche, v éclabousser; (play) patauger.

splendid*, splenn´-dide, a splendide.

splendour, splenn´-d´r, n splendeur f.

splint, splinnte, n (surgical) attelle f.

splinter, splinn´-t´r, n écharde f; ◊ voler en éclats.

split, splitte, v fendre; n fente f.

spoil, spoa'ile, v gâter; (a child, etc); (damage) abîmer.

spoke, spauke, n rayon d'une roue m.

spokesman, spaukce´-mănne, n porte-parole m.

sponge, sponndje, n éponge f; v éponger.

sponsor, sponn´-sor, n garant m; (baptism) parrain m; marraine f.

spontaneous*, sponn-té´-ni-euce, a spontané.

spool, spoule, n bobine f.

spoon, spoune, n cuiller f; **–ful**, cuillerée f.

sport, spaurte, n sport m; **–ing**, a sportif; **-ive**, a gai.

spot, spotte, v tacher; n tache f; (place) endroit

m; **–less**, a sans tache.

spout, spâ'oute, n (gutter) gouttière f; (jug or pot) bec m; v jaillir.

sprain, spréne, v se fouler; n entorse f.

sprat, sprâte, n sprat m.

sprawl, sproale, v s'étaler; se vautrer.

spray, spré, n (branch) ramille f; (water) embrun m; v arroser; pulvériser; atomiser.

sprayer, spré´-eur, n vaporisateur m; atomiseur.

spread, spredde, v étendre; (on bread, etc) étaler; (news) répandre; **– out**, déployer.

sprig, sprigue, n brin m, brindille f.

sprightly, spraîte´-li, a enjoué; vif; gai.

spring, sprinng, n (season) printemps m; (leap) saut m; (water) source f; (metal) ressort m; v sauter; **-y**, a élastique.

sprinkle, sprinng´-k'l, v asperger; saupoudrer.

sprout, sprâ'oute, v germer; n pousse f.

spruce, sprouce, n sapinette f; a pimpant.

spur, speur, n éperon m; v éperonner.

spurious*, spiou´-ri-euce,

a faux.

spurn, speurne, v dédaigner; mépriser.

spy, spâï, n espion, -onne m & f; v espionner.

squabble, scouob´-b'l, v se chamailler.

squad, scouodde, n mil escouade f; **–ron**, mil escadron m; (naval, air) escadre f.

squalid*, scouoll´-ide, a sale; abject.

squall, scouoale, n (wind) rafale f; v (scream) brailler.

squalor, scouoll-eur, n abjection f.

squander, scouonn´-d'r, v dissiper; gaspiller.

square, scouère, n & a carré m; (public) place f.

squash, scouoche, v écraser; n écrasement m.

squat, scouotte, v s'accroupir; a fig trapu.

squeak, scouîke, v crier; (bearings, etc) grincer.

squeeze, scouîze, v serrer; (cuddle) étreindre; (lemon, etc) presser.

squid, scouide, n calmar m.

squint, scouinnte, v loucher; n regard louche m.

squirrel, scouir´-'l, n écureuil m.

squirt, scoueurte, n
seringue f; v seringuer;
faire gicler.

stab, ståbbe, v poignarder;
n coup de poignard m.

stability, stă-bil´-i-ti, n
stabilité f.

stable, sté-b'l, n écurie f;
(cattle) étable f; a
stable.

stack, ståque, n pile f;
(hay) meule f;
(chimney) cheminée f; v
empiler.

stadium, sté-di-eum, n
stade m.

staff, ståffe, n bâton m;
(employees) personnel
m; mil état-major m;
flag-, hampe f.

stag, stågue, n cerf m.

stage, stédje, n (theatre)
scène f; (hall) estrade f;
(period) phase f; v
mettre en scène.

stagger, stagg´-'r, v
chanceler; fig renverser.

stagnate, stagg´-néte, v
croupir.

staid*, stéde, a posé;
sérieux.

stain, sténe, v teindre;
(soil) souiller; n teinture
f; (soil) tache f; **-less**, a
(metal) inoxydable.

stair, stére, n marche f; **-s**,
pl escalier m.

stake, stéque, v garnir de
pieux; (bet) parier; n
pieu m; (wager) enjeu
m; **at the –**, sur le
bûcher.

stale, stéle, a (bread, etc)
rassis; (beer, etc) éventé.

stalk, stoake, n tige f; v
chasser à l'affût.

stall, stoale, n fauteuil
d'orchestre m; (market)
étalage m; (cattle) box
m; v (of engine) caler.

stalwart, stoal´-oueurte, a
fort; robuste.

stamina, stămm´-i-na, n
force de résistance f.

stammer, stămm´-'r, v
bégayer.

stamp, stămmpe, n timbre
m; v timbrer; (foot)
frapper du pied.

stampede, stămm-pîde´, v
fuir en panique; n
débandade f.

stand, stånnde, v être
debout; (place) mettre;
(endure) supporter; n
tribune f; résistance f;
(pedestal) support m;
(market) étalage m;
(exhibition) stand m;
-ing, a permanent; n
rang m; **-ing-room**,
place debout f; **-still**,
arrêt m.

standard, stănn´-deurde, n
étendard m; n & a
modèle m; (weights,

measures) étalon m.

staple, sté-p'l, n crampon
de fer m; agrafe f; a
principal.

star, stårre, n étoile f; **-ry**,
a étoilé.

starboard, stårre´-baurde,
n tribord m.

starch, stårtche, n amidon
m; v empeser.

stare, stére, v regarder
fixement; n regard fixe
m.

starling, står´-linng, n
étourneau m.

start, stårte, n
commencement m;
(shock) coup m; v
commencer;
(machinery) mettre en
marche; (leave) partir.

startle, står-t'l, v
sursauter; effrayer.

starvation, stâr-vé´-ch'n,
n faim f.

starve, stårve, v mourir de
faim; (deprive) affamer.

state, stéte, v déclarer; n
état m; (pomp) apparat
m; **-ly**, a majestueux;
-ment, n déclaration f;
(account) relevé de
compte m.

statesman, stéts´-mănne,
n homme d'Etat m.

station, sté´-ch'n, n
position f; (railway) gare
f; (fire, police) poste m;

v poster.

stationary, sté´-chŏnn-a-ri, *a* stationnaire.

stationer, sté´-cheunn-eur, *n* papetier *m*.

stationery, sté´-cheunn-eur-i, *n* papeterie *f*.

statistics, sta-tiss´-tiks, *n* statistique *f*.

statue, stă´-tiou, *n* statue *f*.

statute, stă´-tioute, *n* statut *m*, loi *f*.

staunch, stânnche, *v* étancher; *a* ferme.

stave, stéve, *n* douve *f*; – **in**, *v* défoncer.

stay, sté, *n* séjour *m*; *v* séjourner; rester.

stays, stéze, *npl* corset *m*.

stead, stedde, *n* place *f*; **in** – **of**, au lieu de.

steadfast, stedd´-fâsste, *a* solide; constant.

steady, stedd´-i, *a* ferme; (reliable) sérieux; (market) ferme.

steak, stéque, *n* bifteck *m*.

steal, stîle, *v* voler; dérober.

stealth, stèlts, **by** –, à la dérobée.

steam, stîme, *n* vapeur *f*; –**er**, bateau à vapeur *m*.

steel, stîle, *n* acier *m*.

steep, stîpe, *a* escarpé; *v* (soak) tremper.

steeple, stî´-p'l, *n* clocher

m.

steer, stîre, *v naut* gouverner; *aero* diriger; (motor) conduire; *n* (ox) bouvillon *m*.

steerage, stîre´-idj, *n* entrepont *m*.

stem, stemme, *n* tige *f*; (glass) pied *m*; (tobacco-pipe) tuyau *m*; *v* refouler.

stench, stenntche, *n* infection *f*; puanteur *f*.

step, steppe, *v* marcher; aller; *n* pas *m*; (stair) marche *f*; (ladder) échelon *m*; –**brother**, *n* demi-frère *m*; –**father**, beau-père *m*; –**ladder**, échelle double *f*; (Brit) escabeau *m*; –**mother**, bellemère *f*; –**sister**, demi-sœur *f*.

stereo, stè´-rî-au, *n* stéréo *f*.

stereophonic, stér-io-fon´-ique, *a* stéréophonique.

sterile, stér-il, *a* stérile.

sterilize, stér´-i-lâîze, *v* stériliser.

sterling, steur´-linng, *a* sterling; pur; de bon aloi.

stern, steurne, *n* arrière *m*. *a** sévère; rébarbatif.

stevedore, stî´-ve-daure, *n* arrimeur *m*.

stew, stioue, *n* ragoût *m*; *v*

mettre en ragoût.

steward, stioue´-eurde, *n* (estate) intendant *m*; (ship) garçon de cabine *m*; –**ess**, (aeroplane) hôtesse (de l'air) *f*; **wine** –, sommelier *m*.

stick, stique, *v* (affix) coller; *n* bâton *m*; (walking) canne *f*; –**y**, *a* collant.

stiff*, stife, *a* raide; –**en**, *v* raidir; (linen) empeser.

stifle, stâî´-f'l, *v* étouffer; suffoquer.

stigmatize, stigg´-ma-tâîze, *v* stigmatiser.

stile, stâîle, *n* barrière *f*; **turn** –, tourniquet *m*.

still, stille, *n* (distil) alambic *m*; *v* calmer; *a* tranquille; *adv* encore; toujours; *conj* (nevertheless) néanmoins.

stimulate, stimm´-iou-léte, *v* stimuler.

sting, stinng, *v* piquer; *n* piqûre *f*.

stink, stinng-k, *v* puer; *n* puanteur *f*.

stint, stinnte, *v* restreindre; rogner.

stipend, stâî´-pennde, *n* traitement *m*.

stipulate, stip´-iou-léte, *v* stipuler.

stipulation, stip-iou-léch'n, n stipulation f.

stir, steur, v remuer; agiter; bouger; n émoi m.

stirrup, stirr´-eupe, n étrier m.

stitch, stitche, v coudre; n point m.

stock, stoque, v avoir en magasin; stocker; n (tree) tronc m; (gun) fût m; (flower) giroflée f; (goods) stock m; (live) animaux vivants mpl; (meat, etc) bouillon m; –**book**, livre d'inventaire m; –**broker**, agent de change m; –**exchange**, bourse f; –**s**, (securities) valeurs fpl; (pillory) pilori m; –**size**, taille normale f; –**taking**, inventaire m.

stocking, stok´-inng, n bas m.

stoke, stauque, v chauffer; –**r**, n chauffeur m.

stolid, stol´-id, a lourd.

stomach, stomm´-aque, n estomac m; –**-ache**, mal d'estomac m; mal au ventre m.

stone, staune, n pierre f; (pebble) caillou m; med calcul m; v lapider; (fruit) enlever les noyaux.

stool, stoule, n tabouret m; med selle f.

stoop, stoupe, v se baisser.

stop, stoppe, n arrêt m; (interruption) pause f; (punctuation) point m; v arrêter, s'arrêter; (payment) suspendre; (teeth) plomber; (cease) cesser; – **up**, boucher.

stopper, stopp´-´r, n bouchon m.

storage, staur´-idj, n magasinage m.

store, staure, n (shop) magasin m.

stores, staur'ze, npl approvisionnements mpl.

stork, stoarque, n cigogne f.

storm, stoarme, n tempête f; v donner l'assaut à.

stormy, stoar´-mi, a orageux.

story, stau´-ri, n histoire f; (untruth) mensonge m; (floor) étage m.

stout, stâ'oute, a gros; (strong) fort.

stove, stauve, n poêle m; (cooking) cuisinière f.

stow, stau, v naut arrimer; (away) ranger.

stowaway, stau´-a-oué, n voyageur clandestin m.

straggle, strägg´-'l, v s'écarter de; (lag) traîner.

straight, stréte, a droit;

direct; –**en**, v redresser; –**forward***, a honorable; franc.

strain, stréne, n effort m; (music) air m; (pull) tension f; v s'efforcer; (stretch) tendre; (tendon) fouler; (liquid) filtrer.

strainer, stré´-neur, n passoire f; filtre m.

straits, strétse, npl (channel) détroit m.

strand, strännde, v naut échouer; n plage f; (rope) brin m.

strange*, stréne'dje, a étrange; –**r**, n étranger, -ère m & f.

strangle, strain´-ng'l, v étrangler.

strap, sträppe, v attacher avec une courroie; n courroie f.

strategy, strä´-ta-djî, n stratégie f.

straw, stroa, n paille f; –**berry**, fraise f.

stray, stré, v s'égarer; s'éloigner; a égaré; perdu.

streak, strîke, n raie f; rayon m; v rayer.

streaky, strîk´-i, a rayé; (meat) entrelardé.

stream, strîme, n ruisseau m; courant m; v couler; –**lined**, a aérodynamique.

street, strîte, n rue f.

street plan, strîte-plănne, n plan (des rues) m.

streetwise, strîte-'ouaïze, a futé; realiste.

strength, strenng-ts, n force f; **–en**, v renforcer.

strenuous*, strenn'-iou-euce, a ardu.

stress, stresse, n accent m; (pressure) pression f; tension f; (urge) urgence f; v accentuer; souligner.

stretch, stretche, v (widen) élargir; (oneself) s'étirer; (pull) tirer; **–er**, n med brancard m; (shoe, etc) forme f.

strew, stroue, v répandre; parsemer.

strict*, stricte, a exact; strict; rigoureux.

stride, strâïde, n enjambée f; v enjamber.

strife, strâïfe, n dispute f; contestation f.

strike, strâïke, v (work) se mettre en grève; (lightning; smite) frapper; (match) frotter; n grève f; **– off**, **– out**, v effacer; (disqualify) rayer; **–r**, n gréviste m & f.

string, strinng, v (beads) enfiler; n ficelle f;

(music) corde f.

stringent, strinn'-djennte, a rigoureux.

strip, strippe, v dénuder; n bande f.

stripe, strâïpe, n raie f; mil galon m; v rayer.

strive, strâïve, v s'efforcer de.

stroke, strauke, n med attaque f; (pen) trait de plume m; (blow) coup m; (piston) course f; v caresser.

stroll, straule, v flâner; faire un tour; n tour m.

strong*, stronng, a fort; solide.

strop, stroppe, n cuir à rasoir m; v repasser.

structure, strok'-tioure, n structure f.

struggle, strogg'-'l, v lutter; n lutte f.

strut, strotte, v se pavaner; n (brace) étai m.

stubborn, stobb'-eurne, a obstiné; opiniâtre.

stud, stodde, n (nail) clou à grosse tête m; (collar) bouton m; (breeding) haras m; v garnir de clous.

student, stioue'-dennte, n étudiant, -e m & f; élève m f.

studio, stioue'-di-ô, n atelier m; studio m.

studious*, stioue'-di-euce, a studieux.

study, stodd'-i, v étudier; n étude f; (room) cabinet de travail m; bureau m.

stuff, stoffe, v rembourrer; (preserve) empailler; (cookery) farcir; n matière f; **–ing**, (cookery) farce f.

stumble, stomm'-b'l, v trébucher.

stump, stommpe, n troncon m; (arm, leg) moignon m; (tooth) racine f; (cricket) bâton m.

stun, stonne, v étourdir.

stunning, stonn'-inng, a fig étourdissant.

stunt, stonnte, n tour de force m; acrobatie f; **–man**, cascadeur m.

stunted, stonn'-tedde, a rabougri.

stupefy, stioue-pi-fâï, v stupéfier.

stupendous*, stiou-penn'-deuce, a prodigieux.

stupid*, stioue'-pide, a stupide; **–ity**, n stupidité f.

stupor, stioue'-peur, n stupeur f.

sturdy, steur'-di, a vigoureux; hardi.

sturgeon, steur'-dj'n, n

esturgeon m.

stutter, stott´-'r, v bégayer; halbutier.

sty, staï, n porcherie f; med compère-loriot m.

style, staïle, n mode f; (manner) style m.

stylish, staïl´-iche, a à la mode; élégant.

subdue, seub-dioue´, v subjuguer; (tame) dompter.

subject, sobb-djecte´, v assujétir; exposer à.

subject, sobb´-djecte, n sujet m.

subjection, sobb-djèque´-ch'n, n dépendance f; soumission f.

subjunctive, sobb-djonngk´-tive, n subjonctif m.

sublime*, seub-laîme´, a sublime.

submarine, sob´-ma-rine, n & a sous-marin m.

submerge, seub-meurdje´, v submerger.

submission, seub-mich´-'n, n soumission f.

submit, seub-mitte´, v soumettre; se soumettre.

subordinate, seub-or´-di-néte, a subordonné.

subpœna, seub-pî´-na, n assignation f; v assigner.

subscribe, seub-scraïbe´, v souscrire; (papers)

s'abonner; **–r,** n souscripteur m; abonné, -ée m & f.

subscription, seub-scrip´-ch'n, n souscription f; (papers, library, etc) abonnement.

subsequent*, seub´-sî-couennte, a subséquent.

subservient, seub-seur´-viennte, a subordonné.

subside, seub-saïde´, v s'affaisser; (water) baisser.

subsidiary, seub-side´-i-a-ri, a subsidiaire.

subsidy, seub´-si-di, n (grant) subvention f.

subsist, seub-cisste´, v subsister; – on, vivre de.

substance, seub´-st'nce, n substance f; fond m.

substantial*, seub-stănn´-cheul, a substantiel.

substantiate, seub-stănn´-chi-éte, v établir.

substantive, seub´-stănn-tive, n substantif m.

substitute, seub´-sti-tioute, v remplacer; n (proxy) remplaçant, -e m & f; **as a –,** à la place de.

subterranean, seub-tèr-ré´-ni-ann, a souterrain.

subtitle, sob´-tî-tl, n cinema sous-titre m.

subtle, seutt´-'l, a subtil;

adroit.

subtract, seub-trăcte´, v soustraire.

suburb, seub´-eurbe, n banlieue f.

subway, seub´-oué, n passage souterrain m.

succeed, seuk-cîde´, v succéder; (achieve) réussir.

success, seuk-cesse´, n succès m; **–ful,** a couronné de succés; (person) heureux; **–ion,** n succession f; **–or,** successeur m.

succour, seuk´-'r, n secours m; v secourir.

succumb, seuk-komme´, v succomber.

such, sotche, a pareil; semblable.

suck, soque, v sucer; (baby) téter; **–le,** allaiter.

suction, soque´-ch'n, n succion f.

sudden*, sod´-'n, a soudain; imprévu.

sue, sioue, v poursuivre en justice.

suede, souéde, n daim m.

suet, sioue´-ette, n graisse de rognon f.

suffer, soff´-'r, v souffrir; supporter; **–ing,** n souffrance f; a patient; **on –ance,** par tolérance.

suffice, *seuf*-fâîce´, v suffire.

sufficient*, *seuf*-fi´- chennte, a suffisant.

suffocate, *sof*-ŏ-quéte, v suffoquer.

suffrage, *seuf*´-frédje, n suffrage m.

sugar, *chou*´-gueur, n sucre m; **–tongs,** pince à sucre f.

suggest, *seudd*-jeste´, v suggérer; (advice) conseiller; **–ion,** n suggestion f; **–ive,** a suggestif.

suicide, *siou*´-i-sâïde, n suicide m.

suit, *sioute*, v convenir; (dress) aller bien; n complet m; costume m; (law) procès m; (cards) couleur f; **–able,** a convenable; **–case,** n valise f; **–or,** (wooer) prétendant m.

suite, *soûîte*, n (retinue) suite f; (rooms) appartement m; (furniture) ameublement m.

sulk, *sollque*, v bouder; **–y,** a boudeur.

sullen*, *soll*´-n, a maussade; morose.

sulphur, *soll*´-f'r, n soufre m.

sultry, *soll*´-tri, a lourd; accablant.

sum, *somme*, n somme f; **– up,** v résumer.

summary, *somm*´-a-ri, n résumé m; a sommaire.

summer, *somm*´-'r, n été m.

summit, *somm*´-itte, n sommet m.

summon, *somm*´-'n, v appeler; (call) convoquer.

summons, *somm*´-eunnze, n sommation f.

sumptuous*, *sommp*´- tiou-euce, a somptueux.

sun, *sonne*, n soleil m; **–beam,** rayon de soleil m; **–bathe,** v prendre un bain de soleil; **–burn,** n coup de soleil m; **–cream,** lait de bronzage m; **–dial,** cadran solaire m; **–glasses,** n lunettes de soleil fpl; **–light,** (lumière du) soleil f; **–ny,** a ensoleillé; **–rise,** n lever du soleil m; **–set,** coucher du soleil m; **–stroke,** coup de soleil m; insolation f; **–tan,** bronzage m.

Sunday, *sonn*´-dé, n dimanche m.

sundries, *sonn*´-drize, npl articles divers mpl.

sundry, *sonn*´-dri, a divers.

sunken, *sonng*´-k'n, a enfoncé, coulé.

sup, *soppe*, v souper; **–per,** n souper m.

super, *sioue*-peur, n (theatrical) figurant m; **–abundant,** a surabondant; **–annuation,** n retraite f; **–cilious,** a hautain; dédaigneux; **–ficial,** a superficiel; **–fin,** surfin; **–intend,** v surveiller; **–intendent,** n contrôleur m; **–market,** n supermarché m; **–natural,** a surnaturel; **–sede,** v supplanter; **–vise,** surveiller; **–vision,** n surveillance f.

superb*, *sioue*-peurbe´, a superbe.

superfluous, *sioue*-peur´- flou-euce, a superflu.

superior, *sioue*-pi´-ri-eur, a supérieur.

superlative, *sioue*-peur´- la-tive, n & a superlatif m.

superstitious*, *sioue*-peur- stich´-euce, a superstitieux.

supplant, *seup*-plânnte´, v supplanter.

supple, *sopp*´-'l, a souple.

supplement, *sopp*´-li-m'nt, n supplément m.

supplier, *seup*-plâï´-eur, n

fournisseur *m*.

supply, *seup*-plâï´, *v* fournir; *n* fourniture *f*.

support, *seup*-paurte´, *n* (prop) support *m*; (moral) appui *m*; (maintenance) entretien *m*; *v* supporter; entretenir; (morally) soutenir.

suppose, *seup*-pauze´, *v* supposer.

supposition, *seup*-pau-ziche´-´n, *n* supposition *f*.

suppress, *seup*-press´, *v* supprimer; (conceal) cacher.

supremacy, sioue-premm´-a-ci, *n* suprématie *f*.

supreme*, sioue-prîme´, *a* suprême.

surcharge, *seur*-tchârdje, *n* surcharge *f*; *v* se surcharger.

sure*, choueur, *a* sûr; certain.

surety, choueur´-ti, *n* (bail, etc) caution *f*.

surf, seurfe, *n* ressac *m*.

surface, *seur*-féce, *n* surface *f*.

surfboard, *seurf*´-baurde, *n* planche de surf *f*.

surfing, *seurf*´-inng, *n* surf *m*.

surge, seurdje, *v* s'enfler; *n* houle *f*.

surgeon, *seur*´-djeune, *n* chirurgien *m*.

surgery, *seur*-djeur-i, *n* chirurgie *f*.

surgical, *seur*´-dji-c'l, *a* chirurgical.

surly, *seur*´-li, *a* bourru; (dog) hargneux.

surmise, *seur*-mâïze´, *v* conjecturer; *n* conjecture *f*.

surmount, *seur*-mâ´ounnte´, *v* surmonter.

surname, *seur*´-néme, *n* nom de famille *m*.

surpass, *seur*-pâsse´, *v* surpasser; l'emporter sur.

surplus, *seur*´-pleuce, *n* excédent *m*, surplus *m*.

surprise, *seur*-prâïze´, *v* surprendre; *n* surprise *f*.

surrender, *seur*-renn´-d´r, *n mil* reddition *f*; *v* se rendre; (cede) céder.

surround, *seur*-râ´ounnde, *v* entourer; *mil* cerner; **-ings,** *npl* environs *mpl*.

survey, *seur*-vé´, *n* (land) arpentage *m*; enquête *f*; *v* mesurer; (look at) inspecter; **-or,** *n* arpenteur *m*; architecte *m*; inspecteur *m*.

survival, *seur*-vâï´-v'l, *n* survivance *f*.

survive, *seur*-vâïve´, *v* survivre.

survivor, *seur*-vâï´-v'r, *n* survivant, -e *m* & *f*.

susceptible, *seuss*-cepp´-ti-b'l, *a* susceptible.

suspect, *seuss*-pecte´, *v* soupçonner; *n* & *a* suspect, -e *m* & *f*.

suspend, *seuss*-pennde´, *v* suspendre; (defer) ajourner; **-ers,** *npl* jarretelles *fpl*.

suspense, *seuss*-pennce´, *n* suspens *m*; incertitude *f*.

suspension, *seuss*-penn´-ch'n, *n* suspension *f*; **— bridge,** pont suspendu *m*.

suspensory, *seuss*-penn´-sor-i, *n* suspensoir *m*.

suspicion, *seuss*-pich´-'n, *n* soupçon *m*.

suspicious*, *seuss*-pich´-euce, *a* méfiant; suspect.

sustain, *seuss*-téne´, *v* soutenir; supporter.

swagger, sou'âgg´-'r, *v* faire le fanfaron.

swallow, sou'oll´-au, *v* avaler; *n* (bird) hirondelle *f*.

swamp, sou'ommpe, *n* marécage *m*; *v* submerger.

swan, sou'onne, *n* cygne *m*.

swarm, sou'oarme, *n* (bees, etc) essaim *m*; (people) multitude *f*; *v*

essaimer; (crowd)
pulluler.

sway, soué, *v* influencer;
osciller; (totter)
chanceler; *n* influence *f*;
(power) pouvoir *m*.

swear, sou'aire, *v* jurer;
(law) prêter serment.

sweat, sou'ète, *n* sueur *f*; *v*
suer; transpirer.

sweep, sou'îpe, *v* balayer;
(chimney) ramoner; *n*
(chimney) ramoner *m*;
–er, balayeur *m*; (carpet)
balai mécanique *m*.

sweet, sou'îte, *a* sucré; *fig*
doux; *n* (confection)
bonbon *m*; (meals)
entremets *m*; **–bread,** ris
de veau d'agneu *m*; **–en,**
v sucrer; **–heart,** *n*
amoureux, -euse *m & f*;
–ness, douceur *f*; **–pea,**
pois de senteur *m*.

swell, sou'elle, *v* enfler;
–ing, *n med* enflure.

swerve, sou'eurve, *v*
dévier; (skid) déraper.

swift, sou'ifte, *a** rapide; *n*
martinet *m*.

swim, sou'imme, *v* nager;
n nage *f*; **–mer,** nageur, -
euse *m & f*; **–ming,**
natation *f*; **–ming-bath,**
piscine *f*; **–ming
costume,** maillot (de
bain); **–ming pool,**
piscine *f*; **–ming trunks,**

maillot (de bain) *m*.

swindle, sou'inn´-d'l, *v*
escroquer; rouler; *n*
escro querie *f*; **–r,** escroc
m.

swine, sou-âîne, *n* cochon
m; porc *m*.

swing, sou'inng, *n*
oscillation *f*; (child's)
balançoire *f*; *v* osciller;
se balancer; (whirl)
tournoyer.

switch, sou'itche, *n*
(riding) cravache *f*;
(electric) commutateur
m; *v* (train) aiguiller; **–
off,** (light) éteindre; **–
on,** (light) allumer.

swivel, sou'ive´-'l, *n*
tourniquet *m*.

swoon, swoune, *v*
s'évanouir; *n*
évanouissement *m*.

swoop, swoupe, *v* fondre
sur.

sword, saurde, *n* épée *f*;
(sabre) sabre *m*.

sworn, sou'aurne, *a*
assermenté.

syllabie, sil´-la-b'l, *n*
syllabe *f*.

syllabus, sil´-la-beuce, *n*
programme *m*.

symbol, simm´-b'l, *n*
symbole *m*.

symmetry, simm´-èt-ri, *n*
symétrie *f*.

sympathetic, simm´-pa-

tsèt´-ique, *a*
sympathique.

sympathize, simm´-pa-
tsâîze, *v* sympathiser.

sympathy, simm´-pa-tsi, *n*
sympathie *f*.

symptom, simmp´-t'm, *n*
symptôme *m*.

synchronize, sinn´-cronn-
âîze, *v* synchroniser.

syndicate, sinn´-di-kéte, *n*
syndicat *m*.

synonymous, si-nonn´-i-
meuce, *a* synonyme.

syphilis, siff´-i-lice, *n*
syphilis *f*.

syringe, sir´-inndje, *n*
seringue *f*; *v* seringuer.

syrup, sir´-oppe, *n* sirop *m*.

system, siss´-t'm *n* système
m.

table, té-´b'l, *n* table *f*;
–**cloth,** nappe *f*; –**land,**
plateau *m*; –**spoon,**
cuiller à bouche *f*; –
tennis, ping-pong *f*.

tablet, tăb´-lette, *n*
tablette *f*; plaque *f*.

tack, tăque, *n* (nail)
semence *f*; *v* clouer;
(sew) faufiler; *naut*
courir une bordée.

tackle, tăque´-'l, *n*
(fishing) articles de
pêche *mpl*; *naut*
apparaux *mpl*; *v*
attaquer.

tact, tăkt, *n* tact *m*; –**ful,** *a*
qui a du tact; –**ics,** *n*
tactique *f*; –**less,** *a* sans
tact.

tadpole, tăde´-pôle, *n*
têtard *m*.

tail, téle, *n* queue *f*; (coat,

short, etc) pan *m*.

tailor, té-´l'r, *n* tailleur *m*.

taint, ténnte, *v* souiller;
infecter; *n* souillure *f*.

take, téque, *v* prendre;
accepter; – **away,** (carry
away) emporter; (clear
away) enlever; (lead
away) emmener; – **away
food,** *n* plats à emporter
mpl; – **care of,** prendre
soin de; avoir soin de; –
off, enlever.

takings, té-´kinngse, *npl*
recettes *fpl*.

talcum powder, tăl-qeum-
pâ'ou-d'r, *n* talc *m*.

tale, téle, *n* récit *m*; (fairy)
conte *m*.

talent, tăl-´ennte, *n* talent
m.

talk, toak, *v* parler; causer;
n conversation *f*.

talkative, toak-´a-tive, *a*
bavard.

tall, toal, *a* grand; haut.

tallow, tăl-´au, *n* suif *m*.

tally, tăl-´i, *v* concorder;
correspondre.

talon, tăl-´onne, *n* serre *f*.

tame, téme, *a* apprivoisé,
domestique; *v*
apprivoiser; (beasts)
dompter; **taming,** *n*
apprivoisement *m*; –**r,**
dompteur *m*.

tamper, tămm-´p'r, –**with,**
v toucher à.

tampon, tămm-´ponne, *n*
med tampon hygiénique
m.

tan, tănne, *v* (leather)
tanner; (sun) bronzer.

tangerine, tănn-´dje-
rinne, *n* mandarine *f*.

tangible, tănn-´dji-b'l, *a*
tangible; palpable.

tangle, tain-´ng'l, *n*
emmêlement *m*; *v*
embrouiller; emmêler.

tank, tain-´ngk, *n* citerne
f; *mil* char d'assaut *m*.

tantalize, tănn-´ta-lăïze, *v*
tenter; torturer.

tap, tăppe, *n* tape *f*; petit
coup *m*; (cock) robinet
m; (cask) cannelle *f*; *v*
taper; (knock) frapper;
(tree) inciser; (cask)
mettre en perce.

tape, tépe, *n* ruban *m*;

–**measure**, mètre à ruban m; –**recorder**, n magnétophone m; –**worm**, ver solitaire m; **red –**, fig bureaucratie f.

taper, tépe´-'r, v effiler.

tapestry, tăp´-'s-tri, n tapisserie f.

tar, târe, n goudron m; v goudronner.

tardy, târe´-di, a lent; (late) tardif.

target, târe´-guette, n cible f.

tariff, tăre´-if, n tarif m.

tarnish, târe´-niche, v ternir.

tarpaulin, târe-poa´-linne, n bâche f.

tart, târte, n tarte f; tourte f. a* acide.

task, tâssque, n tâche f.

tassel, tăss´-'l, n gland m.

taste, téste, v goûter; n goût m; –**ful**, a bon goût; –**less**, sans goût; insipide.

tasty, tést´-i, a savoureux.

tatter, tătt´-'r, n haillon m; lambeau m; –**ed**, a déguenillé.

tattle, tătt´-'l, v jaser; n bavardage m.

tattoo, ta-toue´, v (skin) tatouer; n tatouage m; mil retraite aux flambeaux f.

taunt, toannte, v tancer; n

reproche m.

tavern, tăv´-eurne, n taverne f.

tawdry, toa´-dri, a clinquant.

tax, tăxe, v taxer; n impôt m; –**payer**, contribuable m & f.

taxi, tăk´-si, n taxi m.

tea, tî, n thé m; –**pot**, théière f.

teach, tîtche, v enseigner; –**er**, n professeur m; (primary) maître, -tresse m & f.

teaching, tîtch´-inng, n enseignement m.

team, tîme, n (sport) équipe f; (horses, etc) attelage m.

tear, tère, v (rend) déchirer; n déchirure f.

tear, tîre, n larme f.

tease, tîze, v taquiner; (annoy) agacer.

teat, tîte, n mamelon m; (dummy) tétine f.

technical*, tèque´-ni-c'l, a technique.

tedious*, tî´-di-euce, a ennuyeux; fatigant.

tedium, tî´-di-omme, n ennui m.

teenager, tînn´-é-djeur, n adolescent,-e m & f.

teem, tîme, – **with**, v fourmiller de.

teething, tîdz´-inng, n

dentition f.

teetotaller, tî-tŏ´-t'leur, n abstinent, -ente m & f.

telegram, tell´-i-grămme, n télégramme m.

telegraph, tell´-i-grăfe, v télégraphier.

telephone, tell´-i-faune, v téléphoner; n téléphone m; – **box**, cabine téléphonique f; – **call**, coup de téléphone m; – **number**, numéro de téléphone m.

telescope, tell´-i-scaupe, n télescope m, longue-vue f.

television, tell-i-vij´-'n, n télévision f; – **set**, poste de télévision m.

tell, tell, v dire; (narrate) raconter.

temper, temm´-p'r, n humeur f; colère f; (steel) trempe f; v tremper; –**ance**, n tempérance f; sobriété f; a de tempérance; –**ate***, modéré; sobre; –**ature**, température f; fièvre f.

tempest, temm´-peste, n tempête f.

temple, temm´-p'l, n temple m; (head) tempe f.

temporary, temm´-pŏ-ra-ri, a temporaire.

tempt, temmpte, v tenter;

–ing, *a* tentant.

temptation, temmp-té´ch'n, *n* tentation *f.*

ten, tenne, *n* & *a* dix *m;* –**th,** dixième *m* & *f.*

tenable, tenn´-a-b'l, *a* soutenable; *mil* tenable.

tenacious*, ti-né´-cheuce, *a* tenace.

tenacity, ti-nǎss´-i-ti, *n* ténacité *f.*

tenancy, tenn´-ann-ci, *n* location *f.*

tenant, tenn´-annte, *n* locataire *m* & *f.*

tend, tennde, *v* soigner.

tendency, tenn´-denn-ci, *n* tendance *f.*

tender, tenn´-d'r, *v* offrir; (contract) soumissionner; *n* offre *f;* soumission *f; a** tendre; (painful) sensible; –**hearted,** compatissant; –**ness,** *n* tendresse *f;* sensibilité *f.*

tenement, tenn´-i-m'nt, *n* habitation *f,* logement *m.*

tennis, tenn´-ice, *n* tennis *m;* – **court,** court de tennis *m;* – **racket,** raquette de tennis *f.*

tenor, tenn´-'r, *n* ténor *m;* (purport) teneur *f.*

tense, tennce, *n* (grammar) temps *m; a** tendu.

tension, tenn´-ch'n, *n* tension *f.*

tent, tennte, *n* tente *f.*

tentative*, tenn´-ta-tive, *a* expérimental.

tenure, tenn´-ioure, *n* jouissance *f.*

tepid, tepp´-idde, *a* tiède.

term, teurme, *n* terme *m;* (school) trimestre *m;* (time) durée *f;* –**inate,** *v* terminer; se terminer; –**inus,** *n* terminus *m;* –**s,** *pl* conditions *fpl;* (instalments) à tempérament.

terminal, teurme´-i-neul, *a* terminale, final; *med* en phase terminale; *n* terminal (computer, oil) *m; n* terminus (rail) *m.*

terrace, terr´-ice, *n* terrasse *f.*

terrible, terr´-i-b'l, *a* terrible.

terrific, terr-i´-fique, *a* formidable.

terrify, terr´-i-fâi, *v* terrifier.

territory, terr´-i-tŏr-i, *n* territoire *m.*

terror, terr´-'r, *n* terreur *f,* effroi *m;* –**ize,** *v* terroriser.

terrorist, terr´-a-riste, *n* terroriste *m* & *f.*

terse*, teurse, *a* sec; net.

test, tesste, *v* mettre à l'épreuve; essayer; *n* épreuve, *f,* essai *m;* examen *m;* –**ify,** *v* attester; –**imonial,** *n* certificat *m;* (presentation) témoignage de reconnaissance *m.*

Testament, tess´-ta-m'nt, *n* Testament *m.*

testicle, tess´-ti-k'l, *n* testicule *m.*

testimony, tess´-ti-mo-ni, *n* témoignage *m.*

tether, tèdz´-'r, *n* longe *f; v* mettre à l'attache.

text, texte, *n* texte *m;* –**book,** manuel *m*

textile, tex´-tâïle, *a* textile.

texture, tex´-tioure, *n* tissu *m;* texture *f.*

than, dzànne, *conj* que; de.

thank, tsain-ngk, *v* remercier; – **you!** *interj* merci! –**ful,** *a* reconnaissant; –**less,** (ingrat); –**s,** *npl* remerciements *mpl;* –**s to,** *prep* grâce à.

thanksgiving, tsainngkse´-guiv-inng, *n* actions de grâces *fpl.*

that, dzàtte, *pron* lequel; laquelle; lesquels; lesquelles; cela; *a* ce; cet; cette; *conj* que; afin que; –**one,** *pron* celui-là;

celle-là.

thatch, tsätche, *n* chaume *m*; *v* couvrir de chaume.

thaw, tsoa, *n* dégel *m*; *v* dégeler.

the, dze, *art* le *m*, la *f*, les *mpl* & *fpl*.

theatre, tsî´-a-t'r, *n* théâtre *m*.

theft, tsefte, *n* vol *m*; (petty) larcin *m*.

their, dzère, *poss* a leur; leurs.

theirs, dzèrze, *poss pron* le leur, la leur; les leurs.

them, dzemme, *pron* eux; elles; les; to –, leur; –selves, eux-mêmes; elles-mêmes; *refl* se.

theme, tsîme, *n* thème *m*; texte *m*.

then, dzenne, *adv* alors; ensuite; *conj* donc.

thence, dzennce, *adv* de là; –forth, désormais.

theology, tsî-ol´-ŏdj-i, *n* théologie *f*.

theoretical*, tsî-ŏ-rett´-i-c'l, *a* thérorique.

theory, tsî´-ŏ-ri, *n* théorie *f*.

therapy, tsè´-ra-pî, *n* thérapie *f*.

there, dzair, *adv* là; –by, *adv* par là; –fore, donc; –upon, là-dessus; sur ce.

thermal, tseur´-m'l, *a* thermal.

thermometer, tseur-momm´-i-t'r, *n* thermomètre *m*.

these, dzîze, *pron* ceux-ci, celles-ci; *a* ces; ces ...-ci.

thesis, tsî-sisse, *n* thèse *f*.

they, dzé, *pron* ils; elles; eux.

thick, tsique, *a** épais; (big) gros; –en, *v* épaissir; –et, *n* taillis *m*; –ness, épaisseur *f*.

thief, tsîfe, *n* voleur, -euse *m* & *f*.

thieve, tsîve, *v* voler; (filch) dérober.

thigh, tsaî, *n* cuisse *f*.

thimble, tsimm´-b'l, *n* dé à coudre *m*.

thin, tsinne, *a* mince; maigre; (sparse) clairsemé; *v* amincir; (trees, etc) élaguer; –ness, *n* minceur *f*; maigreur *f*.

thing, tsinng, *n* chose *f*.

think, tsinnque, *v* penser; (believe) croire; – about, (of), penser à, (de); – over, réfléchir.

third, tseurde, *n* & *a** troisième *m* & *f*; (one-third) tiers *m*.

thirst, tseurste, *n* soif *f*; to be –y, *v* avoir soif.

thirteen, tseur´-tîne, *n* & *a* treize *m*; –th, treizième *m* & *f*.

thirtieth, tseur´-ti-its, *n* & *a* trentième *m* & *f*.

thirty, tseur´-ti, *n* & *a* trente *m*.

this, dzice, *pron* ceci; ce; *a* ce; cet; cette.

thistle, tsiss-´'l, *n* chardon *m*.

thong, tsonng, *n* lanière *f*.

thorn, ts oarne, *n* épine *f*; –y, *a* épineux.

thorough*, tsor´-ŏ, *a* entier; parfait; profond; –bred, *n* & *a* pur sang *m*; *a* (dog) de race; –fare, *n* voie *f*; (main) grande artère *f*; no –fare, rue barrée.

those, dzauze, *pron* ceux-là; celles-là; *a* ces; ces ...-là.

thou, dzâ'ou, *pron* tu.

though, dzau, *conj* quoique; bien que.

thought, ts oate, *n* pensée *f*; –ful*, *a* pensif; attentif; –less*, étourdi; inattentif.

thousand, tsâ'ou´-z'nd, *n* & *a* mille *m*; *a* (date) mil.

thousandth, tsâ'ouz´-anndts, *n* & *a* millième *m* & *f*.

thrash, tsräche, *v* battre; (flog) foutter; –ing, *n* raclée *f*; –ing-machine, batteuse *f*.

thread, tsredde, n fil m; v
enfiler; **–bare,** a râpé.

threat, tsrette, n menace f;
–en, v menacer.

threatening*, tsrett´-
ninng, a menaçant.

three, tsrie, n & a trois m;
–fold, a triple.

threshold, tsrèch´-aulde, n
seuil m.

thrift, tsrifte, n économie
f; **–less,** a prodigue.

thrifty, tsrif´-ti, a
économe.

thrill, tsrill, v émouvoir; n
saisissement m.

thrive, tsräïve, v prospérer.

throat, tsraute, n gorge f.

throb, tsrobbe, v vibrer;
(heart) battre.

throes, tsrose, npl douleurs
fpl; fig angoisses fpl.

throne, tsraune, n trône
m.

throng, tsronng, v venir
en foule; n foule f.

throttle, tsrot´-t'l, n larynx
m; mech étrangleur m

through, tsroue, prep par;
à travers; pour cause de;
– out, adv partout; **–
train,** n train direct m.

throw, tsrau, v jeter;
lancer; n coup m.

thrush, tsroche, n grive f.

thrust, tsrosste, v pousser;
(sword) porter un coup
d'épée; n poussée f; coup

d'épée m.

thud, tsodde, n bruit sourd
m.

thumb, tsomme, n pouce
m.

thump, tsommpe, v
frapper du poing; n coup
de poing m.

thunder, tsonn-d'r, v
tonner; n tonnerre m;
–bolt, foudre f; **––storm,**
orage m.

Thursday, tseurz´-dé, n
jeudi m.

thus, dzosse, adv ainsi.

thwart, tsouoarte, v
contrarier; frustrer.

thyme, täïme, n thym m.

tick, tique, v (clock) faire
tic-tac; (check) pointer;
n (cattle) tique f;
(cover) toile à matelas f.

ticket, tik´-ette, n billet
m; (price, etc) étiquette
f; **– office,** guichet m;
season –, carte
d'abonnement f.

tickle, tik´-'l, v
chatouiller.

ticklish, tik´-liche, a
chatouilleux.

tidal, täï´-d'l, a de marée.

tide, täïde, n marée f; **high
–,** marée haute f; **low –,**
marée basse f.

tidings, täï´-inngze, npl
nouvelles fpl.

tidy, täï´-di, a en ordre;

(neat) rangé; v mettre
en ordre.

tie, täï, n (bow) nœud m;
(neck) cravate f; v
ficeler; (a knot) nouer;
(together) attacher;
(surgical) bander.

tier, tire, n rangée f;
gradin m; rang m.

tiger, täï´-gueur, n tigre m.

tight, täïte, a serré;
(tention) tendu; **–en,** v
serrer; (tension) tendre;
–s, n collant m.

tile, täïle, n carreau m;
(roof) tuile f; (slate)
ardoise f; v carreler;
couvrir de ...

till, til, n tiroir caisse m; v
(land) labourer; conj
jusqu'à ce que; prep
jusqu'à.

tiller, till´-eur, n barre du
gouvernail f.

tilt, tilte, v pencher;
incliner.

timber, timm´-b'r, n bois
de construction m.

time, täïme, v contrôler;
(engine) régler; n temps
m; (occasion) fois f;
(hour) heure f; (music)
mesure f; (step) pas m;
–limit, délai m; **–ly,** a &
adv opportun; **–table,** n
horaire m.

timid*, timm´-ide, a
timide.

tin, tinne, n fer blanc m; (pure metal étain m; v étamer; **–box,** n boîte; en fer blanc f; **–foil,** feuille d'étain f; **– ned,** a en boîte, en conserve; **– opener,** n ouvre-boîte m; **–plate,** fer blanc m.

tincture, tinng´-ktioure, n teinture f.

tinge, tinndje, n teinte f; *fig* soupçon m; v teinter.

tingle, tinng´-g´l, v picoter.

tinkle, tinng´-k´l, v tinter; faire tinter; n tintement m.

tinsel, tinn´-s´l, n clinquant m.

tint, tinnte, n teinte f v teinter.

tiny, tâï´-ni, tout petit; minuscule.

tip, tippe, v (give) donner un pourboire; (cart, etc) faire basculer; n pourboire m; (hint) tuyau m; (point) pointe f; **on –toe,** adv sur la pointe des pieds.

tire, tâïeure, v fatiguer; se fatiguer; **– of,** se lasser de; **–some,** a fatigant; *fig* ennuyeux.

tissue, ti´-chiou, n tissu m.

tissue-paper, ti´-chiou-pé´-p´r, n papier de soie m.

tithe, tâïdz, n dîme f.

title, tâï´-t´l, n titre m; **– deed,** titre de propriéte'e m; **–page,** page du titre f.

titter, titt´-´r, v ricaner; n ricanement m.

to, tou, *prep* à; en; vers.

toad, taude, n crapaud m.

toast, tauste, n pain grillé m; toast m; v griller; rôtir.

toast, tauste, n (drink) toast m; v porter un toast à.

tobacco, to-bǎk´-au, n tabac m; **–nist,** marchand de tabac m; **– pouch,** blague à tabac f.

toboggan, tô-bogue´-an, n luge f.

to-day, tou-dé´, adv aujourd'hui.

toddler, tod´-l´r, n tout petit enfant m; toute petite enfante f.

toe, tau, n orteil m, doigt de pied m.

toffee, tof´-i, n caramel m.

together, tou-guèdz´-´r, adv ensemble.

toil, toa´ile, v peiner; n labeur m; **–er,** travailleur m

toilet, toa´il´-ette, n toilette f; (W.C.) lavabo m; **– paper,** papier hygiénique m.

token, tau´-k´n, n marque

f, symbole m.

tolerable, tol´-eur-a-b´l, a tolérable.

tolerance, tol´-eur´-nce, n tolérance f.

tolerant*, tol´-eur-´nt, a tolérant.

tolerate, tol´-eur-éte, v tolérer.

toll, taule, n (knell) glas m; (motorway) péage m; v sonner le glas.

tomato, tŏ-mâ´-tau, n tomate f.

tomb, toum, n tombeau m; **–stone,** pierre tombale f.

to-morrow, tou-morr´-au, adv demain.

tomtit, tomme´-tite, n mésange f.

ton, tonne, n tonne f; **–nage,** tonnage m.

tone, taune, n ton m; accent m; (voice) timbre m.

tongs, tonngze, npl pincettes fpl.

tongue, tonng n langue f.

tonic, tonn´-ique, n & a tonique m; a fortifiant.

to-night, tou-nâîte´, adv cette nuit; ce soir.

tonsil, tonn´-s´l, n amygdale f.

tonsillitis, tonn-sil-âï´-tice, n amygdalite f.

too, toue, adv trop; (also) aussi, **–much,** trop.

tool, toule, n outil m.

tooth, touts, n dent f;
–**ache,** mal de dents m;
–**brush,** brosse à dents f;
–**paste,** pâte dentifrice f;
–**pick,** cure-dents m.

top, toppe, n (upper part)
haut m; (mountain)
sommet m; (of tree)
cime f; (spinning)
toupie f; –**hat,** chapeau
haut de forme m; –**less,**
a aux seins nus mpl on
–, adv par dessus; au-
dessus.

topic, top´-ique, n sujet m.

topple, topp´-'l, – **over,** v
culbuter; (car) verser.

topsy-turvy, topp´-ci-
teur´-vi, adv sens dessus
dessous.

torch, tôrtche, n torche f;
(flaming) flambeau m;
(electric) lampe de
poche f.

torment, tôr´-mennte, n
tourment m; v
tourmenter.

torpedo, tôr-pî´-dau, n
torpille f.

torpedo-boat, tôr-pî´-dau-
baute, n torpilleur m.

torpid, tôr´-pidde, a
engourdi; inerte.

torpor, tôr´-peur, n torpeur
f.

torrent, tôr´-ennte, n
torrent m.

torrid, tôr´-ride, a torride.

tortoise, tôr´-teuce, n
tortue f; –**shell,** écaille
f.

torture, tôr´-tioure, v
torturer; n torture f.

toss, tosse, v lancer en
l'air; (coin) tirer à pile
ou face; – **about,**
s'agiter; naut ballotter.

total, tau´-t'l, n total m; a
total, complet; v
totaliser; –**isator,** n
totalisateur m.

totter, tott´-'r, v
chanceler; –**ing,** a
chancelant.

touch, totche, n contact
m; (talent) doigté m;
(sense) toucher m; v
toucher.

touching, totch´-inng, a
(emotion) touchant.

tough, toffe, a dur;
résistant.

tour, toueur, n tour m;
excursion f; –**nament,** n
tournoi m.

tourist, toueur-iste, n
touriste m & f; –**office,**
syndicat d'initiative m.

tout, tâ´oute, v racoler; n
racoleur m.

tow, tau, v (haul)
remorquer; n (flax)
étoupe f; –**age,**
remorquage m (canal)
halage m; –**ing-path,**

chemin de halage m;
–**line,** corde de
remorque f.

towards, tŏ-ouôrdze´, prep
envers; (direction) vers.

towel, tâ´ou-elle, n
serviette de toilette f.

tower, tâ´ou-eur, n tour f.

town, tâ´oune, n ville f; –
centre, centre de la ville
m; centre-ville m; –**hall,**
hôtel de ville m.

toy, toa´i, n jouet m; v
jouer.

trace, tréce, n trace f;
(trail) piste f; (harness)
trait m; v suivre
la piste; (draw) calquer;
(origin) rechercher.

tracing, tréce´-inng, n
calque m; –**paper,**
papier à calquer m.

track, trăque, n trace f;
(race) piste f; (railway)
voie f; v suivre la piste.

tract, trăkt, n étendue f;
(religious) opuscule m.

tractor, trâk´-t'r, n
tracteur m.

traction, trăk-ch'n, n
traction f.

tractor, trăk´-t'r, n
tracteur m.

trade, tréde, v faire le
commerce; n commerce
m; (craft) métier m;
–**mark,** marque de
fabrique f; –**sman,**

fournisseur m; –union, syndicat (ouvrier) m.

tradition, trä-dich´-eunn, n tradition f.

traditional*, trä-dich´-eunn-al, a traditionnel.

traffic, träf´-ique, n circulation f; (trade) trafic m ; – jam, embouteillage m; – lights, npl feux (de circulation) mpl.

tragedian, tra-djī´-di-anne, n tragédien m.

tragedy, trädj´-i-di, n tragédie f.

tragic, trädj´-ique, a tragique.

trail, tréle, v suivre à la piste; (drag) traîner; n piste f; route f; –er, (van) remorque f.

train, tréne, n train m; (dress) traîne f; (retinue) suite f; v instruire; éduquer; (sport; mil) entraîner; (animals) dresser.

trainers, tréne´-r'z, n chaussures de sport fpl.

training, tré´-ninng, n éducation f; entraînement m.

traitor, tré´-t'r, n traître m.

tram, trämme, n tramway m.

tramp, trämmpe, n clochard, -e m & f; v

aller à pied.

trample, trämm´-p'l, v piétiner.

trance, trânnce, n extase f; med catalepsie f.

tranquil, träng´-kouill, a tranquille; calme.

tranquilizer, träng´-. kouill-î-z'r, n tranquillisant m.

transact, tränn-sâcte´, v traiter; arranger; faire.

transaction, tränn-sâc´-ch'n, n affaire f.

transcribe, tränn-scrãïbe´, v transcrire.

transfer, trännss-feur´, v transférer; transporter; n transport m; billet de correspondance m; (shares) transfert m.

transform, trännss-fôrme´, v transformer.

transgress, trännss-grèsse´, v transgresser.

tranship, tränn-chippe´, v transborder.

transit, tränn´-citte, n transit m.

translate, trännss-léte´, v traduire.

translation, trännss-lé´-ch'n, n traduction f.

translator, trännss-lé´-t'r, n traducteur, -trice m & f.

transmit, trännss-mitte´, v transmettre.

transparent, trännss-pä´-rennte, a transparent.

transpire, trännss-pâïre´, v transpirer.

transport, trännss-pôrte´, v transporter; n transport. m; naut transport m.

transpose, trännss-pause´, v transposer.

trap, träppe, n piège m; v prendre au piège.

trash, träche, n camelote f; –y, a camelote.

travel, träv´-'l, v voyager; – agent, n agent de voyages m; – sickness, mal de la route m.

traveller, n voyageur, -euse m & f; –'s cheque, chèque de voyage m.

traverse, träv´-eurse, v traverser.

trawler, troa´-leur, n chalutier m.

tray, tré, n plateau m; ash –, cendrier m.

treacherous*, trett´-cheur-euce, a tríatre; perfide.

treachery, trett´-cheur-i, n traîtrise f; perfidie f.

treacle, trî´-c'l, n mélasse f.

tread, tredde, n pas m; (stair) marche f; v poser le pied; (accidental) marcher sur.

treason, trî´-z'n, *n* trahison *f.*

treasure, tréj´-*eur*, *n* trésor *m*; *v* garder précieusement.

treasurer, tréj´-*eur-eur*, *n* trésorier *m.*

treasury, tréj´-*eur*-i, *n* Trésor *m.*

treat, trîte, *n* (outing) partie de plaisir *f*; *v* traiter; *fig* régaler; *med* soigner; **–ment,** *n* traitemet *m.*

treatise, trî´-tize, *n* traité *m.*

treaty, trî´-ti, *n* traité *m.*

treble, tréb´-'l, *v* tripler; *n* & *a* triple *m.*

tree, trî, *n* arbre *m.*

trellis, trell´-ice, *n* treillis *m.*

tremble, tremm´-b'l, *v* trembler.

tremendous*, tri-menn´-deuce, *a* prodigieux.

tremor, tremm´-'r, *n* tremblement *m.*

tremulous*, tremm´-iou-leuce, *a* craintif.

trench, trenntche, *n* fossé *m*; *mil* tranchée *f.*

trend, trennde, *n* tendance *f.*

trespass, tress´-pass, *v* empiéter sur.

trespasser, tress´-pass-'r, *n* intrus *m.*

trestle, tress´-'l, *n* tréteau *m.*

trial, trâï´-*al*, *n* épreuve *f*, essai *m*; (law) procès *m.*

triangle, trâï´-ănng-g'l, *n* traingle *m.*

triangular, trâï-ănng´-guiou-lar, *a* triangulaire.

tribe, trâïbe, *n* tribu *f.*

tribunal, trâï-bioue´-n'l, *n* tribunal *m.*

tributary, trib´-iou-ta-ri, *n* affluent *m.*

tribute, trib´-ioute, *n* tribut *m.*

trick, trique, *n* (fraud) ruse *f*; (dexterity) tour *m*; (cards) levée *f*; (joke) farce *f*; *v* duper; **–ery,** *n* duperie *f*; **–ster,** fourbe *m.*

trickle, trique´-'l, *v* dégoutter; (flow) couler.

trifle, trâï-f'l, *v* jouer; badiner; *n* bagatelle *f.*

trifling, trâï´-flinng, *a* insignifiant.

trigger, trigg´-'r, *n* détente *f.*

trill, trile, *v* triller; *n* trille *m.*

trim, trime, *v* (hat, dress) garnir; (hair) couper; égaliser; *a* soigné; **–ming,** *n* garniture *f.*

trinity, trinn´-i-ti, *n* trinité *f.*

trinket, trinng´-kitte, *n* colifichet *m*; breloque *f.*

trio, trî´-au, *n* trio *m.*

trip, trippe, *n* excursion *f*; *v* (stumble) trébucher; **–per,** *n* excursionniste *m* & *f*; **– up,** *v* donner un croc de jambe.

tripe, trâïpe, *n* tripes *fpl.*

triple, tripp´-'l, *a* triple.

triplets, tripp´-lètse, *npl* trois jumeaux *mpl.*

tripod, trâï´-pode, *n* trépied *m.*

triumph, trâï´-eummf, *n* triomphe *m*; *v* triompher.

trivial, triv´-i-al, *a* trivial; insignifiant.

trolley, troll´-i, *n* chariot *m*; (dinner)serveuse *f.*

trombone, tromm´-bône, *n* trombone *m.*

troop, troupe, *n* troupe *f*; **–ship,** transport *m.*

trooper, troup´-*eur*, *n* cavalier *m.*

trophy, trau´-fi, *n* trophée *m.*

tropical, tropp´-i-c'l, *a* tropical.

tropics, tropp´-ikse, *npl* tropiques *mpl.*

trot, trotte, *v* trotter; *n* trot *m*; **–ter,** trotteur *m*; (pig) pied de cochon *m.*

trouble, trobb´-'l, *v* chagriner; (disturb) déranger; *n* (cares)

soucis *mpl*;
(inconvenience)
dérangement *m*;
(disturbance) trouble *m*;
(difficulty) difficulté *f*;
–some, *a* ennuyeux;
difficile.

trough, troffe, *n* pétrin *m*;
(cattle, etc) abreuvoir
m.

trousers, trâ'ou'-zeurce,
npl pantalon *m*.

trout, trâ'oute, *n* truite *f*.

trowel, trâ'ou''l, *n*
(mason's) truelle *f*;
(garden) déplantoir *m*.

truant, troue'-annte, **play
–**, *v* faire l'école
buissonnière.

truce, trouce, *n* trève *f*.

truck, troque, *n* wagon *m*;
(hand) voiture à bras *f*.

truculent*, trok'-iou-
lennte, *a* brutal; féroce.

trudge, trodje, *v* marcher
péniblement.

true, troue, *a* vrai;
(faithful) fidèle.

truffle, troff'-'l, *n* truffe *f*.

truism, troue'-izme, *n*
truisme *m*.

trump, trommpe, *n* atout
m; *v* couper.

trumpet, trommp'-itte, *n*
trompette *f*.

truncheon, tronn'-ch'n, *n*
bâton *m*.

trunk, tronng-k, *n* (tree;

body) tronc *m*;
(elephant) trompe *f*;
(travelling) malle *f*;
–call, appel interurbain
m.

truss, trosse, *n* (hay, etc)
botte *f*; (surgical)
bandage herniaire *m*; *v*
(poultry) trousser.

trust, trosste, *n* confiance
f; (combine) trust *m*; *v*
se fier à; (rely) compter
sur.

trustee, tross-tî', *n*
dépositaire *m*; (public)
curateur *m*;
(liquidation) syndic de
faillite *m*.

trustworthy, trosst'-
oueurdz-i, *a* digne de
confiance.

truth, trouts, *n* vérité *f*;
–ful*, *a* véridique.

try, trâï, *v* essayer; (taste)
goûter; (law) juger;
–ing, *a* pénible; **–on**, *v*
essayer.

T-shirt, tî'-cheurte, *n* tee-
shirt *m*.

tub, tobbe, *n* baquet *m*;
(bath) tub *m*.

tube, tioube, *n* tube *m*;
(railway) métro *m*.

tuck, toque, *n* pli *m*; *v*
faire des plis; **–in**, (rug,
etc) border;
– up, retrousser.

Tuesday, tiouze'-dé, *n*

mardi *m*.

tuft, tofte, *n* (grass) touffe
f; (hair) houppe *f*.

tug, togue, *v* tirer; (boat)
remorquer.

tug-boat, togue'-baute, *n*
remorqueur *m*.

tuition, tiou-i'-ch'n, *n*
enseignement *m*.

tulip, tioue'-lippe, *n* tulipe
f.

tumble, tomm'-b'l, *v* (fall)
dégringoler.

tumbler, tomm'-bl'r, *n*
(glass) grand verre *m*.

tumour, tioue'-m'r, *n*
tumeur *f*.

tumult, tioue'-meulte, *n*
tumulte *m*; (riot)
émeute *f*.

tuna, tioue'-nă, *n* thon *m*.

tune, tioune, *n* air *m*; *v*
accorder.

tuneful, tioune'-foull, *a*
mélodieux.

tunic, tioue'-nique, *n*
tunique *f*.

tuning-fork, tioue'-ninng
forque, *n* diapason *m*.

tunnel, tonn'-'l, *n* tunnel
m; *v* percer un tunnel.

tunny, tonn'-i, *n* thon *m*.

turbine, teur'-bâine, *n*
turbine *f*.

turbot, teur'-beute, *n*
turbot *m*.

turbulence, teur'-biou-
l'nce, *n* turbulence *m*.

turbulent, teur´-biou-
lennte, *a* turbulent.

tureen, tiou-rîne´, *n*
soupière; (sauce)
saucière *f*.

turf, teurfe, *n* (grass) gazon
m; (peat) tourbe *f*.

turkey, teur´-ki, *n* dinde *f*;
dindon *m*.

turkish, teur´-quiche, *a*
turc.

turmoil, teur´-moa'ile, *n*
tumulte *m*; désordre *m*.

turn, teurne, *n* tour *m*; *v*
tourner; – **about,** se
tourner; – **aside,**
détourner; – **back,**
revenir sur ses pas; **–er,** *n*
(artisan) tourneur *m*;
–ing, (corner) tournant
m; **–ing-point,** point
décisif *m*; – **into,** *v* se
changer en; – **off,**
fermer; – **on,** ouvrir; –
out, (expel) renvoyer;
(light) éteindre; – **over,**
se retourner; *n com*
chiffre d'affaires *m*;
–stile, tourniquet *m*; –
to, *v* recourir à.

turnip, teur´-nipe, *n* navet
m.

turpentine, teur´-penn-
tâïne, *n* térébenthine *f*.

turret, teur´-ette, *n*
tourelle *f*.

turtle, teur´-t'l, *n* tortue de
mer *f*; **turn –,** *v* chavirer;

–dove, *n* tourterelle *f*.

tusk, tossque, *n* (long)
défense *f*; (short) croc *m*.

tussle, toss´-'l, *v* lutter; *n*
bagarre *f*.

tutor, tioue´-t'r, *n*
précepteur *m*, professeur
m; *v* instruire.

TV, tî-vi, *n abbr* télé *f*.

twang, touain-ng, *n*
nasillement *m*; (sound)
son *m*.

tweezers, touî´-zeurze, *npl*
pinces *fpl*.

twelfth, tou'elfts, *n* & *a*
douzième *m* & *f*.

twelve, tou'elve, *n* & *a*
douze *f*.

twentieth, tou'enn´-ti-its,
n & *a* vingtième *m* & *f*.

twenty, tou'enn´-ti, *n* & *a*
vingt *m*.

twice, tou'âïce, *adv* deux
fois.

twig, tou'igue, *n* brindille
f.

twilight, tou'âï´-lâïte, *n*
crépuscule *m*.

twill, tou'ile, *n* croisé *m*.

twin, tou'inne, *n* & *a*
jumeau *m*, jumelle *f*; –
bedded room, tou'inne-
bedd-id-roume, *n*
chambre à deux lits *f*.

twine, tou'âïne, *n*
cordonnet *m*; *v*
s'enrouler.

twinge, tou'inndje, *n*

élancement *m*; *fig*
tourment *m*.

twinkle, tou'inng´-k'l, *v*
scintiller; (eyes) cligner.

twirl, tou'eurle, *v*
tournoyer; tourner; *n*
tour *m*.

twist, tou'iste, *v* tordre;
tourner; contourner.

twitch, tou'itche, *v* se
crisper; *n* crispation *f*; tic
m.

twitter, tou'itt´-'r, *v*
gazouiller.

two, toue, *n* & *a* deux *m*;
–fold, *a* double.

type, tâïpe, *n* type *m*;
(print) caractère *m*; *v*
taper à la machine; **–
writer,** *n* machine à
écrire *f*.

typhoid, tâï´-fo'ide, *n*
fièvre typhoïde *f*.

typhoon, tâï-foune´, *n*
typhon *m*.

typical*, tip´-i-c'l, *a*
typique.

typist, tâïp´-iste, *n*
dactylographe *m* & *f*.

typography, ti-pogue´-ra-
fi, *n* typographie *f*.

tyrannical*, ti-rănn´-i-c'l,
a tyrannique.

tyrannize, ti´-ra-nâïze, *v*
tyranniser.

tyrant, tâï´-r'nt, *n* tyran *m*.

tyre, tâïre, *n* bande *f*;
(pneumatic) pneu *m*.

ubiquitous, ioue-bik´-oui-
teuce, a omniprésent.

udder, odd´-'r, *n* pis m.

ugliness, ogg´-li-nesse, *n*
laideur f.

ugly, ogg´-li, *a* laid; vilain.

ulcer, ol´-ceur, *n* ulcère m;
–ate, *v* ulcérer.

ulterior, ol-ti´-ri-eur, *a*
ultérieur.

ultimate*, ol´-ti-méte, *a*
définitif; final.

ultimatum, ol-ti-mé´-
tomm, *n* ultimatum m.

umbrella, omm-brell´-a, *n*
parapluie m; – **stand,**
porte-parapluies m.

umpire, omm´-pâïre, *n*
arbitre m; *v* arbitrer.

unabashed, onn-a-bâshte´,
a sans honte.

unabated, onn-a-bé´-
tedde, *a* continu;

soutenu.

unable, onn-é´-b'l, **to be**
–, *v* être incapable de; ne
pas pouvoir.

unacceptable, onn-ăx-ep´-
ta-b'l, *a* inacceptable.

unaccountable, onn-a-
câ'ounn´-ta-b'l, *a*
inexplicable.

unacquainted, onn-a-
couénn´-tedde, *a*
(person) étranger à;
(subject) être ignorant
de.

unaffected*, onn-a-
fèque´-tedde, *a* naturel;
(unmoved) impassible.

unaided, onn-é´-dedde, *a*
sans aide.

unalterable, onn-oal´-
teur-a-b'l, *a* immuable.

unaltered, onn-oal´-
teurde, *a* pas changé.

unanimous*, ioue-nănn´-
i-*meuce, a* unanime.

unapproachable, onn-a-
prautch´-a-b'l, *a*
inabordable;
inaccessible.

unarmed, onn´ârmde´, *a*
sans armes.

unassailable, onn-a-cél´-
a-b'l, *a* inattaquable.

unassuming, onn-a-
sioue´-minng, *a*
modeste.

unattainable, onn-a-tén´-
a-b'l, *a* inaccessible.

unavoidable, onn-a-vô'ï´-
da-b'l, *a* inévitable.

unaware, onn-a-ouère´, *a*
ignorant.

unawares, onn-a-ouèrze´,
adv à l'improviste.

unbalanced, onn-băl´-
'nsste, *a* déséquilibré.

unbearable, onn-bèr´-a-
b'l, *a* insupportable.

unbelievable, onn-bî-
lîve´-a-b'l, *a* incroyable.

unbending, onn-benn´-
dinng, *a* inflexible.

unbiassed, onn-bâï´-asste,
a impartial.

unbleached, onn-
blîtchte´, *a* écru.

unblemished, onn-blèm´-
ichte, *a* sans tache.

unbounded, onn-
bâ'ounn´-dedde, *a*
illimité.

unbreakable, onn-bréque´-*a*-b'l, *a* incassable.

unburden, onn-beur´-d'n, *v* décharger.

unbutton, onn-bot´-'n, *v* déboutonner.

uncalled for, onn-coalde´ fôr, *a* déplacé.

uncanny, onn-cănn´-i, *a* surnaturel; étrange.

uncared for, onn-cairde´ fôr, *a* négligé.

unceasing, onn-sî´-cinng, *a* incessant.

uncertain*, onn-seur´-tinne, *a* incertain.

unchangeable, onn-tchéne´-dja-b'l, *a* invariable.

unclaimed, onn-clémde´, *a* non réclamé.

uncle, onn´-k'l, *n* oncle *m.*

unclean, onn-clîne´, *a* malpropre; impur.

uncomfortable, onn-comm´-feur-ta-b'l, *a* incommode; (not at ease) mal à l'aise.

uncommon, onn-comm´-'n, *a* peu commun; rare.

unconcern, onn-cŏnn-seurne´, *n* indifférence *f.*

unconditional*, onn-cŏnn-di´-ch'n-al, *a* sans condition.

unconscious*, onn-conn´-cheuce, *a* sans connaissance; *fig* inconscient.

uncontrollable, onn-cŏnn-traul´-a-b'l, *a* incontrôlable.

uncork, onn-corque´, *v* déboucher.

uncouth*, onn-coûts, *a* (manners) grossier.

uncover, onn-cov´-*eur*, *v* découvrir.

uncultivated, onn-col´-ti-vé-tedde, *a* inculte.

undaunted, onn-doann´-tedde, *a* intrépide.

undeceive, onn-di-cîve´, *v* détromper.

undecided, onn-di-sâï´-dedde, *a* indécis.

undelivered, onn-di-liv´-'rde, *a* non livré.

undeniable, onn-di-nâï´-a-b'l, *a* incontestable.

under, onn´-d'r, *prep* sous; au-dessous de. *adv* dessous; – **age,** *a* mineur; –**done,** *a* peu cuit; (beef) saignant; –**estimate,** *v* sousestimer; –**fed,** *a* mal nourri; –**go,** *v* endurer; –**ground,** *a* souterrain; *n* (railway) métro *m*; –**hand,** *a* sous main; –**line,** *v* souligner; –**mine,** miner; –**neath,** *adv* au-dessous; –**rate,** *v* estimer trop bas; –**sell,** vendre à plus bas prix;

–**signed,** *n* & *a* soussigné, -ée *m* & *f*; –**stand,** *v* comprendre; –**standing,** *n* entente *f*; compréhension *f*; –**study,** doublure *f*; –**take,** *v* entreprendre; –**taker,** *n* entrepreneur de pompes funèbres *m*; –**taking,** entreprise *f*; engagement *m*; –**tone,** à voix basse; –**wear,** (men) vêtements de dessous *mpl*; (ladies) dessous *mpl*; –**writer,** assureur *m.*

undeserved, onn-di-zeurvde´, *a* immérité.

undesirable, onn-di-zâï´-ra-b'l, *a* indésirable.

undignified, onn-dig´-ni-fâïde, *a* sans dignité.

undismayed, onn-diss-méde´, *a* sans peur.

undo, onn-doue´, *v* défaire; (untie) délier.

undoing, onn-dou´-inng, *n* (downfall) déchéance *f.*

undoubted*, onn-dâ´outt´-edde, *a* indubitable.

undress, onn-dresse´, *v* déshabiller; se déshabiller.

undulating, onn´-diou-lé-ting, *a* ondulé.

unduly, onn-dioue´-li, *adv*

indûment; à l'excès.

unearned, onn-eurnde´, *a* non gagné; immérité.

unearthly, onn-eurts´-li, *a* surnaturel.

uneasy, onn-î´-zi, *a* inquiet; mal à l'aise.

uneducated, onn-éd´iou-qué-tedde, *a* sans éducation.

unemployed, onn-emm-ploa´ide´, *a* sans travail; *n* les chômeurs *mpl.*

unemployment, onn-emm-ploa´i´-m'nt, *n* chômage *m.*

unequal*, onn-î´-coual, *a* inégal; –led, sans égal.

uneven*, onn-î´-v'n, *a* irrégulier; rugueux; (number) impair.

unexpected*, onn-ex-pec´-tedde, *a* inattendu.

unfailing, onn-fél´-inng, *a* infaillible.

unfair*, onn-fère´, *a* injuste.

unfaithful, onn-féts´-foull, *a* infidèle.

unfasten, onn-fâs´-s'n, *v* défaire; ouvrir.

unfavourable, onn-fé´-veur-a-b'l, *a* défavorable.

unfeeling*, onn-fî´-linng, *a* insensible.

unfit, onn-fite´, *a* impropre à.

unflagging, onn-flâgue´-

inng, *a* soutenu.

unflinching, onn-flinntch´-inng, *a* ferme; résolu.

unfold, onn-faulde´, *v* déplier; (reveal) dévoiler.

unforeseen, onn-fore-cîne´, *a* imprévu.

unfortunate*, onn-fôr´-tiou-néte, *a* malheureux.

unfounded, onn-fâ'ounn´-dedde, *a* sans fondement.

unfriendly, onn-frennde´-li, *a* peu amical; hostile.

unfulfilled, onn-foull-fillde´, *a* inaccompli.

unfurl, onn-feurle´, *v* déployer.

unfurnished, onn-feur´-nichte, *a* non meublé.

ungrateful, onn-gréte´-foull, *a* ingrat.

unguarded, onn-gâre´-dedde, *a fig* inconsidéré.

unhappy, onn-hăpp´-i, *a* malheureux.

unhealthy, onn-hêltz´-i, *a* malsain; (sick) maladif.

unheard, onn-heurde´, –of, *a* inconnu; inouï.

unheeded, onn-hî´-dedde, *a* inaperçu.

unhinge, onn-hinndje´, *v* démonter; déranger.

unhurt, onn-heurte´, *a* sain et sauf.

uniform*, ioue´-ni-fôrme, *n* & *a* uniforme *m.*

uniformity, ioue-ni-fôr´-mi-ti, *n* uniformité *f.*

unimaginable, onn-i-mâdj´-i-na-b'l, *a* inimaginable.

unimpaired, onn-imm-pairde´, *a* intact.

unimportant, onn-imm-por´-t'nt, *a* sans importance.

uninhabitable, onn-inn-hăb´-i-ta-b'l, *a* inhabitable.

uninhabited, onn-inn-hăb´-i-tedde, *a* inhabité.

unintelligible, onn-inn-tel´-i-dji-b'l, *a* inintelligible.

unintentional*, onn-inn-tenn´-ch'n-al, *a* involontaire.

uninviting, onn-inn-vâï´-tinng, *a* peu attrayant.

union, ioue´-ni-eune, *n* union *f;* trade –, syndicat (ouvrier) *m.*

unique*, iou-nique´, *a* unique.

unit, ioue´-nitte, *n* unité *f.*

unite, iou-nâïte´, *v* unir; s'unir.

unity, ioue´-ni-ti, *n* unité *f;* concorde *f.*

universal*, iou-ni-veur´-s'l, *a* universel.

universe, ioue´-ni-veurce,

491

n univers *m*.

university, iou-ni-veur´-ci-ti, *n* université *f*.

unjust*, onn-djosste´, *a* injuste.

unkind*, onn-kaïnnde´, *a* pas gentil; peu aimable.

unknown, onn-naune´, *a* inconnu.

unlawful*, onn-loa´-foull, *a* illégal; illicite.

unleaded, onn-lèdd´-id, *a* sans plomb (petrol, fuel).

unless, onn-lesse´, *conj* à moins que; à moins de.

unlike, onn-lâïque´, *a* différent; **–ly,** improbable.

unlimited, onn-limm´-i-tedde, *a* illimité.

unload, onn-laude´, *v* décharger.

unlock, onn-loque´, *v* ouvrir; *fig* révéler.

unlucky, onn-loque´-i, *a* malheureux; (ill-omened) de mauvais augure; qui porte malheur.

unmanageable, onn-männ´-idj-*a*-b'l, *a* ingouvernable; intraitable.

unmannerly, onn-männ´-'r-li, *a* grossie; mal élevé.

unmarried, onn-mär´-idde, *a* non marié;

célibataire.

unmerciful*, onn-meur´-ci-foull, *a* impitoyable.

unmistakable, onn-mice-téque´-*a*-b'l, *a* évident.

unmoved, onn-mouvde´, *a* impassible.

unnatural, onn-nät´-tiou-r'l, *a* (hard) dénaturé.

unnecessary, onn-nèss´-ess-*a*-ri, *a* inutile.

unnerve, onn-neurve´, *v* effrayer; démonter.

unnoticed, onn-nau´-tisste, *a* inaperçu.

unoccupied, onn-ok´-kiou-pâïde, *a* inoccupé; libre.

unopposed, onn-ŏp-auzde´, *a* sans opposition.

unpack, onn-pâque´, *v* défaire; (case) déballer.

unparalleled, onn-pă´-ral-lelde, *a* sans pareil.

unpardonable, onn-păr´-donn-*a*-b'l, *a* impardonnable.

unpleasant*, onn-plè´-zannte, *a* déplaisant.

unpopular, onn-pop´-iou-lar, *a* impopulaire.

unprecedented, onn-pré´-sid-enn-tedde, *a* sans précédent.

unprepared, onn-pri-pérde´, *a* à l'improviste.

unproductive, onn-pro-

deuc´-tive, *a* improductif.

unprofitable, onn-prof´-i-ta-b'l, *a* peu profitable.

unprotected, onn-pro-tec´-tedde, *a* sans protection; sans défense.

unprovided, onn-prŏ-vâï´-dedde, *a* dépourvu de.

unpunctual, onn-ponngk´-tiou-al, *a* inexact.

unqualified, onn-couoll´-i-fâïde, *a* non qualifié; incapable.

unquestionable, onn-couess´-tieunn-a-b'l, *a* incontestable.

unravel, onn-răv´-'l, *v* démêler.

unreadable, onn-rî´-da-b'l, *a* illisible.

unreasonable, onn-rî´-z'n-a-b'l, *a* déraisonnable.

unrelenting, onn-ri-lenn´-tinng, *a* implacable.

unreliable, onn-ri-lâï´-a-b'l, *a* sur lequel on ne peut pas compter.

unreserved, onn-ri-zeurvde´, *a* non réservé; libre; sans réserve.

unrest, onn-reste´, *n* inquiétude *f*; agitation *f*.

unrestrained, onn-ri-strénnde, *a* sans contrainte; (unruly) désordonné.

unrestricted, onn-ri-stric´-tedde, *a* sans restriction.

unripe, onn-râïpe´, *a* pas mûr; vert.

unroll, onn-raule´, *v* dérouler.

unruly, onn-roue´-li, *a* indiscipliné.

unsafe, onn-séfe´, *a* peu sûr; dangereux.

unsatisfactory, onn-sătt-iss-făque´-t'ri, *a* peu satisfaisant.

unscrew, onn-scroue´, *v* dévisser.

unscrupulous, onn-scroue´-piou-*leuce*, *a* sans scrupule.

unseasonable, onn-sî´-z'n-a-b'l, *a* hors de saison.

unseemly, onn-sîme´-li, *a* inconvenant.

unseen, onn-sîne´, *a* inaperçu.

unselfish, onn-self´-iche, *a* désintéressé.

unsettled, onn-sett´-'lde, *a* incertain; troublé; (accounts) en suspens.

unshaken, onn-chéque´-'n, *a* inébranlable.

unshrinkable, onn-chrinng´-ka-b'l, *a* irrétrécissable.

unsightly, onn-sâïte´-li, *a* déplaisant; laid.

unskilled, onn-skillde, *a* inexpérimenté.

unsociable, onn-sau´-cha-b'l, *a* insociable.

unsold, onn-saulde´, *a* invendu.

unsolicited, onn´sŏ-liss´-itedde, *a* spontané.

unsound, onn-sâ'ounnde´, *a* défectueux; (mind) dément.

unsparing*, onn-spére´-inng, *a* prodigue; impitoyable.

unsteady, onn-stedd´-i, *a* instable.

unsuccessful, onn-*seuk*-cess´-foull, *a* (person) sans succès; (undertaking) infructueux.

unsuitable, onn-sioue´-ta-b'l, *a* déplacé; impropre.

unsupported, onn-seupp-paur´-tedde, *a* sans appui.

unsurpassed, onn-seur-pâsse´, *a* sans égal.

unsuspecting, onn-seuss-pèque´-tinng, *a* confiant.

untamed, onn-témmde´, *a* indompté; sauvage.

untarnished, onn-târe´-nichte, *a* sans tache.

untenable, onn-tenn´-a-b'l, *a* insoutenable.

untidy, onn-tâï´-di, *a* en désordre; (person) négligé.

untie, onn-tâï´, *v* délier; défaire; dénouer.

until, onn-til´, *prep* jusqu'à; jusque. *conj* jusqu'à ce que.

untold, onn-taulde´, *a* non raconté; passé sous silence; *fig* inouï.

untouched, onn-tochte´, *a* intact; non ému.

untranslatable, onn-trănnss-lé´-*ta*-b'l, *a* intraduisible.

untried, onn-trâïde´, *a* non essayé.

untrodden, onn-trode´-'n, *a* non frayé; vierge.

untrue, onn-troue´, *a* faux; pas vrai.

untrustworthy, onn-trosst´-oueurdz-i, *a* indigne de confiance.

untruth, onn-trouts´, *n* mensonge *m*.

untwist, onn-tou'isste´, *v* détordre.

unusual*, onn-ioue´-joue*ul*, *a* rare; peu commun.

unvaried, onn-vair´-idde, *a* uniforme; constant.

unveil, onn-vaile´, *v* dévoiler; inaugurer.

unwarrantable, onn-ouor´-*ann*-ta-b'l, *a* injustifiable; inexcusable.

unwary, onn-ouè´-ri, *a*

imprudent.

unwelcome, onn-ouel´-
k'm, *a* importun;
indésirable.

unwell, onn-ouell´, *a*
indisposé; souffrant.

unwholesome, onn-
haule´-somme, *a*
malsain; insalubre.

unwieldy, onn-ouîld´-i, *a*
lourd; pesant.

unwilling, onn-ouil´-inng,
a de mauvaise volonté.

unwind, onn-ouaînnde´, *v*
dérouler.

unwise, onn-ouâîze´, *a*
peu sage; imprudent.

unwittingly, onn-ouitt´-
inng-li, *adv* sans y
penser.

unworthy, onn-oueurdz´-i,
a indigne.

unwrap, onn-răppe´, *v*
défaire.

unwritten, onn-ritt´-'n, *a*
non écrit; **–laws** *n* droit
coutumier *m*.

unyielding, onn-yîld´-
inng, *a* rigide; inflexible.

up, op, *adv* en haut; en
l'air; (stand up) debout;
(prices) en hausse;
(risen) levé; **–and
down,** de haut en bas; **–
here,** ici; **–side down,**
sens dessus dessous; à
l'envers; **–there,** là-
haut; **–to,** *prep* jusqu'à.

upbraid, op-bréde´, *v*
reprocher.

upheaval, op-hî´-v'l, *n*
(geological)
soulèvement *m*.

uphill, op´-hill, *a* en
montant; *fig* ardu.

uphold, op-haulde´, *v*
soutenir; maintenir.

upholsterer, op-haule´-
steur-'r, *n* tapissier *m*.

upkeep, op´-kîpe, *n*
entretien *m*; soutien *m*.

upland, op´-lännde, *n* pays
élevé *m*.

uplift, op-lifte´, *v* élever.

upon, op-onne´, *prep* sur.

upper, op´-'r, *a* supérieur;
de dessus; **–hand,** *n*
avantage *m*, dessus *m*;
–most, *a* dominant.

upright, op´-râîte, *a* droit;
honorable; (erect)
debout.

uprising, op-râî´-zinng, *n*
soulèvement *m*.

uproar, op´-raure, *n*
tumulte *m*; vacarme *m*.

uproot, op-route´, *v*
déraciner.

upset, op-cette´, *v*
renverser; **to be –,** être
bouleversé.

upstairs, op´-stèrze, *adv* en
haut; **to go –,** *v* aller en
haut.

upstart, op´-stärte, *n*
parvenu, -e *m* & *f*,

nouveau riche *m*.

upwards, op´-oueurdse,
adv en haut; en
montant.

urban, eur´-b'n, *a* urbain.

urchin, eur´-tchinne, *n*
(child) gamin, -e *m* & *f*.

urge, eurdje, *n* désir
ardent *m*; *v* pousser.

urgency, eur´-djenn-ci, *n*
urgence *f*.

urgent, eur´-djennte, *a*
urgent; pressant.

urinate, iou´-ri-néte, *v*
uriner.

urine, iou´-râîne, *n* urine
f.

urn, eurne, *n* urne *f*.

us, osse, *pron* nous.

use, iouze, *v* user de; se
servir de; employer; *n*
usage *m*; utilité *f*; **–ful*,**
a utile; **–less*,** inutile;
–up, *v* consommer.

usher, och´-'r, *n* huissier
m; **– in,** *v* annoncer.

usherette, och-'orette´, *n*
ouvreuse *f*.

usual*, iou´-jou'eul, *a*
usuel; habituel;
ordinaire.

usually, iou´-jioueu-li, *adv*
d'habitude; d'ordinaire.

usurer, iou´-jeu-r'r, *n*
usurier, ère *m* & *f*.

usurp, iou-zeurpe´, *v*
usurper.

usury, iou´-jeu-ri, *n* usure

f.

utensil, iou-tenn´-cil, *n*
ustensile *m.*

utility, iou-til´-i-ti, *n*
utilité *f.*

utilize, ioue´-til-âïze, *v*
utiliser.

utmost, ott´-mauste, *a*
extrême; dernier; *adv* le
plus; *n* comble *m*; tout
son possible *m.*

utter, ott´-'r, *v* (words)
prononcer; (sound, coin,
etc) émettre; (cry)
pousser. *a** entier;
absolu; total.

utterance, ott´-*eur*-'nce, *n*
expression *f*; émission *f.*

uttermost, (see **utmost**).

V

vacancy, vé´-k'n-ci, n vacance f; place vacante f; (emptiness) vide m.

vacant*, vé´-k'nt, a (empty) vide; (free) libre; (mind) distrait.

vacate, va-quéte´, v vider; évacuer; quitter.

vacation, va-qué´-ch'n, n vacances fpl; congé m.

vaccinate, văque´-ci-néte, v vacciner.

vacillate, văss´-il-léte, v vaciller.

vacuum, văque´-iou-'m, n vide m; – **cleaner,** aspirateur m; – **flask,** thermos m.

vagabond, văgue´-a-bonnde, n vagabond, -e m & f.

vagina, va-dji´-na, n vagin m

vague*, végue, a vague.

vain*, véne, a vain; vaniteux; **in –,** adv en vain.

vale, véle, n vallée f; vallon m.

valet, văl´-ette, n valet de chambre m.

valiant*, văl´-i-annte, a vaillant; brave.

valid, văl´-ide, a valable; valide.

valley, văl´-i, n vallée f.

valour, văl´-'r, n bravoure f.

valuable, văl´-iou-a-b'l, a précieux; de valeur.

valuables, văl´-iou-a-b'lze, n objets de valeur mpl.

valuation, văl´-iou-é´-ch'n, n évaluation f.

value, văl´iou, v évaluer; priser; n valeur f.

valuer, văl´-iou-'r, n priseur m; (official) commissaire-priseur m.

valve, vălve, n valve f; soupape f; (radio) lampe f.

vampire, văm´-pâïre, n vampire m.

van, vănne, n camion m; camionnette f; (train) fourgon m.

vane, véne, n girouette f; (windmill) aile f.

vanilla, va-nil´-a, n vanille f.

vanish, vănn´-iche, v disparaître.

vanity, vănn´-i-ti, n vanité f.

vanquish, vaing´-kouiche, v vaincre.

vaporize, vé´-por-âïze, v vaporiser.

vapour, vé´-p'r, n vapeur f.

variable, vé´-ri-a-b'l, a variable; fig inconstant.

variation, vé-ri-é´-ch'n, n variation f; différence f.

varicose vein, văr´-i-kôze véne, n varice f.

varied, vé´-ride, a varié; divers.

variegated, vé´-ri-i-gué-tedde, a panaché; bigarré.

variety, va-râï´-i-ti, n variété f; choix m; – **theatre,** music-hall m.

various, vè´-ri-*euce*, *a* divers; différent.

varnish, vâre´-niche, *n* vernis *m*; *v* vernir.

vary, vé´-ri, *v* varier; changer; dévier.

vase, vâze, *n* vase *m*; (oriental) potiche *f*.

vaseline, vâze´-i-line, *n* vaseline *f*.

vast, vâsste, *a* vaste; immense.

vat, vâtte, *n* cuve *f*; cuvier *m*.

Vatican, vât´-i-k'n, *n* Vatican *m*.

vault, voalte, *n* voûte *f*; (church, etc) crypte *f*; (burial) caveau *m*; (cellar) cave *f*; *v* (jump) sauter.

veal, vîle, *n* veau *m*.

veer, vi´-*eur*, *v* tourner; (wind) changer.

vegetable, vedj´-i-ta-b'l, *n* légume *m*; *a* végétal.

vegetarian, vedj-i-té´-ri-an, *n* végétarien, -ne *m* & *f*.

vegetation, vedj-i-té´-ch'n, *n* végétation *f*.

vehement, vî´-hi-m'nt, *a* véhément.

vehicle, vî´-i-k'l, *n* véhicule *m*.

veil, véle, *n* voile *m*; *v* voiler.

vein, véne, *n* veine *f*;

(geological) filon *m*.

vellum, vell´-'m, *n* vélin *m*.

velocity, vi-loss´-i-ti, *n* vélocité *f*; *mech* vitesse *f*.

velvet, vell´-vett, *n* velours *m*.

velveteen, vell-vè-tine´, *n* velours de coton *m*.

vending machine, vennd-inng-ma-chîne, *n* distributeur automatique *m*.

vendor, venn´-d'r, *n* vendeur, -euse *m* & *f*.

veneer, vi-nieur´, *n* placage *m*; *v* plaquer.

venerable, venn´-*eur*-a-b'l, *a* vénérable.

veneration, venn-*eur*-é´-ch'n, *n* vénération *f*.

venereal, vi-ni´-ri-al, *a* vénérien.

vengeance, venn´-dj'nce, *n* vengeance *f*.

venial*, vî´-ni-al, *a* véniel.

venison, venn´-i-z'n, *n* venaison *f*.

venom, venn´-'m, *n* venin *m*; **–ous**, *a* venimeux.

vent, vennte, *n* issue *f*; (cask) trou de fausset *m*; **give – to**, *v* donner cours à.

ventilate, venn´-ti-léte, *v* aérer.

ventilator, venn´-ti-lé-t'r,

n ventilateur *m*.

ventriloquist, venn-tril´-ŏ-couiste, *n* ventriloque *m* & *f*.

venture, venn´-tioure, *v* aventurer; risquer; (dare) oser; *n* aventure *f*; entreprise *f*; **–some**, *a* aventureux; (daring) osé.

veracity, vi-râss´-i-ti, *n* authenticité *f*; véracité *f*.

veranda, vi-rănn´-da, *n* véranda *f*.

verb, veurbe, *n* verbe *m*; **–al***, *a* verbal; **–atim**, *adv* & *a* mot pour mot.

verbose, veur-bauce´, *a* verbeux; diffus.

verdant, veur´-dannte, *a* verdoyant.

verdict, veur´-dicte, *n* verdict *m*.

verdigris, veur´-di-gri, *n* vert-de-gris *m*.

verge, veurdje, *v* pencher vers; *n* (brink) bord *m*.

verger, veur´-dj'r, *n* bedeau *m*.

verify, vair´-i-fâï, *v* vérifier.

vermilion, veur-mil´-yonne, *n* & *a* vermillon *m*.

vermin, veur´-minne, *n* vermine *f*.

vernacular, veur-năk´-iou-l'r, *n* & *a* vernaculaire

m.

versatile, veur´-sa-tāīle, *a* versatile; apte à tout.

verse, veurce, *n* vers *m*; (song) couplet *m*; (Bible) verset *m*.

versed, veursste, *a* versé.

version, veur´-ch'n, *n* version *f*.

versus, veur´-ceusse, *prep* contre.

vertical*, veur´-ti-k'l, *a* vertical.

vertigo, veur´-ti-gau, *n* vertige *m*; étourdissement *m*.

very, vèr´-i, *adv* très; fort; bien; *a* même.

vessel, vess´-'l, *n* vase *m*; récipient *m*; *naut* vaisseau *m*.

vest, veste, *n* gilet *m*; (under) tricot de corps *m*.

vested, vess´-tedde, *a* (interest, rights) acquis.

vestige, vess´-tidje, *n* vestige *m*.

vestment, vesst´-m'nt, *n* vêtement *m*.

vestry, vess´-tri, *n* sacristie *f*.

vet, vette, *n* vétérinaire *m* & *f*.

veteran, vett´-e-rănn, *n* vétéran *m*.

veterinary, vett´-eur-i-na-ri, *a* vétérinaire; –

surgeon (*pop*: **vet**), *n* vétérinaire *m*.

veto, vî´-tau, *n* veto *m*; *v* mettre le veto à.

vex, vexe, *v* vexer; contrarier.

vexatious, vex-é´-cheuce, *a* vexant; contrariant; irritant; (law) vexatoire.

via, vâï´-a, *prep* via; par.

viaduct, vâï´-a-docte, *n* viaduc *m*.

vibrate, vâï´-bréte, *v* vibrer.

vibration, vâï´-bré´-ch'n, *n* vibration *f*.

vicar, vik´-'r, *n* curé *m*; (protestant) pasteur *m*.

vicarage, vik´-'r-idj, *n* presbytère *m*.

vice, vâïce, *n* vice *m*; *mech* étau *m*.

vice versa, vâïce-veur-să, *adv* vice versa.

vice-admiral, vâïce-ăd´-mi-ral, *n* vice-amiral *m*.

vice-president, vâïce-prèz´-i-dennte, *n* vice-president *m*.

viceroy, vâïce´-roa'i, *n* vice-roi *m*.

vicinity, vi-cinn´-i-ti, *n* voisinage *m*; proximité *f*.

vicious*, vich´-euce, *a* vicieux.

viciousness, vich´-euce-nesse, *n* nature vicieuse *f*.

victim, vic´-time, *n* victime *f*.

victimize, vic´-timm-âïze, *v* rendre victime.

victor, vic´-t'r, *n* vainqueur *m*.

victorious*, vic-tau´-ri-euce, *a* victorieux.

victory, vic´-tŏr-i, *n* victoire *f*.

video, vi´-dî-ô *n* vidéo (film), *f*; *n* vidéo-cassette (video cassette) *f*; *n* magnétoscope (recorder) *m*.

vie, vâï, *v* rivaliser; faire assaut de.

view, vioue, *n* vue *f*; opinion *f*; *v* visiter; examiner.

vigil, vidj´-il, *n* veille *f*; *eccl* vigile *f*.

vigilance, vidj´-i-l'nce, *n* vigilance *f*.

vigilant, vidj´-i-l'nt, *a* vigilant.

vigorous*, vigg´-eur-euce, *a* vigoureux; fort.

vigour, vigg´-'r, *n* vigueur *f*; force *f*.

vile*, vâïle, *a* vil; abject.

vilify, vil´-i-fâï, *v* diffamer; avilir.

village, vil´-idj, *n* village *m*; –**r**, villageois; oise *m* & *f*.

villain, vil´-inne, *n* scélérat *m*; gredin *m*.

villainous, vil´-*a-neuce, a* vil; infâme.

villainy, vil´-*a-ni, n* infamie *f.*

vindicate, vinn´-dik-éte, *v* défendre; justifier.

vindication, vinn-di-ké´-ch'n, *n* justification *f*; défense *f.*

vindictive*, vinn-dic´-tive, *a* vindicatif; rancunier.

vindictiveness, vinn-dic´-tive-nesse, *n* rancune *f.*

vine, vâïne, *n* vigne *f.*

vinegar, vinn´-i-gueur, *n* vinaigre *m.*

vineyard, vinn´-*ieurde, n* vignoble *m.*

vintage, vinn´-tidje, *n* vendange *f*; (year) année *f.*

viola, vi-au´-la, *n* alto *m.*

violate, vâï´-ŏ-léte, *v* violer.

violence, vâï´-ŏ-l'nce, *n* violence *f.*

violent*, vâï´-ŏ-lennte, *a* violent.

violet, vâï´-ŏ-lette, *n* violette *f*; *n & a* violet *m.*

violin, vâï-ŏ-linne´, *n* violon *m.*

violinist, vâï-ŏ-linn´-ist, *n* violoniste *m & f.*

viper, vâï´-p'r, *n* vipère *f.*

virgin, veur´-djinne, *n &*

a vierge *f.*

virile, vi´-râïle, *a* viril.

virtual*, veur´-tiou-al, *a* virtuel.

virtue, veur´-tioue, *n* vertu *f.*

virtuous*, veur´-tiou-euce, *a* vertueux.

virulent, vir´-iou-lennte, *a* virulent.

virus, vî´-reusse, *n* virus *m.*

visa, vî´-*za, n* visa *m.*

viscount, vâï´-câ'ounnte, *n* vicomte *m.*

viscountess, vâï´-câ'ounn-tesse, *n* vicomtesse *f.*

visibility, viz-i-bile´-i-ti, *n* visibilité *f.*

visible, viz´-i-b'l, *a* visible.

visibly, viz´-i-bli, *adv* visiblement.

vision, vij´-'n, *n* vision *f.*

visit, viz´-itte, *v* visiter; aller voir; (a person) rendre visit à; *n* visite *f*; **–ing-card,** carte de visite *f.*

visitor, viz´-itt-'r, *n* visiteur, -euse *m & f.*

visual, vij´-iou-'l, *a* visuel.

vital*, vâï´-t'l, *a* essentiel; vital; **–s,** *npl* organes essentiels *mpl.*

vitality, vâï´-tăl´-i-ti, *n* vitalité *f.*

vitamin, vit´-*a-*minn, *n* vitamine *f.*

vitriol, vite´-ri-ŏle, *n* vitriol *m.*

vivacious*, vi-vé´-cheuce, *a* vif; animé.

vivacity, vi-văss´-i-ti, *n* vivacité *f.*

vivid, viv´-ide, *a* vif, frappant; (colour) éclatant.

vixen, vic´-senn, *n* renarde *f*; *fig* mégère *f.*

viz (namely, némme´-li), *adv* c'est-à-dire.

vocabulary, vau-căb´-iou-la-ri, *n* vocabulaire *m.*

vocal*, vau´-c'l, *a* vocal; **––chords,** *npl* cordes vocales *fpl.*

vocalist, vau´-cal-ist, *n* chanteur *m*; cantatrice *f.*

vocation, vau-qué´-ch'n, *n* vocation *f*; profession *f.*

vociferous*, vŏ-ci´-*feur-euce, a* bruyant.

vogue, vaugue, *n* vogue *f*; mode *f.*

voice, voa'ice, *n* voix *f.*

void, voa'ide, *a* vide; nul; dénué de; *n* vide *m.*

volatile, vol´-*a-*tâïle, *a* volatil; *fig* gai.

volcano, vol-qué´-nau, *n* volcan *m.*

volley, vol´-i, *n* volée *f*; (salute) salve *f.*

volt, volte, *n* (electric) volt *m*; **–age,** tension *f.*

voluble, vol´-iou-b'l, *a*

délié.

volume, vol´-ioume, *n*
volume *m*.

voluminous*, vol-ioue´-
mi-*neuce*, *a*
volumineux.

voluntary, vol´-*eunn*-ta-ri,
a volontaire; spontané.

volunteer, vol-*eunn*-tîre´,
n volontaire *m* & *f*; *v*
s'offrir.

voluptuous*, vol-op´-
tiou-*euce*, *a* voluptueux.

vomit, vomm´-itte, *v*
vomir.

voracious, vŏ-ré´-*cheuce*,
a vorace; dévorant.

vortex, voar´-texe, *n*
tourbillon *m*.

vote, vaute, *n* vote *m*,
scrutin *m*, voix *f*; *v*
voter; **–r,** *n* électeur, -
trice *m* & *f*.

vouch, vâ'outche, *v*
attester; (persons)
répondre de.

voucher, vâ'outch´-'r, *n*
pièce justificative *f*; bon
m.

vow, vâ'ou, *n* vœu *m*/ *v*
faire vœu de; jurer.

vowel, vâ'ou´-'l, *n* voyelle
f.

voyage, voa'i´-idj, *n*
voyage par mer *m*.

vulgar, vol´-gueur, *a*
vulgaire; commun.

vulnerable, vol´-neur-a-

b'l, *a* vulnérable.

vulture, vol´-tioure, *n*
vautour *m*.

wad, ouode, n bourre f; (surgical) tampon m.

wadding, ouodd´-inng, n coton-hydrophile m; (padding) ouate f.

waddle, ouodd´-'l, v se dandiner.

wade, ouéde, v marcher dans.

wafer, oué´-f'r, n (thin biscuit) gaufrette f; (eccl) hostie f.

wag, ouâgue, v remuer, secouer; n farceur m.

wage, ouédje, v (war) faire la guerre à.

wager, oué´-dj'r, n gageure f, pari m; v parier.

wages, oué´-djize, npl (servants) gages mpl; (workmen) salaire m.

waggle, ouâgg´-'l, v remuer; **–about,** v frétiller.

wagon, ouâgg´-'n, n chariot m; (rail) wagon m.

waif, ouéfe, n épave f.

wail, ouéle, v se lamenter; n lamentation f.

waist, ouéste, n taille f; ceinture f.

waistcoat, ouess´-côte, n gilet m.

wait, ouéte, v attendre; (at table) servir; **–er,** n garçon m; **head –,** n maître d'hôtel m; **– for,** v attendre; **–ing,** n attente f; (service) service m; **–ingroom,** salle d'attente f; **–ress,** serveuse f; **– upon,** v servir.

waive, ouéve, v abandonner; renoncer à.

wake, ouéke, v (to awake) se réveiller; (to be called) réveiller; n (ship's) sillage m.

walk, ou'oak, v aller à pied; marcher; (stroll) se promener; n promenade f.

wall, ou'oal, n mur m; **–flower,** giroflée f; **–paper,** papier peint m.

wallet, ouol´-ite, n portefeuille m.

wallow, ouol´-au, v se vautrer.

walnut, ouôl´-notte, n noix f; (tree) noyer m.

walrus, ouôl´-reuce, n morse m.

waltz, ouôlts, v valser; n valse f.

wan, ou'oanne, a pâle; blême.

wander, ou'oann´-d'r, v errer; (mentally) délirer.

wane, ouéne, v décroître; n déclin m.

want, ou'oannte, n (lack) manque m; (distress) dénuement m; **for – of,** faute de; v vouloir; avoir besoin de; avoir envie de.

wanton, ou'onne´-t'n, a (lustful) licencieux; (wicked) criminel; adv de gaieté de cœur.

war, ou'oar, v faire la

guerre; n guerre f; **–like,** a belliqueux; **–office,** ministère de la guerre m; **–ship,** vaisseau de guerre m.

warble, ou'oar´-b'l, v gazouiller.

warbler, ou'oar´-bleur, n fauvette f.

ward, ou'oarde, n (minor) pupille m & f; (hospital) salle f; **–en,** (guard) gardien m; (college) principal m; **–er,** gardien de prison m; **– off,** v parer; **–ress,** n gardienne f; **–robe,** armoire f; **–room,** (naval) carré des officiers m.

ware, ouère, n marchandise f; denrée f.

warehouse, ouère´-hâ'ouce, n entrepôt m; magasin m; v emmagasiner; (furniture, etc) entreposer.

warm, ou'oarme, a* chaud; v chauffer; se chauffer; **–th,** n chaleur f; ardeur f.

warn, ou'oarne, v avertir; notifier; **–ing,** n avertissement m; (caution) avis m.

warp, ou'oarpe, v (wood) jouer; (mind) fausser.

warrant, ouor´-'nte, n (authority) autorisation

f; (for arrest) mandat d'arrêt m; (voucher) mandat m; **–y,** garantie f.

warrior, ouor´-ieur, n guerrier m.

wart, ou'oarte, n verrue f.

wary, oué´-ri, a circonspect, prudent.

wash, ou'oache, v laver; se laver; **–basin,** n cuvette f; **–up,** v faire la vaisselle; **–erwoman,** laveuse f; **–ing,** blanchissage m; **–ing machine,** n machine à laver f; **–ing powder,** lessive f; **–ing up,** vaisselle f; **–ing up liquid,** produit pour la vaisselle m; **–stand,** table de toilette f.

washer, ou'oache´-'r, n mech joint m; rondelle f.

wasp, ou'oaspe, n guêpe f.

waste, ouéste, n gaspillage m; (refuse) rebut m; (land) terrain vague m; v gaspiller; **–away,** dépérir; **–ful,** a gaspilleur; prodigue.

watch, ouotche, v veiller; observer; (vigilance) surveiller; n montre f; (wrist) montre-bracelet f; naut quart m; **–dog,** chien de garde m; **–maker,** horloger m;

–man, veilleur de nuit m; **–over,** v veiller sur; **–word,** n mot d'ordre m.

water, ou'oa´-t'r, v arroser; (cattle, etc) abreuver; n eau f; **hot –bottle,** bouillotte f; **–closet,** cabinets mpl, W.C. mpl; **–colour,** aquarelle f; **–cress,** cresson m; **–fall,** chute d'eau f; **–jug,** cruche f; **–lily,** nénuphar m; **–line,** ligne de flottaison f; **–logged,** a plein d'eau f; **–mark,** n niveau des eaux m; (paper) filigrane f; **–proof,** a imperméable; **–skiing,** n ski nautique m; **–tank,** réservoir m; **–tight,** a étanche; **–works,** npl ouvrages hydrauliques mpl.

watering, ou'oa-teur-inng, n arrosage m; abreuvage m; **–can,** arrosoir m; **–place,** station thermale f.

wave, ouéve, n (sea, etc) vague f; (radio, etc) onde f; v (flags, etc) flotter; agiter; (to somebody) faire signe m; (sway) se balancer; (hair) onduler; **–length,** n longueur d'onde f.

waver, ouéve´-'r, v hésiter; être indécis.

wavering, ouéve´-*eur*-inng, *a* indécis; irrésolu.

wavy, ouéve´-i, *a* onduleux; (hair) ondulé.

wax, ouàxe, *v* cirer; *n* cire *f*; **—works,** musée de figures de cire *m*.

way, oué, *n* chemin *m*; manière *f*; façon *f*; **– in,** entrée *f*; **–lay,** *v* dresser un guetapens; **– out,** *n* sortie *f*; **– through,** passage *m*; **–ward,** *a* entêté; capricieux.

we, oui, *pron* nous.

weak, ouîque, *a** faible; infirme; débile; **–en,** *v* affaiblir; **–ening,** *a* débilitant; **–ling,** *n* être faible *m*; **–ness,** faiblesse *f*.

weal, ouîle, *n* (mark) marque *f*.

wealth, ouèlts, *n* richesse *f*; opulence *f*.

wealthy, ouèlts´-i, *a* riche; opulent.

wean, ouîne, *v* sevrer; *fig* détacher de.

weapon, ouèp´-'n, *n* arme *f*.

wear, ouère, *n* (by use) usage *m*; *v* (carry) porter; (last) durer; **–able,** *a* mettable; **–out** (away), *v* user; (fatigue) épuiser.

weariness, oui´-ri-nesse, *n* lassitude *f*; ennui *m*.

weary, oui´-ri, *a* las; ennuyé; *v* fatiguer; **– of,** se lasser de.

weasel, oui-z´l, *n* belette *f*.

weather, ouèdz´-'r, *n* temps *m*; *v* surmonter; **—bound,** *a* retenu par le mauvais temps; **–cock,** *n* girouette *f*; **– report,** bulletin météorologique *m*.

weave, ouîve, *v* tisser; **–r,** *n* tisserand *m*.

web, ouèbe, *n* (spider) toile *f*.

webbing, ouèbe´-inng, *n* sangle *f*.

web-footed, ouèbe-foutt´-èdde, *a* palmé.

wed, ouède, *v* se marier; épouser; (perform ceremony) marier.

wedding, ouède´-inng, *n* mariage *m*; **–breakfast,** repas de noce *m*; **–ring,** alliance *f*.

wedge, ouèdje, *n* coin *m*; cale *f*; *v* caler; **– in,** serrer; presser.

wedlock, ouède´-loque, *n* mariage *m*.

Wednesday, ou'ennze´-dé, *n* mercredi *m*.

weed, ouîde, *n* mauvaise herbe *f*; *v* sarcler.

week, ouîque, *n* semaine *f*;

–day, jour de semaine *m*; **–end,** fin de semaine *f*; week-end *m*; **–ly,** *a* hebdomadaire.

weep, ouîpe, *v* pleurer.

weevil, ouî´-v'l, *n* charançon *m*.

weigh, oué, *v* peser; (mentally) considérer; **–ing-machine,** *n* bascule *f*.

weight, ouéte, *n* poids *m*; **–y,** *a* pesant; grave.

weir, ouire, *n* barrage *m*.

weird, ouirde, *a* étrange; fantastique.

welcome, ouell´-keume, *n* bienvenue *f*; *a* bienvenu; *v* bien recevoir; accueillir.

weld, ouelde, *v* souder.

welfare, ouell´-fére, *n* bien-être *m*; prospérité *f*.

well, ouell, *n* puits *m*.

well, ouell, *adv* bien; *a* bon; **—being,** *n* bien-être *m*; **—bred,** *a* bien élevé; **–done,** (meat, etc) bien cuit; **—known,** (bien) connu.

welt, ouelte, *n* (shoe, etc) trépointe *f*.

wend, ouennde, *v* aller; se diriger vers.

west, ouesste, *n* ouest *m*; occident *m*.

westerly, ouess´-teur-li, *a* d'ouest; occidental.

wet, ouette, n humidité f; a humide; mouillé; (weather) pluvieux; v mouiller.

wet-nurse, ouette'-neurce, n nourrice f.

wetsuit, ouette'-soute, n combinaison de plongée f.

whack, ouàque, v rosser; battre.

whale, ouélé, n baleine f; **–bone,** baleine f.

whaler, ouél'-eur, n baleinier m.

wharf, ou'oarfe, n quai m; embarcadère m.

what, ouotte, pron ce qui; ce que; que; quoi; qu'est-ce qui, qu'est-ce que; a quel; quelle; quels; quelles.

whatever, ouotte-èv'-'r, pron & a tout ce qui; tout ce que; quel que soit; quelque ... que.

wheat, ouîte, n froment m; blé m.

wheedle, ouîdd'-'l, v cajoler; câliner.

wheel, ouîle, n roue f; v faire rouler; **spinning –,** n rouet m; **–barrow,** brouette f; **– clamp,** n aut sabot (de Denver) m; **–chair,** fauteuil roulant m; **–wright,** charron m.

wheezy, ouîz'-i, a poussif.

whelk, ou'èlque, n buccin m.

when, ouenne, adv quand; lorsque; où; que; **–ce,** d'où; **--ever,** chaque fois que.

where, ouère, adv où; **–about (s),** où; **–as,** conj tandis que; (law) vu que; **–at,** adv sur quoi; **–by,** par quoi; **–fore,** c'est pourquoi; **–in,** dans lequel; **–on,** sur lequel.

wherever, ouère-èv'-'r, adv partout où.

whet, ouette, v aiguiser.

whether, ouèdz'-'r, conj si; soit que; que.

which, ouitche, pron qui; que; lequel; laquelle; lesquels; lesquelles.

whichever, ouitch-èv'-'r, pron lequel; laquelle; lesquels; lesquelles.

while, ouâîle, v passer; conj pendant que.

whim, ouimme, n lubie f; caprice f; **–sical,** a capricieux.

whimper, ouimm'-p'r, v pleurnicher.

whine, ouâîne, v gémir; fig pleurnicher.

whip, ouippe, n fouet m; v fouetter; (riding whip) cravacher; (cream) fouetter.

whirl, ou'eurle, v faire tourner; **–pool,** n tourbillon m; **–wind,** tourbillon m.

whisk, ouisske, n (cookery) fouet m; v (eggs) battre; (cream) fouetter.

whiskers, ouissk'-eurze, npl favoris mpl; (cat) moustaches fpl.

whisky, ouiss'-ki, n whisky m.

whisper, ouiss'-p'r, v chuchoter; n chuchotement m.

whist, ouisste, n (cards) whist m.

whistle, ouiss'-'l, n sifflet m; v siffler.

whistling, ouiss'-linng, n sifflement m.

white, ouâîte, n & a blanc m;– **bait,** n blanchaille f; **–ness,** blancheur f; **–of egg,** blanc d'œuf m; **–wash,** v (lime) blanchir à la chaux.

whither, ouidz'-'r, adv où.

whiting, ouâîte'-inng, n (fish) merlan m.

Whitsuntide, ouitt'-s'n-tâîde, n Pentecôte f.

whiz, ouize, v siffler.

who, oue, pron qui.

whoever, oue-èv'-'r, pron quiconque.

whole, haule, n tout m;

total *m*; *a* tout; entier; –**sale**, *n* vente en gros *f*; *a* en gross; –**some***, sain; salubre.

wholemeal bread, haule-mîle-brède, *a* pain complet *m*.

wholly, haul´-li, *adv* entièrement.

whom, houme, *pron* que; qui; lequel; laquelle; lesquels; lesquelles.

whoop, houpe, *v* huer; *n* cri *m*.

whooping-cough, houpe´-inng-coaf, *n* coqueluche *f*.

whore, haure, *n* prostituée *f*.

whose, houze, *pron* dont.

whosoever, (see **whoever**).

why, ouaî, *adv* pourquoi.

wick, ouique, *n* mèche *f*.

wicked*, ouik´-ide, *a* méchant; mauvais; criminel.

wickedness, ouik´-ide-ness, *n* méchanceté *f*.

wicker, ouik´-'r, *n* osier *m*.

wide, ouâide, *a* large; vaste; étendu; ––**awake**, bien éveillé; *fig* vif; sur ses gardes; –**ly**, *adv* largement; très; –**spread**, *a* répandu.

widen, ouâide´-'n, *v* élargir; s'élargir.

widow, ouid´-au, *n* veuve *f*.

widower, ouid´-au-'r, *n* veuf *m*.

width, ouidts, *n* largeur *f*; (extent) étendue *f*.

wield, ouilde, *v* manier; (power) détenir.

wife, ouâîfe, *n* femme *f*; femme mariée *f*; épouse *f*.

wig, ouigue, *n* perruque *f*.

wild*, ouâîlde, *a* sauvage, farouche; *fig* furieux.

wilderness, ouil´-d'r-ness, *n* désert *m*; solitude *f*.

wildlife, ouâîlde´-laïfe, *n* faune *f*.

wile, ou'âîle, *n* ruse *f*; artifice *m*.

wilful*, ouil´-foull, *a* volontaire; (act) prémédité.

will, ouil, *n* volonté *f*; testament *m*; *v* vouloir; (bequeath) léguer; **good** –, *n com* clientèle *f*.

willing, ouil´-inng, *a* consentant; complaisant; –**ly**, *adv* volontiers; –**ness**, *n* bonne volonté *f*.

will-o'-the-wisp, ouil-ŏ-dzi-ouispe´, *n* feu follet *m*.

willow, ouil´-au, *n* saule *m*; **weeping-** –, saule pleureur *m*.

wily, ou'âî´-li, *a* astucieux; malin.

win, ouinne, *v* gagner; (victory) remporter; –**ner,** *n* gagnant, -e *m* & *f*; –**ning,** *a* (manners) engageant; –**ning-post,** *n* poteau d'arrivée *m*; but *m*; –**nings,** gain *m*.

wince, ouinnce, *v* reculer; tressaillir.

winch, ouinntche, *n* treuil *m*.

wind, ouâînnde, *v* enrouler; (road, river, etc) serpentèr; –**ing,** *a* sinueux; (stairs) en colimaçon; – **up,** *v* rouler; (clock) remonter; (*com*) liquider.

wind, ouinnde, *n* vent *m*; flatulence *f*; –**fall,** (luck) aubaine *f*; –**mill,** moulin à vent *m*; –**pipe,** trachée- artère *f*; –**ward,** côté du vent *m*; **to be** –**y,** *v* (weather) faire du vent.

windlass, ouinnde´-lasse, *n* cabestan *m*.

window, ouinn´-dau, *n* fenêtre *f*; croisée *f*; (car, etc) glace *f*; (shop) vitrine *f*; – **shopping,** *n* lèchevitrines m.

windscreen, ouinnde´-skrîne, *n* pare-brise *m*.

windscreen wiper, ouinnde-skrîne-ouâï-peu, n essuie-glace m.

wine, ouâïne, n vin m.

wine-glass, ouâïne´-glâce, n verre à vin m.

wine list, ouâïne-lisste, n carte des vins f.

wing, ouinng, n aile f; (theatre) coulisse f.

wink, ouinnque, v cligner de l'œil; n clin d'œil m.

winkle, ouinnque´-l, n bigorneau m.

winter, ouinn´-t'r, n hiver m; v passer l'hiver; hiverner.

winter sports, ouinn-t'r-spaurts, npl sports d'hiver mpl.

wipe, ouâïpe, v essuyer; – off, v effacer.

wire, ouâïre, n fil de fer m; –less, sans fil; n (radio) radio; T.S.F.

wisdom, ouiz´-d'm, n sagesse f; prudence f.

wise*, ouâïze, a sage; prudent.

wish, ouiche, n souhait m, vœu m; désir m; v souhaiter; désirer; vouloir.

wishful, ouiche´-foull, a désireux.

wisp, ouisspe, n touffe f; (straw) bouchon de paille m; (hair) mèche f.

wistaria, ouiss-terr´-i'a, n glycine f.

wistful*, ouisst´-foull, a pensif; d'envie; de regret.

wit, ouitte, n esprit m; to –, à savoir; c'est-à-dire.

witch, ouitche, n sorcière f.

witchcraft, ouitche´-crâfte, n sorcellerie f.

with, ouidz, prep avec; chez; de.

withdraw, ouidz-droa´, v retirer; se retirer.

wither, ouidz´-'r, v se faner, se flétrir.

withhold, ouidz-haulde´, v retenir; (sanction) refuser.

within, ouidz-inne´, prep dans; en; adv à l'intérieur.

without, ouidz-â'oute´, prep sans; adv (outside) dehors.

withstand, ouidz-stânnde´, v résister à.

witness, ouitt´-nesse, n témoin m; v témoigner.

wits, ouittse, npl jugement m; to live by one's –, vivre d'expédients.

witticism, ouitt´-i-cizme, n trait d'esprit m.

witty, ouitt´-i, a spirituel.

wizard, ouiz´-eurde, n sorcier m, magicien m.

wobble, ou'obbe´-'l, v branler; vaciller.

woe, ou'au, n malheur m; peine f.

woeful*, ou'au´-foull, a triste; affligé.

wolf, ou'oulf, n loup m; she- –, louve f.

woman, ou'oum´-m'n, n femme f.

womanhood, ou'oum´-m'n-houdde, n état de femme m.

womanly, ou'oum´-m'n-li, a féminin.

womb, ou'oumme, n utérus m; matrice f; fig sein m.

wonder, ou'ounn´-d'r, n merveille f; v s'émerveiller de; s'étonner de; (doubt) se demander.

wonderful, ou'ounn´-d'r-foull, a merveilleux; étonnant.

woo, ou'ou, v faire la cour â; –er, n prétendant m.

wood, ou'oude, n bois m.

woodcock, ou'oude´-coque, n bécasse f.

wooden, ou'oude´-'n, a de bois.

woodpecker, ou'oude-pèque´-'r, n pivert m.

woody, ou'oud´-i, a (trees) boisé.

wool, ou'oul, n laine f.

woollen, ou'oul´-'n, *a* de laine.

woolly, ou'oul´-i, *a* laineux.

word, oueurde, *n* mot *m*, parole *f*; (news) nouvelles *fpl*; *v* (verbal) exprimer; (written) rédiger; – **of honour,** *n* parole d'honneur *f*.

wording, oueurde´-inng, *n* termes *mpl*; style *m*; rédaction *f*.

work, oueurque, *v* travailler; (mine) exploiter; *mech* fonctionner; marcher; *n* travail *m*; ouvrage *m*; (literary) œuvre *f*.

worker, oueurque´-'r, *n* travailleur, -euse *m* & *f*.

workhouse, oueurque´-hâ'ouce, *n* asile des pauvres *m*.

working, oueurque´-inng, *n mech* fonctionnement *m*, marche *f*; (mine) exploitation *f*; (handling) manœuvre *f*; – **expenses,** frais d'exploitation *mpl*.

workman, oueurque´-m'n, *n* ouvrier *m*; –**ship,** exécution *f*; façon *f*.

works, oueurque'se, *npl* usine *f*; *mech* mécanisme *m*.

workshop, oueurque´-choppe, *n* atelier *m*.

world, oueurlde, *n* monde *m*, univers *m*.

worldly, oueurlde´-li, *a* mondain.

worm, oueurme, *n* ver *m*; (screw) filet *m*.

worm-eaten, oueurme´-îtt-'n, *a* vermoulu.

worry, ouorr´-i, *n* tracas *m*; (anxiety) tourment *m*; *v* s'inquiéter; se tracasser; se tourmenter; (bother) ennuyer.

worse, oueurse, *adv* pis; *a* pire.

worship, oueur´-chippe, *v* adorer; *n* adoration *f*; (divine) culte *m*.

worst, oueurste, *a* le pire; *n* le pis *m*.

worsted, ou'ouss´-tèdde, *n* (yarn) fil de laine *m*.

worth, oueurts, *n* valeur *f*; mérite *m*; *a* qui vaut; **to be –,** *v* valoir; mériter; **to be –while,** valoir la peine.

worthily, oueurdz´-i-li, *adv* dignement.

worthless, oueurts´-lesse, *a* sans valeur.

worthy, oueurdz´-i, *a* digne; méritant.

would, ou'oude, *aux v* he – **do** *conditional tense* il ferait; **he – have done** il aurait fait; **I – come**

every day (*used to*) je venais chaque jour; **I – like some tea** je voudrais du thé; – **you come here?** voulez-vous venir ici? **he won't come** il a refusé de venir.

would-be, ou'oude´-bî, *a* soi-disant; prétendu.

wound, ou'ounde, *n* blessure *f*; plaie *f*; *v* blesser.

wrangle, rain-'ng'l, *v* se disputer; *n* querelle *f*.

wrap, răppe, *n* sortie de bal *f*; *v* envelopper; – **up,** (oneself) s'emmitoufler.

wrapper, răppe´-'r, *n* enveloppe *f*; (postal) bande *f*; (book) couverture *f*.

wrapping paper, răppe-inng-pé-p'r, *n* papier d'emballage *m*.

wrath, roats, *n* courroux *m*, colère *f*.

wreath, rits, *n* couronne *f*.

wreathe, ridz, *v* entrelacer.

wreck, rèque, *n* naufrage *m*; *fig* ruine *f*; *v* faire naufrage; *fig* ruiner; –**age,** *n* (pieces of ship, etc) épaves *fpl*.

wrecked, rèkte, *a* naufragé; ruiné.

wren, rène, *n* roitelet *m*.

wrench, renntche, *n*
arrachement violent *m*;
(sprain) entorse *f*; (tool)
clé anglaise *f*; *v* tordre;
(pull) arracher.

wrestle, ress´-'l, *v* lutter.

wrestler, ress´-l'r, *n* lutteur
m.

wretch, rètche, *n*
misérable *m* & *f*.

wretched, rétch´-edde, *a*
triste; (person)
misérable.

wretchedness, rétch´-
edde-ness, *n* misère *f*.

wriggle, rigg´-'l, *v* se
tortiller; – **through,** se
faufiler.

wring, rinng, *v* tordre;
(washing) essorer.

wrinkle, rinng´-k'l, *n* ride
f; *v* rider; (brow) froncer.

wrist, risste, *n* poignet *m*.

writ, rite, *n* assignation *f*;
commandement *m*.

write, râîte, *v* écrire.

writer, râîte´-'r, *n* auteur
m, écrivain *m*.

writhe, râîdz, *v* se tordre.

writing, râîte´-inng, *n*
écriture *f*; inscription *f*;
hand–, écriture *f*; **in –,**
adv par écrit.

writing-pad, râîte´-inng-
pädde, *n* (blotter)
sousmain *m*; (note-
paper) bloc-notes *m*.

writing-paper, râîte´-inng-
pé´-pr, *n* papier à lettres.

written, ritt´-'n, *a* écrit.

wrong, ron-ng, *n* tort *m*;
injustice *f*; *v* faire tort à.
a* faux; mauvais; mal;
injuste; illégal; – **side,** *n*
mauvais côté *m*;
(material) envers *m*; **to
be –,** avoir tort.

wrought iron, roat âî´-
eurne, *n* fer forgé *m*.

wry, râï, *a* de travers
tordu; –**face,** *n* grimace
f.

wryneck, râï´-nèque, *n*
torticolis *m*; (bird)
torcol *m*.

Xmas (Christmas), criss´-
  meusse, *n* Noël *m.*
x-rays, èkce-réze, *npl*
  rayons X *mpl*; (X-ray
  photograph)
  radiographie *f*; *v*
  radiographer.
xylophone, sâï´-lo-faune,
  n xylophone *m.*

yacht, i'ŏte, n yacht m.

yachting, i'ote´-inng, n yachting m.

yard, i'ârde, n cour f; (measure) yard m; (ship, timber, etc) chantier m.

yarn, i'ârne, n fil m; (story) histoire f.

yawn, i'oanne, v bâiller; n bâillement m.

yawning, i'oann´-inng, n bâillement m; a fig béant.

year, i'îre, n an m, année f.

yearly, i'île-li, a annuel; adv annuellement.

yearn, i'eurne, v soupirer après; languir pour.

yearning, i'eurne-inng, n désir m; aspiration f.

yearningly, i'eurne´-inng-li, adv ardemment.

yeast, yi'îste, n levure f, levain m.

yellow, i'ell´-au, n & a jaune m.

yelp, i'elpe, v glapir; japper; n glapissement m.

yes, i'ess, adv oui; (after negative question) si.

yesterday, i'ess´-t'r-dé, adv & n hier m.

yet, i'ette, adv encore; déjà; conj cependant.

yew, i'oue, n if m.

yield, yi'îlde, v céder; produire; (bring in) rapporter; n rapport m; produit m.

yog(h)urt, i'ŏg´-eurte, n yaourt m.

yoke, i'auke, n joug m; fig sujétion f; v mettre au joug; subjuguer.

yokel, i'au´-k'l, n rustre m.

yolk, i'auke, n jaune d'œuf m.

yonder, i'onn´-d'r, adv là-bas; a ce . . . là.

you, i'oue, pron vous; fam tu; te; toi.

young, i'onng, a jeune; n (animals) petits mpl.

youngster, i'onng´-st'r, n jeune garçon, fille.

your, i'our, poss a votre; vos.

yours, i'ourze, poss pron le vôtre; la vôtre; les vôtres.

youth, i'outs, n jeunesse f; (lad) jeune homme m.

youth hostel, i'outs-hosse-tell, n auberge de jeunesse f.

youthful, i'outs´-foull, a jeune; juvénile.

youthfulness, i'outs´-foull-nesse, n jeunesse f.

Yule-tide, i'oule´-tâïde, n temps de Noël m.

Z

zeal, zîle, n zéle m.
zealous, zèl´-euce, a zélé; ardent.
zebra, zî´-bra, n zèbre m; – **crossing,** n passage clouté m.
zenith, zenn´-its, n zénith m.
zephyr, zèf´-'r, n zéphyr m.
zero, zi´-rau, n zéro m.
zest, zeste, n ardeur f; (relish) saveur f.
zinc, zinnque, n zinc m; v zinguer.
zip (fastener), zipe-fâs´-s'n-'r, n fermeture-éclair f.
zone, zaune, n zone f.
zoo, zoue, n zoo m.
zoological, zau-ðl-odj´-i-c'l, a zoologique.
zoology, zau-ol´-odj-i, n zoologie f.